CUMULATIVE RECORD

Definitive Edition

BOOKS BY B. F. SKINNER

- *The Behavior of Organisms.* 1938*
- *Walden Two.* 1948
- *Science and Human Behavior.* 1953
- *Schedules of Reinforcement* (with C. B. Ferster). 1957*
- *Verbal Behavior.* 1957*
- *Cumulative Record.* 1959. (Enlarged Edition: 1961; Third Edition: 1972; Definitive Edition: 1999*)
- *The Analysis of Behavior* (with J. G. Holland). 1961
- *The Technology of Teaching.* 1968
- *Contingencies of Reinforcement.* 1969
- *Beyond Freedom and Dignity.* 1971
- *About Behaviorism.* 1974
- *Particulars of My Life.* 1976
- *Reflections on Behaviorism and Society.* 1978
- *The Shaping of a Behaviorist: Part Two of an Autobiography.* 1979
- *Notebooks* (edited by R. Epstein). 1980
- *Skinner for the Classroom* (edited by R. Epstein). 1982
- *Enjoy Old Age* (with M. E. Vaughan). 1983
- *A Matter of Consequences: Part Three of an Autobiography.* 1983
- *Upon Further Reflection.* 1987
- *The Selection of Behavior: The Operant Behaviorism of B. F. Skinner* (edited by A. C. Catania & S. Harnad). 1988
- *Recent Issues in the Analysis of Behavior.* 1989

* Available from the B. F. Skinner Foundation,
   P. O. Box 825, Cambridge, MA 02238

CUMULATIVE RECORD

RECORD

Definitive Edition

BY

B. F. SKINNER

Copley Publishing Group
Acton, Massachusetts 01720

B. F. Skinner Reprint Series

Edited by Julie S. Vargas

The Editors of this Definitive Edition of
B. F. Skinner's *Cumulative Record* are
Victor G. Laties and A. Charles Catania

To

E. G. Boring

ACKNOWLEDGMENT

Completing this new edition of *Cumulative Record* has been a labor of love. Charlie Catania and Victor Laties undertook that labor. Working from the three original editions of the book, they were confronted with more problems than anyone imagined—certainly more than they themselves anticipated. Many hours were devoted to figuring out the composition of the Definitive Edition, and many discussions were held about what other articles might be included. Vic made several trips to Cambridge to delve into Skinner's papers in the Harvard Archives to find out why the original selections were made, to make sure that restoring material Skinner had omitted in later editions would not violate his wishes were he alive today. The foreword in this edition represents some of what they discovered as well as information from their long association with B. F. Skinner. Words of appreciation fall far short of what is due. I can only offer thanks on behalf of the Foundation and all future readers.

The Foundation is also indebted to Robert Epstein and Julia Becerra who took on the considerable task of creating an index—something that none of the three prior editions contained. Because of the diverse contents of the volume, the particular words to be indexed were not obvious, but required expertise in the field as well as an unusual breadth of intellectual background to match the range of topics discussed. Thus the Foundation was fortunate that they were willing to undertake the job. The resulting index has considerably increased the research value of this Definitive Edition. For the Foundation and all users of this book, I would like to express my appreciation.

Julie S. Vargas, President
B. F. Skinner Foundation
Cambridge, Massachusetts

CONTENTS

FOREWORD

A Matter of *Record*

In the analysis of behavior, a cumulative record is a graph that conveniently shows how behavior changes over time. It is produced in the laboratory by a marking device that moves horizontally at a constant rate over time and vertically with each response in steps of constant size. Thus, the record becomes steeper with faster responding and shallower with slower responding, so that moment-to-moment changes in rate of responding can easily be seen as changes in the slope of the record. As the title for a collection of papers by B. F. Skinner, the person who first used the cumulative recorder in studying behavior, *Cumulative Record* is a pun of sorts, as the author himself noted in the First Edition's Preface, which directly follows this Foreword.

The First Edition. According to a letter to Skinner from Dana Ferrin, the president of Appleton-Century-Crofts, this book was first published on April 27, 1959 [4/5/1960 letter from DHF to BFS]. It included 427 pages with thirty papers, fewer than half of those Skinner had published by then.

Most of the papers were preceded by introductions. These were usually brief, sometimes no more than an acknowledgment of permission to reprint. But on about a dozen occasions the introductions either placed an article in its intellectual context or described the circumstances of its creation. Upon reading them after publication, however, Skinner had strong second thoughts about their appropriateness. In a 1960 letter to Dana Ferrin, his publisher, he had described his concerns this way:

> . . . I am wondering how the sales have gone and how near you are to a reprinting. I am unhappy about the introductory materials. I don't believe the light touch which I intended always comes off, and I hope eventually to see a soberer presentation, possibly with all of the commentaries omitted. During the next two or three years, other papers will be turning up which might be included and which should add to its sales. For example, a

recent paper of mine on our wartime work on pigeon-directed missiles is
attracting attention and would be worth including in a new edition. . . . What would you think of an eventual second edition, . . . adding
a few published papers but four or five unpublished papers? [BFS to DHF,
3/30/1960]

Years later Skinner described his doubts about the introductions, as well
as the origins of the book itself, in *A Matter of Consequences* (1983), the
final volume of his autobiography:

> For years I had had a sublime faith that the truth would prevail. I was
> quite content to get my papers into print somewhere; those who needed
> them would find them. (It was a useful principle, for it permitted me to
> continue working in isolation when isolation was probably more valuable
> than being influential.) I may have been right about a future historian of
> ideas grubbing about in a library, but I was wrong about my contemporar-
> ies. They were not reading all my work, and in taking stock during my
> Putney sabbatical I considered putting together a book of collected papers.
> I could think of eighteen that could be included, but when the manuscript
> went off in October 1958, it contained thirty. I called the book *Cumula-
> tive Record* . . . . (p. 163)

> Perhaps because I was getting a book "for nothing," I went about pre-
> paring *Cumulative Record* in a curiously debonair way. The very title was a
> pun. My preface contained a cumulative curve showing the number of
> words in the papers plotted against the year of publication (and the pub-
> lishers put it on the cover above my name). I wrote a brief introduction for
> each paper and added "A Word about Boxes."

> When I saw my first copy, I knew that something was wrong: I had
> been boasting! I had told the reader that "Freedom and the Control of
> Men" had been reprinted in the French and Italian editions of *Perspectives
> U.S.A.*; that Gertrude Stein had said of me as a psychologist that ". . .
> when he is not too serious he is a pretty good one"; that although my
> chapter in *The Behavior of Organisms* on "The Conceptual Nervous Sys-
> tem" had been "interpreted as showing an anti-physiological or anti-
> neurological bias," I believed the book was "a positive contribution to
> physiology"; that when a questionnaire was sent to seventy-three couples
> who had used baby-tenders for one hundred thirty babies, all but three
> had described the device as "wonderful . . . with physical and psychological
> benefits [which] seemed to warrant extensive research. . . ." (pp. 163–164)

I was dismayed. I was advertising the "Skinner Box," dropping names, and showing off my Latin and my wit by *punning* in Latin. What would the many friends to whom I had sent copies think of me? Dick Herrnstein was one of them, and my anxiety was somewhat assuaged when he was surprised to hear that I was concerned. Had anyone criticized me? He thought the material was charming. But I suffered acutely, and within a year I had persuaded the publishers to bring out an enlarged edition. It was "enlarged" by the addition of only three papers, added without repaginating, but with most of the offending material removed. As I wrote in a note: "Gone are the personal touches . . . gone is my acute shame in thinking about them." (p. 165)

Despite Skinner's unease with some aspects of his book, his fourth in seven years, he could hardly have done better in its reception. The major review, by Harold Schlosberg in the January 1960 issue of the American Psychological Association's *Contemporary Psychology*, began with the flattering words "Long have I regarded Fred Skinner as a potential third member of a trinity, along with Freud and Pavlov." Although Schlosberg quite properly concluded his review by noting that any final evaluation of Skinner's contributions would rest with future generations, he made clear his own admiration for their importance and consistency. He made no comment on the suitability of the introductory material.

The Enlarged Edition. In early April 1960, Dana Ferrin reported to Skinner that about 1,200 copies of *Cumulative Record* had been sold during the 11 months since publication. "Since we printed 2,500 copies, there is little likelihood of our running a new printing in less than two years. However, one can never tell." [4/5/1960 letter from DHF to BFS] Sales must have continued strong because another printing followed in 1961, affording Skinner the opportunity to deal with his misgivings about the introductions as well as to add a few articles. The three papers that he added were "The Design of Cultures," "Why We Need Teaching Machines," and "Pigeons in a Pelican."

He dealt with his "acute shame" in several ways. First, he changed the tone of his prose. Compare the vigorous first paragraph of the original introduction to "The Concept of the Reflex in the Description of Behavior" to his revision. "This paper . . . still seems to me important for three reasons. In the first place, it was an early example of . . . ." was compressed to "This paper . . . was an early example of . . . ." He now avoided writing in first person: "I believe the clue to the definition of reflex came from Bertrand Russell" became "The clue to the definition of reflex may have come from Bertrand Russell." A few sentences later, "I supported the argument with a Machian analysis . . . ." became "The argument could be supported by a Machian analysis . . . ." He sometimes diminished the informality of his prose, discarding a sentence in the introduction to "Psychology in the Understanding of Mental Disease" that stated: "My own scattered comments reveal a concern with the operational definition of terms in the field . . . ."

Not all of the "offending material" that caused him such distress was modified. For example, he did not back off from asserting that ". . . a statement of behavioral facts in a form which most readily makes contact with physiological concepts and methods" constitutes "a positive contribution to physiology." He continued to note that "Freedom and the Control of Men" had been reprinted in the French and Italian editions of *Perspectives U.S.A.* And, in the introduction to "A Case History in Scientific Method," which was his response to a request for a quite formal paper, the mild "My reaction was the present paper" became the stronger and more accurate "The present paper scarcely follows this plan."

The introduction to "Has Gertrude Stein a Secret?" caused Skinner perhaps the most discomfort. He shortened it by half, removing the paragraph on Harvard's Society of Fellows, where he had called attention to the fact that his paper was the first to be published by a Junior Prize Fellow and listed some of the Harvard luminaries with whom the fellows dined weekly, a group that included Alfred North Whitehead as well as the university's president and immediate past-president. He also excised the final paragraph, which was devoted to Miss Stein's reaction to the article itself when it first appeared in the *Atlantic Monthly* and which contained the words of praise he cited in the quotation given above from his autobiography.

The last article in the First Edition was Skinner's contribution to the October 1945 issue of the *Ladies Home Journal,* "Baby in a Box." For the Enlarged Edition, he left unchanged his introduction, where he reported on the overwhelmingly favorable reviews his "Air-Crib" had received from users, but removed the free-standing afterword, "A Word about Boxes," in which he first recounted the origin of the magazine article's title—the editors had supplied it—and the numerous ways in which boxes had entered his life (baby box, Skinner box, even the teaching machine), and then told of the occasion where he was prompted to make the delightful "box populi" Latin pun that later caused him grief when he saw it in print and concluded that he had been "showing off my Latin and my wit."

The Third Edition. In November 1969, Skinner wrote to Jack Burton, his editor at Appleton-Century-Crofts, as follows:

> I am currently at work on three papers given during the past year, each of which is to be published in an appropriate place. I shall then be turning

my attention entirely to book length manuscripts. This seems, therefore, a good time to think of a third edition of *Cumulative Record*. I very much doubt whether I will be writing any other papers during the next five years. A third edition of *Cumulative Record* would, therefore, serve for many years as the one convenient source of all my papers not reprinted elsewhere.

After describing the articles that he wanted to add or delete, Skinner concluded:

> In summary I am proposing to add five substantial papers and several short articles. This seems to me to justify a new edition particularly in view of the fact that there will be no other articles to add for at least many years to come. [BFS to JKB, 11/10/1969]

(Note that Skinner was unduly pessimistic about his subsequent productivity; in addition to his books, he published about four papers per year for the next two decades.)

A few weeks later, Jack Burton agreed that a new edition was appropriate but, noting that they still had "a little over one year's supply on hand," suggested that they aim for publication "early in 1971." [JKB to BFS, 11/25/1969]

The 604-page Third Edition actually appeared in 1972. It contained 18 additional papers, but two articles on teaching machines were deleted because they had been revised and included in *The Technology of Teaching* (1968). Also deleted were the excerpts from "Some Contributions of an Experimental Analysis of Behavior to Psychology as a Whole," which had appeared under the title "The Analysis of Behavior (excerpts)" in the earlier editions. Thus this edition contained 48 papers. Among the additional 18 papers were five that were published prior to 1961 when the Enlarged Edition had appeared. The inclusion of this material plus the addition of a subtitle, "A Selection of Papers," made the nature of the collection more explicit. (Skinner's original selection criteria were set forth in the First Edition's introduction to his paper on alliteration in Shakespeare's sonnets; see page 431 of this volume.)

Almost all introductory material was omitted from the Third Edition; Skinner included no comment on any paper before "Has Gertrude Stein a Secret?," more than half way through the book. There he moved the shortened introduction of the Enlarged Edition to the end, offering it as an epilogue (see the Appendix). Only four papers now contained introductions, all from the more technical sections of the book. He kept the introductions to "Two Types of Conditioned Reflex: A Reply to Konorski and Miller" and "The Processes Involved in the Repeated Guessing of Alternatives," omitting only a single sentence from the latter (see the Note in the Appendix). The already thoroughly massaged introduction to "The Concept of the Reflex in the Description of Behavior" was retained and is included in the Appendix so that it may be compared with the First Edition version, which starts on page 475 of the present volume.

In the introduction to the Estes and Skinner paper, "Some Quantitative Properties of Anxiety," Skinner had originally written that the behavioral technique they described ". . . has proved to be a useful baseline in studying measures which 'relieve anxiety' in human subjects." This was no more than a statement of fact; by that time many pharmaceutical companies were using variants of the procedure as part of their efforts in the rapidly growing field of psychopharmacology. Nevertheless, he dropped this sentence from the Third Edition.

Apart from his 1960 statement in the first letter to Dana Ferrin cited above—"I don't believe the light touch that I intended always comes off, and I hope eventually to see a soberer presentation, possibly with all the commentaries omitted"—nothing we have found in Skinner's correspondence with his publisher alluded to dropping the introductory commentaries. Since it was he who prepared a paste-up manuscript for this revision from cut sheets provided by his editor, Skinner probably simply deleted most of the introductions at that time. [JKB to BFS, 11/25/1969; BFS to JKB, 12/1/1969]

We do know that saving space was not a consideration in the deletions. Acting with remarkable foresight shortly after publication, one of us, near the end of a letter dealing with other matters, asked Skinner why he had made these changes.

> . . . I was disturbed to see that the new edition of *Cumulative Record* does not contain the introductions to the articles that appeared in the earlier editions. I missed them and think that the readers will miss them. I hope you write introductions for some of the articles that you add to the next edition. These are little footnotes to history which are valuable; I hate to see them jettisoned to save a few pennies on the price of a book. [VGL to BFS, 9/1/1972]

Skinner replied:

> The introductory material was not left out of the third edition for reasons of economy. It was my own decision and I thought it had the advantage of cementing the book as such rather than keeping it disjointed as a collection of papers. Maybe I was wrong. [BFS to VGL, 9/14/1972]

A decade later, in the poignant "Epilogue" to *A Matter of Consequences* (1983), some pages after recalling: "I have said that 'I was taught to fear God, the police, and what people will think,'" this is how Skinner addressed his emotional reaction to the first appearance of the introductory material:

I now see that I greatly exaggerated the extent to which the first edition
of *Cumulative Record* was boastful and that I suffered unnecessarily. [p. 410]

––––––––

Four features of previous editions deserve brief mention before we describe the present volume: the revisions made by Skinner in the successive
prefaces, his revisions within articles, his choice of a title, and his use of
quotations.

The three prefaces. The prefaces also reflected their author's attempt to
switch to a more impersonal voice. All three immediately follow this Foreword. In the Preface to the First Edition, Skinner included a figure showing the total words contained in the papers chosen for the book, plotted
cumulatively, for the years between 1930 and 1958, and devoted most of
the Preface to discussing the figure. He had published approximately
160,000 words, averaging about 3,600 words per year through 1955 and
23,000 per year for the next three years, "a period of heightened activity"
that reflected a sharp increase in invited papers. This did not include his
books, which he noted constituted competing behavior for writing other
papers. He used labeled arrowheads on the cumulative record to indicate
when the five books had been written. Also excluded from the graph were
"19 papers which would greatly have increased the slope between 1931
and 1937" but had been used in *The Behavior of Organisms* (1938). He
also pointed out that *Schedules of Reinforcement* (with Charles B. Ferster,
1957) contained material that "would normally have appeared in papers
during the early 50's."

For the much shorter Preface in the 1961 Enlarged Edition, Skinner
updated the cumulative record but removed the book titles and arrowheads. As in the revised introductions, he moved to the passive voice and
excised almost all discussion of his own behavior. He mentioned neither
his editorial changes to the introductions nor his excision of "A Word About
Boxes," the afterword that had accompanied "Baby in a Box."

The Preface to the 1972 Third Edition was only nine lines long and the
cumulative record itself disappeared, the author noting that "there seems
to be no point in extending the cumulative record which appeared in earlier editions to explain my title."

We contemplated preparing an updated cumulative record for this new
edition, but it was not feasible for us to undertake word counts across the
many articles published with different fonts in different formats, nor could
we resolve the problem of units. Publication counts that weigh a single-
paragraph book review as heavily as entire books are inadequate, and even
word counts fail to consider the contribution of figures rich in data. If one

picture is worth a thousand words, then *Schedules of Reinforcement* outweighs all of his other work; it includes more than 900 figures. We leave it for others to explore such quantification when all of Skinner's writings are eventually available in an electronic format that would ease the labor of such a task. (One attempt, displaying cumulative plots of books and other publications separately, appears on the B. F. Skinner Foundation Internet site, in connection with an extensive bibliography originally compiled by Epstein for Todd & Morris (1995).

Skinner's revisions within articles. Skinner's copies of the first two editions have notes in his hand that perhaps were plans for changes to be incorporated into the Third Edition. For example, the third paragraph of "The Operational Analysis of Psychological Terms," which begins with "The operationist . . . ," had been rewritten in the plural, "Operationists . . . ," thereby allowing him to replace the later "He has not . . ." with the ungendered "They have not . . . ." But these and other changes were never made. Perhaps Skinner had reservations about archival problems if the reprinted versions no longer agreed with the originals. He even identified but let stand some substantive and grammatical errors. For example, the seventh paragraph in the section "Complex Learning" in "Are Theories of Learning Necessary?" ends with an example in which the 50 percent success rate by chance of a pigeon's matching-to-sample responses is referred to as fixed ratio reinforcement. Although Skinner corrected his copy to "variable ratio," the text remained as "fixed ratio" in all editions.

In other contexts, Skinner did revise some of his earlier work. For example, when he later prepared some of his classic papers for commentary in the special December 1984 issue of the journal *Behavioral and Brain Sciences* (revised as Catania & Harnad, 1988), he eliminated much of the sexist language and modernized some of the technical vocabulary (e.g., replacing *periodic* with *intermittent*, and *induction* with *generalization*). He also revised some passages in which he had written about the reinforcement of organisms, changing them so that responses were instead reinforced.

Cumulative Record as a title. *Cumulative Record*, first appearing in 1959, was Skinner's sixth book, and its punning title was totally original, at least within psychology.[1] So were the titles of his fourth and fifth books, *Schedules of Reinforcement* and *Verbal Behavior*, both published two years earlier in 1957.

---

[1] *Nature and Use of the Cumulative Record* (Segel, 1938)—a monograph published the same year as *The Behavior of Organisms*—was concerned with record keeping in school guidance programs!

For his first three books, Skinner had used names which resonated with titles used by others. The choice of *The Behavior of Organisms* may have been influenced by Jacques Loeb's *The Organism as a Whole* (1916), which he had read while an undergraduate (Skinner, 1976, p. 296; cf. Catania, 1992, for a discussion of the significance of the term "organism" in Skinner's writings), and perhaps by Herbert S. Jennings' *Behavior of the Lower Organisms* (1906). *Walden Two* (1948), of course, pays tribute to Thoreau's *Walden*. *Science and Human Behavior* (1953) resembles *Science and the Modern World* (1925), the book that attracted him to Alfred North Whitehead's course at Harvard (Skinner, 1979, p. 30) and which, incidentally, contains the statement: "Science is taking on a new aspect that is neither purely physical nor purely biological. It is becoming the study of organisms" (Whitehead, 1925, p. 103).

In choosing *The Analysis of Behavior* (1961) as the title of the programmed text he co-authored with J. G. Holland only two years after *Cumulative Record* appeared, Skinner may have been influenced by the name of a course he took with W. J. Crozier during his first year as a graduate student at Harvard, "The Analysis of Conduct." ("Crozier used 'conduct' because Watson and the psychologists had sullied 'behavior.'"—Skinner, 1979, p. 44)

The use of quotations. Skinner always had an eye for felicitous statements by others and frequently relied upon an apt quotation to help make a point. The very first paragraph of *Science and Human Behavior* contains a long direct quotation from a seventeenth century scientist, Francesco Lana, upon which Skinner bases a discussion of the use and misuse of science. In *Particulars of My Life*, he credits his friend Alf Evers' remark that "Science is the art of the twentieth century" with influencing his turn from literature to science (Skinner, 1976, p. 291). Incidentally, his title is from Shakespeare's *Henry IV*, Part I: "Do thou stand for my father and examine me on the particulars of my life" and he placed the quotation on a page among the front matter. Near the end of *Walden Two*, he quotes a passage from Thoreau's *Walden*, which concludes with the delightful sentence, "The sun is but a morning star." This was his original title for the book, changed at the last minute because another star title was already on the market (Skinner, 1979, p. 330).

Many of Skinner's articles, especially those aimed at general audiences, quote liberally, usually from literary rather than scientific sources. The first paper in this collection, "Freedom and the Control of Men," is especially notable, with quotations from Marcus Aurelius, Dostoevsky, Lord Acton, Ralph Barton Perry, Joseph Wood Krutch, T. H. Huxley, T. S. Eliot, Aldous Huxley, and Dean Acheson.

The earlier editions of *Cumulative Record* contained a single freestanding quotation on a page otherwise blank, from Shakespeare's *Timon of Athens*. It can be found on page 68 of this volume and is one of the only two instances where Shakespeare used a word that Skinner much later claimed for his own: ". . . sauce his palate with thy most operant poison." The other, from *Hamlet*, now appears on page 660 of this edition.

This "Definitive" Edition. *Cumulative Record* was not Skinner's only collection of papers. Just before publishing the Third Edition, he combined nine papers with some other material to produce *Contingencies of Reinforcement: A Theoretical Analysis* (1969). Six years after the Third Edition, *Reflections on Behaviorism and Society* (1978) appeared, containing 18 articles published from 1972 through 1978. *Upon Further Reflection* (1987) included 14 more papers, all but one of which had been published during the 1980's. Finally, *Recent Issues in the Analysis of Behavior* (1989), published the year before he died, contained 12 more from 1986 or later. In the Preface to that final book, he listed only these five collections, apparently not considering *The Technology of Teaching* (1968) to be a collection in the same sense as the others because only four of its 11 chapters had previously been published.

Merely reprinting the Third Edition of *Cumulative Record,* which went out of print some years ago, was a course of action that was entertained briefly but rejected. Given the history as outlined in this Foreword, a more appropriate choice for this volume seemed to be an edition containing significant features from all the prior editions. First, all 48 articles in the Third Edition have been retained and all of those items that Skinner used earlier but then omitted from that edition are again included. Second, two "new" articles (see below) have been added. Third, all of the First Edition's introductions have been restored to their original positions, in light of Skinner's change of heart concerning this material. The two introductions from the 1961 "Enlarged Edition" that Skinner modified most extensively are presented in an Appendix. Lastly, Robert Epstein and Julia Becerra have provided a highly useful Index to this volume. We have also included an index to the pagination of each article in each edition of *Cumulative Record* on pages 698 through 700.

Because any editorial tinkering with the text itself would have produced a flawed archival document, none has been attempted. As it stands, the book exhibits the evolution of Skinner's thinking and writing style and is therefore a cultural and historical document as well as a scientific one.

Reinstated and newly added articles. Three papers that appeared in the first two editions but were deleted from the third have been reinstated: "The Science of Learning and the Art of Teaching," "Teaching Machines," and "The Analysis of Behavior (excerpts)." The short commentary, "A Word About Boxes," which only appeared in the First Edition, now appears on page 620, following "Baby in a Box."

Two articles without a history of inclusion in any earlier edition have been added to this edition. They were published roughly half a century apart.

The first, "The Psychology of Design," appeared in a 1941 issue of *Art Education Today*. It represents an early exercise by Skinner in applying psychological principles to the understanding of visual art. Skinner omitted most of his experimental papers from *Cumulative Record* on the grounds that they had been incorporated in revised form into other books (especially *The Behavior of Organisms*). He also omitted replies that would not stand alone and short technical items of specialized interest. But he included all other papers on topics of general interest such as art and literature. This was the only one we identified from the relevant time period for which there seemed no rationale for exclusion. We found nothing to suggest that Skinner was dissatisfied with the paper (he even briefly discussed it in the second volume of his autobiography—Skinner, 1979, p. 238). Those close to him regard it as unlikely that he lost track of the paper, even given the intervening events of World War II and his subsequent academic moves. One guess is that some technical problem accounts for its omission. For example, if he had included his only copies of the art for the figures when he submitted the article for publication, copies suitable for printing would not have been available at the time when this book was first published.

The second newly added paper is "Can Psychology be a Science of Mind?" The American Psychological Association presented Skinner with its first Citation for Outstanding Lifetime Contribution to Psychology at its 1990 annual meeting in Boston, and this paper was his response to that award. He delivered his talk on August 10. On August 17, in the hospital on the day before he died of leukemia, he put the finishing touches to the written version. This was his most important paper since those collected in *Recent Issues in the Analysis of Behavior*, which had appeared the previous year, and it deserves to conclude this version of *Cumulative Record*.

The current contents. The range of topics included in this collection defies summary and our temptation is to let the articles speak for themselves. Shortly after its publication, the Third Edition of *Cumulative Record* became a main selection of the Behavioral Science Book Service. The Service presciently invited one of us (ACC) to prepare a review for the flier that announced it. The review describes that edition as "a collection of 48 papers by one of the most controversial figures of our time. To say why this collection is worth reading, a reviewer has little more to do than list some of the topics: scientific method; teaching machines; ESP; ethics; the design of cultures; babies; poetry and creativity; pigeons; anxiety; Pavlov; psychoanalysis." Later it continues: "Variety is one remarkable feature of this collection . . . here are such classics as 'The Concept of the Reflex in the Description of Behavior' and 'Are Theories of Learning Necessary?' . . . But poetry and literary analysis are represented also." By including a sample list of topics, the review shares a feature of many of the reviews of *Cumulative Record* that appeared at the time of the earlier editions (Knapp, 1974, pp. 37–38).

The review argues that the variety is important not so much because the book will appeal to different readers, but also because "so many have assumed that the behavioral point of view is necessarily narrow and intellectually confining . . . . The cumulative effect of the papers in this collection will be to set the record straight." The review continues: "It would be misleading to emphasize the variety in these writings without also mentioning their coherence." That coherence can hardly be understated, especially given that the papers in this selection were written over a period of more than forty years—and about sixty if we include the last paper in this edition; cf. Epstein, 1995.

The body of work represented here varies stylistically as well as substantively. As it ranges from the relatively formal prose of "The Generic Nature of the Concepts of Stimulus and Response" to the more informal prose of "How to Teach Animals," and from the implications for literature of "A Lecture on 'Having' a Poem" to the implications for education of "The Science of Learning and the Art of Teaching," Skinner reminds us again and again that behavior is a subject matter in its own right. The analysis of behavior must justify itself in its own terms. It is of course related to other sciences and to other levels of analysis but it need not appeal to them to legitimize its basic units or to verify its taxonomy of behavioral processes. This stance on the primacy of behavior is even more fundamental to the enterprise of behavior analysis than is our understanding of such phenomena as the three-term contingency and the shaping of behavior by its consequences. This singular contribution by Skinner made all of the others possible.

Whether he dealt with pressing levers, behaving ethically, looking at paintings, pecking keys, writing poems, talking, teaching, designing cultures, pushing buttons, doing experiments, or knowing, Skinner offered explanations of behavior in its own terms. Consistent with the opening paragraph of "Are Theories of Learning Necessary?" he did not appeal to "events taking place somewhere else, at some other level of observation, described in different terms, and measured, if at all, in different dimensions." Whenever Skinner dealt with the details of looking and other examples of discriminating, or with talking and thinking in the contexts of education and literature, or with social interactions as instances of cultural practices, or with the role of the environment in mental disease, he extended the boundaries of what we count as behavior. And when he examined his own behavior and scientific behavior in general, as in "A Case History in Scientific Method" or "The Flight from the Laboratory," he even turned behavior analysis upon itself.

The record shows that the earliest paper in this collection, "The Concept of the Reflex in the Description of Behavior," was written during the summer of 1930 (Skinner, 1979, p. 67). The latest, "Can Psychology Be a Science of Mind?" was finished almost exactly 60 years later. These six decades contain a cumulative record of accomplishment that will not soon be matched.

VICTOR G. LATIES
University of Rochester

A. CHARLES CATANIA
University of Maryland Baltimore County

December, 1998

We extend our thanks to the Harvard University Archives for courteously providing access to B. F. Skinner's papers; to John Gach for a helpful discussion of significant features of historic books in psychology; and, above all, to Julie Vargas and the B. F. Skinner Foundation for giving us the opportunity to undertake this labor of love.

References

CATANIA, A. C. (1992). B. F. Skinner, organism, *American Psychologist, 47,* 1521–1530.

CATANIA, A. C. and HARNAD, S. (Eds.). (1988). *The selection of behavior: The operant behaviorism of B. F. Skinner.* Cambridge: Cambridge University Press.

EPSTEIN, R. (1995). An updated bibliography of B. F. Skinner's works. In Todd, J. T. & Morris, E. K. (Eds.) *Modern perspectives on B. F. Skinner and contemporary behaviorism* (pp. 217–226). Westport, CT: Greenwood Press.

FERSTER, C. B. and SKINNER, B. F. (1957). *Schedules of reinforcement.* New York: Appleton-Century-Crofts.

HOLLAND, J. G. AND SKINNER, B. F. (1961). *The analysis of behavior.* New York: McGraw-Hill.

KNAPP, T. J. (1974). *Reference guide to B. F. Skinner: A comprehensive bibliography of published works by and concerning B. F. Skinner from 1929 through 1973.* Reno, NV: Clifford Press.

JENNINGS, H. S. (1906). *Behavior of the lower organisms.* New York: Macmillan.

LOEB, J. (1916). *The organism as a whole.* New York: Putnam's Sons.

SCHLOSBERG, H. (1960). Is this a new Messiah? *Contemporary Psychology, 5,* 35–36.

SEGEL, D. (1938). *Nature and use of the cumulative record.* Bulletin 1938, No. 3. Washington, DC: U.S. Government Printing Office.

SKINNER, B. F. (1938). *The behavior of organisms.* New York: Appleton-Century-Crofts.

SKINNER, B. F. (1948). *Walden two.* New York: Macmillan.

SKINNER, B. F. (1953). *Science and human behavior.* New York: Macmillan.

SKINNER, B. F. (1957). *Verbal behavior.* New York: Appleton-Century-Crofts.

SKINNER, B. F. (1968). *The technology of teaching.* New York: Appleton-Century-Crofts.

SKINNER, B. F. (1969). *Contingencies of reinforcement.* New York: Appleton-Century-Crofts.

SKINNER, B. F. (1976). *Particulars of my life.* New York: Knopf.

SKINNER, B. F. (1978). *Reflections on behaviorism and society.* Englewood Cliffs, NJ: Prentice-Hall.

SKINNER, B. F. (1979). *The shaping of a behaviorist: Part two of an autobiography.* New York: Knopf.

SKINNER, B. F. (1983). *A matter of consequences: Part three of an autobiography.* New York: Knopf.

SKINNER, B. F. (1987). *Upon further reflection.* Englewood Cliffs, NJ: Prentice-Hall.

SKINNER, B. F. (1989). *Recent issues in the analysis of behavior.* Columbus, OH: Merrill.

WHITEHEAD, A. N. (1926). *Science and the modern world.* New York: Macmillan.

PREFACES TO THE EARLIER EDITIONS

First Edition (1959)

The reader who is not familiar with the expression "cumulative record" should take the royal road to knowledge starting on page 178 [p. 212 in this volume]. Further illustrations appear in Part II. As the title of a collection of papers, the expression is not a metaphor, since the behavior of which the papers are a product can be plotted cumulatively. Certain familiar problems arise. It is hard to identify the units of behavior to be counted, and the curve may neglect other behavior of a similar nature occurring at the same time. Rather arbitrary solutions to these problems do not wholly destroy the significance of the result. Plotting total number of pages against the years in which the papers reprinted here were published, we get Figure 1. It reveals a relatively constant slope (a steady output) for the twenty-five year period from 1930 to 1955. A period of heightened activity then follows.

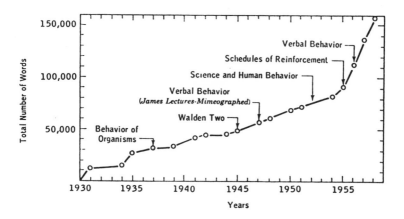

Fig. 1. Cumulative record of the verbal behavior recorded in this book.

The principal competing behavior consisted of writing several books, the manuscripts of which were completed at the points indicated. These will be referred to throughout the present volume by name only. Full citations are as follows:

The Behavior of Organisms. New York: Appleton-Century, 1938.

Walden Two. New York: Macmillan, 1948.

Science and Human Behavior. New York: Macmillan, 1953.

Schedules of Reinforcement (with C. B. Ferster). New York: Appleton-Century-Crofts, 1957.

Verbal Behavior. New York: Appleton-Century-Crofts, 1957.

Some of these books included material previously published in papers not reprinted here (and hence not included in the graph). Thus, the *Behavior of Organisms* contains material from 19 papers which would greatly have increased the slope between 1930 and 1937 if included in the curve. *Schedules of Reinforcement* contains material which would normally have appeared in papers during the early 50's. As a report of my verbal behavior, therefore, the rise in slope after 1954 is unduly delayed. The low slope during the 40's is "real," however, and reflects other activities—principally war research and, later, administration.

The sharply increased slope during the last four years of the graph is due to a change in the variables controlling my behavior. Most of the papers published during this period were "occasional" pieces—that is, they were written because I was asked to write them. Evidently my verbal behavior is strongly controlled by the audience variable (see *Verbal Behavior,* Chapter 7).

My thanks are due to the editors and publishers who have kindly given permission to reprint. Specific acknowledgement is made in the introduction to each article. I also have to thank Mrs. Patricia Pershan for her careful help in preparing the manuscript.

Cambridge, Mass.   B. F. S.

Enlarged Edition (1961)

If the expression "cumulative record" is not familiar to the reader, he may wish to take the royal road to knowledge starting on page 178 [p. 212 in this volume]. Further illustrations appear in Part II. On the principle that turnabout is fair play, the behavior of which the present papers are a product has been plotted cumulatively in Figure 1. Certain familiar problems arise. It is hard to identify units of behavior to be counted, and the curve neglects other behavior of a similar nature occurring at the same time. Arbitrary solutions to these problems do not wholly destroy the significance of the result. When total number of pages is plotted against year of publication, the curve shows a relatively constant slope (indicating a steady output) for the twenty-five year period from 1930 to 1955 and a later period of heightened activity.

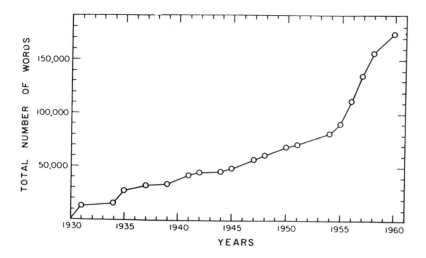

FIG. 1. Cumulative record of the verbal behavior recorded in this book.

The principal competing behavior consisted of the following books, referred to throughout the present volume by name only:

The Behavior of Organisms. New York: Appleton-Century, 1938.

Walden Two. New York: Macmillan, 1948.

Science and Human Behavior. New York: Macmillan, 1953.

Schedules of Reinforcement (with C. B. Ferster). New York: Appleton-Century-Crofts, 1957.

Verbal Behavior. New York: Appleton-Century-Crofts, 1957.

Three papers have been added to this second printing: as an addendum to Part I, "The Design of Cultures;" as an addendum to Part III, "Why We Need Teaching Machines;" and as an addendum to Part VIII, "Pigeons in a Pelican."

Cambridge, Mass.   B. F. S.

Third Edition (1972)

Eighteen papers have been added to this edition, and two which may now be found in *The Technology of Teaching* have been removed. Not all the new material is recent, and there seems to be no point in extending my title.

Preparation of papers 6, 13, 14, 18, 19, 22, and 29 [these correspond to the articles that begin on pp. 58, 254, 271, 322, 329, 379, and 467 in this volume] and editorial work on this edition as a whole have been supported by a Career Award from the National Institutes of Mental Health (Grant K6-MH-21, 775-01).

B. F. Skinner

PART I

The Implications of a Science of Behavior for Human Affairs, Especially for the Concept of Freedom

Freedom and the Control of Men
The Control of Human Behavior (Abstract)
Some Issues Concerning the Control of Human Behavior
The Design of Cultures
"Man"
The Design of Experimental Communities

Freedom and the Control of Men

Originally written for a special issue of The American Scholar (*Winter, 1955-56*) *devoted to "The Human Situation Today," at the suggestion of the editor, Hiram Haydn, this article has been reprinted in* Perspectives U.S.A. *and, in translation, in the French and Italian editions of that quarterly.*

The second half of the twentieth century may be remembered for its solution of a curious problem. Although Western democracy created the conditions responsible for the rise of modern science, it is now evident that it may never fully profit from that achievement. The so-called "democratic philosophy" of human behavior to which it also gave rise is increasingly in conflict with the application of the methods of science to human affairs. Unless this conflict is somehow resolved, the ultimate goals of democracy may be long deferred.

I

Just as biographers and critics look for external influences to account for the traits and achievements of the men they study, so science ultimately explains behavior in terms of "causes" or conditions which lie beyond the individual himself. As more and more causal relations are demonstrated, a practical corollary becomes difficult to resist: it should be possible to *produce* behavior according to plan simply by arranging the proper conditions. Now, among the specifications which might reasonably be submitted to a behavioral technology are these: Let men be happy, informed, skillful, well behaved, and productive.

This immediate practical implication of a science of behavior has a familiar ring, for it recalls the doctrine of human perfectibility of eighteenth- and nineteenth-century humanism. A science of man shares the optimism of that philosophy and supplies striking support for the working faith that men can build a better world and, through it, better men. The support comes just in time, for there has been little optimism of late among those who speak from the traditional point of view. Democracy

3

has become "realistic," and it is only with some embarrassment that one admits today to perfectionistic or utopian thinking.

The earlier temper is worth considering, however. History records many foolish and unworkable schemes for human betterment, but almost all the great changes in our culture which we now regard as worthwhile can be traced to perfectionistic philosophies. Governmental, religious, educational, economic, and social reforms follow a common pattern. Someone believes that a change in a cultural practice—for example, in the rules of evidence in a court of law, in the characterization of man's relation to God, in the way children are taught to read and write, in permitted rates of interest, or in minimal housing standards—will improve the condition of men: by promoting justice, permitting men to seek salvation more effectively, increasing the literacy of a people, checking an inflationary trend, or improving public health and family relations, respectively. The underlying hypothesis is always the same: that a different physical or cultural environment will make a different and better man.

The scientific study of behavior not only justifies the general pattern of such proposals; it promises new and better hypotheses. The earliest cultural practices must have originated in sheer accidents. Those which strengthened the group survived with the group in a sort of natural selection. As soon as men began to propose and carry out changes in practice for the sake of possible consequences, the evolutionary process must have accelerated. The simple practice of making changes must have had survival value. A further acceleration is now to be expected. As laws of behavior are more precisely stated, the changes in the environment required to bring about a given effect may be more clearly specified. Conditions which have been neglected because their effects were slight or unlooked for may be shown to be relevant. New conditions may actually be created, as in the discovery and synthesis of drugs which affect behavior.

This is no time, then, to abandon notions of progress, improvement, or, indeed, human perfectibility. The simple fact is that man is able, and now as never before, to lift himself by his own bootstraps. In achieving control of the world of which he is a part, he may learn at last to control himself.

II

Timeworn objections to the planned improvement of cultural practices are already losing much of their force. Marcus Aurelius was probably right in advising his readers to be content with a haphazard amelioration of mankind. "Never hope to realize Plato's republic," he sighed, ". . . for who can change the opinions of men? And without a change of sentiments what can you make but reluctant slaves and hypocrites?" He was thinking, no doubt, of contemporary patterns of control based upon punishment or the threat of punishment which, as he correctly observed, breed only reluctant slaves of those who submit and hypocrites of those who discover modes of evasion. But we need not share his pessimism, for the opinions of men can be changed. The techniques of indoctrination which were being devised by the early Christian Church at the very time Marcus Aurelius was writing are relevant, as are some of the techniques of psychotherapy and of advertising and public relations. Other methods suggested by recent scientific analyses leave little doubt of the matter.

The study of human behavior also answers the cynical complaint that there is a plain "cussedness" in man which will always thwart efforts to improve him. We are often told that men do not want to be changed, even for the better. Try to help them, and they will outwit you and remain happily wretched. Dostoevsky claimed to see some plan in it. "Out of sheer ingratitude," he complained, or possibly boasted, "man will play you a dirty trick, just to prove that men are still men and not the keys of a piano. . . . And even if you could prove that a man is only a piano key, he would still do something out of sheer perversity—he would create destruction and chaos—just to gain his point. . . . And if all this could in turn be analyzed and prevented by predicting that it would occur, then man would deliberately go mad to prove his point." This is a conceivable neurotic reaction to inept control. A few men may have shown it, and many have enjoyed Dostoevsky's statement because they tend to show it. But that such perversity is a fundamental reaction of the human organism to controlling conditions is sheer nonsense.

So is the objection that we have no way of knowing what changes to make even though we have the necessary techniques. That is one of the great hoaxes of the century—a sort of booby trap left behind in the retreat before the advancing front of science. Scientists themselves have unsuspectingly agreed that there are two kinds of useful prepositions about nature—facts and value judgments—and that science must confine itself to "what is," leaving "what ought to be" to others. But with what special sort of wisdom is the nonscientist endowed? Science is only effective knowing, no matter who engages in it. Verbal behavior proves upon analysis to be composed of many different types of utterances, from poetry and exhortation to logic and factual description, but these are not all equally useful in talking about cultural practices. We may classify useful propositions according to the degrees of confidence with which they may be asserted. Sentences about nature range from highly probable "facts" to sheer guesses. In general, future events are less likely to be correctly described than past. When a scientist talks about a projected experiment, for example, he must often resort to statements having only a moderate likelihood of being correct; he calls them hypotheses.

Designing a new cultural pattern is in many ways like designing an experiment. In drawing up a new constitution, outlining a new educational program, modifying a religious doctrine, or setting up a new fiscal policy, many statements must be quite tentative. We cannot be sure that the practices we specify will have the consequences we predict, or that the consequences will reward our efforts. This is in the nature of such proposals. They are not value judgments—they are guesses. To confuse and delay the improvement of cultural practices by quibbling about the word *improve* is itself not a useful practice. Let us agree, to start with, that health is better than illness, wisdom better than ignorance, love better than hate, and productive energy better than neurotic sloth.

Another familiar objection is the "political problem." Though we know what changes to make and how to make them, we still need to control certain relevant conditions, but these have long since fallen into the hands of selfish men who are not going to relinquish them for such purposes. Possibly we shall be permitted to develop areas which at the moment seem unimportant, but at the first signs of success the strong men will move in. This, it is said, has happened to Christianity, democracy, and communism. There will always be men who are fundamentally selfish and evil, and in the long run innocent goodness cannot have its way. The only evidence here is historical, and it may be misleading. Because of the way in which physical science developed, history could until very recently have "proved" that the unleashing of the energy of the atom was quite unlikely, if not impossible. Similarly, because of the order in which processes in human behavior have become available for purposes of control, history may seem to prove that power will probably be appropriated for selfish purposes. The first techniques to be discovered fell almost always to strong, selfish men. History led Lord Acton to believe that power corrupts, but he had probably never encountered absolute power, certainly not in all its forms, and had no way of predicting its effect.

An optimistic historian could defend a different conclusion. The principle that if there are not enough men of good will in the world the first step is to create more seems to be gaining recognition. The Marshall Plan (as originally conceived), Point Four, the offer of atomic materials to power-starved countries—these may or may not be wholly new in the history of international relations, but they suggest an increasing awareness of the power of governmental good will. They are proposals to make certain changes in the environments of men for the sake of consequences which should be rewarding for all concerned. They do not exemplify a disinterested generosity, but an interest which is the interest of everyone. We have not yet seen Plato's philosopher-king, and may not want to, but the gap between real and utopian government is closing.

III

But we are not yet in the clear, for a new and unexpected obstacle has arisen. With a world of their own making almost within reach, men of good will have been seized with distaste for their achievement. They have uneasily rejected opportunities to apply the techniques and findings of science in the service of men, and as the import of effective cultural design has come to be understood, many of them have voiced an outright refusal to have any part in it. Science has been challenged before when it has encroached upon institutions already engaged in the control of human behavior; but what are we to make of benevolent men, with no special interests of their own to defend, who nevertheless turn against the very means of reaching long-dreamed-of goals?

What is being rejected, of course, is the scientific conception of man and his place in nature. So long as the findings and methods of science are applied to human affairs only in a sort of remedial patchwork, we may continue to hold any view of human nature we like. But as the use of science increases, we are forced to accept the theoretical structure with which science represents its facts. The difficulty is that this structure is clearly at odds with the traditional democratic conception of man. Every discovery of an event which has a part in shaping a man's behavior seems to leave so much the less to be credited to the man himself; and as such explanations become more and more comprehensive, the contribution which may be claimed by the individual himself appears to approach zero. Man's vaunted creative powers, his original accomplishments in art, science, and morals, his capacity to choose and our right to hold him responsible for the consequences of his choice—none of these is conspicuous in this new self-portrait. Man, we once believed, was free to express himself in art, music, and literature, to inquire into nature, to seek salvation in his own way. He could initiate action and make spontaneous and capricious changes of course. Under the most extreme duress some sort of choice remained to him. He could resist any effort to control him, though it might cost him his life. But science insists that action is initiated by forces impinging upon the individual, and that caprice is only another name for behavior for which we have not yet found a cause.

In attempting to reconcile these views it is important to note that the traditional democratic conception was not designed as a description in the scientific sense but as a philosophy to be used in setting up and maintaining a governmental process. It arose under historical circumstances and served political purposes apart from which it cannot be properly understood. In rallying men against tyranny it was necessary that the individual be strengthened, that he be taught that he had rights and could govern himself. To give the common man a new conception of his worth, his dignity, and his power to save himself, both here and hereafter, was often the only resource of the revolutionist. When democratic principles were put into practice, the same doctrines were used as a working formula. This is exemplified by the notion of personal responsibility in Anglo-American law. All governments make certain forms of punishment contingent upon certain kinds of acts. In democratic countries these contingencies are expressed by the notion of responsible choice. But the notion may have no meaning under governmental practices formulated in other ways and would certainly have no place in systems which did not use punishment.

The democratic philosophy of human nature is determined by certain political exigencies and techniques, not by the goals of democracy. But exigencies and techniques change; and a conception which is not supported for its accuracy as a likeness—is not, indeed, rooted in fact at all—may be expected to change too. No matter how effective we judge current democratic practices to be, how highly we value them or how long we expect them to survive, they are almost certainly not the *final* form of government. The philosophy of human nature which has been useful in implementing them is also almost certainly not the last word. The ultimate achievement of democracy may be long deferred unless we emphasize the real aims rather than the verbal devices of democratic thinking. A philosophy which has been appropriate to one set of political exigencies will defeat its purpose if, under other circumstances, it prevents us from applying to human affairs the science of man which probably nothing but democracy itself could have produced.

IV

Perhaps the most crucial part of our democratic philosophy to be reconsidered is our attitude toward freedom—or its reciprocal, the control of human behavior. We do not oppose all forms of control because it is "human nature" to do so. The reaction is not characteristic of all men under all conditions of life. It is an attitude which has been carefully engineered, in large part by what we call the "literature" of democracy. With respect to some methods of control (for example, the threat of force), very little engineering is needed, for the techniques or their immediate consequences are objectionable. Society has suppressed these methods by branding them "wrong," "illegal," or "sinful." But to encourage these attitudes toward objectionable forms of control, it has been necessary to disguise the real nature of certain indispensable techniques, the commonest examples of which are education, moral discourse, and persuasion. The actual procedures appear harmless enough. They consist of supplying information, presenting opportunities for action, pointing out logical relationships, appealing to reason or "enlightened understanding," and so on. Through a masterful piece of misrepresentation, the illusion is fostered that these procedures do not involve the control of behavior; at most, they are simply ways of "getting someone to change his mind." But analysis not only reveals the presence of well-defined behavioral processes, it demonstrates a kind of control no less inexorable, though in some ways more acceptable, than the bully's threat of force.

Let us suppose that someone in whom we are interested is acting unwisely—he is careless in the way he deals with his friends, he drives too fast, or he holds his golf club the wrong way. We could probably help him by issuing a series of commands: don't nag, don't drive over sixty, don't hold your club that way. Much less objectionable would be "an appeal to reason." We could show him how people are affected by his treatment of them, how accident rates rise sharply at higher speeds, how a particular grip on the club alters the way the ball is struck and corrects a slice. In doing so we resort to verbal mediating devices which emphasize and support certain "contingencies of reinforcement"—that is, certain relations between behavior and its consequences—which strengthen the behavior we wish to set up. The same consequences would possibly set up the behavior without our help, and they eventually take control no matter which form of help we give. The appeal to reason has certain advantages over the authoritative command. A threat of punishment, no matter how subtle, generates emotional reactions and tendencies to escape or revolt. Perhaps the controllee merely "feels resentment" at being made to act in a given way, but even that is to be avoided. When we "appeal to reason," he "feels freer to do as he pleases." The fact is that we have exerted *less* control than in using a threat; since other conditions may contribute to the result, the effect may be delayed or, possibly in a given instance, lacking. But if we have worked a change in his behavior at all, it is because we have altered relevant environmental conditions, and the processes we have set in motion are just as real and just as inexorable, if not as comprehensive, as in the most authoritative coercion.

"Arranging an opportunity for action" is another example of disguised control. The power of the negative form has already been exposed in the analysis of censorship. Restriction of opportunity is recognized as far from harmless. As Ralph Barton Perry said in an article which appeared in the Spring, 1953, *Pacific Spectator,* "Whoever determines what alternatives shall be made known to man controls what that man shall choose *from.* He is deprived of freedom in proportion as he is denied access to *any* ideas, or is confined to any range of ideas short of the totality of relevant possibilities." But there is a positive side as well. When we present a relevant state of affairs, we increase the likelihood that a given form of behavior will be emitted. To the extent that the probability of action has changed, we have made a definite contribution. The teacher of history controls a student's behavior (or, if the reader prefers, "deprives him of freedom") just as much in *presenting* historical facts as in suppressing them. Other conditions will no doubt affect the student, but the contribution made to his behavior by the presentation of material is fixed and, within its range, irresistible.

The methods of education, moral discourse, and persuasion are acceptable not because they recognize the freedom of the individual or his right to dissent, but because they make only *partial* contributions to the control of his behavior. The freedom they recognize is freedom from a more coercive form of control. The dissent which they tolerate is the possible effect of other determiners of action. Since these sanctioned methods are frequently ineffective, we have been able to convince ourselves that they do not represent control at all. When they show too much strength to permit disguise, we give them other names and suppress them as energetically as we suppress the use of force. Education grown too powerful is rejected as propaganda or "brain-washing," while really effective persuasion is described as "undue influence," "demagoguery," "seduction," and so on.

If we are not to rely solely upon accident for the innovations which give rise to cultural evolution, we must accept the fact that some kind of control of human behavior is inevitable. We cannot use good sense in human affairs unless someone engages in the design and construction of environmental conditions which affect the behavior of men. Environmental changes have always been the condition for the improvement of cultural patterns, and we can hardly use the more effective methods of science without making changes on a grander scale. We are all controlled by the world in which we live, and part of that world has been and will be constructed by men. The question is this: Are we to be controlled by accident, by tyrants, or by ourselves in effective cultural design?

The danger of the misuse of power is possibly greater than ever. It is not allayed by disguising the facts. We cannot make wise decisions if we continue to pretend that human behavior is not controlled, or if we refuse to engage in control when valuable results might be forthcoming. Such measures weaken only ourselves, leaving the strength of science to others. The first step in a defense against tyranny is the fullest possible exposure of controlling techniques. A second step has already been taken successfully in restricting the use of physical force. Slowly, and as yet imperfectly, we have worked out an ethical and governmental design in which the strong man is not allowed to use the power deriving from his strength to control his fellow men. He is restrained by a superior force created for that purpose—the ethical pressure of the group, or more explicit religious and governmental measures. We tend to distrust superior forces, as we currently hesitate to relinquish sovereignty in order to set up an international police force. But it is only through such counter-control that we have achieved what we call peace—a condition in which men are not permitted to control each other through force. In other words, control itself must be controlled.

Science has turned up dangerous processes and materials before. To use the facts and techniques of a science of man to the fullest extent without making some monstrous mistake will be difficult and obviously perilous. It is no time for self-deception, emotional indulgence, or the assumption of attitudes which are no longer useful. Man is facing a difficult test. He must keep his head now, or he must start again—a long way back.

V

Those who reject the scientific conception of man must, to be logical, oppose the methods of science as well. The position is often supported by predicting a series of dire consequences which are to follow if science is not checked. A recent book by Joseph Wood Krutch, *The Measure of Man,* is in this vein. Mr. Krutch sees in the growing science of man the threat of an unexampled tyranny over men's minds. If science is permitted to have its way, he insists, "we may never be able really to think again." A controlled culture will, for example, lack some virtue inherent in disorder. We have emerged from chaos through a series of happy accidents, but in an engineered culture it will be "impossible for the unplanned to erupt again." But there is no virtue in the accidental character of an accident, and the diversity which arises from disorder can not only be duplicated by design but vastly extended. The experimental method is superior to simple observation just because it multiplies "accidents" in a systematic coverage of the possibilities. Technology offers many familiar examples. We no longer wait for immunity to disease to develop from a series of accidental exposures, nor do we wait for natural mutations in sheep and cotton to produce better fibers; but we continue to make use of such accidents when they occur, and we certainly do not prevent them. Many of the things we value have emerged from the clash of ignorant armies on darkling plains, but it is not therefore wise to encourage ignorance and darkness.

It is not always disorder itself which we are told we shall miss but certain admirable qualities in men which flourish only in the presence of disorder. A man rises above an unpropitious childhood to a position of eminence, and since we cannot give a plausible account of the action of so complex an environment, we attribute the achievement to some admirable faculty in the man himself. But such "faculties" are suspiciously like the explanatory fictions against which the history of science warns us. We admire Lincoln for rising above a deficient school system, but it was not necessarily something *in him* which permitted him to become an educated man in spite of it. His educational environment was certainly unplanned, but it could nevertheless have made a full contribution to his mature behavior. He was a rare man, but the circumstances of his childhood were rare too. We do not give Franklin Delano Roosevelt the same credit for becoming an educated man with the help of Groton and Harvard, although the same behavioral processes may have been involved. The founding of Groton and Harvard somewhat reduced the possibility that fortuitous combinations of circumstances would erupt to produce other Lincolns. Yet the founders can hardly be condemned for attacking an admirable human quality.

Another predicted consequence of a science of man is an excessive uniformity. We are told that effective control—whether governmental, religious, educational, economic, or social—will produce a race of men who differ from each other only through relatively refractory genetic differences. That would probably be bad design, but we must admit that we are not now pursuing another course from choice. In a modern school, for example, there is usually a syllabus which specifies what every student is to learn by the end of each year. This would be flagrant regimentation if anyone expected every student to comply. But some will be poor in particular subjects, others will not study, others will not remember what they have been taught, and diversity is assured. Suppose, however, that we someday possess such effective educational techniques that every student will in fact be put in possession of all the behavior specified in a syllabus. At the end of the year, all students will correctly answer all questions on the final examination and "must all have prizes." Should we reject such a system on the grounds that in making all students excellent it has made them all alike? Advocates of the theory of a special faculty might contend that an important advantage of the present system is that the good student learns *in spite of* a system which is so defective that it is currently producing bad students as well. But if really effective techniques are available, we cannot avoid the problem of design simply by preferring the status quo. At what point should education be made deliberately inefficient?

Such predictions of the havoc to be wreaked by the application of science to human affairs are usually made with surprising confidence. They not only show a faith in the orderliness of human behavior; they presuppose an established body of knowledge with the help of which it can be positively asserted that the changes which scientists propose to make will have quite specific results—albeit not the results they foresee. But the predictions made by the critics of science must be held to be equally fallible and subject also to empirical test. We may be sure that many steps in the scientific design of cultural patterns will produce unforeseen consequences. But there is only one way to find out. And the test must be made, for if we cannot advance in the design of cultural patterns with absolute certainty, neither can we rest completely confident of the superiority of the status quo.

VI

Apart from their possibly objectionable consequences, scientific methods seem to make no provision for certain admirable qualities and faculties which seem to have flourished in less explicitly planned cultures; hence they are called "degrading" or "lacking in dignity." (Mr. Krutch has called the author's *Walden Two* an "ignoble Utopia.") The conditioned reflex is the current whipping boy. Because conditioned reflexes may be demonstrated in animals, they are spoken of as though they were exclusively subhuman. It is implied, as we have seen, that no behavioral processes are involved in education and moral discourse or, at least, that the processes are exclusively human. But men do show conditioned reflexes (for example, when they are frightened by all instances of the control of human behavior because some instances engender fear), and animals do show processes similar to the human behavior involved in instruction and moral discourse. When Mr. Krutch asserts that " 'Conditioning' is achieved by methods which bypass or, as it were, short-circuit those very reasoning faculties which education proposes to cultivate and exercise," he is making a technical statement which needs a definition of terms and a great deal of supporting evidence.

If such methods are called "ignoble" simply because they leave no room for certain admirable attributes, then perhaps the practice of admiration needs to be examined. We might say that the child whose education has been skillfully planned has been deprived of the right to intellectual heroism. Nothing has been left to be admired in the way he acquires an education. Similarly, we can conceive of moral training which is so adequate to the demands of the culture that men will be good practically automatically, but to that extent they will be deprived of the right to moral heroism, since we seldom admire automatic goodness. Yet if we consider the end of morals rather than certain virtuous means, is not "automatic goodness" a desirable state of affairs? Is it not, for example, the avowed goal of religious education? T. H. Huxley answered the question unambiguously: "If some great power would agree to make me always think what is true and do what is right, on condition of being turned into a sort of clock and wound up every morning before I got out of bed, I should instantly close with the offer." Yet Mr. Krutch quotes this as the scarcely credible point of view of a "proto-modern" and seems himself to share T. S. Eliot's contempt for ". . . systems so perfect / That no one will need to be good."

"Having to be good" is an excellent example of an expendable honorific. It is inseparable from a particular form of ethical and moral control. We distinguish between the things we *have* to do to avoid punishment and those we *want* to do for rewarding consequences. In a culture which did not resort to punishment we should never "have" to do anything except with respect to the punishing contingencies which arise directly in the physical environment. And we are moving toward such a culture, because the neurotic, not to say psychotic, by-products of control through punishment have long since led compassionate men to seek alternative techniques. Recent research has explained some of the objectionable results of punishment and has revealed resources of at least equal power in "positive reinforcement." It is reasonable to look forward to a time when man will seldom "have" to do anything, although he may show interest, energy, imagination, and productivity far beyond the level seen under the present system (except for rare eruptions of the unplanned).

What we have to do we do with *effort*. We call it "work." There is no other way to distinguish between exhausting labor and the possibly equally energetic but rewarding activity of play. It is presumably good cultural design to replace the former with the latter. But an adjustment in attitudes is needed. We are much more practiced in admiring the heroic labor of a Hercules than the activity of one who works without having to. In a truly effective educational system the student might not "have to work" at all, but that possibility is likely to be received by the contemporary teacher with an emotion little short of rage.

We cannot reconcile traditional and scientific views by agreeing upon *what* is to be admired or condemned. The question is whether anything is to be so treated. Praise and blame are cultural practices which have been adjuncts of the prevailing system of control in Western democracy. All peoples do not engage in them for the same purposes or to the same extent, nor, of course, are the same behaviors always classified in the same way as subject to praise or blame. In admiring intellectual and moral heroism and unrewarding labor, and in rejecting a world in which these would be uncommon, we are simply demonstrating our own cultural conditioning. By promoting certain tendencies to admire and censure, the group of which we are a part has arranged for the social reinforcement and punishment needed to assure a high level of intellectual and moral industry. Under other and possibly better controlling systems, the behavior which we now admire would occur, but not under those conditions which make it admirable, and we should have no reason to admire it because the culture would have arranged for its maintenance in other ways.

To those who are stimulated by the glamorous heroism of the battlefield, a peaceful world may not be a better world. Others may reject a world without sorrow, longing, or a sense of guilt because the relevance of deeply moving works of art would be lost. To many who have devoted their lives to the struggle to be wise and good, a world without confusion and evil might be an empty thing. A nostalgic concern for the decline of moral heroism has been a dominating theme in the work of Aldous Huxley. In *Brave New World* he could see in the application of science to human affairs only a travesty on the notion of the Good (just as George Orwell, in *1984,* could foresee nothing but horror). Writing in *Esquire* (August, 1955) Huxley has expressed the point this way: "We have had religious revolutions, we have had political, industrial, economic and nationalistic revolutions. All of them, as our descendants will discover, were but ripples in an ocean of conservatism—trivial by comparison with the psychological revolution toward which we are so rapidly moving. *That* will really be a revolution. When it is over, the human race will give no further trouble."

(Footnote for the reader of the future: This was not meant as a happy ending. Up to 1956 men had been admired, if at all, either for causing trouble or alleviating it. Therefore—)

It will be a long time before the world can dispense with heroes and hence with the cultural practice of admiring heroism, but we move in that direction whenever we act to prevent war, famine, pestilence, and disaster. It will be a long time before man will never need to submit to punishing environments or engage in exhausting labor, but we move in that direction whenever we make food, shelter, clothing, and labor-saving devices more readily available. We may mourn the passing of heroes but not the conditions which make for heroism. We can spare the self-made saint or sage as we spare the laundress on the river's bank struggling against fearful odds to achieve cleanliness.

VII

The two great dangers in modern democratic thinking are illustrated in a paper by former Secretary of State Dean Acheson. "For a long time now," writes Mr. Acheson, "we have gone along with some well-tested principles of conduct: That it was better to tell the truth than falsehoods; . . . that duties were older than and as fundamental as rights; that, as Justice Holmes put it, the mode by which the inevitable came to pass was effort; that to perpetuate a harm was wrong no matter how many joined in it . . . and so on. . . . Our institutions are founded on the assumption that most people follow these principles most of the time because they want to, and the institutions work pretty well when this assumption is true. More recently, however, bright people have been fooling with the machinery in the human head and they have discovered quite a lot. . . . Hitler introduced new refinements [as the result of which] a whole people have been utterly confused and corrupted. Unhappily neither the possession of this knowledge nor the desire to use it was confined to Hitler. . . . Others dip from this same devil's cauldron." [1]

The first dangerous notion in this passage is that most people follow democratic principles of conduct "because they want to." This does not account for democracy or any other form of government if we have not explained why people *want* to behave in given ways. Although it is tempting to assume that it is human nature to believe in democratic principles, we must not overlook the "cultural engineering" which produced and con-

[1] *The Pattern of Responsibility.* Boston, 1952. Pages 14–15.

tinues to maintain democratic practices. If we neglect the conditions which produce democratic *behavior,* it is useless to try to maintain a democratic *form* of government. And we cannot expect to export a democratic form of government successfully if we do not also provide for the cultural practices which will sustain it. Our forebears did not discover the essential nature of man; they evolved a pattern of behavior which worked remarkably well under the circumstances. The "set of principles" expressed in that pattern is not the only true set or necessarily the best. Mr. Acheson has presumably listed the most unassailable items; some of them are probably beyond question, but others—concerning duty and effort—may need revision as the world changes.

The second—and greater—threat to the democracy which Mr. Acheson is defending is his assumption that knowledge is necessarily on the side of evil. All the admirable things he mentions are attributed to the innate goodness of man, all the detestable to "fooling with the machinery in the human head." This is reminiscent of the position, taken by other institutions engaged in the control of men, that certain forms of knowledge are in themselves evil. But how out of place in a democratic philosophy! Have we come this far only to conclude that well-intentioned people cannot study the behavior of men without becoming tyrants or that informed men cannot show good will? Let us for once have strength and good will on the same side.

VIII

Far from being a threat to the tradition of Western democracy, the growth of a science of man is a consistent and probably inevitable part of it. In turning to the external conditions which shape and maintain the behavior of men, while questioning the reality of inner qualities and faculties to which human achievements were once attributed, we turn from the ill-defined and remote to the observable and manipulable. Though it is a painful step, it has far-reaching consequences, for it not only sets higher standards of human welfare but shows us how to meet them. A change in a theory of human nature cannot change the facts. The achievements of man in science, art, literature, music, and morals will survive any interpretation we place upon them. The uniqueness of the individual is unchallenged in the scientific view. Man, in short, will remain man. (There will be much to admire for those who are so inclined. Possibly the noblest achievement to which man can aspire, even according to present standards, is to accept himself for what he is, as that is revealed to him by the methods which he devised and tested on a part of the world in which he had only a small personal stake.)

If Western democracy does not lose sight of the aims of humanitarian action, it will welcome the almost fabulous support of its own science of man and will strengthen itself and play an important role in building a better world for everyone. But if it cannot put its "democratic philosophy" into proper historical perspective—if, under the control of attitudes and emotions which it generated for other purposes, it now rejects the help of science—then it must be prepared for defeat. For if we continue to insist that science has nothing to offer but a new and more horrible form of tyranny, we may produce just such a result by allowing the strength of science to fall into the hands of despots. And if, with luck, it were to fall instead to men of good will in other political communities, it would be perhaps a more ignominious defeat; for we should then, through a miscarriage of democratic principles, be forced to leave to others the next step in man's long struggle to control nature and himself.

The Control of Human Behavior (Abstract)

A shortened version of a lecture given at the New York Academy of Sciences on April 18, 1955, this paper appeared in the Transactions of the Academy *(Series II, Vol. 17, No. 7, pp. 547-551) in May of that year.*

We are seldom willing to admit that we are engaged in controlling the behavior of other people. The commonest techniques of control use force or the threat of force and are objectionable to the controllee and have come to be censured by society. But the condoned techniques of education, persuasion, and moral discourse differ only in the behavioral processes through which they operate and in the minimizing of certain side effects. They are still devices through which one man controls the behavior of another in some measure. Cajolery, seduction, incitement, and the various forms of what biographers call "influence" suggest other techniques.

Familiar rules of thumb in controlling men are embedded in folk wisdom and in many great works of literature. This prescientific technology is rapidly being extended by the scientific study of human behavior (there are those who refuse to admit even the possibility of such a science, but I am speaking here to those who are not only aware of the science but share a deep concern for its consequences). In civilized countries, the more powerful controlling techniques have eventually been contained by a sort of ethical counter-control, which prevents exploitation by those in a position to use them. There is a real danger, however, that the rapid development of new techniques will outstrip appropriate measures of counter-control, with devastating results.

We can see how counter-control originates in the case of force or the threat of force. In primitive literature, the hero is often the man who can whip everyone else in the group in open combat. He controls with the techniques of the bully. The relevant processes have been analyzed in the scientific study of behavior under the headings of avoidance and escape. We see these techniques exemplified today in the government of conquered peoples, in despotic governments of all sorts, by religious agencies which lean heavily on the threat of punishment, by many parents in the control of their children, and by most teachers. The technique is psychologically and biologically harmful to the controllee and, for this reason, has generated counter-control. The weak are, at least, more numerous, and we now generally hold it to be "wrong" to control through the use of force or the threat of force (although an impartial observer might not come to this conclusion). Formalized governmental and religious precepts support this containment of the techniques of the bully. The result is called peace—a condition in which men are not permitted to use force in controlling each other.

A later type of popular hero is the cheat, who outwits the strong man by misrepresentation and deceit (in a technical analysis, the relevant processes would be classified under the extinction of conditioned reflexes). But the cheat, eventually, is almost as objectionable as the bully, and ethical control accordingly arises. It is held to be "wrong" to lie, cheat, or cry "Wolf" for one's amusement.

There are techniques which may be as effective as these but may not lead so directly to counter-control. These techniques are becoming more powerful as their processes are better understood. A few examples follow.

1. *Emotional conditioning.* Aldous Huxley, in *Brave New World*, describes a perfectly plausible process through which certain inferior types of citizens are permanently dissuaded from wasting time on books and the beauties of nature. Babies are allowed to crawl toward books and flowers but receive electric shocks just as they touch them. The example appears to be borrowed, not from the science of conditioned reflexes, but from certain forms of moral education in which, for example, a child is spanked for taking an interest in parts of his own body. The same principle is used to generate strong reactions of rage and aggression toward the enemy in preparing servicemen for combat. It is the basis of advertising which shows a product being used by or otherwise associated with pretty girls or admired public figures. The controllee is not likely to revolt against such control, and he may carry the resulting prejudices contentedly to his grave.

2. *Motivational control.* Crude instances, such as the starving of a whole people so that food may be used to reinforce those who begin to support the government, bring their own eventual containment, but the exploitation of prevailing deprivations may be more subtle and possibly equally effective. The deliberate design of art and literature (as in the movies and

"comics") to appeal to people with sadistic tendencies is easily detected, but the subtle design of an automobile so that riding in it is in some measure a sexual experience is not so easily spotted. Neither practice may meet any objection from the people so controlled.

3. *Positive reinforcement.* Wages, bribes, and tips suggest a classical pattern in which we generate behavior in others through reinforcement or reward. Better ways of using reinforcement in shaping up new behavior and in maintaining the condition called interest, or enthusiasm, have been recently discovered. The reinforcing effect of personal attention and affection is coming to be better understood, especially by clinical psychologists. Lord Chesterfield and Dale Carnegie have recommended the use of feigned attention in influencing people.

4. *Drugs.* We are entering the age of the chemical control of human behavior. Drugs have been used for this purpose ever since the first man was deliberately made drunk. But better drugs are now available, not only for allaying anxiety but for other purposes of control. Our government would probably not hesitate to use a drug which, taken by servicemen before combat, would eliminate all signs of fear, thus depriving the individual of the protective reflexes which man has acquired through a long process of evolution. In the not-too-distant future, the motivational and emotional conditions of normal daily life will probably be maintained in any desired state through the use of drugs.

5. *Knowledge of the individual.* Techniques of control can be effective only when certain facts about the controllee are known. Gathering information through eavesdropping, employing spies and informers, opening mail, and wiretapping has, from time to time, come under ethical counter-control, though the present state of this in our culture is uncertain. Meanwhile, new techniques have been developed. Something like the projective tests of clinical psychology, combined with the technique of the political trial balloon, might make it possible to discover information about an individual or a whole people, not only without the knowledge of the controllee but with respect to matters of which the controllee himself has no clear understanding.

The doctrine that there is an absolute moral law applicable to all conditions of human life discourages the analysis of controlling practices and obscures our understanding of the need for counter-control. The methods by which men alter the behavior of other men change, and changing ethical measures are required. A technique need not be immediately objectionable to the controllee to engender counter-control. The gambler, for instance, is possibly the last person to ask for legal or moral restrictions on gambling enterprises. The alcoholic does not usually advocate the control of alcoholic beverages. Few workers object to being paid, even for kinds of work or according to pay schedules which society proscribes. It is the rare man who objects to the tyranny of the beautiful woman. In all these cases, society appeals to long-term consequences to justify measures of counter-control. Unfortunately, such consequences do not supply any hard-and-fast rule. We must continue to experiment in cultural design, as nature has already experimented, testing the consequences as we go. We may deal with cultural practices as a whole, as in "utopian" thinking, or piecemeal by changing one counter-controlling technique at a time. Eventually, the practices which make for the greatest biological and psychological strength of the group will presumably survive, as will the group which adopts them. Survival is not a criterion which we are free to accept or reject, but it is, nevertheless, the one according to which our current decisions will eventually be tested. It is less clear-cut than some absolute criterion of right and wrong, but it is more reassuring in its recognition of the changing needs of society.

Such an experimental attitude is sometimes criticized by those who want to defend some principle appropriate to an earlier stage of our cultural history. An example is the recent book by Joseph Wood Krutch, *The Measure of Man,* which is in considerable part an attack on my utopian novel, *Walden Two.* While arguing that the notion of behavioral engineering is ultimately faulty, because man is in some sense free and hence may escape control, Krutch admits that human freedom is under attack and that, if science is not checked, freedom may vanish altogether. Krutch argues that unless we put a stop to the machinations of scientists "we may never really be able to think again." By freedom, Krutch seems to mean merely a lack of order. The virtues of the prescientific era were the virtues of accident. The great crime of the founder of Walden Two, according to Krutch, was the destruction of the possibility of the happy chance—even such as that which gave rise to the founder himself, before "men's thoughts were controlled with precision." On the same grounds, we might object to the synthetic fibre industry for circumventing the accidental evolutionary processes which produced cotton and wool. If we can arrange better conditions of human life and growth, why should we wait for the happy accident, even if past accidents have brought us to this very point of power?

Krutch's answer is essentially a mystical one: some vague power or faculty has permitted man to transcend his chaotic environment, and this cannot continue to function in less chaotic circumstances. But the existence of such powers or faculties grows more doubtful as man's actual achievements come to be analyzed. Nothing will be lost if science is applied to education or moral discourse. A better way of teaching a child to spell words meets the objection that he is not taught something called "spelling," just as better moral and ethical training meets the objection that the child no longer "has" to be good. In the past, it was natural that some special honor should accrue to the individual who rises above his faulty intellectual and ethical training and is wise and good in spite of it. Men have been at times almost entirely occupied in deciding what is right, intellectually and morally. A world in which education is so successful that one is naturally right in both these senses is criticized because it provides for no heroism in transcending an inadequate environment. One might as well criticize fireproof buildings because the world is thus deprived of brave firemen.

It is easy to object to the control of human behavior by applying the slogans of democracy. But the democratic revolution in government and religion was directed against a certain type of control only. Men were freed from autocratic rulers employing techniques based upon force or the threat of force. It does not follow that men were thus freed of all control, and it is precisely the other forms of control which we must now learn to contain and to which the pattern of the democratic revolution is inappropriate. The democratic concept of "freedom" is no longer effective in international politics because it has lost its point. All major governments profess to be governing *for* the people, and no government will bear close scrutiny of its actual practices. A new conception of the function and practice of government is needed in dealing with the counter-control of techniques against which there is no revolt.

Mr. Krutch is justifiably concerned lest a new type of despotism arise which utilizes the more effective techniques of control provided by the science of human behavior. But his suggestion that we deny the possibility of such a science, or that we abandon it, would deprive us of important help in building adequate safeguards against its misuse. Science poses problems, but it also suggests solutions. In contending that the founder of Walden Two could as easily have been a monster, instead of the fairly benevolent figure he seems to be, Krutch misses the point that, in the long run, the strength of any government depends upon the strength of the governed. Under present conditions of competition, it is unlikely that a government can survive which does not govern in the best interests of everyone.

Unless there is some unseen virtue in ignorance, our growing understanding of human behavior will make it all the more feasible to design a world adequate to the needs of men. But we cannot gain this advantage if we are to waste time defending outworn conceptions of human nature, conceptions which have long since served their original purpose of justifying special philosophies of government. A rejection of science at this time, in a desperate attempt to preserve a loved but inaccurate conception of man, would represent an unworthy retreat in man's continuing effort to build a better world.

Some Issues Concerning the Control of Human Behavior

This is one side of a debate with Carl R. Rogers, held at a meeting of the American Psychological Association on September 4, 1956. Part I was submitted in writing to Dr. Rogers, and his contribution and rebuttal (summarized on pages 34–35) were sent to me before the meeting. Part III is my rebuttal.

Part I

Science is steadily increasing our power to influence, change, mold—in a word, control—human behavior. It has extended our "understanding" (whatever that may be) so that we deal more successfully with people in nonscientific ways, but it has also identified conditions or variables which can be used to predict and control behavior in a new, and increasingly rigorous, technology. The broad disciplines of government and economics offer examples of this, but there is special cogency in those contributions of anthropology, sociology, and psychology which deal with individual behavior. Carl Rogers has listed some of the achievements to date in a recent paper.[1] Those of his examples which show or imply the control of the single organism are primarily due, as we should expect, to psychology. It is the experimental study of behavior which carries us beyond awkward or inaccessible "principles," "factors," and so on, to variables which can be directly manipulated.

It is also, and for more or less the same reasons, the conception of human behavior emerging from an experimental analysis which most directly challenges traditional views. Psychologists themselves often do not seem to be aware of how far they have moved in this direction. But the change is not passing unnoticed by others. Until only recently it was customary to deny the possibility of a rigorous science of human behavior by arguing, either that a lawful science was impossible because man was a free agent, or that merely statistical predictions would always leave room for personal

From *Science* 1956, *124*, 1057–1066. A debate with Carl R. Rogers.
[1] Rogers, C. R. *Teachers College Record*, 1956, *57*, 316.

freedom. But those who used to take this line have become most vociferous in expressing their alarm at the way these obstacles are being surmounted.

Now, the control of human behavior has always been unpopular. Any undisguised effort to control usually arouses emotional reactions. We hesitate to admit, even to ourselves, that we are engaged in control, and we may refuse to control, even when this would be helpful, for fear of criticism. Those who have explicitly avowed an interest in control have been roughly treated by history. Machiavelli is the great prototype. As Macaulay said of him, "Out of his surname they coined an epithet for a knave and out of his Christian name a synonym for the devil." There were obvious reasons. The control which Machiavelli analyzed and recommended, like most political control, used techniques aversive to the controllee. The threats and punishments of the bully, like those of the government operating on the same plan, are not designed—whatever their success—to endear themselves to those who are controlled. Even when the techniques themselves are not aversive, control is usually exercised for the selfish purposes of the controller and, hence, has indirectly punishing effects upon others.

Man's natural inclination to revolt against selfish control has been exploited to good purpose in what we call the philosophy and literature of democracy. The doctrine of the rights of man has been effective in arousing individuals to concerted action against governmental and religious tyranny. The literature which has had this effect has greatly extended the number of terms in our language which express reactions to the control of men. But the ubiquity and ease of expression of this attitude spells trouble for any science which may give birth to a powerful technology of behavior. Intelligent men and women, dominated by the humanistic philosophy of the past two centuries, cannot view with equanimity what Andrew Hacker has called "the specter of predictable man." [2] Even the statistical or actuarial prediction of human events, such as the number of fatalities to be expected on a holiday weekend, strikes many people as uncanny and evil, while the prediction and control of individual behavior is regarded as little less than the work of the devil. I am not so much concerned here with the political or economic consequences for psychology, although research following certain channels may well suffer harmful effects. We ourselves, as intelligent men and women, and as exponents of Western thought, share these attitudes. They have already interfered with the free exercise of a scientific analysis, and their influence threatens to assume more serious proportions.

Three broad areas of human behavior supply good examples. The first

[2] Hacker, A. *Antioch Review,* 1954, *14,* 195.

of these—*personal control*—may be taken to include person-to-person relationships in the family, among friends, in social and work groups, and in counseling and psychotherapy. Other fields are *education* and *government*. A few examples from each will show how nonscientific preconceptions are affecting our current thinking about human behavior.

Personal Control

People living together in groups come to control one another with a technique which is not inappropriately called "ethical." When an individual behaves in a fashion acceptable to the group, he receives admiration, approval, affection, and many other reinforcements which increase the likelihood that he will continue to behave in that fashion. When his behavior is not acceptable, he is criticized, censured, blamed, or otherwise punished. In the first case the group calls him "good"; in the second, "bad." This practice is so thoroughly ingrained in our culture that we often fail to see that it is a technique of control. Yet we are almost always engaged in such control, even though the reinforcements and punishments are often subtle.

The practice of admiration is an important part of a culture, because behavior which is otherwise inclined to be weak can be set up and maintained with its help. The individual is especially likely to be praised, admired, or loved when he acts for the group in the face of great danger, for example, or sacrifices himself or his possessions, or submits to prolonged hardship, or suffers martyrdom. These actions are not admirable in any absolute sense, but they require admiration if they are to be strong. Similarly, we admire people who behave in original or exceptional ways, not because such behavior is itself admirable, but because we do not know how to encourage original or exceptional behavior in any other way. The group acclaims independent, unaided behavior in part because it is easier to reinforce than to help.

As long as this technique of control is misunderstood, we cannot judge correctly an environment in which there is less need for heroism, hardship, or independent action. We are likely to argue that such an environment is itself less admirable or produces less admirable people. In the old days, for example, young scholars often lived in undesirable quarters, ate unappetizing or inadequate food, performed unprofitable tasks for a living or to pay for necessary books and materials or publication. Older scholars and other members of the group offered compensating reinforcement in the form of approval and admiration for these sacrifices. When the modern graduate student receives a generous scholarship, enjoys good living conditions, and has his research and publication subsidized, the grounds for evaluation seem to be pulled from under us. Such a student no longer *needs* admiration to carry him over a series of obstacles (no matter how much he may need it for other reasons), and, in missing certain familiar objects of admiration, we are likely to conclude that such *conditions* are less admirable. Obstacles to scholarly work may serve as a useful measure of motivation—and we may go wrong unless some substitute is found—but we can scarcely defend a deliberate harassment of the student for this purpose. The productivity of any set of conditions can be evaluated only when we have freed ourselves of the attitudes which have been generated in us as members of an ethical group.

A similar difficulty arises from our use of punishment in the form of censure or blame. The concept of responsibility and the related concepts of foreknowledge and choice are used to justify techniques of control using punishment. Was So-and-So aware of the probable consequences of his action, and was the action deliberate? If so, we are justified in punishing him. But what does this mean? It appears to be a question concerning the efficacy of the contingent relations between behavior and punishing consequences. We punish behavior because it is objectionable to us or the group, but in a minor refinement of rather recent origin we have come to withhold punishment when it cannot be expected to have any effect. If the objectionable consequences of an act were accidental and not likely to occur again, there is no point in punishing. We say that the individual was not "aware of the consequences of his action" or that the consequences were not "intentional." If the action could not have been avoided—if the individual "had no choice"—punishment is also withheld, as it is if the individual is incapable of being changed by punishment because he is of "unsound mind." In all these cases—different as they are—the individual is held "not responsible" and goes unpunished.

Just as we say that it is "not fair" to punish a man for something he could not help doing, so we call it "unfair" when one is rewarded beyond his due or for something he could not help doing. In other words, we also object to wasting *reinforcers* where they are not needed or will do no good. We make the same point with the words *just* and *right*. Thus we have no right to punish the irresponsible, and a man has no right to reinforcers he does not earn or deserve. But concepts of choice, responsibility, justice, and so on, provide a most inadequate analysis of efficient reinforcing and punishing contingencies because they carry a heavy semantic cargo of a quite different sort, which obscures any attempt to clarify controlling practices or to improve techniques. In particular, they fail to prepare us for techniques based on other than aversive techniques of control. Most people would object to forcing prisoners to serve as subjects of dangerous medical experiments, but few object when they are induced to serve by the offer of return privileges—even when the reinforcing effect of these privileges has been created by forcible deprivation. In the traditional scheme the right to refuse guarantees the individual against coercion or an unfair bargain. But to what extent *can* a prisoner refuse under such circumstances?

We need not go so far afield to make the point. We can observe our own attitude toward personal freedom in the way we resent any interference with what we want to do. Suppose we want to buy a car of a particular sort. Then we may object, for example, if our wife urges us to buy a less expensive model and to put the difference into a new refrigerator. Or we may resent it if our neighbor questions our need for such a car or our ability to pay for it. We would certainly resent it if it were illegal to buy such a car (remember Prohibition); and if we find we cannot actually afford it, we may resent governmental control of the price through tariffs and taxes. We resent it if we discover that we cannot get the car because the manufacturer is holding the model in deliberately short supply in order to push a model we do not want. In all this we assert our democratic right to buy the car of our choice. We are well prepared to do so and to resent any restriction on our freedom.

But why do we not ask *why* it is the car of our choice and resent the forces which made it so? Perhaps our favorite toy as a child was a car, of a very different model, but nevertheless bearing the name of the car we now want. Perhaps our favorite TV program is sponsored by the manufacturer of that car. Perhaps we have seen pictures of many beautiful or prestigeful persons driving it—in pleasant or glamorous places. Perhaps the car has been designed with respect to our motivational patterns: the device on the hood is a phallic symbol, or the horsepower has been stepped up to please our competitive spirit in enabling us to pass other cars swiftly (or, as the advertisements say, "safely"). The concept of freedom which has emerged as part of the cultural practice of our group makes little or no provision for recognizing or dealing with these kinds of control. Concepts like "responsibility" and "rights" are scarcely applicable. We are prepared to deal with coercive measures, but we have no traditional recourse with respect to other measures which in the long run (and especially with the help of science) may be much more powerful and dangerous.

EDUCATION

The techniques of education were once frankly aversive. The teacher was usually older and stronger than his pupils and was able to "make them learn." This meant that they were not actually taught but were surrounded by a threatening world from which they could escape only by learning. Usually they were left to their own resources in discovering how to do so. Claude Coleman has published a grimly amusing reminder of these older practices.[3] He tells of a schoolteacher who published a careful account of his services during 51 years of teaching, during which he administered: ". . . 911,527 blows with a cane; 124,010 with a rod; 20,989 with a ruler; 136,715 with the hand; 10,295 over the mouth; 7,905 boxes on the ear; [and] 1,115,800 slaps on the head. . . ."

Progressive education was a humanitarian effort to substitute positive reinforcement for such aversive measures, but in the search for useful human values in the classroom it has never fully replaced the variables it abandoned. Viewed as a branch of behavioral technology, education remains relatively inefficient. We supplement it, and rationalize it, by admiring the pupil who learns *for himself;* and we often attribute the learning process, or knowledge itself, to something *inside* the individual. We admire behavior which seems to have inner sources. Thus we admire one who *recites* a poem more than one who simply *reads* it. We admire one who *knows* the answer more than one who *knows where to look it up.* We admire the *writer* rather than the *reader.* We admire the arithmetician who can do a problem in his head rather than with a slide rule or calculating machine, or in "original" ways rather than by a strict application of rules. In general we feel that any aid or "crutch"—except those aids to which we are now thoroughly accustomed—reduces the credit due. In Plato's *Phaedrus,* Thamus, the king, attacks the invention of the alphabet on similar grounds! He is afraid "it will produce forgetfulness in the minds of those who learn to use it, because they will not practice their memories. . . ." In other words, he holds it more admirable to remember than to use a memorandum. He also objects that pupils "will read many things without instruction . . . [and] will therefore seem to know many things when they are for the most part ignorant." In the same vein we are today sometimes contemptuous of book learning, but as educators we can scarcely afford to adopt this view without reservation.

By admiring the student for knowledge and blaming him for ignorance, we escape some of the responsibility of teaching him. We resist any analysis of the educational process which threatens the notion of inner wisdom or questions the contention that the fault of ignorance lies with the student. More powerful techniques which bring about the same changes in behavior

---

[3] Coleman, C. *Bull. Am. Assoc. Univ. Professors,* 1953, *39,* 457.

by manipulating *external* variables are decried as brainwashing or thought control. We are quite unprepared to judge *effective* educational measures. As long as only a few pupils learn much of what is taught, we do not worry about uniformity or regimentation. We do not fear the feeble technique; but we should view with dismay a system under which every student learned everything listed in a syllabus—although such a condition is far from unthinkable. Similarly, we do not fear a system which is so defective that the student must *work* for an education; but we are loath to give credit for anything learned without effort—although this could well be taken as an ideal result—and we flatly refuse to give credit if the student already knows what a school teaches.

A world in which people are wise and good without trying, without "having to be," without "choosing to be," could conceivably be a far better world for everyone. In such a world we should not have to "give anyone credit"—we should not need to admire anyone—for being wise and good. From our present point of view we cannot believe that such a world would be admirable. We do not even permit ourselves to imagine what it would be like.

GOVERNMENT

Government has always been the special field of aversive control. The state is frequently defined in terms of the power to punish, and jurisprudence leans heavily upon the associated notion of personal responsibility. Yet it is becoming increasingly difficult to reconcile current practice and theory with these earlier views. In criminology, for example, there is a strong tendency to drop the notion of responsibility in favor of some such alternative as capacity or controllability. But no matter how strongly the facts, or even practical expedience, support such a change, it is difficult to make the change in a legal system designed on a different plan. When governments resort to other techniques (for example, positive reinforcement), the concept of responsibility is no longer relevant and the theory of government is no longer applicable.

The conflict is illustrated by two decisions of the Supreme Court in the 1930's which dealt with, and disagreed on, the definition of control or coercion.[4] The Agricultural Adjustment Act proposed that the Secretary of Agriculture make "rental or benefit payments" to those farmers who agreed to reduce production. The government argued that the Act would be unconstitutional if the farmer had been *compelled* to reduce production

[4] Freund, P. A. *et al. Constitutional Law: Cases and Other Problems,* Vol. 1. Boston: Little, Brown & Company, 1954.

but was not since he was merely *invited* to do so. Justice Roberts expressed the contrary majority view of the court that "the power to confer or withhold unlimited benefits is the power to coerce or destroy." This recognition of positive reinforcement was withdrawn a few years later in another case in which Justice Cardozo wrote "To hold that motive or temptation is equivalent to coercion is to plunge the law in endless difficulties." We may agree with him, without implying that the proposition is therefore wrong. Sooner or later the law must be prepared to deal with all possible techniques of governmental control.

The uneasiness with which we view government (in the broadest possible sense) when it does not use punishment is shown by the reception of my utopian novel, *Walden Two*. This was essentially a proposal to apply a behavioral technology to the construction of a workable, effective, and productive pattern of government. It was greeted with wrathful violence. *Life* magazine called it "a travesty on the good life," and "a menace . . . a triumph of mortmain or the dead hand not envisaged since the days of Sparta . . . a slur upon a name, a corruption of an impulse." Joseph Wood Krutch devoted a substantial part of his book, *The Measure of Man*,[5] to attacking my views and those of the protagonist, Frazier, in the same vein, and Morris Viteles has recently criticized the book in a similar manner in *Science*.[6] Perhaps the reaction is best expressed in a quotation from *The Quest for Utopia* by Negley and Patrick.[7]

> Halfway through this contemporary utopia, the reader may feel sure, as we did, that this is a beautifully ironic satire on what has been called "behavioral engineering." The longer one stays in this better world of the psychologist, however, the plainer it becomes that the inspiration is not satiric, but messianic. This is indeed the behaviorally engineered society, and while it was to be expected that sooner or later the principle of psychological conditioning would be made the basis of a serious construction of utopia—Brown anticipated it in *Limanora*—yet not even the effective satire of Huxley is adequate preparation for the shocking horror of the idea when positively presented. Of all the dictatorships espoused by utopists, this is the most profound, and incipient dictators might well find in this utopia a guidebook of political practice.

One would scarcely guess that the authors are talking about a world in which there is food, clothing, and shelter for all, where everyone chooses his own work and works on the average only four hours a day, where music and the arts flourish, where personal relationships develop under the most

[5] Krutch, J. W. *The Measure of Man.* Indianapolis: Bobbs-Merrill, 1953.
[6] Viteles, M. *Science,* 1955, *122,* 1167.
[7] Negley, G., and Patrick, J. M. *The Quest for Utopia.* New York: Schuman, 1952.

favorable circumstances, where education prepares every child for the social and intellectual life which lies before him, where—in short—people are truly happy, secure, productive, creative, and forward-looking. What is wrong with it? Only one thing: someone "planned it that way." If these critics had come upon a society in some remote corner of the world which boasted similar advantages, they would undoubtedly have hailed it as providing a pattern we all might well follow—provided that it was clearly the result of a natural process of cultural evolution. Any evidence that intelligence had been used in arriving at this version of the good life would, in their eyes, be a serious flaw. No matter if the planner of *Walden Two* diverts none of the proceeds of the community to his own use, no matter if he has no current control or is, indeed, unknown to most of the other members of the community (he planned that, too), somewhere back of it all he occupies the position of prime mover. And this, to the child of the democratic tradition, spoils it all.

The dangers inherent in the control of human behavior are very real. The possibility of the misuse of scientific knowledge must always be faced. We cannot escape by denying the power of a science of behavior or arresting its development. It is no help to cling to familiar philosophies of human behavior simply because they are more reassuring. As I have pointed out elsewhere [page 19], the new techniques emerging from a science of behavior must be subject to the explicit counter-control which has already been applied to earlier and cruder forms. Brute force and deception, for example, are now fairly generally suppressed by ethical practices and by explicit governmental and religious agencies. A similar counter-control of scientific knowledge in the interests of the group is a feasible and promising possibility. Although we cannot say how devious the course of its evolution may be, a cultural pattern of control and counter-control will presumably emerge which will be most widely supported because it is most widely reinforcing.

If we cannot foresee all the details (as we obviously cannot), it is important to remember that this is true of the critics of science as well. The dire consequences of new techniques of control, the hidden menace in original cultural designs—these need some proof. That the need for proof is so often overlooked is only another example of my present point. Man has got himself into some pretty fixes, and it is easy to believe that he will do so again. But there is a more optimistic possibility. The slow growth of the methods of science, now for the first time being applied to human affairs, *may* mean a new and exciting phase of human life to which historical analogies will not apply and in which earlier political slogans will not be appropriate. If we are to use the knowledge which a science of behavior is now making available with any hope of success, we must look at human nature as it is brought into focus through the methods of science rather than as it has been presented to us in a series of historical accidents.

If the advent of a powerful science of behavior causes trouble, it will not be because science itself is inimical to human welfare but because older conceptions have not yielded easily or gracefully. We expect resistance to new techniques of control from those who have heavy investments in the old, but we have no reason to help them preserve a series of principles which are not ends in themselves but rather outmoded means to an end. What is needed is a new conception of human behavior which is compatible with the implications of a scientific analysis. All men control and are controlled. The question of government in the broadest possible sense is not how freedom is to be preserved but what kinds of control are to be used and to what ends. Control must be analyzed and considered in its proper proportions. No scientist, I am sure, wishes to develop new master-slave relationships or bend the will of the people to despotic rulers in new ways. These are patterns of control appropriate to a world without science. They may well be the first to go when the experimental analysis of behavior comes into its own in the design of cultural practices.

Part II

Dr. Rogers presented his own point of view, together with comments on my paper, which had been submitted to him in manuscript. He argued that "in any scientific endeavor—whether 'pure' or applied science—there is a prior subjective choice of the purpose or value which that scientific work is perceived as serving," and that "this subjective value choice . . . must always lie outside of the scientific endeavor." He attributed certain value choices to me, including the decision to experiment with different choices, and offered some alternative values which might guide scientific research in the field of human behavior. "We might then value: man as a process of becoming, as a process of achieving worth and dignity through the development of his potentialities; the individual human being as a self-actualizing process, moving on to more challenging and enriching experiences; the process by which the individual creatively adapts to an ever-new and changing world. . . ."

He illustrated this with client-centered therapy, where therapists establish "by external control conditions which they predict will be followed by internal control by the individual, in pursuit of internally chosen goals. We can choose to use the behavioral sciences in ways which will free, not control."

Part III

I cannot quite agree that the practice of science *requires* a prior decision about goals or a prior choice of values. The metallurgist can study the properties of steel and the engineer can design a bridge without raising the question of whether a bridge is to be built. But such questions are certainly frequently raised and tentatively answered. Rogers wants to call the answers "subjective choices of values." To me, such an expression suggests that we have had to abandon more rigorous scientific practices in order to talk about our own behavior. In the experimental analysis of other organisms I would use other terms, and I shall try to do so here. Any list of values is a list of reinforcers—conditioned or otherwise. We are so constituted that under certain circumstances food, water, sexual contact, and so on will make any behavior which produces them more likely to occur again. Other things may acquire this power. We do not need to say that an organism chooses to eat rather than to starve. If you reply that it is a very different thing when a man chooses to starve, I am only too happy to agree. If it were not so, we should have cleared up the question of choice long ago. An organism can be reinforced by—can be made to "choose"—almost any given state of affairs.

Rogers is concerned with choices which involve multiple and usually conflicting consequences. I have dealt with some of these in *Science and Human Behavior* in an analysis of self-control. Shall I eat these delicious strawberries today if I will then suffer an annoying rash tomorrow? The decision I am to make used to be assigned to the province of ethics. But we are now studying similar combinations of positive and negative consequences, as well as collateral conditions which affect the result, in the laboratory. Even a pigeon can be taught some measure of self-control! And this work helps us to understand the operation of certain formulas—among them value judgments—which folk-wisdom, religion, and psychotherapy have advanced in the interests of self-discipline. The observable effect of any statement of value is to alter the relative effectiveness of reinforcers. We may no longer enjoy the strawberries for thinking about the rash. If rashes are branded sufficiently shameful, illegal, sinful, maladjusted, or unwise, we may glow with satisfaction as we push the strawberries aside in a grandiose avoidance response which would bring a smile to the lips of Murray Sidman.

People behave in ways which, as we say, conform to ethical, governmental, or religious patterns because they are reinforced for doing so. The resulting behavior may have far-reaching consequences for the survival of the pattern to which it conforms. And whether we like it or not, survival is the ultimate criterion. This is where, it seems to me, science can help—not in choosing a goal, but in enabling us to predict the survival value of cultural practices. Man has too long tried to get the kind of world he wants by glorifying some brand of immediate reinforcement. As science points up more and more of the remoter consequences, he may begin to work to strengthen behavior, not in a slavish devotion to a chosen value, but with respect to the ultimate survival of mankind. Do not ask me why I want mankind to survive. I can tell you why only in the sense in which the physiologist can tell you why I want to breathe. Once the relation between a given step and the survival of my group has been pointed out, I will take that step. And it is the business of science to point out just such relations.

The values I have occasionally recommended (and Rogers has not led me to recant) are transitional. Other things being equal, I am betting on the group whose practices make for healthy, happy, secure, productive, and creative people. And I insist that the values recommended by Rogers are transitional, too, for I can ask him the same kind of question. Man as a process of becoming—*what?* Self-actualization—for what? Inner control is no more a goal than external control.

What Rogers seems to me to be proposing, both here and elsewhere, is this: Let us use our increasing power of control to create individuals who will not need and perhaps will no longer respond to control. Let us solve the problem of our power by renouncing it. At first blush this seems as implausible as a benevolent despot. Yet power has occasionally been foresworn. A nation has burned its Reichstag, rich men have given away their wealth, beautiful women have become ugly hermits in the desert, and psychotherapists have become nondirective. When this happens, I look to other possible reinforcements for a plausible explanation. A people relinquish democratic power when a tyrant promises them the earth. Rich men give away wealth to escape the accusing finger of their fellow men. A woman destroys her beauty in the hope of salvation. And a psychotherapist relinquishes control because he can thus help his client more effectively.

The solution which Rogers is suggesting is thus understandable. But is he correctly interpreting the result? What evidence is there that a client ever becomes truly *self*-directing? What evidence is there that he ever makes a truly *inner* choice of ideal or goal? Even though the therapist does not do the choosing, even though he encourages "self-actualization"—he has not ceased to control as long as he holds himself ready to step in when occasion demands—when, for example, the client chooses the goal of becoming a more accomplished liar or murdering his boss. But supposing the therapist does withdraw completely or is no longer necessary—what about all the other forces acting upon the client? Is the self-chosen goal independent of his early ethical and religious training? of the folk-wisdom of his group? of the opinions and attitudes of others who are important to him? Surely not. The therapeutic situation is only a small part of the world of the client. From the therapist's point of view it may appear to be possible to relinquish control. But the control passes, not to a "self," but to forces in other parts of the client's world. The solution of the therapist's problem of power cannot be *our* solution, for we must consider *all* the forces acting upon the individual.

The child who must be prodded and nagged is something less than a fully developed human being. We want to see him hurrying to his appointment, not because each step is taken in response to verbal reminders from his mother, but because certain temporal contingencies, in which dawdling has been punished and hurrying reinforced, have worked a change in his behavior. Call this a state of better organization, a greater sensitivity to reality, or what you will. The plain fact is that the child passes from a temporary verbal control exercised by his parents to control by certain inexorable features of the environment. I should suppose that something of the same sort happens in successful psychotherapy. Rogers seems to me to be saying this: Let us put an end, as quickly as possible, to any pattern of master-and-slave, to any direct obedience to command, to the submissive following of suggestions. Let the individual be free to adjust himself to more rewarding features of the world about him. In the end, let his teachers and counselors "wither away," like the Marxist state. I not only agree with this as a useful idea, I have constructed a fanciful world to demonstrate its advantages. It saddens me to hear Rogers say that "at a deep philosophic level" *Walden Two* and George Orwell's *1984* "seem indistinguishable." They could scarcely be more unlike—at any level. The book *1984* is a picture of immediate aversive control for vicious selfish purposes. The founder of *Walden Two,* on the other hand, has built a community in which neither he nor any other person exerts any *current* control. His achievement lay in his original *plan,* and when he boasts of this ("It is enough to satisfy the thirstiest tyrant") we do not fear him but only pity him for his weakness.

Another critic of *Walden Two,* Andrew Hacker,[8] has discussed this point in considering the bearing of mass conditioning upon the liberal

[8] Hacker, A. J. *Politics,* 1955, *17,* 590.

notion of autonomous man. In drawing certain parallels between the Grand Inquisitor passage in Dostoevsky's *Brothers Karamazov,* Huxley's *Brave New World,* and *Walden Two,* he attempts to set up a distinction to be drawn in any society between conditioners and conditioned. He assumes that "the conditioner can be said to be autonomous in the traditional liberal sense." But then he notes: "Of course the conditioner has been conditioned. But he has not been conditioned by the conscious manipulation of another *person.*" But how does this affect the resulting behavior? Can we not soon forget the origins of the "artificial" diamond which is identical with the real thing? Whether it is an "accidental" cultural pattern, such as is said to have produced the founder of *Walden Two,* or the engineered environment which is about to produce his successors, we are dealing with sets of conditions generating human behavior which will ultimately be measured by their contribution to the strength of the group. We look to the future, not the past, for the test of "goodness" or acceptability.

If we are worthy of our democratic heritage we shall, of course, be ready to resist any tyrannical use of science for immediate, selfish purposes. But if we value the achievements and goals of democracy, we must not refuse to apply science to the design and construction of cultural patterns, even though we may then find ourselves in some sense in the position of controllers. Fear of control, generalized beyond any warrant, has led to a misinterpretation of valid practices and the blind rejection of intelligent planning for a better way of life. In terms which I trust Rogers will approve, in conquering this fear we shall become more mature and better organized and shall, thus, more fully actualize ourselves as human beings.

The Design of Cultures

A series of three conferences on "Evolutionary Theory and Human Progress" was held at the American Academy of Arts and Sciences in the fall of 1960. The first considered biological problems, the second, anthropological, and the third, psychological. The present paper, part of the third program, was published in Daedalus, *summer issue of 1961. It is reprinted here by permission.*

Anyone who undertakes to improve cultural practices by applying a scientific analysis of human behavior is likely to be told that improvement involves a value judgment beyond the pale of his science and that he is exemplifying objectionable values by proposing to meddle in human affairs and infringe on human freedoms. Scientists themselves often accept this standard contention of Western philosophy, even though it implies that there is a kind of wisdom which is mysteriously denied to them and even though the behavioral scientists among them would be hard pressed to give an empirical account of such wisdom or to discover its sources.

The proposition gains unwarranted strength from the fact that it appears to champion the natural against the artificial. Man is a product of nature, the argument runs, but societies are contrived by men. Man is the measure of all things, and our plans for him—our customs and institutions—will succeed only if they allow for his nature. To this it might be answered that man is more than an immutable product of biological processes; he is a psychological entity, and as such also largely man-made. His cause may be as contrived as society's and possibly as weak. He is, nevertheless, an individual, and his defenders are individuals, too, who may borrow zeal in his defense from their own role in the great conflict between the one and the many. To side with the individual against the state, to take a specific example, is reassuringly to defend one's own, even though it might be answered that mankind has won its battles only because individual men have lost theirs.

These are merely answers in kind, which can no doubt be met with plausible rejoinders. The disputing of values is not only possible, it is interminable. To escape from it we must get outside the system. We can do this by developing an empirical account of the behavior of both protagonists. All objections to cultural design, like design itself, are forms of human behavior and may be studied as such. It is possible that a plausible account of the design of cultures will allay our traditional anxieties and prepare the way for the effective use of man's intelligence in the construction of his own future.

It is reasonable to hope that a scientific analysis will some day satisfactorily explain how cultural practices arise and are transmitted and how they affect those who engage in them, possibly to further the survival of the practices themselves or at least to contribute to their successors. Such an analysis will embrace the fact that men talk about their cultures and sometimes change them. Changing a culture is itself a cultural practice, and we must know as much as possible about it if we are to question it intelligently. Under what circumstances do men redesign—or, to use a discredited term, reform—their way of life? What is the nature of their behavior in doing so? Is the deliberate manipulation of a culture a threat to the very essence of man or, at the other extreme, an unfathomed source of strength for the culture which encourages it?

We need not go into the details of a scientific account of behavior to see how it bears on this issue. Its contribution must, however, be distinguished from any help to be drawn from historical analogy or the extrapolation of historical trends or cycles, as well as from interpretations based on sociological principles or structures. Such an account must make contact with biology, on the one hand, but serve in an interpretation of social phenomena, on the other. If it is to yield a satisfactory analysis of the design and implementation of social practices, it must be free of a particular defect. Evolutionary theory, especially in its appeal to the notion of survival, suffered for a long time from circularity. It was not satisfying to argue that forms of life which had survived must therefore have had survival value and had survived because of it. A similar weakness is inherent in psychologies based on adjustment or adaptation. It is not satisfying to argue that a man adapts to a new environment because of his intelligence and emotional stability if these are then defined in terms of capacities to adapt. It is true that organisms usually develop in directions which maximize, phylogenetically, the survival of the species and, ontogenetically, the adjustment of the individual; but the mechanisms responsible for both kinds of change need to be explained without recourse to the selective effect of their consequences.

In biology this is now being done. Genetics clarifies and supports evolutionary theory with new kinds of facts, and in doing so eliminates the circularity in the concept of survival. A comparable step in the study of human behavior is to analyze the mechanisms of human action apart from their contribution to personal and cultural adjustment. It is not enough to point out that a given form of behavior is advantageous to the individual or that a cultural practice strengthens the group. We must explain the origin and the perpetuation of both behavior and practice.

A scientific analysis which satisfies these conditions confines itself to individual organisms rather than statistical constructs or interacting groups of organisms, even in the study of social behavior. Its basic datum is the probability of the occurrence of the observable events we call behavior (or of inferred events having the same dimensions). The probability of behavior is accounted for by appeal to the genetic endowment of the organism and its past and present environments, described wholly in the language of physics and biology. The laboratory techniques of such an analysis, and their technological applications, emphasize the prediction and control of behavior via the manipulation of variables. Validation is found primarily in the success with which the subject matter can be controlled.

An example of how such an analysis differs from its predecessors is conveniently at hand. An important group of variables which modify behavior have to do with the consequences of action. *Rewards* and *punishments* are variables of this sort, though rather inadequately identified by those terms. We are interested in the fact (apart from any theory which explains it) that by arranging certain consequences—that is, by making certain kinds of events *contingent upon behavior*—we achieve a high degree of experimental control. Our present understanding of the so-called "contingencies of reinforcement" is undoubtedly incomplete, but it nevertheless permits us to construct new forms of behavior, to bring behavior under the control of new aspects of the environment, and to maintain it under such control for long periods of time—and all of this often with surprising ease. Extrapolation to less rigorously controlled samples of behavior outside the laboratory has already led to promising technological developments.

But the importance of the principle is embarrassing. Almost any instance of human behavior involves contingencies of reinforcement, and those who have been alerted to their significance by laboratory studies often seem fanatical in pointing them out. Yet behavior *is* important mainly because of its consequences. We may more readily accept this fact if we recall the ubiquity of the concept of purpose. The experimental study of reinforcing contingencies is nothing more than a nonteleological analysis of the *directed effects* of behavior, of relations which have traditionally been described as purpose. By manipulating contingencies of reinforcement in ways which conform to standard practices in the physical sciences, we study and use them without appealing to final causes.

We can put this reinterpretation of purpose to immediate use, for it bears on a confusion between the phylogenetic and the ontogenetic development of behavior which has clouded our thinking about the origin and growth of cultures. Contingencies of reinforcement are similar to what we might call contingencies of survival. Inherited patterns of behavior must have been selected by their contributions to survival in ways which are not unlike those in which the behavior of the individual is selected or shaped by its reinforcing consequences. Both processes exemplify adaptation or adjustment, but very different mechanisms must be involved.

The evolution of inherited forms of behavior is as plausible as the evolution of any function of the organism when the environment can be regarded as reasonably stable. The internal environment satisfies this requirement, and a genetic endowment of behavior related to the internal economy—say, peristalsis or sneezing—is usually accepted without question. The external environment is much less stable from generation to generation, but some kinds of responses to it are also plausibly explained by evolutionary selection. The genetic mechanisms are presumably similar to those which account for other functions. But environments change, and any process which permits an organism to modify its behavior is then important. The structures which permit modification must have evolved when organisms were being selected by their survival in novel environments.

Although the mechanisms which permit modification of behavior are inherited, learned behavior does not emerge from, and is not an extension of, the unlearned behavior of the individual. The organism does not simply refine or extend a genetic behavioral endowment to make it more effective or more inclusive. Instead, it develops collateral behavior, which must be distinguished from an inherited response system even when both serve similar functions. It is important to remember this when considering social behavior. In spite of certain intriguing analogies, it is not likely that the social institutions of man are founded on or that they emerged from the instinctive patterns of animal societies. They are the achievements of individuals, modifying their behavior as inherited mechanisms permit. The co-ordinated activities of the anthill or beehive operate on very different principles from those of a family, a large company, or a great city. The two kinds of social behavior must have developed through different processes, and they are maintained in force for different reasons.

To take a specific example, verbal behavior is not a refinement upon instinctive cries of alarm, distress, and so on, even though the reinforcing contingencies in the one case are analogous to the conditions of survival in the other. Both may be said to serve similar adaptive functions, but the mechanisms involved in acquiring verbal behavior clearly set it apart from instinctive responses. The innate vocal endowment of an organism is indeed particularly refractory to modification, most if not all verbal responses being modifications of a nonspecific behavioral endowment.

In general, the evolution of man has emphasized modifiability rather than the transmission of specific forms of behavior. Inherited verbal or other social responses are fragmentary and trivial. By far the greater part of behavior develops in the individual through processes of conditioning, given a normal biological endowment. Man becomes a social creature only because other men are important parts of his environment. The behavior of a child born into a flourishing society is shaped and maintained by variables, most of which are arranged by other people. These social variables compose the "culture" in which the child lives, and they shape his behavior in conformity with that culture, usually in such a way that he in turn tends to perpetuate it. The behavioral processes present no special problems. Nevertheless, a satisfactory account calls for some explanation of how a social environment can have arisen from nonsocial precursors. This may seem to raise the hoary question of the origin of society, but we have no need to reconstruct an actual historical event or even a speculative beginning, such as a social compact from which conclusions about the nature of society can be drawn. We have only to show that a social environment could have emerged from nonsocial conditions. As in explaining the origin of life, we cannot discover an actual historical event but must be satisfied with a demonstration that certain structures with their associated functions could have arisen under plausible conditions.

The emergence of a given form of social behavior from nonsocial antecedents is exemplified by imitation. Inherited imitative behavior is hard to demonstrate. The parrot may possibly owe its distinction only to an inherited capacity to be reinforced by the production of imitative sounds. In any case, an inherited repertoire of imitative behavior in man is insignificant, compared with the product of certain powerful contingencies of reinforcement which establish and maintain behaving-as-others-behave. For example, if organism A sees organism B running in obvious alarm, A will probably avoid aversive consequences by running in the same direction. Or, if A sees B picking and eating ripe berries, A will probably be reinforced for approaching the same berry patch. Thousands of instances of this sort compose a general contingency providing for the reinforcement of doing-as-others-do. In this sense, behavior exemplifying imitation is acquired, yet it is practically inevitable whenever two or more organisms live in contact with one another. The essential conditions are not in themselves social.

Most social behavior, however, arises from social antecedents. Transmission is more important than social invention. Unlike the origin of cultural practices, their transmission need not be a matter for speculation, since the process can be observed. Deliberate transmission (that is, transmission achieved because of practices which have been reinforced by their consequences) is not needed. For example, some practices are perpetuated as the members of a group are severally replaced. If *A* has already developed specific controlling behavior with respect to *B*, depending partly upon incidental characteristics of *B*'s behavior, he may impose the same control on a new individual, *C*, who might not himself have generated just the same practices in *A*. A mother who has shaped the vocal responses of her first baby into a primitive verbal repertoire may bring already established contingencies to bear on a second child. A leader who has acquired aversive controlling practices in his interactions with a submissive follower may take by storm a second follower even though, without this preparation, the leader-follower relation might have been reversed in the second case. Overlapping group membership is, of course, only one factor contributing to manners, customs, folkways, and other abiding features of a social environment.

These simple examples are offered not as solutions to important problems but to illustrate an approach to the analysis of social behavior and to the design of a culture. A special kind of social behavior emerges when *A* responds in a definite way *because of the effect on the behavior of B*. We must consider the importance of *B* to *A* as well as of *A* to *B*. For example, when *A* sees *B* looking into a store window, he is likely to be reinforced if he looks too, as in the example of the berry patch. But if this looking is important to *B*, or to a third person who controls *B*, a change may take place in *B*'s behavior. *B* may look into the window in order to induce *A* to do the same. The carnival shill plays on the behavior of prospective customers in this way. *B*'s behavior is no longer controlled by what is seen in the window but (directly or indirectly) by the effect of that behavior on *A*. (The original contingencies for *A* break down: the window may not now be "worth looking into.") Action taken by *B* because of its effect on the behavior of *A* may be called "personal control." An important subdivision is verbal behavior, the properties of which derive from the fact that reinforcements are mediated by other organisms. Another subdivision is cultural design.

In analyzing any social episode from this point of view a complete account must be given of the behaviors of both parties as they contribute to the origin and maintenance of the behavior of each other. For example, in analyzing a verbal episode, we must account for both speaker and listener. This is seldom done in the case of nonverbal personal control. In noticing how the master controls the slave or the employer the worker, we commonly overlook reciprocal effects and, by considering action in one direction only, are led to regard control as exploitation, or at least the gaining of a one-sided advantage; but the control is actually mutual. The slave controls the master as completely as the master the slave, in the sense that the techniques of punishment employed by the master have been selected by the slave's behavior in submitting to them. This does not mean that the notion of exploitation is meaningless or that we may not appropriately ask, *Cui bono?* In doing so, however, we go beyond the account of the social episode itself and consider certain long-term effects which are clearly related to the question of value judgments. A comparable consideration arises in the analysis of any behavior which alters a cultural practice.

We may not be satisfied with an explanation of the behavior of two parties in a social interaction. The slaves in a quarry cutting stone for a pyramid work to escape punishment or death, and the rising pyramid is sufficiently reinforcing to the reigning Pharaoh to induce him to devote part of his wealth to maintaining the forces which punish or kill. An employer pays sufficient wages to induce men to work for him, and the products of their labor reimburse him with, let us say, a great deal to spare. These are on-going social systems, but in thus analyzing them we may not have taken everything into account. The system may be altered by outsiders in whom sympathy with, or fear of, the lot of the slave or exploited worker may be generated. More important, perhaps, is the possibility that the system may not actually be in equilibrium. It may breed changes which lead to its destruction. Control through punishment may lead to increasing viciousness, with an eventual loss of the support of those needed to maintain it; and the increasing poverty of the worker and the resulting increase in the economic power of the employer may also lead to counter-controlling action.

A culture which raises the question of collateral or deferred effects is most likely to discover and adopt practices which will survive or, as conditions change, will lead to modifications which in turn will survive. This is an important step in cultural design, but it is not easily taken. Long-term consequences are usually not obvious, and there is little inducement to pay any attention to them. We may admire a man who submits to aversive stimulation for the sake of later reinforcement or who eschews immediate reinforcement to avoid later punishment, but the contingencies which lead him to be "reasonable" in this sense (our admiration is part of them) are by no means overpowering. It has taken civilized societies a long time to invent the verbal devices—the precepts of morals and ethics—which successfully promote such an outcome. Ultimate advantages seem to be particularly easy to overlook in the control of behavior, where a quick though slight advantage may have undue weight. Thus, although we boast that the birch rod has been abandoned, most school children are still under aversive control—not because punishment is more effective in the long run, but because it yields immediate results. It is easier for the teacher to control the student by threatening punishment than by using positive reinforcement with its deferred, though more powerful, effects.

A culture which has become sensitive to the long-term consequences of its measures is usually supported by a literature or philosophy which includes a set of statements expressing the relations between measures and consequences. To the cultural designer, these statements function as prescriptions for effective action; to the members of the group, they are important variables furthering effective self-management. (To both, and to the neutral observer, they are sometimes said to "justify" a measure, but this may mean nothing more than strengthening the measure by classifying it with certain kinds of events characteristically called "good" or "right.") Thus, a government may induce its citizens to submit to the hardship and tragedy of war by picturing a future in which the world is made safe for democracy or free of Communism, or to a program of austerity by pointing to economic changes which will eventually lead to an abundance of good things for all. In so doing, it strengthens certain behavior on the part of its citizens which is essential to its purposes, and the resulting gain in power reinforces the government's own concern for deferred effects and its efforts to formulate them.

The scientific study of behavior underlines the collateral effects of controlling practices and reveals unstable features of a given interaction which may lead to long-deferred consequences. It may dictate effective remedial or preventive measures. It does not do this, however, by taking the scientist out of the causal stream. The scientist also is the product of a generic endowment and an environmental history. He also is controlled by the culture or cultures to which he belongs. Doing-something-about-human-behavior is a kind of social action and its products and by-products must be understood accordingly. A reciprocal relationship between the knower and the known, common to all the sciences, is important here. A laboratory for the study of behavior contains many devices for controlling the environment and for recording and analyzing the behavior of organisms. With the help of these devices and their associated techniques, we change the behavior of an organism in various ways, with considerable precision. *But note that the organism changes our behavior in quite as precise a fashion.* Our apparatus was designed by the organism we study, for it was the organism which led us to choose a particular manipulandum, particular categories of stimulation, particular modes of reinforcement, and so on, and to record particular aspects of its behavior. Measures which were successful were for that reason reinforcing and have been retained, while others have been, as we say, extinguished. The verbal behavior with which we analyze our data has been shaped in a similar way: order and consistency emerged to reinforce certain practices which were adopted, while other practices suffered extinction and were abandoned. (All scientific techniques, as well as scientific knowledge itself, are generated in this way. A cyclotron is "designed" by the particles it is to control, and a theory is written by the particles it is to explain, as the behavior of these particles shapes the nonverbal and verbal behavior of the scientist.)

A similarly reciprocal effect is involved in social action, especially in cultural design. Governmental, religious, economic, educational, and therapeutic institutions have been analyzed in many ways—for example, as systems which exalt such entities as sovereignty, virtue, utility, wisdom, and health. There is a considerable advantage in considering these institutions simply as behavioral technologies. Each one uses an identifiable set of techniques for the control of human behavior, distinguished by the variables manipulated. The discovery and invention of such techniques and their later abandonment or continued use—in short, their evolution—are, or should be, a part of the history of technology. The issues they raise, particularly with respect to the behavior of the discoverer or inventor, are characteristic of technology in general.

Both physical and behavioral technologies have shown progress or improvement in the sense that new practices have been discovered or invented and tested and that some of them have survived because their effects were reinforcing. Men have found better ways, not only to dye a cloth or build a bridge, but to govern, teach, and employ. The conditions under which all such practices originate range from sheer accident to the extremely complex behaviors called thinking. The conditions under which they are tested and selected are equally diverse. Certain immediate personal advantages may well have been the only important variables in the behavior of the primitive inventors of both physical and cultural devices. But the elaboration of moral and ethical practices has reduced the importance of personal aggrandizement. The honorific reinforcements with which society encourages action for the common weal, as well as the sanctions it applies to selfish behavior, generate a relatively disinterested creativity. Even in the field of personal control, improvements may be proposed, not for immediate exploitation, but—as by religious leaders, benevolent rulers, political philosophers, and educators—for "the good of all."

Only an analysis of moral and ethical practices will clarify the behavior of the cultural designer at this stage. He has faced a special difficulty in the fact that it is easier to demonstrate the right way to build a bridge than the right way to treat one's fellow men (the difference reducing to the immediacy and clarity of the results). The cultural inventor, even though relatively disinterested, has found it necessary to appeal for support to secular or divine authorities, supposedly inviolable philosophical premises, and even to military persuasion. Nothing of the sort has been needed for the greater part of physical technology. The wheel was not propagated by the sword or by promises of salvation—it made its own way. Cultural practices have survived or fallen only in part because of their effect on the strength of the group, and those which have survived are usually burdened with unnecessary impedimenta. By association, the current designer is handicapped by the fact that men look behind any cultural invention for irrelevant, ingenuous, or threatening forces.

There is another step in physical technology, however, which must have a parallel in cultural design. The practical application of scientific knowledge shows a new kind of disinterestedness. The scientist is usually concerned with the control of nature apart from his personal aggrandizement. He is perhaps not wholly "pure," but he seeks control mainly for its own sake or for the sake of furthering other scientific activity. There are practical as well as ethical reasons for this: as technology becomes more complex, for example, the scientist himself is less and less able to pursue the practical implications of his work. There is very little personal reimbursement for the most profitable ideas of modern science. As a result, a new idea may yield immediate technological improvements without bringing the scientist under suspicion of plotting a personal coup. But social technology has not yet reached this stage. A disinterested consideration of cultural practices from which suggestions for improvement may emerge is still often regarded as impossible. This is the price we pay for the fact that men (1) have so often improved their control of other men for purposes of exploitation, (2) have had to bolster their social practices with spurious justifications, and (3) have so seldom shared the attitudes of the basic scientist.

Most people would subscribe to the proposition that there is no value judgment involved in deciding how to build an atomic bomb, but would reject the proposition that there is none involved in deciding to build one. The most significant difference here may be that the scientific practices which guide the designer of the bomb are clear, while those which guide the designer of the culture which builds a bomb are not. We cannot predict the success or failure of a cultural invention with the same accuracy as we do that of a physical invention. It is for this reason that we are said to resort to value judgments in the second case. What we resort to is guessing. It is only in this sense that value judgments take up where science leaves off. When we can design small social interactions and, possibly, whole cultures with the confidence we bring to physical technology, the question of value will not be raised.

So far, men have designed their cultures largely by guesswork, including some very lucky hits; but we are not far from a stage of knowledge in which this can be changed. The change does not require that we be able to describe some distant state of mankind toward which we are moving or "deciding" to move. Early physical technology could not have foreseen the modern world, though it led to it. Progress and improvement are local changes. We better ourselves and our world as we go.

We change our cultural practices because it is in our nature as men to be reinforced in certain ways. This is not an infallible guide. It could, indeed, lead to fatal mistakes. For example, we have developed sanitation and medical science to escape from aversive events associated with illness and death, yet a new virus could conceivably arise to wipe out everyone except those to whom chronic illness and filth had granted immunity. On the present evidence, our decision in favor of sanitation and medicine seems to make for survival, but in the light of unforeseeable developments we may in time look back upon it as having had no survival value.

From time to time, men have sought to reassure themselves about the future by characterizing progress as the working out of some such principle as the general will, universal or collective reason, or the greatest good. Such a principle, if valid, would seem to guarantee an inevitable, if devious, improvement in the human condition. No such principle is clearly supported by a scientific analysis of human behavior. Yet the nature of man tells us something. Just as an ultimate genetic effect cannot be reached if immediate effects are not beneficial, so we must look only to the immediate consequences of behavior for modifications in a cultural pattern. Nevertheless, cultural inventions have created current conditions which have at least a probabilistic connection with future consequences. It is easy to say that men work for pleasure and to avoid pain, as the hedonists would have it. These are, indeed, powerful principles; but in affecting the day-to-day behavior of men, they have led to the construction of cultural devices which extend the range of both pleasure and pain almost beyond recognition. It is the same man, biologically speaking, who acts selfishly or for the good of the group, and it is the same man who, as a disinterested scientist, will make human behavior vastly more effective through cultural invention.

"Man"

Man has long sought to explain his behavior by searching for its causes. Historians and biographers have traced human achievements to conditions of birth, climate, culture, and personal contacts, and some of them have joined philosophers and essayists in more sweeping generalizations. Science has naturally worked in the same direction. The social sciences specialize in statistical demonstrations, but psychology and physiology are closer to history and biography in concentrating on the individual. In any case, more and more of the behavior of organisms, including man, is being plausibly related to events in their genetic and environmental histories. If other sciences are any guide, human behavior may ultimately be accounted for entirely in such terms.

The traditional conception, of course, is very different. It holds that a man behaves as he does because of his wishes, impulses, emotions, attitudes, and so on. His behavior is important only as the expression of an inner life. Many psychologists still subscribe to this view. The good Freudian attributes observable behavior to a drama played in nonphysical space by an immanent triumvirate scarcely to be distinguished from the spirits and demons of early animism. Other psychologists merely divide the inner personae into parts, each of which still carries on its little share of mental life. Thus, where a scientific analysis relates behavior to the physical environment, the mentalist may insist that the mind observes only a none-too-reliable copy of the environment called subjective experience. Where a scientific analysis shows that we react in a given way because similar actions in our past have had particular consequences, the mentalist may insist that we act because we have stored memories of past actions and of their consequences, which we now scan in order to reach certain expectations leading to an act of will which initiates behavior. Where a scientific

From *Proceedings of the American Philosophical Society*, 1964, *108*, 482–485.

analysis traces certain disturbing patterns of behavior to a history of punishment, the mentalist may argue that the disturbance is in the personality and that it is the effect of anxiety, just possibly generated by punishment. The traditional conception of man is an example of an explanatory strategy which was once common in other sciences. It has survived in psychology, possibly because of the extraordinary complexity of the subject matter. As plausible connections with external variables are demonstrated in spite of that complexity, however, the need for inner explanations is reduced. An effective scientific analysis would presumably dispense with them altogether.

That such an analysis will be simpler, more expedient, and more useful will not necessarily mean its adoption, because the older view served other than scientific functions. A behavioristic reinterpretation of mental life is not a fundamental issue for many people, but everyone has a stake in human behavior, and there are other reasons why the scientific picture may not seem to be a picture of man at all. Certain long-admired characteristics of human behavior seem to be neglected, and their absence is more threatening than any implication about the nature of consciousness or the existence of free will.

C. S. Lewis, for example, has gone so far as to argue that science is embarked upon "the abolition of man." [1] He is concerned with the neglect of a familiar feature of the traditional picture—an indwelling sense of justice, a felt standard of rightness, an inner source of values. To the traditionalist a human act is not simply a physical movement, it is a judgment, or the expression of a judgment, reached only by applying certain standards of conduct. It is not the act which is essentially human (morally acceptable though it may be), but the application of the standard. We may condition a man to behave in virtuous ways as we condition animals to behave according to any set of specifications, but such a man will not *be* virtuous. According to this view he can be virtuous only if he has not been conditioned to behave well automatically but has arrived at given forms of virtuous conduct by consulting his sense of rightness. (The argument is reminiscent of the complaint that a rational religion destroys piety, that proof of the existence of God deprives men of the opportunity to demonstrate their faith.)

If this traditional conception of man is to continue to challenge the scientific view, however, some thorny questions need to be answered. What *is* happening when a man refers to a standard of rightness? Can this form of behavior be analyzed? Where do standards come from? If the answer

---

[1] Lewis, C. S. *The Abolition of Man*. New York, 1947.

is that they come from the genetic or environmental history, then the scientific view is not in danger. And this appears to be the case. Lewis, for example, acknowledges that the sentiments he so highly values must be learned. "The little human animal," he says, "would not at first have the right responses"—indeed, in that sense would not yet be human. And he quotes Plato with approval to the effect that such things as taste and compassion must be taught before a child is "of an age to reason." These are the contentions of an environmentalist. The values to which a man must be able to appeal in order to be human are not originally his, and something beyond him is therefore ultimately responsible for his action. (The same unhappy story can be told of all inner explanations of human conduct, for the explanations must themselves be explained—possibly in terms of other inner events but eventually, and necessarily, in terms of forces acting upon a man from without.)

A small issue survives at a technical level. How are we to teach a child to behave well? We can begin by conditioning him to make so many purely automatic, right responses, but we shall find that the number which must thus be taught is distressingly large. It is more efficient, if not actually necessary, to teach him to examine each new occasion as it arises and, by applying certain rules, to arrive at an appropriate response. Such is our practice in teaching multiplication. Up to twelve-times-twelve we condition specific responses, each of which can be quite automatic, implying no understanding of multiplication. Beyond that, we find it expedient to condition certain procedures which permit the child to arrive at a vast number of specific products which it would not be efficient to condition separately.

It is sometimes argued that there is an element of freedom in the application of standards which is lacking in the automatic execution of right responses. But a sense of freedom is another of those inner attributes which lose their force as we more clearly understand man's relation to his environment. Freedom—or, rather, behavior which "feels free"—is also the product of a history of conditioning. In that remarkable book, *Émile*, Jean Jacques Rousseau tried to find replacements for the punitive methods of the schools of his time. He insisted that students should behave as they want, rather than as they are forced to behave through physical coercion. He showed an extraordinary ingenuity in substituting positive inducements for punishment. But he was not turning education over to the pupil himself.

> Let [the child] believe that he is always in control, though it is always you [the teacher] who really controls. There is no subjugation so perfect as that

which keeps the appearance of freedom, for in that way one captures volition itself. The poor baby, knowing nothing, able to do nothing, having learned nothing, is he not at your mercy? Can you not arrange everything in the world which surrounds him? Can you not influence him as you wish? His work, his play, his pleasures, his pains, are not all these in your hands and without his knowing it? Doubtless he ought to do only what he wants; but he ought to want to do only what you want him to do; he ought not to take a step which you have not foreseen; he ought not to open his mouth without your knowing what he will say.²

Thus spoke a great champion of human freedom! Like a sense of rightness or justice, the dispositions which make a given act feel free come from the environment. The surviving question is again technical. What is the best way to bring about those changes which are the object of education? There are many advantages in arranging matters so that the pupil does what he wants to do, but he must be carefully prepared to want to do those things which are required for effective instruction.

Another human attribute which seems to be missing from the scientific picture concerns what one does *not* want to do. In the traditional view a man has duties as well as rights: there are things he must do or suffer the consequences. He is responsible for his conduct in the sense that, if he does not behave in a given way, it is only fair that he be punished. To escape punishment—either the natural punishments of the physical environment or the social punishments of society—he engages in an activity called self-control. When the same ultimate "good" behavior is achieved without using punishment, self-control in this sense is unnecessary.

The omission of personal responsibility from the scientific conception of man has been particularly deplored by Joseph Wood Krutch.³ When we regard a criminal as in need of treatment rather than punishment, for example, we deprive him of "the human attribute of responsibility." Treatment is only one way of generating good behavior without punishment. Preventive steps are likely to be more valuable. For example, we might control stealing by creating a world free of inciting circumstances (for example, a world in which there is nothing one does not already have or where nothing is within reach to be stolen) or by conditioning behavior which is incompatible with stealing or displaces it (for example, we might strongly reinforce "respecting the property of others" or teach easier, legal

---

² Rousseau, Jean Jacques. *Émile ou de L'Éducation.* Amsterdam et Francfort, 1762. Page 121 in the Classiques Garnier Edition.
³ Krutch, Joseph Wood. *The Measure of Man.* Indianapolis: Bobbs-Merrill, 1953.

ways of getting things). When we solve the problem in any of these ways, we leave no room for personal responsibility or self-control. We leave no room for moral struggle; and if to struggle is human, we have indeed destroyed something of man.

The same argument holds for nongovernmental punishments. Smoking cigarettes is "naturally" punished by lung cancer or the threat of lung cancer, as overeating is punished by obesity, illness, and the threat of an early death. Aggressive action is punished by retaliative measures. All these aversive consequences normally lead to some measure of self-control. But we can reduce the inclination to smoke, eat, or act aggressively in other ways—and with it the need to control oneself. Appropriate drugs have this effect. A tranquilizer reduces the need to control aggression, an appetite-suppressant reduces the need to control eating, and a drug which would reduce the tendency to smoke cigarettes would reduce the need to control one's smoking habits. Another form of control would be to build a world in which the positive reinforcements now accorded these behaviors are carefully managed. In such a world a man would be either naturally wise and good or at least easily taught to be wise and good. There would be no place for intellectual and moral struggle.

Any technology, physical or social, which reduces punishing consequences reduces the need for self-control and personal responsibility. If the same acceptable conduct is achieved, it is difficult to see why anyone should object. The trouble is that the characteristics which are thus dismissed have long been admired. We admire people who apply ethical and moral standards, who accept responsibility, and who control themselves. We admire them in part because the results are reinforcing to us, for the individual is thus induced to conform to the interests of others. We also admire such behavior just in order to support it. Admiration is a social practice used to eke out a defective control. There are certain kinds of heroism, for example, which society can engender only by effusively admiring them. We induce men to die for their country by convincing them that it is sweet and decorous to do so. Students work hard to be admired by their teachers. Men undergo exhausting labor and suffer pain with patience because they are admired for doing so. Yet technological progress is directed toward making all this unnecessary. In a world at peace there will be no military heroism to admire. We shall no longer admire patient suffering when men seldom need to suffer. We do not even now give men credit for exhausting labor if the labor can be "saved," and we shall not admire students who work hard when there are techniques of education in which they need not "work" at all. We shall no longer admire wrestling with the devil, if it turns out that the devil is simply a slight disturbance in the hypothalamus which can be allayed by a suitable drug.

In turning to external and manipulable variables, a scientific analysis moves away from supposed inner activities which we have tried to reach through admiration. The inner activity, needing to be admired, naturally seems admirable. Thus we admire a man who can multiply by applying rules more than one who merely recites the multiplication table in an automatic fashion, but we admire the latter far beyond one who simply uses a calculating machine. The calculating machine has been designed to reduce the behavior required in multiplication to external, sharply defined, relatively infallible, and almost effortless responses. It improves multiplication, but makes the multiplier less admirable. Plato records an objection to the invention of the alphabet on similar grounds: if texts were generally available, a man would seem to know things which he had merely read.[4] But the alphabet was invented precisely to enable one man to profit from the direct knowledge of another. Must we destroy all physical and social inventions in order to recapture a man we can wholeheartedly admire?

Two important features often said to be missing from the scientific picture of man are actually emphasized in it. If man has no freedom of choice, if he can initiate no action which alters the causal stream of his behavior, then he may seem to have no control over his own destiny. The scientific view of man according to Krutch is a "dead end."[5] The fact is, however, that men control both their genetic and environmental histories, and in *that* sense they do, indeed, control themselves. Science and technology are concerned with changing the world in which men live, and changes are made precisely because of their effects on human behavior. We have reached the stage, far from a dead end, in which man can determine his future with an entirely new order of effectiveness. C. S. Lewis would still protest; in *The Abolition of Man* he wrote, ". . . the power of man to make himself what he pleases means . . . the power of some men to make other men what *they* please." But it has always been thus. Men control themselves by controlling the world in which they live. They do this as much when they exercise self-control, as when they make changes in their culture which alter the conduct of others.

Another feature of the traditional concept which is emphasized rather than abolished is individuality. Some practices derived from a scientific knowledge of human behavior could no doubt lead to regimentation, as

4 Plato. *Phaedrus*. Jowett translation, III: 274e–275b.

5 Krutch, Joseph Wood. What I learned about existentialism. *Saturday Review*, 45 (April 21, 1962).

practices consonant with traditional conceptions have often done, but there is nothing in the scientific position which makes this inevitable. On the contrary, as the product of a set of genetic and environmental variables man is most reassuringly unique. The uniqueness of the human fingerprint once came as a surprise and, because of its practical usefulness, is still a familiar symbol of individuality. But the body which each man derives from his genetic history is a vast system of unique structures of which the whorls on the ball of the thumb are a ridiculously trivial example. Equally idiosyncratic are all those characteristics which a man derives from his environment. It is true that certain scientific practices are simplified when these sources of individuality are minimized, but there is nothing in scientific practice or theory which threatens individuality or questions the possibility that some collocations of variables arising from these sources will have the outstanding results we attribute to talent or genius.

It is not easy to abandon notions like a sense of justice, a sense of freedom, and personal responsibility or to accept a new interpretation of man's individuality and his power to control his own destiny. Yet it would be remarkable if any conception of man did not occasionally need revision. Human behavior is extraordinarily complex, and it is unlikely that a true definitive account has been reached so soon. The traditional conception has certainly not made us conspicuously successful in dealing with human affairs. The alternative picture which a science of behavior asks us to accept is not really frightening. Man survives unchanged. Physics does not change the nature of the world it studies, and no science of behavior can change the essential nature of man, even though both sciences yield technologies with a vast power to manipulate their subject matters. Science leads us to see man in a different light, but he is nevertheless the same man we once saw in another light. If we must have something to admire, let it be man's willingness to discard a flattering portrait of himself in favor of a more accurate and hence more useful picture. Even here admiration is superfluous. The hard fact is that the culture which most readily acknowledges the validity of a scientific analysis is most likely to be successful in that competition between cultures which, whether we like it or not, will decide all such issues with finality.

The Design of Experimental Communities

A community may be thought of as a small state, even a miniature world, in which some of the problems of implementing a way of life are reduced to manageable size. Many kinds of communities have served this purpose. Although seemingly successful unplanned cultures have often been taken as models (Arcadia by the Greeks, the South Sea islands by the eighteenth-century social philosophers), this article is concerned with communities which have been or might be explicitly designed.

Some of the rules of the Qumran Community were set forth in the Manual of Discipline found among the Dead Sea Scrolls, which the community helped to preserve. The rules of Benedict and Augustine governed life in similar monastic communities. Semireligious and secular communities flourished in the nineteenth century in America (the Oneida Community is a particularly interesting example).[1] Explicitly designed, or intentional, communities of the twentieth century range from the intensely religious Bruderhof to the essentially secular kibbutzim in Israel. The Soviet collectives and *mikroraions* and the Chinese communes, though parts of larger governmental structures, are other examples. Fictional communities—for example, those described in Thomas More's *Utopia*[2] and Francis Bacon's *New Atlantis*[3] have also captured men's imaginations.

From *The International Encyclopedia of the Social Sciences*. David L. Sills, editor. New York: Crowell Collier and Macmillan, 1968.

[1] Noyes, Pierpont. *My Father's House: An Oneida Boyhood*. New York: Farrar & Rinehart, 1937.

[2] More, Thomas (1516). *The Complete Works of St. Thomas More,* vol. 4: Utopia. New Haven: Yale University Press, 1966.

[3] Bacon, Francis (1627). *New Atlantis.*

In its relation to government in the broadest sense, a community, speculative or attempted, serves something of the function of a pilot experiment in science or a pilot model or plant in technology. It is constructed on a small scale. Certain problems arising from sheer size—such as communication and transportation—can then be neglected, but the main advantage is that closer attention can be given to the lives of individual members. Such a community is also almost always geographically isolated. Utopias have often occupied islands, but walls isolate almost as well as water. (The members of a sect, no matter how well organized, are not usually regarded as a community if they are widely dispersed geographically.) There is also a certain isolation from tradition. The eighteenth-century European could expect to abandon much of his culture when he reached Tahiti; life in a monastery may begin with a ritual of rebirth. All this makes it easier to think about such a community as a viable or perishable entity—as an organism with a life of its own. Its success or failure, unlike the rise and fall of eras or nations, is likely to be quick and conspicuous. New ways of doing things are tested for their bearing on its success. Such a community, in short, is an experiment.

Men found, join, or dream of such communities for many reasons. Some are moved by intellectual interests: they want to prove a theory (for example, that men are naturally noble or that they are incomplete without "community" or "love") or to hasten a prophesied stage in history. Others have more immediate personal reasons: they seek simple pleasures, the satisfaction of basic needs, political order, economic stability, help in self-discipline, and so on. Such goals are often formalized as "values." The goal of the community is to maximize happiness, security, sanctity, or personal fulfillment. The more general the goal, however, the more debatable it seems to be. In conceiving of a community as a pilot experiment, the designer may turn directly to two practical questions: What behavior on the part of the members of a community is most likely to contribute to its success? How may that behavior be generated and maintained?

Some answers to the first question are quite obvious. It is important to a community that its members defend it against its enemies, produce the food, shelter, clothing, and other things it needs, and maintain internal order. It is also obviously important that its members teach each other, and, particularly, new members, how to behave in necessary ways. Other kinds of behavior—for example, in the uses of leisure—often figure prominently among expressed goals, but their relevance to the success of a community is not always clear. These behaviors are things members "want to do," and various reasons may be given for doing them, but the designer may proceed most effectively by confining himself to behaviors that are demonstrably related to success or survival.

The second question has usually been answered by appeal to historical analogy. Men have lived peacefully, productively, stably, and happily under many observed systems or structures of government, economics, society, family life, and so on. There is a strong presumption that a given system generates the behavior observed under it, as political science, economics, sociology, and other social disciplines usually contend. We might conclude, therefore, that the designer has only to choose among systems or structures. Should the government of a community be authoritarian or democratic? Should the society be open or closed? Should the social structure be classless or stratified? Should the economy be planned or laissez-faire? Should the family be strong or weak? Questions at this level of analysis offer little practical help in designing a community. Terms like "authoritarian" and "laissez-faire" seldom refer to properties which a designer can build into a social environment, and terms like "peaceful" and "stable" do not sharply characterize behavior which can be shown to contribute to the success of such an environment.

There is a more useful level of analysis. Every developed language contains terms which describe in great detail the social environment and the behavior it generates. Rules of thumb useful in modifying behavior are expressed in such terms. Thus, everyone knows how to attract a man's attention, to arouse him emotionally, to reward and punish him, and so on. Communities are usually designed with an eye to this level of human behavior. The designer is concerned not with a hypothetical type of economic system but with actual working conditions, not with a hypothetical type of government but with ethical practices and instructions in self-discipline, not with a formal conception of social or family structure but with specific interactions among the members of a group.

The relations between behavior and environment at this level have only recently been formulated in a systematic way. It is significant that statements expressing an understanding of human nature or a skill in handling people—for example, in the essays of such men as Bacon or Montaigne or in sporadic comments by political scientists, economists, and others—have remained aphoristic. They have never been brought together in a coherent, consistent account. Psychology is the scientific discipline relevant here, but it has only recently been able to supply an effective alternative to folklore and personal experience. A special branch of psychology has now reached the point at which promising technological applications are becoming feasible. The principles derived from an experimental analysis of behavior offer the designer considerable help in setting up an environment under which behavior which will contribute to the success of the community may be generated.

At any level of analysis, certain conditions either lie beyond the control of the designer or, if used by him to advantage, limit the significance of his design as a general solution. He cannot actually institute a new culture all at once: the earlier social environments of the members of a community will play a role, if only in providing a contrast to a new way of life. Members may show personal idiosyncrasies or background differences. They may have been explicitly selected—and will almost certainly be self-selected—with respect to some such trait as cooperativeness or intelligence. The site of the community—its climate, soil, and existing flora and fauna—will be favorable or unfavorable. The community will begin with a certain amount of starting capital, it will have natural resources, and it may continue to receive outside support in the form of charity or philanthropy. All these conditions limit the significance of a successful result, but there is still scope for extensive design. A few examples must suffice here.

Negative Reinforcement

An important element in any culture is the use of force. The state is often defined primarily in terms of the power to punish. We say that punishment requires force because its imposition is resisted. In political theory the right and power to punish are discussed under some such concept as "sovereignty." The behavioral processes are obvious and easily related to the role of punishment. The term applies, strictly speaking, only to the suppression of unwanted behavior, but the punishing events used for that purpose can be used to generate behavior—to induce people to behave in given ways by "punishing them for not behaving." The technique is particularly useful in offsetting other aversive consequences, as in forcing men to fight or to fill production quotas. Effectively used, punishment in this broad sense can make men law-abiding, obedient, and dutiful.

But there are inevitable side effects. One who is behaving well in order to escape punishment may simply escape in other ways, as exemplified by military desertion and religious apostasy. Extensive use of punishment will cost a community some of its members. It may also lead to counterattack— as in revolution or religious reformation—or to stubborn resistance to all forms of control. These are familiar, predictable reactions upon which an experimental analysis of behavior throws considerable light. A slow, erratic trend toward minimizing aversive control in the design of a community is actually an example of such a by-product. This trend is exemplified when powerful military or police action is replaced by ethical control imposed by those with whom the citizen is in immediate contact or when educational programs are designed to reduce the frequency with which aversive behavior occurs or to prepare the individual to adjust more effectively to any remaining forcible control. An example of a more extreme alternative is the cloister, an environment in which unwanted behavior is unlikely or impossible and in which wanted behavior is particularly likely to occur.

Positive Reinforcement

A very different example of the relevance of an analysis of behavior to the design of a community is the use of so-called rewards. A community may need as much power to reward as to punish, but it is not said to be using force because its operations are not resisted. Reward refers very loosely to the "positive reinforcers" which have been extensively analyzed in laboratory research. It is a basic principle that behavior which is followed by certain kinds of consequences is more likely to occur again, but reinforcements may be contingent on behavior in many subtle and complex ways, and extensive technological knowledge is needed to use the principle effectively in all its ramifications. Although it is generally true that the greater the reinforcement the more it is productive of behavior, the amount of behavior generated is not related in any simple way to the amount of reinforcement. The net gain or utility of an action has little relation to the probability that the action will occur. Indeed, under certain contingencies of reinforcement—for example, in gambling—behavior may be maintained at a high level for long periods of time even though the net monetary gain is negative.

A community may resort to positive reinforcement to generate any behavior important to its success. For example, it may arrange for reinforcement through group approval of accepted behavior as an alternative to coercive legal or ethical control. It will also be interested, of course, in the classical problem of maintaining productive labor. (If there is any established discipline which is most closely concerned with positive reinforcement, it is economics.) The designer of effective working conditions in a small community is in a favorable position to use a technology of reinforcement. The immediate temporal contingencies are crucial. Many communities have given special attention to rewarding productive labor. Some have returned to conditions which prevail in the life of the craftsman

—that is, they have used the natural reinforcing consequences of labor. It is not a very enlightened solution. Furthermore, the use of money as a reinforcement is admittedly not as simple as it may at first appear. The value of money must, of course, be taught—but so must the value of early stages of craftwork. The main difficulty is that wages are artificially contingent upon the behavior which produces them, and it has been difficult to construct contingencies which maintain productive labor without undesirable side effects. It was once thought that the deficiency must be offset by making wages more powerful as reinforcers—for example, by maintaining a hungry labor force. Another solution has been to increase the actual amount of reinforcement (by raising wages). The contingencies of reinforcement have remained poorly analyzed, however. Current systems of rewards are largely aversive, the threatened loss of a standard of living being more important than the receipt of wages. Effective reinforcement of productive labor is one of the more interesting areas in which the designer of an experimental community may apply recent scientific discoveries.

When goods and services which may be used as reinforcers are allowed to become available for other reasons—when, for example, they are supplied by a bountiful nature or a bountiful government concerned with welfare or happiness—much of their reinforcing effect is lost. We make explicit use of this principle when, as an alternative to punishment, we deliberately destroy contingencies by supplying reinforcers gratis—for example, when we give men the things they would otherwise behave illegally to get. If the community does not need productive work, reinforcing contingencies can safely be neglected, but a long-standing conflict between welfare and incentive suggests that the issue has not been wholly resolved.

LEISURE

Positive reinforcement occupies an especially important place in solving the problem of leisure. With modern technology it is conceivable that a man need not spend much time in making his contribution to peace and prosperity. What is he to do with the rest of his time? Perhaps it does not matter. If the community has solved the essential problems of daily life, it may leave each member free to do as he pleases. But he is free only to come under other forms of control. If there are no effective reinforcers, he may spend all his waking hours doing nothing. Or he may come under the sustained control of biological reinforcers, such as food, sex, aggressive damage to others, or drug-induced euphoric states. Weaker reinforcers will take control when they occur on powerful schedules: leisure is often spent in repetitive and compulsive activities, such as solitaire or other simple games.

These are all forms of behavior which flourish when behaviors having a more specific relevance to the success of a community are not needed. A community may be able to afford a certain number of them, but it stands to profit more from other uses of free time. Sports, games, and other forms of complex play; arts and crafts, music, and the dance; literature and the theater; and the contemplation, observation, and exploration of nature which constitute "science" in the broadest sense are important activities to the designer because they bear on the success of the community. Some of them make the community more attractive in the sense that they reinforce supporting behavior and discourage defection. For example, they reinforce the simple behavior of remaining in the community. Other activities develop extraordinary skills which make it possible for members to meet emergencies with maximum effectiveness. Those which advance science yield the physical and cultural technologies needed for the maintenance and improvement of the community as a way of life.

These relations to the success of a community are overlooked in saying that leisure is to be devoted to the pursuit of happiness, for this emphasizes the reinforcers rather than the behaviors reinforced. The concept of "happiness" (or, less frivolously, "fulfillment" or "enrichment") is often felt to be a necessary, if admittedly troublesome, value in explaining man's search for a way of life. From the point of view of an experimental analysis of behavior, it appears to be merely an awkward way of representing the roles of positive and negative reinforcers. Its main fault is its neglect of the contingencies of reinforcement. Asked to describe a world in which he would like to live, a man will often refer directly to reinforcing conditions—freedom from aversive stimulation and an abundance of positive reinforcers—but he then finds himself unprepared for many paradoxes, such as the often encountered unhappiness of those "who have everything" or, in that other field of utopian speculation, man's failure to conceive of an interesting heaven.

In summary, then, a community is much more complex than a laboratory experiment in human behavior but much simpler than the large-scale enterprises analyzed in political science, economics, and other social disciplines. For this reason it is especially helpful in studying the effects of a social environment on human behavior and, in return, the relevance of that behavior to the maintenance and development of the environment. It is a favorable ground for social invention. A surprising number of practices first described in utopian thinking have eventually been adopted on a broader scale. In writing the *New Atlantis* Francis Bacon could imagine that scientists might be organized to solve the problems of the community. Only after he had made such an organization plausible was the Royal Society founded—and quite clearly on Bacon's model. More general principles are also encouraged. The success or failure of a community, for example, is easily seen to mean the success or failure of all its members, whether or not its social structure is egalitarian; but it is hard to reach a similar sense of community in thinking about a nation or the world as a whole.

It has been suggested that the well-governed Greek city-state, by permitting men to conceive of an orderly world of nature, led to the development of Greek science. Little in the world today could have that effect, for the order is now clearly on the side of science. But if the principles which are emerging from the laboratory study of human behavior can be shown to be relevant, then science may repay its debt by bringing order back into human affairs.

PART II

A Method for the Experimental Analysis of Behavior— Its Theory and Practice, Its History, and a Glimpse of Its Future

. . . sauce his palate
With thy most operant poison
TIMON OF ATHENS, IV, iii

Are Theories of Learning Necessary?

This paper, presented at a meeting of the Midwestern Psychological Association in May, 1949, was mainly concerned with the nature and function of theory, with an analysis of the "measures" used in tracing the learning process, with the question of a useful dependent variable, with rate of responding as a measure of probability of response, and with the independent variables which govern behavior. It also provided an opportunity to report illustrative material from a series of experiments carried out during the preceding decade. In some of these, supported by General Mills, Inc., and by the Office of Scientific Research and Development, Keller Breland, Norman Guttman, W. K. Estes, and Marion Breland collaborated. Others were conducted at Indiana University with the assistance of Clayton K. Bishop. The paper was published in Psychological Review, *1950, 57, 193-216 and is reprinted here by permission.*

Certain basic assumptions, essential to any scientific activity, are sometimes called theories. That nature is orderly rather than capricious is an example. Certain statements are also theories simply to the extent that they are not yet facts. A scientist may guess at the result of an experiment before the experiment is carried out. The prediction and the later statement of result may be composed of the same terms in the same syntactic arrangement, the difference being in the degree of confidence. No empirical statement is wholly nontheoretical in this sense because evidence is never complete, nor is any prediction probably ever made wholly without evidence. The term *theory* will not refer here to statements of these sorts but rather to any explanation of an observed fact which appeals to events taking place somewhere else, at some other level of observation, described in different terms, and measured, if at all, in different dimensions.

Three types of theory in the field of learning satisfy this definition. The most characteristic is to be found in the field of physiological psychology. We are all familiar with the changes which are supposed to take place in the nervous system when an organism learns. Synaptic connections are made or broken, electrical fields are disrupted or reorganized, concentrations of ions are built up or allowed to diffuse away, and so on. In the science of neurophysiology statements of this sort are not necessarily theories in the present sense. But in a science of behavior, where we are concerned with whether or not an organism secretes saliva when a bell rings,

69

or jumps toward a gray triangle, or says *bik* when a card reads *tuz,* or loves someone who resembles his mother, all statements about the nervous system are theories in the sense that they are not expressed in the same terms and could not be confirmed with the same methods of observation as the facts for which they are said to account.

A second type of learning theory is in practice not far from the physiological, although there is less agreement about the method of direct observation. Theories of this type have always dominated the field of human behavior. They consist of references to "mental" events, as in saying that an organism learns to behave in a certain way because it "finds something pleasant" or because it "expects something to happen." To the mentalistic psychologist these explanatory events are no more theoretical than synaptic connections to the neurophysiologist, but in a science of behavior they are theories because the methods and terms appropriate to the events to be explained differ from the methods and terms appropriate to the explaining events.

In a third type of learning theory the explanatory events are not directly observed. The writer's suggestion [in *The Behavior of Organisms*] that the letters CNS be regarded as representing, not the Central Nervous System, but the Conceptual Nervous System seems to have been taken seriously. Many theorists point out that they are not talking about the nervous system as an actual structure undergoing physiological or biochemical changes but only as a system with a certain dynamic output. Theories of this sort are multiplying fast, and so are parallel operational versions of mental events. A purely behavioral definition of expectancy has the advantage that the problem of mental observation is avoided and with it the problem of how a mental event can cause a physical one. But such theories do not go so far as to assert that the explanatory events are identical with the behavioral facts which they purport to explain. A statement about behavior may support such a theory but will never resemble it in terms or syntax. Postulates are good examples. True postulates cannot become facts. Theorems may be deduced from them which, as tentative statements about behavior, may or may not be confirmed, but theorems are not theories in the present sense. Postulates remain theories to the end.

It is not the purpose of this paper to show that any of these theories cannot be put in good scientific order, or that the events to which they refer may not actually occur or be studied by appropriate sciences. It would be foolhardy to deny the achievements of theories of this sort in the history of science. The question of whether they are necessary, however, has other implications and is worth asking. If the answer is no, then it may be possible to argue effectively against theory in the field of learning. A science of behavior must eventually deal with behavior in its relation to certain manipulable variables. Theories—whether neural, mental, or conceptual—talk about intervening steps in these relationships. But instead of prompting us to search for and explore relevant variables, they frequently have quite the opposite effect. When we attribute behavior to a neural or mental event, real or conceptual, we are likely to forget that we still have the task of accounting for the neural or mental event. When we assert that an animal acts in a given way because it expects to receive food, then what began as the task of accounting for learned behavior becomes the task of accounting for expectancy. The problem is at least equally complex and probably more difficult. We are likely to close our eyes to it and to use the theory to give us answers in place of the answers we might find through further study. It might be argued that the principal function of learning theory to date has been, not to suggest appropriate research, but to create a false sense of security, an unwarranted satisfaction with the status quo.

Research designed with respect to theory is also likely to be wasteful. That a theory generates research does not prove its value unless the research is valuable. Much useless experimentation results from theories, and much energy and skill are absorbed by them. Most theories are eventually overthrown, and the greater part of the associated research is discarded. This could be justified if it were true that productive research requires a theory— as is, of course, often claimed. It is argued that research would be aimless and disorganized without a theory to guide it. The view is supported by psychological texts which take their cue from the logicians rather than empirical science and describe thinking as necessarily involving stages of hypothesis, deduction, experimental test, and confirmation. But this is not the way most scientists actually work. It is possible to design significant experiments for other reasons, and the possibility to be examined is that such research will lead more directly to the kind of information which a science usually accumulates.

The alternatives are at least worth considering. How much can be done without theory? What other sorts of scientific activity are possible? And what light do alternative practices throw upon our present preoccupation with theory?

It would be inconsistent to try to answer these questions at a theoretical level. Let us therefore turn to some experimental material in three areas in which thories of learning now flourish and raise the question of the function of theory in a more concrete fashion.

The Basic Datum in Learning

What actually happens when an organism learns is not an easy question to answer. Those who are interested in a science of behavior will insist that learning is a change in behavior, but they tend to avoid explicit references to responses or acts as such. "Learning is adjustment or adaptation to a situation." But of what stuff are adjustments and adaptations made? Are they data, or inferences from data? "Learning is improvement." But improvement in what? And from whose point of view? "Learning is restoration of equilibrium." But what is in equilibrium and how is it put there? "Learning is problem solving." But what are the physical dimensions of a problem—or of a solution? Definitions of this sort show an unwillingness to take what appears before the eyes in a learning experiment as a basic datum. Particular observations seem too trivial. An error score falls; but we are not ready to say that this is learning rather than merely the result of learning. An organism meets a criterion of ten successful trials; but an arbitrary criterion is at variance with our conception of the generality of the learning process.

This is where theory steps in. If it is not the time required to get out of a puzzle box which changes in learning, but rather the strength of a bond, or the conductivity of a neural pathway, or the excitatory potential of a habit, then problems seem to vanish. Getting out of a box faster and faster is not learning; it is merely performance. The learning goes on somewhere else, in a different dimensional system. And although the time required depends upon arbitrary conditions, often varies discontinuously, and is subject to reversal of magnitude, we feel sure that the learning process itself is continuous, orderly, and beyond the accidents of measurement. Nothing could better illustrate the use of theory as a refuge from the data.

But we must eventually get back to an observable datum. If learning is the process we suppose it to be, then it must appear so in the situations in which we study it. Even if the basic process belongs to some other dimensional system, our measures must have relevant and comparable properties. But productive experimental situations are hard to find, particularly if we accept certain plausible restrictions. To show an orderly change in the behavior of the *average* rat or ape or child is not enough, since learning is a process in the behavior of the individual. To record the beginning and end of learning of a few discrete steps will not suffice, since a series of cross-sections will not give complete coverage of a continuous process. The dimensions of the change must spring from the behavior itself; they must not be imposed by an external judgment of success or failure or an external criterion of completeness. But when we review the literature with these requirements in mind, we find little justification for the theoretical process in which we take so much comfort.

The energy level or work-output of behavior, for example, does not change in appropriate ways. In the sort of behavior adapted to the Pavlovian experiment (respondent behavior) there may be a progressive increase in the magnitude of response during learning. But we do not shout our responses louder and louder as we learn verbal material, nor does a rat press a lever harder and harder as conditioning proceeds. In operant behavior the energy or magnitude of response changes significantly only when some arbitrary value is differentially reinforced—when such a change is what is learned.

The emergence of a right response in competition with wrong responses is another datum frequently used in the study of learning. The maze and the discrimination box yield results which may be reduced to these terms. But a behavior-ratio of right vs. wrong cannot yield a continuously changing measure in a single experiment on a single organism. The point at which one response takes precedence over another cannot give us the whole history of the change in either response. Averaging curves for groups of trials or organisms will not solve this problem.

Increasing attention has recently been given to latency, the relevance of which, like that of energy level, is suggested by the properties of conditioned and unconditioned reflexes. But in operant behavior the relation to a stimulus is different. A measure of latency involves other considerations, as inspection of any case will show. Most operant responses may be emitted in the absence of what is regarded as a relevant stimulus. In such a case the response is likely to appear before the stimulus is presented. It is no solution to escape this embarrassment by locking a lever so that an organism cannot press it until the stimulus is presented, since we can scarcely be content with temporal relations which have been forced into compliance with our expectations. Runway latencies are subject to this objection. In a typical experiment the door of a starting box is opened and the time which elapses before a rat leaves the box is measured. Opening the door is not only a stimulus, it is a change in the situation which makes the response possible for the first time. The time measured is by no means as simple as a latency and requires another formulation. A great deal depends upon what the rat is doing at the moment the stimulus is presented. Some experimenters wait until the rat is facing the door, but to do so is to tamper with the measurement being taken. If, on the other hand, the door is opened without reference to what the rat is doing, the first major effect is the conditioning of favorable waiting behavior. The rat eventually stays near and facing the door. The resulting shorter starting-time is not due to a reduction in the latency of a response, but to the conditioning of favorable preliminary behavior.

Latencies in a single organism do not follow a simple learning process.

Relevant data on this point were obtained as part of an extensive study of reaction time. A pigeon, enclosed in a box, is conditioned to peck at a recessed disc in one wall. Food is presented as reinforcement by exposing a hopper through a hole below the disc. If responses are reinforced only after a stimulus has been presented, responses at other times disappear. Very short reaction times are obtained by differentially reinforcing responses which occur very soon after the stimulus.[1] But responses also come to be made very quickly without differential reinforcement. Inspection shows that this is due to the development of effective waiting. The bird comes to stand before the disc with its head in good striking position. Under optimal conditions, without differential reinforcement, the mean time between stimulus and response will be of the order of ⅓ second. This is not a true reflex latency, since the stimulus is discriminative rather than eliciting, but it is a fair example of the latency used in the study of learning. The point is that this measure does not vary continuously or in an orderly fashion. By giving the bird more food, for example, we induce a condition in which it does not always respond. But the responses which occur show approximately the same temporal relation to the stimulus (Figure 1, middle curve). In extinction, of special interest here, there is a scattering of latencies because lack of reinforcement generates an emotional condition. Some responses occur sooner and others are delayed, but the commonest value remains unchanged (bottom curve in Figure 1). The longer latencies are easily explained by inspection. Emotional behavior, of which examples will be mentioned later, is likely to be in progress when the ready-signal is presented. It is often not discontinued before the "go" signal is presented, and the result is a long starting-time. Cases also begin to appear in which the bird simply does not respond at all during a specified time. If we average a large number of readings, either from one bird or many, we may create what looks like a progressive lengthening of latency. But the data for an individual organism do not show a continuous process.

Another datum to be examined is the rate at which a response is emitted. Fortunately the story here is different. We study this rate by designing a situation in which a response may be freely repeated, choosing a response (for example, touching or pressing a small lever or key) which may be easily observed and counted. The responses may be recorded on a polygraph, but a more convenient form is a cumulative curve from which rate

---

[1] An experiment on "differential reinforcement with respect to time" was reported at a meeting of the American Psychological Association, September, 1946. An abstract appears in *The American Psychologist*, 1946, *1*, 274–275.

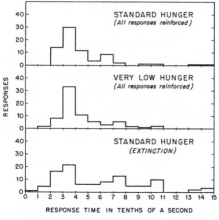

RESPONSE TIME IN TENTHS OF A SECOND

FIG. 1

of responding is immediately read as slope. The rate at which a response is emitted in such a situation comes close to our preconception of the learning process. As the organism learns, the rate rises. As it unlearns (for example, in extinction) the rate falls. Various sorts of discriminative stimuli may be brought into control of the response with corresponding modifications of the rate. Motivational changes alter the rate in a sensitive way. So do those events which we speak of as generating emotion. The range through which the rate varies significantly may be as great as of the order of 1000:1. Changes in rate are satisfactorily smooth in the individual case, so that it is not necessary to average cases. A given value is often quite stable: in the pigeon a rate of four or five thousand responses per hour may be maintained without interruption for as long as fifteen hours.

Rate of responding appears to be the only datum which varies significantly and in the expected direction under conditions which are relevant to the "learning process." We may, therefore, be tempted to accept it as our long-sought-for measure of strength of bond, excitatory potential, etc. Once in possession of an effective datum, however, we may feel little need for any theoretical construct of this sort. Progress in a scientific field usually waits upon the discovery of a satisfactory dependent variable. Until such a variable has been discovered, we resort to theory. The entities which have figured so prominently in learning theory have served mainly as substitutes for a directly observable and productive datum. They have little reason to survive when such a datum has been found.

It is no accident that rate of responding is successful as a datum because it is particularly appropriate to the fundamental task of a science of behavior. If we are to predict behavior (and possibly to control it), we must deal with *probability of response.* The business of a science of behavior is to evaluate this probability and explore the conditions which determine it. Strength of bond, expectancy, excitatory potential, and so on, carry the notion of probability in an easily imagined form, but the additional properties suggested by these terms have hindered the search for suitable measures. Rate of responding is not a "measure" of probability, but it is the only appropriate datum in a formulation in these terms.

As other scientific disciplines can attest, probabilities are not easy to handle. We wish to make statements about the likelihood of occurrence of a single future response, but our data are in the form of frequencies of responses which have already occurred. These responses were presumably similar to each other and to the response to be predicted. But this raises the troublesome problem of response-instance vs. response-class. Precisely what responses are we to take into account in predicting a future instance? Certainly not the responses made by a population of different organisms, for such a statistical datum raises more problems than it solves. To consider the frequency of repeated responses in an individual demands something like the experimental situation just described.

This solution of the problem of a basic datum is based upon the view that operant behavior is essentially an emissive phenomenon. Latency and magnitude of response fail as measures because they do not take this into account. They are concepts appropriate to the field of the reflex, where the all but invariable control exercised by the eliciting stimulus makes the notion of probability of response trivial. Consider, for example, the case of latency. Because of our acquaintance with simple reflexes we infer that a response which is more likely to be emitted will be emitted more quickly. But is this true? What can the word *quickly* mean? Probability of response, as well as prediction of response, is concerned with the moment of emission. This is a point in time, but it does not have the temporal dimension of a latency. The execution may take time after the response has been initiated, but the moment of occurrence has no duration.[2] In recognizing

---

[2] It cannot, in fact, be shortened or lengthened. Where a latency appears to be forced toward a minimal value by differential reinforcement, another interpretation is called for. Although we may differentially reinforce more energetic behavior or the faster execution of behavior after it begins, it is meaningless to speak of differentially reinforcing responses with short or long latencies. What we actually reinforce differentially are (*a*) favorable waiting behavior and (*b*) more vigorous responses. When we ask a subject to respond "as soon as possible" in the human reaction-time experiment, we essentially ask him (*a*) to

the emissive character of operant behavior and the central position of probability of response as a datum, latency is seen to be irrelevant to our present task.

Various objections have been made to the use of rate of responding as a basic datum. For example, such a program may seem to bar us from dealing with many events which are unique occurrences in the life of the individual. A man does not decide upon a career, get married, make a million dollars, or get killed in an accident often enough to make a rate of response meaningful. But these activities are not responses. They are not simple unitary events lending themselves to prediction as such. If we are to predict marriage, success, accidents, and so on, in anything more than statistical terms, we must deal with the smaller units of behavior which lead to and compose these unitary episodes. If the units appear in repeatable form, the present analysis may be applied. In the field of learning a similar objection takes the form of asking how the present analysis may be extended to experimental situations in which it is impossible to observe frequencies. It does not follow that learning is not taking place in such situations. The notion of probability is usually extrapolated to cases in which a frequency analysis cannot be carried out. In the field of behavior we arrange a situation in which frequencies are available as data, but we use the notion of probability in analyzing and formulating instances or even types of behavior which are not susceptible to this analysis.

Another common objection is that a rate of response is just a set of latencies and hence not a new datum at all. This is easily shown to be wrong. When we measure the time elapsing between two responses, we are in no doubt as to what the organism was doing when we started our clock. We know that it was just executing a response. This is a natural zero—quite unlike the arbitrary point from which latencies are measured. The free repetition of a response yields a rhythmic or periodic datum very different from latency. Many periodic physical processes suggest parallels.

We do not choose rate of responding as a basic datum merely from an analysis of the fundamental task of a science of behavior. The ultimate

---

carry out as much of the response as possible without actually reaching the criterion of emission, (*b*) to do as little else as possible, and (*c*) to respond energetically after the stimulus has been given. This may yield a minimal measurable time between stimulus and response, but this time is not necessarily a basic datum nor have our instructions altered it as such. A parallel interpretation of the differential reinforcement of long "latencies" is required. This is easily established by inspection. In the experiments with pigeons previously cited, preliminary behavior is conditioned which postpones the response to the key until the proper time. Behavior which "marks time" is usually conspicuous.

appeal is to its success in an experimental science. The material which follows is offered as a sample of what can be done. It is not intended as a complete demonstration, but it should confirm the fact that when we are in possession of a datum which varies in a significant fashion, we are less likely to resort to theoretical entities carrying the notion of probability of response.

Why Learning Occurs

We may define learning as a change in probability of response, but we must also specify the conditions under which it comes about. To do this we must survey some of the independent variables of which probability of response is a function. Here we meet another kind of learning theory.

An effective classroom demonstration of the Law of Effect may be arranged in the following way. A pigeon, reduced to 80 per cent of its *ad lib* weight, is habituated to a small, semicircular amphitheatre and is fed there for several days from a food hopper, which the experimenter presents by closing a hand switch. The demonstration consists of establishing a selected response by suitable reinforcement with food. For example, by sighting across the amphitheatre at a scale on the opposite wall, it is possible to present the hopper whenever the top of the pigeon's head rises above a given mark. Higher and higher marks are chosen until, within a few minutes, the pigeon is walking about the cage with its head held as high as possible. In another demonstration the bird is conditioned to strike a marble placed on the floor of the amphitheatre. This may be done in a few minutes by reinforcing successive steps. Food is presented first when the bird is merely moving near the marble, later when it looks down in the direction of the marble, later still when it moves its head toward the marble, and finally when it pecks it. Anyone who has seen such a demonstration knows that the Law of Effect is no theory. It simply specifies a procedure for altering the probability of a chosen response.

But when we try to say *why* reinforcement has this effect, theories arise. Learning is said to take place because the reinforcement is pleasant, satisfying, tension reducing, and so on. The converse process of extinction is explained with comparable theories. If the rate of responding is first raised to a high point by reinforcement and reinforcement then withheld, the response is observed to occur less and less frequently thereafter. One common theory explains this by asserting that a state is built up which suppresses the behavior. This "experimental inhibition" or "reaction inhibition" must be assigned to a different dimensional system, since nothing at the level of behavior corresponds to opposed processes of excitation and inhibition. Rate of responding is simply increased by one operation and decreased by another. Certain effects commonly interpreted as showing release from a suppressing force may be interpreted in other ways. Disinhibition, for example, is not necessarily the uncovering of suppressed strength: it may be a sign of supplementary strength from an extraneous variable. The process of spontaneous recovery, often cited to support the notion of suppression, has an alternative explanation, to be noted in a moment.

Let us evaluate the question of why learning takes place by turning again to some data. Since conditioning is usually too rapid to be easily followed, the process of extinction will provide us with a more useful case. A number of different types of curves have been consistently obtained from rats and pigeons using various schedules of prior reinforcement. By considering some of the relevant conditions we may see what room is left for theoretical processes.

The mere passage of time between conditioning and extinction is a variable which has surprisingly little effect. The rat is too short-lived to make an extended experiment feasible, but the pigeon, which may live ten or fifteen years, is an ideal subject. More than five years ago, twenty pigeons were conditioned to strike a large translucent key upon which a complex visual pattern was projected. Reinforcement was contingent upon the maintenance of a high and steady rate of responding and upon striking a particular feature of the visual pattern. These birds were set aside in order to study retention. They were transferred to the usual living quarters, where they served as breeders. Small groups were tested for extinction at the end of six months, one year, two years, and four years. Before the test each bird was transferred to a separate living cage. A controlled feeding schedule was used to reduce the weight to approximately 80 per cent of the *ad lib* weight. The bird was then fed in the dimly lighted experimental apparatus in the absence of the key for several days, during which emotional responses to the apparatus disappeared. On the day of the test the bird was placed in the darkened box. The translucent key was present but not lighted. No responses were made. When the pattern was projected upon the key, all four birds responded quickly and extensively. Figure 2 shows the largest curve obtained. This bird struck the key within two seconds after presentation of a visual pattern which it had not seen for four years, and at the precise spot upon which differential reinforcement had previously been based. It continued to respond for the next hour, emitting

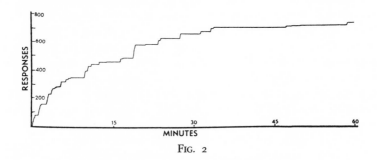

FIG. 2

about 700 responses. This is of the order of one-half to one-quarter of the responses it would have emitted if extinction had not been delayed four years, but otherwise the curve is fairly typical.

Level of motivation is another variable to be taken into account. An example of the effect of hunger has been reported elsewhere.[3] The response of pressing a lever was established in eight rats with a schedule of periodic reinforcement. They were fed the main part of their ration on alternate days so that the rates of responding on successive days were alternately high and low. Two subgroups of four rats each were matched on the basis of the rate maintained under periodic reinforcement under these conditions. The response was then extinguished—in one group on alternate days when the hunger was high, in the other group on alternate days when the hunger was low. (The same amount of food was eaten on the nonexperimental days as before.) The result is shown in Figure 3. The upper graph gives the raw data. The levels of hunger are indicated by the points at P on the abscissa, the rates prevailing under periodic reinforcement. The subsequent points show the decline in extinction. If we multiply the lower curve through by a factor chosen to superimpose the points at P, the curves are reasonably closely superimposed, as shown in the lower graph. Several other experiments on both rats and pigeons have confirmed this general principle. If a given ratio of responding prevails under periodic reinforcement, the slopes of later extinction curves show the same ratio. Level of hunger determines the slope of the extinction curve but not its curvature.

Another variable, difficulty of response, is especially relevant because it

---

[3] The experiment from which the following data are taken was reported at a meeting of the American Psychological Association, September 1940. An abstract appears in the *Psychological Bulletin*, 1940, 37, 243.

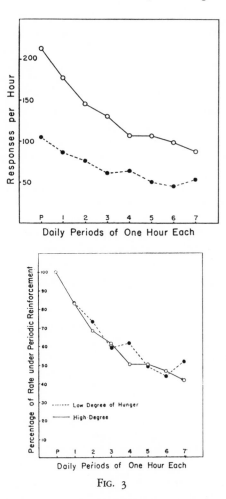

FIG. 3

has been used to test the theory of reaction inhibition,[4] on the assumption that a response requiring considerable energy will build up more reaction inhibition than an easy response and lead, therefore, to faster extinction. The theory requires that the curvature of the extinction curve be altered, not merely its slope. Yet there is evidence that difficulty of response acts

[4] Mowrer, O. H., & Jones, H. M. Extinction and behavior variability as functions of effortfulness of task. *J. exp. Psychol.*, 1943, *33*, 369–386.

like level of hunger simply to alter the slope. A pigeon is suspended in a jacket which confines its wings and legs but leaves its head and neck free to respond to a key and a food magazine.[5] Its behavior in this situation is quantitatively much like that of a bird moving freely in an experimental box, but the use of the jacket has the advantage that the response to the key may be made easy or difficult by changing the distance the bird must reach. In one experiment these distances were expressed in seven equal but arbitrary units. At distance 7 the bird could barely reach the key, at 3 it could strike without appreciably extending its neck. Periodic reinforcement gave a straight baseline upon which it was possible to observe the effect of difficulty by quickly changing position during the experimental period. Each of the five records in Figure 4 covers a fifteen-minute experimental period under periodic reinforcement. Distances of the bird from the key are indicated by numerals above the records. It will be observed that the rate of responding at distance 7 is generally quite low while that at distance 3 is high. Intermediate distances produce intermediate slopes. It should also be noted that the change from one position to another is felt immediately. If repeated responding in a difficult position were to build a considerable amount of reaction inhibition, we should expect the rate to be low for some little time after returning to an easy response. Contrariwise, if an easy response were to build little reaction inhibition, we should expect a fairly high rate of responding for some time after a difficult position is assumed. Nothing like this occurs. The "more rapid extinction" of a difficult response is an ambiguous expression. The slope constant is affected and with it the number of responses in extinction to a criterion, but there may be no effect upon curvature.

One way of considering the question of why extinction curves are curved is to regard extinction as a process of exhaustion comparable to the loss of heat from source to sink or the fall in the level of a reservoir when an outlet is opened. Conditioning builds up a predisposition to respond—a "reserve" —which extinction exhausts. This is perhaps a defensible description at the level of behavior. The reserve is not necessarily a theory in the present sense, since it is not assigned to a different dimensional system. It could be operationally defined as a predicted extinction curve, even though, linguistically, it makes a statement about the momentary condition of a response. But it is not a particularly useful concept, nor does the view that extinction is a process of exhaustion add much to the observed fact that extinction curves are curved in a certain way.

[5] This experiment was reported at a meeting of the Midwestern Psychological Association, March, 1946. An abstract appears in the *American Psychologist*, 1946, *1*, 462.

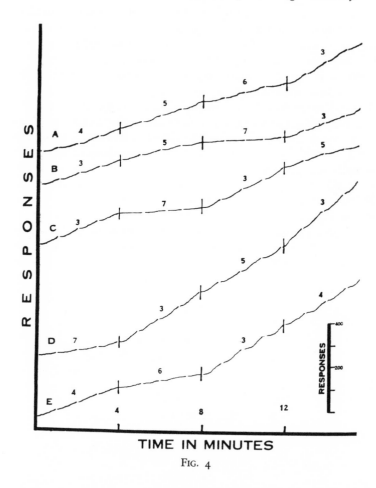

TIME IN MINUTES

Fig. 4

There are, however, two variables which affect the rate, both of which operate during extinction to alter the curvature. One of these falls within the field of emotion. When we fail to reinforce a response which has previously been reinforced, we not only initiate a process of extinction, we set up an emotional response—perhaps what is often meant by frustration. The pigeon coos in an identifiable pattern, moves rapidly about the cage, defecates, or flaps its wings rapidly in a squatting position which suggests treading (mating) behavior. This competes with the response of striking a key and is perhaps enough to account for the decline in rate in early extinction. It is also possible that the probability of a response based upon food deprivation is directly reduced as part of such an emotional reaction. Whatever its nature, the effect of this variable is eliminated through adaptation. Repeated extinction curves become smoother, and in some of the schedules to be described shortly there is little or no evidence of an emotional modification of rate.

A second variable has a much more serious effect. Maximal responding during extinction is obtained only when the conditions under which the response was reinforced are precisely reproduced. A rat conditioned in the presence of a light will not extinguish fully in the absence of the light. It will begin to respond more rapidly when the light is again introduced. This is true for other kinds of stimuli, as the following classroom experiment illustrates. Nine pigeons were conditioned to strike a yellow triangle under intermittent reinforcement. In the session represented by Figure 5 the birds were first reinforced on this schedule for 30 minutes. The combined cumulative curve is essentially a straight line, showing more than 1100 responses per bird during this period. A red triangle was then substi-

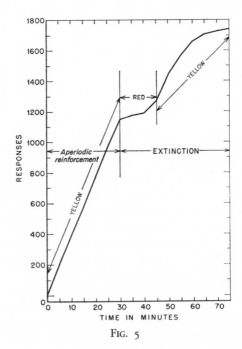

FIG. 5

tuted for the yellow and no responses were reinforced thereafter. The effect was a sharp drop in responding, with only a slight recovery during the next fifteen minutes. When the yellow triangle was replaced, rapid responding began immediately, and the usual extinction curve followed. Similar experiments have shown that the pitch of an incidental tone, the shape of a pattern being struck, or the size of a pattern, if present during conditioning, will to some extent control the rate of responding during extinction. Some properties are more effective than others, and a quantitative evaluation is possible. By changing to several values of a stimulus in random order repeatedly during the extinction process, the gradient for stimulus generalization may be read directly in the rates of responding under each value.

Something very much like this must go on during extinction. Let us suppose that all responses to a key have been reinforced and that each has been followed by a short period of eating. When we extinguish the behavior, we create a situation in which responses are not reinforced, in which no eating takes place, and in which there are probably new emotional responses. The situation could easily be as novel as a red triangle after a yellow. If so, it could explain the decline in rate during extinction. We might have obtained a smooth curve, *shaped like an extinction curve,* between the vertical lines in Figure 5 by *gradually* changing the color of the triangle from yellow to red. This might have happened even though no other sort of extinction were taking place. The very conditions of extinction seem to presuppose a growing novelty in the experimental situation. Is this why the extinction curve is curved?

Some evidence comes from the data of "spontaneous recovery." Even after prolonged extinction an organism will often respond at a higher rate for at least a few moments at the beginning of another session. One theory contends that this shows spontaneous recovery from some sort of inhibition, but another explanation is possible. No matter how carefully an animal is handled, the stimulation coincident with the beginning of an experiment must be extensive and unlike anything occurring in the later part of an experimental period. Responses have been reinforced in the presence of, or shortly following, this stimulation. In extinction it is present for only a few moments. When the organism is again placed in the experimental situation the stimulation is restored; further responses are emitted as in the case of the yellow triangle. The only way to achieve full extinction in the presence of the stimulation of starting an experiment is to start the experiment repeatedly.

Other evidence of the effect of novelty comes from the study of periodic reinforcement. The fact that intermittent reinforcement produces bigger extinction curves than continuous reinforcement is a troublesome difficulty for those who expect a simple relation between number of reinforcements and number of responses in extinction. But this relation is actually quite complex. One result of periodic reinforcement is that emotional changes adapt out. This may be responsible for the smoothness of subsequent extinction curves but probably not for their greater extent. The latter may be attributed to the lack of novelty in the extinction situation. Under periodic reinforcement many responses are made without reinforcement and when no eating has recently taken place. The situation in extinction is therefore not wholly novel.

Periodic reinforcement is not, however, a simple solution. If we reinforce on a regular schedule—say, every minute—the organism soon forms a discrimination. Little or no responding occurs just after reinforcement, since stimulation from eating is correlated with absence of subsequent reinforcement. How rapidly the discrimination may develop is shown in Figure 6, which reproduces the first five curves obtained from a pigeon under periodic reinforcement in experimental periods of fifteen minutes each. In the fifth period (or after about one hour of periodic reinforcement) the discrimination yields a pause after each reinforcement, resulting in a markedly stepwise curve. As a result of this discrimination the bird is almost always responding rapidly when reinforced. This is the basis for another discrimination. Rapid responding becomes a favorable stimulating condition. A good example of the effect upon the subsequent extinction

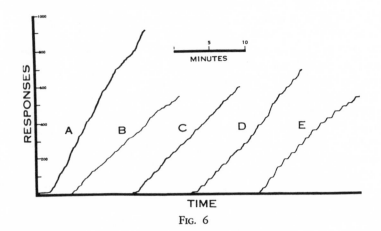

Fig. 6

curve is shown in Figure 7. This pigeon had been reinforced once every minute during daily experimental periods of fifteen minutes each for several weeks. In the extinction curve shown, the bird begins to respond at the rate prevailing under the preceding schedule. A quick positive acceleration at the start is lost in the reduction of the record. The pigeon quickly reaches and sustains a rate which is higher than the over-all rate during periodic reinforcement. During this period the pigeon creates a stimulating condition previously optimally correlated with reinforcement. Eventually, as some sort of exhaustion intervenes, the rate falls off rapidly to a much lower but fairly stable value and then to practically zero. A condition then prevails under which a response is not normally reinforced. The bird is therefore not likely to begin to respond again. When it does respond, however, the situation is slightly improved and, if it continues to respond, the conditions rapidly become similar to those under which reinforcement has been received. Under this "autocatalysis" a high rate is quickly reached, and more than 500 responses are emitted in a second burst. The rate then declines quickly and fairly smoothly, again to nearly zero. This curve is not by any means disorderly. Most of the curvature is smooth. But the burst of responding at forty-five minutes shows a considerable residual strength which, if extinction were merely exhaustion, should have appeared earlier in the curve. The curve may be reasonably accounted for by assuming that the bird is largely controlled by the preceding spurious correlation between reinforcement and rapid responding.

This assumption may be checked by constructing a schedule of reinforcement in which a differential contingency between rate of responding and reinforcement is impossible. In one such schedule of what may be called

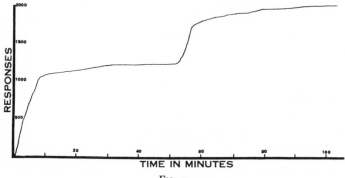

FIG. 7

"aperiodic reinforcement" one interval between successive reinforced responses is so short that no unreinforced responses intervene, while the longest interval is about two minutes.[6] Other intervals are distributed arithmetically between these values, the average remaining one minute. The intervals are roughly randomized to compose a program of reinforcement. Under this program the probability of reinforcement does not change with respect to previous reinforcements, and the curves never acquire the stepwise character of curve *E* in Figure 6. (Figure 9 shows curves from a similar program.) As a result no correlation between different rates of responding and different probabilities of reinforcement can develop.

An extinction curve following a brief exposure to aperiodic reinforcement is shown in Figure 8. It begins characteristically at the rate prevailing

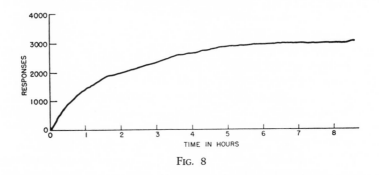

Fig. 8

under aperiodic reinforcement and, unlike the curve following regular periodic reinforcement, does not accelerate to a higher over-all rate. There is no evidence of the "autocatalytic" production of an optimal stimulating condition. Also characteristically, there are no significant discontinuities or sudden changes in rate in either direction. The curve extends over a period of eight hours, as against not quite two hours in Figure 7, and seems to represent a single orderly process. The total number of responses is higher, perhaps because of the greater time allowed for emission. All of this can be explained by the single fact that we have made it impossible for the pigeon to form a pair of discriminations based, first, upon stimulation from eating and, second, upon stimulation from rapid responding.

[6] What is called "periodic reinforcement" in this paper has since come to be known as "fixed-interval reinforcement" and "aperiodic" as "variable-interval." (See *Schedules of Reinforcement.*)

Since the longest interval between reinforcement was only two minutes, a certain novelty must still have been introduced as time passed. Whether this explains the curvature in Figure 8 may be tested to some extent with other programs of reinforcement containing much longer intervals. A geometric progression was constructed by beginning with 10 seconds as the shortest interval and repeatedly multiplying by 1.54. This yielded a set of intervals averaging 5 minutes, the longest of which was more than 21 minutes. Such a set was randomized in a program of reinforcement repeated every hour. In changing to this program from the arithmetic series, the rates first declined during the longer intervals, but the pigeons were soon able to sustain a constant rate of responding under it. Two records in the form in which they were recorded are shown in Figure 9. (The pen resets to zero after every thousand responses. In order to obtain a single cumulative curve it would be necessary to cut the record and piece the sections together to yield a continuous line. The raw form may be reproduced with less reduction.) Each reinforcement is represented by a horizontal dash. The time covered is about three hours. Records are shown for two pigeons which maintained different over-all rates under this program of reinforcement.

Under such a schedule a constant rate of responding is sustained for at least 21 minutes without reinforcement, after which a reinforcement is ceived. Less novelty should therefore develop during succeeding extinction. In Curve 1 of Figure 10 the pigeon had been exposed to several sessions of several hours each with this geometric set of intervals. The number of responses emitted in extinction is about twice that of the curve in Figure 8 after the arithmetic set of intervals averaging one minute, but the curves

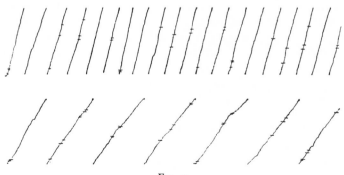

Fig. 9

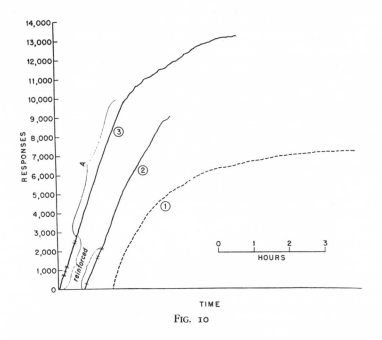

TIME

FIG. 10

are otherwise much alike. Further exposure to the geometric schedule builds up longer runs during which the rate does not change significantly. Curve 2 followed Curve 1 after two and one-half hours of further aperiodic reinforcement. On the day shown in Curve 2 a few aperiodic reinforcements were first given, as marked at the beginning of the curve. When reinforcement was discontinued, a fairly constant rate of responding prevailed for several thousand responses. After another experimental session of two and one-half hours with the geometric series, Curve 3 was recorded. This session also began with a short series of aperiodic reinforcements, followed by a sustained run of more than 6000 unreinforced responses with little change in rate (*A*). There seems to be no reason why other series averaging perhaps more than five minutes per interval and containing much longer exceptional intervals would not carry such a straight line much further.

In this attack upon the problem of extinction we create a schedule of reinforcement which is so much like the conditions which will prevail during extinction that no decline in rate takes place for a long time. In other words we generate extinction with no curvature. Eventually some kind of exhaustion sets in, but it is not approached gradually. The last part of Curve 3 (unfortunately much reduced in the figure) may possibly suggest exhaustion in the slight over-all curvature, but it is a small part of the whole process. The record is composed mainly of runs of a few hundred responses each, most of them at approximately the same rate as that maintained under periodic reinforcement. The pigeon stops abruptly; when it starts to respond again, it quickly reaches the rate of responding under which it was reinforced. This recalls the spurious correlation between rapid responding and reinforcement under regular reinforcement. We have not, of course, entirely eliminated this correlation. Even though there is no longer a differential reinforcement of high against low rates, practically all reinforcements have occurred under a constant rate of responding.

Further study of reinforcing schedules may or may not answer the question of whether the novelty appearing in the extinction situation is entirely responsible for the curvature. It would appear to be necessary to make the conditions prevailing during extinction identical with the conditions prevailing during conditioning. This may be impossible, but in that case the question is academic. The hypothesis, meanwhile, is not a theory in the present sense, since it makes no statements about a parallel process in any other universe of discourse.

It is true that it appeals to stimulation generated in part by the pigeon's own behavior. This may be difficult to specify or manipulate, but it is not theoretical in the present sense. So long as we are willing to assume a one-to-one correspondence between action and stimulation, a physical specification is possible.

The study of extinction after different schedules of aperiodic reinforcement is not addressed wholly to this hypothesis. The object is an economical description of the conditions prevailing during reinforcement and extinction and of the relations between them. In using rate of responding as a basic datum we may appeal to conditions which are observable and manipulable and we may express the relations between them in objective terms. To the extent that our datum makes this possible, it reduces the need for theory. When we observe a pigeon emitting 7000 responses at a constant rate without reinforcement, we are not likely to explain an extinction curve containing perhaps a few hundred responses by appeal to the piling up of reaction inhibition or any other fatigue product. Research which is conducted without commitment to theory is more likely to carry the study of extinction into new areas and new orders of magnitude. By hastening the accumulation of data, we speed the departure of theories. If the theories have played no part in the design of our experiments, we need not be sorry to see them go.

Complex Learning

A third type of learning theory is illustrated by terms like *preferring, choosing, discriminating,* and *matching.* An effort may be made to define these solely in terms of behavior, but in traditional practice they refer to processes in another dimensional system. A response to one of two available stimuli may be called choice, but it is commoner to say that it is the result of choice, meaning by the latter a theoretical pre-behavioral activity. The higher mental processes are the best examples of theories of this sort; neurological parallels have not been well worked out. The appeal to theory is encouraged by the fact that choosing (like discriminating, matching, and so on) is not a particular piece of behavior. It is not a response or an act with specified topography. The term characterizes a larger segment of behavior in relation to other variables or events. Can we formulate and study the behavior to which these terms would usually be applied without recourse to the theories which generally accompany them?

Discrimination is a relatively simple case. Suppose we find that the probability of emission of a given response is not significantly affected by changing from one of two stimuli to the other. We then make reinforcement of the response contingent upon the presence of one of them. The well-established result is that the probability of response remains high under this stimulus and reaches a very low point under the other. We say that the organism now discriminates between the stimuli. But discrimination is not itself an action, or necessarily even a unique process. Problems in the field of discrimination may be stated in other terms. How much induction obtains between stimuli of different magnitudes or classes? What are the smallest differences in stimuli which yield a difference in control? And so on. Questions of this sort do not presuppose theoretical activities in other dimensional systems.

A somewhat larger segment must be specified in dealing with the behavior of choosing one of two concurrent stimuli. This has been studied in the pigeon by examining responses to two keys differing in position (right or left) or in some property like color randomized with respect to position. By occasionally reinforcing a response on one key or the other without favoring either key, we obtain equal rates of responding on the two keys.

The behavior approaches a simple alternation from one key to the other. This follows the rule that tendencies to respond eventually correspond to the probabilities of reinforcement. Given a system in which one key or the other is occasionally connected with the magazine by an external clock, then if the right key has just been struck, the probability of reinforcement via the left key is higher than that via the right since a greater interval of time has elapsed during which the clock may have closed the circuit to the left key. But the bird's behavior does not correspond to this probability merely out of respect for mathematics. The specific result of such a contingency of reinforcement is that changing-to-the-other-key-and-striking is more often reinforced than striking-the-same-key-a-second-time. We are no longer dealing with just two responses. In order to analyze "choice" we must consider a single final response, striking, without respect to the position or color of the key, and in addition the responses of changing from one key or color to the other.

Quantitative results are compatible with this analysis. If we periodically reinforce responses to the right key only, the rate of responding on the right will rise while that on the left will fall. The response of changing-from-right-to-left is never reinforced while the response of changing-from-left-to-right is occasionally so. When the bird is striking on the right, there is no great tendency to change keys; when it is striking on the left, there is a strong tendency to change. Many more responses come to be made to the right key. The need for considering the behavior of changing over is clearly shown if we now reverse these conditions and reinforce responses to the left key only. The ultimate result is a high rate of responding on the left key and a low rate on the right. By reversing the conditions again the high rate can be shifted back to the right key. In Figure 11 a group of eight curves have been averaged to follow this change during six experimental periods of 45 minutes each. Beginning on the second day in the graph responses to the right key (R^R) decline in extinction while responses to the left key (R^L) increase through periodic reinforcement. The mean rate shows no significant variation, since periodic reinforcement is continued on the same schedule. The mean rate shows the condition of strength of the response of striking a key regardless of position. The distribution of responses between right and left depends upon the relative strength of the responses of changing over. If this were simply a case of the extinction of one response and the concurrent reconditioning of another, the mean curve would not remain approximately horizontal since reconditioning occurs much more rapidly than extinction. (Two topo-

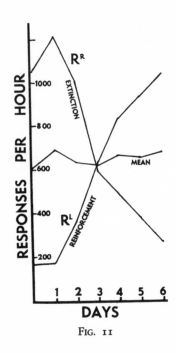

FIG. 11

graphically independent responses, capable of emission at the same time and hence not requiring change-over, show separate processes of reconditioning and extinction, and the combined rate of responding varies.)

The rate with which the bird changes from one key to the other depends upon the distance between the keys. This distance is a rough measure of the stimulus-difference between the two keys. It also determines the scope of the response of changing-over, with an implied difference in sensory feedback. It also modifies the spread of reinforcement to responses supposedly not reinforced, since if the keys are close together, a response reinforced on one side may occur sooner after a preceding response on the other side. In Figure 11 the two keys were about one inch apart. They were therefore fairly similar with respect to position in the experimental box. Changing from one to the other involved a minimum of sensory feedback, and reinforcement of a response to one key could follow very shortly upon a response to the other. When the keys are separated by as much as four inches, the change in strength is much more rapid. Figure 12 shows two curves recorded simultaneously from a single pigeon during one experi-

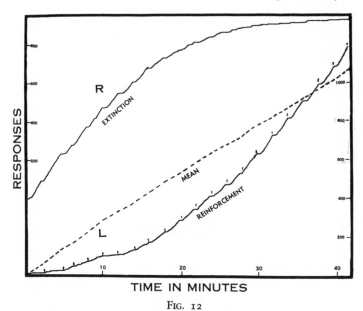

TIME IN MINUTES

FIG. 12

mental period of about 40 minutes. A high rate to the right key and a low rate to the left had previously been established. In the figure no responses to the right were reinforced, but those to the left were reinforced every minute as indicated by the vertical dashes above curve L. The slope of R declines in a fairly smooth fashion while that of L increases, also fairly smoothly, to a value comparable to the initial value of R. The bird has conformed to the changed contingency within a single experimental period. The mean rate of responding is shown by a dotted line, which again shows no significant curvature.

What is called "preference" enters into this formulation. At any stage of the process shown in Figure 12 preference might be expressed in terms of the relative rates of responding to the two keys. This preference, however, is not in striking a key but in changing from one key to the other. The probability that the bird will strike a key regardless of its identifying properties behaves independently of the preferential response of changing from one key to the other. Several experiments have revealed an additional fact. A preference remains fixed if reinforcement is withheld. Figure 13 is an example. It shows simultaneous extinction curves from two keys during seven daily experimental periods of one hour each. Prior to extinction the

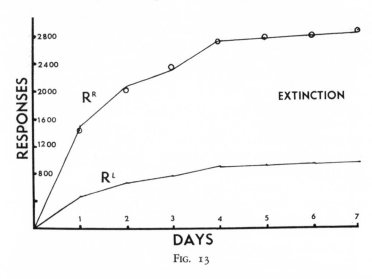

FIG. 13

relative strength of the responses of changing-to-R and changing-to-L yielded a "preference" of about 3 to 1 for R. The constancy of the rate throughout the process of extinction has been shown in the figure by multiplying L through by a suitable constant and entering the points as small circles on R. If extinction altered the preference, the two curves could not be superimposed in this way.

These formulations of discrimination and choosing enable us to deal with what is generally regarded as a much more complex process—matching to sample. Suppose we arrange three translucent keys, each of which may be illuminated with red or green light. The middle key functions as the sample, and we color it either red or green in random order. We color the two side keys one red and one green, also in random order. The "problem" is to strike the side key which corresponds in color to the middle key. There are only four three-key patterns in such a case, and it is possible that a pigeon could learn to make an appropriate response to each pattern. This does not happen, at least within the temporal span of the experiments to date. If we simply present a series of settings of the three colors and reinforce successful responses, the pigeon will strike the side keys without respect to color or pattern and be reinforced 50 percent of the time. This is, in effect, a schedule of "fixed ratio" reinforcement which is adequate to maintain a high rate of responding.

Nevertheless it is possible to get a pigeon to match to sample by reinforcing the discriminative responses of striking-red-after-being-stimulated-by-red and striking-green-after-being-stimulated-by-green while extinguishing the other two possibilities. The difficulty is in arranging the proper stimulation at the time of the response. The sample might be made conspicuous—for example, by having the sample color in the general illumination of the experimental box. In such a case the pigeon would learn to strike red keys in a red light and green keys in a green light (assuming a neutral illumination of the background of the keys). But a procedure which holds more closely to the notion of matching is to induce the pigeon to "look at the sample" by means of a separate reinforcement. We may do this by presenting the color on the middle key first, leaving the side keys uncolored. A response to the middle key is then reinforced (secondarily) by illuminating the side keys. The pigeon learns to make two responses in quick succession—to the middle key and then to one side key. The response to the side key follows quickly upon the visual stimulation from the middle key, which is the requisite condition for a discrimination. Successful matching was readily established in all ten pigeons tested with this technique. Choosing the opposite is also easily set up. The discriminative response of striking-red-after-being-stimulated-by-red is apparently no easier to establish than striking-red-after-being-stimulated-by-green. When the response is to a key of the same color, however, generalization may make it possible for the bird to match a new color. This is an extension of the notion of matching which has not yet been studied with this method.

Even when matching behavior has been well established, the bird will not respond correctly if all three keys are now presented at the same time. The bird does not possess strong behavior of looking at the sample. The experimenter must maintain a separate reinforcement to keep this behavior in strength. In monkeys, apes, and human subjects the ultimate success in choosing is apparently sufficient to reinforce and maintain the behavior of looking at the sample. It is possible that this species difference is simply a difference in the temporal relations required for reinforcement.

The behavior of matching survives unchanged when all reinforcement is withheld. An intermediate case has been established in which the correct matching response is only periodically reinforced. In one experiment one color appeared on the middle key for one minute; it was then changed or not changed, at random, to the other color. A response to this key illuminated the side keys, one red and one green, in random order. A response to a side key cut off the illumination to both side keys, until the middle key had again been srtuck. The apparatus recorded all matching responses on one graph and all non-matching on another. Pigeons which have acquired matching behavior under continuous reinforcement have maintained this behavior when reinforced no oftener than once per minute on the average. They may make thousands of matching responses per hour while being reinforced for no more than sixty of them. This schedule will not necessarily develop matching behavior in a naive bird, for the problem can be solved in three ways. The bird will receive practically as many reinforcements if it responds to (1) only one key or (2) only one color, since the programming of the experiment makes any persistent response eventually the correct one.

A sample of the data obtained in a complex experiment of this sort is given in Figure 14. Although this pigeon had learned to match color under continuous reinforcement, it changed to the spurious solution of a color preference under periodic reinforcement. Whenever the sample was red, it struck both the sample and the red side key and received all reinforcements. When the sample was green, it did not respond and the side keys were not illuminated. The result shown at the beginning of the graph in Figure 14 is a high rate of responding on the upper graph, which records

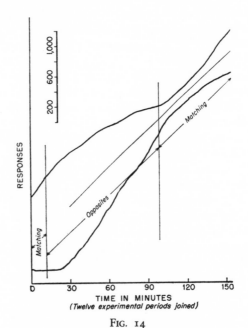

FIG. 14

matching responses. (The record is actually step-wise, following the presence or absence of the red sample, but this is lost in the reduction in the figure.) A color preference, however, is not a solution to the problem of opposites. By changing to this problem, it was possible to change the bird's behavior as shown betwen the two vertical lines in the figure. The upper curve between these lines shows the decline in matching responses which had resulted from the color preference. The lower curve between the same lines shows the development of responding to and matching the opposite color. At the second vertical line the reinforcement was again made contingent upon matching. The upper curve shows the re-establishment of matching behavior while the lower curve shows a decline in striking the opposite color. The result was a true solution: the pigeon struck the sample, no matter what its color, and then the corresponding side key. The lighter line connects the means of a series of points on the two curves. It seems to follow the same rule as in the case of choosing: changes in the distribution of responses between two keys do not involve the over-all rate of responding to a key. This mean rate will not remain constant under the spurious solution achieved with a color preference, as at the beginning of this figure.

These experiments on a few higher processes have necessarily been very briefly described. They are not offered as proving that theories of learning are not necessary, but they may suggest an alternative program in this difficult area. The data in the field of the higher mental processes transcend single responses or single stimulus-response relationships. But they appear to be susceptible to formulation in terms of the differentiation of concurrent responses, the discrimination of stimuli, the establishment of various sequences of responses, and so on. There seems to be no a priori reason why a complete account is not possible without appeal to theoretical processes in other dimensional systems.

Conclusion

Perhaps to do without theories altogether is a *tour de force* which is too much to expect as a general practice. Theories are fun. But it is possible that the most rapid progress toward an understanding of learning may be made by research which is not designed to test theories. An adequate impetus is supplied by the inclination to obtain data showing orderly changes characteristic of the learning process. An acceptable scientific program is to collect data of this sort and to relate them to manipulable variables, selected for study through a common-sense exploration of the field.

This does not exclude the possibility of theory in another sense. Beyond the collection of uniform relationships lies the need for a formal representation of the data reduced to a minimal number of terms. A theoretical construction may yield greater generality than any assemblage of facts. But such a construction will not refer to another dimensional system and will not, therefore, fall within our present definition. It will not stand in the way of our search for functional relations because it will arise only after relevant variables have been found and studied. Though it may be difficult to understand, it will not be easily misunderstood, and it will have none of the objectionable effects of the theories here considered.

We do not seem to be ready for theory in this sense. At the moment we make little effective use of empirical, let alone rational, equations. A few of the present curves could have been fairly closely fitted. But the most elementary preliminary research shows that there are many relevant variables, and until their importance has been experimentally determined, an equation which allows for them will have so many arbitrary constants that a good fit will be a matter of course and cause for very little satisfaction.

The Analysis of Behavior

This discussion of theoretical issues in the analysis of behavior formed the beginning and end of a lecture given on July 17, 1951, in the Riksdaghuset, Stockholm, Sweden, at the Thirteenth International Congress of Psychology. The rest of the lecture was devoted to illustrative experiments on intermittent reinforcement which have since been reported in Schedules of Reinforcement. *Similar material may be found beginning on page 136. The whole lecture was reprinted with adaptations in the* American Psychologist *(1953, 8, 69-79) under the title, "Some Contributions of an Experimental Analysis of Behavior to Psychology as a Whole."*

THE BEHAVIOR of an organism is not an easy thing to describe. It is not an object which may be held still for inspection. It is a process, a continuous change. Even when an accurate account has been given of it as such, a different aspect remains to be treated. A science must achieve more than a description of behavior as an accomplished fact. It must predict future courses of action; it must be able to say that an organism will engage in behavior of a given sort at a given time. But this raises a special problem. We want to believe that a prediction is in some sense a description of a condition at the moment—before the predicted event has taken place. Thus, we speak of tendencies or readinesses to behave as if they corresponded to something in the organism at the moment. We have given this something many names—from the preparatory set of experimental psychology to the Freudian wish. Habits and instincts, dispositions and predispositions, attitudes, opinions—even personality itself—are all ways of representing, in the present organism, something of its future behavior.

This problem cannot be avoided in any scientific account, but it can be expressed much more rigorously. We are dealing here with a question of probability—specifically, the probability that an organism will emit behavior of a given sort at a given time. But probability is always a difficult concept, no matter in what field of science it arises. What is a probability? Where is it? How may we observe it? We have tried to answer these difficult questions by giving probability the status of a thing—by *embodying* it, so to speak, within the organism. We look for neurological or psychic states or events with which habits, wishes, attitudes, and so on, may be identified. In doing so we force extraneous properties on behavior which are not supported by the data and which may be quite misleading.

The practical problem of taking probability as a basic datum may not be as difficult as we suppose. The "physical referent" must be among our data; otherwise the problem would not have been so persistent. The mistake we seem to have made is in looking for it as necessarily a property of a single event, occupying only one point in time. As the mathematicians have pointed out, perhaps not unanimously, a probability is simply a way of representing a frequency of occurrence. We can deal with probability of action by turning our attention to the repeated appearance of an act during an appreciable interval of time.

Some such practice is demanded in defining any of the concepts which have foreshadowed an explicit recognition of probability of response as a basic datum. An organism possesses a "habit" to the extent that a certain form of behavior is observed with a special frequency—in this case attributable to events in the history of the individual. It possesses an "instinct" to the extent that a certain form of behavior is observed with a special frequency—in this case because of membership in a given species. An "attitude" expresses the special frequency of a number of forms of behavior. And so on.

Dozens of less technical terms serve the same purpose, and their existence points to our abiding practical and theoretical interest in frequency as a datum. We say that someone is a tennis "fan" if he frequently plays tennis under appropriate circumstances. He is "enthusiastic" about skating, if he frequently goes skating. He is "greatly interested" in music if he plays, listens to, and talks about music frequently. The "inveterate" gambler gambles frequently. "Highly sexed" people frequently engage in sexual behavior. And so on. The practical problems associated with these aspects of human nature can be expressed also as problems in changing frequencies of response, but in each case we quickly move from an observation of frequency to an inferred *momentary* condition. This is the linguistic effect of terms of this sort, as it is of more technical terms, but a linguistic device should not be allowed to influence the direction of our research. The basic facts about behavior can be discovered only by examining behavior during appreciable intervals of time.

It is possible to study probability—in the light of this interpretation—by designing a laboratory situation in which frequency of response may be easily examined. There are certain considerations to be observed. We must choose a sample of behavior which may be so easily identified that repeated instances may be reliably counted. If our experiment is to be automatic—and we shall see that there are many advantages in making it so—our response must operate an apparatus. The behavior should not require much time, and it should leave the organism ready to respond again. These conditions are rather arbitrary (and our results must be qualified accordingly), but they are easily met. Sometimes such a response is found ready-made—as in studying so-called instinctive behavior. Otherwise it must be, so to speak, constructed. In the case of a rat, for example, we have found it convenient to use a response like depressing a horizontal bar. The movement of the bar is usually clear-cut, and it may be made to operate an apparatus by closing an electric circuit. In the case of a fish, the response of pushing lightly against a plate has proved useful. The fish attacks the plate, backs away, and is then in position to attack it again, the movement of the plate closing a circuit. In birds—for example, the pigeon—a convenient response is pecking a disc through a small hole in the wall of the experimental space. The disc is delicately mounted, and the slightest contact closes a circuit. All these responses are easily specified. They can be readily repeated. In the case of the pigeon, for example, the disc may be pecked as rapidly as fifteen times per sec.

To record frequency of response we could, of course, use the standard polygraph, but another sort of curve has proved to be much more convenient. A pen is arranged to move one step across a strip of paper each time the organism responds (See pages 178-182). The result is a step-like diagonal line. Frequency is converted into slope. Co-ordinates are chosen which convert the commonest frequencies into the most convenient slopes. If the organism is responding rapidly, the line is fairly steep. If it responds slowly, the slope is low. If it does not respond at all, the pen draws a horizontal line. With a little practice it is easy to estimate frequencies from the slopes of such graphs and to follow changes in frequency with fair accuracy. In Figure 1 some actual records show the range of frequencies encountered in the pigeon. The separate steps of the pen cannot be seen on this scale. One record shows a sustained rate of 18,000 responses per hour—five responses per second. Another record, by way of comparison, shows only 300 responds per hour or one response every twelve seconds, yielding a very low slope.

I am concerned here with demonstrating that frequency of response, so recorded, is a useful and significant datum in the experimental analysis of behavior—that it is a sensitive "dependent variable" which is a function of many subtle experimental conditions.

Experiments were described at this point concerning: (1) fixed-interval reinforcement, (2) extinction after fixed-interval reinforcement, (3) fixed-interval reinforcement with "added clock," (4) variable-interval reinforcement, (5) extinction after variable-interval reinforcement, (6) fixed-ratio reinforcement, *(7) fixed-ratio reinforcement with "added counter," (8) two-valued ratio reinforcement, (9) variable-ratio reinforcement, and (10) extinction after variable-ratio reinforcement.*

The following points seem to be justified. First, frequency of response is an extremely orderly datum. The curves which represent its relations to many types of independent variables are encouragingly simple. Secondly, they are

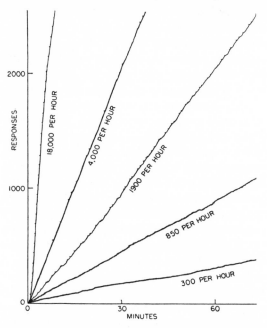

Fɪɢ. ɪ. Cumulative curves showing stable performances at a wide variety of rates of responding.

easily reproduced. It is seldom necessary to resort to groups of subjects at this stage. The method permits a direct view of processes which have hitherto been only inferred, and we often have as little use for statistical control as in the simple observation of objects in the world about us. If the essential features of a given curve are not readily duplicated in a later experiment—in either the same or another organism—we take this, not as a cue to resort to averages, but as a warning that some relevant condition has still to be discovered and controlled. The usual uniformity of the results encourages us to turn—not to sampling procedures—but to more rigorous experimental control.

As a result, thirdly, the concepts and laws which emerge from this sort of study have an immediate reference to the behavior of the individual which is lacking in concepts or laws which are the products of statistical methods. When we extend an experimental analysis to human affairs in general, it is a great advantage to have a conceptual system which refers to the single individual, preferably without comparison with a group. A more direct application to the prediction and control of the individual is thus achieved. The study of frequency of response appears to lead directly to such a system.

Fourthly, frequency of response provides a continuous account of many basic processes. We can follow a curve of extinction, for example, for many hours, and the condition of the response at every moment is apparent in our records. This is in marked contrast to methods and techniques which merely sample a learning process from time to time, where the whole process must be inferred. The samples are often so widely spaced that the kinds of details we have seen here are completely overlooked.

Fifthly, we must not forget the considerable advantage of a datum which lends itself to automatic experimentation. Many processes in behavior cover long periods of time. The records we obtain from an individual organism may cover hundreds of hours and report millions of responses. We characteristically use experimental periods of eight, ten, even fifteen hours. Personal observation of such material is unthinkable.

Finally, and perhaps most important of all, frequency of response is a valuable datum just because it provides a substantial basis for the concept of probability of response—a concept toward which a science of behavior seems to have been groping for many decades. Here is a perfectly good physical referent for that concept. It is true that the momentary condition of the organism as the tangent of a curve is still an abstraction—the very abstraction which became important in the physical sciences with Newton and Leibniz. But we are now able to deal with this in a rigorous fashion. The superfluous trappings of traditional definitions of terms like *habit, attitude, wish,* and so on, may be avoided.

The points illustrated here in a small branch of the field of learning apply equally well to other fields of behavior. Frequency of response has already proved useful in studying the topography of behavior—the shaping of new responses. It permits us to answer such a question as: Does the emission of Response *A* alter the probability of a Response *B* which resembles *A* in certain ways? It has proved to be a useful datum in studying the effect of discriminative stimuli. If we establish a given probability of response under

Stimulus *A*, what is the probability that the response will be made under Stimulus *B*, which resembles *A* in certain ways? Is red as different from orange as green is from blue? We may ask the pigeon a question of this sort quite meaningfully in terms of probability of response. Pattern discrimination and the formation of concepts have been studied with the same method.

Frequency of response is also a useful datum when two responses are being considered at the same time. We can investigate "choice" and follow the development of a preference for one of two stimuli. The datum has proved to be especially useful in studying complex behavior in which two or more responses are related to two or more stimuli—for example, in matching color from sample or in selecting the opposite of a sample. Outside the field of learning considerable work has been done in motivation (where frequency of response varies with degree of deprivation), in emotion (where, for example, rate of responding serves as a useful baseline in observing what we may call "anxiety"), in the effects of drugs (evaluated, for example, against the stable baseline obtained under variable-interval reinforcement), and so on. One of the most promising achievements has been an analysis of the effects of punishment, which confirms much of the Freudian material on repression and reveals many disadvantages in the use of punishment as a technique of control.

The extension of such results to the world at large frequently meets certain objections. In the laboratory we choose an arbitrary response, hold the environment as constant as possible, and so on. Can our results apply to behavior of much greater variety emitted under conditions which are constantly changing? If a certain experimental design is necessary to observe a frequency, can we apply the results to a situation where frequency cannot be determined? The answer here is the answer which must be given by any experimental science. Laboratory experimentation is designed to make a process as obvious as possible, to separate processes one from the other, and to obtain quantitative measures. These are indeed the very heart of an experimental science. The history of science shows that the results can be effectively extended to the world at large. For example, we determine the shape of the cooling curve with the aid of the physical laboratory. We have little doubt that the same process is going on as our breakfast coffee grows cold, but we have no evidence for this and probably could not prove it under genuine breakfast-table conditions. What we transfer from our experiments to a casual world in which satisfactory quantification is impossible is the knowledge that certain basic processes exist, that they are lawful, and that they probably account for the unpleasantly chaotic facts with which we are faced.

The gain in practical effectiveness which is derived from such transferred knowledge may be, as the physical sciences show, enormous.

Another common objection is that if we identify probability of response with frequency of occurrence, we cannot legitimately apply the notion to an event which is never repeated. A man may marry only once. He may engage in a business deal only once. He may commit suicide only once. Is behavior of this sort beyond the scope of such an analysis? The answer here concerns the definition of the unit to be predicted. Complex activities are not always "responses" in the sense of repeated or repeatable events. They are composed of responses, however, which are repeatable and capable of being studied in terms of frequency. The problem is again not peculiar to the field of behavior. Was it possible to assign a given probability to the explosion of the first atomic bomb? The probabilities of many of the component events were soundly based upon data in the form of frequencies. But the explosion of the bomb as a whole was a unique event in the history of the world. Though the probability of its occurrence could not be stated in terms of the frequency of a unit at that level, it could still be evaluated. The problem of predicting that a man will commit suicide is of the same nature.

In summary, then, the basic datum in the analysis of behavior has the status of a probability. The actual observed dependent variable is frequency of response. An experimental situation is required in which frequency may be studied. When this is arranged, important processes in behavior are revealed in a continuous, orderly, and reproducible fashion. Concepts and laws derived from such data are immediately applicable to the behavior of the individual, and they permit us to move on to the interpretation of behavior in the world at large with the greatest possible speed.

A Case History in Scientific Method

In exploring the status and development of psychology in the United States the American Psychological Association, with help from the National Science Foundation, set up Project A under the direction of Sigmund Koch. Among other things the Project sponsored "the preparation of analyses of given systematizations by the actual originators of these formulations." In other words, the proprietors of several current systems of psychology were asked to describe their wares. In the instruction to contributors "systematic formulation" was defined as "any set of sentences formulated as a tool for ordering empirical knowledge with respect to some specifiable domain of events." Topics to be covered included Background Factors and Orienting Attitudes, Initial Evidential Grounds for Assumptions of System, Degree of Programmaticity, and Intermediate and Long Range Strategy for the Development of the System.

My reaction was the present paper. It was written primarily for a meeting of the Eastern Psychological Association in April, 1955, and was published in the American Psychologist *(1956, 11, 221-233). It was submitted with considerable diffidence to the director of Project A, who generously included it in the report of the project,* Psychology: A Study of a Science, *Vol. II (New York, McGraw-Hill, 1958). It is reprinted here by permission.*

In the project report the paper begins with the following paragraph:

A scientist is an extremely complex organism, and his behavior is likely to resist to the very last any effort toward an empirical analysis. Nevertheless, if anything useful is to be said about him, either in trying to understand his behavior or in inculcating similar behavior in others, it will be in the nature of an empirical rather than a formal analysis. As an anti-formalist it would be inconsistent of me to describe my own scientific activity in the formal framework of Project A. I have therefore reacted to the proposal of the director by illustrating my own philosophy of science with a personal history.

———————

It has been said that college teaching is the only profession for which there is no professional training, and it is commonly argued that this is because our graduate schools train scholars and scientists rather than teachers. We are more concerned with the discovery of knowledge than with its dissemination. But can we justify ourselves quite so easily? It is a bold thing

108

to say that we know how to train a man to be a scientist. Scientific thinking is the most complex and probably the most subtle of all human activities. Do we actually know how to shape up such behavior, or do we simply mean that some of the people who attend our graduate schools eventually become scientists?

Except for a laboratory course which acquaints the student with standard apparatus and standard procedures, the only explicit training in scientific method generally received by a young psychologist is a course in statistics— not the introductory course, which is often required of so many kinds of students that it is scarcely scientific at all, but an advanced course which includes "model building," "theory construction," and "experimental design." But it is a mistake to identify scientific practice with the formalized constructions of statistics and scientific method. These disciplines have their place, but it does not coincide with the place of scientific research. They offer *a* method of science but not, as is so often implied, *the* method. As formal disciplines they arose very late in the history of science, and most of the facts of science have been discovered without their aid. It takes a great deal of skill to fit Faraday with his wires and magnets into the picture which statistics gives us of scientific thinking. And most current scientific practice would be equally refractory, especially in the important initial stages. It is no wonder that the laboratory scientist is puzzled and often dismayed when he discovers how his behavior has been reconstructed in the formal analyses of scientific method. He is likely to protest that this is not at all a fair representation of what he does.

But his protest is not likely to be heard. For the prestige of statistics and scientific methodology is enormous. Much of it is borrowed from the high repute of mathematics and logic, but much of it derives from the flourishing state of the art itself. Some statisticians are professional people employed by scientific and commercial enterprises. Some are teachers and pure researchers who give their colleagues the same kind of service for nothing—or at most a note of acknowledgment. Many are zealous people who, with the best of intentions, are anxious to show the nonstatistical scientist how he can do his job more efficiently and assess his results more accurately. There are strong professional societies devoted to the advancement of statistics, and hundreds of technical books and journals are published annually.

Against this, the practicing scientist has very little to offer. He cannot refer the young psychologist to a book which will tell him how to find out all there is to know about a subject matter, how to have the good hunch which will lead him to devise a suitable piece of apparatus, how to develop an efficient experimental routine, how to abandon an unprofitable line of attack, how to move on most rapidly to later stages of his research. The work habits which have become second nature to him have not been formalized by anyone, and he may feel that they possibly never will be. As Richter [1] has pointed out, "Some of the most important discoveries have been made without any plan of research," and "there are researchers who do not work on a verbal plane, who cannot put into words what they are doing."

If we are interested in perpetuating the practices responsible for the present corpus of scientific knowledge, we must keep in mind that some very important parts of the scientific process do not now lend themselves to mathematical, logical, or any other formal treatment. We do not know enough about human behavior to know how the scientist does what he does. Although statisticians and methodologists may seem to tell us, or at least imply, how the mind works—how problems arise, how hypotheses are formed, deductions made, and crucial experiments designed—we as psychologists are in a position to remind them that they do not have methods appropriate to the empirical observation or the functional analysis of such data. These are aspects of human behavior, and no one knows better than we how little can at the moment be said about them.

Some day we shall be better able to express the distinction between empirical analysis and formal reconstruction, for we shall have an alternative account of the behavior of Man Thinking. Such an account will not only plausibly reconstruct what a particular scientist did in any given case, it will permit us to evaluate practices and, I believe, to teach scientific thinking. But that day is some little distance in the future. Meanwhile we can only fall back on examples.

When the director of Project A of the American Psychological Association asked me to describe and analyze my activities as a research psychologist, I went through a trunkful of old notes and records and, for my pains, reread some of my earlier publications. This has made me all the more aware of the contrast between the reconstructions of formalized scientific method and at least one case of actual practice. Instead of amplifying the points I have just made by resorting to a generalized account (principally because it is not available), I should like to discuss a case history. It is not one of the case histories we should most like to have, but what it lacks in importance is perhaps somewhat offset by accessibility. I therefore ask you to imagine that you are all clinical psychologists—a task which becomes easier and easier as the years go by—while I sit across the desk from you or stretch out upon this comfortable leather couch.

The first thing I can remember happened when I was only twenty-two years old. Shortly after I was graduated from college Bertrand Russell

[1] Richter, C. P. Free research versus design. *Science*, 1953, *118*, 91–93.

published a series of articles in the old *Dial* magazine on the epistemology of John B. Watson's Behaviorism. I had had no psychology as an undergraduate but I had had a lot of biology, and two of the books which my biology professor had put into my hands were Loeb's *Physiology of the Brain* and the newly published Oxford edition of Pavlov's *Conditioned Reflexes*. And now here was Russell extrapolating the principles of an objective formulation of behavior to the problem of knowledge! Many years later when I told Lord Russell that his articles were responsible for my interest in behavior, he could only exclaim, "Good Heavens! I had always supposed that those articles had demolished Behaviorism!" But at any rate he had taken Watson seriously, and so did I.

When I arrived at Harvard for graduate study, the air was not exactly full of behavior, but Walter Hunter was coming in once a week from Clark University to give a seminar, and Fred Keller, also a graduate student, was an expert in both the technical details and the sophistry of Behaviorism. Many a time he saved me as I sank into the quicksands of an amateurish discussion of "What is an image?" or "Where is red?" I soon came into contact with W. J. Crozier, who had studied under Loeb. It had been said of Loeb, and might have been said of Crozier, that he "resented the nervous system." Whether this was true or not, the fact was that both these men talked about animal behavior without mentioning the nervous system and with surprising success. So far as I was concerned, they cancelled out the physiological theorizing of Pavlov and Sherrington and thus clarified what remained of the work of these men as the beginnings of an independent science of behavior. My doctoral thesis was in part an operational analysis of Sherrington's synapse, in which behavioral laws were substituted for supposed states of the central nervous system.

But the part of my thesis at issue here was experimental. So far as I can see, I began simply by looking for lawful processes in the behavior of the intact organism. Pavlov had shown the way; but I could not then, as I cannot now, move without a jolt from salivary reflexes to the important business of the organism in everyday life. Sherrington and Magnus had found order in surgical segments of the organism. Could not something of the same sort be found, to use Loeb's phrase, in "the organism as a whole"? I had the clue from Pavlov: control your conditions and you will see order.

It is not surprising that my first gadget was a silent release box, operated by compressed air and designed to eliminate disturbances when introducing a rat into an apparatus. I used this first in studying the way a rat adapted to a novel stimulus. I built a soundproofed box containing a specially structured space. A rat was released, pneumatically, at the far end of a darkened tunnel from which it emerged in exploratory fashion into a well-lighted area. To accentuate its progress and to facilitate recording, the tunnel was placed at the top of a flight of steps, something like a functional Parthenon (Figure 1). The rat would peek out from the tunnel, perhaps glancing suspiciously at the one-way window through which I was watching it, then stretch itself cautiously down the steps. A soft click (carefully calibrated, of course) would cause it to pull back into the tunnel and remain there for some time. But repeated clicks had less and less of an effect. I recorded the rat's advances and retreats by moving a pen back and forth across a moving paper tape.

The major result of this experiment was that some of my rats had babies. I began to watch young rats. I saw them right themselves and crawl about very much like the decerebrate or thalamic cats and rabbits of Magnus. So I set about studying the postural reflexes of young rats. Here was a first principle not formally recognized by scientific methodologists: When you run onto something interesting, drop everything else and study it. I tore up the Parthenon and started over.

If you hold a young rat on one hand and pull it gently by the tail, it will

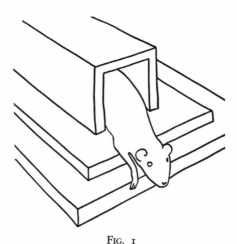

FIG. 1

resist you by pulling forward and then, with a sudden sharp spring which usually disengages its tail, it will leap out into space. I decided to study this behavior quantitatively. I built a light platform covered with cloth and mounted it on tightly stretched piano wires (Figure 2). Here was a version of Sherrington's torsion-wire myograph, originally designed to

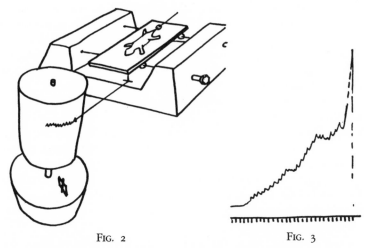

FIG. 2   FIG. 3

record the isometric contraction of the *tibialis anticus* of a cat, but here adapted to the response of a whole organism. When the tail of the young rat was gently pulled, the rat clung to the cloth floor and tugged forward. By amplifying the fine movements of the platform, it was possible to get a good kymograph record of the tremor in this motion and then, as the pull against the tail was increased, of the desperate spring into the air (Figure 3).

Now, baby rats have very little future, except as adult rats. Their behavior is literally infantile and cannot be usefully extrapolated to everyday life. But if this technique would work with a baby, why not try it on a mature rat? To avoid attaching anything to the rat, it should be possible to record, not a pull against the substrate, but the ballistic thrust exerted as the rat runs forward or suddenly stops in response to my calibrated click. So, invoking the first principle of scientific practice again, I threw away the piano-wire platform and built a runway, eight feet long. This was constructed of light wood, in the form of a U girder, mounted rigidly on vertical glass plates, the elasticity of which permitted a very slight longitudinal movement (Figure 4). The runway became the floor of a long tunnel, not shown, at one end of which I placed my soundless release box and at the other end myself, prepared to reinforce the rat for coming down the runway by giving it a bit of wet mash, to sound a click from time to time when it had reached the middle of the runway, and to harvest kymograph records of the vibrations of the substrate.

Now for a second unformalized principle of scientific practice: Some ways of doing research are easier than others. I got tired of carrying the rat back to the other end of the runway. A back alley was therefore added

(Figure 5). Now the rat could eat a bit of mash at point C, go down the back alley A, around the end as shown, and back home by runway B. The experimenter at E could collect records from the kymograph at D in comfort. In this way a great many records were made of the forces exerted against the substratum as rats ran down the alley and occasionally stopped dead in their tracks as a click sounded (Figure 6).

There was one annoying detail, however. The rat would often wait an inordinately long time at C before starting down the back alley on the next run. There seemed to be no explanation for this. When I timed these delays with a stop watch, however, and plotted them, they seemed to show orderly changes (Figure 7). This was, of course, the kind of thing I was looking for. I forgot all about the movements of the substratum and began to run rats for the sake of the delay measurements alone. But there was now no reason why the runway had to be eight feet long and, as the second

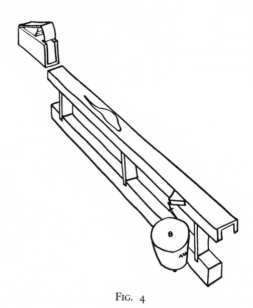

FIG. 4

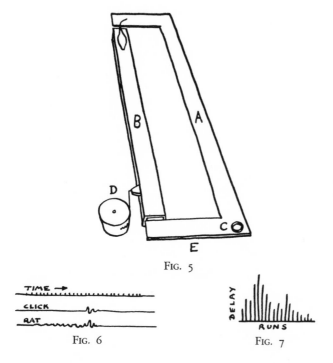

Fig. 5

Fig. 6   Fig. 7

principle came into play again, I saw no reason why the rat could not deliver its own reinforcement.

A new apparatus was built. In Figure 8 we see the rat eating a piece of food just after completing a run. It produced the food by its own action. As it ran down the back alley A to the far end of the rectangular runway, its weight caused the whole runway to tilt slightly on the axis C and this movement turned the wooden disc D, permitting a piece of food in one of the holes around its perimeter to drop through a funnel into a food dish. The food was pearl tapioca, the only kind I could find in the grocery stores in reasonably uniform pieces. The rat had only to complete its journey by coming down the homestretch B to enjoy its reward. The experimenter was able to enjoy *his* reward at the same time, for he had only to load the magazine, put in a rat, and relax. Each tilt was recorded on a slowly moving kymograph.

A third unformalized principle of scientific practice: Some people are lucky. The disc of wood from which I had fashioned the food magazine was taken from a storeroom of discarded apparatus. It happened to have a central spindle, which fortunately I had not bothered to cut off. One day it occurred to me that if I wound a string around the spindle and allowed it to unwind as the magazine was emptied (Figure 9), I would get a different kind of record. Instead of a mere report of the up-and-down movement of the runway, as a series of pips as in a polygraph, I would get a *curve*. And

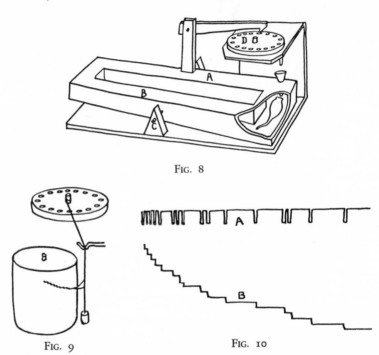

FIG. 8

FIG. 9   FIG. 10

I knew that science made great use of curves, although, so far as I could discover, very little of pips on a polygram. The difference between the old type of record at A (Figure 10) and the new at B may not seem great, but as it turned out the curve revealed things in the rate of responding, and in changes in that rate, which would certainly otherwise have been missed. By allowing the string to unwind rather than to wind, I had got my curve in an awkward Cartesian quadrant, but that was easily remedied. Psychologists have adopted cumulative curves only very slowly, but I think it is fair to say that they have become an indispensable tool for certain purposes of analysis.

Eventually, of course, the runway was seen to be unnecessary. The rat could simply reach into a covered tray for pieces of food, and each movement of the cover could operate a solenoid to move a pen one step in a cumulative curve. The first major change in rate observed in this way was due to indigestion. Curves showing how the rate of eating declined with the time of eating comprised the other part of my thesis. But a refinement was needed. The behavior of the rat in pushing open the door was not a normal part of the ingestive behavior of *Rattus rattus*. The act was obviously learned but its status as part of the final performance was not clear. It seemed wise to add an initial conditioned response connected with ingestion in a quite arbirary way. I chose the first device which came to hand—a horizontal bar or lever placed where it could be conveniently depressed by the rat to close a switch which operated a magnetic magazine. Ingestion curves obtained with this initial response in the chain were found to have the same properties as those without it.

Now, as soon as you begin to complicate an apparatus, you necessarily invoke a fourth principle of scientific practice: Apparatuses sometimes break down. I had only to wait for the food magazine to jam to get an extinction curve. At first I treated this as a defect and hastened to remedy the difficulty. But eventually, of course, I deliberately disconnected the magazine. I can easily recall the excitement of that first complete extinction curve (Figure 11). I had made contact with Pavlov at last! Here was a

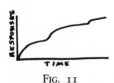

FIG. 11

curve uncorrupted by the physiological process of ingestion. It was an orderly change due to nothing more than a special contingency of reinforcement. It was pure behavior! I am not saying that I would not have got around to extinction curves without a breakdown in the apparatus; Pavlov had given too strong a lead in that direction. But it is still no exaggeration to say that some of the most interesting and surprising results have turned up first because of similar accidents. Foolproof apparatus is no doubt highly desirable, but Charles Ferster and I in recently reviewing the data from a five-year program of research found many occasions to congratulate ourselves on the fallibility of relays and vacuum tubes.

I then built four soundproofed ventilated boxes, each containing a lever and a food magazine and supplied with a cumulative recorder, and was on my way to an intensive study of conditioned reflexes in skeletal behavior. I would reinforce every response for several days and then extinguish for a day or two, varying the number of reinforcements, the amount of previous magazine training, and so on.

At this point I made my first use of the deductive method. I had long since given up pearl tapioca as too unbalanced a diet for steady use. A neighborhood druggist had shown me his pill machine, and I had had one made along the same lines (Figure 12). It consisted of a fluted brass bed across which one laid a long cylinder of stiff paste (in my case a MacCollum formula for an adequate rat diet). A similarly fluted cutter was then lowered onto the cylinder and rolled slowly back and forth, converting the paste into about a dozen spherical pellets. These were dried for a day or so before use. The procedure was painstaking and laborious. Eight rats eating a hundred pellets each per day could easily keep up with production. One pleasant Saturday afternoon I surveyed my supply of dry pellets and,

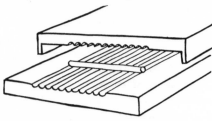

FIG. 12

appealing to certain elemental theorems in arithmetic, deduced that unless I spent the rest of that afternoon and evening at the pill machine, the supply would be exhausted by ten-thirty Monday morning.

Since I do not wish to deprecate the hypothetico-deductive method, I am glad to testify here to its usefulness. It led me to apply our second principle of unformalized scientific method and to ask myself why *every* press of the lever had to be reinforced. I was not then aware of what had happened at the Brown laboratories, as Harold Schlosberg later told the story. A graduate student had been given the task of running a cat through a difficult discrimination experiment. One Sunday the student found the supply of cat food exhausted. The stores were closed, and so, with a beautiful faith in the frequency-theory of learning, he ran the cat as usual and took it back to its living cage unrewarded. Schlosberg reports that the cat howled its protest continuously for nearly forty-eight hours. Unaware of this I decided to reinforce a response only once every minute and to allow all other responses to go unreinforced. There were two results: (*a*) my supply of pellets lasted almost indefinitely; and (*b*) each rat stabilized at a fairly constant rate of responding.

Now, a steady state was something I was familiar with from physical chemistry, and I therefore embarked upon the study of periodic reinforcement. I soon found that the constant rate at which the rat stabilized depended upon how hungry it was. Hungry rat, high rate; less hungry rat, lower rate. At that time I was bothered by the practical problem of controlling food deprivation. I was working half time at the Medical School (on chronaxie of subordination!) and could not maintain a good schedule in working with the rats. The rate of responding under periodic reinforcement suggested a scheme for keeping a rat at a constant level of deprivation. The argument went like this: Suppose you reinforce the rat, not at the end of a given period, but when it has completed the number of responses ordinarily emitted in that period. And suppose you use substantial pellets of food and give the rat continuous access to the lever. Then, except for periods when the rat sleeps, it should operate the lever at a constant rate around the clock. For, whenever it grows slightly hungrier, it will work faster, get food faster, and become less hungry, while whenever it grows slightly less hungry, it will respond at a lower rate, get less food, and grow hungrier. By setting the reinforcement at a given number of responses it should even be possible to hold the rat at any given level of deprivation. I visualized a machine with a dial which one could set to make available, at any time of day or night, a rat in a given state of deprivation. Of course, nothing of the sort happens. This is "fixed-ratio" rather than "fixed-interval" reinforcement and, as I soon found out, it produces a very different type of performance. This is an example of a fifth unformalized principle of scientific practice, but one which has at least been named. Walter Cannon described it with a word invented by Horace Walpole: *serendipity*—the art of finding one thing while looking for something else.

This account of my scientific behavior up to the point at which I published my results in a book called *The Behavior of Organisms* is as exact in letter and spirit as I can now make it. The notes, data, and publications which I have examined do not show that I ever behaved in the manner of Man Thinking as described by John Stuart Mill or John Dewey or in reconstructions of scientific behavior by other philosophers of science. I never faced a Problem which was more than the eternal problem of finding order. I never attacked a problem by constructing a Hypothesis. I never deduced Theorems or submitted them to Experimental Check. So far as I can see, I had no preconceived Model of behavior—certainly not a physiological or mentalistic one and, I believe, not a conceptual one. The "reflex reserve" was an abortive, though operational, concept which was retracted a year or so after publication in a paper at the Philadelphia meeting of the APA. It lived up to my opinion of theories in general by proving utterly worthless in suggesting further experiments. Of course, I was working on a basic Assumption—that there was order in behavior if I could only discover it—but such an assumption is not to be confused with the hypotheses of deductive theory. It is also true that I exercised a certain Selection of Facts but not because of relevance to theory but because one fact was more orderly than another. If I engaged in Experimental Design at all, it was simply to complete or extend some evidence of order already observed.

Most of the experiments described in *The Behavior of Organisms* were done with groups of four rats. A fairly common reaction to the book was that such groups were too small. How did I know that other groups of four rats would do the same thing? Keller, in defending the book, countered with the charge that groups of four were too *big*. Unfortunately, however, I allowed myself to be persuaded of the contrary. This was due in part to my association at the University of Minnesota with W. T. Heron. Through him I came into close contact for the first time with traditional animal psychology. Heron was interested in inherited maze behavior, inherited activity, and certain drugs—the effects of which could then be detected only through the use of fairly large groups. We did an experiment together on the effect of starvation on the rate of pressing a lever and started the new era with a group of sixteen rats. But we had only four boxes, and this was so inconvenient that Heron applied for a grant and built a battery of twenty-four lever-boxes and cumulative recorders. I supplied an attachment which would record, not only the mean performance of all twenty-four rats in a single averaged curve, but mean curves for four subgroups of twelve rats each and four subgroups of six rats each.[2] We thus provided for the design of experiments according to the principles of R. A. Fisher, which were then coming into vogue. We had, so to speak, mechanized the Latin square.

With this apparatus Heron and I published a study of extinction in maze-bright and maze-dull rats using *ninety-five* subjects. Later I published mean extinction curves for groups of twenty-four, and W. K. Estes and I did our work on anxiety with groups of the same size. But although Heron and I could properly voice the hope that "the possibility of using large groups of animals greatly improves upon the method as previously reported, since tests of significance are provided for and properties of behavior not apparent in single cases may be more easily detected," in actual practice that is not what happened. The experiments I have just mentioned are almost all we have to show for this elaborate battery of boxes. Undoubtedly more work could be done with it and would have its place, but something had happened to the natural growth of the method. You cannot easily make a change in the conditions of an experiment when twenty-four apparatuses have to be altered. Any gain in rigor is more than matched by a loss in flexibility. We were forced to confine ourselves to processes which could be studied with the baselines already developed in earlier work. We could not move on to the discovery of other processes or even to a more refined analysis of those we were working with. No matter

[2] Heron, W. T., & Skinner, B. F. An apparatus for the study of behavior. *Psychol. Rec.*, 1939, *3*, 166–176.

how significant might be the relations we actually demonstrated, our statistical Leviathan had swum aground. The art of the method had stuck at a particular stage of its development.

Another accident rescued me from mechanized statistics and brought me back to an even more intensive concentration on the single case. In essence, I suddenly found myself face to face with the engineering problem of the animal trainer. When you have the responsibility of making absolutely sure that a given organism will engage in a given sort of behavior at a given time, you quickly grow impatient with theories of learning. Principles, hypotheses, theorems, satisfactory proof at the .05 level of significance that behavior at a choice point shows the effect of secondary reinforcement—nothing could be more irrelevant. No one goes to the circus to see the average dog jump through a hoop significantly oftener than untrained dogs raised under the same circumstances, or to see an elephant demonstrate a principle of behavior.

Perhaps I can illustrate this without giving aid and comfort to the enemy by describing a Russian device which the Germans found quite formidable. The Russians used dogs to blow up tanks. A dog was trained to hide behind a tree or wall in low brush or other cover. As a tank approached and passed, the dog ran swiftly alongside it, and a small magnetic mine attached to the dog's back was sufficient to cripple the tank or set it afire. The dog, of course, had to be replaced.

Now I ask you to consider some of the technical problems which the psychologist faces in preparing a dog for such an act of unintentional heroism. The dog must wait behind the tree for an indefinite length of time. Very well, it must therefore be intermittently reinforced for waiting. But what schedule will achieve the highest probability of waiting? If the reinforcement is to be food, what is the absolutely optimal schedule of deprivation consistent with the health of the dog? The dog must run to the tank—that can be arranged by reinforcing it with a practice tank—but it must start instantly if it is to overtake a swift tank, and how do you differentially reinforce short reaction times, especially in counteracting the reinforcement for sitting and waiting? The dog must react only to tanks, not to a refugee driving his oxcart along the road, but what are the defining properties of a tank so far as a dog is concerned?

I think it can be said that a functional analysis proved adequate in its technological application. Manipulation of environmental conditions alone made possible a wholly unexpected practical control. Behavior could be shaped up according to specifications and maintained indefinitely almost at will. One behavioral technologist who worked with me at the time

(Keller Breland) is now specializing in the production of behavior as a salable commodity and has described this new profession in the *American Psychologist*.[3]

There are many useful applications within psychology itself. Ratliff and Blough have recently conditioned pigeons to serve as psychophysical observers. In their experiment a pigeon may adjust one of two spots of light until the two are equally bright or it may hold a spot of light at the absolute threshold during dark adaptation. The techniques which they have developed to induce pigeons to do this are only indirectly related to the point of their experiments and hence exemplify the application of a behavioral science.[4] The field in which a better technology of behavior is perhaps most urgently needed is education. I cannot describe here the applications which are now possible, but perhaps I can indicate my enthusiasm by hazarding the guess that educational techniques at all age levels are on the threshold of revolutionary changes (see page 217).

The effect of a behavioral technology on scientific practice is the issue here. Faced with practical problems in behavior, you necessarily emphasize the refinement of *experimental* variables. As a result, some of the standard procedures of statistics appear to be circumvented. Let me illustrate. Suppose that measurements have been made on two groups of subjects differing in some detail of experimental treatment. Means and standard deviations for the two groups are determined, and any difference due to the treatment is evaluated. If the difference is in the expected direction but is not statistically significant, the almost universal recommendation would be to study larger groups. But our experience with practical control suggests that we may reduce the troublesome variability by changing the conditions of the experiment. By discovering, elaborating, and fully exploiting every relevant variable, we may eliminate *in advance of measurement* the individual differences which obscure the difference under analysis. This will achieve the same result as increasing the size of groups, and it will almost certainly yield a bonus in the discovery of new variables which would not have been identified in the statistical treatment.

The same may be said of smooth curves. In our study of anxiety, Estes and I published several curves, the reasonable smoothness of which was obtained by averaging the performances of twelve rats for each curve. The individual curves published at that time show that the mean curves do not

[3] Breland, K., & Breland, Marion. A field of applied animal psychology. *Amer. Psychologist*, 1951, 6, 202–204.

[4] Ratliff, F., & Blough, D. S. Behavioral studies of visual processes in the pigeon. Report of Contract N50ri-07663, Psychological Laboratories, Harvard University, September, 1954.

faithfully represent the behavior of any one rat. They show a certain tendency toward a change in slope which supported the point we were making, and they may have appeared to warrant averaging for that reason.

But an alternative method would have been to explore the individual case until an equally smooth curve could be obtained. This would have meant not only rejecting the temptation to produce smoothness by averaging cases, but manipulating all relevant conditions as we later learned to manipulate them for practical purposes. The individual curves which we published at that time point to the need not for larger groups but for improvement in experimental technique. Here, for example, is a curve the smoothness of which is characteristic of current practice. Such curves were shown in the making in a demonstration which Ferster and I arranged at the Cleveland meeting of the American Psychological Association (Figure 13). Here, in a single organism, three different schedules of reinforcement

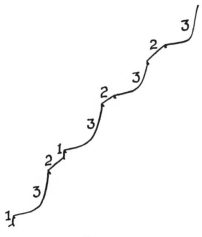

FIG. 13

are yielding corresponding performances with great uniformity under appropriate stimuli alternating at random. One does not reach this kind of order through the application of statistical methods.

In *The Behavior of Organisms* I was content to deal with the over-all slopes and curvature of cumulative curves and could make only a rough classification of the properties of behavior shown by the finer grain. The grain has now been improved. The resolving power of the microscope has been greatly increased, and we can see fundamental processes of behavior in sharper and sharper detail. In choosing rate of responding as a basic datum and in recording this conveniently in a cumulative curve, we make important temporal aspects of behavior *visible*. Once this has happened, our scientific practice is reduced to simple looking. A new world is opened to inspection. We use such curves as we use a microscope, X-ray camera, or telescope. This is well exemplified by recent extensions of the method. These are no longer part of my case history, but perhaps you will permit me to consult you about what some critics have described as a *folie à deux* or group neurosis.

An early application of the method to the behavior of avoidance and escape was made by Keller in studying the light aversion of the rat. This was brilliantly extended by Murray Sidman in his shock-avoidance experiments. It is no longer necessary to describe avoidance and escape by appeal to "principles," for we may *watch* the behavior develop when we have arranged the proper contingencies of reinforcement, as we later watch it change as these contingencies are changed.

Hunt and Brady have extended the use of a stable rate in the study of anxiety-producing stimuli and have shown that the depression in rate is eliminated by electroconvulsive shock and by other measures which are effective in reducing anxiety in human patients. O. R. Lindsley has found the same thing for dogs, using insulin-shock therapy and sedatives. Brady has refined the method by exploring the relevance of various schedules of reinforcement in tracing the return of the conditioned depression after treatment. In these experiments you *see* the effect of a treatment as directly as you see the constriction of a capillary under the microscope.

Early work with rats on caffeine and Benzedrine has been extended by Lindsley with dogs. A special technique for evaluating several effects of a drug in a single short experimental period yields a record of behavior which can be read as a specialist reads an electrocardiogram. Dr. Peter Dews of the Department of Pharmacology at the Harvard Medical School is investigating dose-response curves and the types and effects of various drugs, using pigeons as subjects. In the Psychological Laboratories at Harvard additional work on drugs is being carried out by Morse, Herrnstein, and Marshall, and the technique is being adopted by drug manufacturers. There could scarcely be a better demonstration of the experimental treatment of variability. In a *single* experimental session with a *single* organism one observes the onset, duration, and decline of the effects of a drug.

The direct observation of *defective* behavior is particularly important.

Clinical or experimental damage to an organism is characteristically unique. Hence the value of a method which permits the direct observation of the behavior of the individual. Lindsley has studied the effects of near-lethal irradiation, and the effects of prolonged anesthesia and anoxia are currently being examined by Thomas Lohr in co-operation with Dr. Henry Beecher of the Massachusetts General Hospital. The technique is being applied to neurological variables in the monkey by Dr. Karl Pribram at the Hartford Institute. The pattern of such research is simple: establish the behavior in which you are interested, submit the organism to a particular treatment, and then look again at the behavior. An excellent example of the use of experimental control in the study of *motivation* is some work on obesity by J. E. Anliker in collaboration with Dr. Jean Mayer of the Harvard School of Public Health, where abnormalities of ingestive behavior in several types of obese mice can be compared by direct inspection.

There is perhaps no field in which behavior is customarily described more indirectly than psychiatry. In an experiment at the Massachusetts State Hospital, O. R. Lindsley is carrying out an extensive program which might be characterized as a quantitative study of the temporal properties of psychotic behavior.[5] Here again it is a question of making certain characteristics of the behavior visible.

The extent to which we can eliminate sources of variability before measurement is shown by a result which has an unexpected significance for comparative psychology and the study of individual differences. Figure 14 shows tracings of three curves which report behavior in response to a multiple fixed-interval fixed-ratio schedule. The hatches mark reinforcements. Separating them in some cases are short, steep lines showing a high constant rate on a fixed-ratio schedule and, in others, somewhat longer "scallops" showing a smooth acceleration as the organism shifts from a very low rate just after reinforcement to a higher rate at the end of the fixed interval. The values of the intervals and ratios, the states of deprivation, and the exposures to the schedules were different in the three cases, but except for these details the curves are quite similar. Now, one of them was made by a *pigeon* in some experiments by Ferster and me, one was made by a *rat* in an experiment on anoxia by Lohr, and the third was made by a *monkey* in Karl Pribram's laboratory at the Hartford Institute. Pigeon, rat, monkey, which is which? It doesn't matter. Of course, these three species have behavioral repertoires which are as different as their

[5] Lindsley, O. R. Operant conditioning methods applied to research in chronic schizophrenia. *Psychiat. Res. Rep.*, 1956, *5*, 118–139.

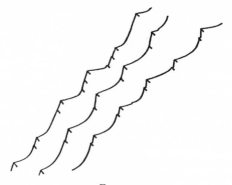

FIG. 14

anatomies. But once you have allowed for differences in the ways in which they make contact with the environment, and in the ways in which they act upon the environment, what remains of their behavior shows astonishingly similar properties. Mice, cats, dogs, and human children could have added other curves to this figure. And when organisms which differ as widely as this nevertheless show similar properties of behavior, differences between members of the same species may be viewed more hopefully. Difficult problems of idiosyncrasy or individuality will always arise as products of biological and cultural processes, but it is the very business of the experimental analysis of behavior to devise techniques which reduce their effects except when they are explicitly under investigation.

We are within reach of a science of the individual. This will be achieved, not by resorting to some special theory of knowledge in which intuition or understanding takes the place of observation and analysis, but through an increasing grasp of relevant conditions to produce order in the individual case.

A second consequence of an improved technology is the effect upon behavior theory. As I have pointed out elsewhere, it is the function of learning theory to create an imaginary world of law and order and thus to console us for the disorder we observe in behavior itself. Scores on a T maze or jumping stand hop about from trial to trial almost capriciously. Therefore we argue that if learning is, as we hope, a continuous and orderly process, it must be occurring in some other system of dimensions—perhaps in the nervous system, or in the mind, or in a conceptual model of behavior. Both the statistical treatment of group means and the averaging of curves encourage the belief that we are somehow going behind the individual case to an otherwise inaccessible, but more fundamental, process. The whole tenor of our paper on anxiety, for example, was to imply that the change we observed was not necessarily a property of behavior, but of some theoretical state of the organism ("anxiety") which was merely *reflected* in a slight modification of performance.

When we have achieved a practical control over the organism, theories of behavior lose their point. In representing and managing relevant variables, a conceptual model is useless; we come to grips with behavior itself. When behavior shows order and consistency, we are much less likely to be concerned with physiological or mentalistic causes. A datum emerges which takes the place of theoretical fantasy. In the experimental analysis of behavior we address ourselves to a subject matter which is not only manifestly the behavior of an individual and hence accessible without the usual statistical aids but also "objective" and "actual" without recourse to deductive theorizing.

Statistical techniques serve a useful function, but they have acquired a purely honorific status which may be troublesome. Their presence or absence has become a shibboleth to be used in distinguishing between good and bad work. Because measures of behavior have been highly variable, we have come to trust only results obtained from large numbers of subjects. Because some workers have intentionally or unconsciously reported only selected favorable instances, we have come to put a high value on research which is planned in advance and reported in its entirety. Because measures have behaved capriciously, we have come to value skillful deductive theories which restore order. But although large groups, planned experiments, and valid theorizing are associated with significant scientific results, it does not follow that nothing can be achieved in their absence. Here are two brief examples of the choice before us.

How can we determine the course of dark adaptation in a pigeon? We move a pigeon from a bright light to a dark room. What happens? Presumably the bird is able to see fainter and fainter patches of light as the process of adaptation takes place, but how can we follow this process? One way would be to set up a discrimination apparatus in which choices would be made at specific intervals after the beginning of dark adaptation. The test patches of light could be varied over a wide range, and the percentages of correct choices at each value would enable us eventually to locate the threshold fairly accurately. But hundreds of observations would be needed to establish only a few points on the curve and to prove that these show an actual change in sensitivity. In the experiment by Blough already mentioned, the pigeon holds a spot of light close to the threshold throughout

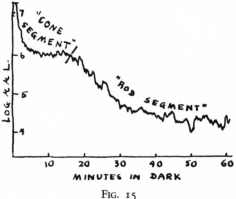

the experimental period. A single curve, such as the one sketched in Figure 15, yields as much information as hundreds of readings, together with the means and standard deviations derived from them. The information is more accurate because it applies to a single organism in a single experimental session. Yet many psychologists who would accept the first as a finished experiment because of the tables of means and standard deviations would boggle at the second or call it a preliminary study. The direct evidence of one's senses in observing a process of behavior is not trusted.

As another example, consider the behavior of several types of obese mice. Do they all suffer from a single abnormality in their eating behavior or are there differences? One might attempt to answer this with some such measure of hunger as an obstruction apparatus. The numbers of crossings of a grid to get to food, counted after different periods of free access to food, would be the data. Large numbers of readings would be needed, and the resulting mean values would possibly not describe the behavior of any one mouse in any experimental period. A much better picture may be obtained with one mouse of each kind in single experimental sessions, as Anliker has shown.[6] In an experiment reported roughly in Figure 16, each mouse was reinforced with a small piece of food after completing a short "ratio" of responses. The hypothalamic-obese mouse shows an exaggerated but otherwise normal ingestion curve. The hereditary-obese mouse eats slowly but for an indefinite length of time and with little change in rate.

[6] Anliker, J., and Mayer, J. Operant conditioning technique for studying feeding patterns in normal and obese mice. *J. Appl. Physiol.,* 1956, 8, 667–670.

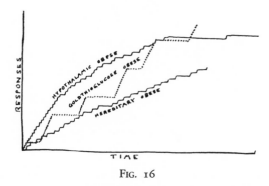

FIG. 16

The gold-poisoned obese mouse shows a sharp oscillation between periods of very rapid responding and no responding at all. These three individual curves contain more information than could probably ever be generated with measures requiring statistical treatment, yet they will be viewed with suspicion by many psychologists because they are single cases.

It is perhaps natural that psychologists should awaken only slowly to the possibility that behavioral processes may be directly observed, or that they should only gradually put the older statistical and theoretical techniques in their proper prospective. But it is time to insist that science does not progress by carefully designed steps called "experiments" each of which has a well-defined beginning and end. Science is a continuous and often a disorderly and accidental process. We shall not do the young psychologist any favor if we agree to reconstruct our practices to fit the pattern demanded by current scientific methodology. What the statistician means by the design of experiments is design which yields the kind of data to which *his* techniques are applicable. He does not mean the behavior of the scientist in his laboratory devising research for his own immediate and possibly inscrutable purposes.

The organism whose behavior is most extensively modified and most completely controlled in research of the sort I have described is the experimenter himself. The point was well made by a cartoonist in the Columbia *Jester* (Figure 17). The caption read: "Boy, have I got this guy conditioned! Every time I press the bar down he drops in a piece of food." The subjects we study reinforce us much more effectively than we reinforce them. I have been telling you simply how I have been conditioned to behave. And of course it is a mistake to argue too much from

FIG. 17

one case history. My behavior would not have been shaped as it was were it not for personal characteristics which all psychologists fortunately do not share. Freud has had something to say about the motivation of scientists and has given us some insight into the type of person who achieves the fullest satisfaction from precise experimental design and the intricacies of deductive systems. Such a person tends to be more concerned with his success as a scientist than with his subject matter, as is shown by the fact that he often assumes the role of a roving ambassador. If this seems unfair, let me hasten to characterize my own motivation in equally unflattering terms. Several years ago I spent a pleasant summer writing a novel called *Walden Two*. One of the characters, Frazier, said many things which I was not yet ready to say myself. Among them was this:

I have only one important characteristic, Burris: I'm stubborn. I've had only one idea in my life—a true *idée fixe* . . . to put it as bluntly as possible, the idea of having my own way. "Control" expresses it, I think. The control of human behavior, Burris. In my early experimental days it was a frenzied, selfish desire to dominate. I remember the rage I used to feel when a prediction went awry. I could have shouted at the subjects of my experiments, "Behave, damn you, behave as you ought!" Eventually I realized that the subjects were always right. They always behaved as they ought. It was I who was wrong. I had made a bad prediction.

(In fairness to Frazier and the rest of myself, I want to add his next remark: "And what a strange discovery for a would-be tyrant, that the only effective technique of control is unselfish." Frazier means, of course, positive reinforcement.)

We have no more reason to say that all psychologists should behave as I have behaved than that they should all behave like R. A. Fisher. The scientist, like any organism, is the product of a unique history. The practices which he finds most appropriate will depend in part upon this history. Fortunately, personal idiosyncrasies usually leave a negligible mark on science as public property. They are important only when we are concerned with the encouragement of scientists and the prosecution of research. When we have at last an adequate empirical account of the behavior of Man Thinking, we shall understand all this. Until then, it may be best not to try to fit all scientists into any single mold.

The Experimental Analysis of Behavior

A Sigma Xi National Lecture, given in November and December of 1956 before thirty-one chapters of the Society of the Sigma Xi or the Research Engineers Society of America, the following paper was written primarily for the non-psychological scientist. It was published in the American Scientist *(1957, 45, 343-371) and is reprinted with permission.*

Not so long ago the expression "a science of behavior" would have been regarded as a contradiction in terms. Living organisms were distinguished by the fact that they were spontaneous and unpredictable. If you saw something move without being obviously pushed or pulled, you could be pretty sure it was alive. This was so much the case that mechanical imitations of living things—singing birds which flapped their wings, figures on a clock tolling a bell—had an awful fascination which, in the age of electronic brains and automation, we cannot recapture or fully understand. One hundred and fifty years of science and invention have robbed living creatures of this high distinction.

Science has not done this by creating truly spontaneous or capricious systems. It has simply discovered and used subtle forces which, acting upon a mechanism, give it the direction and apparent spontaneity which make it seem alive. Similar forces were meanwhile being discovered in the case of the living organism itself. By the middle of the seventeenth century it was known that muscle, excised from a living organism and out of reach of any "will," would contract if pinched or pricked or otherwise stimulated, and during the nineteenth century larger segments of the organism were submitted to a similar analysis. The discovery of the reflex, apart from its neurological implications, was essentially the discovery of stimuli —of forces acting upon an organism which accounted for part of its behavior.

For a long time the analysis of behavior took the form of the discovery and collection of reflex mechanisms. Early in the present century, the Dutch physiologist Rudolph Magnus,[1] after an exhaustive study of the reflexes involved in the maintenance of posture, put the matter this way: when a cat

---

[1] Magnus, R. *Köperstellung.* Berlin, 1924.

hears a mouse, turns toward the source of the sound, sees the mouse, runs toward it, and pounces, its posture at every stage, even to the selection of the foot which is to take the first step, is determined by reflexes which can be demonstrated one by one under experimental conditions. All the cat has to do is to decide whether or not to pursue the mouse; everything else is prepared for it by its postural and locomotor reflexes.

To pursue or not to pursue is a question, however, which has never been fully answered on the model of the reflex, even with the help of Pavlov's principle of conditioning. Reflexes—conditioned or otherwise—are primarily concerned with the internal economy of the organism and with maintaining various sorts of equilibrium. The behavior through which the individual deals with the surrounding environment and gets from it the things it needs for its existence and for the propagation of the species cannot be forced into the simple all-or-nothing formula of stimulus and response. Some well-defined patterns of behavior, especially in birds, fish, and invertebrates are controlled by "releasers" which suggest reflex stimuli,[2] but even here the probability of occurrence of such behavior varies over a much wider range, and the conditions of which that probability is a function are much more complex and subtle. And when we come to that vast repertoire of "operant" behavior which is shaped up by the environment in the lifetime of the individual, the reflex pattern will not suffice at all.

In studying such behavior we must make certain preliminary decisions. We begin by choosing an organism—one which we hope will be representative but which is first merely convenient. We must also choose a bit of behavior—not for any intrinsic or dramatic interest it may have, but because it is easily observed, affects the environment in such a way that it can be easily recorded, and for reasons to be noted subsequently may be repeated many times without fatigue. Thirdly, we must select or construct an experimental space which can be well controlled.

These requirements are satisfied by the situation shown in Figure 1. A partially sound-shielded aluminum box is divided into two compartments. In the near compartment a pigeon, standing on a screen floor, is seen in the act of pecking a translucent plastic plate behind a circular opening in the partition. The plate is part of a delicate electric key; when it is pecked, a circuit is closed to operate recording and controlling equipment. Colored lights can be projected on the back of the plate as stimuli. The box is ventilated, and illuminated by a dim ceiling light.

We are interested in the probability that in such a controlled space the

[2] Tinbergen, N. *The Study of Instinct.* Oxford, 1951.

FIG. 1.   An experimental space showing a pigeon in the act of pecking a plastic key.

organism we select will engage in the behavior we thus record. At first blush, such an interest may seem trivial. We shall see, however, that the conditions which alter the probability, and the processes which unfold as that probability changes, are quite complex. Moreover, they have an immediate, important bearing on the behavior of other organisms under other circumstances, including the organism called man in the everyday world of human affairs.

Probability of responding is a difficult datum. We may avoid controversial issues by turning at once to a practical measure, the *frequency* with which a response is emitted. The experimental situation shown in Figure 1 was designed to permit this frequency to vary over a wide range. In the experiments to be described here, stable rates are recorded which differ by a factor of about 600. In other experiments, rates have differed by as much as 2000:1. Rate of responding is most conveniently recorded in a cumulative curve. A pen moves across a paper tape, stepping a short uniform distance with each response. Appropriate paper speeds and unit steps are chosen so that the rates to be studied give convenient slopes.

Operant Conditioning

Among the conditions which alter rate of responding are some of the consequences of behavior. Operant behavior usually affects the environment and generates stimuli which "feed back" to the organism. Some feedback may have the effects identified by the layman as reward and punishment. Any consequence of behavior which is rewarding or, more technically, *reinforcing* increases the probability of further responding. Unfortunately, a consequence which is punishing has a much more complex result.[3] Pecking the key in our experimental space has certain natural consequences. It stimulates the bird tactually and aurally, and such stimulation may be slightly reinforcing. We study the effect more expediently, however, by arranging an arbitrary consequence which is clearly reinforcing. Food is reinforcing to a hungry pigeon (for our present purposes we need not inquire why this is so), and we therefore arrange to present food with a special magazine. When a solenoid is energized, a tray containing a mixture of grains is brought into position in the square opening below the key in Figure 1, where the pigeon has access to the grain for, say, four seconds.

We can demonstrate the effect of operant reinforcement simply by connecting the key which the pigeon pecks to the solenoid which operates the food tray. A single presentation of food, following immediately upon a response, increases the rate with which responses to the key are subsequently emitted so long as the pigeon remains hungry. By reinforcing several responses, we may create a high probability of responding. If the magazine is now disconnected, the rate declines to, and may even go below, its original level. These changes are the processes of operant conditioning and extinction, respectively. More interesting phenomena are generated when responses are merely *intermittently* reinforced. It is characteristic of everyday life that few of the things we do always "pay off." The dynamic characteristics of our behavior depend upon the actual schedules of reinforcement.

The effects of intermittent reinforcement have been extensively studied

---

[3] See *The Behavior of Organisms*.

in the laboratory.[4] A common sort of intermittency is based on time. Reinforced responses can be spaced, say, ten minutes apart. When one reinforcement is received, a timer is started which opens the reinforcing
circuit for ten minutes; the first response after the circuit is closed is reinforced. When an organism is exposed to this schedule of reinforcement for
many hours, it develops a characteristic performance which is related in a
rather complex way to the schedule. A short sample of such a performance
is shown in Figure 2, obtained with a cumulative recorder. The scales and

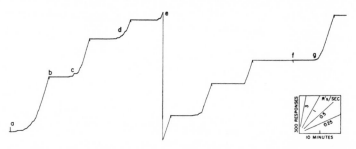

FIG. 2.   Characteristic performance by pigeon under fixed-interval reinforcement.

a few representative speeds are shown in the lower right-hand corner. The
experimental session begins at *a*. The first reinforcement will not occur
until ten minutes later, and the bird begins at a very low rate of responding. As the 10-minute interval passes, the rate increases, accelerating fairly
smoothly to a terminal rate at reinforcement at *b*. The rate then drops to
zero. Except for a slight abortive start at *c*, it again accelerates to a high
terminal value by the end of the second 10-minute interval. A third fairly
smooth acceleration is shown at *d*. (At *e* the pen instantly resets to the
starting position on the paper.) The over-all pattern of performance on a
"fixed-interval" schedule is a fairly smoothly accelerating scallop in each
interval, the acceleration being more rapid the longer the initial pause.
Local effects due to separate reinforcements are evident, however, which
cannot be discussed here for lack of space.

If the intervals between reinforcements are not fixed, the performance
shown in Figure 2 cannot develop. If the length of interval is varied essen-

---

[4] Much of the research from which the following examples are drawn has been supported
by the Office of Naval Research and the National Science Foundation. It is reported in
Schedules of Reinforcement.

tially at random, responding occurs at a single rate represented by a constant slope in the cumulative record. Two examples are shown in Figure 3. In the upper curve, a hungry pigeon is reinforced with grain on a *variable-interval schedule,* where the mean interval between reinforcements is 3 minutes. Reinforcements occur where marked by pips. In the lower curve a hungry chimpanzee, operating a toggle switch, is reinforced on the same schedule with laboratory food. The over-all rate under variable-interval reinforcement is a function of the mean interval, the level of food-deprivation, and many other variables. It tends to increase slowly under prolonged exposure to any one set of conditions. The constant rate itself eventually becomes an important condition of the experiment and resists any change to other values. For this reason the straight lines of Figure 3 are not as suitable for baselines as might be supposed.

Reinforcements may be scheduled with a *counter* instead of a timer. For example, we may maintain a *fixed ratio* between responses and reinforcements. In industry this schedule is referred to as piecework or piece-rate pay. Anyone who has seen workers paid on such a schedule is familiar with

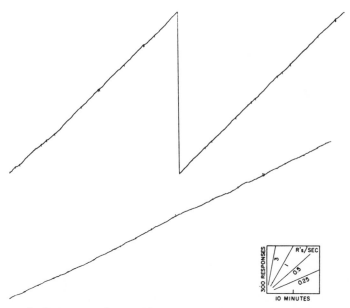

FIG. 3. Performance under variable-interval reinforcement for a pigeon (upper curve) and a chimpanzee (lower curve).

some features of the performance generated: a high rate is sustained for long periods of time. For this reason, the schedule is attractive to employers, but it is generally recognized that the level of activity generated is potentially dangerous and justified only in seasonal or other periodic employment.

Performances of a pigeon under fixed-ratio reinforcement are shown in Figure 4. In the left-hand record reinforcements occur every 210 responses

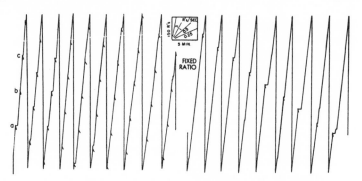

FIG. 4. Typical performance by a pigeon under fixed-ratio reinforcement. At the left every 210th response is reinforced; at the right every 900th response.

(at *a, b, c,* and elsewhere). The over-all rate is high. Most of the pauses occur immediately after reinforcement. At the right is the performance generated when the pigeon pecks the key 900 times for each reinforcement. This unusually high ratio was reached in some experiments in the Harvard Psychological Laboratories by W. H. Morse and R. J. Herrnstein. A short pause after reinforcement is the rule.

A *variable-ratio* schedule programmed by a counter corresponds to the variable-interval schedule programmed by a timer. Reinforcement is contingent on a given *average* number of responses but the numbers are allowed to vary roughly at random. We are all familiar with this schedule because it is the heart of all gambling devices and systems. The confirmed or pathological gambler exemplifies the result: a very high rate of activity is generated by a relatively slight net reinforcement. Where the "cost" of a response can be estimated (in terms, say, of the food required to supply the energy needed, or of the money required to play the gambling device), it may be demonstrated that organisms will operate at a net loss.

When the food magazine is disconnected after intermittent reinforcement, many responses continue to occur in greater number and for a longer time than after continuous reinforcement. After certain schedules, the rate may decline in a smoothly accelerated extinction curve. After other schedules, when the rate itself enters prominently into the experimental conditions, it may oscillate widely. The potential responding built up by reinforcement may last a long time. We have obtained extinction curves six years after prolonged reinforcement on a variable-ratio schedule.[5] Ratio schedules characteristically produce large numbers of responses in extinction. After prolonged exposure to a ratio of 900:1 (Figure 4) the bird was put in the apparatus with the magazine disconnected. During the first 4½ hours it emitted 73,000 responses.

Interval and ratio schedules have different effects for several reasons. When a reinforcement is scheduled by a timer, the probability of reinforcement increases during any pause, and the first responses after pauses are especially likely to be reinforced. On ratio schedules responses which are part of short runs are likely to be reinforced. Moreover, when a given schedule of reinforcement has had a first effect, the performance which develops becomes itself an important part of the experimental situation. This performance, in combination with the schedule, arranges certain probable conditions at the moment of reinforcement. Sometimes a schedule produces a performance which maintains just those conditions which perpetuate the performance. Some schedules generate a progressive change. Under still other schedules the combination of schedule and performance yields conditions at reinforcement which generate a different performance, which in turn produces conditions at reinforcement which restore the earlier performance.

In *Schedules of Reinforcement* Charles B. Ferster and I checked this explanation of the effect of schedules by controlling conditions more precisely at the moment of reinforcement. For example, we guaranteed that all reinforced responses would be preceded by pauses instead of making this condition merely probable under an interval schedule. In a variable-interval performance, such as that shown in Figure 3, it is not difficult to find responses which are preceded by, say, 3-second pauses. We can arrange that only such responses will be reinforced without greatly disturbing the schedule. When this is done, the slope of the record immediately drops. On the other hand, we may choose to reinforce responses which occur during short rapid bursts of responding, and we then note an immediate increase in rate.

If we insist upon a very long pause, we may be able to reinforce *every*

---

[5] A curve after four years appears on page 80.

response satisfying these conditions and still maintain a very low rate. The differential reinforcement of low rates was first studied by Douglas Anger in the Harvard Laboratories. Wilson and Keller at Columbia have reported an independent investigation.[6] Recently W. H. Morse and I have studied the effect of relatively long enforced pauses. Figure 5 shows the perform-

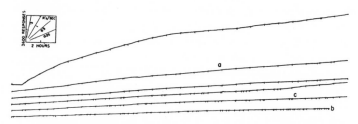

FIG. 5.   Very slow sustained responding when only responses preceded by a 3-minute pause are reinforced.

ance obtained in one such experiment. Any response which followed a pause at least 3 minutes in duration was reinforced. Whenever a response was made before 3 minutes had elapsed, the timer was reset and another 3-minute pause required. Under these conditions a very low stable rate of responding obtains. The figure shows a continuous performance (cut into segments for easier reproduction) in a single experimental session of 143 hours, during which time the pigeon received approximately 250 reinforcements. At no time did it pause for more than 15 minutes, and it seldom paused for more than 5 minutes.

The situation under this schedule is inherently unstable. Rate of responding increases with the severity of food deprivation and decreases as the bird becomes satiated. Let us assume that at some time during the experiment—say, at *a* in Figure 5—reinforcements are occurring too infrequently to maintain the bird's weight. The bird is operating, so to speak, at a loss. The increasing deprivation then increases the rate of responding and makes it even less likely that the pigeon will wait 3 minutes in order to respond successfully for reinforcement. Nothing but starvation lies ahead in that direction. If, on the other hand, the bird is receiving slightly more reinforcements than necessary to maintain body weight, the level of deprivation will be decreased. This will produce a lower rate of responding,

[6] Wilson, M. P. and Keller, F. S. On the selective reinforcement of spaced responses. *J. Comp. and Physiol. Psychol.*, 1953, *46*, 190–193.

which in turn means that the 3-minute pause is more frequently satisfied and reinforcements still more frequently received. In such a case the result is a fully satiated bird, and the experiment must be brought to a close. This actually happened at *b* in Figure 5, where reinforcements had become so frequent that the bird was rapidly gaining weight. This inherent instability can be corrected by changing the required pause in terms of the organism's performance. If the over-all rate of reinforcement begins to drift in either direction, the required pause may be appropriately changed. Thus the experiment in Figure 5 could have been continued if at point *c,* say, the required interval had been increased to 4 minutes. By an appropriate adjustment of the interval, we have been able to keep a pigeon responding continuously for 1500 hours—that is, 24 hours a day, 7 days a week, for approximately 2 months. Wendell Levi [7] has advanced the thesis that pigeons never sleep (roosting is merely a precautionary device against blind flying), and the statement seems to be confirmed by experiments of the present sort.

By differentially reinforcing high rates of responding, pigeons have been made to respond as rapidly as 10 to 15 responses per second. Here technical problems become crucial. It is not difficult to construct a key which will follow rapid responding, but the topography of the behavior itself changes. The excursions of head and beak become very small, and it is doubtful whether any single "response" can be properly compared with a response at a lower rate.

In our study of different kinds of schedules of reinforcement, Ferster and I found that it was possible to set up several performances in a single pigeon by bringing each one of them under stimulus control. Several different colored lights were projected on the translucent key, and responses were reinforced on several corresponding schedules. Figure 6 shows a typical performance under such a multiple schedule of reinforcement. When the key was red, the pigeon was reinforced on a 6-minute fixed-interval schedule. The usual interval scallops are seen, as at *a* and *b.* When the key was green, the pigeon was reinforced upon completing 60 responses (a fixed ratio of 60:1). The usual high ratio rate is shown as at *c* and *d.* When the key was yellow, reinforcements followed a variable-interval schedule where a pause of 6 seconds was required. The resulting low steady performance is shown at *e, f,* and elsewhere. In one experiment we were able to show nine different performances under the control of nine different

---

[7] Levi, Wendell. *The Pigeon.* Sumter, S. C., 1941.

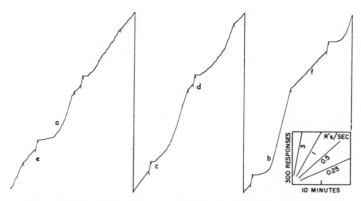

FIG. 6.   Performance under a multiple schedule of reinforcement.

patterns on the key. (The performance shown in Figure 5 is actually one part of a multiple schedule. Once per hour during the 154-hour session the key color changed to one of two other colors. In one case a single ratio was run off, in the other a single interval. All reinforcements are indicated in Figure 5. The number of reinforcements obtained under the differential reinforcement of a low rate was therefore much smaller than Figure 5 indicates. The additional schedules were inserted in an effort to detect increasing "mental fatigue" during such a long sustained session.)

The experiment may be complicated still further by introducing more than one key and by reinforcing on two or more schedules concurrently. An example of the resulting performances is shown in Figure 7, from some research by Ferster, at the Yerkes Laboratories for Primate Biology at Orange Park, Florida. In Ferster's experiment, a chimpanzee operates two toggle switches, one with each hand. Responses with the right hand are reinforced on a fixed ratio of approximately 210:1, and the performance recorded from the right toggle switch is shown in the upper part of Figure 7. As usual in many ratio performances, pauses occur after reinforcements. Responses with the left hand are at the same time being reinforced on a variable-interval schedule with a mean interval of 5 minutes, and the performance is shown in the lower part of the figure. There is some interaction between the performances, for reinforcements in the variable-interval record usually correspond to slight pauses in the ratio performance. In general, however, the experiment shows a remarkable independence of two response systems in a single organism.

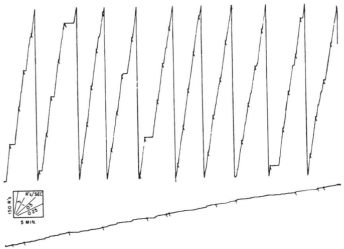

FIG. 7.   Simultaneous records of the performances by a chimpanzee reinforced for operating a toggle switch with its right hand on a fixed-ratio schedule and for operating another switch with its left hand on a variable-interval schedule (lower curve).

Stimulus Control

In speaking about colors projected on the key or the fact that a key is on the right or left, we are, of course, talking about stimuli. Moreover, they are stimuli which act prior to the appearance of a response and thus occur in the temporal order characteristic of the reflex. But they are not *eliciting* stimuli; they merely modify the probability that a response will occur, and they do this over a very wide range. The general rule seems to be that the stimuli present at the moment of reinforcement produce a maximal probability that the response will be repeated. Any change in the stimulating situation reduces the probability. This relationship is beautifully illustrated in some experiments by Norman Guttman [8] and his colleagues at Duke University on the so-called stimulus generalization gradient. Guttman makes use of the fact that, after a brief exposure to a variable-interval schedule, a large number of responses will be emitted by the organism without further reinforcement (the usual extinction curve) and that, while

8 Guttman, N., The pigeon and the spectrum and other perplexities. *Psychol. Reports*, 1956, *2*, 449–460.

these are being emitted, it is possible to manipulate the stimuli present and to determine their relative control over the response without confusing the issue by further reinforcement. In a typical experiment, for example, a monochromatic light with a wave length of 550 millimicrons was projected on the key during variable-interval reinforcement. During extinction, monochromatic lights from other parts of the visible spectrum were projected on the key for short periods of time, each wave length appearing many times and each being present for the same total time. Simply by counting the number of responses made in the presence of each wave length, Guttman and his colleagues have obtained stimulus generalization gradients similar to those shown in Figure 8. The two curves represent separate experiments. Each is an average of measurements made on six pigeons. It will be seen that during extinction responding was most rapid

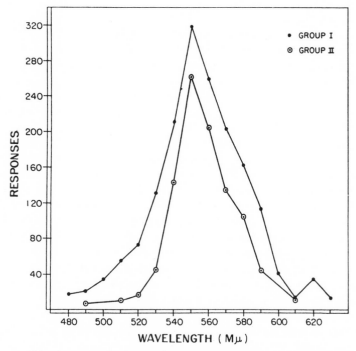

Fig. 8. Stimulus generalization gradients given by pigeons reinforced under a monochromatic light of 550 millimicrons and then extinguished under the other wave lengths shown (Guttman).

at the original wave length of 550 millimicrons. A color differing by only 10 millimicrons controls a considerably lower rate of responding. The curves are not symmetrical. Colors toward the red end of the spectrum control higher rates than those equally distant on the violet end. With this technique Guttman and his colleagues have studied gradients resulting from reinforcement at two points in the spectrum, gradients surviving after a discrimination has been set up by reinforcing one wave length and extinguishing another, and so on.

The control of behavior achieved with methods based upon rate of responding has given rise to a new psychophysics of lower organisms. It appears to be possible to learn as much about the sensory processes of the pigeon as from the older introspective methods with human subjects. An important new technique of this sort is due to D. S. Blough.[9] His ingenious procedure utilizes the apparatus shown in Figure 9. A pigeon, behaving most of the time in total darkness, thrusts its head through an opening in a partition at *a*, which provides useful tactual orientation. Through the small opening *b*, the pigeon can sometimes see a faint patch of light indicated by the word *Stimulus*. (How this appears to the pigeon is shown at the right.) The pigeon can reach and peck two keys just below the opening *b*, and it is sometimes reinforced by a food magazine which rises within reach at *c*. Through suitable reinforcing contingencies Blough conditions the pigeon to peck Key B whenever it can see the light and Key A whenever it cannot. The pigeon is occasionally reinforced for pecking Key A by the presentation of food (in darkness). Blough guarantees that the pigeon cannot see the spot of light at the time this response is made because no light at all is then on the key. By a well-established principle of "chaining," the pigeon is reinforced for pecking Key B by the disappearance of the spot of light. This suffices to keep responses to both keys in strength.

A further fact about the apparatus is that Key B automatically reduces the intensity of the spot of light, while Key A increases it. Suppose, now, that a pigeon is placed in a brightly lighted space for a given interval of time and then put immediately into the apparatus. The spot of light is at an intensity in the neighborhood of the bright-adapted threshold. If the pigeon can see the spot, it pecks Key B until it disappears. If it cannot see the spot, it pecks Key A until it appears. In each case it then shifts to the other key. During an experimental session of one hour or more, it holds the spot of light very close to its threshold value, occasionally being rein-

[9] Blough, D. S. Dark adaptation in the pigeon. *J. Comp. and Physiol. Psychol.*, 1956, *49*, 425–430.

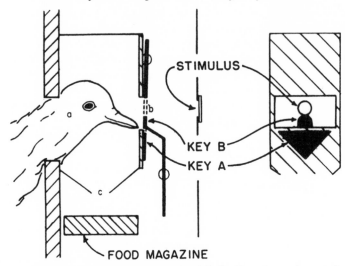

FIG. 9.   Blough's apparatus for the study of dark-adaptation and spectral sensitivity in the pigeon.

forced with food. The intensity of the light is recorded automatically. The result is the "dark-adaptation curve" for the pigeon's eye. Typical curves show a break as the dark-adaptation process shifts from the cone elements in the retina to the rods.

By repeating the experiment with a series of monochromatic lights, Blough has been able to construct spectral sensitivity curves for the pigeon which are as precise as those obtained with the best human observers. An example is shown in Figure 10, where data for the pigeon are compared with data for an aphakic human [10]—one who has had a crystalline lens removed for medical reasons. Such a person sees violet light more sensitively than normal subjects because the light is not absorbed by the lens. Even with this advantage the human observer is no more sensitive to light at the violet end of the spectrum than the pigeon. The discontinuities in the photopic curves (the lower set of open circles) of the pigeon appear to be real. The surprising correspondence in the scotopic curves (after dark adaptation, and presumably mediated by the rods) is remarkable when we recall that the avian and mammalian eye parted company in the evolutionary scale of things many millions of years ago.

[10] Wald, G. *J. Gen. Physiol.*, 1954, *38*, 623–681.

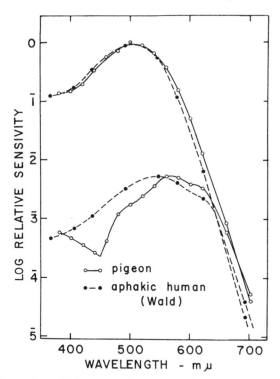

FIG. 10. Spectral sensitivity curves for scotopic (upper curves) and photopic (lower curves) vision in the pigeon and aphakic human.

Avoidance

So far our data have been taken from the pleasanter side of life—from be-havior which produces positive consequences. There are important conse-quences of another sort. Much of what we do during the day is done not because of the positive reinforcements we receive but because of aversive consequences we avoid. The whole field of escape, avoidance, and punish-ment is an extensive one, but order is slowly being brought into it. An important contribution has been the research of Murray Sidman [11] on avoidance behavior. In the Sidman technique, a rat is placed in a box the floor of which is an electric grid through which the rat can be shocked. The

[11] Sidman, M. Avoidance conditioning with brief shock and no exteroceptive warning signal. *Science*, 1953, *118*, 157–158.

pattern of polarity of the bars of the grid is changed several times per second so that the rat cannot find bars of the same sign to avoid the shock. In a typical experiment a shock occurs every 20 seconds unless the rat presses the lever, but such a response postpones the shock for a full 20 seconds. These circumstances induce a rat to respond steadily to the lever, the only reinforcement being the postponement of shock. The rat must occasionally receive a shock—that is, it must allow 20 seconds to pass without a response—if the behavior is to remain in strength. By varying the intervals between shocks, the time of postponement, and various kinds of warning stimuli, Sidman has revealed some of the important properties of this all-too-common form of behavior.

A sample of behavior which W. H. Morse and the writer obtained with the Sidman procedure is shown in Figure 11. Here both the interval between shocks and the postponement time were 8 seconds. (White space has been cut out of the record and the separate segments brought together to facilitate reproduction.) The records report a 7-hour experimental session during which about 14,000 responses were emitted. Occasional shocks are indicated by the downward movements of the pen (not to be confused with the fragments of the reset line). A significant feature of the performance is the warm-up at *a*. When first put into the apparatus the rat "takes" a number of shocks before entering upon the typical avoidance pattern. This occurs whenever a new session is begun. It may indicate that an emotional condition is required for successful avoidance behavior. The condition disappears between sessions and must be reinstated. The figure shows considerable variation in over-all rate and many local irregularities. At times small groups of shocks are taken, suggesting a return to the warm-up condition.

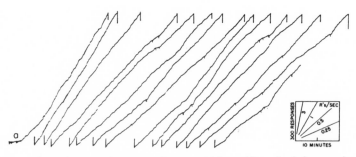

FIG. 11.   Seven-hour performance of a rat which avoids a shock by pressing a lever under the Sidman procedure.

Motivation

The consequences of behavior, whether positive or negative, and the control acquired by various stimuli related to them do not exhaust the variables of which behavior is a function. Others lie in the field commonly called motivation. Food is a reinforcement only to a hungry organism. In practice this means an organism whose weight has been reduced substantially below its value under free feeding. Reinforcing stimuli are found in other motivational areas. Responding to a key can be reinforced with water when the organism is deprived of water, with sexual contact when the organism has been sexually deprived, and so on. The level of deprivation is in each case an important condition to be investigated. How does food deprivation increase the rate of eating or of engaging in behavior reinforced with food? How does satiation have the opposite effect? The first step toward answering such questions is an empirical study of rate of responding as a function of deprivation. An analysis of the internal mechanisms responsible for the relations thus discovered may require techniques more appropriately employed in other scientific disciplines.

An example of how the present method may be applied to a problem in motivation is an experiment by Anliker and Mayer [12] on the familiar and important problem of obesity. Obese animals eat more than normal, but just how is their ingestive behavior disrupted? Anliker and Mayer have studied several types of normal and obese mice. There are strains of mice in which the abnormality is hereditary: some members of a litter simply grow fat. A normal mouse may be made obese by poisoning it with goldthioglucose or by damaging the hypothalamus. The food-getting behavior of all these types of obese mice can be observed in the apparatus shown in Figure 12. A fat mouse is shown depressing a horizontal lever which projects from the partition in the box. On a fixed-ratio schedule every 25th response produces a small pellet of food, delivered by the dispenser seen behind the partition. A supply of water is available in a bottle.

Each mouse was studied continuously for several days. The resulting cumulative curves (Figure 13) show striking differences among the patterns of ingestion. Curve C shows normal cyclic changes in rate. The non-obese mouse eats a substantial part of its daily ration in a single period (as at *a* and *b*) and for the rest of each day responds only at a low over-all rate.

---

[12] Anliker, J., and Mayer, J. Operant conditioning technique for studying feeding patterns in normal and obese mice. *J. Appl. Physiol.*, 1956, *8*, 667–670.

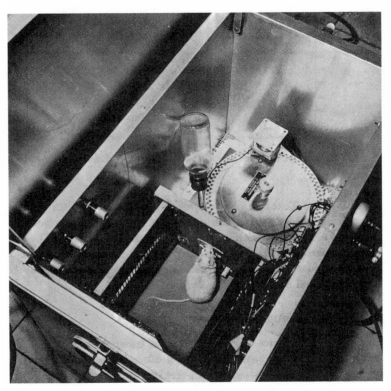

FIG. 12.   Obese mouse pressing a lever for food.

The result is a wave-like cumulative curve with 24-hour cycles. A mouse of the same strain made obese by goldthioglucose poisoning does not show this daily rhythm but continues to respond at a fairly steady rate (Curve A). The slope is no higher than parts of Curve C, but the mechanism which turns off ingestive behavior in a normal mouse appears to be inoperative. Curve B is a fairly similar record produced by a mouse of the same strain made obese by a hypothalamic lesion. Curves D and E are for litter mates from a strain containing an hereditary-obese factor. E is the performance of the normal member. Curve D, showing the performance of the obese member, differs markedly from Curves A and B. The hereditary obese mouse eats at a very high rate for brief periods, which are separated by pauses of the order of one or two hours. A different kind of disturbance in the physiological mechanism seems to be indicated.

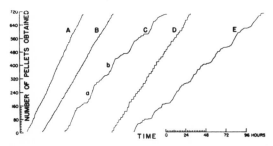

FIG. 13. Ingestive patterns for several types of normal and obese mice (Anliker and Mayer).

Williams and Teitelbaum [13] have recently produced a fourth kind of obese animal, with an apparatus in which a rat must eat a small amount of liquid food to avoid a shock. The avoidance contingencies specified by Sidman and illustrated in Figure 11 are used to induce the rat to ingest unusually large amounts of even unpalatable food. A condition which may be called "behavioral obesity" quickly develops.

The Effects of Drugs on Behavior

Other powerful variables which affect operant behavior are found in the field of pharmacology. Some drugs which affect behavior—alcohol, caffeine, nicotine, and so on—were discovered by accident and have had a long history. Others have been produced explicitly to yield such effects. The field is an active one (partly because of the importance of pharmacotherapy in mental illness), and available compounds are multiplying rapidly. Most of the behavioral drugs now available have effects which would be classified in the fields of motivation and emotion. There is no reason, however, why the effects of various contingencies of reinforcement could not be simulated by direct chemical action—why "intelligence" could not be facilitated or confusion or mental fatigue reduced. In any case, the behavior generated by various contingencies of reinforcement (including the control of that behavior via stimuli) are the baselines against which motivational and emotional effects are felt. The present technique for the study of operant behavior offers a quantitative, continuous record of the behavior of an individual organism, which is already being widely used—in industry as well as the research laboratory—in screening psycho-

13 Williams, D. R., and Teitelbaum, P. Control of drinking behavior by means of an operant-conditioning technique. *Science*, 1956, *124*, 1294–1296.

pharmacological compounds and investigating the nature of pharmacological effects.

An example is some research by Peter B. Dews,[14] of the Department of Pharmacology of the Harvard Medical School. Dews has studied the effect of certain sedatives on the pigeon's performance under a multiple fixed-interval fixed-ratio schedule. A standard baseline obtained in a short daily experimental session is shown in the upper half of Figure 14. The pigeon is reinforced on a fixed-interval schedule when the key is red and on a fixed-ratio schedule when the key is green, the two schedules being presented in the order: one interval, one ratio, two intervals, ten ratios, two intervals, four ratios. In addition to the usual characteristics of the multiple performance, this brief program shows local effects which add to its usefulness as a baseline. For example, the period of slow responding after reinforcement is greater when the preceding reinforcement has been on a ratio schedule— that is, the scallops at *a* and *b* are shallower than those at *c* and *d*. The effect of moderate doses of barbiturates, bromides, and other sedatives under a multiple fixed-interval fixed-ratio schedule is to destroy the interval performance while leaving the ratio performance essentially untouched. The lower half of Figure 14 was recorded on the day following the upper half. Three milligrams of chlorpromazine had been injected 2.5 hours prior to the experiment. The tranquilizing effect of chlorpromazine develops only with repeated doses; what is shown here is the immediate effect of a dose of this magnitude, which is similar to that of a sedative. It will be seen that the ratios survive (at *e, f,* and *g*) but that the interval performances are greatly disturbed. There is responding where none is expected, as at *h,* but not enough where a rapid rate usually obtains. This fact provides a useful screening test, but it also throws important light on the actual nature of sedation. The difference between intervals and ratios may explain some instances in which sedatives appear to have inconsistent effects on human subjects.

The interval performance is also damaged by chlorpromazine in a different type of compound schedule. Ferster and I have studied the effect of concurrent schedules in which two or more controlling circuits set up reinforcements independently. In one experiment a rat was reinforced with food at fixed intervals of 10 minutes and also by the avoidance of shock, where a shock occurred every 20 seconds unless postponed for 20 seconds by a response to a lever. The normal result of this concurrent schedule is

[14] Dews, P. B. Modification by drugs of performance on simple schedules of positive reinforcement. *Ann. N. Y. Acad. Sci.,* 1956, *65,* 268–281.

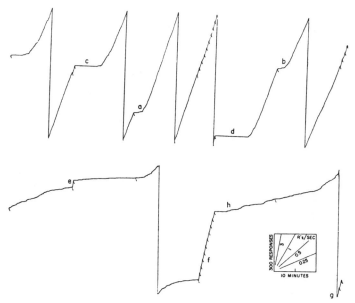

FIG. 14. Performance of a pigeon on a multiple fixed-interval fixed-ratio sched-ule in a control (upper curve) and after an injection of chlorpromazine (lower curve).

shown in the upper part of Figure 15. When the rat is "working for food and to avoid a shock," its performance suggests the usual interval scallop tilted upward so that instead of pausing after reinforcement, the rat re-sponds at a rate sufficient to avoid most shocks. A one-milligram dose of chlorpromazine immediately before the experiment has the effect shown in the lower part of the figure. The interval performance is eliminated, leaving the slow steady responding characteristic of avoidance conditioning.

Drugs which alter emotional conditions may be studied by examining the effect of the emotional variable upon operant behavior. An example is the condition usually called "anxiety." Many years ago Estes and I (see page 558) showed that the normal performance under fixed-interval rein-forcement was suppressed by a stimulus which characteristically preceded a shock. In our experiment, a rat was reinforced on a fixed-interval schedule until a stable baseline developed. A stimulus was then introduced for 3 minutes and followed by a shock to the feet of the rat. In later presenta-tions the stimulus began to depress the rate of responding—an effect com-parable to the way in which "anxiety" interferes with the daily behavior of

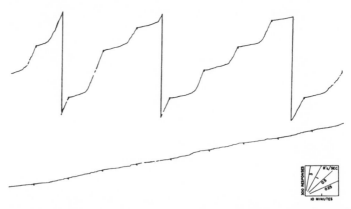

FIG. 15.   Performance of a rat on a concurrent fixed-interval and avoidance schedule in a control session (upper curve) and after being injected with chlorpromazine (lower curve).

a man. Hunt and Brady [15] have shown that some of the "treatments" for human anxiety (for example, electro-convulsive shock) temporarily eliminate the conditioned suppression in such experiments.

Brady [16] has recently applied this technique to the study of tranquilizing drugs. In his experiment, a rat is reinforced on a variable-interval schedule until responding stabilizes at a constant intermediate rate. Stimuli are then presented every 10 minutes. Each stimulus lasts for 3 minutes and is followed by a shock. Conditioned suppression soon appears. In Figure 16 each simple arrow shows the onset of the stimulus. In order to isolate the performance in the presence of the stimulus, the record is displaced downward. In the saline control, shortly after the onset of the stimulus, the rate falls to zero, as shown by the horizontal portions of the displaced segments. As soon as the shock is received (at the broken arrows, where the pen returns to its normal position), responding begins almost immediately at the normal rate. The baseline between stimuli is not smooth because a certain amount of chronic anxiety develops under these circumstances. A suitable dose of a stimulant such as amphetamine has the effect of increasing the over-all rate, as seen in the middle part of Figure 16. The suppressing stimulus is, if anything, more effective. A course of treatment with reserpine, another tranquilizer, has the effect of slightly depressing

15 Hunt, H. F., and Brady, J. V. Some effects of electro-convulsive shock on a conditioned emotional response ("anxiety"). *J. Comp. and Physiol. Psychol.,* 1955, *48,* 305.
16 Brady, J. V. Assessment of drug effects on emotional behavior. *Science,* 1956, *123,* 1033–1034.

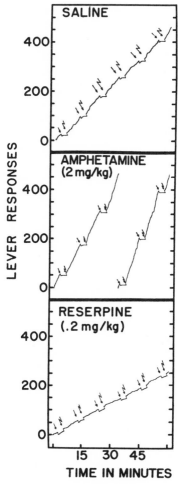

Fig. 16.   Effect of a stimulant and a tranquilizer on conditioned suppression in the rat (Brady).

the over-all rate but restoring responding during the formerly suppressing stimulus. Thus, in the lower part of Figure 16, the slopes of the displaced segments of the record are of the same order as the over-all record itself. The reserpine has eliminated an effect which, from a similarity of inciting causes, we may perhaps call anxiety.

Another field in which important variables affecting behavior are studied is neurology. Performances under various schedules of reinforcement supply baselines which are as useful here as in the field of psychopharmacology. The classical pattern of research is to establish a performance containing features of interest, then to remove or damage part of the nervous system, and later to have another look at the behavior. The damaged performance shows the effect of the lesion and helps in inferring the contribution of the area to normal behavior.

The procedure is, of course, negative. Another possibility is that neurological conditions may be arranged which will have a positive effect. A step in this direction has been taken by James Olds [17] with his discovery that weak electrical stimulation of certain parts of the brain, through permanently implanted electrodes, has an effect similar to that of positive reinforcement. In one of Olds' experiments, a rat presses a lever to give itself mild electrical stimulation in the anterior hypothalamus. When every response is so "reinforced," behavior is sustained in strength for long periods of time. One of Olds' results is shown in Figure 17. The electrical "rein-

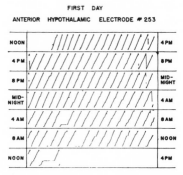

FIRST DAY

ANTERIOR HYPOTHALAMIC ELECTRODE # 253

FIG. 17.   Performance of a rat pressing a level to shock itself in the anterior hypothalamus (Olds).

forcement" was begun shortly after noon. The rat responded at approximately 2000 responses per hour throughout the day and night until the following noon. There are only three or four brief pauses during this period. When the experiment was continued the following day, however, the rat fell asleep and slept for 20 hours. Then it awoke and began again at approximately the same rate. Although there remain some puzzling differences between behavior so reinforced and behavior reinforced with food,

[17] Olds, J. Pleasure centers in the brain. *Scient. Amer.*, 1956, *195*, 105–116.

Olds' discovery in an important step toward our understanding of the physiological mechanisms involved in the operation of the environmental variable. A similar reinforcing effect of brain stimulation has been found in cats by Sidman, Brady, Boren, and Conrad [18] and in monkeys by Lilly, of the National Institutes of Health, and Brady, in the laboratories of the Walter Reed Army Institute of Research.

Human Behavior

What about man? Is rate of responding still an orderly and meaningful datum here, or is human behavior the exception in which spontaneity and and caprice still reign? In watching experiments of the sort described above, most people feel that they could "figure out" a schedule of reinforcement and adjust to it more efficiently than the experimental organism. In saying this, they are probably overlooking the clocks and calendars, the counters, and the behavior of counting with which man has solved the problem of intermittency in his environment. But if a pigeon is given a clock or a counter, it works more efficiently, and without these aids man shows little if any superiority.

Parallels have already been suggested between human and infra-human behavior in noting the similarity of fixed-ratio schedules to piece-rate pay and of variable ratios to the schedules in gambling devices. These are more than mere analogies. Comparable effects of schedules of reinforcement in man and the other animals are gradually being established by direct experimentation. An example is some work by James Holland [19] at the Naval Research Laboratories on the behavior of observing. We often forget that looking at a visual pattern or listening to a sound is itself behavior, because we are likely to be impressed by the more important behavior which the pattern or sound controls. But any act which brings an organism into contact with a discriminative stimulus, or clarifies or intensifies its effect, is reinforced by this result and must be explained in such terms. Unfortunately mere "attending" (as in reading a book or listening to a concert) has dimensions which are difficult to study. But behavior with comparable effects is sometimes accessible, such as turning the eyes toward a page, tilting a page to bring it into better light, or turning up the volume of a phonograph. Moreover, under experimental conditions, a specific response

[18] Sidman, M., Brady, J. V., Boren, J. J., and Conrad, D. G. Reward schedules and behavior maintained by intracranial self-stimulation. *Science*, 1955, *122*, 830–831.

[19] Holland, J. G. Technique for behavioral analysis of human observing. *Science*, 1957, *125*, 348–350.

can be reinforced by the production or clarification of a stimulus which controls other behavior. The matter is of considerable practical importance. How, for example, can a radar operator or other "lookout" be kept alert? The answer is: by reinforcing his looking behavior.

Holland has studied such reinforcement in the following way. His human subject is seated in a small room before a dial. The pointer on the dial occasionally deviates from zero, and the subject's task is to restore it by pressing a button. The room is dark, and the subject can see the dial only by pressing another button which flashes a light for a fraction of a second. Pressing the second button is, then, an act which presents to the subject a stimulus which is important because it controls the behavior of restoring the pointer to zero.

Holland has only to *schedule* the deviations of the pointer to produce changes in the rate of flashing the light comparable to the performances of lower organisms under comparable schedules. In Figure 18, for example, the upper curve shows a pigeon's performance on a fairly short fixed-interval. Each interval shows a rather irregular curvature as the rate passes from a low value after reinforcement to a high, fairly constant, terminal rate. In the lower part of the figure is one of Holland's curves obtained when the pointer deflected from zero every three minutes. After a few hours of exposure to these conditions, the subject flashed the light ("looked at the pointer") only infrequently just after a deflection, but as the interval passed, his rate accelerated, sometimes smoothly, sometimes abruptly, to a fairly constant terminal rate. (An interesting feature of this curve is the tendency to "run through" the reinforcement and to continue at a high rate for a few seconds after reinforcement before dropping to the low rate from which the terminal rate then emerges. Examples of this are seen at *a, b,* and *c.* Examples in the case of the pigeon are also seen at *d* and *e.* In our study of schedules, Ferster and I had investigated this effect in detail long before the human curves were obtained.)

Other experiments on human subjects have been conducted in the field of psychotic behavior. In a project at the Behavior Research Laboratories of the Metropolitan State Hospital, in Waltham, Massachusetts,[20] a psychotic subject spends one or more hours each day in a small room containing a chair and an instrument panel as seen in Figure 19. At the right of the instrument board is a small compartment (*a*) into which reinforcers (candy, cigarettes, coins) are dropped by an appropriate magazine. The

[20] Lindsley, O. R. Operant conditioning methods applied to research in chronic schizophrenia. *Psychiat. Res. Rep.,* 1956, *5,* 118–139.

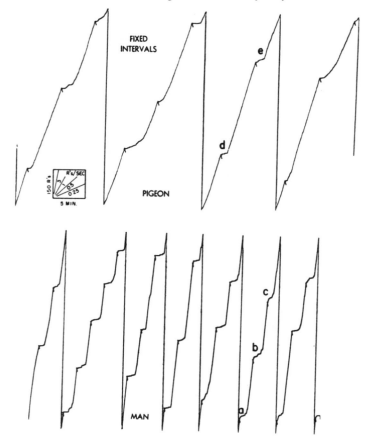

FIG. 18. Fixed-interval performance by a human subject compared with that of a pigeon.

board contains a plunger (*b*), similar to that of a vending machine. The controlling equipment behind a series of such rooms is shown in Figure 20. Along the wall at left, as at *a,* are seen four magazines, which can be loaded with various objects. Also seen are periscopes (as at *b*) through which the rooms can be observed through one-way lenses. At the right are cumulative recorders and behind them panels bearing the controlling equipment which arranges schedules.

It has been found that even deteriorated psychotics of long standing can,

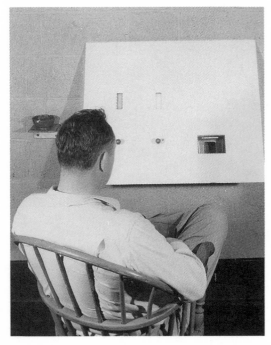

FIG. 19. Arrangement for the study of the behavior of a psychotic subject (Lindsley).

through proper reinforcement, be induced to pull a plunger for a variety of reinforcers during substantial daily experimental sessions and for long periods of time. Schedules of reinforcement have the expected effects, but the fact that these organisms are sick is also apparent. In Figure 21, for example, the record at *A* shows a "normal" human performance on a variable-interval schedule where the subject (a hospital attendant) is reinforced with nickels on an average of once per minute. A straight line, similar to the records of the pigeon and chimpanzee in Figure 3, is obtained. Records *B, C,* and *D* are the performances of three psychotics on the same schedule working for the same reinforcers. Behavior is sustained during the session (as it is during many sessions for long periods of time), but there are marked deviations from straight lines. Periods of exceptionally rapid responding alternate with pauses or periods at a very low rate.

That a schedule is nevertheless effective in producing a characteristic

FIG. 20.   Controlling equipment used in research on psychotic behavior at the Metropolitan State Hospital, Waltham, Massachusetts.

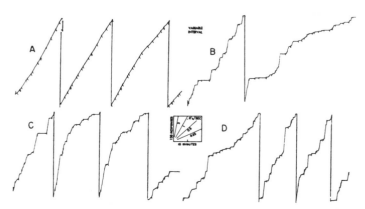

FIG. 21.   One normal (*A*) and three psychotic (*B, C, D*) performances on a variable-interval schedule.

performance is shown by Figure 22. A fixed-ratio performance given by a pigeon under conditions in which there is substantial pausing after reinforcement is shown at A. In spite of the pauses, the general rule holds: as soon as responding begins, the whole ratio is quickly run off. Fixed-ratio curves for two psychotic subjects, both severely ill, are shown at *B* and *C*. Only small ratios can be sustained (40 and 20, respectively), and pauses follow all reinforcements. Nevertheless, the performance is clearly the result of a ratio schedule: once responding beings, the complete ratio is run off.

Conclusion

It is unfortunate that a presentation of this sort must be confined to mere examples. Little more can be done than to suggest the range of application of the method and the uniformity of results over a fairly wide range of species. The extent of which we are moving toward a unified formulation of this difficult material cannot be properly set forth. Perhaps enough has

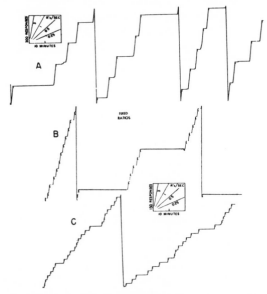

FIG. 22.   A "breaking" fixed-ratio performance by a pigeon (*A*) and two fixed-ratio performances by psychotic subjects (*B, C*).

been said, however, to make one point—that in turning to probability of response or, more immediately, to frequency of responding we find a datum which behaves in an orderly fashion under a great variety of conditions. Such a datum yields the kind of rigorous analysis which deserves a place in the natural sciences. Several features should not be overlooked. Most of the records reproduced here report the behavior of single individuals; they are not the statistical product of an "average organism." Changes in behavior are followed continuously during substantial experimental sessions. They often reveal changes occurring within a few seconds which would be missed by any procedure which merely samples behavior from time to time. The properties of the changes seen in the cumulative curves cannot be fully appreciated in the non-instrumental observation of behavior. The reproducibility from species to species is a product of the method. In choosing stimuli, responses, and reinforcers appropriate to the species being studied, we eliminate the sources of many species differences.

Have we been guilty of an undue simplification of conditions in order to obtain this level of rigor? Have we really "proved" that there is comparable order outside the laboratory? It is difficult to be sure of the answers to such questions. Suppose we are observing the rate at which a man sips his breakfast coffee. We have a switch concealed in our hand, which operates a cumulative recorder in another room. Each time our subject sips, we close the switch. It is unlikely that we shall record a smooth curve. At first the coffee is too hot, and sipping is followed by aversive consequences. As it cools, positive reinforcers emerge, but satiation sets in. Other events at the breakfast table intervene. Sipping eventually ceases not because the cup is empty but because the last few drops are cold.

But although our behavioral curve will not be pretty, *neither will the cooling curve for the coffee in the cup.* In extrapolating our results to the world at large, we can do no more than the physical and biological sciences in general. Because of experiments performed under laboratory conditions, no one doubts that the cooling of the coffee in the cup is an orderly process, even though the actual curve would be very difficult to explain. Similarly, when we have investigated behavior under the advantageous conditions of the laboratory, we can accept its basic orderliness in the world at large even though we cannot there wholly demonstrate law.

In turning from an analysis of this sort many familiar aspects of human affairs take on new significance. Moreover, as we might expect, scientific analysis gives birth to technology. The insight into human behavior gained from research of this sort has already proved effective in many areas. The application to personnel problems in industry, to psychotherapy, to "human relations" in general, is clear. The most exciting technological extension at the moment appears to be in the field of education. The principles emerging from this analysis, and from a study of verbal behavior based upon it, are already being applied in the design of mechanical devices to facilitate instruction in reading, spelling, and arithmetic in young children, and in routine teaching at the college level.

In the long run one may envisage a fundamental change in government itself, taking that term in the broadest possible sense. For a long time men of good will have tried to improve the cultural patterns in which they live. It is possible that a scientific analysis of behavior will provide us at last with the techniques we need for this task—with the wisdom we need to build a better world and, through it, better men.

Reinforcement Today

This paper was part of a symposium on reinforcement held at a meeting of the American Psychological Association, in September, 1957. It was published in The American Psychologist *(1958, 13, 94-99) and is reprinted here by permission.*

During the past twenty-five years the role of reinforcement in human affairs has received steadily increasing attention—not through any changing fashion in learning theory but as the result of the discovery of facts and practices which have increased our power to predict and control behavior and in doing so have left no doubt of their reality and importance. The scope of reinforcement is still not fully grasped, even by those who have done most to demonstrate it, and elsewhere among psychologists cultural inertia is evident. This is understandable because the change has been little short of revolutionary: scarcely anything in traditional learning theory is left in recognizable form. In this paper I shall try to characterize some of the changes in our conception of reinforcement which have been forced upon us and to suggest why it has been so hard to accept them and to recognize their import.

The Acquisition of Behavior

In 1943 Keller Breland, Norman Guttman, and I were working on a wartime project sponsored by General Mills, Inc. Our laboratory was the top floor of a flour mill in Minneapolis, where we spent a good deal of time waiting for decisions to be made in Washington. All day long, around the mill, wheeled great flocks of pigeons. They were easily snared on the window sills and proved to be an irresistible supply of experimental subjects. We built a magnetic food-magazine, which dispensed grain on the principle of an automatic peanut vendor, and conditioned pigeons to turn at the sound it made and eat the grain it discharged into a cup. We used the device to condition several kinds of behavior. For example, we built a gauge to measure the force with which a pigeon pecked a horizontal block,

165

and by differentially reinforcing harder pecks we built up such forceful blows that the base of the pigeon's beak quickly became inflamed. This was serious research, but we had our lighter moments. One day we decided to teach a pigeon to bowl. The pigeon was to send a wooden ball down a miniature alley toward a set of toy pins by swiping the ball with a sharp sideward movement of the beak. To condition the response, we put the ball on the floor of an experimental box and prepared to operate the food-magazine as soon as the first swipe occurred. But nothing happened. Though we had all the time in the world, we grew tired of waiting. We decided to reinforce any response which had the slightest resemblance to a swipe—perhaps, at first, merely the behavior of looking at the ball—and then to select responses which more closely approximated the final form. The result amazed us. In a few minutes, the ball was caroming off the walls of the box as if the pigeon had been a champion squash player. The spectacle so impressed Keller Breland that he gave up a promising career in psychology and went into the commercial production of behavior.

Why had the pigeon learned with such surprising speed? Three points seem relevant:

1. In *magazine-training* the pigeon—that is, in getting it to respond to the sound of the magazine by turning immediately and approaching the food tray—we had created an auditory *conditioned reinforcer*. This is a great help in operant conditioning because it can follow a response instantly. When a rat runs down an alley and finds food at the end, or when a performing seal bounces a ball off its nose and is thrown a fish, behavior is reinforced under relatively loose temporal conditions. The rat may not immediately find the food, and the trainer may take a moment to throw the fish. Organisms will, of course, learn and continue to behave when reinforcement is substantially delayed, but only when certain temporal contingencies have been strengthened. Unless the gap between the behavior and the ultimate reinforcer is bridged with a sequence of conditioned reinforcers, other behavior will occur and receive the full force of the reinforcement. If the seal has time to turn toward the trainer before receiving the visual reinforcement of the approaching fish, its behavior in turning is most powerfully reinforced and may interfere with the behavior the trainer is trying to set up. Eventually a discrimination is formed so that the seal turns only after having executed the proper behavior, but this can be a slow process. A delay of even a fraction of a second is sometimes important, as we have found in designing equipment for the study of operant behavior in the pigeon. When the response is pecking a plastic disc, the controlling circuit must act so rapidly that the sound of the maga-

zine, as a conditioned reinforcer, will coincide with striking the disc rather than pulling the head away from it. This is a matter of perhaps a twentieth of a second, but such a delay produces disturbing changes in the topography of the response.

2. In early experiments on lever pressing, a quick response to the food-magazine was always set up before the lever was introduced. This was done for another reason—to permit emotional responses to the noise of the magazine to adapt out—but it must have been important in providing instantaneous reinforcement. The explicit conditioning of an auditory reinforcer was, therefore, not new; there must have been something else in the bowling experiment. In most experiments on learning, an organism produces reinforcement by direct action: a rat pushes over the door of a jumping stand and discovers food, or a monkey lifts a cup and exposes a grape. Electrical circuits greatly increase the possibilities, but even then the organism is usually left to close the circuit by mechanical contact. In *The Behavior of Organisms* I describe an experiment in which a rat was conditioned to pull a string to get a marble from a rack, pick up the marble with its forepaws, carry it across the cage to a vertical tube rising two inches above the floor, lift the marble, and drop it into the tube. The behavior was set up through successive approximations, but every stage was reached by constructing mechanical and electrical systems operated by the rat. In the experiment on bowling, however, we held the reinforcing switch in our hand and could reinforce any given form of behavior without constructing a mechanical or electrical system to report its occurrence. *The mechanical connection between behavior and reinforcement was greatly attenuated.*

3. But this was not new, either. Thorndike had reinforced a cat when it licked its paw, and animal trainers use hand reinforcement. The surprising result in our bowling experiment may have been due to the combination of the temporal precision of reinforcement provided by a conditioned reinforcer and the free selection of topography resulting from hand reinforcement. In any event this combination must have enhanced the effect of the third, and main, feature of the experiment: the gradual *shaping* of behavior by reinforcing crude approximations of the final topography instead of waiting for the complete response.

The technique of shaping behavior is now a familiar classroom demonstration, but the principle it demonstrates has not yet found a secure place in textbook discussions of learning. Curiously enough, the acquisition of behavior has never been directly attacked in classical research. The study of memory, from Ebbinghaus on, has not been primarily concerned with how behavior is acquired but only with how it is retained or how one form interferes with another in retention. Why does the subject sit in front of the memory drum, why does he vouchsafe anticipatory guesses, and how (not when) does he eventually arrive at that first correct response? These questions have not been the primary concern of research on memory. Animal research has almost always left the shaping of behavior to mechanical devices. In both fields the acquisition of behavior has been reported by learning curves or, worse, by something called *the* learning curve. When one has watched the actual shaping of behavior, it is obvious that such curves do not reflect any important property of the change in behavior brought about by operant reinforcement. They summarize the arbitrary and often accidental consequences which arise when complex and largely unanalyzed conditions of reinforcement act upon large samples of behavior. There are probably as many learning curves as there are apparatuses for the study of learning, and mathematicians will strive in vain to pull a useful order out of this chaos. Yet the prestige of the learning curve is so great that psychologists are unable to believe their eyes when the process of learning is made visible.

The Maintenance of Behavior

An obvious fact about behavior is that it is almost never invariably reinforced. Not so obvious is the fact that the pattern of intermittent reinforcement controls the character and level of a performance. Why this is so cannot be explained in a few words. In *Schedules of Reinforcement* Charles B. Ferster and I have argued as follows.

A schedule of reinforcement is arranged by a programming system which can be specified in physical terms. A clock is introduced into the circuit between key and magazine so that the first response made to the key after a given interval of time will be reinforced. A counter introduced into the circuit establishes a contingency in terms of number of responses emitted per reinforcement. Various settings of clock and counter and combinations of these generate almost unlimited possibilities.

A selected schedule usually generates a characteristic performance, expressed in terms of rate of responding and changes in rate. Once this has happened, the organism is characteristically reinforced at the end of a particular pattern of responding. Its behavior at the moment of reinforcement and during the period preceding reinforcement is part of the stimulating environment, aspects of which acquire control over subsequent behavior. To take a very simple example: if an organism is characteristically responding at a high rate at the moment of reinforcement, behavior at that rate becomes an optimal stimulating condition, comparable to the presence of the reinforced stimulus in a discrimination, and the probability of further responding is therefore maximal. When the organism is not responding at all, the probability is minimal. Other rates and patterns of changes in rate come to serve similar discriminative functions. Ferster and I have checked this explanation of the performances characteristic of schedules in several ways. For example, instead of letting a schedule generate a condition *most* of the time, we have added special devices to *assure* a given condition of behavior at every reinforcement. Thus, where a fixed-interval performance *usually* arranges a moderately high rate at the moment of reinforcement, a special device will guarantee that reinforcements occur *only* at that rate. We have also added stimuli to the physical environment which are correlated with, and hence amplify, the aspects of the organism's behavior appealed to in such an explanation.

This, then, is what happens under intermittent reinforcement: A scheduling system sets up a performance, and the performance generates stimuli which enter into the control of the rate of responding, either maintaining the performance or changing it in various ways. Some schedules produce performances which guarantee reinforcement under conditions which continue to maintain that performance. Others produce progressive changes. Still others yield oscillations: the first performance generates conditions which eventually produce a different performance, which in turn generates conditions restoring the earlier performance, and so on.

Both the circuit and the behavior, then, contribute to the reinforcing contingencies. It follows that the effect of any circuit depends upon the behavior the organism brings to it. Some complex schedules can be studied only by taking the organism through a series of simpler schedules into the final performance. The performance, as well as the topography of a response, may need to be "shaped." This does not mean that schedule-performances vary greatly because of individual histories, for only a few of the effects of schedules are not readily reversible. Once a performance is reached, it usually shows a high order of uniformity, even between species. The fact that it is the *combination* of schedule and performance which generates reinforcing contingencies can easily be overlooked. A physiologist once asked to borrow one of our apparatuses to show his class the behavioral effects of certain drugs. We sent him an apparatus which reinforced a pigeon on a multiple fixed-ratio fixed-interval schedule, together with two pigeons showing beautifully stable performances. When one pigeon died through an overdose of a drug, the physiologist simply bought another pigeon and put it into the apparatus. To his surprise, nothing happened.

The same mistake is made in much traditional work on learning and problem solving. In the usual study of problem solving, for example, the experimenter constructs a complex set of contingencies and simply waits for it to take hold. This is no test of whether the organism can adjust to these contingencies with a performance which would be called a solution. All we can properly conclude is that the experimenter has not constructed an adequate succession of performances. The ability of the experimenter rather than that of the organism is being tested. It is dangerous to assert that an organism of a given species or age *cannot* solve a given problem. As the result of careful scheduling, pigeons, rats, and monkeys have done things during the past five years which members of their species have never done before. It is not that their forebears were incapable of such behavior; nature had simply never arranged effective sequences of schedules.

What we have learned about the shaping of response-topography and about the techniques which bring an organism under the control of complex schedules has made it possible to study the behavior generated by arrangements of responses, stimuli, and reinforcements once classified as the "higher mental processes." An experiment can be designed in which two or more responses are emitted concurrently or in rapid alternation, under the control of multiple stimuli, often under two or more schedules of reinforcement or two or more types of reinforcement under appropriate conditions of motivation. It has been found that a schedule, or rather the stimuli present when a schedule is in force, has reinforcing or aversive properties. An organism will respond on one schedule to reach or avoid another. We can determine which of two schedules a pigeon "prefers" by comparing how fast it will respond on a variable-interval schedule to get into Schedule A with how fast it will respond on the same variable-interval schedule to get into Schedule B. The analysis of avoidance and escape behavior in the hands of Sidman, Brady, and others has made it possible to study combinations of positive and negative reinforcers in many interrelated patterns. The analysis of punishment in such terms has permitted a reformulation of the so-called Freudian dynamisms.[1]

The technology resulting from the study of reinforcement has been extended into other fields of psychological inquiry. It has permitted Blough, Guttman, and others to convert pigeons into sensitive psychophysical observers. It has allowed pharmacologists and psychologists in pharmacological laboratories to construct behavioral baselines against which the effects of drugs on the so-called higher mental processes can be evaluated.

---

[1] See *Science and Human Behavior*.

It has enabled Lindsley and his co-workers to test the limits of the environmental control of psychotic subjects. And so on, in a long list. The technology is difficult. It cannot conveniently be learned from books; something resembling an apprenticeship is almost necessary. Possibly we may explain the fact that psychologists in general have only slowly accepted these new methods by noting that under such conditions knowledge is diffused slowly.

Many psychologists may never wish to acquire the competence necessary for detailed research on reinforcement, but there is another application which is of broader significance. A clinical psychologist recently complained [2] that learning theory told him nothing about important aspects of human behavior. It would not explain, for example, why a man would seek "little bits of punishment in order to accept a big punishment." He may be right in saying that learning *theory* does not tell him much, but the example he chose is just the kind of complex arrangement of contingencies which is now under intensive investigation. And he is asking for just the kind of interpretation of human affairs which is emerging from this work. The world in which man lives may be regarded as an extraordinarily complex set of positive and negative reinforcing contingencies. In addition to the physical environment to which he is sensitively attuned and with which he carries on an important interchange, we have (as he has) to contend with social stimuli, social reinforcers, and a network of personal and institutional control and countercontrol—all of amazing intricacy. The contingencies of reinforcement which man has made for man are wonderful to behold.

But they are by no means inscrutable. The parallel between the contingencies now being studied in the laboratory and those of daily life cry for attention—and for remedial action. In any social situation we must discover *who* is reinforcing *whom* with *what* and to *what effect*. As a very simple example, take the aggressive child. When two young children are left alone in a room with a few toys, conditions are almost ideal for shaping selfish and aggressive behavior. Under these circumstances one child's reinforcement is the other child's punishment, and vice versa. When I once discussed this example with a group of teachers, one of them exclaimed: "Yes, and that's why in the nursery schools of the Soviet Union the toys are so big it takes two children to play with them!" Possibly that is one solution. Certainly there are many others. When contingencies of reinforcement are properly understood, we cannot thoughtlessly allow damag-

2 Sheehan, J. G. The marital status of psychoanalysis and learning theory. *Amer. Psychologist*, 1957, *12*, 277–278.

ing contingencies to arise or go unremedied. By taking a little thought it is now possible to design social situations which have happier consequences for everyone.

I am not saying that any one set of contingencies explains aggression in children or that it takes a long apprenticeship in reinforcement research to understand that case. It is the very existence of reinforcing contingencies which must first be recognized—and that is not always easy. Here is a slightly less obvious example. The current nationwide problem of school discipline is frequently, though possibly erroneously, attributed to progressive education. Whatever its explanation, it is a serious problem. How can we recapture the orderly conduct once attributed to "discipline" without reinstating all the undesirable by-products of an inhumane aversive control? The answer is: use positive reinforcement instead of punishment. But how? A first step is to analyze the reinforcing contingencies in the classroom. In particular, what reinforcers are available to the teacher? The answer to that question is sometimes discouraging, but even in the worst possible case she can at least reinforce a class by dismissing it. The point is that she must understand that dismissal is reinforcing if she is not to throw away the small measure of power it offers her. The "natural" thing is for a teacher to dismiss the class when its conduct is most aversive to her. But this is exactly the wrong thing to do, for she then differentially reinforces the very behavior she wants to suppress. A teacher who understands reinforcement will survey the class during the final minutes of a period and choose for dismissal the moment at which things are going as well as can be expected. The effect will not be evident the first day, it may not be evident the second or third, and it may never be enough to solve all her problems; but a careful husbanding of small reinforcers and the nurturing of proper contingencies is a program well worth exploring.

As a final and more technical example of the use of reinforcement in interpreting human affairs, take the always interesting form of behavior called gambling. Gamblers appear to violate the law of effect because they continue to play even though their net reward is negative. Hence it is often argued that they must be gambling for other reasons. To the psychoanalyst the gambler may simply be punishing himself. Others may insist that the attraction is not money but excitement, or that people gamble to get away from a humdrum life. Now, all gambling devices arrange a variable-ratio schedule of reinforcement, and our explanation of the performance generated by that schedule embraces the behavior of the gambler. It happens to be relatively *excited* behavior, but this, as well as the fact that there is no net gain, is irrelevant in accounting for the performance. A pigeon, too, can become a pathological gambler, and it is unlikely that it does so to punish itself, or for the excitement, or to get away from it all.

Such expressions may not be meaningless. The complex contingencies involved in "self-punishment" may well be involved, although quantitative evidence would be needed to show this. "Getting away from it all" reminds us that some schedules are aversive. Herrnstein and Morse have shown that a pigeon can be conditioned to peck one key if this is occasionally followed by the opportunity to take time off from another key. In turning to a variable-ratio system of reinforcement, then, the gambler may well be escaping from other schedules. Moreover, a variable-ratio schedule at suitable values is reinforcing. These facts account for any behavior which brings an organism under a variable-ratio schedule, but they do not explain the performance once this schedule is in force. The conditions which prevail under the schedule are the relevant facts.

These are necessarily fragmentary examples of the contribution of an experimental analysis of intermittent reinforcement to our understanding of human behavior, but they may serve to make an important point. The relevance of reinforcement is often quite unexpected. These examples are not part of the classical field of learning; they are matters of *motivation!* One expects to see them discussed by dynamic psychologists, psychologists of personality, or psychoanalysts, not by people who study white rats and pigeons. True, learning theory has long been applied to psychotherapy, but traditional research in learning has not made a very helpful contribution. Suddenly, reinforcement takes on new dimensions. When Freud was once asked whether psychoanalysis and psychology were the same, he insisted that psychoanalysis embraced all of psychology except the physiology of the sense organs.[3] This was an ambitious statement, and perhaps a similar claim for reinforcement would be equally unjustified. Yet the facts of human behavior fall to the psychoanalyst and the student of reinforcement alike for explanation. But where the analyst has studied behavior in a given environment as the manifestation of hidden (even if eventually-to-be-revealed) forces, we can now interpret the same behavior and environment as a set of reinforcing contingencies. In doing so we gain a tremendous advantage, for all terms necessary for such an analysis lie within an observable and often manipulable universe. Beyond the prediction and control made possible by recent research in reinforcement lies the broader field of interpretation. And it is a kind of interpretation so closely

[3] Wortis, J. *Fragments of an analysis with Freud.* New York: Simon & Schuster, 1954.

allied with prediction and control that positive and successful action are frequently within easy reach.

If I have suggested to psychologists in general that they will find much of interest in the modern study of reinforcement, it will be appropriate to end with a few words of caution.

1. This kind of research is difficult and relatively expensive. In our book on schedules of reinforcement, Ferster and I report on 70,000 hours of continuously recorded behavior composed of about one quarter of a *billion* responses. The personal observation of behavior on such a scale is unthinkable. The research must be heavily instrumented. The programming of complex schedules demands not only a large budget but considerable skill in relay engineering, neither of which is common in psychological laboratories.

2. It is usually single-organism research. Any other experimental method is often impossible. When an experiment on one pigeon runs to thousands of hours, it cannot be repeated on even a modest group of, say, ten subjects —at least if one wants to get on with other matters. Fortunately, a statistical program is *unnecessary*. Most of what we know about the effects of complex schedules of reinforcement has been learned in a series of discoveries no one of which could have been proved to the satisfaction of a student in Statistics A. Moreover, a statistical approach is just *wrong*. The curves we get cannot be averaged or otherwise smoothed without destroying properties which we know to be of first importance. These points are hard to make. The seasoned experimenter can shrug off the protests of statisticians, but the young psychologist should be prepared to feel guilty, or at least stripped of the prestige conferred upon him by statistical practices, in embarking upon research of this sort.

3. The research is not theoretical in the sense that experiments are designed to test theories. As I have pointed out elsewhere [see page 69], when lawful changes in behavior take place before our very eyes—or, at most, only one step removed in a cumulative curve—we lose the taste, as we lose the need, for imagined changes in some fanciful world of neurones, ideas, or intervening variables. Here again tradition throws up a roadblock. Certain people—among them psychologists who should know better—have claimed to be able to say how the scientific mind works. They have set up normative rules of scientific conduct. The first step for anyone interested in studying reinforcement is to challenge that claim. Until a great deal more is known about thinking, scientific or otherwise, a sensible man will not abandon common sense. Ferster and I were impressed by the wisdom of this course of action when, in writing our book, we reconstructed our own

scientific behavior. At one time we intended—though, alas, we changed our minds—to express the point in this dedication: "To the mathematicians, statisticians, and scientific methodologists with whose help this book would never have been written."

The difficulties which have stood in the way of the advancing study of reinforcement will undoubtedly continue to cause trouble, but they will be more than offset by the powerful reinforcing consequences of work in this field. Techniques are now available for a new and highly profitable exploration of the human behavior at issue in education, commerce and industry, psychotherapy, religion, and government. A program of cultural design in the broadest sense is now within reach. Sociologists, anthropologists, political scientists, economists, theologians, psychotherapists, and psychologists have long tried to reach an understanding of human behavior which would be useful in solving practical problems. In that technological race a dark horse is coming up fast. The new principles and methods of analysis which are emerging from the study of reinforcement may prove to be among the most productive social instruments of the twentieth century.

PART III

The Technology of Education

The Science of Learning
and the Art of Teaching

In March, 1954, the Annual Conference on Current Trends in Psychology at the University of Pittsburgh was devoted to "Psychology and the Behavioral Sciences." It provided an opportunity to report some recent reflections on the technology of education and to describe an early device designed to mechanize certain forms of instruction. The paper was published in the Harvard Educational Review *(1954, 24, 86-97) and in* Psychology and the Behavioral Sciences *(Pittsburgh, University of Pittsburgh Press, 1955), and is reprinted here with the permission of the University of Pittsburgh Press.*

SOME PROMISING ADVANCES have recently been made in the field of learning. Special techniques have been designed to arrange what are called "contingencies of reinforcement"—the relations which prevail between behavior on the one hand and the consequences of that behavior on the other—with the result that a much more effective control of behavior has been achieved. It has long been argued that an organism learns mainly by producing changes in its environment, but it is only recently that these changes have been carefully manipulated. In traditional devices for the study of learning—in the serial maze, for example, or in the T-maze, the problem box, or the familiar discrimination apparatus—the effects produced by the organism's behavior are left to many fluctuating circumstances. There is many a slip between the turn-to-the-right and the food-cup at the end of the alley. It is not surprising that techniques of this sort have yielded only very rough data from which the uniformities demanded by an experimental science can be extracted only by averaging many cases. In none of this work has the behavior of the individual organism been predicted in more than a statistical sense. The learning processes which are the presumed object of such research are reached only through a series of inferences. Current preoccupation with deductive systems reflects this state of the science.

Recent improvements in the conditions which control behavior in the field of learning are of two principal sorts. The Law of Effect has been taken seriously; we have made sure that effects *do* occur and that they occur under conditions which are optimal for producing the changes called learning. Once we have arranged the particular type of consequence called a reinforcement, our techniques permit us to shape up the behavior of an organism almost at will. It has become a routine exercise to demonstrate this in classes in elementary psychology by conditioning such an organism as a pigeon. Simply by presenting food to a hungry pigeon at the right time, it is possible to shape up three or four well-defined responses in a single demonstration period—such responses as turning around, pacing the floor in the pattern of a figure-8, standing still in a corner of the demonstration apparatus, stretching the neck, or stamping the foot. Extremely complex performances may be reached through successive stages in the shaping process, the contingencies of reinforcement being changed progressively in the direction of the required behavior. The results are often quite dramatic. In such a demonstration one can *see* learning take place. A significant change in behavior is often obvious as the result of a single reinforcement.

A second important advance in technique permits us to maintain behavior in given states of strength for long periods of time. Reinforcements continue to be important, of course, long after an organism has learned *how* to do something, long after it has acquired behavior. They are necessary to maintain the behavior in strength. Of special interest is the effect of various schedules of intermittent reinforcement. Most important types of schedules have now been investigated, and the effects of schedules in general have been reduced to a few principles.[1] On the theoretical side we now have a fairly good idea of why a given schedule produces its appropriate performance. On the practical side we have learned how to maintain any given level of activity for daily periods limited only by the physical exhaustion of the organism and from day to day without substantial change throughout its life. Many of these effects would be traditionally assigned to the field of motivation, although the principal operation is simply the arrangement of contingencies of reinforcement.

These new methods of shaping behavior and of maintaining it in strength are a great improvement over the traditional practices of professional animal trainers, and it is not surprising that our laboratory results are already being applied to the production of performing animals for commercial purposes. In a more academic environment they have been used for demonstration purposes which extend far beyond an interest in learning as such. For example, it is not too difficult to arrange the complex contingencies which produce many types of social behavior. Competition is exemplified by two

[1] See *Schedules of Reinforcement.*

pigeons playing a modified game of ping-pong. The pigeons drive the ball back and forth across a small table by pecking at it. When the ball gets by one pigeon, the other is reinforced. The task of constructing such a "social relation" is probably completely out of reach of the traditional animal trainer. It requires a carefully designed program of gradually changing contingencies and the skillful use of schedules to maintain the behavior in strength. Each pigeon is separately prepared for its part in the total performance, and the "social relation" is then arbitrarily constructed. The sequence of events leading up to this stable state are excellent material for the study of the factors important in nonsynthetic social behavior. It is instructive to consider how a similar series of contingencies could arise in the case of the human organism through the evolution of cultural patterns.

Co-operation can also be set up, perhaps more easily than competition. We have trained two pigeons to co-ordinate their behavior in a co-operative endeavor with a precision which equals that of the most skillful human dancers. In a more serious vein these techniques have permitted us to explore the complexities of the individual organism and to analyze some of the serial or co-ordinate behaviors involved in attention, problem solving, various types of self-control, and the subsidiary system of responses within a single organism called "personalities." Some of these are exemplified in what we call multiple schedules of reinforcement. In general, a given schedule has an effect upon the rate at which a response is emitted. Changes in the rate from moment to moment show a pattern typical of the schedule. The pattern may be as simple as a constant rate of responding at a given value, it may be a gradually accelerating rate between certain extremes, it may be an abrupt change from not responding at all to a given stable high rate, and so on. It has been shown that the performance characteristic of a given schedule can be brought under the control of a particular stimulus and that different performances can be brought under the control of different stimuli in the same organism. At a recent meeting of the American Psychological Association, C. B. Ferster and I demonstrated a pigeon whose behavior showed the pattern typical of "fixed-interval" reinforcement in the presence of one stimulus and, alternately, the pattern typical of the very different schedule called "fixed ratio" in the presence of a second stimulus. In the laboratory we have been able to obtain performances appropriate to *nine* different schedules in the presence of appropriate stimuli in random alternation. When Stimulus 1 is present, the pigeon executes the performance appropriate to Schedule 1. When Stimulus 2 is present, the pigeon executes the performance appropriate to Schedule 2. And so on. This result is important because it makes the extrapolation of our laboratory results to daily life much more plausible. We are all constantly shifting from schedule to schedule as our immediate environment changes, but the dynamics of the control exercised by reinforcement remain essentially unchanged.

It is also possible to construct very complex *sequences* of schedules. It is not easy to describe these in a few words, but two or three examples may be mentioned. In one experiment the pigeon generates a performance appropriate to Schedule A where the reinforcement is simply the production of the stimulus characteristic of Schedule B, to which the pigeon then responds appropriately. Under a third stimulus, the bird yields a performance appropriate to Schedule C where the reinforcement in this case is simply the production of the stimulus characteristic of Schedule D, to which the bird then responds appropriately. In a special case, first investigated by L. B. Wyckoff, Jr., the organism responds to one stimulus where the reinforcement consists of the *clarification* of the stimulus controlling another response. The first response becomes, so to speak, an objective form of "paying attention" to the second stimulus. In one important version of this experiment, as yet unpublished, we could say that the pigeon is telling us whether it is "paying attention" to the *shape* of a spot of light or to its *color*.

One of the most dramatic applications of these techniques has recently been made in the Harvard Psychological Laboratories by Floyd Ratliff and Donald S. Blough, who have skillfully used multiple and serial schedules of reinforcement to study complex perceptual processes in the infrahuman organism. They have achieved a sort of psychophysics without verbal instruction. In a recent experiment by Blough, for example, a pigeon draws a detailed dark-adaptation curve showing the characteristic breaks of rod and cone vision. The curve is recorded continuously in a single experimental period and is quite comparable with the curves of human subjects. The pigeon behaves in a way which, in the human case, we would not hesitate to describe by saying that it adjusts a very faint patch of light until it can just be seen [see page 145].

In all this work, the species of the organism has made surprisingly little difference. It is true that the organisms studied have all been vertebrates, but they still cover a wide range. Comparable results have been obtained with pigeons, rats, dogs, monkeys, human children, and most recently, by the author in collaboration with Ogden R. Lindsley, human psychotic subjects. In spite of great phylogenetic differences, all these organisms show amazingly similar properties of the learning process. It should be emphasized that this has been achieved by analyzing the effects of reinforcement and by designing techniques which manipulate reinforcement with considerable precision. Only in this way can the behavior of the individual organism be brought under such precise control. It is also important to note that through a gradual advance to complex interrelations among responses, the same degree of rigor is being extended to behavior which would usually be assigned to such fields as perception, thinking, and personality dynamics.

From this exciting prospect of an advancing science of learning, it is a great shock to turn to that branch of technology which is most directly concerned with the learning process—education. Let us consider, for example, the teaching of arithmetic in the lower grades. The school is concerned with imparting to the child a large number of responses of a special sort. The responses are all verbal. They consist of speaking and writing certain words, figures, and signs which, to put it roughly, refer to numbers and to arithmetic operations. The first task is to shape up these responses—to get the child to pronounce and to write responses correctly, but the principal task is to bring this behavior under many sorts of stimulus control. This is what happens when the child learns to count, to recite tables, to count while ticking off the items in an assemblage of objects, to respond to spoken or written numbers by saying "odd," "even," "prime," and so on. Over and above this elaborate repertoire of numerical behavior, most of which is often dismissed as the product of rote learning, the teaching of arithmetic looks forward to those complex serial arrangements of responses involved in original mathematical thinking. The child must acquire responses of transposing, clearing fractions, and so on, which modify the order or pattern of the original material so that the response called a solution is eventually made possible.

Now, how is this extremely complicated verbal repertoire set up? In the first place, what reinforcements are used? Fifty years ago the answer would have been clear. At that time educational control was still frankly aversive. The child read numbers, copied numbers, memorized tables, and performed operations upon numbers to escape the threat of the birch rod or cane. Some positive reinforcements were perhaps eventually derived from the increased efficiency of the child in the field of arithmetic, and in rare cases some automatic reinforcement may have resulted from the sheer manipulation of the medium—from the solution of problems or the discovery of the intricacies of the number system. But for the immediate purposes of education the child acted to avoid or escape punishment. It was part of the reform movement known as progressive education to make the positive consequences more immediately effective, but anyone who visits the lower grades of the average school today will observe that a change has been made, not from aversive to positive control, but from one form of aversive stimulation to another. The child at his desk, filling in his workbook, is behaving primarily to escape from the threat of a series of minor aversive events—the teacher's displeasure, the criticism or ridicule of his classmates, an ignominious showing in a competition, low marks, a trip to the office "to be talked to" by the principal, or a word to the parent who may still resort to the birch rod. In this welter of aversive consequences, getting the right answer is in itself an insignificant event, any effect of which is lost amid the anxieties, the boredom, and the aggressions which are the inevitable by-products of aversive control.

Secondly, we have to ask how the contingencies of reinforcement are arranged. When is a numerical operation reinforced as "right"? Eventually, of course, the pupil may be able to check his own answers and achieve some sort of automatic reinforcement, but in the early stages the reinforcement of being right is usually accorded by the teacher. The contingencies she provides are far from optimal. It can easily be demonstrated that, unless explicit mediating behavior has been set up, the lapse of only a few seconds between response and reinforcement destroys most of the effect. In a typical classroom, nevertheless, long periods of time customarily elapse. The teacher may walk up and down the aisle, for example, while the class is working on a sheet of problems, pausing here and there to say right or wrong. Many seconds or minutes intervene between the child's response and the teacher's reinforcement. In many cases—for example, when papers are taken home to be corrected—as much as 24 hours may intervene. It is surprising that this system has any effect whatsoever.

A third notable shortcoming is the lack of a skillful program which moves forward through a series of progressive approximations to the final complex behavior desired. A long series of contingencies is necessary to bring the organism into the possession of mathematical behavior most efficiently. But the teacher is seldom able to reinforce at each step in such a series because she cannot deal with the pupil's responses one at a time. It is usually necessary to reinforce the behavior in blocks of responses—as in correcting a worksheet or page from a workbook. The responses within such a block must not be interrelated. The answer to one problem must not depend upon the answer to another. The number of stages through which one may progressively approach a complex pattern of behavior is therefore small, and the task so much the more difficult. Even the most modern workbook in beginning arithmetic is far from exemplifying an efficient program for shaping up mathematical behavior.

Perhaps the most serious criticism of the current classroom is the relative infrequency of reinforcement. Since the pupil is usually dependent upon the teacher for being right, and since many pupils are usually dependent upon the same teacher, the total number of contingencies which may be arranged during, say, the first four years is of the order of only a few thousand. But a very rough estimate suggests that efficient mathematical behavior at this level requires something of the order of 25,000 contingencies. We may suppose that even in the brighter student a given contingency must be arranged several times to place the behavior well in hand. The responses to be set up are not simply the various items in tables of addition, subtraction, multiplication, and division; we have also to consider the alternative forms in which each item may be stated. To the learning of such material we should add hundreds of responses concerned with factoring, identifying primes, memorizing series, using short-cut techniques of calculation, constructing and using geometric representations or number forms, and so on. Over and above all this, the whole mathematical repertoire must be brought under the control of concrete problems of considerable variety. Perhaps 50,000 contingencies is a more conservative estimate. In this frame of reference the daily assignment in arithmetic seems pitifully meagre.

The result of all this is, of course, well known. Even our best schools are under criticism for their inefficiency in the teaching of drill subjects such as arithmetic. The condition in the average school is a matter of widespread national concern. Modern children simply do not learn arithmetic quickly or well. Nor is the result simply incompetence. The very subjects in which modern techniques are weakest are those in which failure is most conspicuous, and in the wake of an ever-growing incompetence come the anxieties, uncertainties, and aggressions which in their turn present other problems to the school. Most pupils soon claim the asylum of not being "ready" for arithmetic at a given level or, eventually, of not having a mathematical mind. Such explanations are readily seized upon by defensive teachers and parents. Few pupils ever reach the stage at which automatic reinforcements follow as the natural consequences of mathematical behavior. On the contrary, the figures and symbols of mathematics have become standard emotional stimuli. The glimpse of a column of figures, not to say an algebraic symbol or an integral sign, is likely to set off—not mathematical behavior—but a reaction of anxiety, guilt, or fear.

The teacher is usually no happier about this than the pupil. Denied the opportunity to control via the birch rod, quite at sea as to the mode of operation of the few techniques at her disposal, she spends as little time as possible on drill subjects and eagerly subscribes to philosophies of education which emphasize material of greater inherent interest. A confession of weakness is her extraordinary concern lest the child be taught something unnecessary. The repertoire to be imparted is carefully reduced to an essential minimum. In the field of spelling, for example, a great deal of time and energy has gone into discovering just those words which the young child is going to use, as if it were a crime to waste one's educational power in teaching an unnecessary word. Eventually, weakness of technique emerges in the disguise of a reformulation of the aims of education. Skills are minimized in favor of vague achievements—educating for democracy, educating the whole child, educating for life, and so on. And there the matter ends; for, unfortunately, these philosophies do not in turn suggest improvements in techniques. They offer little or no help in the design of better classroom practices.

There would be no point in urging these objections if improvement were impossible. But the advances which have recently been made in our control of the learning process suggest a thorough revision of classroom practices and, fortunately, they tell us how the revision can be brought about. This is not, of course, the first time that the results of an experimental science have been brought to bear upon the practical problems of education. The modern classroom does not, however, offer much evidence that research in the field of learning has been respected or used. This condition is no doubt partly due to the limitations of earlier research. But it has been encouraged by a too hasty conclusion that the laboratory study of learning is inherently limited because it cannot take into account the realities of the classroom. In the light of our increasing knowledge of the learning process we should, instead, insist upon dealing with those realities and forcing a substantial change in them. Education is perhaps the most important branch of scientific technology. It deeply affects the lives of all of us. We can no longer allow the exigencies of a practical situation to suppress the tremendous improvements which are within reach. The practical situation must be changed.

There are certain questions which have to be answered in turning to the study of any new organism. What behavior is to be set up? What reinforcers are at hand? What responses are available in embarking upon a program of progressive approximation which will lead to the final form of the behavior? How can reinforcements be most efficiently scheduled to maintain the behavior in strength? These questions are all relevant in considering the problem of the child in the lower grades.

In the first place, what reinforcements are available? What does the school have in its possession which will reinforce a child? We may look first to the material to be learned, for it is possible that this will provide considerable automatic reinforcement. Children play for hours with mechanical toys, paints, scissors and paper, noise-makers, puzzles—in short, with almost anything which feeds back significant changes in the environment and is reasonably free of aversive properties. The sheer control of nature is itself reinforcing. This effect is not evident in the modern school because it is masked by the emotional responses generated by aversive control. It is true that automatic reinforcement from the manipulation of the environment is probably only a mild reinforcer and may need to be carefully husbanded, but one of the most striking principles to emerge from recent research is that the *net* amount of reinforcement is of little significance. A very slight reinforcement may be tremendously effective in controlling behavior if it is wisely used.

If the natural reinforcement inherent in the subject matter is not enough, other reinforcers must be employed. Even in school the child is occasionally permitted to do "what he wants to do," and access to reinforcements of many sorts may be made contingent upon the more immediate consequences of the behavior to be established. Those who advocate competition as a useful social motive may wish to use the reinforcements which follow from excelling others, although there is the difficulty that in this case the reinforcement of one child is necessarily aversive to another. Next in order we might place the good will and affection of the teacher, and only when that has failed need we turn to the use of aversive stimulation.

In the second place, how are these reinforcements to be made contingent upon the desired behavior? There are two considerations here—the gradual elaboration of extremely complex patterns of behavior and the maintenance of the behavior in strength at each stage. The whole process of becoming competent in any field must be divided into a very large number of very small steps, and reinforcement must be contingent upon the accomplishment of each step. This solution to the problem of creating a complex repertoire of behavior also solves the problem of maintaining the behavior in strength. We could, of course, resort to the techniques of scheduling already developed in the study of other organisms but in the present state of our knowledge of educational practices, scheduling appears to be most effectively arranged through the design of the material to be learned. By making each successive step as small as possible, the frequency of reinforcement can be raised to a maximum, while the possibly aversive consequences of being wrong are reduced to a minimum. Other ways of designing material would yield other programs of reinforcement. Any supplementary reinforcement would probably have to be scheduled in the more traditional way.

These requirements are not excessive, but they are probably incompatible with the current realities of the classroom. In the experimental study of learning it has been found that the contingencies of reinforcement which are most efficient in controlling the organism cannot be arranged through the personal mediation of the experimenter. An organism is affected by subtle details of contingencies which are beyond the capacity of the human organism to arrange. Mechanical and electrical devices must be used. Mechanical help is also demanded by the sheer number of contingencies which may be used efficiently in a single experimental session. We have recorded many millions of responses from a single organism during thousands of experimental hours. Personal arrangement of the contingencies and personal observation of the results are quite unthinkable. Now, the human organism is, if anything, more sensitive to precise contingencies than the other organisms we have studied. We have every reason to expect, therefore, that the most effective control of human learning will require instrumental aid. The simple fact is that, as a mere reinforcing mechanism, the teacher is out of date. This would be true even if a single teacher devoted all her time to a single child, but her inadequacy is multiplied manyfold when she must serve as a reinforcing device to many children at once. If the teacher is to take advantage of recent advances in the study of learning, she must have the help of mechanical devices.

The technical problem of providing the necessary instrumental aid is not particularly difficult. There are many ways in which the necessary contingencies may be arranged, either mechanically or electrically. An inexpensive device which solves most of the principal problems has already been constructed. It is still in the experimental stage, but a description will suggest the kind of instrument which seems to be required. The device consists of a box about the size of a small record player. On the top surface is a glazed window through which a question or problem printed on a paper tape may be seen. The child answers the question by moving one or more sliders upon which the digits 0 through 9 are printed. The answer appears in square holes punched in the paper upon which the question is printed. When the answer has been set, the child turns a knob. The operation is as simple as adjusting a television set. If the answer is right, the knob turns freely and can be made to ring a bell or provide some other conditioned reinforcement. If the answer is wrong, the knob will not turn. A counter may be added to tally wrong answers. The knob must then be reversed slightly and a second attempt at a right answer made. (Unlike the flash-card, the device reports a wrong answer without giving the right answer.) When the answer is right, a further turn of the knob engages a clutch which moves the next problem into place in the window. This movement cannot be completed, however, until the sliders have been returned to zero.

The important features of the device are these: Reinforcement for the right answer is immediate. The mere manipulation of the device will probably be reinforcing enough to keep the average pupil at work for a suitable period each day, provided traces of earlier aversive control can be wiped out. A teacher may supervise an entire class at work on such devices at the same time, yet each child may progress at his own rate, completing as many problems as possible within the class period. If forced to be away from school, he may return to pick up where he left off. The gifted child will advance rapidly, but can be kept from getting too far ahead either by being excused from arithmetic for a time or by being given special sets of problems which take him into some of the interesting bypaths of mathematics.

IBM

Fig. 1. A recent model of a teaching machine for the lower grades. The machine operates on the principles described in the accompanying article. Material is presented in a window with a few letters or figures missing. The pupil moves sliders which cause letters or figures to appear. When an answer has been composed, the pupil turns a crank. If the answer was right, a new frame of material moves into the window and the sliders return to their home position. If the material was wrong, the sliders return but the frame remains and must be completed again.

The device makes it possible to present carefully designed material in which one problem can depend upon the answer to the preceding and where, therefore, the most efficient progress to an eventually complex repertoire can be made. Provision has been made for recording the commonest mistakes so that the tapes can be modified as experience dictates. Additional steps can be inserted where pupils tend to have trouble, and ultimately the material will reach a point at which the answers of the average child will almost always be right.

If the material itself proves not to be sufficiently reinforcing, other reinforcers in the possession of the teacher or school may be made contingent upon the operation of the device or upon progress through a series of problems. Supplemental reinforcement would not sacrifice the advantages gained from immediate reinforcement and from the possibility of constructing an optimal series of steps which approach the complex repertoire of mathematical behavior most efficiently.

A similar device in which the sliders carry the letters of the alphabet has been designed to teach spelling. In addition to the advantages which can be gained from precise reinforcement and careful programming, the device will teach reading at the same time. It can also be used to establish the large and important repertoire of verbal relationships encountered in logic and science. In short, it can teach verbal thinking. As to content instruction, the device can be operated as a multiple-choice self-rater.

Some objections to the use of such devices in the classroom can easily be foreseen. The cry will be raised that the child is being treated as a mere animal and that an essentially human intellectual achievement is being analyzed in unduly mechanistic terms. Mathematical behavior is usually regarded, not as a repertoire of responses involving numbers and numerical operations, but as evidences of mathematical ability or the exercise of the power of reason. It is true that the techniques which are emerging from the experimental study of learning are not designed to "develop the mind" or to further some vague "understanding" of mathematical relationships. They are designed, on the contrary, to establish the very behaviors which are taken to be the evidences of such mental states or processes. This is only a special case of the general change which is under way in the interpretation of human affairs. An advancing science continues to offer more and more convincing alternatives to traditional formulations. The behavior in terms of which human thinking must eventually be defined is worth treating in its own right as the substantial goal of education.

Of course the teacher has a more important function than to say right or wrong. The changes proposed would free her for the effective exercise of that function. Marking a set of papers in arithmetic—"Yes, nine and six *are* fifteen; no, nine and seven *are not* eighteen"—is beneath the dignity of any intelligent individual. There is more important work to be done—in which the teacher's relations to the pupil cannot be duplicated by a mechanical device. Instrumental help would merely improve these relations. One might say that the main trouble with education in the lower grades today is that the child is obviously not competent and *knows it* and that the teacher is unable to do anything about it and *knows that too*. If the advances which have recently been made in our control of behavior can give the child a genuine competence in reading, writing, spelling, and arithmetic, then the teacher may begin to function, not in lieu of a cheap machine, but through intellectual, cultural, and emotional contacts of that distinctive sort which testify to her status as a human being.

Another possible objection is that mechanized instruction will mean technological unemployment. We need not worry about this until there are enough teachers to go around and until the hours and energy demanded of the teacher are comparable to those in other fields of employment. Mechanical devices will eliminate the more tiresome labors of the teacher but they will not necessarily shorten the time during which she remains in contact with the pupil.

A more practical objection: Can we afford to mechanize our schools? The answer is clearly yes. The device I have just described could be produced as cheaply as a small radio or phonograph. There would need to be far fewer devices than pupils, for they could be used in rotation. But even if we suppose that the instrument eventually found to be most effective would cost several hundred dollars and that large numbers of them would be required, our economy should be able to stand the strain. Once we have accepted the possibility and the necessity of mechanical help in the classroom, the economic problem can easily be surmounted. There is no reason why the schoolroom should be any less mechanized than, for example, the kitchen. A country which annually produces millions of refrigerators, dish-washers, automatic washing-machines, automatic clothes-driers, and automatic garbage disposers can certainly afford the equipment necessary to educate its citizens to high standards of competence in the most effective way.

There is a simple job to be done. The task can be stated in concrete terms. The necessary techniques are known. The equipment needed can easily be provided. Nothing stands in the way but cultural inertia. But what is more characteristic of America than an unwillingness to accept the traditional as inevitable? We are on the threshold of an exciting and revolutionary period, in which the scientific study of man will be put to work in man's best interests. Education must play its part. It must accept the fact that a sweeping revision of educational practices is possible and inevitable. When it has done this, we may look forward with confidence to a school system which is aware of the nature of its tasks, secure in its methods, and generously supported by the informed and effective citizens whom education itself will create.

Teaching Machines

This paper, published in Science *(1958, 128, 969-977) and reprinted here by permission, was part of a report to the Fund for the Advancement of Education which had sponsored a two-year test of machine instruction at the high-school and college levels.*

THERE ARE MORE people in the world than ever before, and a far greater part of them want an education. The demand cannot be met simply by building more schools and training more teachers. Education must become more efficient. To this end curricula must be revised and simplified, and textbooks and classroom techniques improved. In any other field a demand for increased production would have led at once to the invention of labor-saving capital equipment. Education has reached this stage very late, possibly through a misconception of its task. Thanks to the advent of television, however, the so-called audio-visual aids are being re-examined. Film projectors, television sets, phonographs, and tape recorders are finding their way into American schools and colleges.

Audio-visual aids supplement and may even supplant lectures, demonstrations, and textbooks. In doing so they serve one function of the teacher: they present material to the student and, when successful, make it so clear and interesting that the student learns. There is another function to which they contribute little or nothing. It is best seen in the productive interchange between teacher and student in the small classroom or tutorial situation. Much of that interchange has already been sacrificed in American education in order to teach large numbers of students. There is a real danger that it will be wholly obscured if use of equipment designed simply to *present* material becomes widespread. The student is becoming more and more a mere passive receiver of instruction.

Pressey's Teaching Machines

There is another kind of capital equipment which will encourage the student to take an active role in the instructional process. The possibility was recognized in the 1920's, when Sidney L. Pressey designed several machines for the automatic testing of intelligence and information. A recent model of one of these is shown in Figure 1. In using the device the student refers to a numbered item in a multiple-choice test. He presses the button corresponding to his first choice of answer. If he is right, the device moves on to the next item; if he is wrong, the error is tallied, and he must continue to make choices until he is right.[1] Such machines, Pressey pointed out,[2] could not only test and score, they could *teach*. When an examination is corrected and returned after a delay of many hours or days, the student's behavior is not appreciably

Fig. 1. Pressey's self-testing machine. The device directs the student to a particular item in a multiple-choice test. The student presses the key corresponding to his choice of answer. If correct, the device advances to the next item. Errors are totaled.

modified. The immediate report supplied by a self-scoring device, however, can have an important instructional effect. Pressey also pointed out that such machines would increase efficiency in another way. Even in a small classroom the teacher usually knows that he is moving too slowly for some students and too fast for others. Those who could go faster are penalized, and those who

---

[1] The Navy's "Self-Rater," is a larger version of Pressey's machine. The items are printed on code-punched plastic cards fed by the machine. The time required to answer is taken into account in scoring.

[2] Pressey, S. L. *School and Society, 23,* 586 (1926).

should go slower are poorly taught and unnecessarily punished by criticism and failure. Machine instruction would permit each student to proceed at his own rate.

The "industrial revolution in education" which Pressey envisioned stubbornly refused to come about. In 1932 he expressed his disappointment.[1] "The problems of invention are relatively simple," he wrote. "With a little money and engineering resource, a great deal could easily be done. The writer has found from bitter experience that one person alone can accomplish relatively little and he is regretfully dropping further work on these problems. But he hopes that enough may have been done to stimulate other workers, that this fascinating field may be developed."

Pressey's machines succumbed in part to cultural inertia; the world of education was not ready for them. But they also had limitations which probably contributed to their failure. Pressey was working against a background of psychological theory which had not come to grips with the learning process. The study of human learning was dominated by the "memory drum" and similar devices originally designed to study forgetting. Rate of learning was observed, but little was done to change it. Why the subject of such an experiment bothered to learn at all was of little interest. "Frequency" and "recency" theories of learning, and principles of "massed and spaced practice," concerned the conditions under which responses were remembered.

Pressey's machines were designed against this theoretical background. As versions of the memory drum, they were primarily testing devices. They were used after a certain amount of learning had already taken place elsewhere. By confirming correct responses and by weakening responses which should not have been acquired, a self-testing machine does, indeed, teach; but it is not designed primarily for that purpose. Nevertheless, Pressey seems to have been the first to emphasize the importance of immediate feedback in education and to propose a system in which each student could move at his own pace. He saw the need for capital equipment in realizing these objectives. Above all he conceived of a machine which (in contrast with the audio-visual aids which were beginning to be developed) permitted the student to play an active role.

Another Kind of Machine

The learning process is now much better understood. Much of what we know has come from studying the behavior of lower organisms, but the results hold surprisingly well for human subjects. The emphasis in this re-

[1] Pressey, S. L. *School and Society, 36,* 934 (1932).

search has not been on proving or disproving theories but on discovering and controlling the variables of which learning is a function. This practical orientation has paid off, for a surprising degree of control has been achieved. By arranging appropriate "contingencies of reinforcement," specific forms of behavior can be set up and brought under the control of specific classes of stimuli. The resulting behavior can be maintained in strength for long periods of time. A technology based on this work has already been put to use in neurology, pharmacology, nutrition, psychophysics, psychiatry, and elsewhere [see page 132].

The analysis is also relevant to education. A student is "taught" in the sense that he is induced to engage in new forms of behavior and in specific forms upon specific occasions. It is not merely a matter of teaching him *what* to do; we are as much concerned with the probability that appropriate behavior will, indeed, appear at the proper time—an issue which would be classed traditionally under motivation. In education the behavior to be shaped and maintained is usually verbal, and it is to be brought under the control of both verbal and nonverbal stimuli. Fortunately, the special problems raised by verbal behavior can be submitted to a similar analysis.[1]

If our current knowledge of the acquisition and maintenance of verbal behavior is to be applied to education, some sort of teaching machine is needed. Contingencies of reinforcement which change the behavior of lower organisms often cannot be arranged by hand; rather elaborate apparatus is needed. The human organism requires even more subtle instrumentation. An appropriate teaching machine will have several important features. The student must *compose* his response rather than select it from a set of alternatives, as in a multiple-choice self-rater. One reason for this is that we want him to recall rather than recognize—to make a response as well as see that it is right. Another reason is that effective multiple-choice material must contain plausible wrong responses, which are out of place in the delicate process of "shaping" behavior because they strengthen unwanted forms. Although it is much easier to build a machine to score multiple-choice answers than to evaluate a composed response, the technical advantage is outweighed by these and other considerations.

A second requirement of a minimal teaching machine also distinguishes it from earlier versions. In acquiring complex behavior the student must pass through a carefully designed sequence of steps, often of considerable length. Each step must be so small that it can always be taken, yet in taking it the student moves somewhat closer to fully competent behavior. The machine must make sure that these steps are taken in a carefully prescribed order.

[1] See *Verbal Behavior*.

Several machines with the required characteristics have been built and tested. Sets of separate presentations or "frames" of visual material are stored on disks, cards, or tapes. One frame is presented at a time, adjacent frames being out of sight. In one type of machine the student composes a response by moving printed figures or letters [see page 189]. His setting is compared by the machine with a coded response. If the two correspond, the machine automatically presents the next frame. If they do not, the response is cleared, and another must be composed. The student cannot proceed to a second step until the first has been taken. A machine of this kind is being tested in teaching spelling, arithmetic, and other subjects in the lower grades.

For more advanced students—from junior high school, say, through college —a machine which senses an arrangement of letters or figures is unnecessarily rigid in specifying form of response. Fortunately, such students may be asked to compare their responses with printed material revealed by the machine. In the machine shown in Figure 2, material is printed in 30 radial frames on a 12-inch disk. The student inserts the disk and closes the machine. He cannot proceed until the machine has been locked, and, once he has begun, the machine cannot be unlocked. All but a corner of one frame is visible through a window. The student writes his response on a paper strip exposed through a second opening. By lifting a lever on the front of the machine, he moves what he has written under a transparent cover and uncovers the correct response in the remaining corner of the frame. If the two responses correspond, he moves the lever horizontally. This movement punches a hole in the paper opposite his response, recording the fact that he called it correct, and alters the machine so that the frame will not appear again when the student works around the disk a second time. Whether the response was correct or not, a second frame appears when the lever is returned to its starting position. The student proceeds in this way until he has responded to all frames. He then works around the disk a second time, but only those frames appear to which he has not correctly responded. When the disk revolves without stopping, the assignment is finished. (The student is asked to repeat each frame until a correct response is made to allow for the fact that, in telling him that a response is wrong, such a machine tells him what is right.)

The machine itself, of course, does not teach. It simply brings the student into contact with the person who composed the material it presents. It is a labor-saving device because it can bring one programmer into contact with an indefinite number of students. This may suggest mass production, but the effect upon each student is surprisingly like that of a private tutor. The comparison holds in several respects. (i) There is a constant interchange

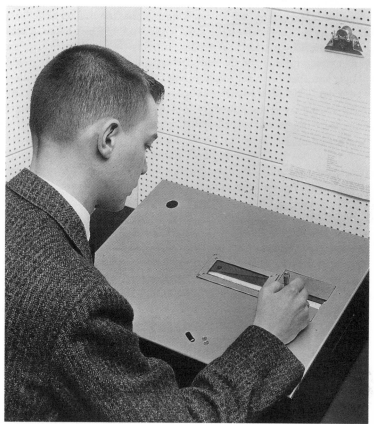

FIG. 2. Student at work in the self-instruction room. One frame of material is partly visible in the left-hand window. The student writes his response on a strip of paper exposed at the right. He then lifts a lever with his left hand, advancing his written response under a transparent cover and uncovering the correct response in the upper corner of the frame. If he is right, he moves the lever to the right, punching a hole alongside the response he has called right and altering the machine so that that frame will not appear again when he goes through the series a second time. A new frame appears when the lever is returned to its starting position.

between program and student. Unlike lectures, textbooks, and the usual audio-visual aids, the machine induces sustained activity. The student is always alert and busy. (ii) Like a good tutor, the machine insists that a given point be thoroughly understood, either frame by frame or set by set, before the student moves on. Lectures, textbooks, and their mechanized equivalents, on the other hand, proceed without making sure that the student understands and easily leave him behind. (iii) Like a good tutor, the machine presents just that material for which the student is ready. It asks him to take only that step which he is at the moment best equipped and most likely to take. (iv) Like a skillful tutor, the machine helps the student to come up with the right answer. It does this in part through the orderly construction of the program and in part with techniques of hinting, prompting, suggesting, and so on, derived from an analysis of verbal behavior. (v) Lastly, of course, the machine, like the private tutor, reinforces the student for every correct response, using this immediate feedback not only to shape his behavior most efficiently but to maintain it in strength in a manner which the layman would describe as "holding the student's interest."

Programming Material

The success of such a machine depends on the material used in it. The task of programming a given subject is at first sight rather formidable. Many helpful techniques can be derived from a general analysis of the relevant behavioral processes, verbal and nonverbal. Specific forms of behavior are to be evoked and, through differential reinforcement, brought under the control of specific stimuli.

This is not the place for a systematic review of available techniques, or of the kind of research which may be expected to discover others. However, the machines themselves cannot be adequately described without giving a few examples of programs. We may begin with a set of frames (see Table 1) designed to teach a third- or fourth-grade pupil to spell the word *manufacture*. The six frames are presented in the order shown and the pupil moves sliders to expose letters in the open squares.

The word to be learned appears in bold face in frame 1, with an example and a simple definition. The pupil's first task is simply to copy it. When he does so correctly, frame 2 appears. He must now copy selectively: he must identify *fact* as the common part of *manufacture* and *factory*. This helps him to spell the word and also to acquire a separable "atomic" verbal operant. In frame 3 another root must be copied selectively from *manual*. In frame 4 the pupil must for the first time insert letters without copying. Since he is asked to insert the same letter in two places, a wrong response will be doubly conspicuous, and the chance of failure is thereby minimized. The same principle governs frame 5. In frame 6 the pupil spells the word to complete the sentence used as an example in frame 1. Even a poor student is likely to do this correctly because he has just composed or completed the word five times, has made two important root-responses, and has learned that two letters occur in the word twice. He has probably learned to spell the word without having made a mistake.

Teaching spelling is mainly a process of shaping complex forms of behavior. In other subjects—for example, arithmetic—responses must be brought under the control of appropriate stimuli. Unfortunately, the material which has been prepared for teaching arithmetic, with the help of Susan R. Meyer, does not lend itself to excerpting. The numbers 0 through 9 are generated

TABLE 1

A SET OF FRAMES DESIGNED TO TEACH A THIRD- OR FOURTH-GRADE PUPIL TO SPELL THE WORD *manufacture*

---

1. **Manufacture** means to make or build. *Chair factories manufacture chairs.* Copy the word here:

   □ □ □ □ □ □ □ □ □ □ □

2. Part of the word is like part of the word **factory**. Both parts come from an old word meaning *make* or *build*.

   m a n u □ □ □ □ u r e

3. Part of the word is like part of the word **manual**. Both parts come from an old word for *hand*. Many things used to be made by hand.

   □ □ □ □ f a c t u r e

4. The same letter goes in both spaces:
   m □ n u f □ c t u r e

5. The same letter goes in both spaces:
   m a n □ f a c t □ r e

6. **Chair factories** □ □ □ □ □ □ □ □ □ □ chairs.

---

in relation to objects, quantities, and scales. The operations of addition, subtraction, multiplication, and division are thoroughly developed before the number 10 is reached. In the course of this the pupil composes equations and expressions in a great variety of alternative forms. He completes not only $5+4=\square$, but $\square+4=9$, $5\square4=9$, and so on, aided in most cases by illustrative materials. No appeal is made to rote memorizing, even in the later acquisition of the tables. The student is expected to arrive at $9\times7=63$, not by memorizing it as he would memorize a line of poetry, but by putting into practice such principles as that nine times a number is the same as ten times the number minus the number (both of these being "obvious" or already well learned), that the digits in a multiple of nine add to nine, that in composing successive multiples of nine one counts backwards (*nine, eighteen, twenty-seven, thirty-six,* and so on), that nine times a single digit is a number beginning with one less than the digit (nine times *six* is *fifty* something), and possibly even that the product of two numbers separated by only one number is equal to the square of the separating number minus one (the square of eight already being familiar from a special series of frames concerned with squares).

Programs of this sort run to great length. At five or six frames per word, four grades of spelling may require 20,000 or 25,000 frames, and three or four grades of arithmetic as many again. If these figures seem large, it is only because we are thinking of the normal contact between teacher and pupil. Admittedly, a teacher cannot supervise 10,000 or 15,000 responses made by each pupil per year. But the pupil's time is not so limited. In any case, surprisingly little time is needed. Fifteen minutes per day on a machine should suffice for each of these programs, the machines being free for other students for the rest of each day. (It is probably because traditional methods are so inefficient that we have been led to suppose that education requires such a prodigious part of a young person's day.)

A simple technique used in programming material at the high-school or college level, by means of the machine shown in Figure 2, is exemplified in teaching a student to recite a poem. The first line is presented with several unimportant letters omitted. The student must read the line "meaningfully" and supply the missing letters. The second, third, and fourth frames present succeeding lines in the same way. In the fifth frame the first line reappears with other letters also missing. Since the student has recently read the line, he can complete it correctly. He does the same for the second, third, and fourth lines. Subsequent frames are increasingly incomplete, and eventually —say, after 20 or 24 frames—the student reproduces all four lines without external help, and quite possibly without having made a wrong response. The technique is similar to that used in teaching spelling: responses are first controlled by a text, but this is slowly reduced (colloquially, "vanished") until the responses can be emitted without a text, each member in a series of responses being now under the "intraverbal" control of other members.

"Vanishing" can be used in teaching other types of verbal behavior. When a student describes the geography of part of the world or the anatomy of part of the body, or names plants and animals from specimens or pictures, verbal responses are controlled by nonverbal stimuli. In setting up such behavior the student is first asked to report features of a fully labeled map, picture, or object, and the labels are then vanished. In teaching a map, for example, the machine asks the student to describe spatial relations among cities, countries, rivers, and so on, as shown on a fully labeled map. He is then asked to do the same with a map in which the names are incomplete or, possibly, lacking. Eventually he is asked to report the same relations with no map at all. If the material has been well programmed, he can do so correctly. Instruction is sometimes concerned not so much with imparting a new repertoire of verbal responses as with getting the student to describe something accurately in any available terms. The machine can "make sure the student understands" a graph, diagram, chart, or picture by asking him to identify and explain its features—correcting him, of course, whenever he is wrong.

In addition to charts, maps, graphs, models, and so on, the student may have access to auditory material. In learning to take dictation in a foreign language, for example, he selects a short passage on an indexing phonograph according to instructions given by the machine. He listens to the passage as often as necessary and then transcribes it. The machine then reveals the correct text. The student may listen to the passage again to discover the sources of any error. The indexing phonograph may also be used with the machine to teach other language skills, as well as telegraphic code, music, speech, parts of literary and dramatic appreciation, and other subjects.

A typical program combines many of these functions. The set of frames shown in Table 2 is designed to induce the student of high-school physics to talk intelligently, and to some extent technically, about the emission of light from an incandescent source. In using the machine the student will write a word or phrase to complete a given item and then uncover the corresponding word or phrase shown here in the column at the right. The reader who wishes to get the "feel" of the material should cover the right-hand column with a card, uncovering each line only after he has completed the corresponding item.

Several programming techniques are exemplified by the set of frames in Table 2. Technical terms are introduced slowly. For example, the familiar term *fine wire* in frame 2 is followed by a definition of the technical term *filament* in frame 4; *filament* is then asked for in the presence of the non-scientific synonym in frame 5 and without the synonym in frame 9. In the same way *glow, give off light,* and *send out light* in early frames are followed by a definition of *emit* with a synonym in frame 7. Various inflected forms of *emit* then follow, and *emit* itself is asked for with a synonym in frame 16. It is asked for without a synonym but in a helpful phrase in frame 30, and *emitted* and *emission* are asked for without help in frames 33 and 34. The relation between temperature and amount and color of light is developed in several frames before a formal statement using the word *temperature* is asked for in frame 12. *Incandescent* is defined and used in frame 13, is used again in frame 14, and is asked for in frame 15, the student receiving a thematic prompt from the recurring phrase "incandescent source of light." A formal prompt is supplied by *candle*. In frame 25 the new response *energy* is easily

TABLE 2

PART OF A PROGRAM IN HIGH SCHOOL PHYSICS. THE MACHINE PRESENTS ONE ITEM AT A TIME. THE STUDENT COMPLETES THE ITEM AND THEN UNCOVERS THE CORRESPONDING WORD OR PHRASE SHOWN AT THE RIGHT

Sentence to be completed	Word to be supplied
1. The important parts of a flashlight are the battery and the bulb. When we "turn on" a flashlight, we close a switch which connects the battery with the ——.	bulb
2. When we turn on a flashlight, an electric current flows through the fine wire in the —— and causes it to grow hot.	bulb
3. When the hot wire glows brightly, we say that it gives off or sends out heat and ——.	light
4. The fine wire in the bulb is called a filament. The bulb "lights up" when the filament is heated by the passage of a(n) —— current.	electric
5. When a weak battery produces little current, the fine wire, or ——, does not get very hot.	filament
6. A filament which is *less* hot sends out or gives off —— light.	less
7. "Emit" means "send out." The amount of light sent out, or "emitted," by a filament depends on how —— the filament is.	hot
8. The higher the temperature of the filament the —— the light emitted by it.	brighter, stronger
9. If a flashlight battery is weak, the —— in the bulb may still glow, but with only a dull red color.	filament
10. The light from a very hot filament is colored yellow or white. The light from a filament which is not very hot is colored ——.	red
11. A blacksmith or other metal worker sometimes makes sure that a bar of iron is heated to a "cherry red" before hammering it into shape. He uses the —— of the light emitted by the bar to tell how hot it is.	color
12. Both the color and the amount of light depend on the —— of the emitting filament or bar.	temperature
13. An object which emits light because it is hot is called "incandescent." A flashlight bulb is an incandescent source of ——.	light
14. A neon tube emits light but remains cool. It is, therefore, not an incandescent —— of light.	source
15. A candle flame is hot. It is a(n) —— source of light.	incandescent
16. The hot wick of a candle gives off small pieces or particles of carbon which burn in the flame. Before or while burning, the hot particles send out, or ——, light.	emit
17. A long candlewick produces a flame in which oxygen does not reach all the carbon particles. Without oxygen the particles cannot burn. Particles which do not burn rise above the flame as ——.	smoke

18. We can show that there are particles of carbon in a candle flame, even when it is not smoking, by holding a piece of metal in the flame. The metal cools some of the particles before they burn, and the unburned carbon —— collect on the metal as soot. particles

19. The particles of carbon in soot or smoke no longer emit light because they are —— than when they were in the flame. cooler, colder

20. The reddish part of a candle flame has the same color as the filament in a flashlight with a weak battery. We might guess that the yellow or white parts of a candle flame are —— than the reddish part. hotter

21. "Putting out" an incandescent electric light means turning off the current so that the filament grows too —— to emit light. cold, cool

22. Setting fire to the wick of an oil lamp is called —— the lamp. lighting

23. The sun is our principal —— of light, as well as of heat. source

24. The sun is not only very bright but very hot. It is a powerful —— source of light. incandescent

25. Light is a form of energy. In "emitting light" an object changes, or "converts," one form of —— into another. energy

26. The electrical energy supplied by the battery in a flashlight is converted to —— and ——. heat, light; light, heat

27. If we leave a flashlight on, all the energy stored in the battery will finally be changed or —— into heat and light. converted

28. The light from a candle flame comes from the —— released by chemical changes as the candle burns. energy

29. A nearly "dead" battery may make a flashlight bulb warm to the touch, but the filament may still not be hot enough to emit light —in other words, the filament will not be —— at that temperature. incandescent

30. Objects, such as a filament, carbon particles, or iron bars, become incandescent when heated to about 800 degrees Celsius. At that temperature they begin to —— ——. emit light

31. When raised to any temperature above 800 degrees Celsius, an object such as an iron bar will emit light. Although the bar may melt or vaporize, its particles will be —— no matter how hot they get. incandescent

32. About 800 degrees Celsius is the lower limit of the temperature at which particles emit light. There is no upper limit of the —— at which emission of light occurs. temperature

33. Sunlight is —— by very hot gases near the surface of the sun. emitted

34. Complex changes similar to an atomic explosion generate the great heat which explains the —— of light by the sun. emission

35. Below about —— degrees Celsius an object is not an incandescent source of light. 800

evoked by the words *form of* . . . because the expression "form of energy" is used earlier in the frame. *Energy* appears again in the next two frames and is finally asked for, without aid, in frame 28. Frames 30 through 35 discuss the limiting temperatures of incandescent objects, while reviewing several kinds of sources. The figure 800 is used in three frames. Two intervening frames then permit some time to pass before the response *800* is asked for.

Unwanted responses are eliminated with special techniques. If, for example, the second sentence in frame 24 were simply "It is a(n)——source of light," the two *very's* would frequently lead the student to fill the blank with *strong* or a synonym thereof. This is prevented by inserting the word *powerful* to make a synonym redundant. Similarly, in frame 3 the words *heat and* pre-empt the response *heat,* which would otherwise correctly fill the blank.

The net effect of such material is more than the acquisition of facts and terms. Beginning with a largely unverbalized acquaintance with flashlights, candles, and so on, the student is induced to talk about familiar events, together with a few new facts, with a fairly technical vocabulary. He applies the same terms to facts which he may never before have seen to be similar. The emission of light from an incandescent source takes shape as a topic or field of inquiry. An understanding of the subject emerges which is often quite surprising in view of the fragmentation required in item building.

It is not easy to construct such a program. Where a confusing or elliptical passage in a textbook is forgivable because it can be clarified by the teacher, machine material must be self-contained and wholly adequate. There are other reasons why textbooks, lecture outlines, and film scripts are of little help in preparing a program. They are usually not logical or developmental arrangements of material but stratagems which the authors have found successful under existing classroom conditions. The examples they give are more often chosen to hold the student's interest than to clarify terms and principles. In composing material for the machine, the programmer may go directly to the point.

A first step is to define the field. A second is to collect technical terms, facts, laws, principles, and cases. These must then be arranged in a plausible developmental order—linear if possible, branching if necessary. A mechanical arrangement, such as a card filing system, helps. The material is distributed among the frames of a program to achieve an arbitrary density. In the final composition of an item, techniques for strengthening asked-for responses and for transferring control from one variable to another are chosen from a list according to a given schedule in order to prevent the establishment of irrelevant verbal tendencies appropriate to a single technique. When one set of frames has been composed, its terms and facts are seeded mechanically among succeeding sets, where they will again be referred to in composing later items to make sure that the earlier repertoire remains active. Thus, the technical terms, facts, and examples in Table 2 have been distributed for reuse in succeeding sets on reflection, absorption, and transmission, where they are incorporated into items dealing mainly with other matters. Sets of frames for explicit review can, of course, be constructed. Further research will presumably discover other, possibly more effective, techniques. Meanwhile, it must be admitted that a considerable measure of art is needed in composing a successful program.

Whether good programming is to remain an art or to become a scientific technology, it is reassuring to know that there is a final authority—the student. An unexpected advantage of machine instruction has proved to be the feedback to the *programmer*. In the elementary school machine, provision is made for discovering which frames commonly yield wrong responses, and in the high-school and college machine the paper strips bearing written answers are available for analysis. A trial run of the first version of a program quickly reveals frames which need to be altered, or sequences which need to be lengthened. One or two revisions in the light of a few dozen responses work a great improvement. No comparable feedback is available to the lecturer, textbook writer, or maker of films. Although one text or film may seem to be better than another, it is usually impossible to say, for example, that a given sentence on a given page or a particular sequence in a film is causing trouble.

Difficult as programming is, it has its compensations. It is a salutary thing to try to guarantee a right response at every step in the presentation of a subject matter. The programmer will usually find that he has been accustomed to leave much to the student—that he has frequently omitted essential steps and neglected to invoke relevant points. The responses made to his material may reveal surprising ambiguities. Unless he is lucky, he may find that he still has something to learn about his subject. He will almost certainly find that he needs to learn a great deal more about the behavioral changes he is trying to induce in the student. This effect of the machine in confronting the programmer with the full scope of his task may in itself produce a considerable improvement in education.

Composing a set of frames can be an exciting exercise in the analysis of knowledge. The enterprise has obvious bearings on scientific methodology. There are hopeful signs that the epistemological implications will induce experts to help in composing programs. The expert may be interested for another reason. We can scarcely ask a topflight mathematician to write a primer in second-grade arithmetic if it is to be used by the average teacher in the average classroom. But a carefully controlled machine presentation and the resulting immediacy of contact between programmer and student offer a very different prospect, which may be enough to induce those who know most about the subject to give some thought to the nature of arithmetical behavior and to the various forms in which such behavior should be set up and tested.

Can Material Be Too Easy?

The traditional teacher may view these programs with concern. He may be particularly alarmed by the effort to maximize success and minimize failure. He has found that students do not pay attention unless they are worried about the consequences of their work. The customary procedure has been to maintain the necessary anxiety by inducing errors. In recitation, the student who obviously knows the answer is not too often asked; a test item which is correctly answered by everyone is discarded as nondiscriminating; problems at the end of a section in a textbook in mathematics generally include one or two very difficult items; and so on. (The teacher-turned-programmer may be surprised to find this attitude affecting the construction of items. For example, he may find it difficult to allow an item to stand which "gives the point away." Yet if we can solve the motivational problem with other means, what is more effective than giving a point away?) Making sure that the student knows he doesn't know is a technique concerned with motivation, not with the learning process. Machines solve the problem of motivation in other ways. There is no evidence that what is easily learned is more readily forgotten. If this should prove to be the case, retention may be guaranteed by subsequent material constructed for an equally painless review.

The standard defense of "hard" material is that we want to teach more than subject matter. The student is to be challenged and taught to "think." The argument is sometimes little more than a rationalization for a confusing presentation, but it is doubtless true that lectures and texts are often inadequate and misleading by design. But to what end? What sort of "thinking" does the student learn in struggling through difficult material? It is true that those who learn under difficult conditions are better students, but are they better because they have surmounted difficulties or do they surmount them because they are better? In the guise of teaching thinking we set difficult and confusing situations and claim credit for the students who deal with them successfully.

The trouble with deliberately making education difficult in order to teach thinking is (i) that we must remain content with the students thus selected, even though we know that they are only a small part of the potential supply of thinkers, and (ii) that we must continue to sacrifice the teaching of subject matter by renouncing effective but "easier" methods. A more sensible program is to analyze the behavior called "thinking" and produce it according to specifications. A program specifically concerned with such behavior could be composed of material already available in logic, mathematics, scientific method, and psychology. Much would doubtless be added in completing an effective program. The machine has already yielded important relevant by-products. Immediate feedback encourages a more careful reading of pro-grammed material than is the case in studying a text, where the consequences of attention or inattention are so long deferred that they have little effect on reading skills. The behavior involved in observing or attending to detail—as in inspecting charts and models or listening closely to recorded speech—is efficiently shaped by the contingencies arranged by the machine. And when an immediate result is in the balance, a student will be more likely to learn how to marshal relevant material, to concentrate on specific features of a presentation, to reject irrelevant materials, to refuse the easy but wrong solu-tion, and to tolerate indecision, all of which are involved in effective thinking.

Part of the objection to easy material is that the student will come to de-pend on the machine and will be less able than ever to cope with the inefficient presentations of lectures, textbooks, films, and "real life." This is indeed a problem. All good teachers must "wean" their students, and the machine is no exception. The better the teacher, the more explicit must the weaning pro-cess be. The final stages of a program must be so designed that the student no longer requires the helpful conditions arranged by the machine. This can be done in many ways—among others by using the machine to discuss mate-rial which has been studied in other forms. These are questions which can be adequately answered only by further research.

No large-scale "evaluation" of machine teaching has yet been attempted. We have so far been concerned mainly with practical problems in the design and use of machines, and with testing and revising sample programs. The machine shown in Figure 2 was built and tested with a grant from the Fund for the Advancement of Education. Material has been prepared and tested with the collaboration of Lloyd E. Homme, Susan R. Meyer, and James G. Holland.[1] The self-instruction room shown in Figure 3 was set up under

[1] Dr. Homme prepared sets of frames for teaching part of college physics (kinematics), and Mrs. Meyer has prepared and informally tested material in remedial reading and vocabulary building at the junior high school level. Others who have contributed to the development of teaching machines should be mentioned. Nathan H. Azrin cooperated with me in testing a version of a machine to teach arithmetic. C. B. Ferster and Stanley M. Sapon used a simple "machine" to teach German [see "An application of recent developments in psychology to the

this grant. It contains ten machines and was recently used to teach part of a course in human behavior to Harvard and Radcliffe undergraduates. Nearly 200 students completed 48 disks (about 1400 frames) prepared with the collaboration of Holland. The factual core of the course was covered, corresponding to about 200 pages of the text.[1] The median time required to finish 48 disks was 14½ hours. The students were not examined on the material but were responsible for the text which overlapped it. Their reactions to the material and to self-instruction in general have been studied through in-

FIG. 3. Self-instruction room in Sever Hall at Harvard. Ten booths contain teaching machines, some equipped with indexing phonographs.

terviews and questionnaires. Both the machines and the material are now being modified in the light of this experience, and a more explicit evaluation will then be made.

Meanwhile, it can be said that the expected advantages of machine instruction were generously confirmed. Unsuspected possibilities were revealed

teaching of German," *Harvard Educational Rev. 28, 1* (1958)]. Douglas Porter, of the Graduate School of Education at Harvard, has made an independent schoolroom test of machine instruction in spelling [see "Teaching machines," *Harvard Graduate School of Educ. Assoc. Bull. 3, 1* (1958)]. Devra Cooper has experimented with the teaching of English composition for freshmen at the University of Kentucky. Thomas F. Gilbert, of the University of Georgia, has compared standard and machine instruction in an introductory course in psychology, and with the collaboration of J. E. Jewett has prepared material in algebra.

[1] *Science and Human Behavior.*

which are now undergoing further exploration. Although it is less convenient to report to a self-instruction room than to pick up a textbook in one's room or elsewhere, most students felt that they had much to gain in studying by machine. Most of them worked for an hour or more with little effort, although they often felt tired afterwards, and they reported that they learned much more in less time and with less effort than in conventional ways. No attempt was made to point out the relevance of the material to crucial issues, personal or otherwise, but the students remained interested. (Indeed, one change in the reinforcing contingencies suggested by the experiment is intended to *reduce* the motivational level.) An important advantage proved to be that the student always knew where he stood, without waiting for an hour test or final examination.

Some Questions

Several questions are commonly asked when teaching machines are discussed. Cannot the results of laboratory research on learning be used in education without machines? Of course they can. They should lead to improvements in textbooks, films, and other teaching materials. Moreover, the teacher who really understands the conditions under which learning takes place will be more effective, not only in teaching subject matter but in managing the class. Nevertheless, some sort of device is necessary to arrange the subtle contingencies of reinforcement required for optimal learning if each student is to have individual attention. In nonverbal skills this is usually obvious; texts and instructor can guide the learner but they cannot arrange the final contingencies which set up skilled behavior. It is true that the verbal skills at issue here are especially dependent upon social reinforcement, but it must not be forgotten that the machine simply mediates an *essentially verbal* relation. In shaping and maintaining verbal knowledge we are not committed to the contingencies arranged through immediate personal contact.

Machines may still seem unnecessarily complex compared with other mediators such as workbooks or self-scoring test forms. Unfortunately, these alternatives are not acceptable. When material is adequately programmed, adjacent steps are often so similar that one frame reveals the response to another. Only some sort of mechanical presentation will make successive frames independent of each other. Moreover, in self-instruction an automatic record of the student's behavior is especially desirable, and for many purposes it should be fool-proof. Simplified versions of the present machines have been found useful—for example, in the work of Ferster and Sapon, of Porter, and of Gilbert—but the mechanical and economic problems are so easily solved that a machine with greater capabilities is fully warranted.

Will machines replace teachers? On the contrary, they are capital equipment to be used by teachers to save time and labor. In assigning certain mechanizable functions to machines, the teacher emerges in his proper role as an indispensable human being. He may teach more students than heretofore—this is probably inevitable if the world-wide demand for education is to be satisfied—but he will do so in fewer hours and with fewer burdensome chores. In return for his greater productivity he can ask society to improve his economic condition.

The role of the teacher may well be changed, for machine instruction will affect several traditional practices. Students may continue to be grouped in "grades" or "classes," but it will be possible for each to proceed at his own level, advancing as rapidly as he can. The other kind of "grade" will also change its meaning. In traditional practice a *C* means that a student has a smattering of a whole course. But if machine instruction assures mastery at every stage, a grade will be useful only in showing *how far* a student has gone. *C* might mean that he is halfway through a course. Given enough time he will be able to get an *A*; and since *A* is no longer a motivating device, this is fair enough. The quick student will meanwhile have picked up *A*'s in other subjects.

Differences in ability raise other questions. A program designed for the slowest student in the school system will probably not seriously delay the fast student, who will be free to progress at his own speed. (He may profit from the full coverage by filling in unsuspected gaps in his repertoire.) If this does not prove to be the case, programs can be constructed at two or more levels, and students can be shifted from one to the other as performances dictate. If there are also differences in "types of thinking," the extra time available for machine instruction may be used to present a subject in ways appropriate to many types. Each student will presumably retain and use those ways which he finds most useful. The kind of individual difference which arises simply because a student has missed part of an essential sequence (compare the child who has no "mathematical ability" because he was out with the measles when fractions were first taken up) will simply be eliminated.

Other Uses

Self-instruction by machine has many special advantages apart from educational institutions. Home study is an obvious case. In industrial and military training it is often inconvenient to schedule students in groups, and individual instruction by machine should be a feasible alternative. Programs can also be constructed in subjects for which teachers are not available—for example, when new kinds of equipment must be explained to operators and repairmen, or where a sweeping change in method finds teachers unprepared.[1] Education sometimes fails because students have handicaps which make a normal relationship with a teacher difficult or impossible. (Many blind children are treated today as feeble-minded because no one has had the time or patience to make contact with them. Deaf-mutes, spastics, and others suffer similar handicaps.) A teaching machine can be adapted to special kinds of communication—as, for example, Braille—and, above all, it has infinite patience.

Conclusions

An analysis of education within the framework of a science of behavior has broad implications. Our schools, in particular our "progressive" schools, are often held responsible for many current problems—including juvenile delinquency and the threat of a more powerful foreign technology. One remedy frequently suggested is a return to older techniques, especially to a greater "discipline" in schools. Presumably this is to be obtained with some form of punishment, to be administered either with certain classical instruments of physical injury—the dried bullock's tail of the Greek teacher or the cane of the English schoolmaster—or as disapproval or failure, the frequency of which is to be increased by "raising standards." This is probably not a feasible solution. Not only education but Western culture as a whole is moving away from aversive practices. We cannot prepare young people for one kind of life in institutions organized on quite different principles. The discipline of the birch rod may facilitate learning, but we must remember that it also breeds followers of dictators and revolutionists.

In the light of our present knowledge a school system must be called a failure if it cannot induce students to learn except by threatening them for not learning. That this has always been the standard pattern simply emphasizes the importance of modern techniques. John Dewey was speaking for his culture and his time when he attacked aversive educational practices and appealed to teachers to turn to positive and humane methods. What he threw out should have been thrown out. Unfortunately he had too little to put in its place. Progressive education has been a temporizing measure which can now be effectively supplemented. Aversive practices can not only be replaced, they can be replaced with far more powerful techniques. The possibilities should be thoroughly explored if we are to build an educational system which will meet the present demand without sacrificing democratic principles.

[1] Menger, K. New approach to teaching intermediate mathematics. *Science, 127* 3310 (1958).

The material in Table 3 is taken from the program for the author's course in Human Behavior mentioned in the preceding article. It is added here as a further illustration and for purposes mentioned in the Preface.

TABLE 3

A Set of Frames Designed to Teach a Student to Read a Cumulative Record

Material presented to the student	*Responses to be made*

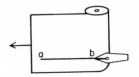

FIG. 1

1. Fig. 1. A broad strip of paper is unwinding from a roll. The end of the strip is moving slowly and steadily toward the left. A pen held against the paper in a fixed position has drawn a line beginning at (1)———— and ending at (2)————.   (1)*a* (2)*b*

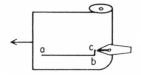

FIG. 2

2. Fig. 2. The slow movement of the paper under the fixed pen has drawn the horizontal line from (1)———— to (2)————. At *b* the pen suddenly moved a short distance upward to (3)————.   (1)*a* (2)*b* (3)*c*

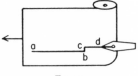

FIG. 3

3. In Fig. 3 the paper has moved a short distance beyond the position shown in Fig. 2. The fixed pen has drawn a second horizontal line from ———— to ————.   *c d*

TABLE 3 (*Continued*)

Material presented to the student	Responses to be made
4. In Fig. 3 the pen has been in the four positions *a, b, c, d.* It occupied position (1)_____ first and (2)_____ last.	(1)*a* (2)*d*
5. Fig. 3. The time which elapsed between *c* and *d* was _____ than the time which elapsed beween *a* and *b*.	shorter, less

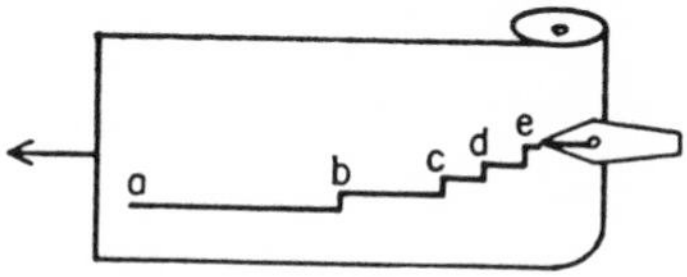

Fig. 4

6. In recording the responses made by an organism, the pen moves upward and draws a short vertical line each time a response is made. In Fig. 4, an experiment began when the pen was at *a*. The first response was made at _____.	*b*
7. In Fig. 4 three responses were made fairly quickly, and at a steady rate, at _____, _____, and _____.	*c d e.*

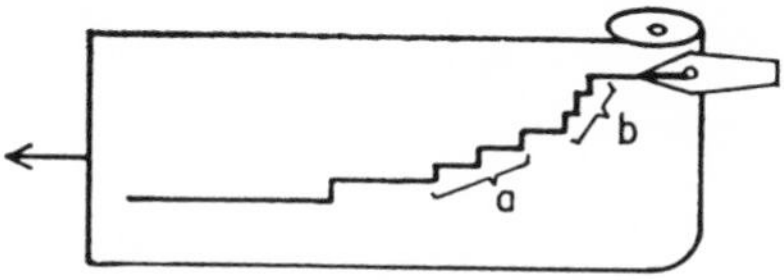

Fig. 5

8. In Fig. 5 the three responses recorded at *a* were emitted _____ rapidly then the three at *b*.	less
9. The more rapid the responding, the _____ the pauses between responses.	shorter
10. The higher the rate of responding, the _____ the horizontal line drawn by the pen between successive responses.	shorter
11. In Fig. 5 the more rapid the responding, the _____ the slope of the step-like line.	steeper
12. Rate of responding is shown by the _____ of the step-like line.	slope

TABLE 3 (*Continued*)

Material presented to the student	Responses to be made

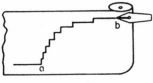

Fig. 6

13. Fig. 6. Responding begins at a relatively high rate at *a*.
The time between successive responses grows progressively ———.

longer, greater

14. In Fig. 6 the slope of the first part of the curve drawn by
the pen beginning at *a* is relatively ———.

steep, great

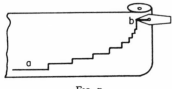

Fig. 7

15. In Fig. 7 the rate increases fairly steadily from a low value
near (1)——— to a high value near (2)———.

(1)*a* (2)*b*

16. An *increase* in rate is called *positive acceleration*. Positive
acceleration is shown in Fig. ——— (6 or 7).

7

17. Negative acceleration refers to a(n) ——— in rate.

decrease

18. Negative acceleration is shown in Fig ——— (6 or 7).

6

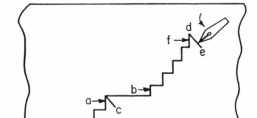

Fig. 8

TABLE 3 (*Continued*)

Material presented to the student	*Responses to be made*
19. To record other events which occur while an animal is responding, the pen swings quickly "to the southeast" and back again. In Fig. 8 the pen has just drawn a line from (1)——— to (2)———. The point of the pen will immediately return to (3)———.	(1)*d* (2)*e* (3)*d*
20. Fig. 8. The short mark ("hatch" or "pip") at ——— was made by the same movement of the pen as shown at *d-e.*	*c*
21. The "southeast" mark or hatch is often used to indicate that a response has been reinforced (rewarded). In Fig. 8 reinforced *responses* were recorded by the *vertical* marks at ——— and ———.	*a* and *f.*
22. In Fig. 10, below, a response was reinforced at ———.	*d*
23. In practice, the vertical mark made by a single response is too small to be easily identified. However, we can still use the ——— of the curve at any point as a valid indicator of rate of responding.	slope
24. In Fig. 10, below, the rate was highest between (1) ——— and ———, zero between (2)——— and ———, and of an intermediate value between (3)——— and ———.	(1)*a b* (2)*b c* (3)*c d*

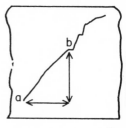

Fig. 9

25. When the steps are so small that we cannot count responses, we can still determine the number of responses between two points on the record by using a scale. In Fig. 9 the scale at the right tells us that approximately ——— responses were made between *a* and *b* in the cumulative record at the left.

100

26. If the paper moves very slowly, we may not be able to measure accurately the time between two responses, but we can still determine the time elapsing between two

TABLE 3 (*Continued*)

Material presented to the student	Responses to be made
chosen points. In Fig. 9 the scale at the right tells us that responses at *a* and *b* in the cumulative record at the left occurred approximately ——— minutes apart.	5

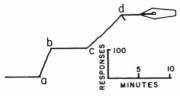

FIG. 10

27. In Fig. 10 after completing about 100 responses, between *a* and *b*, the animal paused for a short period, (1)——— to (2)———, and then emitted about (3)——— responses between *c* and *d*.   *t*   (1)*b* (2)*c* (3)100

28. When a cumulative curve is used to record animal behavior the slope indicates ———.   rate of responding, response rate.

29. "Rate of responding" means number of responses per unit time. In a cumulative record, number of responses can be determined from the distance traversed by the pen in a ——— direction.   vertical

30. In a cumulative record, time is indicated by the distance traversed by the pen in a ——— direction.   horizontal

Why We Need Teaching Machines

Current suggestions for improving education are familiar to everyone. We need more and better schools and colleges. We must pay salaries which will attract and hold good teachers. We should group students according to ability. We must bring textbooks and other materials up-to-date, particularly in science and mathematics. And so on. It is significant that all this can be done without knowing much about teaching or learning. Those who are most actively concerned with improving education seldom discuss what is happening when a student reads a book, writes a paper, listens to a lecture, or solves a problem, and their proposals are only indirectly designed to make these activities more productive. In short, there is a general neglect of educational method. (Television is no exception, for it is only a way of amplifying and extending *old* methods, together with their shortcomings.)

It is true that the psychology of learning has so far not been very helpful in education. Its learning curves and its theories of learning have not yielded greatly improved classroom practices. But it is too early to conclude that nothing useful is to be learned about the behavior of teacher and student. No enterprise can improve itself very effectively without examining its basic processes. Fortunately, recent advances in the experimental analysis of behavior suggest that a true technology of education is feasible. Improved techniques are available to carry out the two basic assignments of education: constructing extensive repertoires of verbal and nonverbal behavior and generating that high probability of action which is said to show interest, enthusiasm, or a strong "desire to learn."

The processes clarified by an experimental analysis of behavior have, of course, always played a part in education, but they have been used with little understanding of their effects, wanted or unwanted. Whether by intention or necessity, teachers have been less given to teaching than to

From *Harvard Educational Review*, 1961, *31*, 377–398.

holding students responsible for learning. Methods are still basically aversive. The student looks, listens, and answers questions (and, incidentally, sometimes learns) as a gesture of avoidance or escape. A good teacher can cite exceptions, but it is a mistake to call them typical. The birch rod and cane are gone, but their place has been taken by equally effective punishments (criticism, possibly ridicule, failure) used in the same way: the student must learn, or else!

By-products of aversive control in education range from truancy, early drop-outs, and school-vandalism to inattention, "mental fatigue," forgetting, and apathy. It does not take a scientific analysis to trace these to their sources in educational practice. But more acceptable techniques have been hard to find. Erasmus tells of an English gentleman who tried to teach his son Greek and Latin without punishment. He taught the boy to use a bow and arrow and set up targets in the shape of Greek and Latin letters, rewarding each hit with a cherry. Erasmus suggested cutting letters ("from delicious biscuits"). As a result, we may assume that the boy salivated slightly upon seeing a Greek or Latin text and that he was probably a better archer; but any effect on his knowledge of Greek and Latin is doubtful.

Current efforts to use rewards in education show the same indirection. Texts garnished with pictures in four colors, exciting episodes in a scientific film, interesting classroom activities—these will make a school interesting and even attractive (just as the boy probably liked his study of Greek and Latin), but to generate specific forms of behavior these things must be related to the student's behavior in special ways. Only then will they be truly rewarding or, technically speaking, "reinforcing."

We make a reinforcing event contingent on behavior when, for example, we design a piece of equipment in which a hungry rat or monkey or chimpanzee may press a lever and immediately obtain a bit of food. Such a piece of equipment gives us a powerful control over behavior. By scheduling reinforcements, we may maintain the behavior of pressing the lever in any given strength for periods of time. By reinforcing special kinds of responses to the lever—for example, very light or very heavy presses or those made with one hand or the other—we "shape" different forms or topographies of behavior. By reinforcing only when particular stimuli or classes of stimuli are present, we bring the behavior under the control of the environment. All these processes have been thoroughly investigated, and they have already yielded standard laboratory practices in manipulating complex forms of behavior for experimental purposes. They are obviously appropriate to educational design.

In approaching the problem of the educator we may begin by surveying available reinforcers. What positive reasons can we give the student for studying? We can point to the ultimate advantages of an education—to the ways of life which are open only to educated men—and the student himself may cite these to explain why he wants an education, but ultimate advantages are not contingent on behavior in ways which generate action. Many a student can testify to the result. No matter how much he may *want* to become a doctor or an engineer, say, he cannot force himself to read and remember the page of text in front of him at the moment. All notions of ultimate utility (as, for example, in economics) suffer from the same shortcoming: they do not specify effective contingencies of reinforcement.

The gap between behavior and a distant consequence is sometimes bridged by a series of "conditioned reinforcers." In the laboratory experiment just described a delay of even a fraction of a second between the response to the lever and the appearance of food may reduce the effectiveness of the food by a measurable amount. It is standard practice to let the movement of a lever produce some visual stimulus, such as a change in the illumination in the apparatus, which is then followed by food. In this way the change in illumination becomes a conditioned reinforcer which can be made immediately contingent on the response. The marks, grades, and diplomas of education are conditioned reinforcers designed to bring ultimate consequences closer to the behavior reinforced. Like prizes and medals, they represent the approval of teachers, parents, and others; and they show competitive superiority, but they are mainly effective because they signalize progress through the system—toward some ultimate advantage of, or at least freedom from, education. To this extent they bridge the gap between behavior and its remote consequences; but they are still not contingent on behavior in a very effective way.

Progressive education tried to replace the birch rod, and at the same time avoid the artificiality of grades and prizes, by bringing the reinforcers of everyday life into the schools. Such natural contingencies have a kind of guaranteed effectiveness. But a school is only a small part of the student's world, and no matter how real it may seem, it cannot provide natural reinforcing consequences for all the kinds of behavior which education is to set up. The goals of progressive education were shifted to conform to this limitation, and many worthwhile assignments were simply abandoned.

Fortunately, we can solve the problem of education without discovering or inventing additional reinforcers. We merely need to make better use of those we have. Human behavior is distinguished by the fact that it is affected by small consequences. Describing something with the right word is often reinforcing. So is the clarification of a temporary puzzlement, or the solution of a complex problem, or simply the opportunity to move forward after completing one stage of an activity. We need not stop to explain *why* these things are reinforcing. It is enough that, when properly contingent upon behavior, they provide the control we need for successful educational design. Proper contingencies of reinforcement, however, are not always easily arranged. A modern laboratory for the study of behavior contains elaborate equipment designed to control the environment of individual organisms during many hours or days of continuous study. The required conditions and changes in conditions cannot be arranged by hand, not only because the experimenter does not have the time and energy, but because many contingencies are too subtle and precise to be arranged without instrumental help. The same problem arises in education.

Consider, for example, the temporal patterning of behavior called "rhythm." Behavior is often effective only if properly timed. Individual differences in timing, ranging from the most awkward to the most skillful performances, affect choice of career and of artistic interests and participation in sports and crafts. Presumably a "sense of rhythm" is worth teaching, yet practically nothing is now done to arrange the necessary contingencies of reinforcement. The skilled typist, tennis player, lathe operator, or musician is, of course, under the influence of reinforcing mechanisms which generate subtle timing, but many people never reach the point at which these natural contingencies can take over.

The relatively simple device shown in Figure 1 supplies the necessary contingencies. The student taps a rhythmic pattern in unison with the device. "Unison" is specified very loosely at first (the student can be a little early or late at each tap) but the specifications are slowly sharpened. The process is repeated for various speeds and patterns. In another arrangement, the student echoes rhythmic patterns sounded by the machine, though not in unison, and again the specifications for an accurate reproduction are progressively sharpened. Rhythmic patterns can also be brought under the control of a printed score.

Another kind of teaching machine generates sensitivity to properties of the environment. We call an effective person "discriminating." He can tell the difference between the colors, shapes, and sizes of objects, he can identify three-dimensional forms seen from different aspects, he can find patterns concealed in other patterns, he can identify pitches, intervals, and musical themes and distinguish between different tempos and rhythms— and all of this in an almost infinite variety. Subtle discriminations of this

Fig. 1. A machine to teach "a good sense of rhythm."

sort are as important in science and industry and in everyday life as in identifying the school of a painter or the period of a composer.

The ability to make a given kind of discrimination can be taught. A pigeon, for example, can be *made* sensitive to the color, shape, and size of objects, to pitches, and rhythms, and so on—simply by reinforcing it when it responds in some arbitrary way to one set of stimuli and extinguishing responses to all others. The same kinds of contingencies of reinforcement are responsible for human discriminative behavior. *The remarkable fact is that they are quite rare in the environment of the average child.* True, children are encouraged to play with objects of different sizes, shapes, and colors, and are given a passing acquaintance with musical patterns; but they are seldom exposed to the precise contingencies needed to build subtle discriminations. It is not surprising that most of them move into adulthood with largely undeveloped "abilities."

The number of reinforcements required to build discriminative behavior in the population as a whole is far beyond the capacity of teachers. Too many teachers would be needed, and many contingencies are too subtle to be mediated by even the most skillful. *Yet relatively simple machines will suffice.* The apparatus shown in Figure 2 is adapted from research on lower organisms. It teaches an organism to discriminate selected properties of stimuli while "matching to sample." Pictures or words are projected on translucent windows which respond to a touch by closing circuits. A child can be made to "look at the sample" by reinforcing him for pressing the top window. An adequate reinforcement for this response is simply the appearance of material in the lower windows, from which a choice is to be made.

The child identifies the material which corresponds to the sample in some prescribed way by pressing one of the lower windows, and he is then

Will Rapport

FIG. 2.   A machine to teach the matching of colors, shapes, sizes, as well as correspondences between pictures and words, words and other words, and so on.

reinforced again—possibly simply because a new set of materials now appears on the windows. If he presses the wrong window, all three choices disappear until the top window has been pressed again—which means until he has again looked at the sample. Many other arrangements of responses and reinforcements are, of course, possible. In an auditory version, the child listens to a sample pattern of tones and then explores other samples to find a match.

If devices similar to these shown in Figures 1 and 2 were generally available in our nursery schools and kindergartens, our children would be far more skillful in dealing with their environments. They would be more productive in their work, more sensitive to art and music, better at sports, and so on. They would lead more effective lives. We cannot assert all this with complete confidence on the present evidence, but there is no doubt whatsoever *that the conditions needed to produce such a state of affairs are now lacking*. In the light of what we know about differential contingencies of reinforcement, the world of the young child is shamefully impoverished. And only machines will remedy this, for the required frequency and subtlety of reinforcement cannot otherwise be arranged.

The teacher is, of course, at a disadvantage in teaching skilled and discriminative behavior because such instruction is largely nonverbal. It may be that the methods of the classroom, in which the teacher is said to "communicate" with the student, to "impart information," and to build "verbal abilities," are better adapted to standard subject matters, the learning of which is usually regarded as more than the acquisition of forms of behavior or of environmental control. Yet a second look may be worthwhile. Traditional characterizations of verbal behavior raise almost insuperable problems for a teacher, and a more rigorous analysis suggests another possibility. We can define terms like "information," "knowledge," and "verbal ability" by reference to the behavior from which we infer their presence. *We may then teach the behavior directly.* Instead of "transmitting information to the student" we may simply set up the behavior which is taken as a sign that he possesses information. Instead of teaching a "knowledge of French" we may teach the behavior from which we infer such knowledge. Instead of teaching "an ability to read" we may set up the behavioral repertoire which distinguishes the child who knows how to read from one who does not.

To take the last example, a child reads or "shows that he knows how to read" by exhibiting a behavioral repertoire of great complexity. He finds a letter or word in a list on demand; he reads aloud; he finds or identifies objects described in a text; he rephrases sentences; he obeys written instructions; he behaves appropriately to described situations; he reacts emotionally to described events; and so on, in a long list. He does none of this before learning to read and all of it afterwards. To bring about such a change is an extensive assignment, and it is tempting to try to circumvent it by teaching something called "an ability to read" from which all these specific behaviors will flow. But this has never actually been done. "Teaching reading" is always directed toward setting up specific items in such a repertoire.

It is true that parts of the repertoire are not independent. A student may acquire some kinds of responses more readily for having acquired others, and he may for a time use some in place of others (for example, he may follow written directions not by responding directly to a text but by following his own spoken instructions as he reads the text aloud). In the long run all parts of the repertoire tend to be filled in, not because the student is rounding out an ability to read, but simply because all parts are in their several ways useful. They all continue to be reinforced by the world at large after the explicit teaching of reading has ceased.

Viewed in this way, reading can also be most effectively taught with instrumental help. A pupil can learn to distinguish among letters and groups of letters in an alphabet simply as visual patterns in using the device and procedures just described. He can be taught to identify arbitrary correspondences (for example, between capitals and lower-case letters, or between handwritten and printed letters) in a more complex type of stimulus control which is within reach of the same device. With a phonographic attachment, correspondences between printed letters and sounds, between sounds and letters, between words and sounds, between sounds and printed words, and so on, can be set up. (The student could be taught all of this without pronouncing a word, and it is possible that he would learn good pronunciation more quickly if he had first done so.)

The same device can teach correspondences between words and the properties of objects. The pupil selects a printed or spoken word which corresponds in the language to, say, a pictured object or another printed or spoken word. These semantic correspondences differ in important respects from formal matches, but the same processes of programming and reinforcement can—indeed, must—be used. Traditional ways of teaching reading establish all these repertoires, but they do so indirectly and, alas, inefficiently. In "building a child's need to read," in motivating "his mental readiness," in "sharing information," and so on, the teacher arranges, sometimes almost surreptitiously, many of the contingencies just listed, and these are responsible for whatever is learned. An explicit treatment clarifies the program, suggests effective procedures, and guarantees a coverage which is often lacking with traditional methods. Much of what is called reading has not been covered, of course, but it may not need to be taught, for once these basic repertoires have been established, the child begins to receive automatic reinforcement in responding to textual material.

The same need for a behavioral definition arises in teaching other verbal skills (for example, a second language) as well as the traditional subjects of education. In advancing to that level, however, we must transcend a limitation of the device in Figure 2. The student can *select* a response without being able to speak or write, but we want him to learn to *emit* the response, since this is the kind of behavior which he will later find most useful. The emission of verbal behavior is taught by another kind of machine (see *The Technology of Teaching,* page 25). A frame of textual material appearing in a square opening is incomplete: in place of certain letters or figures there are holes. Letters or figures can be made to appear in these holes by moving sliders (a keyboard would be an obvious improvement). When the material has been completed, the student checks his response by turning a crank. The machine senses the settings of the sliders and, if they are correct, moves a new frame of material into place, the sliders returning to their home position. If the response is wrong, the sliders return home, and a second setting must be made.

The machine can tell the student he is wrong without telling him what is right. This is an advantage, but it is relatively costly. Moreover, correct behavior is rather rigidly specified. Such a machine is probably suitable only for the lower grades. A simpler and cheaper procedure, with greater flexibility, is to allow the student to compare his written response with a revealed text. The device shown in Figure 3 uses this principle. It is suitable for verbal instruction beyond the lower primary grades—that is, through junior high school, high school, and college, and in industrial and professional education. Programmed material is stored on fan-folded paper tapes. One frame of material, the size of which may be varied with the nature of the material, is exposed at a time. The student writes on a separate paper strip. He cannot look at unauthorized parts of the material without recording the fact that he has done so, because when the machine has been loaded and closed, it can be opened only by punching the strip of paper.

The student sees printed material in the large window at the left. This may be a sentence to be completed, a question to be answered, or a problem to be solved. He writes his response in an uncovered portion of a paper strip at the right. He then moves a slider which covers the response he has written with a transparent mask and uncovers additional material in the larger opening. This may tell him that his response is wrong without telling

FIG. 3.   A machine to teach "verbal knowledge."

him what is right. For example, it may list a few of the commonest errors.
If the response he wrote is among them, he can try again on a newly uncovered portion of the paper strip. A further operation of the machine
covers his second attempt and uncovers the correct response. The student
records a wrong response by punching a hole alongside it, leaving a record

for the instructor who may wish to review a student's performance, and operating a counter which becomes visible at the end of the set. Then the student records the number of mistakes he has made and may compare it with a par score for the set.

Exploratory research in schools and colleges indicates that what is now taught by teacher, textbook, lecture, or film can be taught in half the time with half the effort by a machine of this general type. One has only to see students at work to understand why this is a conservative estimate. The student remains active. If he stops, the program stops (in marked contrast with classroom practice and educational television); but there is no compulsion for he is not inclined to stop. Immediate and frequent reinforcement sustains a lively interest. (The interest, incidentally, outlasts any effect of novelty. Novelty may be relevant to interest, but the material in the machine is always novel.) Where current instructional procedures are highly efficient, the gain may not be so great. In one experiment involving industrial education there was approximately a 25% saving in the time required for instruction and something of the order of a 10% increase in retention, and about 90% of the students preferred to study by the machine. In general, the student generally likes what he is doing; he makes no effort to escape—for example, by letting his attention wander. He need not force himself to work and is usually free of the feeling of effort generated by aversive control. He has no reason to be anxious about impending examinations, for none are required. Both he and his instructor know where he stands at all times.

No less important in explaining the success of teaching machines is the fact that each student is free to proceed at his own rate. Holding students together for instructional purposes in a class is probably the greatest source of inefficiency in education. Some efforts to mechanize instruction have missed this point. A language laboratory controlled from a central console presupposes a group of students advancing at about the same rate, even though some choice of material is permitted. Television in education has made the same mistake on a colossal scale. A class of twenty or thirty students moving at the same pace is inefficient enough, but what must we say of all the students in half a dozen states marching in a similar lock step?

In trying to teach more than one student at once we harm both fast and slow learners. The plight of the good student has been recognized, but the slow learner suffers more disastrous consequences. The effect of pressure to move beyond one's natural speed is cumulative. The student who has not fully mastered a first lesson is less able to master a second. His ultimate failure may greatly exaggerate his shortcoming; a small difference in speed has grown to an immense difference in comprehension. Some of those most active in improving education have been tempted to dismiss slow students impatiently as a waste of time, but it is quite possible that many of them are capable of substantial, even extraordinary, achievements if permitted to move at their own pace. Many distinguished scientists, for example, have appeared to think slowly.

One advantage of individual instruction is that the student is able to follow a program without breaks or omissions. A member of a class moving at approximately the same rate cannot always make up for absences, and limitations of contact time between student and teacher make it necessary to abbreviate material to the point at which substantial gaps are inevitable. Working on a machine, the student can always take up where he left off or, if he wishes, review earlier work after a longer absence. The coherence of the program helps to maximize the student's success, for by thoroughly mastering one step he is optimally prepared for the next. Many years ago, in their *Elementary Principles of Education,* Thorndike and Gates considered the possibility of a book "so arranged that only to him who had done what was directed on page one would page two become visible, and so on." With such a book, they felt, "much that now requires personal instruction could be managed by print." The teaching machine is, of course, such a book.

In summary, then, machine teaching is unusually efficient because (1) the student is frequently and immediately reinforced, (2) he is free to move at his natural rate, and (3) he follows a coherent sequence. These are the more obvious advantages, and they may well explain current successes. But there are more promising possibilities: the conditions arranged by a good teaching machine make it possible to apply to education what we have learned from laboratory research and to extend our knowledge through rigorous experiments in schools and colleges.

The conceptions of the learning process which underlie classroom practices have long been out of date. For example, teachers and textbooks are said to "impart information." They expose the student to verbal and non-verbal material and call attention to particular features of it, and in so doing they are said to "tell the student something." In spite of discouraging evidence to the contrary, it is still supposed that if you tell a student something, he then knows it. In this scheme, teaching is the transmission of information, a notion which, through a false analogy, has acquired undue prestige from communication engineering. Something is undoubtedly transmitted by teacher to student, for if communication is interrupted, instruction ceases; but the teacher is not merely a source from which knowledge flows into the student. We cannot necessarily improve instruction by altering the conditions of transmission—as, for example, by changing to a different sensory modality. This is a mistake made by some so-called teaching machines which, accepting our failure to teach reading, have tried to restore communication by using recorded speech. The student no longer pores over a book, as in the traditional portrait; he stares into space with earphones on his head. For the same reasons, improvements in the coding of information may not be immediately relevant.

The student is more than a receiver of information. He must take some kind of action. The traditional view is that he must "associate." The stream of information flowing from teacher to student contains pairs of items which, being close together or otherwise related, become connected in the student's mind. This is the old doctrine of the association of ideas, now strengthened by a scientific, if uncritical, appeal to conditioned reflexes: two things occurring together in experience somehow become connected so that one of them later reminds the student of the other. The teacher has little control over the process except to make sure that things occur together often and that the student pays attention to them—for example, by making the experiences vivid or, as we say, memorable. Some devices called teaching machines are simply ways of presenting things together in ways which attract attention. The student listens to recorded speech, for example, while looking at pictures. The theory is that he will associate these auditory and visual presentations.

But the action demanded of the student is not some sort of mental association of contiguous experiences. It is more objective and, fortunately, more controllable than that. To acquire behavior, *the student must engage in behavior.* This has long been known. The principle is implied in any philosophy of "learning by doing." But it is not enough simply to acknowledge its validity. Teaching machines provide the conditions needed to apply the principle effectively.

Only in the early stages of education are we mainly interested in establishing *forms* of behavior. In the verbal field, for example, we teach a child to speak, eventually with acceptable accent and pronunciation, and later to write and spell. After that, topography of behavior is assumed; the student can speak and write and must now learn to do so appropriately—that is, he must speak or write in given ways under given circumstances. How he comes to do so is widely misunderstood. Education usually begins by establishing so-called formal repertoires. The young child is taught to "echo" verbal behavior in the sense of repeating verbal stimuli with reasonable accuracy. A little later he is taught to read—to emit verbal behavior under the control of textual stimuli. These and other formal repertoires are used in later stages of instruction to evoke new responses without "shaping" them.

In an important case of what we call instruction, control is simply transferred from so-called formal to thematic stimuli. When a student learns to memorize a poem, for example, it is clearly inadequate to say that by reading the poem he presents to himself its various parts contiguously and then associates them. He does not simply read the poem again and again until he knows it. (It is possible that he could never learn the poem in that way.) Something else must be done, as anyone knows who has memorized a poem from the text. The student must make tentative responses while looking away from the text. He must glance at the text from time to time to provide fragmentary help in emitting a partially learned response. If a recalled passage makes sense, it may provide its own automatic confirmation, but if the passage is fragmentary or obscure, the student must confirm the correctness of an emitted response by referring to the text after he has emitted it.

A teaching machine facilitates this process. It presents the poem line by line and asks the student to read it. The text is then "vanished"—that is, it becomes less and less clear or less and less complete in subsequent presentations. Other stimuli (arising from the student's own behavior in this case) take over. In one procedure a few unimportant letters are omitted in the first presentation. The student reads the line without their help and indicates his success by writing down the omitted letters, which are confirmed by the machine. More of the line is missing when it again appears, but because he has recently responded to a fuller text, the student can nevertheless read it correctly. Eventually, no textual stimulus remains, and he can "recite" the poem.

(If the reader wishes to try this method on a friend or member of his family without a machine, he may do so by writing the poem on a chalk board in a clear hand, omitting a few unimportant letters. He should ask his subject to read the poem aloud but to make no effort to memorize it. He should then erase another selection of letters. He will have to guess at how far he can go without interfering with his subject's success on the next reading, but under controlled conditions this could be determined for the average student quite accurately. Again the subject reads the poem aloud, making no effort to memorize, though he may have to make some effort to recall. Other letters are then erased and the process repeated. For a dozen lines of average material, four or five readings should suffice to eliminate the text altogether. The poem can still be "read.")

Memorized verbal behavior is a valuable form of knowledge which has played an important role in classical education. There are other, and generally more useful, forms in which the same processes are involved. Consider, for example, a labeled picture. To say that such an instructional device "tells the student the name of the pictured object" is highly elliptical —and dangerous if we are trying to understand the processes involved. Simply showing a student a labeled picture is no more effective than letting him read a poem. He must take some sort of action. As a formal stimulus, the label evokes a verbal response, not in this case in the presence of other verbal behavior on the part of the student, but in the presence of the picture. The control of the response is to pass from the label to the picture; the student is to give the name of the pictured object without reading it.

The steps taken in teaching with labeled pictures can also be arranged particularly well with a machine. Suppose we are teaching medical-school anatomy at the textbook level. Certain labeled charts represent what is to be learned in the sense that the student will eventually (1) give the names of indicated parts and describe relations among them and (2) be able to point to, draw, or construct models of parts, or relations among them, given their names. To teach the first of these, we induce the student to describe relations among the parts shown on a fully labeled chart. One effect of this is that he executes the verbal behavior at issue—he writes the names of the parts. More important, he does this while, or just after, looking at corresponding pictured details. He will be able to write the names again while looking at a chart which shows only incomplete names, possibly only initial letters. Finally, he will be able to supply the complete names of parts identified only by number on still another chart. His verbal responses have passed from the control of textual stimuli to that of pictured anatomical details. Eventually, as he studies a cadaver, the control will pass to the actual anatomy of the human body. In this sense he then "knows the names of the parts of the body and can describe relations among them."

(The device shown in Figure 3 is designed to skip one or two steps in "vanishing" textual stimuli. A fully labeled chart may be followed by a merely numbered one. The student writes the name corresponding to a number in the first space. If he cannot do this, he operates the machine to uncover, not merely some indication that he is right or wrong, but additional help—say, a few letters of the correct response.)

Learning a poem or the names of pictured objects is a relatively straightforward task. More complex forms of knowledge require other procedures. At an early point, the main problem becomes that of analyzing knowledge. Traditionally, for example, something called a "knowledge of French" is said to permit the student who possesses it to do many things. One who possesses it can (1) repeat a French phrase with a good accent, (2) read a French text in all the senses of reading listed above, (3) take dictation in French, (4) find a word spoken in French on a printed list, (5) obey instructions spoken in French, (6) comment in French upon objects or events, (7) give orders in French, and so on. If he also "knows English," he can give the English equivalents of French words or phrases or the French equivalents of English words or phrases.

The concept of "a knowledge of French" offers very little help to the would-be teacher. As in the case of reading, we must turn to the behavioral repertoires themselves, for these are all that have ever been taught when education has been effective. The definition of a subject matter in such terms may be extraordinarily difficult. Students who are "competent in first-year college physics," for example, obviously differ from those who are not—but in what way? Even a tentative answer to that question should clarify the problem of teaching physics. It may well do more. In the not-too-distant future much more general issues in epistemology may be approached from the same direction. It is possible that we shall fully understand the nature of knowledge only after having solved the practical problems of imparting it.

Until we can define subject matters more accurately and until we have improved our techniques of building verbal repertoires, writing programs for teaching machines will remain something of an art. This is not wholly satisfactory, but there is some consolation in the fact that an impeccable authority on the excellence of a program is available. The student himself can tell the programmer where he has failed. By analyzing the errors made by even a small number of students in a pilot study, it is usually possible to work a great improvement in an early version of a program. (The machine shown in Figure 3 is designed to supply the necessary feedback to the programmer in a convenient form. When a student punches an error, he marks the back of the printed material, which eventually carries an item-by-item record of the success or failure of the programmer. This is obviously valuable during the experimental stages of programming, but it will also be desirable when machines are widely used in schools and colleges, since publishers can then periodically call in programs to be studied and improved by their authors. The information supplied might be compared to a record showing the percentage of students who have misunderstood each sentence in a text.)

The teaching machine shown in Figure 3 falls far short of the "electronic classrooms" often visualized for the schools and colleges of the future.

Many of these, often incorporating small computers, are based on misunderstandings of the learning process. They are designed to duplicate current classroom conditions. When instruction is badly programmed, a student often goes astray, and a teacher must come to his rescue. His mistakes must be analyzed and corrected. This may give the impression that instruction is largely a matter of correcting errors. If this were the case, an effective machine would, indeed, have to follow the student into many unprofitable paths and take remedial action. But under proper programming nothing of this sort is required. It is true that a relatively important function of the teacher will be to follow the progress of each student and to suggest collateral material which may be of interest, as well as to outline further studies, to recommend changes to programs of different levels of difficulty, and so on, and to this extent a student's course of study will show "branching." But changes in level of difficulty or in the character of the subject need not be frequent and can be made as the student moves from one set of material to another.

Teaching machines based on the principle of "multiple choice" also often show a misunderstanding of the learning process. When multiple-choice apparatuses were first used, the organism was left to proceed by "trial and error." The term does not refer to a behavioral process but simply to the fact that contingencies of reinforcement were left to chance: some responses happened to be successful and others not. Learning was not facilitated or accelerated by procedures which increased the probability of successful responses. The results, like those of much classroom instruction, suggested that errors were essential to the learning process. But when material is carefully programmed, both subhuman and human subjects can learn while making few errors or even none at all. Recent research by Herbert S. Terrace, for example, has shown that a pigeon can learn to discriminate colors practically without making mistakes. The control exerted by color may be passed, via a vanishing technique, to more difficult properties of stimuli—again without error. Of course we learn something from our mistakes—for one thing, we learn not to make them again—but we *acquire* behavior in other ways.

The teaching machines of S. J. Pressey, the first psychologist to see the "coming industrial revolution in education," were mechanical versions of self-scoring test forms, which Pressey and his students also pioneered. They were not designed for programmed instruction in the present sense. The student was presumed to have studied a subject before coming to the machine. By testing himself, he consolidated what he had already partially learned. For this purpose a device which evaluated the student's selection from an array of multiple-choice items was appropriate. For the same purpose multiple-choice material can, of course, be used in all the machines described above. But several advantages of programmed instruction are lost when such material is used in straightforward instruction.

In the first place, the student should *construct* rather than *select* a response, since this is the behavior he will later find useful. Secondly, he should advance to the level of being able to emit a response rather than merely recognize a given response as correct. This represents a much more considerable achievement, as the difference between the sizes of reading and writing vocabularies in a foreign language demonstrates. Thirdly, and more important, multiple-choice material violates a basic principle of good programming by inducing the student to engage in erroneous behavior. Those who have written multiple-choice tests know how much time, energy, and ingenuity are needed to construct plausible wrong answers. (They must be plausible or the test will be of little value.) In a multiple-choice *test,* they may do no harm, since a student who has already learned the right answer may reject wrong answers with ease and possibly with no undesirable side-effects. The student who is *learning,* however, can scarcely avoid trouble. Traces of erroneous responses survive in spite of the correction of errors or the confirmation of a right answer. In multiple-choice material designed to teach "literary appreciation," for example, the student is asked to consider three or four plausible paraphrases of a passage in a poem and to identify the most acceptable. But as the student reads and considers inacceptable paraphrases, the very processes which the poet himself used in making his poem effective are at work to destroy it. Neither the rigorous correction of wrong choices nor the confirmation of a right choice will free the student of the verbal and nonverbal associations thus generated.

Scientific subjects offer more specific examples. Consider an item such as the following, which might be part of a course in high school physics:

As the pressure of a gas increases, volume decreases. This is because:
  (a) *the space between the molecules grows smaller*
  (b) *the molecules are flattened*
  (c) etc. . . .

Unless the student is as industrious and as ingenious as the multiple-choice programmer, it will probably not have occurred to him that molecules may be flattened as a gas is compressed (within the limits under consideration). If he chooses item (b) and is corrected by the machine, we may say that he "has learned that it is wrong," but this does not mean that the sentence will never occur to him again. And if he is unlucky enough to select the right answer first, his reading of the plausible but erroneous answer will be corrected only "by implication"—an equally vague and presumably less effective process. In either case, he may later find himself recalling that "somewhere he has read that molecules are flattened when a gas is compressed." And, of course, somewhere he has.

Multiple-choice techniques are appropriate when the student is to learn to compare and choose. In forming a discrimination (as with the device shown in Figure 2), an organism must be exposed to at least two stimuli, one of which may be said to be wrong. Similarly, in learning to "troubleshoot" equipment there may be several almost equally plausible ways of correcting a malfunction. Games offer other examples. A given hand at bridge may justify several bids or plays, no one of which is wholly right and all the others wrong. In such cases, the student is to learn the most expedient course to be taken among a natural array of possibilities. This is not true in the simple acquisition of knowledge—particularly verbal knowledge—where the task is only rarely to discriminate among responses in an array. In solving an equation, reporting a fact of history, restating the meaning of a sentence, or engaging in almost any of the other behavior which is the main concern of education, the student is to *generate* responses. He may generate and reject, but only rarely will he generate a set of responses from which he must then make a choice.

It may be argued that machines which provide for branching and decision-making are designed to teach more than verbal repertoires—in particular, that they will teach thinking. There are strategies in choosing from an array, for example, which require kinds of behavior beyond the mere emission of correct responses. We may agree to this without questioning the value of knowledge in the sense of a verbal repertoire. (The distinction is not between rote and insightful learning, for programmed instruction is especially free of rote memorizing in the etymological sense of wearing down a path through repetition.) If an "idea" or "proposition" is defined as something which can be expressed in many ways, then it may be taught by teaching many of these "ways." What is learned is more likely to generalize to comparable situations than a single syntactical form, and generalization is what distinguishes so-called deeper understanding.

But not all thinking is verbal. There are, first of all, alternative, parallel nonverbal repertoires. The mathematician begins with a verbal problem and ends with a verbal solution, but much of his intervening behavior may be of a different nature. The student who learns to follow or construct a proof entirely by manipulating symbols may not engage in this kind of thinking. Similarly, a merely verbal knowledge of physics, as often seen in the student who has "memorized the text," is of little interest to the serious educator. Laboratories and demonstrations sometimes supply contingencies which build some nonverbal knowledge of physics. Special kinds of teaching machines could help, for machines are not only not confined to verbal instruction, they may well make it possible to reduce the emphasis on verbal communication between teacher and student.

A more clear-cut example of the distinction between verbal and nonverbal thinking is musical composition. The composer who "thinks musically" does more than perform on an instrument or enjoy music. He also does more than use musical notation. In some sense he "thinks" pitches, intervals, melodies, harmonic progressions, and so on. It should not surprise us that individuals differ greatly in their abilities to do this, since the necessary contingencies are in very short supply. One might attack the problem by setting up an explicit kinesthetic repertoire in which "thinking a pitch" takes the form of identifying a position on a keyboard. A device which arranges the necessary contingencies is under development. With its help we may discover the extent to which students can in general learn (and at what ages they can learn most effectively) to strike a key which produces a tone which has just been heard. Similar devices might generate important forms of nonverbal mathematical behavior or the behavior exhibited, say, by an inventor conceiving of a device in three dimensions, as well as creative repertoires in other forms of art. Here is an extraordinary challenge to the technology of instrumentation.

There is another sense in which the student must learn to think. Verbal and nonverbal repertoires may prepare him to behave in effective ways, but he will inevitably face novel situations in which he cannot at first respond appropriately. He may solve such problems, not by exercising some mental ability, but by altering either the external situation or the relative probabilities of an adequate response.

In this sense, thinking consists of a special repertoire which we may call self-management. For example, the student may alter the extent to which the environment affects him by "attending to it in different ways. As one step in teaching thinking we must teach effective attending. The phrase "Pay attention!" is as common on the lips of teachers as "Open, please" on those of dentists—and for much the same reason: both phrases set up working conditions. The student may pay attention to avoid punishment and in doing so many learn to pay attention, but where aversive sanctions have been given up, teachers have resorted to attracting and holding attention.

The techniques of the publication and entertainment industries are extensively invoked. Primers are usually decorated with colored pictures, and high school textbooks are sometimes designed to resemble picture magazines. Films dramatize subject matters in competition with noneducational films and television.

Attention which is captured by attractive stimuli must be distinguished from attention which is "paid." Only the latter must be learned. Looking and listening are forms of behavior, and they are strengthened by reinforcement. A pigeon can learn to match colors, for example, only if it "pays attention to them." The experimenter makes sure that it does so, not by attracting its attention, but by reinforcing it for looking. Similarly, a well-taught student pays attention to sentences, diagrams, samples of recorded speech and music, and so on, not because they are attractive but because something interesting occasionally happens *after* he has paid attention.

Most audio-visual devices fail to teach attention because they stimulate the student *before* he looks or listen closely. No matter how well a four-colored text or a dramatically filmed experiment in physics attracts attention, it prepares the student only for comics, advertising, picture magazines, television programs, and other material which is *interesting on its face.* What is wanted is an adult who, upon seeing a page of black-and-white text, will read it because it may *prove* interesting. Unfortunately, the techniques associated with captured and paid attention are incompatible. Whenever a teacher attracts the attention of a student, he deprives him of an opportunity to learn to pay attention. Teaching machines, with their control over the consequences of action, can make sure that paying attention will be effectively reinforced.

Another activity associated with thinking is studying—not merely looking at a text and reading it but looking and reading *for the sake of future action.* Suppose we show a child a picture and later, in the absence of the picture, reinforce him generously for correct answers to questions about it. If he has done nothing like this before, he will probably not be very successful. If we then show him another picture, he may begin to behave in a different way: he may engage in behavior which will increase the probability that he will later answer questions correctly. It will be to his advantage (and to ours as educators) if this kind of behavior is taught rather than left to chance. We teach a student "how to study" when we teach him to take notes, to rehearse his own behavior, to test himself, to organize, outline, and analyze, to look for or construct mnemonic patterns, and so on.

Some of these behaviors are obvious, but others are of more subtle dimensions and admittedly hard to teach. Machines have an advantage in maintaining the contingencies required for indirect or mediated reinforcement.

Other aspects of thinking, including the solution of personal problems, can also be analyzed and directly programmed. This is not current practice, however. Students are most often "taught to think" simply by thrusting them into situations in which already established repertoires are inadequate. Some of them modify their behavior or the situation effectively and come up with solutions. They may have learned, but they have not necessarily been taught, how to think.

Logicians, mathematicians, and scientists have often tried to record and understand their own thinking processes, but we are still far from a satisfactory formulation of all relevant behaviors. Much remains to be learned about how a skillful thinker examines a situation, alters it, samples his own responses with respect to it, carries out specific verbal manipulations appropriate to it, and so on. It is quite possible that we cannot teach thinking adequately until all this has been analyzed. Once we have specified the behavior, however, we have no reason to suppose that it will then be any less adaptable to programmed instruction than simple verbal repertoires.

Teaching machines and the associated practices of programmed instruction will have proved too successful if their practical consequences are allowed to overshadow their promise for the future. We need teaching machines to help solve a very pressing problem, but we also need them to utilize our basic knowledge of human behavior in the design of entirely new educational practices.

Teaching machines are an example of the technological application of basic science. It is true that current machines might have been designed in the light of classroom experience and common sense, and that explanations of why they are effective can be paraphrased in traditional terms. The fact remains that more than half a century of the self-conscious examination of instructional processes had worked only moderate changes in educational practices. The laboratory study of learning provided the confidence, if not all the knowledge, needed for a successful instrumental attack on the *status quo*. Traditional views may not have been actually wrong, but they were vague and were not entertained with sufficient commitment to work substantial technological changes.

As a technology, however, education is still immature, as we may see from the fact that it defines its goals in terms of traditional achievements. Teachers are usually concerned with reproducing the characteristics and achievements of already educated men. When the nature of the human organism is better understood, we may begin to consider not only what man has already shown himself to be, but what he may become under carefully designed conditions. The goal of education should be nothing short of the fullest possible development of the human organism. An experimental analysis of behavior, carried out under the advantageous conditions of the laboratory, will contribute to progress toward that goal. So will practical experiments conducted in schools and colleges with the help of adequate instrumentation.

Reflections on a Decade
of Teaching Machines

To the general public, and to many educators as well, the nature and scope of teaching machines are by no means clear. There is an extraordinary need for more and better teaching, and any enterprise which may help to meet it will not be left to develop normally. The demand for information about teaching machines has been excessive. Articles and books have been published and lectures given; symposia have been arranged, and conferences and workshops have been held and courses taught. Those who have had anything useful to say have said it far too often, and those who have had nothing to say have been no more reticent.

Education is big business. Teaching machines were soon heralded as a growth industry, and fantastic predictions of the sales of programed texts were circulated. Devices have been sold as teaching machines which were not well built or designed with any understanding of their function or the practical exigencies of their use. No author was ever more warmly received by a publisher than the author of a programed text. Many programs, to be used either with machines or in textbook form, have been marketed without adequate evaluation.

Teachers and Devices

The "mechanizing of education" has been taken literally in the sense of doing by machine what was formerly done by people. Some of the so-called computer-based teaching machines are designed simply to duplicate the behavior of teachers. To automate education with mechanical teachers is like automating banking with mechanical tellers and bookkeepers. What is

From *Teachers College Record*, 1963, *65*, 168–177.

needed in both cases is an analysis of the functions to be served, followed by the design of appropriate equipment. Nothing we now know about the learning process calls for very elaborate instrumentation.

Educational specialists have added to the confusion by trying to incorporate the principles upon which teaching machines are based into older theories of learning and teaching.

In the broadest sense, teaching machines are simply devices which make it possible to apply our technical knowledge of human behavior to the practical field of education.[1] Teaching is the expediting of learning. Students learn without teaching, but the teacher arranges conditions under which they learn more rapidly and effectively. In recent years, the experimental analysis of behavior has revealed many new facts about relevant conditions. The growing effectiveness of an experimental analysis is still not widely recognized, even within the behavioral sciences themselves, but the implications of some of its achievements for education can no longer be ignored.

An important condition is the relation between behavior and its consequences; learning occurs when behavior is "reinforced." The power of reinforcement is not easily appreciated by those who have not had firsthand experience in its use or have not at least seen some sort of experimental demonstration. Extensive changes in behavior can be brought about by arranging so-called contingencies of reinforcement. Various kinds of contingencies are concealed in the teacher's discussions with his students, in the books he gives them to read, in the charts and other materials he shows them, in the questions he asks them, and in the comments he makes on their answers. An experimental analysis clarifies these contingencies and suggests many improvements.

Shaping by Program

An important contribution has been the so-called "programing" of knowledge and skills—the construction of carefully arranged sequences of contingencies leading to the terminal performances which are the object of education. The teacher begins with whatever behavior the student brings to the instructional situation; by selective reinforcement, he changes that behavior so that a given terminal performance is more and more closely approximated. Even with lower organisms, quite complex behaviors can be "shaped" in this way with surprising speed; the human organism is

---

[1] Skinner, B. F. The Science of Learning and the Art of Teaching. *Harvard Educational Review*, 1954, *24*, 86–97. [This volume, pp. 179–191.]

presumably far more sensitive. So important is the principle of programing that it is often regarded as the main contribution of the teaching-machine movement, but the experimental analysis of behavior has much more to contribute to a technology of education.

The direct contact which often exists between teacher and student favors the construction of programed sequences, and the teacher who understands the process can profit from the opportunity to improvise programs as he goes. Programs can be constructed in advance, however, which will successfully shape the behavior of most students without local modifications, and many of them can conveniently be mediated by mechanical devices. Laboratory studies have shown that contingencies emphasizing subtle properties of behavior can often be arranged *only* through instrumentation. There are potentially as many different kinds of teaching machines as there are kinds of contingencies of reinforcement.

Teaching machines which present material to the student and differentially reinforce his responses in well constructed programs differ in several ways from self-testing devices and self-scoring test forms, as well as from the training devices which have long been used by industry and the armed services. As Pressey pointed out many years ago,[2] a student will learn while taking a multiple-choice test if he is told immediately whether his answers are right or wrong. He learns not to give wrongs answers again, and his right answers are strengthened. But testing has traditionally been distinguished from teaching for good reason. Before using a self-testing device, the student must already have studied the subject and, presumably, learned most of what he is to learn about it. Tests usually occupy only a small part of his time. Their main effect is motivational: A poor score induces him to study harder and possibly more effectively. Materials designed to be used in self-testing devices have recently been programed, but the contingencies which prevail during a test are not favorable to the shaping and maintaining of behavior.

Conventional training devices arrange conditions under which students learn, usually by simulating the conditions under which they eventually perform. Their original purpose was to prevent injury or waste during early stages of learning, but attention has recently been given to programing the actual behaviors they are designed to teach. To the extent that they expedite learning, they are teaching machines. Terminal performances have usually been selected for practical reasons, but a more promising

[2] Pressey, S. J. A simple device for teaching testing, and research in learning. *Sch. & Soc.*, 1926, *23*, 373–376.

possibility is the analysis and programing of basic motor and perceptual skills—a goal which should have an important place in any statement of educational policy.

In arranging contingencies of reinforcement, machines do many of the things teachers do; in that sense, they teach. The resulting instruction is not impersonal, however. A machine presents a program designed by someone who knew what was to be taught and could prepare an appropriate series of contingencies. It is most effective if used by a teacher who knows the student, has followed his progress, and can adapt available machines and materials to his needs. Instrumentation simply makes it possible for programer and teacher to provide conditions which maximally expedite learning. Instrumentation is thus secondary, but it is nevertheless inevitable if what is now known about behavior is to be used in an effective technology.

The New Pedagogy

Any practical application of basic knowledge about teaching and learning is, of course, pedagogy. In the United States at least, the term is now discredited, but by emphasizing an analysis of learning processes, teaching machines and programed instruction have been responsible for some improvement in its status. The significance of the teaching machine movement can be indicated by noting the astonishing lack of interest which other proposals for the improvement of education show in the teaching process.

Find better teachers. In his *Talks to Teachers,* William James insisted that there was nothing wrong with the American school system which could not be corrected by "impregnating it with geniuses." [3] It is an old formula: If you cannot solve a problem, find someone who can. If you do not know how to teach, find someone who knows or can find out for himself. But geniuses are in short supply, and good teachers do not come ready-made. Education would no doubt be improved if, as Conant [4] has repeatedly pointed out, good teachers who know and like the subjects they teach could be attracted and retained. But something more is needed. It is not true that "the two essentials of a good teacher are (a) enthusiasm and (b) thorough knowledge of an interest in his subject." [5] A third essential is knowing how to teach.

Emulate model schools. Rickover's criticism of the present American

---

[3] James, W. *Talks to Teachers.* New York: Holt, 1899.
[4] Conant, J. B. *The Education of American Teachers.* New York: McGraw-Hill, 1963.
[5] Helwig, J. Training of college teachers. *Science,* 1960, *132,* 845.

school system is well known.[6] His only important positive suggestion is to set up model schools, staffed by model teachers. The implication is that we already have, or at least can have for the asking, schools which need no improvement and whose methods can be widely copied. This is a dangerous assumption if it discourages further inquiry into instruction.

Simplify what is to be learned. Unsuccessful instruction is often blamed on refractory subject matters. Difficulties in teaching the verbal arts are often attributed to the inconsistencies and unnecessary complexities of a language. The pupil is taught manuscript handwriting because it more closely resembles printed forms. He is taught to spell only those words he is likely to use. Phonetic alphabets are devised to help him learn to read. It may be easier to teach such materials, but teaching itself is not thereby improved. Effective teaching would correct these pessimistic estimates of available instructional power.

Reorganize what is to be learned. The proper structuring of a subject matter is perhaps a part of pedagogy, but it can also serve as a mode of escape. Proposals for improving education by reorganizing what is to be learned usually contain an implicit assumption that students will automatically perceive and remember anything which has "good form"—a doctrine probably traceable to Gestalt psychology. Current revisions of high school curricula often seem to lean heavily on the belief that if what the student is to be taught has been "structured," he cannot help understanding and remembering it.[7] Other purposes of such revisions cannot be questioned: Materials should be up to date and well organized. But a high school presentation acceptable to a current physicist is no more easily taught or easily remembered than the out-of-date and erroneous material to be found in texts of a decade or more ago. Similarly, the accent of a native speaker encountered in a language laboratory is no more easily learned than a bad accent. No matter how well structured a subject matter may be, it must still be taught.

Improve presentation. Pedagogy can also be avoided if what is to be learned can be made memorable. Audio-visual devices are often recommended for this purpose. Many of their other purposes are easily defended. It is not always easy to bring the student into contact with the things he is to learn about. Words are easily imported into the classroom, and books, lectures, and discussions are therefore staples of education; but this is often an unfortunate bias. Audio-visual devices can enlarge the

---

[6] Rickover, H. G. *Education and Freedom.* New York: Dutton, 1959.

[7] Bruner, J. S. *The Process of Education.* Cambridge: Harvard University Press, 1960.

student's nonverbal experience. They can also serve to present material clearly and conveniently. Their use in attracting and holding the student's attention and in dramatizing a subject matter in such a way that it is almost automatically remembered must be questioned, however. It is especially tempting to turn to them for these purposes when the teacher does not use punitive methods to "make students study." But the result is not the same. When a student observes or attends to something in order to see it more clearly or remember it more effectively, his behavior must have been shaped and maintained by reinforcement. The temporal order was important. Certain reinforcing events must have occurred *after* the student looked at, read, and perhaps tested himself on the material. But when colored displays, attractive objects, filmed episodes, and other potentially reinforcing materials are used to attract attention, they must occur *before* the student engages in these activities. Nothing can reinforce a student for *paying* attention if it has already been used to *attract* his attention. Material which attracts attention fails to prepare the student to attend to material which is not interesting on its face, and material which is naturally memorable fails to prepare him to study and recall things which are not, in themselves, unforgettable. A well prepared instructional film may appear to be successful in arousing interest in a given subject, and parts of it may be remembered without effort, but it has not taught the student that a subject may *become* interesting when more closely examined or that intensive study of something which is likely to be overlooked may have reinforcing consequences.

Multiply contacts between teacher and students. Audio-visual devices, particularly when adapted to television, are also used to improve education by bringing one teacher into contact with an indefinitely large number of students. This can be done, of course, without analyzing how the teacher teaches, and it emphasizes a mode of communication which has two serious disadvantages: The teacher cannot see the effect he is having on his students, and large numbers of students must proceed at the same pace. Contributions to pedagogy may be made in designing programs for educational television, but the mere multiplication of contacts is not itself an improvement in teaching.

Expand the educational system. Inadequate education may be corrected by building more schools and recruiting more teachers so that the total quantity of education is increased, even though there is no change in efficiency.

Raise standards. Least effective in improving teaching are demands for higher standards. We may agree that students will be better educated when they learn more, but how are they to be induced to do so? Demands for higher standards usually come from critics who have least to offer in improving teaching itself.

The movement symbolized by the teaching machine differs from other proposals in two ways. It emphasizes the direct improvement of teaching on the principle that no enterprise can improve itself to the fullest extent without examining its basic processes. In the second place, it emphasizes the implementation of basic knowledge. If instructional practices violate many basic principles, it is only in part because these principles are not widely known. The teacher cannot put what he knows into practice in the classroom. Teaching machines and programed instruction constitute a direct attack on the problem of implementation. With appropriate administrative changes, they may bridge the gap between an effective pedagogical theory and actual practice.

Educational Goals

An effective technology of teaching calls for a re-examination of educational objectives. What is the teacher's actual assignment? Educational policy is usually stated in traditional terms: The teacher is to "impart knowledge," "improve skills," "develop rational faculties," and so on. That education is best, says Dr. Hutchins,[8] which develops "intellectual power." The task of the teacher is to change certain inner processes or states. He is to improve the mind.

The role of the teacher in fostering mental prowess has a certain prestige. It has always been held superior to the role of the trainer of motor skills. And it has the great advantage of being almost invulnerable to criticism. In reply to the complaint that he has not produced observable results, the teacher of the mind can lay claim to invisible achievements. His students may not be able to read, but he has only been trying to make sure they wanted to learn. They may not be able to solve problems, but he has been teaching them simply to think creatively. They may be ignorant of specific facts, but he has been primarily concerned with their general interest in a field.

Traditional specifications of the goals of education have never told the teacher what to do upon a given occasion. No one knows how to alter a mental process or strengthen a mental power, and no one can be sure that

[8] Hutchins, R. M. *On Education.* Santa Barbara: Center for the Study of Democratic Institutions, 1963.

he has done so when he has tried. There have been many good teachers who have supposed themselves to be working on the minds of their students, but their actual practices and the results of those practices can be analyzed in other ways. The well educated student is distinguished by certain characteristics. What are they, and how can they be produced? Perhaps we could answer by redefining traditional goals: Instead of imparting knowledge, we could undertake to bring about those changes in behavior which are said to be the conspicuous manifestations of knowledge, or we could set up the behavior which is the mark of a man possessing well-developed rational power. But mentalistic formulations are warped by irrelevant historical accidents. The behavior of the educated student is much more effectively analyzed directly as such.

Contrary to frequent assertions, a behavioristic formulation of human behavior is not a crude positivism which rejects mental processes because they are not accessible to the scientific public.[9] It does not emphasize the rote learning of verbal responses. It does not neglect the complex systems of verbal behavior which are said to show that a student has had an idea, or developed a concept, or entertained a proposition. It does not ignore the behavior involved in the intellectual and ethical problem solving called "thinking." It does not overlook the value judgments said to be invoked when we decide to teach one thing rather than another or when we defend the time and effort given to education. It is merely an effective formulation of those activities of teacher and student which have always been the concern of educational specialists.[10]

Not all behavioristic theories of learning are relevant, however. A distinction is commonly drawn between learning and performance. Learning is said to be a change in some special part of the organism, possibly the nervous system, of which behavior is merely the external and often erratic sign. With modern techniques, however, behavior can be much more successfully studied and manipulated than any such inner system, even when inferences about the latter are drawn from the behavior with the help of sophisticated statistics. An analysis of learning which concentrates on the behavior applies most directly to a technology, for the task of the teacher is to bring about changes in the student's behavior. His methods are equally conspicuous: He makes changes in the environment. A teaching method is simply a way of arranging an environment which expedites learning.

---

[9] Skinner, B. F. Behaviorism at fifty. *Science,* 1963, *140,* 951–958.
[10] Skinner, B. F. Why we need teaching machines. (See page 217.)

Managing Contingencies

Such a formulation is not easily assimilated with the traditional psychology of learning. The teacher may arrange contingencies of reinforcement to set up new *forms* of response, as in teaching handwriting and speech or nonverbal forms of behavior in the arts, crafts, and sports. He may arrange contingencies to bring responses under new kinds of *stimulus control,* as in teaching the student to read or draw from copy, or to behave effectively upon other kinds of occasions. Current instructional programs designed to fulfill such assignments are mainly verbal, but comparable contingencies generate nonverbal behavior, including perceptual and motor skills and various kinds of intellectual and ethical self-management.

A second kind of programing maintains the student's behavior in strength. The form of the response and the stimulus control may not change; the student is simply more likely to respond. Some relevant methods are traditionally discussed under the heading of motivation. For example, we can strengthen behavior by introducing new reinforcers or making old ones more effective, as in giving the student better reasons for getting an education. The experimental analysis of behavior suggests another important possibility: Schedule available reinforcers more effectively. Appropriate terminal schedules of reinforcement will maintain the student's interest, make him industrious and persevering, stimulate his curiosity, and so on; but less demanding schedules, carefully designed to maintain the behavior at every stage, must come first. The programing of schedules of reinforcement is a promising alternative to the aversive control which, in spite of repeated reforms, still prevails in educational practice.

In neglecting programing, teaching methods have merely followed the lead of the experimental psychology of learning, where the almost universal practice has been to submit an organism immediately to terminal contingencies of reinforcement.[11] A maze or a discrimination problem, for example, is learned only if the subject acquires appropriate behavior before the behavior he brings to the experiment has extinguished. The intermediate contingencies are largely accidental. The differences in behavior and in rate of learning which appear under these conditions are often attributed to inherited differences in ability.

In maximizing the student's success, programed instruction differs from so-called trial-and-error learning where the student is said to learn from

[11] Skinner, B. F. Operant behavior. *American Psychologist,* 1963, *18,* 503–515.

his mistakes. At best, he learns not to make mistakes again. A successful response may survive, but trial-and-error teaching makes little provision for actually strengthening it. The method seems inevitably committed to aversive control. For the same reason, programed instruction does not closely resemble teaching patterned on everyday communication. It is usually not enough simply to tell the student something or induce him to read a book; he must be told or must read and then be questioned. In this "tell-and-test" pattern, the test is not given to measure what he has learned, but to show him what he has not learned and thus induce him to listen and read more carefully in the future. A similar basically aversive pattern is widespread at the college level, where the instructor assigns material and then examines on it. The student may learn to read carefully, to make notes, to discover for himself how to study, and so on, because in doing so he avoids aversive consequences, but he has not necessarily been taught. Assigning-and-testing is not teaching. The aversive by-products, familiar to everyone in the field of education, can be avoided through the use of programed positive reinforcement.

Many facts and principles derived from the experimental analysis of behavior are relevant to the construction of effective programs leading to terminal contingencies. The facts and principles are often difficult, but they make up an indispensable armamentarium of the effective teacher and educational specialist. We have long since passed the point at which our basic knowledge of human behavior can be applied to education through the use of a few general principles.

Principle and Practice

The difference between general principles and an effective technology can be seen in certain efforts to assimilate the principles of programed instruction with earlier theories. Programed instruction has, for example, been called "Socratic." It is true that Socrates proceeded by small steps and often led his students through an argument with a series of verbal prompts, but the example often cited to illustrate his method suggests that he was unaware of an important detail—namely, that prompts must eventually be "vanished" in order to put the student on his own. In the famous scene in the *Meno*, Socrates demonstrates his theory that learning is simply recollection by leading an uneducated slave boy through Pythagoras's Golden Theorem. The boy responds with the rather timid compliance to be expected under the circumstances and never without help. Although Socrates himself and some of those among his listeners who were already familiar with the theorem may have understood the proof better at the end of the scene, there is no evidence whatsoever that the boy understood it or could reconstruct it. In this example of Socratic instruction, at least, the student almost certainly learned nothing. The program of the *Meno* episode constructed by Cohen [12] is an improvement in that the student responds with less prompting.

A seventeenth-century anticipation of programed instruction has also been found in the work of Comenius, who advocated teaching in small steps, no step being too great for the student who was about to take it. Programing is sometimes described simply as breaking material into a large number of small pieces, arranged in a plausible genetic order. But size of step is not enough. Something must happen to help the student take each step, and something must happen as he takes it. An effective program is usually composed of small steps, but the whole story is not to be found in Comenius's philosophy of education.

Another venerable principle is that the student should not proceed until he has fully understood what he is to learn at a given stage. Several writers have quoted E. L. Thorndike [13] to this effect, who wrote in 1912, "If, by a miracle of mechanical ingenuity, a book could be so arranged that only to him who had done what was directed on page one would page two become visible, and so on, much that now requires personal instruction could be managed by print." In commenting on this passage, Finn and Perrin [14] have written, ". . . Here are the insights of a genius. History can very often teach us a lesson in humility—and it does here. The interesting question is: Why couldn't we see it then?" We might also ask, why couldn't Thorndike see it then? He remained active in education for at least 30 years, but he turned from this extraordinarily promising principle to another and—as it proved—less profitable approach to educational psychology.

It is always tempting to argue that earlier ideas would have been effective if people had only paid attention to them. But a good idea must be more than right. It must command attention; it must make its own way because of what it does. Education does not need principles which will improve education as soon as people observe them; it needs a technology so powerful that it cannot be ignored. No matter how insightful the anticipation of modern principles in earlier writers may seem to have been,

[12] Cohen, I. S. Programed learning and the Socratic dialogue. *American Psychologist,* 1962, *17,* 772–775.

[13] Thorndike, E. L. *Education.* New York: Macmillan, 1912.

[14] Finn, J. D., and Perrin, D. G. *Teaching Machines and Programmed Learning: A Survey of the Industry, 1962.* Washington, D.C.: U.S. Office of Education, 1962.

something was lacking or education would be much further advanced. We are on the threshold of a technology which will be not only right but effective.[15]

Criteria of Research

A science of behavior makes its principal contribution to a technology of education through the analysis of useful contingencies of reinforcement. It also suggests a new kind of educational research. Thorndike never realized the potentialities of his early work on learning because he turned to the measurement of mental abilities and to matched-group comparisons of teaching practices. He pioneered in a kind of research which, with the encouragement offered by promising new statistical techniques, was to dominate educational psychology for decades. It led to a serious neglect of the process of instruction.

There are practical reasons why we want to know whether a given method of instruction is successful or whether it is more successful than another. We may want to know what changes it brings about in the student, possibly in addition to those it was designed to effect. The more reliable our answers to such questions, the better. But reliability is not enough. Correlations between test scores and significant differences between group means tell us less about the behavior of the student in the act of learning than results obtained when the investigator can manipulate variables and assess their effects in a manner characteristic of laboratory research. The practices evaluated in studies of groups of students have usually not been suggested by earlier research of a similar nature, but have been drawn from tradition, from the improvisations of skillful teachers, or from suggestions made by theorists working intuitively or with other kinds of facts. No matter how much they may have stimulated the insightful or inventive researcher, the evaluations have seldom led directly to the design of improved practices.

The contrast between statistical evaluation and the experimental analysis of teaching has an illuminating parallel in the field of medicine. Various drugs, regimens, surgical procedures, and so on, must be examined with respect to a very practical question: Does the health of the patient improve? But "health" is only a general description of specific physiological processes, and "improvement" is, so to speak, merely a by-product of the changes in these processes induced by a given treatment. Medicine has

15 Skinner, B. F. *The Technology of Teaching.* New York: Appleton-Century-Crofts, 1968.

reached the point where research on specific processes is a much more fertile source of new kinds of therapy than evaluations in terms of improvement in health. Similarly, in education, no matter how important improvement in the student's performance may be, it remains a by-product of specific changes in behavior resulting from the specific changes in the environment wrought by the teacher. Educational research patterned on an experimental analysis of behavior leads to a much better understanding of these basic processes. Research directed toward the behavior of the individual student has, of course, a long history, but it can still profit greatly from the support supplied by an experimental analysis of behavior.

This distinction explains why those concerned with experimental analyses of learning are not likely to take matched-group evaluations of teaching machines and programed instruction very seriously. It is not possible, of course, to evaluate either machines or programs *in general* because only specific instances can be tested, and available examples by no means represent all the possibilities; but even the evaluation of a given machine or program in the traditional manner may not give an accurate account of its effects. For example, those who are concerned with improvement are likely to test the student's capacity to give right answers. Being right has, of course, practical importance, but it is only one result of instruction. It is a doubtful measure of "knowledge" in any useful sense. We say that a student "knows the answer" if he can select it from an array of choices, but this does not mean that he could have given it without help. The right answer to one question does not imply right answers to all questions said to show the "possession of the same fact." Instructional programs are often criticized as repetitious or redundant when they are actually designed to put the student in possession of a number of different responses "expressing the same proposition." Whether such instruction is successful is not shown by any one right answer.

Correct or Educated?

A preoccupation with correct answers has led to a common misunderstanding of programed materials. Since a sentence with a blank to be filled in by the student resembles a test item, it is often supposed that the response demanded by the blank is what is learned. In that case, a student could not be learning much because he may respond correctly in 19 out of 20 frames and must therefore already have known 95 per cent of the answers. The instruction which occurs as he completes an item comes from having responded to other parts of it. The extent of this instruction cannot be estimated from the fact that he is right 19 out of 20 times, either while pursuing a program *or on a subsequent test.* Nor will this statistic tell us whether other conditions are important. Is it most profitable for the student to execute the response by writing it out, by speaking it aloud, by speaking it silently, or by reading it in some other way? These procedures may or may not have different effects on a selected "right-answer" statistic, but no one statistic will cover all their effects.

Research in teaching must not, of course, lose sight of its main objective —to make education more effective. But improvement as such is a questionable dimension of the behavior of either teacher or student. Dimensions which are much more intimately related to the conditions the teacher arranges to expedite learning must be studied even though they do not contribute to improvement or contribute to it in a way which is not immediately obvious.

The changes in the behavior of the individual student brought about by manipulating the environment are usually immediate and specific. The results of statistical comparisons of group performances usually are not. From his study of the behavior of the individual student, the investigator gains a special kind of confidence. He usually knows what he has done to get one effect and what he must do to get another.

Confidence *in* education is another possible result of an effective technology of teaching. Competition between the various cultures of the world, warlike or friendly, is now an accepted fact, and the role played by education in strengthening and perpetuating a given way of life is clear. No field is in greater need of our most powerful intellectual resources. An effective educational technology based upon an experimental analysis will bring it support commensurate with its importance in the world today.

Teaching Science in High School —What Is Wrong?

The scientific community faces a serious problem. Science and technology are growing at an ever-increasing rate, but the number of young men and women going into science is not keeping pace. Only a fairly small percentage of high school students go to college expressing an interest in becoming scientists, and many of these eventually shift to other fields. There is already an acute shortage, which could prove disastrous not only for science itself but for a way of life which becomes more and more dependent on science as the years pass.

A possible explanation is that the life of the scientist has lost some of its glamour. It may offer less chance for individual achievement, and its exciting moments may be reserved only for those who have had a very extensive preparation. Even so, the main fault must lie with education. Good teaching should give an accurate account of what science is and does, of what a single scientist may contribute to the world, and of the genuine excitement of those who enjoy science for what it is—the great art of the 20th century. Above all, education should recruit the scientists of the future, finding the right people, giving them the knowledge and skills they need, and providing the satisfactions which will make them creative and dedicated men and women. Only if it does so can we hope to find those who will practice science in our universities and in industrial and governmental laboratories, and who will teach science in our schools and colleges to keep the enterprise going. Only effective teaching will create that large pool from which, in each generation, a few great scientists are drawn.

The problem has not gone unnoticed. For the past 10 or 15 years education as a whole has been sharply criticized, and many constructive sug-

From *Science*, 1968, *159*, 704–710.

254

gestions have been made. We are all familiar with proposed remedies. Education needs support, and support means money, and the money is to be used in a variety of ways. We need more and better schools. We need to recruit and hold better teachers, selecting them through better systems of qualification and making them more competent in the fields in which they teach. We need to give all qualified students a chance, selecting them impartially, supporting them financially, and removing social and racial barriers. We need more and better capital equipment—texts, workbooks, films, and audiovisual devices, including teaching machines and television. We need to change our curricula, making a sensible selection among the things to be taught and bringing what is taught up-to-date.

High school science teaching has been singled out for special effort, and there is no doubt that important steps have been taken, but there is not yet any great change. The curve showing the number of students going into science, particularly physics, has not turned sharply upward. Possibly it is too soon to expect results. Educational practices change slowly, and we may yet see progress. But some possible reasons why improvement has not been more dramatic may be pointed out.

There is a curious omission in this list of educational needs. Nothing is said about a better understanding of the processes involved in learning and teaching. No suggestion is made that we should learn more about what is happening when a teacher teaches and a student learns. On the contrary, the issue is avoided in almost all current proposals for the improvement of education. Pedagogy is a dirty word, and courses in "method" are discounted, if not ridiculed. This is a serious mistake. As science itself has so abundantly demonstrated, the power of any technology depends upon an understanding of its basic processes. We cannot really improve teaching until we know what it is.

The most casual attitude toward a better understanding of instruction is evident at all levels. You will not find anything like a medical school, law school, or business school for those who want to be college teachers. No professional training is felt to be necessary. Preparation for grade and high school teaching is scarcely more explicit. Schools of education no longer actively promote pedagogy or method as formalized practice. Instead, the beginning teacher serves an apprenticeship. He watches other teachers and learns to behave as they behave, and eventually he may profit from his own classroom experience. In the long run, high school teachers, like college teachers, teach as they themselves have been taught, as they have seen others teach, or as experience dictates.

Classroom Experience

What is learned from classroom experience is perhaps likely to be more useful than formalized rules and prescriptions, but the classroom is nevertheless not an ideal source of educational wisdom. On the contrary, it can be seriously misleading. Francis Bacon once formulated his famous Idols —the false notions or fallacies which led to bad thinking. I have suggested [1] that we should add another to his list: the Idols of the School. The Idol or Fallacy of the Good Teacher is the belief that what a good teacher can do, any teacher can do. Some people are socially skillful; they are good judges of character and get along well with people. They make good teachers. The trouble is, we do not know why. Like the old-time doctor, they practice an art which has not been analyzed and can seldom be communicated. In the hands of a good teacher a new text, a new set of materials, or a new method may be dramatically successful, but it does not follow that it will be successful in the hands of teachers at large. The complementary Fallacy of the Good Student is the belief that what a good student can learn, any student can learn. Some students are highly intelligent and well motivated. They know how to study, and they learn without being taught or even when taught by a bad teacher. But a text, a set of materials, or a method which works well with them will not necessarily be a success with all students.

For many years educational journals, school bulletins, and the popular media have reported examples of effective teaching. They have portrayed lively classes in which teachers and students work together in harmony and the students obviously learn a great deal. Everyone is pleased. The teachers take satisfaction in what they are doing, the students enjoy themselves and make progress, and administrators and parents are delighted. But is it not time to ask why these examples are not more widely copied? Why, by this time, is not all teaching equally pleasant and profitable? The answer is probably to be found in the Idols of the School. We are looking at good teachers or good students or both, but not at practices which have been analyzed or can be communicated. We cannot improve education to any great extent by finding more good teachers and more good students. We need to find practices which permit all teachers to teach well and under which all students learn as efficiently as their talents permit.

A first step is to recognize how misleading classroom experience is as a source of educational wisdom. Its outstanding defect is that the teacher sel-

[1] In *The Technology of Teaching.*

dom sees the effects of what he has done. The significant results of teaching lie in that distant future in which students make use of what they have learned, and it is a future usually closed to the teacher. He knows nothing of what happens to most of his students. He is influenced instead only by short-term results, and many of these not only contribute nothing to long-term gains but may actually conflict with them.

Classroom Games

No teacher enjoys students who are disorganized, inattentive, lethargic, or resentful. But students may be lively and attentive in ways which have little to do with what or how much they are learning. In a familiar—perhaps too familiar—classroom practice, the teacher asks questions and the students answer. The students are rewarded for right answers and punished for wrong, and anything a student does to be called on when he knows the answer or overlooked when he does not will be reinforced. The teacher is reinforced either by right answers if they show that he has been teaching successfully or by wrong if he must control the class through a threat of punishment, and anything he may do to get a right answer when he wants a right answer or a wrong one when he wants a wrong will be reinforced.

These are the essential conditions for a complex game in which teacher and students attempt to outguess each other. The student who knows an answer waves his hand, and a teacher who wants a right answer calls on him, but he calls on someone else if he wants a wrong answer, and the student who does not know the answer then raises his hand to avoid being called on and the student who knows the answer keeps his hand down, hoping to get a chance. The class is excited, the teacher is in control, and everyone may be having a good time. But the game is quite unrelated to the subject being taught—it is the same for all subjects—and its educational value may be questioned. It may induce some students to engage in more profitable activities, but it is not characteristic of thoughtful discussion or study, and its long-term effects may be negligible or even harmful. A dull, lethargic class is no doubt the sign of a bad teacher, but an excited class is not necessarily the sign of a good one.

Hand-waving may seem too trivial to mention, but the same kind of game is played with verbal interchanges. The modern Socrates, like his famous predecessor, plays cat and mouse with his students, pretending to misunderstand, constructing absurd paraphrases, making suggestions which lead his listeners into error, making ironic comments which amuse some of his listeners at the expense of others, and so on. If he is skillful, he may induce his students to protest, disagree, insist, and defend themselves in a lively fashion. All this is valuable in teaching students to argue and in giving them reasons for acquiring facts to be used in an argument but, like the hand-waving game, it is unrelated to subject matter and it gives the student a wrong impression of scientific thinking. It is true that scientists occasionally discuss things among themselves, but the creative interchanges are more likely to be between men and things than between men and men. The Great Conversation which has been going on for more than 2000 years has not been notably productive of useful information or wisdom. To suggest to high school students that science is a kind of running debate is to risk selecting potential debaters rather than potential scientists.

Both teacher and student can be similarly misled by practices designed primarily to make science interesting. Students who take an interest in things are likely to learn something about them, and making a subject interesting is no doubt worthwhile, but it is a mistake to confuse arousing interest with teaching. In a recent review of a book on the mathematics curriculum [2] the reviewer insisted that remarks on the psychology of teaching should *"confine themselves* [my italics] to observing that mathematics teaching (indeed, all teaching) must make the subject matter attractive." And how often do we hear it said that the good teacher is simply one who knows his field and can make it interesting! But teaching is much more than arousing interest, and materials and techniques designed to generate interest may conflict with good teaching.

Attention

A student who is not paying attention is obviously not learning, and the teacher is therefore reinforced when he behaves in ways which attract attention. Audiovisual materials, texts with colored pictures and charts, animated films, and demonstration experiments full of surprises are often used for this reason. Advertisers and the entertainment industry face a similar problem and solve it in similar ways. But to *attract* attention is to deprive the student of the chance to learn to *pay* attention. The important thing is for the student to discover that interesting things happen when he attends to something which, on its face, is not interesting at all. We do not want students who read books only when they are printed in four colors, or who watch films or demonstrations only when something interesting is always happening. We want students who read black-and-white pages because something interesting happens when they do, and who

[2] Hilton, P. J. *Science, 147* (1965), 138.

watch films and demonstrations which seem no more interesting than nature itself, until close observation shows how fascinating they really are. Materials miscarry in the same way when they are designed to appeal to a student's interests outside the classroom—the physics of the tennis court, the chemistry of the kitchen. Faraday became interested in electricity when he read an article in the encyclopedia, and it was not entitled "Electricity for young Britons."

I am not saying that a student should not be interested in what he is doing or that interesting aspects of a subject should not be pointed out, but in relying too heavily on the attractions of science we give the student a wrong impression of what he is to find when he pursues science further, and we should not be surprised that he drops out when he discovers the actual state of affairs. The things which commit the mature scientist to a lifetime of dedicated research are not the kinds of things which interest the layman or the beginning student. It is characteristic of the successful scientist, for example, that he continues to work for long periods when nothing interesting is happening. That kind of dedication can be instilled in the student, as we shall see, but not by making a subject interesting.

Discovery

Another practice which has the effect of immediately rewarding the teacher even though the ultimate consequences are questionable is letting the student discover science for himself. This was the great principle which Rousseau developed in his book *Emile.* Let the student learn from nature, not from what others have said about nature. Let him go directly to the facts, to *things,* which alone are incorruptible. The principle is supported by Pascal's earlier observation that the arguments we discover for ourselves are better understood and remembered than those we get from others. The principle seems particularly appropriate in teaching science, where the great achievements take the form of discoveries. The scientist works in order to discover, and he continues to work so long as he has a chance to discover. Why should the student not have the same motivation?

We cannot mean, however, that the student is to discover all of science for himself, or even any appreciable part of it. Science is a vast accumulation of the discoveries of a great many men. It must be transmitted from one generation to another—either in the form of books, charts, tables, and so on, or in the form of behavior taught to new members of a culture. Education is charged with the transmission of knowledge in the second sense, and it cannot possibly fulfill its obligation simply by arranging for rediscovery. Whether we like it or not, a great deal of science must be taught. We raise a serious obstacle to teaching when we suggest to the student that it is beneath his dignity to learn what someone else already knows. How much of science is to be taught, how much is simply to be made available in recorded form, and how much is to be left for rediscovery are questions concerning the available time and energy of teachers and students. The answers must take into account the efficiency of teaching methods.

The problem is particularly difficult because scientific knowledge changes so rapidly. Textbooks and other records go out-of-date, and so do the behavioral repertoires imparted through instruction, but we cannot solve that problem by refusing to write books or to teach. We must be prepared to change our books and to teach in such a way that the behavior of our students can change as occasion demands. It is no solution to this problem to let the student discover things for himself, because what he discovers will also soon be out-of-date.

Of course we want to encourage students to inquire, explore, and discover things, and we want to teach them to do so efficiently. We must teach a wide range of scientific methods as well as facts. Many of the verbal practices of science have been carefully formulated by mathematicians, logicians, statisticians, and others, and they are usually part of a science curriculum. The nonverbal day-to-day behavior of the scientist in his laboratory has in contrast been sadly neglected, and it is here that techniques of discovery are more likely to be relevant. We no doubt need to know more about them if we are to teach them well, but even so there is no reason why they should be taught by the discovery method.

Indeed, it is not likely that they *are* taught well by that method. The guided discoveries of the classroom bear only a vague resemblance to genuine scientific discoveries. The archetypal pattern of this kind of teaching is the scene in Plato's *Meno* in which Socrates leads the slave boy through Pythagoras' theorem for doubling the square. This is still hailed as a great educational innovation, but the fact is that the slave boy learned nothing. There was not the remotest chance that he could go through the proof himself when Socrates had finished with him, and even if he could have done so, his behavior in assenting to Socrates' suggestions almost certainly had nothing in common with the steps which led Pythagoras to his discovery of the theorem. Polya [3] has published a delightful account of how one might tease out the formula for the diagonal of a parallelepiped from a class of high school students, but the hints, sugges-

---

[3] Polya, G. *How to Solve It*. Princeton: Princeton University Press, 1945.

tions, corrections, and heuristic exhortations he uses do not give a very convincing picture of the conditions under which the original discovery must have been made. A few students no doubt benefit from this kind of teaching in the hands of a good teacher. They experience some of the delight of making a discovery, which may sustain them in further work. Even so, they are not necessarily then more likely to make other discoveries by themselves, and meanwhile all the other students in the class have received a particularly confusing presentation. Although the moment of discovery is important in the life of a scientist and may explain his dedication, it is necessarily a rare event and cannot explain the quality or nature of most of his behavior.

Aversive Control

These, then, are a few examples of classroom practices which flourish because their immediate effects are reinforcing to students and teachers in spite of the fact that long-term effects may be weak, lacking, or actually undesirable. There are no doubt other reasons why the practices flourish. Education is in transition. It is a transition in the right direction, but it has a long way to go. We are in the process of rejecting methods which have long dominated the field, in which students study primarily to avoid punishment and which impose upon the teacher the necessity of maintaining a sustained threat. A dictatorial, despotic teacher—an "authority" in a political as well as a scholarly sense—is out of place in modern life. We want learning to mean more than practice, drill, or rote memorizing, which are the commonest products of such a system. It is not surprising, therefore, that we should turn first to making science attractive, engaging the student in discussion, giving him materials which arouse his interest, and letting him discover things for himself. But as enjoyable as these practices may be—for teacher and student alike—the fact remains that they are not really effective alternatives. The proof is that the teacher is forced back again and again upon the old coercive pattern. In spite of all our efforts, it is still true that students learn mainly to avoid the consequences of not learning. The commonest practice in high school as well as college is still "assign and test." We tell the student what he is to learn and hold him responsible for learning it by making a variety of unhappy consequences contingent upon his failure. In doing so we may give him some reason to learn, but we do not teach.

Our failure is clear in the frequency with which educators conclude that a teacher cannot really teach but can only help the student learn. This is a disastrous philosophy. It can be asserted, of course, only of methods which have actually been tried, but it tends to be used as an argument against trying new ones. It is not only a confession of failure but a form of exculpation. By admitting that we cannot teach, we avoid confessing that we have failed to do so, and we thus continue to maintain, as teachers have maintained for centuries, that it is always the student who fails, not the teacher. We can discard coercive practices only when we have found satisfactory replacements, and the present state of education is proof that we have not yet been successful.

What Does Teaching Mean?

An important first step in searching for better ways of teaching is to define our terms. What is happening when a student learns? Traditional theories of education almost always answer that question in mentalistic ways. The student is said to begin with a desire to learn, a natural curiosity, of which the teacher must take advantage. The teacher must exercise the student's faculties, strengthen his reasoning powers, develop his cognitive styles and skills, let him discover strategies of inquiry. The student must acquire concepts, come to see relations, and have ideas. He must take in and store information in such a form that it can be quickly retrieved when needed. Statements of educational policy are replete with expressions of this sort. It would be a mistake to underestimate their power, for they are supported by ancient systems of psychology imbedded in our language and by vestigial cognitive theories. It is therefore hard to realize that they are either metaphors which inadequately represent the changes taking place in the student's behavior or explanatory fictions which really explain nothing. Their most serious shortcoming is that they do not tell the teacher what to do in order to bring about changes in his students or give him any satisfactory way of knowing whether he has done so. If these are indeed the tasks of the teacher, we must agree that he cannot really teach. It is even doubtful whether he can help the student learn.

A much more promising approach is to look at the student's behavior—the behavior from which mentalistic states and processes are inferred and which they so inadequately describe and explain. The basic question, in its crudest form, is this: *what do we want the student to do as the result of having been taught?* (It is no answer to cite the examinations he is to pass, for they are only samples of his behavior, and no matter how reliable they may be, they are, we hope, very small samples indeed of what he will actually learn.) To say that we want the student to "behave like a scientist" is on the right track, but it is only a start. For how *does* a scientist behave? The answer will be nothing less than an epistemology, a theory of scientific knowledge. It must in fact be more: we need an empirical description of the behavior of the scientist at work, in all its myriad forms.

Such a description is not to be had for the asking. Scientific thinking is an extraordinarily difficult field, and we have not advanced very far in analyzing it, possibly just because we have so often been seduced by metaphor. If we announce that we are interested in giving the student a thorough knowledge of a science, a grasp of its structure, an understanding of its basic relations, we shall be endlessly admired. If, instead, we specify the things we want him to *do,* verbally and nonverbally, we risk being called mechanical and shallow, even though the things we list are precisely the things from which an understanding or grasp of the structure of the science is inferred. There is nothing about behavior which evokes the mystery which has always attached to mind, but it is important to remember that we stand in awe of mind just because we have been able to do so little about it.

Programmed Instruction

To remove the mystery, we must define our goals in the most explicit way. And we can then begin to teach. Having specified the terminal behavior our students are to exhibit, we can proceed to generate it. One way is through programmed instruction, a contribution to education which has been widely misunderstood. Many educational theorists have insisted that it is nothing new and have tried to assimilate it to earlier theories and practices. We are told that it is simply a matter of breaking the material to be learned into easy steps, arranging steps in a logical order with no gaps, making sure the student understands one step before moving on to another, and thus, incidentally, making sure that he is frequently successful. All these things are done in constructing a good program, but the central point has still not been reached.

Programmed instruction is primarily a way of using recent advances in our understanding of human behavior. We want to strengthen certain kinds of behavior in our students and so far as we know, there is only one way of doing so. Behavior is strengthened when it is followed by certain kinds of consequences. To be more precise, a response which produces a so-called positive reinforcer or terminates a negative is more likely to occur again under similar circumstances. We use this principle of "operant conditioning" to strengthen behavior by arranging reinforcing consequences—by making available reinforcers contingent on behavior.

This is often said to be nothing more than reward and punishment, and there is certainly a connection. But the traditional concepts of reward and punishment are about as close to operant conditioning as traditional concepts of heat, space, or matter are to contemporary scientific treatments. Only a detailed experimental analysis of contingencies of reinforcement will supply the principles we need in the design of effective instructional practices.

Teaching is the arrangement of contingencies of reinforcement which expedite learning. Learning occurs without teaching, fortunately, but improved contingencies speed the process and may even generate behavior which would otherwise never appear. Programmed instruction is designed to solve a special problem. We cannot simply wait for our student to behave in a given way, particularly in the complex ways characteristic of a scientist, in order to reinforce him. Somehow or other we must get him to behave. Our culture has devised relevant techniques for other than educational purposes. We resort to verbal instruction, for example, when we simply tell the student what to do, or we show him what to do and let him imitate us. If we induce the student to engage in terminal behavior in that way, however, he will be much too dependent upon being shown or told. He will not have learned. We begin instead with whatever behavior the student has available—with behavior which does not call for much help. We selectively reinforce any part which contributes to the terminal pattern or makes it more likely that the student will behave in other ways which contribute to it. The devices we use to evoke the behavior can then be easily withdrawn, so that the terminal behavior appears upon appropriate occasions without help. A high degree of technical knowledge is needed to do this.

Many instructional programs have been written by those who do not understand the basic principle, and it is an unhappy reflection on the state of education today that they are still probably better than unprogrammed materials, but they give a wrong impression. Even a good program may be misleading to anyone who is already proficient in a field because he cannot easily appreciate its effect on a new learner. Anyone who wants to get the feel of programmed instruction should try his hand at a good program in an unfamiliar subject. A colleague whose work had begun to move in the direction of biochemistry worked through an excellent program in that field. "In 3 days," he told me, "I knew biochemistry!" He was exaggerating, of course, as we both knew, but he was expressing very well the almost miraculous effect of a good program.

A further misunderstanding has arisen from the fact that industry and the Armed Services have taken up programmed instruction much more rapidly than schools and colleges. There are some obvious reasons. For one thing, teaching techniques in these organizations can be easily changed. For another, there are people in industry and the Armed Services whose job it is to see that no possible improvement in teaching is overlooked. Unfortunately they have no counterparts in school and college administrations. Explanations of this sort have not prevented the erroneous conclusion that there is another reason why instruction is particularly suited to industry and the Services. Instruction there is said to be of a special nature, a matter of training rather than teaching. This is a very dubious distinction. Training once meant nonverbal instruction, usually through the use of training devices, but that is no longer true. Industry and the Services teach many of the things taught in schools and colleges, although the terminal behavior admittedly comes in smaller packages. The important thing is that it can be more easily specified. The traditional distinction comes down to this: when we know what we are doing, we are training; when we do not know what we are doing, we are teaching. Once we have taken the important first step and specified what we want the student to do as the result of having been taught, we can begin to teach in ways with respect to which this outworn distinction is meaningless.

In doing so we need not abandon any of our goals. We must simply define them. Any behavior which can be specified can be programmed. An experimental analysis has much more to offer in this direction than is generally realized. It is far from a crude stimulus-response theory and is not committed to rote memorizing or the imparting of monolithic, unchanging truth. It has as much to say about solving problems, inductive or deductive reasoning, and creative insight as about learning facts. We have only to define these terms and a technology of teaching becomes applicable. Specification, of course, is only the first step. Good programs must be constructed. At the moment only a few people have the necessary competence, but this is one of the points at which educational reform should start. Scientists, as subject matter specialists, must play a major role.

Classroom Management

Another important application is in classroom management. The teacher who understands reinforcement and is aware of the reinforcing effects of his own behavior can control his class. Those who are interested in the intellectual side of education have tended to neglect classroom discipline, but at great cost. Much of the time of both student and teacher is now spent in ways which contribute little to education. Students who are particularly hard to manage are often in effect abandoned, although there are probably geniuses among them.

It is here that the transition from older aversive practices is most conspicuous. Many educational reformers—Admiral Rickover among them, for example—look with envy on the disciplined classroom of European schools. It appears to be a background against which the student uses his time most profitably. But punitive techniques have objectionable by-products, and we are led to explore the possibility of creating an equally favorable background in other ways. Special skills on the part of the teacher are needed, not only in maintaining discipline but in teaching the kinds of nonverbal behavior which figure so prominently in such fields as laboratory experimentation. It is a particularly difficult problem because we must compete with other contingencies in the student's daily life involving sex, aggression, competitive sports, and so on. Too often the good student is simply one who is unsuccessful in other ways. He responds to our instructional contingencies only because he has not come under the control of others. The result, of course, is poor selection. We need to recruit scientists from those who could be successful in any walk of life. To do so we must take the design of classroom behavior seriously.

Effective instructional contingencies in the classroom are more difficult to arrange than those in programmed instruction. Curiously enough, the nature of the enterprise is clearest with respect to a more difficult kind of student. Institutions for the care of autistic or retarded children and training schools for juvenile delinquents have begun to make effective use of operant conditioning. Because of either their heredity or their early environments, certain people do not respond well to normal contingencies of reinforcement. A special environment must be constructed. Ogden R. Lindsley has called it a prosthetic environment. Eyeglasses and hearing aids are prosthetic devices which compensate for defective sense organs, as crutches and artificial limbs compensate for defective organs of response. A prosthetic environment compensates for a defective sensitivity to contingencies of reinforcement. In such an environment reinforcers may be clarified; many institutions reinforce students with tokens, exchangeable for other reinforcers such as sweets or privileges, which can be made contingent on behavior in conspicuous ways. Many of these defective people will always require a prosthetic environment, but others can be brought under the control of the reinforcers in daily life, such as personal approval or the successful manipulation of the physical environment, and can thus be prepared for life outside an institution.

Contrived reinforcers intended to have a similar effect are by no means new in education. Marks, grades, diplomas, honors, and prizes, not to mention the teacher's personal approval, are seldom the natural consequences of the student's behavior. They are used on the assumption that natural consequences will not induce the student to learn. Several objections may be leveled against them. In the first place, as conditioned reinforcers they are likely to lose their power. This is even true of personal reinforcers if they are not genuine. When our telephone says to us, "I'm sorry. The number you have reached is not in service at this time," we may respond at first to the "I'm sorry" as if it were spoken, say, by a friend. Eventually, we may stop to ask, "*Who* is sorry?" and look forward to the day when machines will be permitted to behave like machines. The computers used in computer-aided instruction are particularly likely to "get personal" in this way. They call the young student by name and type out exclamations of delight at his progress. But the natural consequences which made these expressions reinforcing in the first place are not forthcoming, and the effects extinguish. What is not so obvious is that personal approval may be equally spurious. George Bernard Shaw is responsible for a principle which may be stated in this way: never strike a child except in anger. A complementary principle in the classroom is this: never admire a student except when he is behaving admirably. Contrived admiration is self-defeating.

But the objection to grades, prizes, and synthetic personal approval is not that they are contrived, but that the contingencies in which they are used are bad. An experimental analysis is most valuable at just this point. To bring a class under control, the teacher must begin by making available reinforcers explicitly contingent on the desired behavior. Some students may need reinforcers as conspicuous as tokens or points exchangeable for goods or privileges. Money is a token reinforcer which should not be ruled out of account. (It could solve the high school dropout problem if the contingencies were right.) But once a classroom has been brought under control, a teacher must move to more subtle contingencies and eventually to those inherent in the everyday physical and social environment of the student.

Techniques of reinforcement are now available which can replace the aversive techniques which have dominated education for thousands of years. We can have students who pay attention not because they are afraid of the consequences if they do not, or because they are attracted by fascinating if often meretricious features, but because paying attention has proved to be worthwhile. We can have students who are interested in their work not because work has been chosen which is interesting or because its relation to interesting things has been stressed, but because the complex behavior we call taking an interest has been abundantly reinforced. We can have students who learn not because they will be punished for not learning, but because they have begun to feel the natural advantages of knowledge over ignorance. We can have students who will continue to behave effectively after instruction has ceased because the contingencies which have been used by their teachers find counterparts in daily life.

Above all, we can have dedicated students who will become dedicated men and women. Many interesting aspects of human behavior, often attributed to something called motivation, are the results of various schedules of reinforcement [4] to which almost no attention has been given in educational theory. A common criticism of programmed instruction, for example, is that frequent reinforcement leaves the student unprepared for a world in which reinforcers may be scarce, and this would be true if the possibility were neglected. But programming techniques are available which permit us to sustain the behavior of the student even when reinforcers are very rare indeed. One of the most powerful schedules, the so-called variable-ratio schedule, is characteristic of all gambling systems. The gambler cannot be sure the next play will win, but a certain mean ratio of plays to wins is maintained by the system. A high ratio will not take control if it is encountered without preparation, because any available behavior will extinguish during a long run, but a low ratio will be effective and can be "stretched" as the behavior builds up. This is the way a dishonest gambler hooks his victim. At first the victim is permitted to win fairly often, but as the probability that he will continue to play increases, the ratio is increased. Eventually he continues to play when he is not winning at all. The power of the schedule is most obvious when it produces a pathological gambler, but pigeons, rats, monkeys, and other lowly organisms have become pathological gamblers on the same schedule.

And so have scientists. The prospector, the explorer, the investigator, the experimenter—all meet with success on a variable-ratio schedule. The dedicated scientist continues to work even though the ratio of responses to reinforcement is very high, but he would not have become a dedicated scientist if he had started at that ratio. It would not be correct to say that we can always arrange a program which starts with frequent successes and leads inevitably to a high ratio, but at least we know the kind of schedule needed. In any case, the extraordinary effects of scheduled reinforcements

[4] See, for example, pages 132–134.

should not be overlooked. In designing a laboratory course, for example, if we keep an eye on the student's successes and particularly on the way in which they are spaced, we are more likely to produce a student who not only knows how to conduct experiments but shows an uncontrollable enthusiasm for doing so.

The new materials which have been made available for teaching science in high school are genuinely exciting, but the fact remains that classroom practice has not really changed very much. The forces which make practices traditional make them easy to transmit to new teachers. The relations between student and teachers demanded by such practices arouse no anxiety. The practices can be justified to parents, policy-makers, supporters of education, and students themselves. They call for no extensive changes in administration. And of course they have their occasional successes—particularly with good students or in the hands of good teachers. All this favors the *status quo*.

The change which is needed must overcome many handicaps. Much more is known about the basic processes of learning and teaching than is generally realized, but we need to know still more. What is known has not yet been put to use very effectively. The design and construction of methods and materials is a difficult enterprise which demands a kind of specialist who is, at the moment, in short supply. New practices need to be thoroughly tested. And when, at last, we have devised more effective methods, we must convince educators that they should be used. Extensive administrative changes must be made. (The changes required simply to permit the individual student to progress at his own rate are prodigious.) Teachers need to be retrained as skillful behavioral engineers. The common complaint that new materials do not work because the teachers are incompetent is not only unfair, it shows a failure to recognize another point at which the improvement of teaching might begin. Materials are good only if they can be used by available teachers. It is quite possible that materials can be designed which will permit teachers to teach well even in fields in which they have no special competence.

The Improvement of Teaching

Scientists are wary of being asked about their "values." They hesitate to speak of progress because they are likely to be asked, "Progress toward what?" They are uneasy in suggesting improvements. "Improvements in what sense?" The current fashion is to speak only of educational *innovation*. All that is claimed for a new practice is that it is new. We need a much more positive attitude. The efficiency of current methods of teaching is deplorably low. The change which occurs in a student as the result of spending one day in high school is discouragingly small. We need to improve education in the simple sense of making it possible to teach more in the same time and with the same effort on the part of teacher and student. It is a difficult assignment—possibly as difficult, say, as the control of population or resolving the threat of nuclear war, but there is no more important problem facing America today because its solution will advance all other solutions.

It is the sort of challenge that scientists are accustomed to accept. They, above all others, should appreciate the need to define objectives—to know, in this instance, what it means to teach science. They should be quick to recognize the weaknesses of casual experience and of folk wisdom based on that experience. They, above all others, should know that no enterprise can improve itself to any great extent without analyzing its basic processes. They should be best able to gage the importance of science in the immediate and distant future and therefore the extent of the disaster which will follow if we fail to recruit for science large numbers of our most intelligent and dedicated men and women. It is no time for half-hearted measures. The improvement of teaching calls for the most powerful methods which science has to offer.

Contingency Management
in the Classroom

Why do students go to school? Why do they behave themselves in class? Why do they study and learn and remember? These are important questions, but they are seldom asked—possibly because we are not proud of the answers. Whether we like it or not, most students still come to school, behave themselves, and study in order to avoid the consequences of not doing so. True, most teachers have abandoned the birch rod (though its return is called for in some quarters), but there are many ingenious, less violent replacements. Violent or not, punitive methods have serious consequences, among them truancy, apathy, resentment, vandalism, and ultimately an anti-intellectualism which includes an unwillingness to support education. These are the great problems of the educational establishment, and they can be traced in large part to the techniques of the establishment itself.

Few teachers are happy about punitive methods (most of them would like to be friends with their students), but alternatives have seldom proved fruitful. Simply to abandon punishment and allow students to do as they please is to abandon the goals of education. A "free school" was recently described in a newspaper article as follows:

> The middle school classroom I saw was full of children working in an endless variety of subjects, the life cycle of the beetle, action painting, physical properties of water, mathematics (by choice), making dressing-up clothes, writing poetry. Some of them wandered up and started a conversation. They were confident and articulate. I was asked to join various games, give an honest opinion on a painting, listen to poetry. Ten year old Michael is writing poetry nearly all the time now. . . . Another child is coaxing a woodworm out of a piece of rotting wood.

From *Education*, 1969, *90*, 93–100.

271

It is no doubt an attractive picture—until we start to think about what a school is for.

Men have been dreaming of the permissive or free school for at least two hundred years. The idea first appeared in close association with the idea of political freedom, and one man—Jean Jacques Rousseau—was largely responsible for both. He has been credited with inspiring not only the French Revolution but, in his great work *Émile*, a revolution of perhaps comparable magnitude in education. He was interested, quite justly, in abolishing the punitive methods of his time, and so were the disciples who followed him—Pestalozzi, Froebel and his kindergarten, Montessori, John Dewey, and (*ad absurdum*) Neill with his Summerhill.

With Rousseau the proposal was clearly a dream, for Émile was an imaginary student with, as we now know, imaginary learning processes. When Pestalozzi tried Rousseau's principles on his own child, he came to grief. And, sooner or later, the dream is almost always followed by a rude awakening. Secondary schools are founded by well-intentioned people who want their students to be free, but the schools. grow steadily more disciplined as the exigencies of teaching make themselves felt. When prospective parents begin to ask "How many of your students go on to college?" and "What colleges do they go to?" the goal of the free student is abandoned. Courses show the same pattern. Language instruction begins painlessly with the direct method, but sooner or later the student will be found memorizing vocabulary lists and grammatical paradigms. And one of the freedoms enjoyed by the students in Summerhill was the freedom to treat their fellows punitively.

Occasionally the dream comes true. In any generation there are a few outstanding teachers, just as there are a few outstanding artists, writers, executives, and personalities in films and television. There are also many exceptional students—students who scarcely need to be taught at all. An outstanding teacher and a few good students compose a picture that we should all like to copy, but it is not a model for the teaching of ordinary students by ordinary teachers.

Nor can we replace punishment simply by telling our students about long-term advantages. We make a great deal of the "dollar value" of an education (conveniently overlooking the fact that truck drivers and carpenters make as much as most teachers), but the ultimate consequences of an education are too remote to have any important effect on the student as he reads a textbook or listens to a lecture. The gold stars, marks, grades, honors, promotion, and prizes which we think of as alternatives to punitive sanctions also lack a necessary immediacy. Nor can we solve the problem by bringing real life into the classroom so that students will come into contact with things which are naturally rewarding, for we cannot find interesting things relevant to everything we want to teach. "Real life" philosophies of education have also meant the abandonment of important goals.

All these measures fail because they do not give the student adequate reasons for studying and learning. Punishment gave him a reason (we can say that for it), but if we are to avoid unwanted by-products, we must find nonpunitive forms. It is not an impossible assignment. The "reasons" why men behave are to be found among the consequences of their behavior —what, to put it roughly, they "get out of behaving in given ways." And these have been carefully studied. Behavior which acts upon the environment to produce consequences—"operant" behavior—has been experimentally analyzed in great detail. Certain kinds of consequences called reinforcers (among them the things the layman calls rewards) are made contingent upon what an organism is doing and upon the circumstances under which it is doing it. Changes in behavior are then observed.

The contingencies, rather than the reinforcers, are the important things. It has long been obvious that men act to achieve pleasure and avoid pain (at least most of the time), but the fact to be emphasized is what they are doing at the moment they achieve these results. Special equipment is used to arrange so-called "contingencies of reinforcement" (and if teaching can be defined as the expediting of learning, then this equipment is a kind of teaching machine). The complexity of the equipment to be found in hundreds of laboratories throughout the world is not a bad indicator of the complexity of the contingencies now under investigation. Few people outside the field are aware of how far the analysis has gone. As more and more complex contingencies have been arranged, it has been possible to study more and more complex kinds of behavior, including behavior once attributed to higher mental processes.

An application to education was inevitable, but it has not been unopposed. The fact that much of the early work involved the behavior of lower animals such as rats and pigeons has often been held against it. But man is an animal, although an extraordinarily complex one, and shares many basic behavioral processes with other species. Human behavior must nevertheless be studied in its own right, and human subjects are in fact now commonly used in experimental analyses. When comparable contingencies of reinforcement can be arranged, they yield comparable results; but the contingencies to which the human organism can adjust are extraordinarily complex. Efforts currently under analysis have the subtlety, variety, and intricacy which characterize human behavior in the world at large.

That the methods of an experimental analysis of operant behavior are appropriate to human subjects is confirmed by the success with which they have been put to work in practical ways. Psychotherapy, for example, has undergone an important change. A recent book by Ayllon and Azrin, *The Token Economy,* shows how a hospital for psychotics can be converted into a community in which patients care for themselves and their possessions, avoid trouble with their associates, and (within the limits imposed by their illness) enjoy life. Such an arrangement of contingencies of reinforcement has been called a "prosthetic" environment. Like eye glasses, hearing aids, and artificial limbs, it permits people to behave successfully in spite of defects. In the psychotic the defect is often an insensitivity to contingencies of reinforcements.

The principles of operant conditioning were first applied to education in programmed instruction. The step-by-step shaping of complex behavior was first demonstrated in an experimental analysis, and the technique is probably still best seen in experiments with animals. A hungry pigeon, for example, can be induced through reinforcement with food to respond in specified ways. Quite complex forms of behavior can be generated, often with surprising speed, through a series of stages leading to the terminal specifications. One actually "sees learning take place," and the visibility is important. When a teacher can bring about conspicuous changes in behavior, changes which do not need to be confirmed by a statistical treatment of test scores, he knows immediately what he has done, and he is then most likely to learn to teach effectively. Traditional research in learning has seldom been very useful in education, and in part because it has neglected the process of shaping. Subjects have been plunged into terminal contingencies and left to struggle toward adequate forms of behavior through "trial and error." (Although shaping is important, it is not always necessary. There are effective ways of evoking complex behavior so that it can be directly reinforced, and there is often a great gain in efficiency. Relevant techniques can also be attributed to the experimental analysis of behavior.)

Programmed instruction has been largely responsible for the current emphasis on behavioral specifications. A program can be written only when certain basic questions have been answered. What is the student to do as the result of having been taught? To say that a program is to "impart knowledge," "train rational powers," or "make students creative" is not to identify the changes which are actually to be brought about. Something more specific is needed to design effective programmed contingencies (as it is needed in order to teach well in the classroom). We do not teach the skills students are said to display when they behave skillfully, we teach skillful behavior. We do not impart knowledge, we generate behavior said to show the possession of knowledge. We do not improve abilities or strengthen rational powers; we make it more likely that the student will show the behavior from which abilities and powers are inferred. When goals are properly specified, the teacher knows what he is to do and, later, whether he has done it. Behavioral objectives remove much of the mystery from education, and teachers may feel demeaned when their task is reduced to less awesome dimensions. But the loss is more than offset by a greater sense of achievement.

Many early programs were constructed by writers who missed some of the implications of the basic analysis. They were encouraged to do so by educational philosophers who tried to assimilate programming to traditional theories of learning. Programming was said to be simply a matter of proceeding in small steps, of asking the student to master one step before moving on to the next, of arranging steps in a logical sequence with no gaps, and so on. This was true enough, and programs designed on these principles were better than no programs at all, but other points need to be considered. An important example has to do with "motivation."

Studies of operant reinforcement differ from earlier studies of learning by emphasizing the maintenance as well as the acquisition of behavior. Acquisition is the conspicuous change brought about by reinforcement, but the maintenance of behavior in a given state of strength is an equally important effect. A good program reinforces the student abundantly and at just the right times. It shapes new forms of behavior under the control of appropriate stimuli, but the important thing is that it maintains the student's behavior. It holds his attention; it keeps him at work.

Traditional studies of learning have paid little attention to why the student learns, and this has encouraged the belief that men have a natural curiosity or love of learning, or that they naturally want to learn. We do not say that about a pigeon; we say only that under the conditions we have arranged, a pigeon learns. We should say the same thing about human students. Given the right conditions men will learn—not because they want to, but because, as the result of the genetic endowment of the species, contingencies bring about changes in behavior. One of the main differences between a textbook and a program is that a textbook teaches only when students have been given some extraneous reason for studying it. A program contains its own reasons. Fortunately for us all, the human organism is reinforced by many things. Success is one of them. A baby shakes a rattle because the production of noise is reinforcing, and adults put jigsaw puzzles together and work crossword puzzles for no more obvious reason than that they come out right. In a good program the student makes things come out right; he makes things work; he brings order out of chaos. A good program helps him do so. It makes right responses highly probable —just short of telling him what they are. Again the motivational issue may be missed. Many people resist making a student's task easy, and the beginning programmer may find himself unwilling to "give a response away." As a teacher he has felt the need to keep students under aversive control, and he may not yet be fully aware of his power to control them in other ways.

A program is also reinforcing because it clarifies progress. It has a definite size. The student knows when he is half-way through and when he has finished. Because of all this a good program pulls the student forward. He may feel exhausted when he has finished, but he does not need to force himself to work.

There is another problem in education which operant reinforcement helps to solve. In primary and secondary schools (and to some extent at other levels) a teacher not only teaches, he has custody of his students for an appreciable part of the day. Their behavior in the classroom, quite apart from what they are learning, is part of his assignment. Coming to class, behaving well toward other students, attending to the teacher, entering into discussions, studying—these are as essential to education as what is being learned, and here the teacher plays a different role. He is not a source of knowledge or an evaluator of what a student knows; he is in a sense the governor of a community.

It should be a community in which learning takes place expeditiously, and the teacher can meet that assignment if he knows how to use reinforcement. But he must first answer an important question: what reinforcers are available? To put it roughly, what does he possess that his students want? It is often an embarrassing question, but almost never wholly unanswerable. The built-in reinforcers of programmed materials will not suffice, but other things are available.

The physical aspect of a school may or may not be reinforcing, and this will have a bearing on what happens when a student turns a corner and comes in sight of the school. If the building is not attractive, he will be less likely to turn that corner again and may go in some other direction. The appearance of a building is usually beyond the teacher's control, but reinforcing features of a classroom may not be. Business enterprises understand the principle. A well-run store smells good; it is tastefully decorated and pleasantly lighted; there may be music in the background. The behavior of entering the store is therefore reinforced, and customers are more likely to enter it again. To "reduce absenteeism" the teacher should take similar steps to make sure that his students are reinforced when they enter his classroom.

What goes on in the room is also relevant. The aversive techniques of the birch rod or cane are not likely to reinforce coming to school, and students so treated are likely to play truant or become drop-outs when they can legally do so. Social contingencies are important. A child is more likely to come to school if he gets along with his peers and his teacher; he is not likely to come if he is frequently criticized, attacked, or ostracized.

Unfortunately, social contingencies are often hard to arrange. To induce the members of a classroom community to behave well with respect to each other, additional reinforcers may be needed. The teacher may have some control over what food children eat at lunchtime, what supplies they are permitted to use, what privileges they can enjoy (such as access to play areas), whom they may associate with, when they may turn to preferred activities, and what field trips they may take. Personal commendation is often a powerful reinforcer, but a merely synthetic approval or affection has its dangers.

The main problem is to make these reinforcers contingent on the desired behavior. They are often not available on the spur of the moment. The teacher cannot conveniently reinforce a child when he sits quietly by sending him off on a field trip, or when he stops fighting by handing him an ice cream cone. A "generalized reinforcer" is needed—something which is exchangeable for reinforcing things. Money shows the archetypal pattern. We pay people even though at the time they receive our money they are not hungry for the food they will buy with it or in the mood for the film they will use it to go to see. Credit points or tokens can be used as money in the classroom. They are relatively independent of the deprivations which make them reinforcing and of the circumstances under which the things they are exchanged for will be consumed.

In one procedure the behavior of the students is sampled from time to time. A student is chosen with some mechanical system such as spinning a dial or drawing a name from a bowl, and his behavior is sampled for, say, 20 or 30 seconds. He is then told that he has been observed and that he has or has not received a token or credit. A day or two of this is often enough to make a great change: the room grows quiet as the students go to work. Sampling can then become less frequent. Eventually, as the students begin to be reinforced in other ways when they find themselves working more effectively in a quiet room, they will construct their own social contingencies, which may eventually replace those arranged by the teacher.

No one procedure will work well in every classroom, and a certain ingenuity is needed to devise the right system in the right place, but the principle of contingency management is sound and it is proving effective in a rapidly increasing number of experiments. Research conducted in a classroom is not always impressive "statistically," but enough has been done to warrant further experimentation on a broad scale.

There are objections, however, and some of them call for comment. Reinforcement is sometimes called bribery. (To say this is to make a confession: a bribe is paid to induce a person to do something he is for some reason inclined not to do, and it is tragic that we are so ready to see school work in that light.) The point of a bribe is an implied contract ("Do this and I will give you that"), but a contract tends to destroy the effect of a reinforcer. Contingencies of reinforcement are most effective when there is no prior agreement as to terms.

A more valid objection is that contingencies of this sort are artificial. In real life one does not sit quietly in order to take a field trip to the zoo or stop annoying one's neighbor in order to get an ice cream cone. The connection between the behavior and its consequence is contrived. (It is curious that no one raises the same objection with respect to punishment, for there is no natural connection between solving a problem in arithmetic and avoiding the cane. And good marks, promotion, honors, and prizes are not only artificial reinforcers, they are artificially and ineffectively contingent on behavior.) But artificiality is not the issue. We use contrived contingencies to set up behavior which will, we hope, be reinforced naturally under the contingencies of daily life. The problem is to make sure that the behavior we set up will indeed be effective in the world at large.

There have often been great discrepancies between what is taught and what students eventually use. Verbal materials are easily imported into the classroom (in the form of discussions, lectures, and testbooks), and they have often been overemphasized. Students spend a great deal of time answering questions, but answering questions is only a small part of daily life. Nonverbal behavior also needs to be taught. But this does not mean that we should get rid of verbal teaching altogether. The value of verbal programs in such a field as medical school anatomy may well be questioned. Nothing but a cadaver will teach the would-be doctor what the human body is like or permit him to acquire the special behaviors he needs.

One would certainly not want to be operated upon by a surgeon who had merely worked through a programmed text in human anatomy. But there is a great deal to be said for programmed instruction before turning to a cadaver. What one learns in verbal or pictorial form facilitates learning about things themselves. There is nothing unreal about verbal material.

Another objection is that reinforcers in daily life are not always immediate, and that the student must be prepared to behave for the sake of remote consequences. No one is ever actually reinforced by remote consequences, but rather by mediating reinforcers which have acquired their power through some connection with them. Mediating reinforcers can be set up, however, and the student can be taught with available principles and techniques to find or construct them for himself.

A rather similar objection is that in daily life a student is not always reinforced when he behaves, and that he should become accustomed to nonreinforcement. But this is a subject which has been studied with particular care. High levels of activity can be sustained by intermittent reinforcement, particularly if the schedule of reinforcement has been suitably programmed. A gambler is reinforced on what is called a "variable-ratio schedule." It may sustain his behavior to the point at which he loses all his money, but it will not have this effect unless the mean ratio of responses to reinforcements has been extended gradually. Students reinforced on a variable-ratio schedule will show a fantastic dedication if the schedule has been properly programmed. They will work for long periods of time with no reinforcement whatsoever, and are thus well prepared for a world in which reinforcements may indeed be rare.

Current applications of operant conditioning to education are no doubt crude, but they are a beginning, and a beginning must be made. The task is particularly difficult because we must contend with theories and practices which are deeply entrenched. There is nothing very new in prevailing educational theories, and it will be a long time before we can properly estimate the harm they have done. Most teachers today teach essentially as teachers have taught for centuries. The best of them are simply people who have a knack in getting along with others. All this must change, and the change will take time. But we are on the verge of a new educational "method"— a new pedagogy—in which the teacher will emerge as a skilled behavioral engineer. He will be able to analyze the contingencies which arise in his classes, and design and set up improved versions. He will know what is to be done and will have the satisfaction of knowing that he has done it.

The training of a teacher should begin with basic principles. Everyone who intends to be a teacher should have a chance to see learning take place or, better, to produce visible learning himself, as by shaping the behavior of a rat or a pigeon. It is a heartening experience to discover that one can produce behavior of specified topography and bring it under the control of specified stimuli. Some such experience is particularly valuable because the effects of positive reinforcement are somewhat delayed in contrast with punishment, which tends to be used in part just because the results are quick. Laboratory or classroom practice in operant conditioning gives the teacher the confidence he needs to change behavior in less immediate but more effective ways.

It also clarifies the mistakes teachers make when they are careless about reinforcement. Many problems in classroom management arise because the teacher reinforces students when they behave in objectionable ways. For example, the teacher may pay special attention when the student uses obscenities or moves about or talks at inappropriate times. The teacher tends to do so "naturally," and he will be dissuaded from doing so only when the effects of reinforcement have been made clear to him.

An example of the misuse of operant reinforcement in the classroom has been analyzed elsewhere. No matter how bad a teacher may be, he has at least one available reinforcer—dismissing his class. If, near the end of a period, he is free to tell his students that they may leave (if there is no routine signal such as a bell), he can use dismissal as a powerful reinforcer. He should wait until the behavior of the class is as acceptable as it is likely to be and then dismiss. But almost inevitably he will do the wrong thing: he will tend to dismiss the class when trouble is brewing. A surreptitious fight is starting in the back of the room, and so he says "That's enough for today." In doing so he gets out of today's trouble, but a fight will be more likely to start tomorrow.

Another natural mistake is to shift to a more interesting topic when a discussion or lecture appears to be boring the listener. A more interesting topic is a reinforcer, and by shifting to it we reinforce expressions of boredom. Another common mistake is to distract the attention of a likely troublemaker. A distraction is by definition reinforcing, and it reinforces what the student is doing when we distract him—namely, making trouble. We make mistakes of this sort until a greater familiarity with the principles of reinforcement induces us to stop.

In England a "black paper" recently criticized the educational establishment. It performed a service by bringing into the open a growing dissatisfaction with current methods. We have been too ready to assume that the student is a free agent, that he wants to learn, that he knows best what he should learn, that his attitudes and tastes should determine what he learns, and that he should discover things for himself rather than learn what others have already discovered. These principles are all wrong, and they are responsible for much of our current trouble. Education is primarily concerned with the transmission of a culture—with teaching new members what others have already learned—and it is dangerous to ignore this function. But the black paper took the wrong line by suggesting that we return to what are essentially punitive techniques. The teacher must regain control, but he must do so in ways which are not only more efficient but free of the undesirable by-products of older practices. Progressive education made an honest effort to dispense with punishment, but it never found the alternatives it needed. Effective alternatives are now available.

The classroom is a kind of community, with a culture of its own, and we can design such a culture while respecting the standards of dignity and freedom which we value in the world at large. The assignment is important because in the long run education must take its place as the method of choice in all forms of social control. It must replace the aversive sanctions of government, both international and domestic, and the unduly compelling economic sanctions of business and industry. The by-products are all too visible today, in part because of the violence with which they are attacked. The sooner we find effective means of social control, the sooner we shall produce a culture in which man's potential is fully realized. Those who are genuinely trying to improve education have, therefore, a frightening responsibility, but they face a tremendous opportunity.

PART IV

The Analysis and Management of Neurotic, Psychotic, and Retarded Behavior

A Critique of Psychoanalytic Concepts and Theories

At the annual meeting of the American Association for the Advancement of Science in 1953, the Institute for the Unity of Science, the Philosophy of Science Association, and Section L of AAAS sponsored a series of papers subsequently published in The Scientific Monthly *and later under the editorship of Philipp G. Frank in* The Validation of Scientific Theories *(Boston, 1956). The present paper appeared in* The Scientific Monthly *in November, 1954, and is reprinted here by permission of the editor.*

Freud's great contribution to Western thought has been described as the application of the principle of cause and effect to human behavior. Freud demonstrated that many features of behavior hitherto unexplained—and often dismissed as hopelessly complex or obscure—could be shown to be the product of circumstances in the history of the individual. Many of the causal relationships he so convincingly demonstrated had been wholly unsuspected—unsuspected, in particular, by the very individuals whose behavior they controlled. Freud greatly reduced the sphere of accident and caprice in our considerations of human conduct. His achievement in this respect appears all the more impressive when we recall that he was never able to appeal to the quantitative proofs characteristic of other sciences. He carried the day with sheer persuasion—with the massing of instances and the delineation of surprising parallels and analogies among seemingly diverse materials.

This was not, however, Freud's own view of the matter. At the age of 70 he summed up his achievement in this way: "My life has been aimed at one goal only: to infer or guess how the mental apparatus is constructed and what forces interplay and counteract in it." [1] It is difficult to describe the mental apparatus he refers to in noncontroversial terms, partly because Freud's conception changed from time to time and partly because its very nature encouraged misinterpretation and misunderstanding. But it is perhaps not too wide of the mark to indicate its principal features as follows: Freud conceived of some realm of the mind, not necessarily having physical extent, but nevertheless capable of topographic description and of subdivision into regions of the conscious, co-conscious, and unconscious.

---

[1] Jones, E. *Life and Work of Sigmund Freud.* New York: Basic Books, 1953, Vol. 1.

Within this space, various mental events—ideas, wishes, memories, emotions, instinctive tendencies, and so on—interacted and combined in many complex ways. Systems of these mental events came to be conceived of almost as subsidiary personalities and were given proper names: the Id, the Ego, and the Superego. These systems divided among themselves a limited store of psychic energy. There were, of course, many other details.

No matter what logicians may eventually make of this mental apparatus, there is little doubt that Freud accepted it as real rather than as a scientific construct or theory. One does not at the age of 70 define the goal of one's life as the exploration of an explanatory fiction. Freud did not use his "mental apparatus" as a postulate system from which he deduced theorems to be submitted to empirical check. If there was any interaction between the mental apparatus and empirical observations, it took the form of modifying the apparatus to account for newly discovered facts. To many followers of Freud the mental apparatus appears to be equally as real, and the exploration of such an apparatus is similarly accepted as the goal of a science of behavior. There is an alternative view, however, which holds that Freud did not discover the mental apparatus but rather invented it, borrowing part of its structure from a traditional philosophy of human conduct but adding many novel features of his own devising.

There are those who will concede that Freud's mental apparatus was a scientific construct rather than an observable empirical system but who, nevertheless, attempt to justify it in the light of scientific method. One may take the line that metaphorical devices are inevitable in the early stages of any science and that although we may look with amusement today upon the "essences," "forces," "phlogistons," and "ethers" of the science of yesterday, these nevertheless were essential to the historical process. It would be difficult to prove or disprove this. However, if we have learned anything about the nature of scientific thinking, if mathematical and logical researches have improved our capacity to represent and analyze empirical data, it is possible that we can avoid some of the mistakes of adolescence. Whether Freud could have done so is past demonstrating, but whether we need similar constructs in the future prosecution of a science of behavior is a question worth considering.

Constructs are convenient and perhaps even necessary in dealing with certain complicated subject matters. As Frenkel-Brunswik shows,[2] Freud was aware of the problems of scientific methodology and even of the metaphorical nature of some of his own constructs. When this was the case, he justified the constructs as necessary or at least highly convenient.

---

[2] Frenkel-Brunswik, E. P. *Scientific Monthly*, 1954, 79, 293.

But awareness of the nature of the metaphor is no defense of it, and if modern science is still occasionally metaphorical, we must remember that theorywise it is also still in trouble. The point is not that metaphor or construct is objectionable but that particular metaphors and constructs have caused trouble and are continuing to do so. Freud recognized the damage worked by his own metaphorical thinking, but he felt that it could not be avoided and that the damage must be put up with. There is reason to disagree with him on this point.

Freud's explanatory scheme followed a traditional pattern of looking for a cause of human behavior inside the organism. His medical training supplied him with powerful supporting analogies. The parallel between the excision of a tumor, for example, and the release of a repressed wish from the unconscious is quite compelling and must have affected Freud's thinking. Now, the pattern of an inner explanation of behavior is best exemplified by doctrines of animism, which are primarily concerned with explaining the spontaneity and evident capriciousness of behavior. The living organism is an extremely complicated system behaving in an extremely complicated way. Much of its behavior appears at first blush to be absolutely unpredictable. The traditional procedure had been to invent an inner determiner, a "demon," "spirit," "homunculus," or "personality" capable of spontaneous change of course or of origination of action. Such an inner determiner offers only a momentary explanation of the behavior of the outer organism, because it must, of course, be accounted for also, but it is commonly used to put the matter beyond further inquiry and to bring the study of a causal series of events to a dead end.

Freud, himself, however, did not appeal to the inner apparatus to account for spontaneity or caprice because he was a thoroughgoing determinist. He accepted the responsibility of explaining, in turn, the behavior of the inner determiner. He did this by pointing to hitherto unnoticed external causes in the environmental and genetic history of the individual. He did not, therefore, need the traditional explanatory system for traditional purposes; but he was unable to eliminate the pattern from his thinking. It led him to represent each of the causal relationships he had discovered as a series of three events. Some environmental condition, very often in the early life of the individual, leaves an effect upon the inner mental apparatus, and this in turn produces the behavioral manifestation or symptom. Environmental event, mental state or process, behavioral symptom—these are the three links in Freud's causal chain. He made no appeal to the middle link to explain spontaneity or caprice. Instead he used it to bridge the gap in space and time between the events he had proved to be causally related.

A possible alternative, which would have had no quarrel with established science, would have been to argue that the environmental variables leave *physiological* effects which may be inferred from the behavior of the individual, perhaps at a much later date. In one sense, too little is known at the moment about physiological processes to make them useful in a legitimate way for this purpose. On the other hand, too much is known of them, at least in a negative way. Enough is known of the nervous system to place certain dimensional limits upon speculation and to clip the wings of explanatory fictions. Freud accepted, therefore, the traditional fiction of a mental life, avoiding an out-and-out dualism by arguing that eventually physiological counterparts would be discovered. Quite apart from the question of the existence of mental events, let us observe the damage which resulted from this maneuver.

We may touch only briefly upon two classical problems which arise once the conception of a mental life has been adopted. The first of these is to explain how such a life is to be observed. The introspective psychologists had already tried to solve this problem by arguing that introspection is only a special case of the observation upon which all science rests and that man's experience necessarily stands between him and the physical world with which science purports to deal. But it was Freud himself who pointed out that not all of one's mental life was accessible to direct observation— that many events in the mental apparatus were necessarily inferred. Great as this discovery was, it would have been still greater if Freud had taken the next step, advocated a little later by the American movement called Behaviorism, and insisted that conscious, as well as unconscious, events were inferences from the facts. By arguing that the individual organism simply reacts to its environment, rather than to some inner experience of that environment, the bifurcation of nature into physical and psychic can be avoided.[3]

A second classical problem is how the mental life can be manipulated. In the process of therapy, the analyst necessarily acts upon the patient only through physical means. He manipulates variables occupying a position in the first link of Freud's causal chain. Nevertheless, it is commonly assumed that the mental apparatus is being directly manipulated. Sometimes it is argued that processes are initiated within the individual himself, such as those of free association and transference, and that these in turn act directly

---

[3] Although it was Freud himself who taught us to doubt the face value of introspection, he appears to have been responsible for the view that another sort of direct experience is required if certain activities in the mental apparatus are to be comprehended. Such a requirement is implied in the modern assertion that only those who have been psychoanalyzed can fully understand the meaning of transference or the release of a repressed fear.

upon the mental apparatus. But how are these mental processes initiated by physical means? The clarification of such a causal connection places a heavy and often unwelcome burden of proof upon the shoulders of the dualist.

The important disadvantages of Freud's conception of mental life can be described somewhat more specifically. The first of these concerns the environmental variables to which Freud so convincingly pointed. The cogency of these variables was frequently missed because the variables were transformed and obscured in the course of being represented in mental life. The physical world of the organism was converted into conscious and unconscious experience, and these experiences were further transmuted as they combined and changed in mental processes. For example, early punishment of sexual behavior is an observable fact which undoubtedly leaves behind a changed organism. But when this change is represented as a state of conscious or unconscious anxiety or guilt, specific details of the punishment are lost. When, in turn, some unusual characteristic of the sexual behavior of the adult individual is related to the supposed guilt, many specific features of the relationship may be missed which would have been obvious if the same features of behavior had been related to the punishing episode. Insofar as the mental life of the individual is used as Freud used it to represent and to carry an environmental history, it is inadequate and misleading.

Freud's theory of the mental apparatus had an equally damaging effect upon his study of behavior as a dependent variable. Inevitably, it stole the show. Little attention was left to behavior per se. Behavior was relegated to the position of a mere mode of expression of the activities of the mental apparatus or the symptoms of an underlying disturbance. Among the problems not specifically treated in the manner which was their due, we may note five.

1. The nature of the act as a unit of behavior was never clarified. The simple *occurrence* of behavior was never well represented. "Thoughts" could "occur" to an individual; he could "have" ideas according to the traditional model; but he could "have" behavior only in giving expression to these inner events. We are much more likely to say that "the thought occurred to me to ask him his name" than that "the act of asking him his name occurred to me." It is the nature of thoughts and ideas that they occur to people, but we have never come to be at home in describing the emission of behavior in a comparable way. This is especially true of verbal behavior. In spite of Freud's valuable analysis of verbal slips and of the techniques of wit and verbal art, he rejected the possibility of an analysis of verbal behavior in its own right rather than as the expression of ideas,

feelings, or other inner events, and therefore missed the importance of this field for the analysis of units of behavior and the conditions of their occurrence.

The behavioral nature of perception was also slighted. To see an object as an object is not mere passive sensing; it is an act, and something very much like it occurs when we see an object although no object is present. Fantasy and dreams were for Freud not the perceptual *behavior* of the individual but pictures painted by an inner artist in some atelier of the mind which the individual then contemplated and perhaps then reported. This division of labor is not essential when the behavioral component of the act of seeing is emphasized.

2. The dimensions of behavior, particularly its dynamic properties, were never adequately represented. We are all familiar with the fact that some of our acts are more likely to occur upon a given occasion than others. But this likelihood is hard to represent and harder to evaluate. The dynamic changes in behavior which are the first concern of the psychoanalyst are primarily changes in probability of action. But Freud chose to deal with this aspect of behavior in other terms—as a question of "libido," "cathexis," "volume of excitation," "instinctive or emotional tendencies," "available quantities of psychic energy," and so on. The delicate question of how probability of action is to be quantified was never answered, because these constructs suggested dimensions to which the quantitative practices of science in general could not be applied.

3. In his emphasis upon the genesis of behavior, Freud made extensive use of processes of learning. These were never treated operationally in terms of changes in behavior but rather as the acquisition of ideas, feelings, and emotions later to be expressed by, or manifested in, behavior. Consider, for example, Freud's own suggestion that sibling rivalry in his own early history played an important part in his theoretical considerations as well as in his personal relationships as an adult.

An infant brother died when Freud himself was only 1½ years old, and as a young child Freud played with a boy somewhat older than himself and presumably more powerful, yet who was, strangely enough, in the nominally subordinate position of being his nephew. To classify such a set of circumstances as sibling rivalry obscures, as we have seen, the many specific properties of the circumstances themselves regarded as independent variables in a science of behavior. To argue that *what was learned* was the effect of these circumstances upon unconscious or conscious aggressive tendencies or feelings of guilt works a similar misrepresentation of the dependent variable. An emphasis upon behavior would lead us to inquire into the specific acts plausibly assumed to be engendered by these childhood episodes. In very specific terms, how was the behavior of the young Freud *shaped* by the special reinforcing contingencies arising from the presence of a younger child in the family, by the death of that child, and by later association with an older playmate who nevertheless occupied a subordinate family position? What did the young Freud *learn to do* to achieve parental attention under these difficult circumstances? How did he avoid aversive consequences? Did he exaggerate any illness? Did he feign illness? Did he make a conspicuous display of behavior which brought commendation? Was such behavior to be found in the field of physical prowess or intellectual endeavor? Did he learn to engage in behavior which would in turn increase the repertoires available to him to achieve commendation? Did he strike or otherwise injure young children? Did he learn to injure them verbally by teasing? Was he punished for this, and if so, did he discover other forms of behavior which had the same damaging effect but were immune to punishment?

We cannot, of course, adequately answer questions of this sort at so late a date, but they suggest the kind of inquiry which would be prompted by a concern for the *explicit shaping of behavioral repertoires* under childhood circumstances. What has survived through the years is not aggression and guilt, later to be manifested in behavior, but rather patterns of behavior themselves. It is not enough to say that this is "all that is meant" by sibling rivalry or by its effects upon the mental apparatus. Such an expression obscures, rather than illuminates, the nature of the behavioral changes taking place in the childhood learning process. A similar analysis could be made of processes in the fields of motivation and emotion.

4. An explicit treatment of behavior as a datum, of probability of response as the principal quantifiable property of behavior, and of learning and other processes in terms of changes of probability is usually enough to avoid another pitfall into which Freud, in common with his contemporaries, fell. There are many words in the layman's vocabulary which suggest the activity of an organism yet are not descriptive of behavior in the narrower sense. Freud used many of these freely—for example, the individual is said to discriminate, remember, infer, repress, decide, and so on. Such terms do not refer to specific acts. We say that a man discriminates between two objects when he behaves differently with respect to them; but discriminating is not itself behavior. We say that he represses behavior which has been punished when he engages in other behavior *just because* it displaces the punished behavior; but repressing is not action. We say that he decides upon a course of conduct either when he enters upon one course to the

exclusion of another, or when he alters some of the variables affecting his own behavior in order to bring this about; but there is no other "act of deciding." The difficulty is that when one uses terms which suggest an activity, one feels it necessary to invent an actor, and the subordinate personalities in the Freudian mental apparatus do, indeed, participate in just these activities rather than in the more specific behavior of the observable organism.

Among these activities are conspicuous instances involving the process of self-control—the so-called "Freudian mechanisms." These need not be regarded as activities of the individual or any subdivision thereof—they are not, for example, what happens when a skillful wish evades a censor—but simply as ways of representing relationships among responses and controlling variables. I have tried to demonstrate this by restating the Freudian mechanisms without reference to Freudian theory [in *Science and Human Behavior*].

5. Since Freud never developed a clear conception of the behavior of the organism and never approached many of the scientific problems peculiar to that subject matter, it is not surprising that he misinterpreted the nature of the observation of one's own behavior. This is admittedly a delicate subject, which presents problems which no one, perhaps, has adequately solved. But the act of self-observation can be represented within the framework of physical science. This involves questioning the reality of sensations, ideas, feelings, and other states of consciousness which many people regard as among the most immediate experiences of their life. Freud himself prepared us for this change. There is, perhaps, no experience more powerful than that which the mystic reports of his awareness of the presence of God. The psychoanalyst explains this in other ways. He himself, however, may insist upon the reality of certain experiences which others wish to question. There are other ways of describing what is actually seen or felt under such circumstances.

Each of us is in particularly close contact with a small part of the universe enclosed within his own skin. Under certain limited circumstances, we may come to react to that part of the universe in unusual ways. But it does not follow that that particular part has any special physical or nonphysical properties or that our observations of it differ in any fundamental respect from our observations of the rest of the world. I have tried to show elsewhere [4] how self-knowledge of this sort arises and why it is likely to be subject to limitations which are troublesome from the point of view of physical science. Freud's representations of these events was a particular

[4] See page 416 below.

personal contribution influenced by his own cultural history. It is possible that science can now move on to a different description of them. If it is impossible to be wholly nonmetaphorical, at least we may improve upon our metaphors.

The crucial issue here is the Freudian distinction between the conscious and unconscious mind. Freud's contribution has been widely misunderstood. The important point was not that the individual was often unable to describe important aspects of his own behavior or identify important causal relationships but that his ability to describe them was irrelevant to the occurrence of the behavior or to the effectiveness of the causes. We begin by attributing the behavior of the individual to events in his genetic and environmental history. We then note that because of certain cultural practices, the individual may come to describe some of that behavior and some of those causal relationships. We may say that he is conscious of the parts he can describe and unconscious of the rest. But the act of self-description, as of self-observation, plays no part in the determination of action. It is superimposed upon behavior. Freud's argument that we need not be aware of important causes of conduct leads naturally to the broader conclusion that awareness of cause has nothing to do with causal effectiveness.

In addition to these specific consequences of Freud's mental apparatus in obscuring important details among the variables of which human behavior is a function and in leading to the neglect of important problems in the analysis of behavior as a primary datum, we have to note the most unfortunate effect of all. Freud's methodological strategy has prevented the incorporation of psychoanalysis into the body of science proper. It was inherent in the nature of such an explanatory system that its key entities would be unquantifiable in the sense in which entities in science are generally quantifiable, but the spatial and temporal dimensions of these entities have caused other kinds of trouble.

One can sense a certain embarrassment among psychoanalytic writers with respect to the primary entities of the mental apparatus. There is a predilection for terms which avoid the embarrassing question of the spatial dimensions, physical or otherwise, of terms at the primary level. Although it is occasionally necessary to refer to mental events and their qualities and to states of consciousness, the analyst usually moves on in some haste to less committal terms such as *forces, processes, organizations, tensions, systems,* and *mechanisms.* But all these imply terms at a lower level. The notion of a conscious or unconscious "force" may be a useful metaphor, but if this is analogous to force in physics, what is the analogous mass which is analogously accelerated? Human behavior is in a state of flux and undergoing changes which we call "processes," but what is changing in what direction when we speak of, for example, an affective process? Psychological "organizations," "mental systems," "motivational interaction" —these all imply arrangements or relationships among *things,* but what are the things so related or arranged? Until this question has been answered the problem of the dimensions of the mental apparatus can scarcely be approached. It is not likely that the problem can be solved by working out independent units appropriate to the mental apparatus, although it has been proposed to undertake such a step in attempting to place psychoanalysis on a scientific footing.

Before one attempts to work out units of transference or scales of anxiety, or systems of mensuration appropriate to the regions of consciousness, it is worth asking whether there is not an alternative program for a *rapprochement* with physical science which would make such a task unnecessary. Freud could hope for an eventual union with physics or physiology only through the discovery of neurological mechanisms which would be the analogs of, or possibly only other aspects of, the features of his mental apparatus. Since this depended upon the prosecution of a science of neurology far beyond its current state of knowledge, it was not an attractive future. Freud appears never to have considered the possibility of bringing the concepts and theories of a psychological science into contact with the rest of physical and biological science by the simple expedient of an operational definition of terms. This would have placed the mental apparatus in jeopardy as a life goal, but it would have brought him back to the observable, manipulable, and preeminently physical variables with which he was in the last analysis dealing.

Psychology in the Understanding of Mental Disease

Two conferences on the "Etiology of Mental Disease" were held in 1953 and 1954 under the auspices of the Committee on Public Health of the New York Academy of Medicine. The present paper was given at the second conference. It appears in Integrating the Approaches to Mental Disease *(New York, Paul B. Hoeber, Inc., 1957) and is reprinted here by permission. That volume also reports much of the discussion which followed the papers. My own scattered comments reveal a concern with the operational definition of terms in the field of mental disease later clarified in the paper on page 303. A sample is included at the end of the following paper.*

Any survey of the contributions which psychology can make to our understanding of mental disease will depend upon how psychology is defined. In practice, the methods and concepts of all four of the disciplines represented at this Conference overlap extensively. Narrowly considered, however, the special province of psychology may be taken to be the description of the behavior of the individual as a whole and the explanation of that behavior in terms of environmental factors and conditions. More specifically, psychology is concerned with recording and measuring human behavior and its various aspects, and with relating the quantities so measured to variables in the past and current environment. Many psychologists, of course, have broader interests. In addition to forces which are currently acting upon the organism, or have acted upon it in the past, they may be concerned with variables in its genetic history, the physiology of its parts, or, at the other extreme, its social environment or cultural history. A narrower delineation of the field is, though arbitrary, desirable for our present purposes.

Mental disease appears to refer to modes of behavior which are troublesome or dangerous either to the individual himself or to others. Behavior may be troublesome or dangerous by its very nature or because of the circumstances under which it occurs. It is not strictly correct to describe such behavior as "atypical," since extreme or unrepresentative values of many properties of behavior do not always present problems appropriately described as the result of disease. Genius is atypical but, presumably, healthy. It is probably also not of any great value to characterize troublesome or dangerous behavior as "nonadaptive," or as violating some principle of "homeostasis" or "equilibrium." The problems of mental disease arise when an individual shows behavior which, because of its character or the circumstances under which it appears, causes trouble. One problem is to explain this behavior, and another is to change it.

One contribution which experimental psychology has to offer, by virtue of its methods and concepts, is a precise description of the behavior under examination. Psychological techniques are peculiarly designed to provide the clearest possible record of behavioral manifestations, together with a rigorous demonstration of relations to causal factors. The behavior of the mentally diseased is often so obviously troublesome or dangerous that precise measurement is felt to be unnecessary, but it is possible that such behavior differs from what might be called normal merely by occupying an extreme position on a continuum. Lesser conditions, not so easily detected, may offer a clue to the causal factors involved. Further advances in the study of the mentally diseased may create a demand for the type of description which can be established only by more careful measurement.

In other words, the first question to which psychology may address itself is, What *is* neurotic, psychotic, or defective behavior? We cannot answer this with a logical definition of terms. The question is more specific. Given an agreed-upon example of neurotic, psychotic, or defective behavior, what are its significant properties? The commoner manifestations of mental disease may not at the present time require detailed description, but an eventual account of these phenomena will almost certainly need to lean upon the methods and terms of a science primarily concerned with the behavior of the whole organism.

Among the special topics to which psychology has addressed itself, for example, is the *sensory control* of behavior. Gross instances of hallucinations, anesthesias, confusions, or defective categorizations can often be accepted as symptoms of mental disease without further inquiry, but a comprehensive account of such phenomena, which would relate them to "normal" manifestations, requires the techniques of sensory psychology.

Psychology has also been especially concerned with *motor behavior*. The study of gross instances of paralysis, ataxia, loss of skill, or confusion may not require the precise techniques of the laboratory, but here again a full description of these "symptoms" may.

Emotional behavior is also a subject to which psychology has given considerable attention. The emotional behavior of the mentally diseased is, again, often so gross that no appeal is made to the methods of the laboratory. But as further precision in characterizing abnormal behavior is required, and as the experimental study of emotion progresses, the psychological characterization of the emotional pattern of the psychotic should become more important.

Motivation has only recently been studied on a substantial scale in the case of human subjects, but much has been learned from the study of animals with respect to the effects of deprivation, satiation, and aversive stimulation. Here again the extreme conditions manifested by the mentally diseased—behaviors which suggest excessive deprivation, or complete satiation, or a failure to avoid or escape from powerfully aversive conditions— may seem to make the precise methods of experimental psychology irrelevant, but an improved account of the psychotic condition must eventually be based upon the relationships demonstrated in such a science.

Lastly, in the field of *learning,* quantitative properties of processes have been demonstrated against which the unusual conditions of the mentally diseased must eventually be evaluated. Many deficiencies in the field of learning are at the present time measured indirectly through intelligence tests, but methods which are more appropriate to a laboratory science are available. The speed with which behavior is acquired in conditioning, the complexity of the behavior which may be so acquired, the rate at which such behavior will be extinguished, and the precision with which behavior may be brought under stimulus control, all enter into many of the characteristics of mental disease. Although a gross effect, such as a conspicuous loss of memory, may not at the moment require precise measurement, an eventual detailed account of the nature of such a difficulty may need to appeal to the methods and results of the experimental laboratory.

Of special importance in the field of mental disease are many forms of behavior resulting from the use of punishment as a measure of control. It is now clear that in punishing a response, we do not simply lower the probability that it will be emitted. Punishment acts by letting up certain aversive conditions from which the organism may escape, or which it may avoid, through many different types of behavior. Among such avoidance or escape responses are frequently found the troublesome or dangerous responses characteristic of mental disease.

The methods and concepts of experimental psychology which are likely to be useful in the precise description of the behavior characteristic of mental disease cannot be described in detail. The present point is simply that, among the four disciplines here represented,[1] it is primarily experimental psychology which has concerned itself with the problem of describing and explaining the behavior of the intact organism in the above sense. The

[1] The conference at which this paper was given began with statements from four points of view: organic, psychological, psychodynamic, and psychosocial.

advantage which psychology has gained from the laboratory control of the variables it has studied should be emphasized, even though it may reasonably be objected that the variables so far manipulated are by no means comprehensive or entirely representative.

These are not, strictly speaking, contributions to the etiology of mental disease but merely to the investigation of that etiology. In exploring the *causes* of the behavior characteristic of mental disease, the technical contributions of psychology are frequently joined with the methods and concepts of other disciplines. For example, to investigate *hereditary factors* in the causation of mental disease, we must combine the methods and concepts of genetics with those of experimental psychology. Similarly, if we are to investigate *organic causes,* we need to combine the methods and terms of physiology and experimental psychology. Much the same relation prevails in the study of endocrinological and pharmacological effects. In each case the psychologist is reaching beyond the variables which are usually taken to be characteristic of his special field. His peculiar contribution is to provide, so to speak, a baseline upon which the effect of genetic, organic, and other variables may be observed.

Causal factors important in understanding mental disease are, however, to be found among the independent variables to which the psychologist characteristically turns. An excessive emotional condition, a dangerous mode of escape from anxiety, a troublesome preoccupation with sex, or an excessive enthusiasm for gambling may be nothing more than extreme cases of the effects of environmental conditions. These aspects of the personal history and the current environment of the individual are commonly taken to be in the realm of psychology and within reach of the psychologist's techniques. Modes of behavior characteristic of mental disease may be simply the result of a history of reinforcement, an unusual condition of deprivation or satiation, or an emotionally exciting circumstance. Except for the fact that they are troublesome or dangerous, they may not be distinguishable from the rest of the behavior of the individual. Insofar as this is the case, the etiology of mental disease and the possibility of analysis and therapy lie within the field of psychology proper. (At this point an overlap with psychodynamics is obvious. The distinction between the psychological and psychodynamic view is not basically a distinction in subject matter or in the range of factors studied. The distinction is primarily one of method, and it is possible that these two fields will eventually fuse or at least become very closely associated.)

Recent work in the field of learning has enabled the psychologist to achieve an extensive control over the behavior of an organism, and to bring this behavior under the control of complex environmental conditions. By manipulating the event called a reinforcement, it is possible not only to shape up many novel forms of behavior but also to sustain almost any given level of activity for long periods of time. In the field of Pavlovian conditioning, comparable advances have been made in the understanding of the origins of emotional patterns. It is reasonable to suppose that such an experimental science will eventually produce a technology capable of modifying and sustaining any given pattern of behavior almost at will. Suppose it can be shown that an organism with a given genetic history and a given organic condition can be induced to engage in the kinds of behavior characteristic of mental disease through the manipulation of environmental variables. Then in order to demonstrate one type of cause of mental disease, it will remain only to show that comparable environmental variables *could* have been operative upon a given person showing neurotic, psychotic, or defective characteristics. Another technological extension of such an experimental science would be to change the behavior of the mentally diseased, in the direction usually referred to as therapy, through the arrangement of environmental variables.

If experimental psychology continues in its current direction, it may reasonably be expected to show how some of the behavioral characteristics of mental disease can be generated and how they can be corrected. By appealing only to environmental variables (while assuming a given set of genetic and organic variables), psychology may make this contribution entirely within its own traditional field. That there are etiological factors lying beyond this field is doubtless true. Here psychology can make only the kind of co-operative contribution previously described. A certain practical hierarchy of causes may, however, be pointed out. Although genetic and organic factors can be efficiently evaluated only by holding environmental factors constant, and although environmental factors can be correctly evaluated only against a stable genetic and organic condition, it is probably a useful practice to explore environmental factors first to see whether any behavioral manifestations remain to be attributed to genetic and organic causes.

Summary

In a narrow, though traditional sense, psychology is concerned with describing and measuring the behavior of the individual and with relating that behavior to environmental factors. The techniques and concepts which it has developed for this purpose may contribute to the study of the etiology of mental disease by providing a more precise characterization of the forms of behavior at issue. The contributions of psychology in this respect will become more important when the gross disorders which first attract our attention are no longer adequate in characterizing a diseased condition. The methods and concepts of experimental psychology are required in the investigation of genetic, physiological, endocrinological, and pharmacological factors in the causation of neurotic and psychotic behavior, although the methods and techniques of other disciplines are here also required. Some etiological factors are to be found within the narrower province of psychology itself. Some of the *emotional* and *motivational* conditions which are taken to be symptoms of mental disease may be nothing more than extreme values of the effects of variables encountered in the analysis and control of the normal organism. Behavior which is so troublesome or dangerous as to be said to characterize mental disease may also simply be *learned*—that is, it may be the product of reinforcing contingencies which affect the organism according to the learning processes encountered in the behavior of the normal individual. It is a reasonable expectation that a developing experimental psychology will find itself increasingly more effective in producing behavior which would be said to reflect mental disease, and in changing the behavior of the actually mentally diseased in the direction known as therapy—and all of this by manipulating environmental variables traditionally assigned to the field of psychology. In this latter approach to the problem of the causation of mental disease, it is clear that psychology and psychodynamics overlap, these two fields being distinguished not in terms of subject matter or the causal factors to which appeal is made, but only in technique—a distinction which may be lost as the two sciences are further developed.

The following comment on some remarks of Dr. Franz Alexander was made at the conference at which the preceding paper was given.

Dr. Alexander has developed a theory of knowledge with the intention, I think, of justifying analytic practices and theories. It is a theory of knowledge which has very deep historical and traditional philosophical roots. He seems to be willing to base the matter eventually on a pragmatic test. We cannot ask any more than that. I am perfectly willing to let him or anyone who so desires use that conception of knowledge to show how useful it is. However, he does seem to imply that it is the only theory or interpretation of human knowledge, and that alternative views will necessarily miss something which is fundamental and particularly important.

The notion that knowledge consists of sense impressions and concepts derived from sense impressions was, of course, the view of British empiricism and is still held by many people. But others, including myself, believe that it is incapable of representing human knowledge adequately. Even a simple idea is not, as Locke supposed, an assemblage of sensory materials in response to stimulation. To suppose that physical knowledge exists in the mind of a physicist as psychic or mental material—as the way he looks at the world—seems to me quite absurd. At no time is a physical theory a psychic event in the sense of an image or sensation.

To say that physics always gets back to sense impression is simply to say that the organism is in contact with the environment only through its sense organs—a very obvious axiom. But the organism does more than soak up the environment. It reacts with respect to the environment, and throughout its lifetime it learns more and more varied ways of reacting. An alternative conception of knowledge, which many of us hold, is that knowledge is action rather than sensing, and that a formulation of knowledge should be in terms of behavior. It is true that we may be aware of our own behavior in the sense that we can see ourselves seeing something. Some of the time we know when we are reacting to the world around us, but, as Freud pointed out, at other times we do not know. When we do know, we are reacting to ourselves as we react to the world about us.

The notion of knowledge as response is useful in enabling us to formulate the assembled knowledge of physics in terms of the equations and laws which comprise the verbal behavior of the scientist, rather than his mental states. It also gives a much more plausible view of the insight which is apparently so useful to the analyst. We acquire the vocabulary which describes our own behavior under great difficulty. The verbal community which can easily teach a child to distinguish colors, for example, cannot with the same technique teach him to distinguish aches, pains, feelings, and emotions. As physical states in the individual, these are a part of the physical world, but the individual himself has a special connection with them. My aching tooth is mine in a very real sense because none of you can possibly get nerves into it, but that does not make it different in nature from the ceiling light which we all react to in more or less the same way. As a result of this physical privacy, the subjective vocabulary, such as was used by introspective psychology and seems to be used today by some analysts, has limitations in precision which no one has been able to surmount.

When the analyst states that he can predict what a patient is going to do, I accept the fact that he can make that prediction. But I challenge the statement that he does it by experiencing the same sensations or feelings. I do not see any distinction between predicting what an individual is going to do and predicting what, let us say, a sailboat is going to do. A person who is familiar with a sailboat and knows how it will take the waves has a high predictive knowledge of how to handle the tiller. That seems to me to be parallel to what the skilled analyst does in knowing what to expect and what to do next in the course of an analysis. We do not need to assume that the skillful sailor must be experiencing something which the boat is experiencing. It is obvious that he is not. The analysts have tended to conceptualize certain ways of dealing with the behavior of themselves and their patients which may be convenient or inconvenient, but need not be evaluated accordingly.

Those of us who work with verbal behavior per se, rather than with the expression of meanings, become suspicious of efforts to improve vocabularies for talking about what is going on inside the individual. It will be recalled that the old introspective psychologist had a trained observer, but it is now clear that in training him the psychologist was definitely shaping the way in which the observer reacted to stimuli and was to some extent creating the very data which he was trying to collect. Something of the same sort may very well happen in the training analysis. It is necessary to be on guard lest the interchange between the patient and the therapist result in building up a very particular vocabulary which will lead to quite spurious results.

Several experiments are now in the literature in which an interviewer has skillfully shaped, by very slight reinforcements and punishments, the verbal behavior of the person being interviewed. It is fairly easy to get another person onto an arbitrarily chosen topic during a conversation by showing attention when the topic is being approached and inattention when it is being left. The same process could generate a misleading community of vocabulary in the personal interaction between two people.

What Is Psychotic Behavior?

A scientific program on "Newer Aspects of the Theory, Etiology, and Treatment of the Psychoses" marked the opening of the Renard Hospital, a psychiatric unit of the Washington University School of Medicine and the Barnes and Affiliated Hospitals, in St. Louis on October 10, 1955. As part of that program this paper was addressed primarily to psychiatrists and others concerned with mental health. The analysis, particularly as represented by the four figures and the accompanying text, has proved useful in a broader context. In characterizing the traditional method of describing and explaining behavior and suggesting a more profitable operational definition of common psychological terms, the paper amplifies points made in "The operational analysis of psychological terms" (page 416).

Since my field of specialization lies some distance from psychiatry, it may be well to begin with credentials. The first will be negative. In the sense in which my title is most likely to be understood, I am wholly unqualified to discuss the question before us. The number of hours I have spent in the presence of psychotic people (assuming that I am myself sane) is negligible compared with what many of you might claim, and the time I have spent in relevant reading and discussion would suffer equally from the same comparison. I am currently interested in some research on psychotic subjects, to which I shall refer again later, but my association with that program in no way qualifies me as a specialist.

Fortunately, I am not here to answer the question in that sense at all. A more accurate title would have been "What is *behavior?*—with an occasional reference to psychiatry." Here I will list such positive credentials as seem appropriate. I have spent a good share of my professional life in the experimental analysis of the behavior of organisms. Almost all my subjects have been below the human level (most of them rats or pigeons) and all, so far as I know, have been sane. My research has not been designed to test any theory of behavior, and the results cannot be evaluated in terms of the statistical significance of such proofs. The object has been to discover the functional relations which prevail between measurable aspects of behavior and various conditions and events in the life of the organism. The success of such a venture is gauged by the extent to which behavior can, as a result of the relationships discovered, actually be predicted and controlled. Here we have, I think, been fortunate. Within a limited experimental arrangement, my colleagues and I have been able to demonstrate a lawfulness in behavior which seems to us quite remarkable. In more recent research it has been possible to maintain—actually, to sharpen—this degree of lawfulness while slowly increasing the complexity of the behavior studied. The extent of the prediction and control which have been achieved is evident not only in "smoothness of curves" and uniformity of results from individual to individual or even species to species, but in the practical uses which are already being made of the techniques—for example, in providing baselines for the study of pharmacological and neurological variables, or in converting a lower organism into a sensitive psychophysical observer.

Although research designed in this way has an immediate practical usefulness, it is not independent of one sort of theory. A primary concern has been to isolate a useful and expedient measure. Of all the myriad aspects of behavior which present themselves to observation, which are worth watching? Which will prove most useful in establishing functional relations? From time to time many different characteristics of behavior have seemed important. Students of the subject have asked how well organized behavior is, how well adapted it is to the environment, how sensitively it maintains a homeostatic equilibrium, how purposeful it is, or how successfully it solves practical problems or adjusts to daily life. Many have been especially interested in how an individual compares with others of the same species or with members of other species in some arbitrary measure of the scope, complexity, speed, consistency, or other property of behavior. All these aspects may be quantified, at least in a rough way, and any one may serve as a dependent variable in a scientific analysis. But they are not all equally productive. In research which emphasizes prediction and control, the topography of behavior must be carefully specified. Precisely what is the organism doing? The most important aspect of behavior so described is its probability of emission. How likely is it that an organism will engage in behavior of a given sort, and what conditions or events change this likelihood? Although probability of action has only recently been explicitly recognized in behavior theory, it is a key concept to which many classical notions, from reaction tendencies to the Freudian wish, may be reduced. Experimentally we deal with it as the *frequency* with which an organism behaves in a given way under specified circumstances, and our methods are designed to satisfy this requirement. Frequency of response has proved to be a remarkably sensitive variable, and with its aid the exploration of causal factors has been gratifyingly profitable.

One does not engage in work of this sort for the sheer love of rats or pigeons. As the medical sciences illustrate, the study of animals below the level of man is dictated mainly by convenience and safety. But the primary object of interest is always a man. Such qualifications as I have to offer in approaching the present question spring about equally from the experimental work just mentioned and from a parallel preoccupation with human behavior, in which the principles emerging from the experimental analysis have been tested and put to work in the interpretation of empirical facts. The formal disciplines of government, education, economics, religion, and psychotherapy, among others, together with our everyday experience with men, overwhelm us with a flood of facts. To interpret these facts with the formulation which emerges from an experimental analysis has proved to be strenuous but healthful exercise. In particular, the nature and function of *verbal* behavior have taken on surprisingly fresh and promising aspects when reformulated under the strictures of such a framework.

In the long run, of course, mere interpretation is not enough. If we have achieved a true scientific understanding of man, we should be able to prove this in the actual prediction and control of his behavior. The experimental practices and the concepts emerging from our research on lower organisms have already been extended in this direction, not only in the experiments on psychotic subjects already mentioned, but in other promising areas. The details would take us too far afield, but perhaps I can indicate my faith in the possibilities in a single instance by hazarding the prediction that we are on the threshold of a revolutionary change in methods of education, based not only upon a better understanding of learning processes, but upon a workable conception of knowledge itself.

Whether or not this brief personal history seems to you to qualify me to discuss the question before us, there is no doubt that it has created a high probability that I will do so, as shown by the fact that I am here. What I have to say is admittedly methodological. I can understand a certain impatience with such discussion particularly when, as in the field of psychiatry, many pressing problems call for action. The scientist who takes time out to consider human nature when so many practical things need to be done for human welfare is likely to be cast in the role of a Nero, fiddling while Rome burns. (It is quite possible that the fiddling referred to in this archetypal myth was a later invention of the historians, and that in actual fact Nero had called in his philosophers and scientists and was discussing "the fundamental nature of combustion" or "the epidemiology of conflagration.") But I should not be here if I believed that what I have to say is remote from practical consequences. If we are now entering an era of research in psychiatry which is to be as extensive and as productive as other types of medical research, then a certain detachment from immediate problems, a fresh look at human behavior in general, a survey of applicable formulations, and a consideration of relevant methods may prove to be effective practical steps with surprisingly immediate consequences.

The study of human behavior is, of course, still in its infancy, and it would be rash to suppose that anyone can foresee the structure of a well-developed and successful science. Certainly no current formulation will seem right fifty years hence. But although we cannot foresee the future clearly, it is not impossible to discover in what direction we are likely to change. There are obviously great deficiencies in our present ways of thinking about men; otherwise we should be more successful. What are they, and how are they to be remedied? What I have to say rests upon the assumption that the behavior of the psychotic is simply part and parcel of human behavior, and that certain considerations which have been emphasized by the experimental and theoretical analysis of behavior in general are worth discussing in this special application.

It is important to remember that I am speaking as an experimental scientist. A conception of human behavior based primarily on clinical information and practice will undoubtedly differ from a conception emanating from the laboratory. This does not mean that either is superior to the other, or that eventually a common formulation will not prove useful to both. It is possible that questions which have been suggested by the exigencies of an experimental analysis may not seem of first importance to those of you who are primarily concerned with human behavior under therapy. But as psychiatry moves more rapidly into experimental research and as laboratory results take on a greater clinical significance, certain problems in the analysis of behavior should become common to researcher and therapist alike, and should eventually be given common and cooperative solutions.

The study of behavior, psychotic or otherwise, remains securely in the company of the natural sciences so long as we take as our subject matter the observable activity of the organism, as it moves about, stands still, seizes objects, pushes and pulls, makes sounds, gestures, and so on. Suitable instruments will permit us to amplify small-scale activities as part of the same subject matter. Watching a person behave in this way is like watching any physical or biological system. We also remain within the framework of the natural sciences in explaining these observations in terms of external forces and events which act upon the organism. Some of these are to be

found in the hereditary history of the individual, including his membership in a given species as well as his personal endowment. Others arise
from the physical environment, past or present. We may represent the
situation as in Figure 1. Our organism emits the behavior we are to account

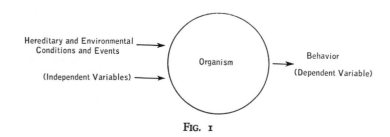

FIG. 1

for, as our dependent variable, at the right. To explain this, we appeal to
certain external, generally observable, and possibly controllable hereditary
and environmental conditions, as indicated at the left. These are the
independent variables of which behavior is to be expressed as a function.
Both input and output of such a system may be treated with the accepted
dimensional systems of physics and biology. A complete set of such relations would permit us to predict and, insofar as the independent variables
are under our control, to modify or generate behavior at will. It would
also permit us to *interpret* given instances of behavior by inferring plausible variables of which we lack direct information. Admittedly the data
are subtle and complex, and many relevant conditions are hard to get at,
but the program as such is an acceptable one from the point of view of
scientific method. We have no reason to suppose in advance that a complete account cannot be so given. We have only to try and see.

It is not, however, the subtlety or complexity of this subject matter which
is responsible for the relatively undeveloped state of such a science. Behavior has seldom been analyzed in this manner. Instead, attention has been
diverted to activities which are said to take place within the organism. All
sciences tend to fill in causal relationships, especially when the related
events are separated by time and space. If a magnet affects a compass needle
some distance away, the scientist attributes this to a "field" set up by the
magnet and reaching to the compass needle. If a brick falls from a chimney, releasing energy which was stored there, say, a hundred years ago
when the chimney was built, the result is explained by saying that the brick

has all this time possessed a certain amount of "potential energy." In order to fill such spatial and temporal gaps between cause and effect, nature has from time to time been endowed with many weird properties, spirits, and essences. Some have proved helpful and have become part of the subject matter of science, especially when identified with events observed in other ways. Others have proved dangerous and damaging to scientific progress. Sophisticated scientists have usually been aware of the practice and alert to its dangers. Such inner forces were, indeed, the hypotheses which Newton refused to make.

Among the conditions which affect behavior, hereditary factors occupy a primary position, at least chronologically. Differences between members of different species are seldom, if ever, disputed, but differences between members of the same species, possibly due to similar hereditary factors, are so closely tied up with social and ethical problems that they have been the subject of seemingly endless debate. In any event, the newly conceived organism begins at once to be influenced by its environment; and when it comes into full contact with the external world, environmental forces assume a major role. They are the only conditions which can be changed so far as the individual is concerned. Among these are the events we call "stimuli," the various interchanges between organism and environment such as occur in breathing or eating, the events which generate the changes in behavior we call emotional, and the coincidences between stimuli or between stimuli and behavior responsible for the changes we call learning. The effects may be felt immediately or only after the passage of time—perhaps of many years. Such are the "causes"—the independent variables —in terms of which we may hope to explain behavior within the framework of a natural science.

In many discussions of human behavior, however, these variables are seldom explicitly mentioned. Their place is taken by events or conditions within the organism for which they are said to be responsible (see Figure 2). Thus, the species status of the individual is dealt with as a set of instincts, not simply as patterns of behavior characteristic of the species, but as biological drives. As one text puts it, "instincts are innate biological forces, urges, or impulsions driving the organism to a certain end." The individual genetic endowment, if not carried by body type or other observable physical characteristic, is represented in the form of inherited traits or abilities, such as temperament or intelligence. As to the environmental variables, episodes in the past history of the individual are dealt with as memories and habits, while certain conditions of interchange between organism and environment are represented as needs or wants. Certain

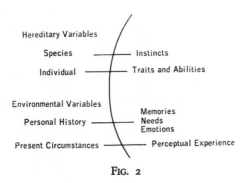

Hereditary Variables
Species —— Instincts
Individual —— Traits and Abilities

Environmental Variables
Personal History —— Memories / Needs / Emotions
Present Circumstances —— Perceptual Experience

FIG. 2

inciting episodes are dealt with as emotions, again in the sense not of patterns but of active causes of behavior. Even the present environment as it affects the organism is transmuted into "experience," as we turn from what is the case to what "seems to be" the case to the individual.

The same centripetal movement may be observed on the other side of the diagram (see Figure 3). It is rare to find behavior dealt with as a subject matter in its own right. Instead it is regarded as evidence for a mental life, which is then taken as the primary object of inquiry. What the individual does—the topography of his behavior—is treated as the functioning of one or more personalities. It is clear, especially when personalities are multiple, that they cannot be identified with the biological organism as such, but are conceived of, rather, as inner behavers of doubtful status and dimensions. The act of behaving in a given instance is

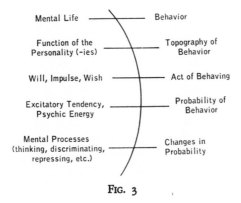

Mental Life —— Behavior
Function of the Personality (-ies) —— Topography of Behavior
Will, Impulse, Wish —— Act of Behaving
Excitatory Tendency, Psychic Energy —— Probability of Behavior
Mental Processes (thinking, discriminating, repressing, etc.) —— Changes in Probability

FIG. 3

neglected in favor of an impulse or wish, while the probability of such an act is represented as an excitatory tendency or in terms of psychic energy. Most important of all, the changes in behavior which represent the fundamental behavioral processes are characterized as mental activities —such as thinking, learning, discriminating, reasoning, symbolizing, projecting, identifying, and repressing.

The relatively simple scheme shown in the first figure does not, therefore, represent the conception of human behavior characteristic of most current theory. The great majority of students of human behavior assume that they are concerned with a series of events indicated in the expanded diagram of Figure 4. Here the hereditary and environmental conditions are assumed to generate instincts, needs, emotions, memories, habits, and so on, which in turn lead the personality to engage in various activities characteristic of the mental apparatus, and these in turn generate the observable behavior of the organism. All four stages in the diagram are accepted as proper objects of inquiry. Indeed, far from leaving the inner events to other specialists while confining themselves to the end terms, many psychologists and psychiatrists take the mental apparatus as their primary subject matter.

Perhaps the point of my title is now becoming clearer. Is the scientific study of behavior—whether normal or psychotic—concerned with the behavior of the observable organism under the control of hereditary and environmental factors, or with the functioning of one or more personalities engaged in a variety of mental processes under the promptings of instincts, needs, emotions, memories, and habits? I do not want to raise the question of the supposed *nature* of these inner entities. A certain kinship between such an explanatory system and primitive animism can scarcely be missed,

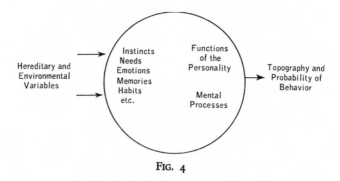

FIG. 4

but whatever the historical sources of these concepts, we may assume that they have been purged of dualistic connotations. If this is not the case, if there are those who feel that psychiatry is concerned with a world beyond that of the psychobiological or biophysical organism, that conscious or unconscious mind lacks physical extent, and that mental processes do not affect the world according to the laws of physics, then the following arguments should be all the more cogent. But the issue is not one of the nature of these events, but of their usefulness and expedience in a scientific description.

It can scarcely be denied that the expansion of subject matter represented by Figure 4 has the unfortunate effect of a loss of physical status. This is more than a question of prestige or "face." A subject matter which is unquestionably part of the field of physics and biology has been relinquished for one of doubtful characteristics. This cannot be corrected merely by asserting our faith in the ultimately physical nature of inner processes. To protest that the activities of the conscious and unconscious mind are only in some sense an aspect of the biological functioning of the organism will not answer the practical question. In abandoning the dimensional systems of physics and biology, we abandon the techniques of measurement which would otherwise be a natural heritage from earlier achievements in other sciences. This is possibly an irreparable loss. If we come out flatly for the existence of instincts, needs, memories, and so on, on the one hand, and the mental processes and functions of the personality on the other, then we must accept the responsibility of devising methods of observing these inner events and of discovering dimensional systems according to which they can be measured. The loss of the opportunity to measure and manipulate in the manner characteristic of the physical sciences would be offset only by some extraordinary advantage gained by turning to inner states or conditions.

It is possible, however, to argue that these inner events are merely ways of representing the outer. Many theorists will contend that a habit is only a sort of notation useful in reporting a bit of the history of the individual, just as so-called "mental processes" are ways of talking about changes in behavior. This is a tempting position, for we may then insist that the only dimensional systems required are those appropriate to the terminal events. But if we are to take that line, a great deal still needs to be done to put our house in scientific order. The concepts which one encounters in current behavior theory represent the observable events in an extremely confusing way. Most of them have arisen from theoretical or practical considerations which have little reference to their validity or usefulness as scientific constructs, and they bear the scars of such a history. For example, Freud pointed to important relationships between the behavior of an adult and certain episodes in early childhood, but he chose to bridge the very considerable gap between cause and effect with activities or states of the mental apparatus. Conscious or unconscious wishes or emotions in the adult represent the earlier episodes and are said to be directly responsible for their effect upon behavior. The adult is said, for example, to be suffering from conscious or unconscious anxiety generated when as a child he was punished for aggressive behavior toward a sibling. But many details of the early episode are glossed over (and may, as a result, be neglected) in attributing the disturbances in his behavior to a current anxiety rather than to the earlier punishment. The number of references to anxiety in treatises on behavior must greatly exceed the number of references to punishing episodes, yet we must turn to the latter for full details. If the details are not available, nothing can take their place.

Other kinds of independent variables provide similar examples. Everyone is familiar with the fact that, in general, organisms eat or do not eat depending upon a recent history of deprivation or ingestion. If we can establish that a child does not eat his dinner because he has recently eaten other food, there may seem to be no harm in expressing this by saying that "he is not hungry," provided we explain this in turn by pointing to the history of ingestion. But the concept of hunger represents quite inadequately the many features of schedules of deprivation and other conditions and events which alter the behavior of eating. In the same way the inner surrogates of hereditary variables function beyond the line of duty. We often have no other explanation of a given bit of behavior than that, like other features of anatomy and physiology, it is characteristic of a species; but when we choose instead to attribute this behavior to a set of instincts, we obscure the negative nature of our knowledge and suggest more active causes than mere species status warrants. Similarly, we accept the fact that individuals differ in their behavior, and we may, in some instances, show a relation between aspects of the behavior of successive generations, but these differences and relationships are optimistically misrepresented when we speak of hereditary traits and abilities. Again, the term *experience* incorrectly represents our information about a stimulating field. It has often been observed, for example, that some trivial incident generates a reaction altogether out of proportion to its magnitude. A person seems to be reacting, not to the physical world as such, but to what the world "means to him." Eventually, of course, the effect must be explained—for example, by pointing to some earlier connection with more important events. But whatever the explanation, it is almost certainly not adequately expressed by the notion of a momentary experience. There are obvious difficulties involved in representing a physical environment *plus a personal history* as a current psychological environment alone.

So far as our independent variables are concerned, then, the practice we are examining tends to gloss over many important details and complexities. The conceptual structure conceals from us the inadequacy of our present knowledge. Much the same difficulty is encountered with respect to the dependent variable, when observable behavior takes second place to mental functionings of a personality. Just as the physical environment is transmuted into experience, so physical behavior comes to be described in terms of its purpose or meaning. A man may walk down the street in precisely the same way upon two occasions, although in one instance he is out for exercise and in another he is going to mail a letter. And so it is thought necessary to consider, not the behavior itself, but "what it means" to the behaving individual. But the additional information we are trying to convey is not a property of behavior but of an independent variable. The behavior we observe in the two cases *is* the same. In reading meaning or intention into it, we are speculating about some of its causes. To take another example, it is commonly said that we can "see" aggression. But we "see" it in two steps: (1) we observe the behavior of an organism, and (2) we relate it to observed or inferred variables having to do with injurious consequences and with the kinds of circumstances which make such behavior probable. No behavior is itself aggressive by nature, although some forms of behavior are so often a function of variables which make them aggressive that we are inclined to overlook the inferences involved. Similarly, when we observe two or more behavioral systems in the same individual and attribute them to different personalities, we gain a considerable advantage for certain descriptive purposes. For example, we can then describe oppositions between such systems as we would between different persons. But we have almost certainly suggested a unity which is not justified by the observed systems of behavior, and we have probably made it more difficult to represent the actual extent of any conflicts as well as to explain its origins. And when we observe that the behavior of a person is characterized by a certain responsiveness or probability of responding and speak instead of a given amount of psychic energy, we neglect many details of the actual facts and dodge the responsibility of finding a dimensional system. Lastly, mental processes are almost always conceived of as simpler and more orderly than the rather chaotic material from which they are inferred and which they are used to explain. The "learning process" in experimental psychology, for example, does not give us an accurate account of measured changes in behavior.

We look inside the organism for a *simpler* system, in which the causes of behavior are less complex than the actual hereditary and environmental events and in which the behavior of a personality is more meaningful and orderly than the day-to-day activity of the organism. All the variety and complexity of the input in our diagram seems to be reduced to a few relatively amorphous states, which in turn generate relatively amorphous functions of the personality, which then suddenly explode into the extraordinary variety and complexity of behavior. But the simplification achieved by such a practice is, of course, illusory, for it follows only from the fact that a one-to-one correspondence between inner and outer events has not been demanded. It is just this lack of correspondence which makes such an inner system unsuitable in the experimental analysis of behavior. If "hunger" is something which is produced by certain schedules of deprivation, certain drugs, certain states of health, and so on, and if in turn it produces changes in the probability of a great variety of responses, then it must have very complex properties. It cannot be any simpler than its causes or its effects. If the behavior we observe simply expresses the functioning of a personality, the personality cannot be any simpler than the behavior. If some common learning process is responsible for the changes observed in a number of different situations, then it cannot be any simpler than these changes. The apparent simplicity of the inner system explains the eagerness with which we turn to it, but from the point of view of scientific method it must be regarded as a spurious simplicity, which foreshadows ultimate failure of such an explanatory scheme.

There is another objection. Although speculation about what goes on within the organism seems to show a concern for completing a causal chain, in practice it tends to have the opposite effect. Chains are left incomplete. The layman commonly feels that he has explained behavior when he has attributed it to something in the organism—as in saying "He went *because* he wanted to go," or "He could not work *because* he was worried about his health." Such statements may have value in suggesting the relevance of one set of causes as against another, but they do not give a full explanation until it is explained *why* the person wanted to go, or why he was worried. Frequently this additional step is taken, but perhaps just as often these incomplete explanations bring inquiry to a dead stop.

No matter how we may wish to represent such a sequence of causal events, we cannot satisfy the requirements of interpretation, prediction, or control unless we go back to events acting upon the organism from without

—events, moreover, which are observed as any event is observed in the physical and biological sciences. It is only common sense, therefore, as well as good scientific practice, to make sure that the concepts which enter into a theory of behavior are explicitly and carefully related to such events. What is needed is an operational definition of terms. This means more than simple translation. The operational method is commonly misused to patch up and preserve concepts which are cherished for extraneous and irrelevant reasons. Thus it might be possible to set up acceptable definitions of instincts, needs, emotions, memories, psychic energy, and so on, in which each term would be carefully related to certain behavioral and environmental facts. But we have no guarantee that these concepts will be the most useful when the actual functional relationships are better understood. A more reasonable program at this stage is to attempt to account for behavior without appeal to inner explanatory entities. We can do this within the accepted framework of biology, gaining thereby not only a certain personal reassurance from the prestige of a well-developed science but an extensive set of experimental practices and dimensional systems. We shall be prevented from oversimplifying and misrepresenting the available facts because we shall not transmute our descriptions into other terms. The practical criteria of prediction and control will force us to take into account the complete causal chain in every instance. Such a program is not concerned with establishing the existence of inferred events, but with assessing the state of our knowledge.

This does not mean, of course, that the organism is conceived of as actually empty, or that continuity between input and output will not eventually be established. The genetic development of the organism and the complex interchanges between organism and environment are the subject matters of appropriate disciplines. Some day we shall know, for example, what happens when a stimulus impinges upon the surface of an organism, and what happens inside the organism after that, in a series of stages the last of which is the point at which the organism acts upon the environment and possibly changes it. At that point we lose interest in this causal chain. Some day, too, we shall know how the ingestion of food sets up a series of events, the last of which to engage our attention is a reduction in the probability of all behavior previously reinforced with similar food. Some day we may even know how to bridge the gap between the behavioral characteristics common to parents and offspring. But all these inner events will be accounted for with techniques of observation and measurement appropriate to the physiology of the various parts of the organism, and the account will be expressed in terms appropriate to that subject matter. It would be a remarkable coincidence if the concepts now used to refer inferentially to inner events were to find a place in that account. The task of physiology is not to find hungers, fears, habits, instincts, personalities, psychic energy, or acts of willing, attending, repressing, and so on. Nor is that task to find entities or processes of which all these could be said to be other aspects. Its task is to account for the causal relations between input and output which are the special concern of a science of behavior. Physiology should be left free to do this in its own way. Just to the extent that current conceptual systems fail to represent the relationships between terminal events correctly, they misrepresent the task of these other disciplines. A comprehensive set of causal relations stated with the greatest possible precision is the best contribution which we, as students of behavior, can make in the co-operative venture of giving a full account of the organism as a biological system.

But are we not overlooking one important source of knowledge? What about the direct observation of mental activity? The belief that the mental apparatus is available to direct inspection anticipated the scientific analysis of human behavior by many hundreds of years. It was refined by the introspective psychologists at the end of the nineteenth century into a special theory of knowledge which seemed to place the newly created science of consciousness on a par with natural science by arguing that all scientists necessarily begin and end with their own sensations and that the psychologist merely deals with these in a different way for different purposes. The notion has been revived in recent theories of perception, in which it has been suggested that the study of what used to be called "optical illusions," for example, will supply principles which help in understanding the limits of scientific knowledge. It has also been argued that the especially intimate empathic understanding which frequently occurs in psychotherapy supplies a kind of direct knowledge of the mental processes of other people. Franz Alexander and Lawrence Kubie have argued in this manner in defense of psychoanalytic practices. Among clinical psychologists Carl Rogers has actively defended a similar view. Something of the same notion may underlie the belief that the psychiatrist may better understand the psychotic if, through the use of lysergic acid, for example, he may temporarily experience similar mental conditions.

Whether the approach to human behavior which I have just outlined ignores some basic fact, whether it is unable to take into account the "stubborn fact of consciousness," is part of a venerable dispute which will not be settled here. Two points may be made, however, in evaluating the evidence from direct "introspection" of the mental apparatus. Knowledge is not to be identified with how things look to us, but rather with what we do about them. Knowledge is power because it is action. How the surrounding world soaks into the surface of our body is merely the first chapter of the story and would be meaningless were it not for the parts which follow. These are concerned with behavior. Astronomy is not how the heavens look to an astronomer. Atomic physics is not the physicist's perception of events within the atom, or even of the macroscopic events from which the atomic world is inferred. Scientific knowledge is what people *do* in predicting and controlling nature.

The second point is that knowledge depends upon a personal history. Philosophers have often insisted that we are not aware of a difference until it makes a difference, and experimental evidence is beginning to accumulate in support of the view that we should probably not know anything at all if we were not forced to do so. The discriminative behavior called knowledge arises only in the presence of certain reinforcing contingencies among the things known. Thus, we should probably remain blind if visual stimuli were never of any importance to us, just as we do not hear all the separate instruments in a symphony or see all the colors in a painting until it is worthwhile for us to do so.

Some interesting consequences follow when these two points are made with respect to our knowledge of events within ourselves. That a small part of the universe is enclosed within the skin of each of us, and that this constitutes a private world to which each of us has a special kind of access can scarcely be denied. But the world with which we are in contact does not for that reason have any special physical or metaphysical status. Now, it is presumably necessary to learn to observe or "know" events within this private world just as we learn to observe or "know" external events, and our knowledge will consist of doing something about them. But the society from which we acquire such behavior is at a special disadvantage. It is easy to teach a child to distinguish between colors by presenting different colors and reinforcing his responses as right or wrong accordingly, but it is much more difficult to teach him to distinguish between different aches or pains, since the information as to whether his responses are right or wrong is much less reliable. It is this limited accessibility of the world within the skin, rather than its nature, which has been responsible for so much metaphysical speculation.

Terms which refer to private events tend to be used inexactly. Most of them are borrowed in the first place from descriptions of external events. (Almost all the vocabulary of emotion, for example, has been shown to be metaphorical in origin.) The consequences are well known. The testimony of the individual regarding his mental processes, feelings, needs, and so on, is, as the psychiatrist above all others has insisted, unreliable. Technical systems of terms referring to private events seldom resemble each other. Different schools of introspective psychology have emphasized different features of experience, and the vocabulary of one may occasionally be unintelligible to another. This is also true of different dynamic theories of mental life. The exponent of a "system" may show extraordinary conviction in his use of terms and in his defense of a given set of explanatory entities, but it is usually easy to find someone else showing the same conviction and defending a different and possibly incompatible system. Just as introspective psychology once found it expedient to train observers in the use of terms referring to mental events, so the education of experimental psychologists, educators, applied psychologists, psychotherapists, and many others concerned with human behavior is not always free from a certain element of indoctrination. Only in this way has it been possible to make sure that mental processes will be described by two or more people with any consistency.

Psychiatry itself is responsible for the notion that one need not be aware of the feelings, thoughts, and so on, which are said to affect behavior. The individual often behaves *as if* he were thinking or feeling in a given way although he cannot himself say that he is doing so. Mental processes which do not have the support of the testimony supplied by introspection are necessarily defined in terms of, and measured as, the behavioral facts from which they are inferred. Unfortunately, the notion of mental activity was preserved in the face of such evidence with the help of the notion of an unconscious mind. It might have been better to dismiss the concept of mind altogether as an explanatory fiction which had not survived a crucial test. The modes of inference with which we arrive at knowledge of the unconscious need to be examined with respect to the conscious mind as well. Both are conceptual entities, the relations of which to observed data need to be carefully reexamined.

In the long run the point will not be established by argument, but by the effectiveness of a given formulation in the design of productive research. An example of research on psychotic subjects which emphasizes the end terms in our diagram is the project already mentioned. This is not the place for technical details,[1] but the rationale of this research may be relevant. In

---

[1] Dr. Harry Solomon of the Boston Psychopathic Hospital has served as co-director of the project, although the preceding arguments do not necessarily represent his views. Dr. Ogden R. Lindsley is in immediate charge and responsible for much of the overall experimental design as well as for the actual day-to-day conduct of the experiments. Support has been provided by the Office of Naval Research and by the National Institute of Mental Health. The work is being carried out at the Metropolitan State Hospital in Waltham, Massachusetts, with the cooperation of Dr. William McLaughlin, Superintendent, and Dr. Meyer Asakoff, Director of Research. [See reference on page 158.]

these experiments a patient spends one or more hours daily, alone, in a small pleasant room. He is never coerced into going there and is free to leave at any time. The room is furnished with a chair, and contains a device similar to a vending machine, which can be operated by pushing a button or pulling a plunger. The machine delivers candies, cigarettes, or substantial food, or projects colored pictures on a translucent screen. Most patients eventually operate the machine, are "reinforced" by what it delivers, and then continue to operate it daily for long periods of time—possibly a year or more. During this time the behavior is reinforced on various "schedules"—for example, once every minute or once for every thirty responses—in relation to various stimuli. The behavior is recorded in another room in a continuous curve which is read somewhat in the manner of an electrocardiogram and which permits a ready inspection and measurement of the rate of responding.

The isolation of this small living space is, of course, not complete. The patient does not leave his personal history behind as he enters the room, and to some extent what he does there resembles what he does or has done elsewhere. Nevertheless, as time goes on, the conditions arranged by the experiment begin to compose, so to speak, a special personal history, the important details of which are known. Within this small and admittedly artificial life space, we can watch the patient's behavior change as we change conditions of reinforcement, motivation, and to some extent emotion. With respect to these variables the behavior becomes more and more predictable and controllable or—as characteristic of the psychotic subject—fails to do so in specific ways.

The behavior of the patient may resemble that of a normal human or infrahuman subject in response to similar experimental conditions, or it may differ in a simple quantitative way—for example, the record may be normal except for a lower over-all rate. On the other hand, a performance may be broken by brief psychotic episodes. The experimental control is interrupted momentarily by the intrusion of extraneous behavior. In some cases it has been possible to reduce or increase the time taken by these interruptions, and to determine where during the session they will occur. As in similar work with other organisms, this quantitative and continuous account of the behavior of the individual under experimental control provides a highly sensitive baseline for the observation of the effects of drugs and of various forms of therapy. For our present purposes, however, the important thing is that it permits us to apply to the psychotic a fairly rigorous formulation of behavior based upon much more extensive work under the much more propitious control of conditions obtained with other species. This formulation is expressed in terms of input and output without reference to inner states.

The objection is sometimes raised that research of this sort reduces the human subject to the status of a research animal. Increasing evidence of the lawfulness of human behavior only seems to make the objection all the more cogent. Medical research has met this problem before, and has found an answer which is available here. Thanks to parallel work on animals, it has been possible, in some cases at least, to generate healthier behavior in men, even though at this stage we may not be directly concerned with such a result.

Another common objection is that we obtain our results only through an oversimplification of conditions, and that they are therefore not applicable to daily life. But one always simplifies at the start of an experiment. We have already begun to make our conditions more complex and will proceed to do so as rapidly as the uniformity of results permits. It is possible to complicate the task of the patient without limit, and to construct not only complex intellectual tasks but such interactions beween systems of behavior as are seen in the Freudian dynamisms.

One simplification sometimes complained of is the absence of other human beings in this small life space. This was, of course, a deliberate preliminary measure, for it is much more difficult to control social than mechanical stimulation and reinforcement. But we are now moving on to situations in which one patient observes the behavior of another working on a similar device, or observes that the other patient receives a reinforcement whenever he achieves one himself, and so on. In another case the patient is reinforced only when his behavior corresponds in some way to the behavior of another. Techniques for achieving extraordinarily precise competition and co-operation between two or more individuals have already been worked out with lower organisms, and are applicable to the present circumstances.

This project has, of course, barely scratched the surface of the subject of psychotic behavior. But so far as it has gone, it seems to us to have demonstrated the value of holding to the observable data. Whether or not you will all find them significant, the data we report have a special kind of simple objectivity. At least we can say that this is what a psychotic subject did under these circumstances, and that this is what he failed to do under circumstances which would have a had a different effect had he not been psychotic.

Although we have been able to describe and interpret the behavior observed in these experiments without reference to inner events, such references, are of course, not interdicted. Others may prefer to say that what we are actually doing is manipulating habits, needs, and so on, and observing changes in the structure of the personality, in the strength of the ego, in the amount of psychic energy available, and so on. But the advantage of this over a more parsimonious description becomes more difficult to demonstrate as evidence of the effectiveness of an objective formulation accumulates. In that bright future to which research in psychiatry is now pointing, we must be prepared for the possibility that increasing emphasis will be placed on immediately observable data and that theories of human behavior will have to adjust themselves accordingly. It is not inconceivable that the mental apparatus and all that it implies will be forgotten. It will then be more than a mere working hypothesis to say—to return at long last to my title—that psychotic behavior, like all behavior, is part of the world of observable events to which the powerful methods of natural science apply and to the understanding of which they will prove adequate.

From *Theory and Treatment of the Psychoses: Some Newer Aspects.* F. Glidea, editor. Washington University Studies, 1956. The research described at the end of this article was carried out at the Metropolitan State Hospital at Waltham, Massachusetts. Dr. Harry Solomon, then of the Boston Psychopathic Hospital, collaborated with the author in setting up the laboratory. Dr. Ogden R. Lindsley took immediate charge and was responsible for much of the overall experimental design and the day-to-day conduct of the experiments.

Some Relations Between Behavior Modification and Basic Research

The first scientific laws were probably the rules of craftsmen. In other words, science seems to have emerged from efforts to solve practical problems. There are examples of this in psychology. Binet's invention of a way to place children in schools led to intelligence testing, and the problem of selecting personnel in industry led to other measures in what later became the psychology of individual differences. Clinical problems led Freud to invent the mental apparatus of psychoanalytic theory. Even the physiological psychology of Fechner and Wundt arose from efforts to solve certain philosophical problems concerning the nature of knowledge and the relation between mind and body. As science advances, however, the direction changes. Subject matters become too complex to yield to lay wisdom or rules of thumb, and it is the scientist who sees the useful implications of his discoveries. Most improvements in technology now come from what is essentially basic research. Behavior modification is an example. Its origins lay in a relatively "pure" experimental analysis.

The shaping of behavior through a step-by-step approximation to a final topography is a case in point. As a distinction began to be made between operant and respondent conditioning, or between emitted and elicited behavior, the role of the controlling stimulus changed, and problems arose. The experimenter had no control over the first instance of an operant response; he could only wait for it to appear. It seemed to follow that complex forms of behavior which seldom if ever occurred were essentially out of reach of operant conditioning. But the possibility remained that the component parts of a complex pattern might occur separately and that larger patterns might be constructed bit by bit.

From *Cumulative Record* (3rd ed.). New York: Appleton-Century-Crofts, 1972, pp. 276–282.

An early effort to shape complex behavior was suggested by an experiment in which a chimpanzee used poker chips to operate a sort of vending machine.[1] It was implied by some writers that in doing so the chimpanzee demonstrated certain higher mental processes—in which, for example, the poker chip served a symbolic function. To show that operant conditioning could explain the behavior, I conditioned a rat to behave in a similar way. As originally reported in *The Behavior of Organisms,*[2] "every step in the process had to be worked out through a series of approximations, since the component responses were not in the original repertoire of the rat." Following the practice in early experiments on operant conditioning, and in other experiments on learning at that time, I made reinforcers contingent on behavior by constructing mechanical systems. To begin with, a number of marbles were strewn on the floor of the rat's cage. The sides of the cage were clear of the floor so that a marble could roll off any edge. Whenever a marble dropped off the floor, it tripped a switch and operated a food dispenser. When responses which caused marbles to roll about the floor became more frequent, three edges of the floor were blocked so that a marble could fall off only one edge, and movements which caused marbles to move in other directions underwent extinction. Later, only a small section of one edge was left clear, and the edge was then slightly raised. By this time the rat was pushing the marbles with its forepaws or nose, and a strong directed response would force a marble up and over the edge and would be reinforced. Eventually the rat grasped and lifted the marble over the edge.

A new problem then arose. Evidently it is hard for a rat to acquire the operant of "letting go." It lets go of an object when it is either punished or not reinforced for holding on, but apparently it learns only with difficulty to do so "to produce an effect." The rat would hold the marble over the edge, showing a considerable tremor because of the unnatural posture, and eventually the marble would fall from its hands. (At one stage, it learned to knock the marble out of its paws with its nose, often shooting it some distance, and a sort of backstop had to be built to make sure the marble would not miss the triggering platform below.) Eventually an appropriate response of letting go appeared.

The edge and the backstop were then changed to form a slot, which grew smaller in cross section and taller until it was eventually a tube less than one inch in diameter extending two inches above the floor. A rack was then added from which a marble could be obtained by pulling a chain

---

[1] Cowles, J. T. *Comp. Psychol. Monogr.,* 1937, *14,* No. 5.

[2] Skinner, B. F. *Behavior of Organisms.* New York: Appleton-Century-Crofts, 1938.

that hung from the top of the cage. In the final performance the rat would pull the chain, pick up the marble thus discharged, walk on its hind legs across the cage, lift the marble tremblingly to the top of the tube, and drop it in.

The curious thing about this experiment, seen in retrospect, is that every step in the shaping process was taken by *changing the equipment.* Mechanical contingencies have the advantage that they work in the absence of the experimenter, and in spite of much evidence to the contrary I may have been under the influence of early learning theories in which it was assumed that a great many trials were needed to teach a rat anything. (I made the same mistake with my students; I assumed that they would always need to go over material more than once, and the first teaching machine designed for their use allowed for the presentation of each item until two correct responses had been made.[3]

I well remember the day when Norman Guttman, Keller Breland, and I discovered how wrong all this was by dispensing with mechanical contingencies and reinforcing successive approximations to a complex response by hand. By operating a food dispenser with a hand switch we taught a pigeon to strike a wooden ball with a swiping motion of its beak and to knock the ball about its cage, rather in the manner of a squash player. Shaping complex behavior through a programmed sequence of contingencies is now so commonplace that it is hard to understand why we should have been amazed at the speed with which this was done.

Another useful principle discovered in basic research has to do with the maintenance of behavior. Early experiments on learning concentrated on certain conspicuous facts—the acquisition of new forms of behavior (in learning) and the disappearance of old ones (in forgetting). "Overlearning" was studied, but there was no recognition of the fact that behavior could be maintained in various states of strength by appropriate schedules of reinforcement. Schedules are now widely used to solve what are essentially practical problems—for example, in generating baselines to show drug effects and emotional changes such as the conditioned suppression called "anxiety"—but the implications for behavior modification have not been fully explored. Although the maintenance of available behavior in strength through intermittent reinforcement is an important practical problem, the emphasis is still on the production of new behavior. But this will change as practical implications are discovered. The behavior modification

[3] Skinner, B. F. *The Technology of Teaching.* New York: Appleton-Century-Crofts, 1968. See page 36, Figure 4.

of the future will also make a far more extensive use of the control exerted by the current environment, of deprivation and satiation, of the conditioning of new reinforcers, and of the explicit design of instructional repertoires (of which imitation is an example).

Not all innovations in behavior modification are traceable to a basic analysis, of course, and traditional rules of thumb for shaping and maintaining behavior which use the same principles arose long before any research had been done. The analysis is nevertheless important in interpreting and explaining the effect of a method, whatever its provenance. It is hard to see the contingencies of reinforcement which prevail in daily life and hence to understand the behavior they generate.[4] Laboratory research tells us what to look for and, equally important, what to ignore, and in doing so it leads to the improvement of practical contingencies.

It is not always easy to maintain a distinction between basic and applied research, since both may use the same methods and equipment and come up with the same kinds of results, but an important difference lies in the reasons why research is undertaken and supported. The applied researcher is under the influence of a special kind of consequence. He carries on, in part, because he will make someone healthier or wealthier rather than simply wiser. This is not a reflection on his "purity" or any other trait of character. It is simply a fact which bears on certain characteristics of his practice, and for that reason some further relations between applied and basic research are worth considering.

One obvious value of practical results is illustrated by the history of the experimental analysis of behavior. Operant research was not at first generously supported by departments of psychology, and many young researchers took jobs in laboratories—in pharmaceutical companies, for example— which were supported because of practical consequences. It was not always necessary to design research under the influence of such consequences, however, and many important basic experiments were carried out. Even when the practical consequences were stressed, there was often a gain in basic knowledge.

Behavior modification supplies another example. Its practical implications have led to the support of work from which contributions to basic knowledge are being made. Practical consequences often force the scientist to deal with variables he would otherwise put off for later consideration. To improve the lives of institutionalized retardates or psychotics, for example, it is usually necessary to deal with more variables than convenience

---

[4] Skinner, B. F. *Contingencies of Reinforcement: A Theoretical Analysis.* New York: Appleton-Century-Crofts, 1969.

dictates, and the simplifying practices of the laboratory are not feasible. As a result, discoveries are made which standard experimental practice would, in a sense, put out of reach.

A contribution in the other direction—from basic to applied—would traditionally be described as the "confidence" with which contingencies are now designed in solving practical problems. Laboratory successes generalize to daily life. The effects of reinforcement are often deferred and need to be mediated, and this is particularly true when reinforcement is used in place of punishment because the latter has quicker effects. The amenable conditions of the laboratory are likely to bring the researcher under the control of deferred consequences and to maintain his behavior when it is only intermittently reinforced. A practical method may continue to be used because of its success, but help from basic research is often needed in its early development. Techniques of behavior modification often seem, after the fact, like the plainest of common sense, but we should remember that they remained undiscovered or unused for a long time and that the same "common sense" still leads to many violations of the basic principles.

The theory which accompanies an experimental analysis is particularly helpful in justifying practice because behavior modification often means a vast change in the way in which we deal with people. It is vast not only in scope (touching fields as diverse as education, psychotherapy, economics, and government) but in its very nature, as the states of mind, feelings, and other attributes of the inner man who figures in traditional explanations of human behavior are rejected in favor of antecedent circumstances in a person's genetic and individual histories. The genetic history is at the moment beyond control, but the environmental history, past and present, can be supplemented and changed, and that is what is done in a genuine technology of behavior. Behavior modification is environment modification, but this is not widely recognized. Very little current "behavioral science" is really behavioral, because prescientific modes of explanation still flourish, but behavior modification is an outstanding exception.

One practical contribution of an experimental analysis is easily overlooked. It is derived from the scientific methodology upon which the analysis is based. Applied psychologists have usually found themselves in a subordinate position. They have served as fact-finders rather than decision-makers. More than any other science, psychology has had to move against a weight of folklore, superstition, and error, and it is not surprising that psychologists have put a premium on the factual and objective. They have struggled to escape from the limitations of personal experience. To know what a man actually hears or sees they have controlled the stimulating environment. To know what he does or says they have recorded his behavior as precisely as possible and quantified it with inventories, questionnaires, and tests. To discover what he is inclined to do or say they have sampled his opinions and beliefs.

This "objectivity" has no doubt been valuable, but it has cast the psychologist in a merely supportive role. Clinical psychologists and psychometricians find themselves testing patients and supplying the information to the psychiatrist who carries on with therapy. The school psychologist reports to a teacher or administrator, who is the one who takes appropriate action. The results of opinion polls are used by statesmen or politicians, not by the pollsters, and it is the directors who plan the future of a company in the light of a market analysis. When a psychologist moves into a decision-making spot, it is generally felt that he is no longer acting as a psychologist. Something of the same sort holds for all the behavioral sciences, and the relationship has, in fact, been given semi-official status. An "Advisory Committee on Government Programs in the Behavioral Sciences," appointed by the National Academy of Sciences and the National Research Council in 1965, has been careful to point out that "there is no assumption . . . that knowledge is a substitute for wisdom or common sense or for decision-making." [5]

The wisdom, common sense, or decision-making faculty thus denied to social scientists is probably a remnant of a prescientific autonomous man. It is not supported by the conception of human behavior which emerges from an experimental analysis, and this fact explains the unique characteristic of behavior modification that it *is* directly concerned with decision-making and control. When we have specified the goals to which "wisdom and common sense" are to be applied, we may go straight to the design of relevant contingencies. The experimental analysis of behavior is more than measurement. It is more than testing hypotheses. It is an empirical attack upon the manipulable variables of which behavior is a function. As a result the behavior modifier plays an exceptional role.

Even so, he may find it difficult to move into a position where important decisions are made. Changes in practice do not usually come about in the center of power. It is not the administrator or teacher who is likely to make a major contribution to instruction, but rather those who analyze teaching and learning experimentally. It is not the employer or worker who is likely

[5] Quoted in a review by Albert D. Biderman (*Science,* 1970, 169, 1064–1067) of the report of the Young Committee, appointed by NAS-NRC in 1965 as "Advisory Committee on Government Programs in the Behavior Sciences." The report was published under the title *Politics of Social Research,* by Ralph L. Beals (Chicago: Aldine, 1969).

to propose better incentive systems but rather someone who has examined the effects of reinforcers on human behavior in general. We have become used to this fact in medicine, where major improvements come from sciences peripheral to medicine itself rather than from practicing physicians. But unlike the physician, who has learned to accept new practices originating elsewhere, the administrator, teacher, psychiatrist, or industrialist may feel that he has a special kind of wisdom arising from familiarity with his field and may resist the application of a basic science or a new method closely associated with such a science. The current condition of American elementary and high school education is a tragic example. Prevailing practices are derived from unscientific "philosophies of education" and from the personal experiences of administrators and teachers, and the results are particularly disturbing to those who know what might be done instead. The first behavior which needs to be modified is obviously that of the teacher, administrator, or philosopher of education.

Another practical consequence of basic research remains to be emphasized. Our culture has made us all sensitive to the good of others, and we are generously reinforced when we act for their good, but the display of gratitude which reinforces the teacher or therapist who is in immediate contact with another person is often dangerous. Those who are especially sensitive to the good of others are often induced to go into teaching or therapy rather than basic research. Progress would be more rapid if the same kind of reinforcement could be brought to bear on the researcher, if he could be appropriately affected by the extraordinary extent to which he is also acting for good of others. The basic researcher has, in fact, a tremendous advantage. Any slight advance in our understanding of human behavior which leads to improved practices in behavior modification will eventually work for the good of *billions* of people.

Compassion and Ethics in the Care of the Retardate

We all know what it means to *feel* that something is right or wrong, or good or bad, but do we *behave* ethically because we do what we feel is right or good, or is what we feel a mere by-product? If our feelings do not explain our behavior, some other explanation for right or wrong or good or bad conduct must be found. Ethical and moral principles must then be derived from the reasons why people behave (and only incidentally feel) as they do. The point is important because we can change reasons more directly than feelings, and a reformulation may therefore improve our chances of inducing people to behave ethically.

Prominent among the reasons why a person behaves in a given way are the consequences which follow when he does so. Relevant consequences are usually described in terms of feelings. Thus, a person is said to behave in a given way because the effect is "satisfying" or "pleasant" or because he thus avoids an effect which is "annoying" or "unpleasant." (It is clear that we are already close to a question of ethics, because we call one kind of consequence "good" and say that behavior followed by it is "right," and another kind "bad" and that behavior followed by it "wrong." These are elemental value judgments.) The laymen calls such consequences rewarding, but the word "reinforcing" is an improvement. It emphasizes the fact that reinforced behavior is *strengthened* in the sense that it becomes more likely to be repeated. The reinforcing or strengthening effects have been exhaustively studied in the experimental analysis of operant behavior.

We use the terms good and bad, or right and wrong, even when speaking of a solitary person whose behavior does not affect others. There are many natural ways in which the human organism is reinforced: food rein-

To be published by the Joseph P. Kennedy, Jr., Foundation for Mental Retardation.
[From *Cumulative Record* (3rd ed.). We have no evidence to show whether the publication described in the footnote above ever took place.]

forces the hungry, water the thirsty, sexual contact the sexually deprived, and escape from pain those who are in pain. Why this is so is a question about the evolution of the species; organisms have been more likely to survive when such consequences have strengthened the behaviors they were contingent upon. But these natural values do not explain much of the behavior of a civilized person. Nonsocial reinforcement produces at best only a feral child—a child who has grown up untouched by human care—or Rousseau's noble savage, uncorrupted by civilization, perhaps, but not really very noble and still a savage.

People living together in groups are sensitive to other kinds of values because they are subject to other kinds of consequences. Their behavior is shaped and maintained because its effects are good or bad *for others*. We call the behavior of another person good or bad according to its effect upon us, and we also take more positive action; we reinforce such behavior when its consequences are reinforcing to us (thus inducing the person to act in the same way again) and punish it when it is punishing to us (so that the person will henceforth avoid acting in that way again). The words "Good!" and "Bad!" eventually become social reinforcers in their own right. Comparable social contingencies are implied by the concepts of duty and obligation. We are likely to speak of a "sense of duty" or a "feeling of obligation," but the basic facts concern social reinforcement. The terms refer to what is *due* to others (who may demand their due) and to what others *oblige* us to do.

A behavioristic reformulation does not ignore feelings; it merely shifts the emphasis from the feeling to what is felt. A person responds to the physical world around him and, with a rather different set of nerves, to the no less physical world within his skin. What he feels is his own body, and among the things he feels is his own behavior as it has been affected by its consequences. He may feel it as right or wrong. When he is walking from one place to another in a city, he may feel that he is or is not on the right street. He takes one street or another depending upon how well he knows the city or, in other words, how well his behavior has been shaped and maintained by its earlier consequences. He does not take a particular street because he feels it is right; he feels it is right because he is inclined to take it, and he is so inclined because he has been reinforced for doing so. Similarly, in dealing with other people he feels that he is or is not doing the right thing, but he does not do it because he feels it is right; he feels it is right because it is what he tends to do, and he tends to do it because it has had consequences which were reinforcing first to others and then in turn to him.

When someone mistreats us, we may feel angry or enraged, but if we call him bad and his behavior wrong or take more effective action, it is not because of our feelings but because of the mistreatment. But why do we protest mistreatment when we ourselves are not directly involved? Again, the traditional explanation is sought in the world of feeling: we are said to respond to the mistreatment of others out of sympathy or compassion, in the etymological sense of *suffering with* the mistreated person. If that were true, we could scarcely deny that feelings can serve as the causes of action. But the explanation is not satisfactory. Compassion will not explain action until the compassion has in turn been explained. Why we act in the interest of others is no harder to explain than why we feel their feelings.

To say that it is human nature to be compassionate is to appeal to the human genetic endowment, which must eventually be explained by showing that it has had survival value for the species. A tendency to feel compassionate would contribute to the survival of the species if it induced people to protect and help each other, but it is the *behavior* of protecting and helping others which is selected by the contingencies of survival. We do not say that a female rat has an innate tendency to feel compassionate and that the feeling then induces her to care for her helpless young; instead we speak of the survival value of maternal behavior. The human mother will feel the condition of her body as she cares for her child (if her culture has induced her to feel it), and she may call it compassion (if her culture has taught her to do so), but what she feels is a by-product, not the cause of her behavior.

When people call it wrong to mistreat an animal or child or helpless person or when they take more positive action, they may feel accompanying conditions of their bodies, which they have learned to call, say, anger, but it is their behavior which is to be explained. The process of generalization may be relevant. What we see when a person is mistreating others resembles what we see when he is mistreating us. The physical aspects of mistreatment *become* aversive, and we may act to escape or attack even though the original reasons no longer prevail. We kill the mosquito on our arm and through generalization on the arm of a friend. We attack those who attack us and through generalization those who attack others. Verbal practices offer support. A culture teaches its members to call those who mistreat others bad and their behavior wrong. It establishes rules for dealing with the mistreatment of others and maintains appropriate sanctions to induce people to follow them. There are other reasons why we protest mistreatment, and they explain as well the condition we feel as compassion or sympathy when we do so.

Such an explanation may not be wholly convincing to those who insist upon the priority of feelings, but it must be remembered that it would be at least equally difficult to explain the feelings. Moreover, no very powerful explanation is needed, because the behavior itself is likely to be weak. The action we take with respect to the mistreatment of others is less vigorous than when we ourselves are mistreated, and our feelings are correspondingly weaker. The point has an important bearing on some classical examples of mistreatment in which any countercontrolling action must be taken by a third party who is not directly affected and is therefore less inclined to act and to have the feelings associated with action.

Consider, first, the care of small children in orphanages or in schools to which children are sent by people who soon lose contact with them. Charles Dickens described typical examples of the abuse which has been characteristic of such institutions throughout their long history, and he was responsible for a certain measure of reform, but there is still much to be done. The trouble arises because those who exert control are subject to little or no countercontrol. Children are too small and weak to protest and can only occasionally turn to that archetypal response to mistreatment, escape. In the absence of effective countercontrol those in charge begin to change—from being perhaps merely careless to being callous or even cruel. In the end they almost necessarily behave in ways we call ethically wrong. They do not do so because they lack compassion, but because reciprocal action has been weak or absent. What they may at first have felt as compassion grows weak or vanishes altogether.

The care of the chronically ill or the aged is subject to the same deterioration. Nursing homes and homes for the elderly are often supported by the state or by relatives who take little further interest in what happens in them. The ill or the aged cannot protest effectively, nor can they escape, and little or no countercontrol is therefore exerted. Under these conditions those in charge begin to behave in ways we call ethically wrong. They do so not because they lack compassion but because there is no adequate countercontrol, and as their behavior deteriorates, nothing is left to be felt as compassion.

Prisons offer a rather different example. A prison is itself a device for the countercontrol of unlawful behavior, and its practices are at the start almost always punitive. Those who establish prisons and incarcerate people in them usually take little further interest in what happens, and prisons have therefore been notorious for inhumane treatment. The prisoner escapes if he can, but no other action is possible short of extreme violence, which tends to be suppressed by even more violent means. It is usually obvious that the mistreatment of a prisoner is due to inability to protest, and we are not likely to look to the compassion of prison authorities for reform.

The care of psychotics has also shown a long history of inhumane treatment. It would be difficult for any sane person to avoid becoming psychotic under many forms of institutional care. The institutions are usually run by the state, and those who commit patients to them often lose interest or accept the care they provide as somehow inevitable. The psychotic cannot protest effectively and, if he escapes, he is usually easily caught. Countercontrol is negligible, and the behavior of those in charge therefore tends to become careless, callous, or cruel. Feelings change accordingly.

We are especially concerned here with a fifth field in which there has also been a long history of mistreatment, the care of the retardate. It would be difficult for a normal child to develop normally under many forms of institutional care. Like the psychotic, the retardate cannot escape or protest effectively. Those in charge easily fall into modes of conduct we call ethically wrong, and their feelings presumably change accordingly.

Fortunately, there are those who are inclined to do something about the mistreatment of children, the aged, prisoners, psychotics, and retardates. We say that they *care,* but it is important to make clear that caring is first of all a matter of acting and only secondarily a matter of feeling. From time to time, energetic action has been taken, but reform has nevertheless remained episodic. Programs designed to correct mistreatment wax and wane, and compassion waxes and wanes too. The trouble lies in the weakness of the contingencies which induce a third party to undertake reform. Professional ethics (a significant expression!) shows the problem. A code of ethics states that it is wrong for a professional person to behave in certain ways and that those who do so will be censured or stripped of professional privileges. The people protected by such a code do not exert countercontrol because they do not know that they have been injured. A third party enters because the good of the profession suffers; but the good of the profession is a remote gain, and only well-organized professions are able to bring it to bear on the conduct of their members. More remote and more difficult to make effective is the "good" which induces a third party to act in the interests of children, the aged, prisoners, psychotics, and retardates.

One step which might be taken to correct the contingencies under which treatment tends to deteriorate is to make sure that the care of others is adequately supported. Mistreatment is often a matter of poor conditions and of underpaid and overworked personnel. But making good care as easy as possible will not redress the imbalance which is causing trouble. Affluence alone has never made people particularly concerned for the welfare of others.

Another possibility is to recruit people who already tend to treat other people well. They do so, and presumably also feel compassionate, not because they are compassionate people but because they have been exposed to countercontrolling contingencies elsewhere. We recruit them in the hope that they will continue to behave well even under the effective contingencies of a custodial institution. But unfortunately the effects of contingencies are not permanent. When there is no current countercontrol, compassionate people often find themselves becoming careless or cruel, often to their dismay. Good behavior borrowed from other environments will not last; we need sustained contingencies which continue to induce people to behave well.

An obvious step is to correct the imbalance by exerting countercontrol on behalf of those who cannot exert it themselves. We may act toward those in charge of children, old people, prisoners, psychotics, and retardates as if we were ourselves aggrieved and thus subject them to normal countercontrol. But precisely what are we to do? A version of the golden rule may be relevant: we may insist that those who are in charge of others do unto them as we should have them do unto us. But the rule is not infallible; it does not, for example, specify the degree of countercontrol to be supplied. What is to keep the balance from swinging too far the other way? Given unlimited power it is possible that we should all become selfish monsters. The main trouble with the rule, however, is that we do not always know what we should want if we were children, old, in prison, or, in particular, psychotic or retarded. "Shared feelings" will not help. The rule may serve to prevent gross mistreatment, but it will not prescribe a detailed plan of action. What, after all, is the good life for such people?

In using our feelings—or, technically speaking, our own susceptibilities to reinforcement—as a guide, we make a mistake which is inherent in the very notion of *caring*—of *caritas* or charity in the Biblical sense. We feed the hungry, heal the sick, and visit the lonely—and possibly because these are things we like others to do to us. But the pattern will not suffice for the design of a better world. Something is missing in the formula "to each according to his need." It is missing in both an affluent and a welfare state. We imagine, wish for, and pray for a world—or heaven—in which reinforcers are available without effort, and we do so because any behavior which brings us into such a world is abundantly reinforced. But what is to be done when we are once there? All that remains is the consumption of gratifiers. The important thing is not what a person gets, but what he is doing when he gets it, and this is almost always neglected by those who wish for a better way of life.

Those who argue against caring for people by fulfilling their needs are likely to fall under suspicion. They seem to be saying that people "ought" to deserve or appreciate what they get or "ought not" to sponge on others. That is often the view of those from whom goods have been taken—who have been exploited in the pursuit of affluence or taxed to build a welfare state. But in improving custodial care, we must take into account the good of those who receive rather than those who give. The human organism has evolved under conditions in which great effort has been needed for survival, and a person is in a very real sense less than human when he is merely consuming things supplied to him *gratis*.

We see the problem in the world at large. We have developed more and more efficient ways of getting the things we need, and in doing so we have deprived ourselves of some powerful reinforcers. We have built a world in which we less and less often engage in strongly reinforced behavior. We feel the resulting condition and call it boredom. It is the problem of leisure. When we do not "have" to do anything, we seem to be free to engage in art, music, literature, and science, but we are much more likely to fall under the control of other kinds of weak reinforcers which get their chance when the powerful reinforcers have been attenuated. Our forefathers put it in the form of an aphorism: "The devil always has something for idle hands to do." Leisure classes have characteristically gambled, used alcohol and drugs, and enjoyed themselves by watching other people behave seriously. The problem is particularly acute in an institutional environment, where those who do not "have" to do anything (in part because they are being cared for) have nothing to do and are therefore likely to behave in particularly troublesome ways. The charitable fulfillment of needs can be justified only for those who cannot fulfill their needs themselves. Help is charity only for the helpless. We do not help those who can help themselves when we make it unnecessary for them to do so. Instead, we deprive them of the chance to behave in ways which are said to show an interest in life or possibly even excitement or enthusiasm.

Sympathetic understanding may suggest the design of a reinforcing environment, but it will not specify details. What is needed is technical knowledge of the effects of the environment on human behavior. Fortunately, the ways in which reinforcers can be made contingent upon behavior have been extensively studied, and the results have been put to use in a technology of behavior modification, which is concerned with the design of effective contingencies of reinforcement.

That technology has much to contribute to custodial care, but it will make its contribution only when certain ethical questions have been answered. One of these brings us back to the problem we have just considered. In creating a better world for the institutionalized retardate should we be limited to the reinforcers which remain when basic needs have been satisfied? A strong position was taken by a committee of psychiatrists who issued some principles governing the use of token economies in state hospitals for psychotics: "Deprivation is never to be used. No patient is to be deprived of expected goods and services or ordinary rights . . . that he had before the program started. In addition, deficit rewarding must be avoided; that is, rewards must not consist of the restoration of objects or privileges that were taken away from the patient or that he should have had to begin with." But what should he have had to begin with?

A program of contingency management which begins by taking something away from people suggests a lack of compassion if compassion is associated with giving people what they need. But although a state in which all needs are satisfied may appeal to those who have struggled to satisfy needs, it is in a curious sense a state of deprivation, a state in which people are deprived of reinforcements which induce them to behave productively. We honor and admire normal people who do things for themselves. Psychotics and retardates have failed to do so in the past, but it is a mistake to suppose that they cannot do so in the future. Through the proper use of what is known about contingencies of reinforcement, we can construct simplified environments in which defective people can to some extent take care of themselves. In doing so, we could be said to give them some measure of self-reliance and dignity.

Other "values" which may help us decide what the retardate *should* be doing can also be derived from practices concerning normal people. What a person does when he does not "have" to do anything may be judged in terms of the extent to which he exhibits all the behavior of which he is capable. The behaviors most characteristic of leisure tend to be repetitious (as in gambling), stupefying (as in the use of alcohol or other drugs), and passive (as in being a mere spectator). They are characteristic of leisure just because they demand very little of a person. A person may spend a lifetime doing these things and be very little changed at the end of it. Both the individual and his culture suffer. Other activities characteristic of leisure, however, lead to the development of extensive, varied, and subtle repertoires—among them the arts and crafts, sports, scholarship, scientific investigation, exploration, and the maintenance of good relations with others who are also changing. When activities of that sort are encouraged, the retardate leads the fullest life of which he is capable.

The design of such a world needs more than compassion or sympathy; it needs a highly developed science of behavior. We do not yet have a science which can solve all our problems, and that fact points to something else which the retardate could be doing which raises an ethical question. A science of behavior needs research which necessarily involves people. But under what conditions is it ethical to force or induce people to serve as subjects? It is generally held that participants must be aware of all possible consequences and must give their consent, but this is obviously not possible for psychotics and retardates. The consent of those to whom they have been entrusted for custodial care is required. And unfortunately it is often hard to get. Administrative problems are bad enough without making further adjustments in support of research. Nevertheless, anyone who is concerned with the ultimate welfare of those who must live in the care of others should insist that such people contribute to research. Personal safety should, of course, be protected, but guidelines are not hard to set up. Psychotics and retardates have an opportunity to contribute to a world in which others like themselves will lead better lives. They may not know that they are doing so, but those who do know should insist that they be given the chance. In that way they can share one other commonly admired feature of normal behavior: they can be controlled by remote consequences having to do with the good of others.

We shall not bring about major changes in custodial management by appealing to compassion, sympathy, or ethical principles. The contingencies affecting those who manage custodial institutions must be changed. Environments can be designed in which those who are in the care of others will lead better lives, and it may just happen that those who construct and maintain them will as a result feel compassionate and follow ethical principles.

PART V

For Experimental Psychologists Only

Current Trends in
Experimental Psychology

This lecture was given in March, 1947, at the first annual conference on Current Trends in Psychology at the University of Pittsburgh. It appeared in Current Trends in Psychology *(Pittsburgh, University of Pittsburgh Press, 1947) and is reprinted by permission of the University of Pittsburgh Press.*

There is a familiar caricature of the experimental psychologist which runs something like this: He is first of all an apparatus man, who spends a good share of his time tinkering with sundry pieces of equipment which never quite work to his satisfaction. He investigates only problems which he calls appropriate to the laboratory. He cannot study learning as part of the complex and subtle interplay of behavior and environment in everyday life, so he confines himself to the memorizing of meaningless words presented with clocklike regularity in a standard aperture. He cannot bring love or hate or envy into the laboratory, so he investigates reactions to garter snakes and pistol shots. The only strong motives he knows are his own, for his subjects perform merely to oblige him or because they are required to do so as part of a course they are taking. (In an exceptional case, if he "has a grant," they may be paid seventy-five cents an hour.) He remains an experimental psychologist only so long as his problems have no practical value; that is how he stays pure. If his field suddenly becomes important for industry or the public weal, then he becomes an industrial or applied psychologist and does the whole thing over again in no time at all with better and more expensive apparatus. He works only with amenable subjects—that is to say, with subjects in whom no one is really interested: white rats or dogs or human beings who have stepped out of their normal lives and into a laboratory frame as standard organisms.

The picture is not as amusing as it may seem. Parts of it are perhaps too close to the truth to be funny, and whether justified or not the general tone is disturbing. It supports a conviction, which most of us have reached on the strength of other evidence, that experimental psychology is passing

341

through a critical phase in its history, and that it is under close and not always sympathetic scrutiny. Psychologists who take a broader interest in the affairs of men have grown impatient with their experimental colleagues, if not openly critical. They often appear to resent the historical seniority of the experimental field and the prestige which seniority has engendered. The experimental psychologists themselves have grown uncertain of their scientific position. Their confidence has been shaken, and desertions from the ranks occur more and more frequently.

This does not mean that a great deal of what may properly be called experimental psychology is not still going on, or that the results are not duly published in the journals. It would be possible to write a paper on "Current Trends in Experimental Psychology" by describing the latest improvements in techniques, by reporting the most important recent advances, and so on, and such a paper would not suffer from any shortage of material. But the important issue is the survival of the field itself, or at least its ultimate position with respect to other branches of the science. This ought to have first claim upon our attention.

The very definition of experimental psychology is in doubt. It is always easy to overemphasize some incidental or superficial feature. For example, there is no reason why we should suppose that experimental psychology is concerned with a special subdivision of human behavior. At one time, it is true, experimentalists were dedicated to a limited subject matter, particularly the fields of sensory processes, reaction times, and certain limited learning situations, but this is no longer so. Experimentation is now common in every field of human behavior. Nor is the experimental psychologist any longer distinguished by the fact that he uses apparatus. It is characteristic of him that he is not satisfied to observe behavior with his eyes and ears alone, but must connect his subjects to amplifiers and recorders of one sort or another. Characteristically, too, he does not take the environment simply as he finds it, but modifies it in various ways with various ingenious devices. He was once almost alone in these practices, but virtually every sort of investigator now adopts them from time to time. The use of apparatus may improve an experiment, but it must not be confused with experimentation itself. It is possible to be an experimentalist without using apparatus at all. It is also not true that experimental psychology necessarily deals with something less than the whole man in something less than the real world. To simplify the material of a science is one of the purposes of a laboratory, and simplification is worthwhile whenever it does not actually falsify. But the experimental psychologist has no corner on simplification. The psychoanalytic couch is a simplified world, and so is any test situation.

Since the experimental psychologist is no longer distinguished by a special field of research, or by his technical equipment, or by laboratory simplification, still another historical distinction must be given up: his statements are not necessarily more reliable than those of anyone else. At one time this might have been regarded as the essential difference. Experimental psychology stood for precision versus casual observation, for experimental validation versus general impression, for fact versus opinion. Most of what was said about human behavior in education, public affairs, industry, letters, and so on, was on the other side. The experimental psychologist was distinguished by the fact that one could trust his statements, no matter how limited their application. Elsewhere one expected nothing more than casual or philosophical discourse. But this is no longer true. Statements of comparable validity are characteristic of most of the fields represented in this conference and may be found in other and still larger spheres of human behavior. Rigorous definition, careful measurement, and validation no longer comprise a sufficient criterion; and even the consolation that the experimental psychologist was at least first to take these matters seriously will not suffice for a current definition.

We can make some progress toward delimiting a field of experimental psychology which is not merely an historical accident by looking more closely at the word *experimental.* In psychology, as in any science, the heart of the experimental method is the direct control of the thing studied. When we say, "Let us try an experiment," we mean, "Let us do something and see what happens." The order is important: we do something first and then see what happens. In more formal terms we manipulate certain "independent variables" and observe the effect upon a "dependent variable." In psychology the dependent variable, to which we look for an effect, is behavior. We acquire control over it through the independent variables. The latter, the variables which we manipulate, are found in the environment. We manipulate them when we stimulate an organism, when we alter conditions of motivation or learning, and so on. The great majority of psychological experiments can be reduced to this form. There may be variations on the theme: in sensory psychology, for example, we may wish to see how far we can change the environment *without* changing behavior, as when we study difference limens. But the basic pattern of control remains the same.

This is a narrow definition of an experimental science. It does not identify "experimental" with "scientific." Physics, chemistry, physiology, and genetics are experimental sciences in this sense. Astronomy, geology, and taxonomical biology would not generally qualify. This is no reflection upon the latter. We are merely classifying them according to methodology. The classification is worth making because the psychologist is more likely to find common problems and common solutions among sciences which have the same formal structure.

One interesting consequence of defining experimental psychology as a branch of the science in which we control the variables which govern behavior is that we thus exclude most investigations using correlational methods. It may be possible to prove the existence of a functional relation of the sort here in question by running a correlation between some aspect of behavior and some aspect of the environment, but if we are able to manipulate the aspect of the environment, letting it take different values at different times, we can get a much more complete account of the relation. The experimental control or elimination of a variable is the heart of a laboratory science, and, in general, it is to be preferred to manipulation through statistical treatment. It is not a question of a choice of methods, however. The two approaches represent different scientific plans and lead to different results. It is curious that our definition should single out the kind of result which has been traditionally accepted as characteristic of the field of experimental psychology. A possible explanation of why it does so will appear later.

A line drawn between functional and correlational analyses will run approximately along the accepted boundary between pure and applied psychology. If this were not an accident we might seize upon it in order to replace the distinction between the useful and the useless—a distinction which is not exactly flattering to the pure scientist. But the agreement is rough and accidental. Correlational techniques have been extensively used in pure research, and the reason they have dominated the science of psychology in its application to education, industry, public affairs, and elsewhere is not that the processes to be dealt with in those fields are of any special nature, but that it has generally been impossible to give an account of relevant factors in any other way.

The special problem of the applied psychologist is a practical one. He must gain control of certain relatively complex material—if not directly, as in the laboratory, then indirectly and frequently after-the-fact through statistical procedures. He is not confronted with any special sort of psychological fact for which a special method is required. The preference for correlational techniques in applied psychology may therefore change. It has been true of technology in general that as the basic engineering problem is solved, as the applied scientist gains control of his material, the connection with pure or laboratory science is strengthened. Common methods and common terms can be adopted. Something of this sort may be expected in psychology as engineering control is improved.

It is a familiar complaint that the kind of control possible in the laboratory is impossible in the world at large. The argument is that we cannot modify a natural environment in subtle ways or measure normal unhampered behavior to thousandths of a second. The complaint is especially loud with respect to the laboratory study of animal behavior. The fact that sciences like physiology, embryology, and genetics are very largely concerned with the study of animals and yet yield results constantly applied to men is dismissed as beside the point. Even though behavioral processes may be essentially similar in man and rat, it is argued that men cannot be similarly controlled, and that the results of the animal laboratory are therefore worthless when applied to the larger problems of human behavior.

This position is bound to grow weaker as the applied sciences grow stronger. It is not true that human behavior is not controlled. At least we cannot proceed very far as scientists on that assumption. To have a science of psychology at all, we must adopt the fundamental postulate that human behavior is a lawful datum, that it is undisturbed by the capricious acts of any free agent—in other words, that it is completely determined. The genetic constitution of the individual and his personal history to date play a part in this determination. Beyond that, the control rests with the environment. The more important forces, moreover, are in the social environment, which is man-made. Human behavior is therefore largely under human control.

Except for the trivial case of physical restraint or coercion, the control is, of course, indirect. It follows the general pattern of altering a dependent variable by manipulating the independent variables. Now, there are many cases in which the independent variables are freely manipulable with respect to human behavior. In the nursery, in certain types of schools, in corrective and penal institutions the degree of control may be very great. Although there are certain legal and ethical restrictions, the kind of manipulation characteristic of the laboratory is quite feasible. Elsewhere—in education, industry, law, public affairs, and government—the control is not so likely to be lodged in a single person or agency. Here, the basic engineering problem is to acquire control. But we must remember that the problem has frequently been solved—perhaps as often as not to our sorrow.

Since human behavior is controlled—and controlled, moreover, by men —the pattern of an experimental science is not restricted in any way. It is not a matter of bringing the world into the laboratory, but of extending the practices of an experimental science to the world at large. We can do this as soon as we wish to do it. At the moment psychologists are curiously diffident in assuming control where it is available or in developing it where it is not. In most clinics the emphasis is still upon psychometrics, and this is in part due to an unwillingness to assume the responsibility of control which is implied in guidance and counseling. Most personnel psychologists still obtain men with desired capacities or personalities by selecting them from a larger population rather than by creating them through training and guidance. In education we design and re-design our curricula in a desperate attempt to provide a liberal education while steadfastly refusing to employ available engineering techniques which would efficiently build the interests and instill the knowledge which are the goals of education. In some curious way, we feel compelled to leave the active control of human behavior to those who grasp it for selfish purposes: to advertisers, propagandists, demagogues, and the like.

This diffidence in accepting control has had far-reaching consequences. It is doubtless to some extent responsible for the continued effort to analyze behavior into traits, abilities, factors, and so on. The end result of such a program is a description of behavior in terms of aspect rather than process. It is a static rather than a dynamic description, and again it is primarily correlational rather than functional. No one doubts the value of investigating relations between ability and age, intellect and socio-economic status, emotionality and body type, and so on. The results may have important engineering applications. But so far as the single individual is concerned, we do not then proceed to *alter* age, or body type, or socio-economic status. Relations of this sort may make us more skillful in using the instruments of control already in our possession, but they do not help us to acquire new instruments. No matter how satisfactorily we may demonstrate the reality of abilities, traits, factors, and so on, we must admit that there is little we can do about them. They give us an aspect description of behavior which may have a practical value in classifying or selecting the members of a group, but they do not carry us very far toward the control of the behavior of the individual. That control requires techniques which are peculiarly experimental in nature, according to the present limited definition, and we may therefore anticipate that as soon as applied psychology emphasizes active control, the experimental pattern will emerge.

Our definition of the experimental field is therefore not yet complete, since it does not exclude the applied interest in functional control. But a final distinction can now be made. It concerns the use to which the control is put. What the experimental psychologist is up to when he is being essentially experimental is disinguished from other fields of psychology by the fact that he has a special goal. We need not blush to express this in rather general terms. The experimental psychologist is fundamentally interested in *accounting for* behavior, or *explaining* behavior, or in a very broad sense *understanding* behavior. If these are synonymous expressions I have been redundant and I apologize. If each carries its own special shade of meaning, then all three, taken together, will come nearer to an adequate statement. In any event, we must try to be more precise.

We do not understand a thing simply by becoming familiar with it. Nor is it enough to be able describe it, no matter how specific or subtle our terms may be. We make some progress toward understanding anything when we discover how it is related to other things, especially to antecedent events. This is what the layman means by cause and effect, and the satisfaction which he feels when he discovers the cause of an event is probably not to be distinguished from the satisfaction which the scientist takes in demonstrating a functional relationship. The discovery that the environment, in acting upon the organism, could be regarded as a causal agent in the direction and control of behavior, and the realization that it was therefore possible to dispense with fictitious inner controls marked the beginning of a science of behavior. This was as much the spirit of the sensory analysis of mind begun by the British Empiricists as it was the spirit of Descartes and the later analysts of action.

But the cataloguing of functional relationships is not enough. These are the basic facts of a science, but the accumulation of facts is not science itself. There are scientific handbooks containing hundreds of thousands of tabulated facts—perhaps the most concentrated knowledge in existence— but these are not science. Physics is more than a collection of physical constants, just as chemistry is more than a statement of the properties of elements and compounds. There is no better proof of this than the failure of simple fact-collecting to inspire the scientific worker. Most of the facts entered in our scientific handbooks are virtually hack work. Some were collected in the course of more rewarding scientific pursuits, but the tables are filled out only by the type of man who might otherwise be found collecting stamps or old coins. There is no more pathetic figure in psychology today than the mere collector of facts, who operates, or thinks he operates, with no basis for selecting one fact as against another. In the end, he is usually to be found doing something else, or perhaps nothing at all.

Behavior can only be satisfactorily understood by going beyond the facts themselves. What is needed is a theory of behavior, but the term *theory* is in such bad repute that I hasten to explain. Psychology has had no worse theories than any other science, but it has had them more recently, and they have suffered in the light of our improved understanding of scientific method. No one today seriously uses a fictional explanation as a theory, but all sciences have done so at one time or another. That mercury stands at a certain height in a barometer because nature abhors a vacuum to exactly that extent, or that certain bodies move because they are possessed by a *vis viva,* or that a substance burns by giving off phlogiston are the kinds of theories whose demise marks the progress of a science. They are the sort of hypotheses which Newton refused to make, and most scientists have followed his example. But Newton himself demonstrated the value of a proper scientific theory.

A theory, as I shall use the term here, has nothing to do with the presence or absence of experimental confirmation. Facts and theories do not stand in opposition to each other. The relation, rather, is this: theories are based upon facts; they are statements about organizations of facts. The atomic theory, the kinetic theory of gases, the theory of evolution, and the theory of the gene are examples of reputable and useful scientific theories. They are all statements about facts, and with proper operational care they need be nothing more than that. But they have a generality which transcends particular facts and gives them a wider usefulness. Every science eventually reaches the stage of theory in this sense.

Whether particular experimental psychologists like it or not, experimental psychology is properly and inevitably committed to the construction of a theory of behavior. A theory is essential to the scientific understanding of behavior as a subject matter. But if we are to consider the current status of experimental psychology rather than its destiny, we must admit that it is at the moment in the midst of theoretical chaos. This is, in fact, the explanation of the present crisis. Many experimentalists obviously lack motivation and direction and find it difficult to impart either one to their students. Many of them have lost interest and are turning to other fields. This is not due to any lack of financial support. Our universities can still win out against industrial offers when that is the only thing at issue. Nor is it a question of the support of research, although many universities have not fully understood their responsibility in generating as well as imparting knowledge. The real difficulty is that the experimental psychologist is unable to do anything with the facts he has accumulated, and he sees no reason to accumulate any more. He lacks a professional goal.

Part of this difficulty can be traced to the fact that the two great explanatory systems which have held the psychological field for a hundred years are no longer paying their way. They have lost their power to integrate and illuminate the facts of the science and to inspire and motivate the scientific worker. The only research to which they now lead is a sort of desperate patchwork to keep the theories intact, and this is unsatisfying.

One of these explanatory theories is the notion of a controlling mind. From our modern vantage point the essentially fictional nature of this explanation is clear. It is on a par with the abhored vacuum or the *vis viva* or phlogiston. Most of us like to feel that the ghost has been laid, and that we are free of mentalistic explanations. But the inner man, constructed of such stuff as dreams are made on, still flourishes. At least half the textbooks in psychology still talk about mental life, and few are successful in convincing the student that this can be reduced to the stuff which is dealt with in the physical sciences. In psychiatry the score would be almost a hundred to one in favor of an appeal to psychic determiners of behavior. Psychoanalysis has assigned names to at least three of these inner men, and it is the exceptional psychoanalyst who is willing to regard them as physical entities.

We cannot break away from these hoary practices simply by resolving to avoid theory altogether. We need a better theory. But this will be of a different sort and cannot be reached by patching up an old model. One current practice, for example, is to make the inner man more respectable by stripping him of what we may call his personification. He no longer exists as a complete person, but only as small fractions of his old self—as wants, drives, attitudes, interests, and so on. It is the exceptional writer who convincingly defines terms of this sort in a nonmentalistic way; and even if an operational re-definition is successful, the old theory may leave its mark in the structure surviving.

The other current explanatory theory flourishes with greater prestige and presumably in more robust health. This is the physiological theory of behavior. The inner man is given neurological properties, with a great gain in scientific respectability. Psychiatry becomes neuropsychiatry, and psychology the study of the nervous system. It is difficult to attack this theory without seeming to criticize the physiological psychologist, but no criticism is involved. There are many precedents in the history of science for borderline disciplines. To integrate the facts of two sciences is an interesting and profitable endeavor. Eventually, we may assume, the facts and principles of psychology will be reducible not only to physiology but through biochemistry and chemistry to physics and subatomic physics. But this reduction is undoubtedly a long way off. The current theoretical practice which is objectionable is the use of a hypothetical neural structure, the conceptual nervous system, as a theory of behavior. The neurological references introduced into such a theory, like references to mental states, interfere with free theory building, and they produce a structure which is not optimal for the organization of behavioral facts.

The traditional physiological theory, too, eventually fails to motivate the psychologist. Valid neurological explanations of important psychological laws are not arrived at with a very rewarding frequency, and the investigations which they inspire have a tendency to lead to such a jumble of details that the original plan is lost sight of. We are all familiar with the type of graduate student who comes to study psychology full of enthusiasm for a science of behavior, who climbs the physiological family tree through Berkeley, Hume, Wundt, and the moderns, and finds himself studying some detailed physiological mechanism. His motivation eventually flags when he sees that his current activities have only the most tenuous connection with his original interest in human behavior. Such a case history is only a scale model of the history of experimental psychology. No matter how critically we may now view the original program of a science of mind, we must admit that a great driving force was lost when the nervous system had to be brought in. Instead of the basic psychophysical relation, the object of research became the operation of specific physiological mechanisms. Generalized brain theories of the Gestalt variety and dimensional analyses of consciousness are efforts to bring together again the fragments of a science of mind, and to add something of theoretical interest to the study of the physiology of end-organs. But the spark has been lost.

If we try to put these two great explanatory systems in good scientific order through operational re-definition, we only succeed in dealing the *coup de grâce*. We can, of course, define "mind" in behavioral terms, and we can set up a conceptual nervous system for the representation of behavioral facts, leaving the specification of the actual neural properties until some later date. But in this way we eliminate all the explanatory force of the theories. An operational definition is possible in every case, but it does not necessarily lead to a satisfactory theoretical construct. Whatever its success, it spoils the explanatory fun.

The appeal to what we may call naive physiologizing, like the appeal to psychic determiners, is made in an attempt to explain behavior by shifting to a different level of observation. These are "outside" theories, which account for one thing by pointing to something which is going on somewhere else at the same time. For this reason they cannot fill the need for a theory of behavior, no matter how carefully they may be extended or repaired. What is emerging in psychology, as it has emerged at some point in the history of most sciences, is a theory which refers to facts at a single level of observation. The logic of this is simple enough. We begin with behavior as a subject matter and devise an appropriate vocabulary. We express the basic protocol facts of the science in the terms of this vocabulary. In the course of constructing a theory we may invent new terms, but they will not be invented to describe any new sort of fact. At no time will the theory generate terms which refer to a different subject matter—to mental states, for example, or neurones. It is not the purpose of such a theory to explain behavior by turning to "outside" determiners.

The real achievement of such theory building is not easy to demonstrate because of the present confused condition in psychology. There is no generally accepted theory of behavior which will serve as an example. But the situation is not quite hopeless. A scientific theory is never fully subscribed to by all the practitioners of a science; if it were, there would be no further need for scientific effort. And while no explicit theory in experimental psychology today has more than a handful of adherents, in practice most psychologists respect certain underlying assumptions which constitute the beginning of an implicit theory. We realize how extensive this implicit theory is when we observe non-psychologists dealing with the same subject matter and see how they repeatedly violate our assumptions. We have, then, something to begin with by way of actual theoretical practice. We may also get a plausible glimpse of the future, for some of the features of an effective theory can be inferred from the nature of behavior as a subject matter and from comparable theories in other fields. It should, therefore, also be possible to evaluate the present status of psychology with respect to theory construction.

The first step in building a theory is to identify the basic data. It may be easy or difficult, depending upon the science. It was relatively easy, for example, to decide what events were to be taken into account in the Copernican theory of the solar system. Astronomers had observed the positions of the planets at given times; the theoretical problem was to relate these facts, not to identify them. In genetics, on the other hand, it is relatively difficult to discover what characteristics of an organism are valid genetic units. Psychology faces an even more difficult problem: what are the parts of behavior and environment between which orderly relations may be demonstrated?

The layman has little difficulty in analyzing the behavior of himself and his fellow men. He breaks it into discrete acts. He may report, for example, that someone "watched a car until it passed out of sight." The statement conveys useful information at the level of casual discourse, but is it necessarily a valid scientific description? The language of the kitchen may be of no use to the chemist, though the cook finds it meaningful enough. Anyone who has tried to analyze pursuit behavior knows the problem involved in orienting the eyes toward a moving object, and very much more than that is covered by the word *watch*. And when the layman, with what seems like breathless daring, reports that someone "chose to remain silent," he stakes out a field which might suffice for a lifetime of research. The statement may be quite effective for practical purposes, but it will not necessarily suffice for a scientific description. For what is "choice"? Even the behavior involved in choosing between simple objects like cigarettes or neckties is complex enough. But what is happening when one "chooses to remain silent"? And in what sense is remaining silent to be regarded as behavior at all?

In practice psychologists define "response" in many ways—from muscle twitch to telic effect. In the latter case they present the physiologist with the baffling problem of how two responses executed by different parts of the body can be mutually replaceable in a lawful physiological train of events. It is a common current practice to dodge the problem by accepting some practical measure of behavior, often limited to a particular measuring device, such as "maze performance" or some arbitrary criterion of "success." The physiologist has also been appealed to, but in vain, since an indication of the presence or absence of activity in a particular effector is of little help.

We cannot continue to leave the problem unsolved if we are to construct an effective theory. It may be that the notion of a unit of response is at fault and that a final statement will reflect the fluidity and continuity of behavior as a whole. This would require more powerful analytical tools, but it may be necessary. A further requirement must also be recognized; it is not the mere form of behavior which we undertake to predict but rather its occurrence. Expressions like "reaction tendency" or "excitatory potential" have attempted to take account of this fact. The end term in a theory of behavior, in short, is the probability of action.

In the companion problem of environment, the layman again shows an enviable talent, for he describes and analyzes the environment with no hesitation whatsoever. The world to him is simply a collection of *things*. But his success gives the case away. He has analyzed the environment in terms of its practical importance. This is justifiable for his purposes; and in so far as various aspects of the environment have common practical consequences for everyone, the lay vocabulary might even be adopted for scientific use. But a complete scientific account must go back to properties of the environment which are effective before any consequences have been felt, and it must account for the process by which consequences alter the effectiveness of these properties.

Current practices are again diverse. Some psychologists, as in psychophysics, deal with stimuli one dimension at a time. Others, at the other extreme, refer to the "total situation"—an expression which seems safe because it can scarcely overlook anything, but which is unpleasantly vague. Our present knowledge of the physiology of the receptors offers little if any help in deciding upon an effective practice.

Since we have not clearly identified the significant data of a science of behavior, we do not arrive well prepared at the second stage of theory building, at which we are to express relations among data. Observed relations of this sort are the facts of a science—or, when a sufficient degree of generality has been reached, its laws. The general form of laws of behavior can be inferred from the nature of our program, but examples are not very abundant among the achievements to date. A weakness at the first stage of theory construction cannot be corrected at the second. In psychophysics the stimulus is defined rigorously, if not very comprehensively, and an arbitrary definition of response seems to suffice. Consequently, some generality at the second stage has been achieved. In the field of learning, on the other hand, we have collected thousands of separate learning curves, but they represent changes in hundreds of different aspects of behavior in hundreds of different situations. As a result, we have no valid general expressions for learning processes. This is characteristic of most of the facts of experimental psychology, and the next step in the construction of a satisfactory theory is therefore very difficult.

This step—at the third stage in theory building—can be exemplified by a simple example from the science of mechanics. Galileo, with the help of his predecessors, began by restricting himself to a limited set of data. He proposed to deal with the positions of bodies at given times, rather than with their color or hardness or size. This decision, characteristic of the first stage in building a theory, was not so easy as it seems to us today. Galileo then proceeded to demonstrate a relation between position and time—the position of a ball on an inclined plane and the time which had elapsed since its release. Something else then emerged—namely, the concept of acceleration. Later, as other facts were added, other concepts appeared—mass, force, and so on. Third-stage concepts of this sort are something more than the second-stage laws from which they are derived. They are peculiarly the product of theory-making in the best sense, and they cannot be arrived at through any other process.

There are few, if any, clear-cut examples of comparable third-stage concepts in psychology, and the crystal ball grows cloudy. But the importance of the stage is indicated by the fact that terms like *wants, faculties, attitudes, drives, ideas, interests,* and *capacities* properly belong there.

When it is possible to complete a theoretical analysis at this stage, concepts of this sort will be put in good scientific order. This will have the effect of establishing them in their own right. At present they need external support. Some of them, like wants and attitudes, come to us trailing clouds of psychic glory, and a wisp or two of the psychic can usually be detected when they are used. Other concepts, like drives and motives, borrow physiological support in certain favorable cases. Still others, like abilities and traits, have been made respectable through correlational analyses, which give them the status of "individual differences." Although most psychologists think of an ability as something which has meaning in the behavior of a single individual, current techniques of measurement find it necessary to make use of the position of the individual in a population. Magnitudes are assigned to the abilities and traits of the individual in terms of his relation to the group rather than through direct measurement. A proper theory at this stage would characterize the behavior of an individual in such a way that measurement would be feasible if he were the only individual on earth. This would be done by determining the values of certain constants in equations describing his behavior—clearly a third-stage enterprise.

From all of this should emerge a new conception of the individual as the locus of a system of variables. Fortunately for psychology it has been possible to deal with behavior without a clear understanding of who or what is behaving, just as it seems to be possible to deal with personality without defining "person." The integrity or unity of the individual has been assumed, perhaps because the organism is a biological unit. But it is quite clear that more than one person, in the sense of an integrated and organized system of responses, exists within one skin. The individual proves to be no more undividable than the atom was uncuttable. Many sorts of metaphorical schemes have been devised to represent this fact. A single personality may be regarded as moving about from one level of consciousness to another, or personalities may be frankly multiple. A proper theory must be able to represent the multiplicity of response systems. It must do something more: it must abolish the conception of the individual as a doer, as an originator of action. This is a difficult task. The simple fact is that psychologists have never made a thoroughgoing renunciation of the inner man. He is surreptitiously appealed to from time to time in all our thinking, especially when we are faced with a bit of behavior which is difficult to explain otherwise.

Eventually we may expect the main features of a behavioral theory to have physiological significance. As the science of physiology advances, it will presumably be possible to show what is happening in various structures within the organism during particular behavioral events, and the theoretical systems of the two sciences may also be seen to correspond. An example of this rapprochement is the way in which facts and principles of genetics arrived at from the study of the characteristics of parents and offspring are seen to correspond to facts and principles of cell structure. The science of genetics has already reached the stage at which it is profitable to investigate both subject matters at the same time. Terms which originally described relations between the characteristics of parents and offspring may now carry additional cytological references.

A similar day may come in psychology. That is up to the physiologist and the physiological psychologist. But the eventual correspondence should not be allowed to obscure the present need for a behavioral theory. The hypothetical physiological mechanisms which inspire so much research in psychology are not acceptable as substitutes for a behavioral theory. On the contrary, because they introduce many irrelevant matters, they stand in the way of effective theory building. There is a tendency in some quarters to admit this while insisting upon compensating advantages. It is argued that the solidity of the nervous system gives it the strength to dispossess psychic fictions which a purely behavioral theory may lack. It is also thought to be a necessary intellectual crutch—an ever-present help in time of theoretical need. Many people cannot think of the origination of an act without thinking of a motor center. They cannot conceive of learning without thinking of changes in synaptic resistance or some other protoplasmic change. They cannot contemplate a derangement of behavior without thinking of damaged tissue. Moreover, it is often pointed out that the histories of other sciences show many examples of theories which, under a proper operational analysis, would have been found to contain unwarranted references to other kinds of data but which made it possible to think more effectively about relevant data than would have been possible with a purely conceptual scheme. But this remains to be proved. It is not necessarily true that physiological theories have in the long run directed the energies of psychologists into the most profitable channels. An enlightened scientific methodology should enable us to improve upon the practices exemplified by the history of science. In any event an independent theory of behavior is not only possible, it is highly desirable, and such a theory is in no sense opposed to physiological speculation or research.

Because of the unhappy fate of so many psychological theories of the past, a sound theory of behavior must work itself out against a weight of indifference and even active opposition. Very few psychologists understand the nature of such a theory or are aware that it has a counterpart in most established sciences. Many of them deny the possibility of a respectable theory. It is encouraging to recall, however, that a good tentative theory has usually proved to be autocatalytic; a demonstration of what can be done, even within a limited sphere, draws attention to theory-building, and the process is accelerated.

There is usually no need to justify a theory of behavior when its potentialities are made clear, for these are very great. Consider the case of the social sciences, for example. The current practice of the sociologist is either to express his facts and theories without referring to individual behavior at all, or to construct a psychology of his own—devoting at least an introductory chapter (if not an entire treatise) to the motives and habits which lead men to live together and behave together as they do. The sociologist may or may not agree that the behavior of the group is to be predicted from a study of the psychology of the individual, but he has no hesitation in using the behavior of the individual to expound, if not to explain, sociological facts. The economist, whether professional or professorial, faces the same alternatives. Either he must state laws and make predictions without mentioning human behavior, or he must devise a special psychology to explain the activities of the great-grandchildren of Adam Smith's "economic man." It is the exceptional economist who does not account for facts about goods or money or labor or capital by pointing to what men will typically do under certain circumstances. Similarly, the political scientist, whether or not he hopes to derive the principles of government or the characteristics of political struggles from psychology, usually continues to talk about some species of "political man," to whom he assigns just the motives and capacities needed to account for his political facts.

Whatever his field, the social scientist does not currently find in the science of psychology a conceptual scheme with which he can talk about human behavior consistently and effectively. Economic man, political man, the group mind—these are crude explanatory fictions which need to be replaced by a sound behavioral theory. That such a theory need not be essential to a true social science is beside the point. There is no question that it would be enormously helpful.

There is a greater need for such a theory in those broad fields of human endeavor in which rigorous scientific practices are not yet feasible. For example, a widespread critical examination of our educational practices is currently in progress. This is basically a program of psychological engineering. Yet it is being projected and carried through with a quite unrealistic conception of human behavior. Ancient theories of the nature of man recur again and again with their familiar cant—"an integrated view of life," "a sense of personal responsibility," "a capacity to experience and understand life as a related whole," "the development of the mind," and so on. Educators are not wholly to blame, for we have not yet put forth a workable conception of human behavior suitable for their purposes.

Our legal system, to take another example, is based upon an even older form of the traditional theory. It is becoming more and more difficult to reconcile our modern conception of man and society with the legal notion of personal responsibility, of a will capable of conscious motion and dominated from time to time by ideas, feelings, and influences. But an alternative theory is apparently not yet in workable form.

The lack of an adequate understanding of human behavior is most cruelly felt in the field of government and world affairs. We are faced with the disheartening spectacle of hundreds of men of good will drawing up blueprints for the world of the future, while making assumptions about human nature which most of us know to be invalid. Two world wars have not been fought over anything as simple as world trade or boundaries. We are in transition from one conception of man to another and to an effective understanding of the possible relationships which may exist between men. We have paid a terrible price for knowledge which could conceivably be acquired through the peaceful and profitable methods of science, and as yet we have little to show for it. A great deal may depend upon whether we can reach in the near future a workable theory of human behavior.

One important role of a scientific theory of behavior, then, is to replace the theories which now pervade our thinking, which are part of our everyday speech, which influence all our dealings with our fellow men, and which stand in the way of applying the methods of science to human affairs. As everyone knows, many technical procedures which would improve our practices in education, law, politics, and so on are now available. The contributions which the science of psychology can make in these matters is very great. Psychologists have been powerful advocates of an objective attitude and will undoubtedly continue to insist that the methods of science be applied to human behavior and human society wherever possible. If we are to talk about behavior, let us be precise. If we are to insist that two facts are related, let us prove the relation. Psychology can offer better ways of describing and measuring behavior, better methods of guaranteeing the validity of statements, and so on. But nothing of this sort is any longer exclusively a psychological contribution. The main task is to make these technical contributions felt, to put them into the hands of the people who need them; and we can do this only when we make it clear that a science is more than method, more than facts. The most important contribution that psychology can make today is a workable theory of behavior in the present sense—a conception of man which is in accord with all the facts of human behavior and which has been crucially tested in the experimental laboratory. Only an effective and progressive theory of behavior can bring about the proper change in attitude which will make it possible to apply the methods of science to human affairs in every field.

The survival of the traditional conception of man as a free and responsible agent is an excellent example of the general principle that a theory is never overthrown by facts, but only by another theory. There are facts which have been well established for centuries which are incompatible with the traditional theories of human behavior, and these theories move about in the modern world in a welter of contradiction. But their proponents work busily to patch them up, and somehow they survive. A new interpretation here, a conspiracy of silence there, and the trick is turned; and this will continue to be so until a new and effective theory is worked out.

We cannot remedy the situation by mere dialectic. We need to arrive at a theory of human behavior which is not only plausible, not only sufficiently convincing to be "sold" to the public at large, but a theory which has proved its worth in scientific productivity. It must enable us, not only to talk about the problems of the world, but to do something about them, to achieve the sort of control which it is the business of a science of behavior to investigate. The superiority of such a theory will then be clear and we shall not need to worry about its acceptance.

The important trend in experimental psychology, then, is toward a satisfactory theory of behavior. Perhaps we should not be surprised at this, since the field was defined in such a way that it would necessarily be true. But the field had to be defined in that way. Experimental psychology is more than a tradition; it is more than an assemblage of practices and interests passed along from generation to generation without respect to a changing world. A tradition needs to be reviewed and justified, and this is especially true in experimental psychology, where it has been easy to lose the main theme. The trend, then, is toward a clarification of this theme, toward a sort of self-realization. The experimental psychologist is not using method for method's sake. He is not following an interest to which he has been led by indulging in one idle curiosity after another. He does not seize upon a field of research because the practical-minded have left it untouched. In so far as he is behaving as an experimental psychologist, he is trying to understand behavior. In this work he must discover and collect facts, and he must construct an adequate theory.

A clear realization of this aim should be helpful. There is nothing wrong with experimental psychology which a clear-cut objective will not cure. The development of an effective theory of behavior is ideal for this purpose. The science of experimental psychology will presumably remain in the hands of the professors. Critical issues in applied fields may lead to important contributions to theory; methods will be devised and facts discovered in industry, education, the clinic, and so on, which are relevant to a central science. But the husbanding of facts, the sifting of information from all fields of human behavior, the special study of questions which are theoretically crucial, and the working out of a satisfactory conceptual system will presumably remain the function of the psychologists in our universities. This is still so, at least, in older sciences with much more extensive technological applications. It is appropriate, too, that a concern for theory in this sense should remain closely associated with instruction.

But the academic psychologist is limited in the time and facilities available for research, and at the moment he may be rather bewildered by, if not envious of, the glittering technical advantages of his erstwhile colleagues. In theory-construction, however, he finds a field which is not only exclusively his own, but one in which he can experiment effectively and to some purpose with relatively limited resources. He will not need to confine himself to facts which have been neglected by those who can experiment more efficiently. He will be able to explore key positions of the greatest importance. The *experimentum crucis* is his field, and in it he may usually rest content with one subject for every hundred studied by his applied colleagues and with one chronoscope or pursuitmeter or cathode-ray oscillograph in place of dozens.

This is not a gesture of escape. It is not a conclusion that the grapes are sour. The experimental psychologist is above all a scientist, and this is the proper field of science—the discovery and ordering and understanding of nature. This is Faraday and Maxwell rather than the laboratories of General Electric or Westinghouse. It is Mendel and T. H. Morgan rather than an agricultural breeding station. It is Pasteur and Koch rather than research laboratories of great pharmaceutical houses. This is good company. To understand human behavior in the sense in which any part of nature is understood by science is truly an exciting and satisfying goal.

The Flight from the Laboratory

The circumstances under which this paper was written are described in the first paragraphs. It was given at the University of Pittsburgh in January, 1958, and is reprinted here by permission of the University of Pittsburgh Press.

An experimental psychologist sometimes invites a man into a laboratory, asks him to memorize a list of nonsense syllables or learn to keep a pointer on a moving target, and sends him on his way quite unaware that he will be asked to come back later for a second series of observations. The experiment will not succeed unless he is ignorant of the future test. I do not know whether the originator of these conferences was conducting such an experiment ten years ago, but I can now report what it feels like to be invited back for the second session. It is mainly a feeling of regret. If, when I was preparing my earlier paper, I had known that I would be asked to compare my prediction of trends in experimental psychology with a decade of actual historical fact, I should have confined myself to statements which could have been more easily twisted to accommodate the eventualities. I should have prepared a much more palatable dish of humble pie.

It is obvious now, after the fact, that the trends I described were scarcely more than my hopes for the future of experimental psychology. Possibly my behavior could be defended as a gesture appropriate to the intellectual climate of 1947. Experimental psychology was then at the nadir of its popularity. Graduate students were turning to social, personal, clinical, and applied psychology in ever-increasing numbers, and defections from the ranks among older men were common. The practical contributions which experimental psychologists had made during World War II had not offset a growing impatience with their stubborn dedication to seemingly unimportant aspects of human behavior. But was there not a bright spot on this murky horizon? If the history of science were any guide, an effective psychology would eventually develop a central conception of human behavior which not only would be fundamentally "right" in the sense of enabling us to *understand* behavior, whatever that might mean, but would generate

From *Current Trends in Psychological Theory*. Pittsburgh: University of Pittsburgh Press, 1961.

powerful techniques having important applications in every field of human affairs. No theory of behavior had yet come close to that achievement. Psychoanalysis was the only discipline which had spread beyond its original boundaries, and it had gone no further than some of the social sciences and literary criticism. Elsewhere—in government, economics, religion, education, and all the natural sciences—provincial theories of human behavior were eked out by the tattered theory which had been bequeathed to the English language by a long line of outmoded philosophies. It was as if each of the technologies of physical science had its own scientific conception of nature—as if specialists in synthetic fibers used one theory of molecular structure, pharmacologists another, and biochemists still another, while the layman carried on with a commonsense view of the structure of matter untouched by any of these technical treatments. Such a state of affairs was far from satisfactory. After all, it was the same man who was of interest to psychologists, political scientists, theologians, psychotherapists, economists, educators, literary critics, and scientific methodologists. Why should there be a different theory of human behavior in each case?

Into this power vacuum, it seemed to me, experimental psychology must eventually move. A general theory of human behavior was needed, and only an experimental science could supply it. Separate technologies of behavior could temporize with particular theories, but the special control of variables attainable only in laboratory experimentation would ultimately supply the account which, being in closest accord with the actual properties of the human organism, would be most useful in every field of human affairs. The close check with reality characteristic of experimental analysis would be most likely to expose the fictional entities which had played so devastating a role in what passed for psychological explanation and would permit us to escape from the inaccessible, hypothetical constructs emerging from statistical analyses. This extrapolation of the history of science was intended to give the experimental psychologist a broader horizon. In pointing out the potential significance of an effective theory of human behavior and the special place of a laboratory science in developing such a theory, I was trying to alter the contingencies of reinforcement of my colleagues in the hope of stemming what seemed to be a perpetually ebbing tide.

It is tempting to argue that this proved, indeed, to be an actual trend. It is possible that theories of behavior derived from the clinic or from field studies, rather than from the laboratory, are on the wane. A strict Freudian psychology, for example, is no longer stoutly defended. Certain general points have been made—in some sense we are all Freudians—but the facts and principles which have been salvaged can be stated in relatively non-technical language. Even the patient under therapy is no longer likely to be burdened with technical references to the structure and function of the psyche. Experimental psychologists are not responsible for this change, but if the common heritage of psychoanalysis is to be put in good scientific order, if an effective technology is to be more than a general understanding of the motives and emotions of oneself and one's fellow men, experimental psychologists will play an important role. The Freudian dynamisms can be subjected to experimental analysis, and the resulting changes in definition reveal the experimental method at work.[1] The Freudian explanatory system seldom traces the causal linkage far enough. We do not really explain "disturbed behavior" by attributing it to "anxiety" until we have also explained the anxiety. The extra step required is in the spirit of an experimental science: it is a search for a manipulable variable rather than a verbal explanation. Psychoanalysis itself has identified some of the conditions which must be changed in order to modify behavior in psychotherapy, and to bring about other behavioral effects, but its methodology is not adapted to the manipulation and control of these conditions. In contrast, experimental psychology is becoming more and more successful in dealing with the variables to which one must eventually turn for a full account of behavior and for effective control.

There are other signs of a change. The layman's way of talking about behavior, deeply entrenched in our everyday vocabulary though it is, has lost ground. It is viewed with greater uneasiness by those who use it. Ten years ago the physiologist, neurologist, or pharmacologist whose research involved behavior was likely to set up his own experiments and to describe his results in non-technical terms. He now accepts the experimental psychologist as a specialist to whom he must turn for help. To take a very different example, the lay terminology is now more often used with apologies (or in quotation marks) by political scientists. The ultimate danger of arguing from historical analogy, and of predicting or recommending courses of action by deducing theorems from axiomatic principles or governmental stereotypes, is more likely to be recognized. The ideological use of the work of Pavlov by Soviet propagandists has little to recommend it, but we probably make the same mistake when we counter by expressing contempt for techniques of government based on conditioned reflexes. In the long run all this will have a salutary effect if it leads us to ask whether a more adequate science of behavior may not be relevant to the design of governmental practices. A conception of human behavior will eventually

[1] See *Science & Human Behavior,* Chapter 24.

prove workable, not because it fits a momentary predilection for a philosophy of government, but because it survives the test of experimental analysis.

Somewhere between the extremes of physiology and government lies a third bit of evidence for a possible trend. Educational psychologists have long been devotees of research, but the pattern of a laboratory science has not been closely followed. Their experiments have seldom come to grips with the behavior of the individual student in the act of learning. On the other hand, the experimental psychology of learning, though once a staple in textbooks on education, has been receiving less and less attention. But we have learned a great deal about learning in the past decade. A proposal to put this to use in education was made at an earlier conference in this series. The principles of an experimental analysis are now being extended to the field of verbal behavior, and it is inconceivable that the results will not be used to improve instructional procedures. And with fabulous results. Enough has already been done to justify the prediction that what is now learned by the average college student will someday be learned in half the time with half the effort.

There is, then, evidence of a renaissance in experimental psychology which might be attributed in part to a realization of the potential contribution of the experimental method. But it does not warrant the claim that I correctly predicted a major trend. A general theory of human behavior in this sense has appealed to only a "happy few." As one can easily discover by glancing at the tables of contents of our journals, experimental psychology as a whole has not shown much change. Very little current research is reported in the frame of reference of a comprehensive theory. Nor has the point of view of an experimental analysis yet reached far afield. Many social sciences remain untouched, and among natural scientists there is almost complete ignorance of the promise and achievement of the scientific study of behavior. Dr. Neils Bohr, one of the most distinguished living physicists, recently discussed certain issues in psychology as follows:

> Quite apart from the extent to which the use of words like "instinct" and "reason" in the description of animal behavior is necessary and justifiable, the word "consciousness," applied to oneself as well as to others, is indispensable when describing the human situation. . . . The use of words like "thought" and "feeling" does not refer to a firmly connected causal chain, but to experiences which exclude each other because of different distinctions between the conscious content and the background which we loosely term ourselves. . . . We must recognize that psychical experience cannot be subjected to physical measurements and that the very concept of volition does not refer to a gen-

eralization of a deterministic description, but from the outset points to characteristics of human life. Without entering into the old philosophical discussion of freedom of the will, I shall only mention that in an objective description of our situation the use of the word "volition" corresponds closely to that of words like "hope" and "responsibility," which are equally indispensable to human communications.[2]

These terms and issues would have been at home in psychological discussions fifty years ago. (Indeed, one commentator mentioned the similarity of Dr. Bohr's views to those of William James.)

How shocked Dr. Bohr would be if a distinguished psychologist were to discuss modern problems in physical science in terms which were current at the beginning of the century! Psychology in general, and experimental psychology in particular, is still a long way from providing a conception of human behavior which is as readily accepted by those who deal with men as the views of physics are accepted by those who deal with the physical world. And psychologists themselves are not doing much about it.

I therefore return to the attack. (In doing so I assert my membership in a species distinguished by the fact that, at least when psychotic, its members sometimes fail to show extinction.)[3] But I shall not doggedly repeat my exhortations or promises of a decade ago. It is evidently not enough to strengthen the scientific behavior of psychologists by giving them a glimpse of an exciting future. Fortunately, as one achievement of the intervening decade, the problem can now be attacked with a better brand of behavioral engineering. I propose to analyze the behavior of psychologists. Why are they not currently developing the pure science of human behavior from which such tremendous technological advances would certainly flow? How are we to explain the continuing flight from the experimental field? Where have the experimental psychologists gone, and what are they doing instead? And why? And, above all, what steps can be taken to remedy the situation? Such questions clarify the engineering task which faces us if we are to *produce* the trend in experimental psychology which I insist upon predicting.

So stated, the problem has an analogy in a type of experiment which is growing in importance in the experimental analysis of behavior. When we have studied the performances generated by various contingencies of reinforcement in a single arbitrary response, we can move on to two or more concurrent responses. Instead of one lever to be pressed by a rat or one key to be pecked by a pigeon, our experimental space now frequently contains two or three levers or keys, each with its own set of reinforcing contingen-

[2] Bohr, N. *Atomic physics and human knowledge.* New York, 1958.
[3] See reference page 158.

cies. In the present experiment, we are to account for the fact that psychologists have stopped pressing the experimental lever and have turned to other available manipulanda. To explain this two questions must be asked: (1) What has happened to the reinforcing contingencies on the experimental lever? and (2) What contingencies compete so effectively elsewhere? Once these questions have been answered, we can proceed to the engineering task of increasing the relative effectiveness of the experimental contingencies. It would probably be unfair to do this by attacking competing conditions, for any source of scientific zeal should be respected, but it is possible that some of the reinforcements responsible for activity on other levers can be made contingent upon the response in which we are primarily interested.

Some deficiencies in the rewards of the experimental psychologist were analyzed in my earlier paper. All sciences undergo changes in fashion. Problems lose interest even though they remain unsolved. In psychology many green pastures have been glimpsed on the other side of the experimental fence. The very success of a science may force it to become preoccupied with smaller and smaller details, which cannot compete with broad new issues. The philosophical motivation of the pioneers of a "mental science" has been lost. Although idealism is evidently still a fighting word in some parts of the world, dualism is no longer a challenging issue in American psychology. Classical research on the relation between the psychic and the physical has been transmuted into the study of the physiological and physical actions of end-organs. This is a scientific step forward, but an important source of inspiration has been left behind.

Some of the most effective rewards contingent upon experimental practice have been inadvertently destroyed in another way. We owe most of our scientific knowledge to methods of inquiry which have never been formally analyzed or expressed in normative rules. For more than a generation, however, our graduate schools have been building psychologists on a different pattern of Man Thinking. They have taught statistics in lieu of scientific method. Unfortunately, the statistical pattern is incompatible with some major features of laboratory research. As now taught, statistics plays down the direct manipulation of variables and emphasizes the treatment of variation after the fact. If the graduate student's first result is not significant, statistics tells him to increase the size of his sample; it does not tell him (and, because of self-imposed restrictions on method, it cannot tell him) how to achieve the same result by improving his instruments and his methods of observation. Bigger samples mean more work, the brunt of which the young psychologist may have to bear. When he gets his degree (and a grant), he may pass the labor on to someone else, but in doing so he himself loses contact with the experimental organism he is studying. What statisticians call experimental design (I have pointed out elsewhere that this means design which yields data to which the methods of statistics are appropriate) usually generates a much more intimate acquaintance with a calculating machine than with a behaving organism. One result is a damaging delay in reinforcement. An experiment may "pay off" only after weeks of routine computation. A graduate student who designs an experiment according to accepted statistical methods may survive the ordeal of the calculating room by virtue of his youthful zeal, but his ultimate reinforcement as a scientist may be so long deferred that he will never begin another experiment. Other levers then beckon.

The psychologist who adopts the commoner statistical methods has at best an indirect acquaintance with the "facts" he discovers—with the vectors, factors, and hypothetical processes secreted by the statistical machine. He is inclined to rest content with rough measures of behavior because statistics shows him how to "do something about them." He is likely to continue with fundamentally unproductive methods, because squeezing something of significance out of questionable data discourages the possibly more profitable step of scrapping the experiment and starting again.

Statistics offers its own brand of reinforcement, of course, but this is often not contingent upon behavior which is most productive in the laboratory. One destructive effect is to supply a sort of busy work for the compulsive. In the early stages of any inquiry the investigator often has to weather a period of ignorance and chaos during which apparent progress is slight, if not lacking altogether. This is something he must be taught to endure. He must acquire a kind of faith in the ultimate value of ostensibly undirected exploration. He must also learn to be indifferent to the criticism that he is not getting anywhere. If he has accepted funds in support of his research, he must learn to tolerate a gnawing anxiety about the annual report. At such times statistics offers consoling comfort and, what is worse, an all-too-convenient escape-hatch. How simple it is to match groups of subjects, devise a crude measure of the behavior at issue, arrange for tests to be administered, and punch the scores into IBM cards! No matter what comes of it all, no one can say that work has not been done. Statistics will even see to it that the result will be "significant" even if it is proved to mean nothing.

The intention of the statistician is honorable and generous. He wants the experimental scientist to be sure of his results and to get the most out of them. But, whether or not he understands the essence of laboratory practice, his recommendations are often inimical to it. Perhaps against his will, he has made certain essential activities in good laboratory research no longer respectable. The very instrument which might have made an experimental science more rewarding has, instead, all but destroyed its basic features. In the long run the psychologist has been deprived of some of his most profitable, and hence eventually most reinforcing, achievements.

The resulting flight from the laboratory can be stopped by pointing to alternative methods of research. If all psychologists are to be required to take courses in statistics, they should also be made familiar with laboratory practices and given the chance to behave as scientists rather than as the robots described by scientific methodologists. In particular, young psychologists should learn how to work with single organisms rather than with large groups. Possibly with that one step alone we could restore experimental psychology to the vigorous health it deserves.

But it will be worthwhile to examine the competing contingencies. Psychologists have fled from the laboratory, and perhaps for good reason. Where have they gone?

The Flight to Real People

Laboratories can be dull places, and not only when furnished with calculating machines. It is not surprising that psychologists have been attracted by the human interest of real life. The experimental subject in the laboratory is only part of a man, and frequently an uninteresting part, while the whole individual is a fascinating source of reinforcement. Literature flourishes for that reason. Psychologists have long since learned to borrow from the literary domain. If a lecture flags, or a chapter seems dull, one has only to bring in a case history and everything literally "comes to life." The recipe is so foolproof that the lecture or text which consists of nothing but case histories has been closely approximated. But in resorting to this device for pedagogical or therapeutic effect psychologists have themselves been influenced by these reinforcers; their courses of action as scientists have been deflected. They often recognize this and from time to time have felt the need for a special theory of scientific knowledge (based, for example, on empathy or intuition) to justify themselves. They seldom seem to feel secure, however, in the belief that they have regained full citizenship in the scientific commonwealth.

The reinforcements which flow from real people are not all related to, on the one hand, an intellectual conviction that the proper study of mankind is man or, on the other, the insatiable curiosity of a Paul Pry. In a world in which ethical training is widespread, most men are reinforced when they succeed in reinforcing others. In such a world personal gratitude is a powerful generalized reinforcer. We can scarcely hold it against psychologists that, like other men of good will, they want to help their fellow men— either one by one in the clinic or nation by nation in, say, studies of international good will. We may agree that the world would be a better place if more men would concern themselves with personal and political problems. But we must not forget that the remedial step is necessarily a short-term measure and that it is not the only step leading to the same goal. The lively prosecution of a science of behavior, applied to the broad problem of cultural design, could have more sweeping consequences. If such a promising alternative is actually feasible, anyone who is capable of making a long-term contribution may wisely resist the effect of other consequences which, no matter how important they may be to him personally, are irrelevant to the scientific process and confine him to short-term remedial action. A classical example from another field is Albert Schweitzer. Here is a brilliant man who, for reasons we need not examine, dedicated his life to helping his fellow men—one by one. He has earned the gratitude of thousands, but we must not forget what he might have done instead. If he had worked as energetically for as many years in a laboratory of tropical medicine, he would almost certainly have made discoveries which in the long run would help—not thousands—but literally *billions* of people. We do not know enough about Schweitzer to say why he took the short-term course. Could he not resist the blandishments of gratitude? Was he freeing himself from feelings of guilt? Whatever his reasons, his story warns us of the danger of a cultural design which does not harness some personal reinforcement in the interests of pure science. The young psychologist who wants above all to help his fellow men should be made to see the tremendous potential consequences of even a small contribution to the scientific understanding of human behavior. It is possibly this understanding alone, with the improved cultural patterns which will flow from it, which will eventually alleviate the anxieties and miseries of mankind.

The Flight to Mathematical Models

The flight from the experimental method has sometimes gone in the other direction. If the human being studied in the laboratory has been too drab and unreal for some, he has been just the opposite for others. In spite of our vaunted control of variables, the experimental subject too often remains capricious. Sometimes he is not only warm but, as baseball players say, too hot to handle. Even the "average man," when captured in the statistical net, may be unpleasantly refractory. Some psychologists have therefore fled to an ivory image of their own sculpturing, mounted on a mathematical pedestal. These Pygmalions have constructed a Galatea who always behaves as she is supposed to behave, whose processes are orderly and relatively simple, and to whose behavior the most elegant of mathematical procedures may be applied. She is a creature whose slightest blemish can be erased by the simple expedient of changing an assumption. Just as political scientists used to simplify their problems by talking about an abstract Political Man, and the economists theirs by talking about Economic Man, so psychologists have built the ideal experimental organism—the Mathematical Model.

The effect of this practice on so-called learning theory has been pointed out elsewhere (page 69). Early techniques available for the study of learning—from the nonsense syllables of Ebbinghaus, through the problem boxes of Thorndike and the mazes of Watson, to the discrimination apparatuses of Yerkes and Lashley—always yielded learning curves of disturbing irregularity. In experiments with these instruments an orderly change in the behavior of a single organism was seldom seen. Orderly processes had to be generated by averaging data, either for many trials or many organisms. Even so, the resulting "learning curves" varied in a disturbing way from experiment to experiment. The theoretical solution to this problem was to assume that an orderly learning process, which always had the same properties regardless of the particular features of a given experiment, took place somewhere inside the organism. A given result was accounted for by making a distinction between learning and performance. Though the performance might be chaotic, the psychologist could continue to cherish the belief that learning was always orderly. Indeed, the mathematical organism seemed so orderly that model builders remained faithful to techniques which consistently yielded disorderly data. An examination of mathematical models in learning theory will show that no degree of disorder in the facts has placed any restriction on the elegance of the mathematical treatment.

The properties which (to drop to a two-dimensional figure of speech) make a paper doll [4] more amenable than a living organism are crucial in a scientific account of behavior. No matter how many of the formulations derived from the study of a model eventually prove useful in describing reality (remember wave-mechanics!), the questions to which answers are

[4] The reference, of course, is to the well-known song by Johnny S. Black, in which the lyricist expresses his preference for "a paper doll to call his own" rather than a "fickleminded real live girl."

most urgently needed concern the correspondence between the two realms. How can we be sure that a model is a model of *behavior?* What *is* behavior, and how is it to be analyzed and measured? What are the relevant features of the environment, and how are they to be measured and controlled? How are these two sets of variables related? The answers to these questions cannot be found by constructing models. (Nor is a model likely to be helpful in furthering the necessary empirical inquiry. It is often argued that some model, hypothesis, or theory is essential because the scientist cannot otherwise choose among the facts to be studied. But there are presumably as many models, hypotheses, or theories as facts. If the scientific methodologist will explain how he proposes to choose among them, his answer will serve as well to explain how one may choose among empirical facts.)

What sort of behavioral engineering will reduce the rate of responding to the mathematical lever and induce distinguished psychologists to get back to the laboratory? Two steps seem to be needed. First, it must be made clear that the formal properties of a system of variables can be profitably treated only after the dimensional problems have been solved. The detached and essentially tautological nature of mathematical models is usually frankly admitted by their authors, particularly those who come into experimental psychology from mathematics, but for the psychologist these disclaimers are often lost among the integral signs. Secondly, the opportunity to be mathematical in dealing with factual material should be clarified. To return to the example of learning theory, the psychologist should recognize that with proper techniques one can *see learning take place,* not in some inner recess far removed from the observable performance of an organism, but as a change in that performance itself. Techniques are now available for the experimental analysis of very subtle behavioral processes, and this work is ready for the kind of mathematical theory which has always been productive at the proper stage in the history of science. What is needed is not a mathematical model, constructed with little regard for the fundamental dimensions of behavior, but a mathematical treatment of experimental data. Mathematics will come into its own in the analysis of behavior when appropriate methods yield data which are so orderly that there is no longer any need to escape to a dream world.

The Flight to the Inner Man

Experimental psychology has suffered perhaps its greatest loss of manpower because competent investigators, beginning with a *descriptive* interest in behavior, have passed almost immediately to an *explanatory* preoccupation with what is going on inside the organism. In discussing this flight to the inner man I should like to believe that I am whipping a dead horse, but the fact remains that human behavior is still most commonly discussed in terms of psychic or physiological processes. A dualistic philosophy is not necessarily implied in either case for it may be argued, on the one hand, that the data of physics reduce at last to the direct experience of the physicist or, on the other, that behavior is only a highly organized set of biological facts. The nature of any real or fancied inner cause of behavior is not at issue; investigative practices suffer the same damage in any case.

Sometimes, especially among psychoanalysts, the inner men are said to be organized personalities whose activities lead at last to the behavior of the organism we observe. The commoner practice is to dissect the inner man and deal separately with his traits, perceptions, experiences, habits, ideas, and so on. In this way an observable subject matter is abandoned in favor of an inferred. It was Freud himself who insisted that mental processes could occur without "conscious participation" and that, since they could not always be directly observed, our knowledge of them must be inferential. Much of the machinery of psychoanalysis is concerned with the process of inference. In the analysis of behavior we may deal with *all* mental processes as inferences, whether or not they are said to be conscious. The resulting re-definition (call it operational if you like) conveniently omits the mentalistic dimension. At the same time, however, the explanatory force is lost. Inner entities or events do not "cause" behavior, nor does behavior "express" them. At best they are mediators, but the causal relations between the terminal events which are mediated are inadequately represented by traditional devices. Mentalistic concepts may have had some heuristic value at one stage in the analysis of behavior, but it has long since been more profitable to abandon them. In an acceptable explanatory scheme the ultimate causes of behavior must be found *outside* the organism.

The *physiological* inner man is, of course, no longer wholly inferential. New methods and instruments have brought the nervous system and other mechanisms under direct observation. The new data have their own dimensions and require their own formulations. The behavioral facts in the field of learning, for example, are dealt with in terms appropriate to behavior, while electrical or chemical activities occurring at the same time demand a different conceptual framework. Similarly, the effects of deprivation and satiation on behavior are not the same as the events seen through a gastric fistula. Nor is emotion, studied as behavioral predisposition, capable of being analyzed in terms appropriate to pneumographs and electrocardiographs. Both sets of facts, and their appropriate concepts, are important—

but they are *equally* important, not dependent one upon the other. Under the influence of a contrary philosophy of explanation, which insists upon the reductive priority of the inner event, many brilliant men who began with an interest in behavior, and might have advanced our knowledge of that field in many ways, have turned instead to the study of physiology. We cannot dispute the importance of their contributions, we can only imagine with regret what they might have done instead.

If we are to make a study of behavior sufficiently reinforcing to hold the interest of young men in competition with inner mechanisms, we must make clear that behavior is an acceptable subject matter in its own right, and that it can be studied with acceptable methods and without an eye to reductive explanation. The responses of an organism to a given environment are physical events. Modern methods of analysis reveal a degree of order in such a subject matter which compares favorably with that of any phenomena of comparable complexity. Behavior is not simply the result of more fundamental activities, to which our research must therefore be addressed, but an end in itself, the substance and importance of which are demonstrated in the practical results of an experimental analysis. We can predict and control behavior, we can modify it, we can construct it according to specifications—and all without answering the explanatory questions which have driven investigators into the study of the inner man. The young psychologist may contemplate a true science of behavior without anxiety.

The Flight to Laymanship

Experimental psychology has also had to contend with what is in essence a rejection of the whole scientific enterprise. In a recent review of a study of the psychological problems of aging, the reviewer comments upon "a tendency in psychological thought which is returning to prominence after some years of relative disfavor. The statements have a certain refreshing directness and 'elegance' in their approach to the study of human behavior. The sterile arguments of so-called 'learning theory,' the doctrinaire half-truths of the 'schools,' the panacea treatments of 'systems,' and the high-sounding, empty technical terms often found in psychological writings are conspicuous by their absence." No one will want to defend "*sterile* arguments," "half-truths," "panaceas," or "*empty* technical terms," no matter what their sources, but the force of the passage is more than this. The author is rejecting all efforts to improve upon the psychology of the layman in approaching the problems of the aged. And many psychologists agree with him.

"Enough of the lingo of the laboratory!" the argument runs. "Enough of clinical jargon! Enough of frightening equations! A plague on all your houses! Let us go back to commonsense! Let us say what we want to say about human behavior in the well-worn but still useful vocabulary of the layman!" Whether this is a gesture of fatigue or impatience, or the expression of a desire to get on with practical matters at the expense of a basic understanding, it must be answered by anyone who defends a pure science. It would be easier to find the answer if experimental psychology had moved more rapidly toward a helpful conception of human behavior.

Some progress has been made in proving the superiority of scientific concepts over those of traditional usage. Consider, for example, two psychological accounts written in the vulgar tongue. First, a sample in the field of emotional behavior:

> The emotional temper of the type of juvenile delinquent just mentioned is as extraordinary as it is well-known. Far from being naturally peaceful, sympathetic, or generous, men who are excluded from the society of their fellow men become savage, cruel, and morose. The wanton destructiveness of the delinquent is not due to sudden bursts of fury, but to a deliberate and brooding resolve to wage war on everything.

The second has to do with intellect. It is an explanation of how a child learns to open a door by depressing a thumb-latch and pushing against the door with his legs.

> Of course the child may have observed that doors are opened by grownups placing their hands on the handles, and having observed this the child may act by what is termed imitation. But the process as a whole is something more than imitative. Observation alone would be scarcely enough to enable the child to discover that the essential thing is not to grasp the handle but to depress the latch. Moreover, the child certainly never saw any grownup push the door with his legs as it is necessary for the child to do. This pushing action must be due to an originally deliberate intention to open the door, not to accidentally having found this action to have this effect.

Both passages make intelligible points and would conceivably be helpful in discussing juvenile delinquency or the teaching of children. But there is a trap. Actually the heroes of these pieces were not human at all. The quotations are slightly altered passages from Romanes' *Animal Intelligence,* published about seventy-five years ago. The first describes the behavior of the prototype of all delinquents—the rogue elephant. The "child" of the second was a cat—possibly the very cat which set Thorndike to work to discover how animals do, indeed, learn to press latches.

The experimental analysis of behavior has clearly shown the practical and theoretical value of abandoning a commonsense way of talking about behavior and has demonstrated the advantages of an alternative account of emotion and intelligence. That is to say, it has done this for cats, rats, pigeons, and monkeys. Its successes are only slowly reaching into the field of human behavior—not because we any longer assume that man is fundamentally different but in part because an alternative method of analysis is felt to be available because of the scientist's membership in the human species. But the special knowledge resulting from self-observation can be given a formulation which preserves intact the notion of the continuity of species. Experimental methods can be applied first to the behavior of the Other One, and only later to the analysis of the behavior of the scientist himself. The value of this practice is demonstrated in the consistency of the resulting account and the effectiveness of the resulting technological control.

It is not difficult to explain the strength of traditional concepts. Many of those who discuss human behavior are speaking to laymen and must adapt their terms to their audience. The immediate effect of the lay vocabulary also gains strength from its deep intrenchment in the language. Our legal system is based on it, and the literature of ideas is couched in it. Moreover, from time to time efforts are made to rejuvenate the philosophical systems from which it came. Aristotle, through Thomas Aquinas, still speaks to some students of behavior. The very fact that Aristotle's psychology, scarcely modified, can be seriously championed in behavioral science today shows how little it has done to advance our understanding. Aristotelian physics, chemistry, and biology have enjoyed no such longevity. We may look forward to the early demise of this sole survivor of Greek science.

A return to the lay vocabulary of behavior cannot be justified. The move is a matter of motivation, competence, or the accessibility of goals. These are all irrelevant to the long-term achievement of a scientific account of behavior. No doubt, many pressing needs can still be most readily satisfied by casual discussion. In the long run, however, we shall need an effective understanding of human behavior—so that, in the example cited, we shall know the nature of the changes which take place as men and women grow old and shall, therefore, be in the most favorable position to do something about them. To reach that understanding we must recognize the limitations of the remedial patchwork which emerges from commonsense discussion and must be willing to resort to experiments which quite possibly involve complicated techniques and to theoretical treatments quite possibly expressed in difficult terms.

Conclusion

We have glanced briefly at four *divertissements* in the growth of a science of human behavior. Real Men, Mathematical Men, Inner Men, and Everyday Men—it would be a mistake to underestimate their seductive power. Together they constitute a formidable array of rival suitors, and to groom the Experimental Organism for this race may seem a hopeless enterprise. But he has a chance, for in the long run he offers the greatest net reinforcement to the scientist engaged in the study of behavior. I doubt whether this fact will affect many of those who have already flown from the laboratory, but I am not speaking to them. A story about William James is appropriate. James was much in demand as a lecturer and one day discovered that he was scheduled to address a ladies' literary society in a suburb of Boston. He set off to keep his appointment after having picked up from his desk the first lecture which came to hand. It happened to be a lecture he had prepared for one of his Radcliffe classes. His audience, in contrast, was composed of elderly New England matrons. James was reading his paper, possibly thinking of other things, when to his horror he heard himself saying, ". . . and so, my fair young friends. . . ." He looked out upon a sea of startled faces and—failing utterly in this pragmatic test of a psychologist —blurted out, "I should explain that this lecture was written for a very different audience."

I wish I could say, and also with more tact, what audience *this* lecture was prepared for. No matter how strong my conviction that we are close to an effective science of human behavior, with all which such a science implies, I do not expect to recapture the interest and enthusiasm of those who have fled from the laboratory to pleasurable dalliance elsewhere. But some of you, I hope, are not yet committed. For you the possibility of an adequate theory of behavior, in the sense in which any empirical science leads eventually to a theoretical formulation, together with its enormous technical potential, may be enough to tip the balance. And if such of you there be, I look to you to restore to experimental psychology the energy, enthusiasm, and productivity which characterized it in an earlier epoch.

We are living in an age in which science fiction is coming true. The thrilling spectacle of man-made satellites has turned our eyes toward outer space. What we shall find there only time will tell. Meanwhile, we are confronted by far more important problems on the surface of the earth. A possible solution is in the spirit of another kind of science fiction: the eighteenth-century utopian dream of Perfectionism with its basic contention that, if human nature is determined by environment and if environment can be changed, human nature can be changed. Like an artificial satellite or a rocket to the moon, this was once a foolish dream. But science moves forward at a breathless pace. We may shortly be designing the world in which men will henceforth live. But how is it to be designed, and to what end? These are difficult questions, to which nothing short of an effective science of man will provide the answers. The methods of science no longer need verbal defense; one cannot throw a moon around the earth with dialectic. Applied to human behavior, the same methods promise even more thrilling achievements. That prospect will, I still believe, determine the trend in experimental psychology in the years to come.

PART VI

Creative Behavior

Creating the Creative Artist

There are many reasons why we may want to give art a more important place in our culture. Perhaps we simply want more art to be available to be enjoyed. Perhaps we believe that a culture in which art flourishes is stronger because it attracts and holds people who can solve practical problems. But our reasons, whatever they may be, are by no means as important as our prospects. What can be done to further the production and consumption of art?

Art and Leisure

A relation between art and leisure has long been recognized. Early man had to free himself from a constant preoccupation with food, shelter, and safety before he could begin to decorate his clothing, his dwelling, his weapons, and his body, and eventually create things with no other function than to be decorative. When civilizations reach the stage at which many people enjoy leisure, great periods of art often begin. We acknowledge the connection when we encourage artists by giving them leisure—through patronage, fellowships, grants, or sinecures. The archetypal connection between art and bohemianism or between art and life in a garret is in the same pattern, for these are devices through which the artist gives himself leisure, by avoiding commitments and living cheaply.

The relation is easily misunderstood. Certainly not everyone becomes an artist as soon as he is free to do so. And the artist will be the first to insist that just because he has managed to dispose of the things we say he "has" to do, he is not in any real sense free. The serious, dedicated artist must do what he does as earnestly and as compellingly as other men struggle for food, shelter, or safety. The difference is merely in the conspicuousness of the causes. We usually know why people behave as they do when they

From *On the Future of Art*. New York: Viking Press, 1970.

"have" to do so, but less compelling reasons are usually less obvious. They exist, however, and if we are going to encourage people to be artists (or, for that matter, consumers of art), we ought to know what they are.

The Reasons for Art

Why, indeed, do artists paint pictures? The traditional answers are not very helpful. They refer to events supposedly taking place inside the artist himself. The artist who has been freed from the pressures of the world around him is said to be able to express his individuality, his creative impulses, his love of beauty, the agony and ecstasy of his inner struggles. These are engaging theories. They represent the artist as a complex person living a dramatic life, and they give him exclusive credit for the beautiful things he creates. But we have not really explained the artist's achievement in terms of his inner life if we have learned about that life only from his achievements.

It is true that artists talk about themselves and very often about their inner lives. They are no doubt in an excellent position to observe the behavior of artists, but we must accept their accounts with caution. When they talk about their emotions, thoughts, ideas, and impulses, they necessarily use a vocabulary that they have learned from people who have had no contact with these things and who, therefore, cannot teach them to describe what they observe accurately. As a result, every artist gives his own idiosyncratic account, and his answer to the question "Why does the artist paint as he does?" is probably no more helpful than that of anyone else.

Nor does the traditional view help us in furthering the production and enjoyment of art. We have no direct contact with the mind or emotions of the artist. Only indirectly, if at all, can we induce him to have strong feelings or original ideas. If art springs from an inner life which is truly original, in the sense that it *begins* with the artist, then there is nothing to be done beyond giving the artist an opportunity. It is much more promising, however, to argue that the achievements of the artist can be traced to the world in which he lives, for we can then begin to examine that world not only to explain the achievements but also to find the means of taking practical steps.

The colloquial "what for" is often a useful synonym for "why." What do artists paint pictures *for?* What do people look at pictures *for?* The term points to the future, and emphasizes an important fact. Artists paint pictures *because of the consequences,* and people look at pictures *because of the consequences.* In traditional terms, the consequences may be said to define the purposes of art, but there is a more important implication. The relation between behavior and its consequences has recently been studied in considerable detail. In hundreds of laboratories throughout the world, in a special scientific discipline called the experimental analysis of behavior, various kinds of consequences are made contingent upon behavior in complex ways, and the effects observed. Certain kinds of consequences are said to "reinforce" behavior in the sense that they make it more likely to occur. We need not go into detail here, but if we can discover the reinforcers which are contingent upon the artist's behavior when he paints a picture, and upon the behavior of others when they look at a picture, we can not only explain their behavior but also use our knowledge to give art a more important role in our culture.

The word "reinforcing," though technical, is useful as a rough synonym for "interesting," "attractive," "pleasing," and "satisfying," and all these terms are commonly applied to pictures. For our present purposes it is particularly useful as a synonym for "beautiful." Pictures are by definition reinforcing in the sense that they are responsible for the fact that artists paint them and people look at them. It is a mistake to suppose that they do this because of how people feel about them. Feelings are mere by-products; the important thing is what a picture does to behavior. The artist puts paint on canvas and is or is not reinforced by the result. If he is reinforced, he goes on painting. Others look at the picture and are or are not reinforced when they do so. If they are reinforced, they continue to look and to seek other pictures to look at.

To some extent we are reinforced by pictures for idiosyncratic reasons. Consumers of art have different preferences and so have artists. The integrity of an artist's work is in part a matter of what features have reinforced him. If he is unduly reinforced when his pictures sell, he may begin to paint pictures which are likely to sell. The reinforcing effect of a picture is, however, significant for another reason.

The Competitors of Art

Let us look again at the relation between art and leisure. Things we "have to do" are under the control of powerful reinforcers. When hungry, we are dominated by behavior which has been reinforced by food. When under a threat, we are absorbed in avoidance or escape. But when free of powerful reinforcers, *we are simply more vulnerable to weak ones.* Leisure brings the artist under the control of inconspicuous reinforcers.

But works of art are not the only reinforcers which take over when serious consequences have been eliminated. Members of the leisure class are not all artists. On the contrary, the leisure to be observed in either an affluent society or a welfare state has a variety of quite different effects. It may lead, for example, to play—to behavior resembling serious behavior but exhibited for less than serious reasons (as in hunting and fishing, when what is caught, captured, or killed is not eaten) or to playing games in which trivial consequences have been made critical (will the ball fall into the hole?). Gambling is characteristic of leisure, and all gambling systems are designed to make their consequences particularly effective by making them contingent on behavior in unpredictable ways. Sexual behavior is characteristic of leisure because it is concerned with the survival of the species rather than the individual, and is not subject to long-term satiation; in a sense it cannot be made unimportant. Synthetic reinforcers, such as alcohol or marijuana, are among the nonessentials which take over in leisure. Spectatorship is a common feature, and recent technological advances have made it possible for vast numbers of people to watch others engage in the serious business of life, as they undergo crucial personal experiences in drama, are hurt in football and other games, or run the risks of exploration in space.

These are the natural competitors of art. How can we give art a chance against them? If art needs leisure, then leisure needs art. In essence, how can we induce the artist to paint more pictures and everyone else to look at them? The obvious answer is this: make sure that painting and looking are abundantly reinforced. And here we see the advantage in substituting "reinforcing" for "beautiful." No matter what other aspects of beauty the critic may wish to emphasize, we are for the moment interested simply in the reinforcing effect of a picture. What is it about a picture that makes the artist more inclined to continue painting it and the viewer to look at it and to continue to do so?

Why a Picture Is Reinforcing

From time to time answers have been sought in pictures themselves. Beauty, it has been said, is in the object, and we have only to analyze a large number of beautiful objects to discover it. But different people in different ages and in different cultures have found different things beautiful, and if there are indeed objective properties which make a thing beautiful or reinforcing, they must be less important than other reasons.

We say that a picture is reinforcing because of its content, but this is not a full explanation of why we look at it. It is reinforcing because it resembles real things, but these are reinforcing for other reasons. An exhaustive account would explain all of human behavior. Contingencies of survival in the evolution of the human race have made the human form an important visual reinforcer, and the human figure is, of course, common subject matter in the art of many cultures. Foodstuffs become reinforcing for other biological reasons, and it should occasion no surprise that people have, from time to time, hung pictures of fruit, fish, and game in their living rooms. Portraits of people we love or admire permit us to look at the people in absentia, and when the young lover kisses the portrait of his beloved, he is only exemplifying in a conspicuous way the kind of thing we all do when we look at a portrait: we behave toward the portrait to some slight extent as we should behave toward the person portrayed. The artist who relies mainly on content to make his pictures reinforcing is usually held deficient in other respects.

We turn from content to abstract form in a search for other kinds of reinforcing things which are less obviously traceable to the history of the individual or species. But we must not forget that what we *do* about an abstraction is still the important thing. Denman Ross pointed this out in 1907 in his *Theory of Pure Design*,[1] a book which, though not particularly influential, could be regarded as the manifesto of abstractionism. A design induces the viewer to look at it in a particular way. What he does may be common to so many visual presentations that we divorce it from content altogether and regard it as possibly close to an essential artistic process. But if an abstract picture induces a painter to finish painting it and viewers to look at it, it is because it has reinforcing properties. (The loss of content is to some extent a loss of power, and some contemporary artists offset this with a use of abstract material which is as exaggerated as the most maudlin sentimentality in representational art.)

Other issues commonly encountered in discussions of art can be restated in terms of reinforcement. The history of art is to a large extent the history of what artists and viewers have found reinforcing. Universality is the universality of reinforcing effects. Changes in fashion come about as some reinforcers lose power and others gain. The emphasis is important in its bearing upon the practical problem of improving the place of art in a culture.

There is not much the nonartist can do to make art itself more reinforcing. That is the artist's own field, and it must be left to him. It is he who must discover new kinds of reinforcers in the sense of new forms of

[1] Ross, Denman W. (1907). New York: Peter Smith, 1933.

beauty. But there are other things to be done. There are ways in which the nonartist can make it more likely that the artist will be reinforced by the pictures he paints. To become an artist (or, in the course of a career, to become a different kind of artist) is a form of learning. The "instruction" responsible for it may be entirely accidental. Can it be deliberate? Can we teach a person to be an artist? So far as technique goes, the answer is yes. And that fact is relevant to the present issue. The more competent the artist, the more reinforcing his work is likely to be—other things being equal. But what about the "other things"? Can we actually teach an artist how to discover or invent new forms of beauty in the sense of new kinds of reinforcers?

The easy answer is "no," and it is usually given by those who continue to regard artistic achievement as the expression of an inner life. Such a life is not directly within reach of a teacher; genius must be left to work its way out. And if that is the nature of art, then, apart from technique, the teacher cannot teach but only help the artist learn. Moreover, he must think twice about teaching technique lest he interfere with untaught creative expression. The position has the support of many educational philosophies outside the field of art where subject matter is abandoned in order to strengthen an inquiring spirit. The position is in essence a renunciation of teaching: the student is somehow better off if he is left to discover things for himself.

The "discovery method" is particularly attractive to those who are interested in producing original artists, but we should first be sure that it works. It is by definition not a method of instruction at all. It arose, in fact, from a concern with motivation. When teachers abandoned older forms of discipline, they lost control, and to the extent that they have not found suitable substitutes, it is quite correct to say that they can no longer teach. And they have, therefore, been tempted to let students discover knowledge for themselves.

But we do not need to abandon subject matter in order to teach discovery. It is not true that if we fill the student's head with facts he will be unable to think for himself. He is not damaged by facts but only by the ways in which facts have been taught. There is no reason why methods of discovery must be taught by the discovery method. Learning the techniques of others does not interfere with the discovery of techniques of one's own. On the contrary, the artist who has acquired a variety of techniques from his predecessors is in the best possible position to make truly original discoveries. And he is most likely to be original if he has been taught how to do so.

The very assignment of producing a *creative* artist may seem contradictory. How can behavior be original or creative if it has been "produced"? Production presupposes some form of external control, but creativity, taken literally, denies such control. That is why we tend to associate it with an inner life. Arthur Koestler has taken this line in his book, *The Act of Creation.* For Koestler a behavioral analysis of creativity is not only impossible but ludicrous, since novelty cannot arise in a "mechanistic" system. A creative *mind* must be at work. But a creative mind explains nothing. It is an appeal to the miraculous: mind is brought in to do what the body cannot do. But we must then explain how the mind does it, and if we accept that assignment, we discover that we have merely restated our original problem in much more difficult terms.

Novelty or originality can occur in a wholly deterministic system. A convenient archetypal pattern is the theory of evolution. The living forms on the earth show a variety far beyond that of works of art. The diversity was once attributed to the whims and vagaries of a creative Mind, but Darwin proposed an alternative explanation. The word "origin" in *The Origin of Species* is important, for the book is essentially a study of originality. The multiplicity of living forms is accounted for in terms of mutation and selection, without appealing to any prior design. There are comparable elements in the behavior of the artist who produces original works.

The artist facing a clean canvas is in much the same position as the writer facing a clean sheet of paper. What is to be put on it, and where is it to come from? (Those who insist that artists, like writers, must first have ideas must rephrase the question accordingly: What ideas are to be put on the clean slate of the mind, and where do they come from?) There are some simple answers. If the artist has already successfully put paint on canvas, he is likely to do the same thing again. If he has learned to copy things which are reinforcing, he can convert his clean canvas into a reinforcing object by copying something which has proved reinforcing elsewhere. It is tempting, of course, to copy other pictures, but when the other pictures have been painted by other artists, the copies will be the source of little satisfaction or approval. It is legitimate, however, for artists to copy themselves. Only the first Picasso was not derivative: all the others were derived from earlier Picassos.

What we call an original or creative painting must arise for other reasons. We must look for "mutations." Many of these are accidental in the sense that they arise from conditions which we cannot now identify in the genetic and environmental histories of the artist and from unpredictable details of his working methods and conditions. We may not like to credit any aspect of a successful painting to chance, but, if we are willing to admit that chance does make a contribution, we can take steps to improve the chances. Mutations may be made more probable by making the control of a medium less precise or by encouraging disturbances. During the Second World War new types of electronic equipment were used which could not be made wholly reliable in the available time, and an element was therefore sometimes introduced to keep the equipment in constant vibration. If a relay stuck, it would be instantly shaken loose. The vibration was called "dither." The artist introduces a source of dither when he adds an extra length of handle to his brush, or paints with bits of sponge instead of a brush, or pours paint on a horizontal canvas. He can generate mutations by changing his working conditions, by working when he is tired, cold, discouraged, or drunk. He can generate other kinds of mutations by deliberately doing what he has been taught not to do; he can violate standards, conventions, and taboos, as a mathematician denies self-evident axioms or as a composer uses previously forbidden harmonies. Randomness is most obviously deliberate when the artist spins a dial, throws dice, or consults a table of random numbers and puts paint on canvas as the results dictate.

Mutation must, however, be followed by selection. Not every product of carelessness—a cold studio, the deliberate rejection of a convention, or the roll of dice—is art. Putting paint on canvas is no more important than letting it stand, changing it, or scraping it off. The picture eventually left on the canvas is only one product of the combined processes of mutation and selection. An artist who will henceforth paint in a different way is another. The selective side of the artist's role emphasizes his uniqueness and the almost infinite variety of the circumstances under which he lives and paints. But selection is also learned and can presumably be taught. The young artist may be taught, for example, to tolerate effects he once rejected, to permit some features to stand for the sake of others, to stop painting in time, and so on.

The Role of the Consumer

Apart from the idiosyncratic factors which play a part in mutation and selection, an artist is to some extent reinforced when others enjoy his work. We can help by making sure that his work will be enjoyed. We should be explicit about this: we want to induce more people to look at more pictures and for longer periods of time—to seek out pictures to look at, as by going to museums, and to buy pictures in order that they may be looked at. People do all this when pictures are reinforcing. How can they be made so?

The artist himself is concerned with producing consumers. Whether or not he paints primarily because of effects upon himself, he constructs pictures which are reinforcing to others when they look at them. As nonartists we can help. We want pictures to be more valuable to those who look at them in the sense of being more effective in inducing them to continue to look. That is one of the functions of art education: people are taught to look at pictures in ways which are more likely to be reinforced. "Art appreciation" is an apt expression, for it is a matter of increasing the reinforcing value of art, and it is appropriate to use the same term to speak of an appreciation in price.

We can scarcely be proud of what is now being done, however. Only a small part of the average school curriculum is devoted to the enjoyment of art—or, for that matter, music or literature. It is the misfortune of all three fields to be taught as mysteries to which effective methods of instruction are held not to apply. Very little beyond simple communication and conspicuous enjoyment is attempted. The emphasis is on the feelings engendered by books, music, and pictures. Students may not read books, listen to music, or look at pictures without feelings, but an increased likelihood that they will do these things should be the goal of education.

An important opportunity to encourage creative art by multiplying consumers is often overlooked. A comparison with music is instructive. A generation or two ago very few people could hear good music. For everyone who heard a symphony orchestra or opera, thousands heard no more than the brass band on the village green or the parlor piano. The phonograph and radio made a prodigious difference. Vast numbers of people now hear music of unlimited variety and excellent quality. A recorded performance is often better than an actual symphony heard from many of the seats in a symphony hall. If there is not yet a Golden Age in musical composition, the stage is certainly set for one. As Roy Harris has said, the long-playing record "is to music what the printing press was to literature." There is nothing like it yet in the field of art. Those who are engaged in reproducing pictures lack the power and zeal of the electronics industry. Most copies of paintings are fragile, awkward to handle, and hard to store or display. Fidelity is generally low. How little attention is paid to this is evident in the fact that new issues of reproductions are not reviewed in the popular press as new records are.

What is needed, however, is not only better reproductions but a basic change in attitude. Copies of works of art are suspect. No one is bothered by the fact that a good phonograph is not actually an orchestra, but many people are bothered by the fact that a picture is not genuine. Indeed, a very good copy suggests a forgery. Another difficulty is that people seldom change the pictures on their walls. Pictures are regarded as part of the decoration of a room, or they are permanently displayed as valuable possessions. They then either cease to be noticed or become as objectionable as background music. (It may be argued that one need not look at a picture while one cannot help listening to music, but background music is not always heard.) Pictures should be enjoyed as music is enjoyed, and they should be as easily "played."

Dedication

The proper reinforcement of artistic behavior can have another important effect. Life is greater than art, and both producer and consumer of art are, as we have seen, under the control of relatively weak reinforcers. But it is significant that the natural competitors of art are also weakly reinforced. Far more people visit race tracks than museums, buy lottery tickets than pictures, and look at televised football games than pictures, but the competing *reinforcers* are not actually stronger. The net reinforcement at the race track or in a lottery is indeed almost always negative (the gambler eventually loses), and the victory of a favorite team could scarcely be less important in itself. Something has *made* these reinforcers effective, and thanks to recent research we know what it is. A weak reinforcer exerts a powerful control when effectively scheduled. All gambling systems and all games and sports "pay off" in a special unpredictable way. The behavior of placing a bet or playing a game is reinforced on a so-called variable-ratio schedule, and the schedule generates a high level of activity. Under such schedules pigeons as well as men become pathological gamblers. We can create "pathological" artists and viewers of art with the same system.

A person who, as we say, lives for art, for whom art is the most important thing in the world, is not so much one who finds art reinforcing as one who has enjoyed a favorable history of painting or looking at pictures. The technique with which a dishonest gambler "hooks" his victim shows what needs to be done. The first reinforcements must be quick and easy, but the average amount of behavior demanded for each reinforcement must then slowly increase. Eventually the behavior is maintained for long periods of time, possibly without any reinforcement whatsoever. Instruction in the enjoyment of art should begin with arrangements in which reinforcement is generous, and perhaps "cheap." Even the meretricious may have its place. More difficult ("better") materials should be introduced with care as instruction proceeds. It is often hard to arrange effective programs, but the teacher must not neglect the possibility of doing so. The dedicated artist, like the dedicated hunter, fisherman, explorer, or scientist, is the product of a probably accidental but happy program of successes. An effective program may arise naturally as an artist strives for more and more difficult effects or as a viewer turns to reinforcing features of a picture which are to be found less and less often.

Philistinism?

We have considered only some of the more obvious reasons why people paint and look at pictures. We have scarcely touched on the many different kinds of things to be found in pictures or on the effects they have on artist or viewer. (And we have not, of course, considered other forms of art than painting.) We have not traced the effects of pictures to personal histories. It is easy, therefore, to say that this account is oversimplified. But the central point deserves consideration. People paint and look at pictures for good reasons—which can be investigated. Prominent among the reasons are certain reinforcing consequences, and recent advances in the experimental analysis of behavior have shown their importance. There is a practical implication: when consequences can be manipulated, behavior can be changed. Technological applications are already well advanced in other fields. Why should we not use this knowledge to induce more people to take an interest in art?

Perhaps it is a kind of Philistinism to suppose that we can "produce" artists, as if they were some sort of commodity. Certainly such a position is incompatible with many traditional conceptions. But is it unrealistic? Art is produced by a culture or a mixture of cultures. People commonly act to change the culture in which they live, and they do so in order to change its effects. We change our culture in an effort to further art when we subsidize artists, teach or encourage the teaching of art, make works of art more generally available, and so on, and some of these measures can now be greatly improved. Even so, they will affect only a small part of the conditions responsible for any artist, let alone any great artist. These are circumstances over which we have no control, but we can give them a better chance. The occasional chess genius is most likely to appear in a culture in which many people play chess, and a great artist is most likely to arise when the production and consumption of art are important parts of a way of life.

If we are willing to accept the assignment of making our culture more effective in this way, then we should turn to a formulation of human behavior which points to things to be done. Traditional explanations have seldom led to effective action; they are supported primarily by the weight of tradition and the fascination of the inexplicable. Perhaps nothing less than a resolute Philistinism will permit us to build the background from which, for reasons we admit we do not fully understand, more creative artists will emerge.

A Lecture on "Having" a Poem

What I am going to say has the curious property of illustrating itself. The quotation marks in my title are intended to suggest that there is a sense in which having a poem is like having a baby, and in that sense I am in labor; I am having a lecture. In it I intend to raise the question of whether I am responsible for what I am saying, whether I am actually originating anything, and to what extent I deserve credit or blame. That is one issue in *Beyond Freedom and Dignity,*[1] but since I am having a verbal baby, the argument goes back to an earlier book.

In his review of *Beyond Freedom and Dignity* in *The New York Times,*[2] Christopher Lehmann-Haupt begins with two sentences dear to the hearts of my publishers, and they have not allowed them to become hidden under a bushel. But later in the review, unhappy about some of the implications, he tries to fault me. "Well then," he writes, "what about the most serious (and best advertised) attack that has been leveled against behaviorism in recent years—namely, Noam Chomsky's attempts to demonstrate man's innate linguistic powers, which began with Chomsky's famous review of Skinner's book *Verbal Behavior*. Skinner says nothing explicit on the matter in *Beyond Freedom and Dignity*. Indeed, Chomsky's name is never brought up (which seems disingenuous on Skinner's part). Have we got him there?"

Let me tell you about Chomsky. I published *Verbal Behavior* in 1957. In 1958 I received a 55-page typewritten review by someone I had never heard of named Noam Chomsky. I read half a dozen pages, saw that it missed the point of my book, and went no further. In 1959, I received a reprint from the journal *Language.*[3] It was the review I had already seen, now reduced to 32 pages in type, and again I put it aside. But then, of

This lecture was given at the Poetry Center in New York City on October 13, 1971.
[1] *Beyond Freedom and Dignity.* New York: Knopf, 1971.
[2] *The New York Times,* September 22, 1971.
[3] *Language,* 1959, *35*, 26–58.

course, Chomsky's star began to rise. Generative grammar became the thing—and a very big thing it seemed to be. Linguists have always managed to make their discoveries earthshaking. In one decade everything seems to hinge on semantics, in another decade on the analysis of the phoneme. In the sixties, it was grammar and syntax, and Chomsky's review began to be widely cited and reprinted and became, in fact, much better known than my book.

Eventually the question was asked, why had I not answered Chomsky? My reasons, I am afraid, show a lack of character. In the first place I should have had to read the review, and I found its tone distasteful. It was not really a review of my book but of what Chomsky took, erroneously, to be my position. I should also have had to bone up on generative grammar, which was not my field, and to do a good job I should have had to go into structuralism, a theory which Chomsky, like Claude Lévi-Strauss, acquired from Roman Jakobson. According to the structuralists we are to explain human behavior by discovering its organizing principles, paying little or no attention to the circumstances under which it occurs. If anything beyond structure is needed by way of explanation, it is to be found in a creative mind—Lévi-Strauss's savage mind or Chomsky's innate rules of grammar. (Compare the recent analysis of Shakespeare's sonnet "Th' expence of spirit" by Jakobson and Lawrence Jones [4] with my earlier analysis in *Verbal Behavior*. Where Jakobson and Jones confine themselves to the structure or pattern of the poem as it appears to the reader, I used the same features to illustrate the behavioral processes of formal and thematic strengthening which, to put it roughly, made words available to the poet as he wrote.) No doubt I was shirking a responsibility in not replying to Chomsky, and I am glad an answer has now been supplied by Kenneth MacCorquodale in the *Journal of the Experimental Analysis of Behavior*.[5]

A few years ago *Newsweek* magazine carried the disagreement further, going beyond linguistics and structuralism to the philosophy of the seventeenth century. I was said to be a modern disciple of John Locke, for whom the mind began as a clean slate or *tabula rasa* and who thought that knowledge was acquired only from experience, while Chomsky was said to represent Descartes, the rationalist, who was not sure he existed until he thought about it. *Newsweek* suggested that the battle was going my way, and the reaction by the generative grammarians was so violent that the magazine found it necessary to publish four pro-Chomsky letters. Each

---

[4] *Shakespeare's Verbal Art in "Th' Expence of Spirit."* The Hague: Mouton, 1970.
[5] *Journal of the Experimental Analysis of Behavior*, 1970, *13*, 83–99.

one repeated a common misunderstanding of my position. One implied that I was a stimulus-response psychologist (which I am not) and another that I think people are very much like pigeons (which I do not). One had at least a touch of wit. Going back to our supposed seventeenth-century progenitors, the writer advised *Newsweek* to "Locke up Skinner and give Chomsky Descartes blanche." (But Chomsky cannot use a *carte blanche,* of course; it is too much like a *tabula rasa.*)

Ironically, Chomsky was later invited to give the John Locke Lectures at Oxford. I was at Cambridge University at the time, and the BBC thought it would be interesting if we were to discuss our differences on television. I don't know what excuse Chomsky gave, but I agreed to participate only if the moderator could guarantee equal time. I suggested that we use chess clocks. My clock would be running when I was talking, and Chomsky's when he was talking, and in that way I planned to have the last fifteen or twenty minutes to myself. The BBC thought that my suggestion would not make for a very interesting program.

Verbal Behavior was criticized in a different way by an old friend, I. A. Richards, whose interest in the field goes back, of course, to the *Meaning of Meaning.* For nearly forty years Ivor Richards and I have respected each other while disagreeing rather violently. I have never been able to understand why he feels that the works of Coleridge make an important contribution to our understanding of human behavior, and he has never been able to understand why I feel the same way about pigeons. He has at times been deeply distressed. He once asked me to lecture to his freshman course in General Education. I turned up at the appointed hour, he made a few announcements, and then he said, "I now present the Devil," and sat down. And I had not yet published *Verbal Behavior,* that outrageous invasion of Richards' territory which might indeed have borne the subtitle, *The Meaninglessness of Meaning.*

When my book appeared, and in turn Chomsky's review, Ivor Richards sent me a poem. It was prefaced by two quotations, one from my book and one from the review, and it proceeded to document the extraordinary extent to which each of us believed that he was absolutely right. The poem began:

> Confidence with confidence oppose.
> Knowledge ducks under in between two No's
> So firmly uttered. Look again. You'll see
> Uncertainty beside uncertainty.

Some unacknowledged uncertainties were then cited and analyzed.

A few months later I received a second poem. It was called "Verbal Behaviour" and began as follows:

> No sense in fretting to be off the ground,
> There's never hurry whither we are bound,
> Where all's behaviour—and the rest is naught,
> Not even rest, but void beyond all thought.

It went on to argue that behaviorism will mean the death of the individual, the end of man's divine image of himself. The behaviorist contends that

> The Angels are a sketch
> *They* made long since to comfort the sore wretch
> Cast out of Paradise he knew not why
> To start his long climb back into the sky.

But he will never reach paradise again because the behaviorist will tear off his wings, crying, to set him free:

> These gleaming sails are but the flattering means,
> (Theologic gear, Pythagorean beans!)
> Whereby grubs flit and feed and lay their eggs,
> By metaphor, beyond the reach of legs.
> No psyche more! Homunculus-theory, out!
> Verbal behaviour's all it's all about.

It seemed to me that this had gone far enough, and so I replied—in kind—as follows:

For Ivor Richards

> Yes, "all's behavior—and the rest is naught."
>
> And thus compressed
> Into "the rest
> Of all,"
> A thought
> Is surely neither bad nor wrong.
>
> Or right or good?
> No, no.
> Define
> And thus expunge
> The *ought,*
> The *should!*
> Nothing is so
> (See History.)

Let not the strong
Be cozened
By *Is* and *Isn't,*
Was and *Wasn't.*
Truth's to be sought
In *Does* and *Doesn't.*

Decline
To be.

And call
Him neither best
Nor blessed
Who wrought
That silly jest,
The Fall.

(It was a Plunge.)

A few days later Ivor Richards phoned. Why not publish our poems?
I had no objection, and so he sent them to an American magazine. The
editor agreed that they were interesting but that, since we were both at
Harvard, it was a sort of in-house joke which might not appeal to their
West Coast readers. Stephen Spender, however, had no West Coast readers
to worry about, and our poems were eventually published in *Encounter.*[6]

That is the only poem I have published since college, and it must serve
as my only credential in discussing the present topic. I am unwilling to let
it stand without comment, and so I offer the following exegesis, as it
might be written by some future candidate for a Ph.D. in English literature.

The poet begins with a quotation from his friend's poem, picking up a
slight redundancy. If all's behavior, then of course the rest is naught. And it
is perhaps just as well, since a thought reduced to nothing can scarcely be bad
or wrong. But what about the possibility that it might be right or good? No,
logical positivism will take care of that. By defining our values we expunge
them.

A new theme then appears, perhaps best stated in the immortal words of
Henry Ford, "History is bunk," but here extended to the present as well as the
past, as the poet attacks existentialism as well as the uses of history. The theme
is broached in the contemptuous lines

Nothing is so
(See History.)

but developed more explicitly when we are warned not to be deceived by *Is* and *Isn't* (so much for the Existentialists) or *Was* and *Wasn't* (so much for the Historians). Then follows that stirring behavioristic manifesto:

> Truth's to be sought
> In *Does* and *Doesn't*.

At this point, almost as if exhausted, the poet enters upon a new mood. Behaviorism has squeezed thought to death and with it consciousness and mind. George Kateb made the point later in his review of *Beyond Freedom and Dignity* in the *Atlantic Monthly*,[7] insisting that "Skinner foresees and condones the atrophy of consciousness." But since foreseeing and condoning are conscious acts, the behaviorist is engaged in a kind of intellectual suicide. To use a strangely inept expression, mind is to die by its own hand. The position is stated with stunning economy:

> Decline
> *To be.*

(We note here a certain infelicity. *To be* is a verb, and as such can be conjugated but not declined. But we must remember that an intentional suicide is likely to be distraught and an unintentional one at least careless. One thinks of Ophelia. The semantic blemish therefore simply adds to the tone of the passage.)

The theme of suicide becomes clear when the poet turns to his friend's reference to the fallen Angel and warns us against accepting uncritically "that silly jest, The Fall." (Note in passing that *silly* is cognate with the German *selig,* meaning holy or sacred.) "Fall" is wrong because it suggests chance. (Chance, of course, comes from the Latin *cadere* meaning *to fall*—the fall of a die or penny—and is it entirely irrelevant that "jest" is etymologically related to "cast," as in casting dice?) Make no mistake; the Fall was not an accident. It was a deliberate plunge.

Thus might some beknighted graduate student of the future write in search of partial fulfillment. Whether or not he will thus establish my competence in discussing poetry, I cannot say. If not, I must fall back upon that stock reply of the critic when the playwright who has received a bad review points out that the critic has never written a play, and the critic replies, "Neither have I laid an egg, but I am a better judge of an omelet than any hen." It is a stale and musty joke, and I should not allow it to injure the tone of my lecture if it did not serve the important function of bringing me to my point. I am to compare having a poem with having a baby, and it will do no harm to start with a lower class of living things. Samuel Butler suggested the comparison years ago when he said that a poet writes a poem as a hen lays an egg, and both feel better afterwards.

But there are other points of similarity, and on one of them Butler

---

[7] *Atlantic Monthly,* Oct. 1971.

built a whole philosophy of purposive evolution. The statement was current in early post-Darwinism days that "a hen is only an egg's way of making another egg." It is not, of course, a question of which comes first, though that is not entirely irrelevant. The issue is who *does* what, who *acts* to produce something and therefore deserves credit. Must we give the hen credit for the egg or the egg for the hen? Possibly it does not matter, since no one is seriously interested in defending the rights of hen or egg, but something of the same sort can be said about a poet, and then it does matter. Does the poet create, originate, initiate the thing called a poem, or is his behavior merely the product of his genetic and environmental histories?

I raised that question a number of years ago with a distinguished poet at a conference at Columbia University. I was just finishing *Verbal Behavior* and could not resist summarizing my position. I thought it was possible to account for verbal behavior in terms of the history of the speaker, without reference to ideas, meanings, propositions, and the like. The poet stopped me at once. He could not agree. "That leaves no place for me as a poet," he said, and he would not discuss the matter further. It was a casual remark which, I am sure, he has long since forgotten, and I should hesitate to identify him if he had not recently published something along the same lines.

When Jerome Weisner was recently inaugurated as President of Massachusetts Institute of Technology, Archibald MacLeish read a poem.[8] He praised Dr. Weisner as:

A good man in a time when men are
scarce, when the intelligent foregather,
follow each other around in the fog like
sheep, bleat in the rain, complain
because Godot never comes; because
all life is a tragic absurdity—Sisyphus
sweating away at his rock, and the rock
won't; because freedom and dignity . . .

Oh, weep, they say, for freedom and dignity!
You're not free: it's your grandfather's itch you're scratching.
You have no dignity: you're not a man,
you're a rat in a vat of rewards and punishments,
you think you've chosen the rewards, you haven't:
the rewards have chosen you.
                    Aye! Weep!

[8] Boston *Globe,* October 9, 1971.

I am just paranoid enough to believe that he is alluding to *Beyond Freedom and Dignity*. In any case, he sums up the main issue rather effectively: "You think you've chosen the rewards; you haven't. The rewards have chosen you." To put it more broadly, a person does not act upon the environment, perceiving it and deciding what to do about it; the environment acts upon him, determining that he will perceive it and act in special ways. George Eliot glimpsed the issue: "Our deeds determine us, as much as we determine our deeds," though she did not understand *how* we are determined by our deeds. Something does seem to be taken away from the poet when his behavior is traced to his genetic and personal histories. Only a person who truly initiates his behavior can claim that he is free to do so and that he deserves credit for any achievement. If the environment is the initiating force, he is not free, and the environment must get the credit.

The issue will be clearer if we turn to a biological parallel—moving from the oviparous hen to the viviparous human mother. When we say that a woman "bears" a child, we suggest little by way of creative achievement. The verb refers to carrying the fetus to term. The expression "gives birth" goes little further; a bit of a platonic idea, birth, is captured by the mother and given to the baby, which then becomes born. We usually say simply that a woman "has" a baby where "has" means little more than possess. To have a baby is to come into possession of it. The woman who does so is then a mother, and the child is her child. But what is the nature of her contribution? She is not responsible for the skin color, eye color, strength, size, intelligence, talents, or any other feature of her baby. She gave it half its genes, but she got those from *her* parents. She could, of course, have damaged the baby. She could have aborted it. She could have caught rubella at the wrong time or taken drugs, and as a result the baby would have been defective. *But she made no positive contribution.*

A biologist has no difficulty in describing the role of the mother. She is a place, a locus in which a very important biological process takes place. She supplies protection, warmth, and nourishment, but she does not design the baby who profits from them. The poet is also a locus, a place in which certain genetic and environmental causes come together to have a common effect. Unlike a mother, the poet has access to his poem during gestation. He may tinker with it. A poem seldom makes its appearance in a completed form. Bits and pieces *occur* to the poet, who rejects or allows them to stand, and who puts them together to *compose* a poem. But they come from his past history, verbal and otherwise, and he has had to learn how to put them together. The act of composition is no more an act of creation than "having" the bits and pieces composed.

But can this interpretation be correct if a poem is unquestionably new? Certainly the plays of Shakespeare did not exist until he wrote them. Possibly all their parts could be traced by an omniscient scholar to Shakespeare's verbal and nonverbal histories, but he must have served some additional function. How otherwise are we to explain the creation of something new?

The answer is again to be found in biology. A little more than a hundred years ago the act of creation was debated for a very different reason. The living things on the surface of the earth show a fantastic variety—far beyond the variety in the works of Shakespeare—and they had long been attributed to a creative Mind. The anatomy of the hand, for example, was taken as evidence of a prior design. And just as we are told today that a behavioral analysis cannot explain the "potentially infinite" number of sentences composable by a speaker, so it was argued that no physical or biological process could explain the potentially infinite number of living things on the surface of the earth. (Curiously enough the creative behavior invoked by way of explanation was verbal: "In the beginning was the word . . . ," supplemented no doubt by a *generative* grammar.)

The key term in Darwin's title is Origin. Novelty could be explained without appeal to prior design if random changes in structure were selected by their consequences. It was the contingencies of survival which created new forms. Selection is a special kind of causality, much less conspicuous than the push-pull causality of nineteenth-century physics, and Darwin's discovery may have appeared so late in the history of human thought for that reason. The selective action of the consequences of behavior was also overlooked for a long time. It was not until the seventeenth century that any important initiating action by the environment was recognized. People acted upon the world, but the world did not act upon them. The first evidence to the contrary was of the conspicuous push-pull kind. Descartes's (*pace* Chomsky) theoretical anticipation of the reflex and the reflex physiology of the nineteenth century gave rise to a stimulus-response psychology in which behavior was said to be triggered by the environment. There is no room in such a formulation for a more important function. When a person acts, the consequences may strengthen his tendency to act in the same way again. The Law of Effect, formulated nearly three quarters of a century ago by Edward L. Thorndike, owed a great deal to Darwinian theory, and it raised very similar issues. It is not some prior purpose, intention, or act of will which accounts for novel behavior; it is the "contingencies of reinforcement." (Among the behaviors thus explained are techniques of self-management, once attributed to "higher mental processes," which figure in the gestation of new topographies.)

The poet often knows that some part of his history is contributing to the poem he is writing. He may, for example, reject a phrase because he sees that he has borrowed it from something he has read. But it is quite impossible for him to be aware of all his history, and it is in this sense that he does not know where his behavior comes from. Having a poem, like having a baby, is in large part a matter of exploration and discovery, and both poet and mother are often surprised by what they produce. And because the poet is not aware of the origins of his behavior, he is likely to attribute it to a creative mind, an "unconscious" mind, perhaps, or a mind belonging to someone else—to a muse, for example, whom he has invoked to come and write his poem for him.

A person produces a poem and a woman produces a baby, and we call the person a poet and the woman a mother. Both are essential as loci in which vestiges of the past come together in certain combinations. The process is creative in the sense that the products are new. Writing a poem is the sort of thing men and women do as men and women, having a baby is the sort of thing a woman does as a woman, and laying an egg is the sort of thing a hen does as a hen. To deny a creative contribution does not destroy man *qua* man or woman *qua* woman any more than Butler's phrase destroys hen *qua* hen. There is no threat to the essential humanity of man, the muliebrity of woman, or the gallity of *Gallus gallus*.

What is threatened, of course, is the autonomy of the poet. The autonomous is the uncaused, and the uncaused is miraculous, and the miraculous is God. For the second time in a little more than a century a theory of selection by consequences is threatening a traditional belief in a creative mind. And is it not rather strange that although we have abandoned that belief with respect to the creation of the world, we fight so desperately to preserve it with respect to the creation of a poem?

But is there anything wrong with a supportive myth? Why not continue to believe in our creative powers if the belief gives us satisfaction? The answer lies in the future of poetry. To accept a wrong explanation because it flatters us is to run the risk of missing a right one—one which in the long run may offer more by way of "satisfaction." Poets know all too well how long a sheet of paper remains a *carte blanche*. To wait for genius or a genie is to make a virtue of ignorance. If poetry is a good thing, if we want more of it and better, and if writing poems is a rewarding experience, then we should look afresh at its sources.

Perhaps the future of poetry is not that important, but I have been using a poem simply as an example. I could have developed the same theme in art, music, fiction, scholarship, science, invention—in short, wherever we speak of *original* behavior. We say that we "have" ideas and again in the simple sense of coming into possession of them. An idea "occurs to us" or "comes to mind." And if for idea we read "the behavior said to express an idea," we come no closer to an act of creation. We "have" behavior, as the etymology of the word itself makes clear. It "occurs to us" to act in a particular way, and it is not any prior intention, purpose, or plan which disposes us to do so. By analyzing the genetic and individual histories responsible for our behavior, we may learn how to be more original. The task is not to think of new forms of behavior but to create an environment in which they are likely to occur.

Something of the sort has happened in the evolution of cultures. Over the centuries men and women have built a world in which they behave much more effectively than in a natural environment, but they have not done so by deliberate design. A culture evolves when new practices arise which make it more likely to survive. We have reached a stage in which our culture induces some of its members to be concerned for its survival. A kind of deliberate design is then possible, and a scientific analysis is obviously helpful. We can build a world in which men and women will be better poets, better artists, better composers, better novelists, better scholars, better scientists—in a word, better people. We can, in short, "have" a better world.

And that is why I am not much disturbed by the question with which George Kateb concludes his review of *Beyond Freedom and Dignity.* He is attacking my utopianism, and he asks, "Does Skinner not see that only silly geese lay golden eggs?" The question brings us back to the oviparous again, but it does not matter, for the essential issue is raised by all living things. It is characteristic of the evolution of a species, as it is of the acquisition of behavior and of the evolution of a culture, that ineffective forms give rise to effective. Perhaps a goose is silly if, because she lays a golden egg, she gets the ax; but, silly or not, she has laid a golden egg. And what if that egg hatches a golden goose? There, in an eggshell, is the great promise of evolutionary theory. A silly goose, like Butler's hen, is simply the way in which an egg produces a *better* egg.

And now my labor is over. I have had my lecture. I have no sense of fatherhood. If my genetic and personal histories had been different, I should have come into possession of a different lecture. If I deserve any credit at all, it is simply for having served as a place in which certain processes could take place. I shall interpret your polite applause in that light.

PART VII

Literary and Verbal Behavior

Has Gertrude Stein a Secret?

I first heard about the Autobiography of Alice B. Toklas *from Mary Louise White (Aswell). It had reached her desk in the editorial offices of the* Atlantic Monthly *as a bona fide autobiography, but the last paragraph had come as no surprise: "About six weeks ago Gertrude Stein said, it does not look to me as if you were ever going to write that autobiography. You know what I am going to do. I am going to write it for you. I am going to write it as simply as Defoe did the autobiography of Robinson Crusoe. And she has and this is it."*

Miss White was to be the only Atlantic *reader to enjoy Gertrude Stein's little joke for when parts of the book were published in that magazine during the summer of 1933, the author's name appeared on the title page. I read the reference to Miss Stein's psychological experiments while vacationing on Monhegan Island, Maine. Upon returning to Cambridge I made at once for the library and that evening reported my "discovery" to Miss White, who suggested the present article. I called it "Gertrude Stein and Automatic Writing." The editor of the* Atlantic, *Ellery Sedgwick, had a less pedantic suggestion.*

The article had the accidental distinction of being the first published by a Junior Prize Fellow in the Society of Fellows at Harvard. The Society had been conceived by Lawrence J. Henderson and established with an "anonymous" gift from A. Lawrence Lowell, then just retiring from the presidency of Harvard. Its object was to bring young scholars in various fields into contact with each other and with some of the distinguished members of the Harvard faculty. In addition to Henderson and Lowell, the first Senior Fellows included Alfred North Whitehead, John Livingston Lowes, James B. Conant, Kenneth B. Murdock, and Charles P. Curtis. We were to meet weekly for an excellent dinner (Professor Henderson had stocked the cellar of the Society with an honest Burgundy from the vineyards of a friend at the University of Dijon) and for the cross-fertilization of ideas.

The mountain labored and brought forth an article on Gertrude Stein. It proved to be an offspring not easily concealed. Conrad Aiken, writing in the New Republic, *reviewed the prevailing attitude toward Miss Stein's experiment—"Like the splitting of the atom, or the theory of relativity, Miss Stein's destruction of meaning was inevitably going to change, if not the world, at any rate the word"—and expressed the opinion that the present article made of the whole thing a very cruel joke. "What becomes of all this precise and detached and scientific experimentation with rhythm and mean-*

From *Atlantic Monthly,* January 1984.

ing, if, after all, it has been nothing on earth but automatic writing? Is it merely one more instance of the emperor's new clothes? Have we been duped, and has Miss Stein herself, perhaps, been duped? It looks very like it—though of course it is not impossible that Miss Stein has been pulling our legs." Among those who came to the defense was Sherwood Anderson, who quite properly rejoined that "all good writing is, in a sense, automatic." But partisans of Gertrude Stein have been afraid of this answer and have generally denied that her published work was written automatically. Fortunately, we have Gertrude Stein's own version of the facts, expressed in a letter to Ellery Sedgwick:

"No it is not so automatic as he thinks. If there is anything secret it is the other way too. I think I achieve by xtra consciousness, xcess, but then what is the use of telling him that, he being a psychologist and I having been one. Besides when he is not too serious he is a pretty good one."

In the *Autobiography of Alice B. Toklas* Gertrude Stein tells in the following way of some psychological experiments made by her at Harvard:

> She was one of a group of Harvard men and Radcliffe women and they all lived very closely and very interestingly together. One of them, a young philosopher and mathematician who was doing research work in psychology, left a definite mark on her life. She and he together worked out a series of experiments in automatic writing under the direction of Münsterberg. The results of her own experiments, which Gertrude Stein wrote down and which was printed in the *Harvard Psychological Review,* was the first writing of hers ever to be printed. It is very interesting to read because the method of writing to be afterwards developed in *Three Lives* and *The Making of Americans* already shows itself.

There is a great deal more in this early paper than Miss Stein points out. It is, as she says, an anticipation of the prose style of *Three Lives* and is unmistakably the work of Gertrude Stein in spite of the conventional subject matter with which it deals. Many turns of speech, often commonplace, which she has since then in some subtle way made her own are already to be found. But there is much more than this. The paper is concerned with an early interest of Miss Stein's which must have been very important in her later development, and the work which it describes cannot reasonably be overlooked by anyone trying to understand this remarkable person.

Since the paper is hard to obtain, I shall summarize it briefly. It was published in the *Psychological Review* for September, 1896, under the title, "Normal Motor Automatism," by Leon M. Solomons and Gertrude Stein, and it attempted to show to what extent the elements of a "second personality" (of the sort to be observed in certain cases of hysteria) were to be found in a normal being. In their experiments the authors investigated the limits of their own normal motor automatism; that is to say, they undertook to see how far they could "split" their own personalities in a deliberate and purely artificial way. They were successful to the extent of being able to perform many acts (such as writing or reading aloud) in an automatic manner, while carrying on at the same time some other activity such as reading an interesting story.

II

In the experiments with automatic writing a planchette of the ouija board type was originally used, but as soon as the authors had satisfied themselves that spontaneous writing movements do occur while the attention is directed elsewhere, an ordinary pencil and paper were used instead. The subject usually began by making voluntary random writing movements or by writing the letter *m* repeatedly. In one experiment this was done while the subject read an interesting story at the same time, and it was found that some of the words read in the story would be written down in an automatic way. At first there was a strong tendency to notice this as soon as it had begun to happen and to stop it, but eventually the words could be written down unconsciously as well as involuntarily. (I shall use Miss Stein's psychological terminology throughout.) "Sometimes the writing of the word was completely unconscious, but more often the subject knew what was going on. His knowledge, however, was obtained by sensations *from the arm.* He was conscious that he just had written a word, not that he was about to do so."

In other experiments the subject read an interesting story as before, and single words were dictated to him to be written down at the same time. These were difficult experiments, but after considerable practice they were successful. The subject was eventually able to write down "five or six" words spoken by another person, without being conscious of either the heard sounds or the movement of the arm. If his attention were not sufficiently well distracted, he might become aware that his hand was writing something. The information came from the arm, not from the sound of the dictated word. "It is never the sound that recalls us. This, of course, may be an individual peculiarity to a certain extent. . . . Yet, Miss Stein has a strong auditory consciousness, and sounds usually determine the direction of her attention."

In a third group of experiments the subject read aloud, preferably from an uninteresting story, while being read to from an interesting one. "If he does not go insane during the first few trials, he will quickly learn to concentrate his attention fully on what is being read to him, yet go on reading just the same. The reading becomes completely unconscious for periods of as much as a page." Automatic reading of this sort is probably part of the experience of everyone.

The fourth and last group brings out the relevance of the experiments to the later work of Gertrude Stein. I shall let Miss Stein describe the result.

Spontaneous automatic writing.—This became quite easy after a little practice. We had now gained so much control over our habits of attention that distraction by reading was almost unnecessary. Miss Stein found it sufficient distraction often to simply read what her arm wrote, but following three or four words behind her pencil.

A phrase would seem to get into the head and keep repeating itself at every opportunity, and hang over from day to day even. The stuff written was grammatical, and the words and phrases fitted together all right, but there was not much connected thought. The unconsciousness was broken into every six or seven words by flashes of consciousness, so that one cannot be sure but what the slight element of connected thought which occasionally appeared was due to these flashes of consciousness. But the ability to write stuff that sounds all right, without consciousness, was fairly well demonstrated by the experiments. Here are a few specimens:

"Hence there is no possible way of avoiding what I have spoken of, and if this is not believed by the people of whom you have spoken, then it is not possible to prevent the people of whom you have spoken so glibly. . . ."

Here is a bit more poetical than intelligible:

"When he could not be the longest and thus to be, and thus to be, the strongest."

And here is one that is neither:

"This long time when he did this best time, and he could thus have been bound, and in this long time, when he could be this to first use of this long time. . . ."

III

Here is obviously an important document. No one who has read *Tender Buttons* or the later work in the same vein can fail to recognize a familiar note in these examples of automatic writing. They are quite genuinely in the manner which has so commonly been taken as characteristic of Gertrude Stein. Miss Stein's description of her experimental result is exactly that of the average reader confronted with *Tender Buttons* for the first time: "The stuff is grammatical, and the words and phrases fit together all right, but there is not much connected thought." In short, the case is so good, simply on the grounds of style, that we are brought to the swift conclusion that the two products have a common origin, and that the work of Gertrude Stein in the *Tender Buttons* manner is written automatically and unconsciously in some such way as that described in this early paper.

This conclusion grows more plausible as we consider the case. It is necessary, of course, to distinguish between the Gertrude Stein of *Three Lives* and the *Autobiography* and the Gertrude Stein of *Tender Buttons,* a distinction which is fairly easily made, even though, as we shall see in a moment, there is some of the first Gertrude Stein in the latter work. If we confine ourselves for the present to the second of these two persons, it is clear that the hypothetical author who might be inferred from the writing itself possesses just those characteristics which we should expect to find if a theory of automatic writing were the right answer. Thus there is very little intellectual content discoverable. The reader—the ordinary reader, at least—cannot infer from the writing that its author possesses any consistent point of view. There is seldom any intelligible expression of opinion, and there are enough capricious reversals to destroy the effect of whatever there may be. There are even fewer emotional prejudices. The writing is cold. Strong phrases are almost wholly lacking, and it is so difficult to find a well-rounded emotional complex that if one is found it may as easily be attributed to the ingenuity of the seeker. Similarly, our hypothetical author shows no sign of a personal history or of a cultural background; *Tender Buttons* is the stream of consciousness of a woman without a past. The writing springs from no literary sources. In contrast with the work of Joyce, to whom a superficial resemblance may be found, the borrowed phrase is practically lacking.

When memorized passages occur, they are humdrum—old saws or simple doggerel recovered from childhood and often very loosely paraphrased: "If at first you don't succeed try try again," or "Please pale hot, please cover rose, please acre in the red. . . ." If there is any character in the writing whatsoever, it is due to this savor of the schoolroom, and the one inference about the author which does seem plausible is that she has been to grammar school. Her sentences are often cast as definitions ("What is a spectacle a spectacle is the resemblance . . ." or "A sign is the specimen spoken") or as copy-book aphorisms ("An excuse is not dreariness, a single plate is not butter," or "There is coagulation in cold and there is none in prudence") or as grammatical paradigms ("I begin you begin we begin they began we began you began I began"). This heavy dose of grammar school is especially strongly felt in *An Elucidation,* Miss Stein's first attempt to explain herself, and a piece of writing in which there are many evidences of a struggle on the part of the conscious Gertrude Stein to accept the origin of the *Tender Buttons* manner. Miss Stein wanted the volume *Lucy Church Amiably* to be bound like a schoolbook, but I shall leave it to a more imaginative mind to elaborate this metaphor further.

This is apparently as much of the writing as will help to illuminate the character of the writer. For the rest, it is what Miss Stein describes as sounding all right without making sense. There is no paradox about this, there is no secret about how it is done; but it gives us very little information about the author. Grammar is ever present—that is the main thing. We are presented with sentences ("sentences and always sentences"), but we often recognize them as such only because they show an accepted order of article, substantive, verb, split infinitive, article, substantive, connective, and so on. The framework of a sentence is there, but the words tacked upon it are an odd company. In the simplest type of case we have a nearly intelligible sentence modified by the substitution for a single word of one sounding much the same. This sort of substitution was reported by Miss Stein in connection with her experiments in automatic reading: "Absurd mistakes are occasionally made in the reading of words—substitutions similar in sound but utterly different in sense." The reader will recognize it as the sort of slip which is made when one is very tired. In more complex cases it cannot, of course, be shown that the unintelligibility is due to substitution; if most of the words are replaced, we have nothing to show that a word is a slip. We must be content to characterize it, as Miss Stein herself has done: "We have made excess return to rambling."

IV

From this brief analysis it is apparent that, although it is quite plausible that the work is due to a second personality successfully split off from Miss Stein's conscious self, it is a very flimsy sort of personality indeed. It is intellectually unopinionated, is emotionally cold, and has no past. It is unread and unlearned beyond grammar school. It is as easily influenced as a child; a heard word may force itself into whatever sentence may be under construction at the moment, or it may break the sentence up altogether and irremediably. Its literary materials are the sensory things nearest at hand—objects, sounds, tastes, smells, and so on. The reader may compare, for the sake of the strong contrast, the materials of "Melanctha" in *Three Lives,* a piece of writing of quite another sort. In her experimental work it was Miss Stein's intention to avoid the production of a true second personality, and she considered herself to be successful. The automatism she was able to demonstrate possessed the "elements" of a second personality, it was able to do anything which a second personality could do, but it never became the organized *alter ego* of the hysteric. The superficial character of the inferential author of *Tender Buttons* consequently adds credibility to the theory of automatic authorship.

The Gertrude Stein enthusiast may feel that I am being cruelly unjust in this estimate. I admit that there are passages in *Tender Buttons* which elude the foregoing analysis. But it must be made clear that the two Gertrude Steins we are considering are not kept apart by the covers of books. There is a good deal of the Gertrude Stein of the *Autobiography* in *Tender Buttons,* in the form of relatively intelligible comment, often parenthetical in spirit. Thus at the end of the section on Mutton (which begins "A letter which can wither, a learning which can suffer and an outrage which is simultaneous is principal") comes this sentence: "A meal in mutton mutton why is lamb cheaper, it is cheaper because so little is more," which is easily recognized as a favorite prejudice of the Gertrude Stein of the *Autobiography.* Similarly such a phrase as "the sad procession of the un-killed bull," in *An Elucidation,* is plainly a reference to another of Miss Stein's interests. But, far from damaging our theory, this occasional appearance of Miss Stein herself is precisely what the theory demands. In her paper in the *Psychological Review* she deals at length with the inevitable alternation of conscious and automatic selves, and in the quotation we have given it will be remembered that she comments upon these "flashes of consciousness." Even though the greater part of *Tender Buttons* is automatic, we should expect an "element of connected thought," and our only problem is that which Miss Stein herself has considered—namely, are we to attribute to conscious flashes all the connected thought which is present?

There is a certain logical difficulty here. It may be argued that, since we dispense with all the intelligible sentences by calling them conscious flashes, we should not be surprised to find that what is left is thin and meaningless. We must therefore restate our theory, in a way which will avoid this criticism. We first divide the writings of Gertrude Stein into two parts on the basis of their ordinary intelligibility. I do not contend that this is a hard and fast line, but it is a sufficiently real one for most persons. It does not, it is to be understood, follow the outlines of her works. We then show that the unintelligible part has the characteristics of the automatic writing produced by Miss Stein in her early psychological experiments, and from this and many other considerations we conclude that our division of the work into two parts is real and valid and that one part is automatic in nature.

I cannot find anything in the *Autobiography* or the other works I have read which will stand against this interpretation. On the contrary, there are many bits of evidence, none of which would be very convincing in itself, which support it. Thus (1) *Tender Buttons* was written on scraps of paper, and no scrap was ever thrown away; (2) Miss Stein likes to write in the presence of distracting noises; (3) her handwriting is often more legible to Miss Toklas than to herself (that is, her writing is "cold" as soon as it is produced); and (4) she is "fond of writing the letter *m*," with which, the reader will recall, the automatic procedure often began. In *An Elucidation,* her "first effort to realize clearly just what her writing meant and why it was as it was," there are many fitful allusions to the experimental days: "Do you all understand extraneous memory," "In this way my researches are easily read," a suddenly interpolated "I stopped I stopped myself," which recalls the major difficulty in her experiments, and so on.

V

It is necessary to assume that when Gertrude Stein returned to the practice of automatic writing (about 1912?) she had forgotten or was shortly to forget its origins. I accept as made in perfectly good faith the statement in the *Autobiography* that "Gertrude Stein never had subconscious reactions, nor was she a successful subject for automatic writing," even though the evidence to the contrary in her early paper is incontrovertible. She has forgotten it, just as she forgot her first novel almost immediately after it was completed and did not remember it again for twenty-five years. It is quite possible, moreover, that the manner in which she writes the *Tender Buttons* sort of thing is not unusual enough to remind her of its origins or to be remarked by others. One of the most interesting statements in the excerpt quoted from her early paper is that Gertrude Stein found it sufficient distraction simply to follow what she was writing some few words behind her pencil. If in the course of time she was able to bring her attention nearer and nearer to the pencil, she must eventually have reached a point at which there remained only the finest distinction between "knowing what one is going to write and knowing that one has written it." This is a transitional state to which Miss Stein devotes considerable space in her paper. It is therefore reasonable for us to assume that the artificial character of the experimental procedure has completely worn off, and that there remains only a not-far-from-normal state into which Miss Stein may pass unsuspectingly enough and in which the *Tender Buttons* style is forthcoming.

Having begun to produce stuff of this sort again, however, Miss Stein could not have failed to notice its peculiarities. We have her own opinion that the sentences quoted from her automatic writing do not show much connected thought, and I believe we are fully justified in our characterization of the greater part of *Tender Buttons* as "ordinarily unintelligible." I know that it would be quite possible for an industrious and ingenious person to find any number of meanings in it, just as it is possible to find meanings in any chance arrangement of words. But the conclusion to which we are now led is that the work with which we are dealing is very probably unintelligible in any ordinary sense, not only to other readers, but to Miss Stein herself. Why, then, did she publish?

It is important for our theory that between 1896 and 1912 Miss Stein had come to know Picasso and Matisse and was already long in the practice of defending their work against the question, "What does it mean?" With such an experience behind one, it is not difficult to accept as art what one has hitherto dismissed as the interesting and rather surprising result of an experiment. It was, I believe, only because Gertrude Stein had already prepared the defense as it applied to Picasso that she could put forth her own unintelligible product as a serious artistic experiment. For a person of the sound intelligence of Miss Stein there is a great natural resistance against the production of nonsense. It was the major problem in her experimental technique: "I stopped I stopped myself." But the writing succeeded in this case, because the resistance had been broken down, first by the procedure of the experiments, which permitted the sustained production of meaningless sentences, and later by the championing of Picasso, which permitted their publication. This was a fortunate combination of circumstances. "I could explain," she says in *An Elucidation,* "how it happened accidentally that fortunately no explanation was necessary."

Miss Stein has not, however, freed herself from the problem of the meaning of the things she writes. She is not above being bothered by criticism on the score of unintelligibility. She often characterizes her work in this vein as experimental, but that is in no sense an explanation. Beyond this her answer seems to be that the writing is its own justification.

It was not a question, she told her Oxford audience, of whether she was right in doing the kind of writing she did. "She had been doing as she did for about twenty years and now they wanted to hear her lecture." And she had previously dealt with the matter in *An Elucidation:*

> If it is an event just by itself is there a question
> Tulips is there a question
> Pets is there a question
> Furs is there a question
> Folds is there a question
> Is there anything in question.

I think we must accept this answer to the ethical question of whether she is doing right by Oxford and the King's English. The final test of whether it is right is whether anyone likes it. But a literary composition is not "an event just by itself," and the answer to Miss Stein's query is that there certainly *are* questions, of a critical sort, which may legitimately be raised. Meaning is one of them.

One kind of meaning which might be found if our theory is valid is psychological. In noting the presence of verbal slips ("substitutions similar in sound but utterly different in sense") we lay ourselves open to the criticism of the Freudian, who would argue that there are no true slips. According to this view, there is always some reason why the substitution is made, and the substituted word will have a deeper significance if we can find it. But we are here not primarily concerned with such psychological significances.

Of literary significances it may be urged that for the initiated or sympathetic reader there is an intellectual content in this part of Miss Stein's work which we have overlooked. Now, either this will be of such a sort that it could also be expressed normally, or it will be a special kind of content which requires the form given to it by Miss Stein. A partisan could so easily prove the first case by translating a representative passage that we may assume it not to be true. The second case requires a very difficult theory of knowledge in its defense, and we shall not need to inquire into it any more closely. It is quite true that something happens to the conscientious reader of *Tender Buttons*. Part of the effect is certainly due either to repetition or to surprise. These are recognized literary devices, and it may be argued that still a third kind of meaning, which we may designate as emotional, is therefore to be found. But in ordinary practice these devices are supplementary to expressions of another sort. The mere generation of the effects of repetition and surprise is not in itself a literary achievement.

VI

We have allowed for the presence of any or all of these kinds of meaning by speaking only of ordinary intelligibility. I do not think that a case can be made out for any one of them which is not obviously the invention of the analyzer. In any event the present argument is simply that the evidence here offered in support of a theory of automatic writing makes it *more probable* that meanings are not present, and that we need not bother to look for them. A theory of automatic writing does not, of course, necessarily exclude meanings. It is possible to set up a second personality which will possess all the attributes of a conscious self and whose writings will be equally meaningful. But in the present case it is clear that, as Miss Stein originally intended, a true second personality does not exist. This part of her work is, as she has characterized her experimental result, little more than "what her arm wrote." And it is an arm which has very little to say. This is, I believe, the main importance of the present theory for literary criticism. It enables one to assign an origin to the unintelligible part of Gertrude Stein which puts one at ease about its meanings.

There are certain aspects of prose writing, such as rhythm, which are not particularly dependent upon intelligibility. It is possible to experiment with them with meaningless words, and it may be argued that this is what is happening in the present case. Considering the freedom which Miss Stein has given herself, I do not think the result is very striking, although this is clearly a debatable point. It is a fairer interpretation, however, to suppose, in accordance with our theory, that there is no experimentation at the time the writing is produced. There may be good reason for publishing the material afterward as an experiment. For example, I recognize the possibility of a salutary, though accidental, effect upon Gertrude Stein's conscious prose or upon English prose in general. In *Composition as Explanation,* for example, there is an intimate fusion of the two styles, and the conscious passages are imitative of the automatic style. This is also probably true of parts of the *Autobiography.* It is perhaps impossible to tell at present whether the effect upon her conscious prose is anything more than a loss of discipline. The compensating gain is often very great.

We have no reason, of course, to estimate the literary value of this part of Miss Stein's work. It might be considerable, even if our theory is correct. It is apparent that Miss Stein believes it to be important and has accordingly published it. If she is right, if this part of her work is to become historically as significant as she has contended, then the importance of the document with which we began is enormous. For the first time we should then have an account by the author herself of how a literary second personality has been set up.

I do not believe this importance exists, however, because I do not believe in the importance of the part of Miss Stein's writing which does not make sense. On the contrary, I regret the unfortunate effect it has had in obscuring the finer work of a very fine mind. I welcome the present theory because it gives one the freedom to dismiss one part of Gertrude Stein's writing as a probably ill-advised experiment and to enjoy the other and very great part without puzzlement.

The Operational
Analysis of Psychological Terms

The symposium on operationism conducted in the September, 1945, issue of the Psychological Review *was suggested by Edwin G. Boring, who proposed a set of eleven questions to which participants might address themselves. In the present version of my contribution several references to these questions by number have been omitted and others replaced by brief paraphrases. Part of the material appears in slightly modified form in both* Verbal Behavior *and* Science and Human Behavior, *but its bearing on the issue of operationism may make it worth including here. It is reprinted with the permission of the* Psychological Review.

"Is operationism more than a renewed and refined emphasis upon the experimental method (as understood already by Galileo, if not even by Archimedes)—that is, a formulation of modern scientific empiricism and pragmatism (especially of the Peirce-Dewey variety), mainly of criteria of factual meaningfulness and empirical validity?" An answer to this question will define the position to be taken in what follows. Operationism is not regarded as a new theory or mode of definition. The literature has emphasized certain critical or hitherto neglected instances, but no new kind of operation has been discovered and none should be singled out. There is no reason to restrict operational analysis to high-order constructs; the principle applies to all definitions. This means that we must explicate an operational definition for every term unless we are willing to adopt the vague usage of the vernacular.

Operationism may be defined as the practice of talking about (1) one's observations, (2) the manipulative and calculational procedures involved in making them, (3) the logical and mathematical steps which intervene between earlier and later statements, and (4) *nothing else.* So far, the major contribution has come from the fourth provision and, like it, is negative. We have learned how to avoid troublesome references by showing that they are artifacts which may be variously traced to history, philosophy, linguistics, and so on. No very important positive advances have been made in connection with the first three provisions because operation-

From *Psychological Review,* 1945, *52,* 270–277.

ism has no good definition of a definition, operational or otherwise. It has not developed a satisfactory formulation of the effective verbal behavior of the scientist.

The operationist, like most contemporary writers in the field of linguistic and semantic analysis, is on the fence between logical "correspondence" theories of reference and empirical formulations of language in use. He has not improved upon the mixture of logical and popular terms usually encountered in casual or even supposedly technical discussions of scientific method or the theory of knowledge (e.g., Bertrand Russell's recent *An inquiry into meaning and truth*). *Definition* is a key term but is not rigorously defined. Bridgman's original contention that the "concept is synonymous with the corresponding set of operations" cannot be taken literally, and no similarly explicit but satisfactory statement of the relation is available. Instead, a few roundabout expressions recur with rather tiresome regularity whenever this relation is mentioned. We are told that a concept is to be defined *"in terms of"* certain operations, that propositions are to be *"based upon"* operations, that a term denotes something only when there are *"concrete criteria for its applicability,"* that operationism consists in *"referring any concept for its definition* to . . . concrete operations . . . ,"* and so on. We may accept expressions of this sort as outlining a program, but they do not provide a general scheme of definition, much less an explicit statement of the relation between concept and operation.

The weakness of current theories of language may be traced to the fact that an objective conception of human behavior is still incomplete. The doctrine that words are used to express or convey meanings merely substitutes "meaning" for "idea" (in the hope that meanings can then somehow be got outside the skin) and is incompatible with modern psychological conceptions of the organism. Attempts to derive a symbolic function from the principle of conditioning (or association) have been characterized by a very superficial analysis. It is simply not true that an organism reacts to a sign "as it would to the object which the sign supplants." [1] Only in a very limited area (mainly in the case of autonomic responses) is it possible to regard the sign as a simple substitute stimulus in the Pavlovian sense. Modern logic, as a formalization of "real" languages, retains and extends this dualistic theory of meaning and can scarcely be appealed to by the psychologist who recognizes his own responsibility in giving an account of verbal behavior.

[1] Stevens, S. S. Psychology and the science of science. *Psychol. Bull.*, 1939, 36, 221–263.

It is not my intention to attempt a more adequate formulation here. The fundamental revision is too sweeping to be made hastily. I should like, however, to try to make a small but positive contribution to this symposium by considering a few points which arise in connection with the operational definition of psychological terms. Much of the material which follows is adapted from a much longer work now in preparation, in which the necessary groundwork is more carefully prepared.

The operational attitude, in spite of its shortcomings, is a good thing in any science but especially in psychology because of the presence there of a vast vocabulary of ancient and non-scientific origin. It is not surprising that the broad empirical movement in the philosophy of science, which Stevens has shown to be the background of operationism, should have had a vigorous and early representation in the field of psychology—namely, behaviorism. In spite of the differences which Stevens claims to find, behaviorism has been (at least to most behaviorists) nothing more than a thoroughgoing operational analysis of traditional mentalistic concepts. We may disagree with some of the answers (such as Watson's disposition of images), but the *questions* asked by behaviorism were strictly operational in spirit. I also cannot agree with Stevens that American behaviorism was "primitive." The early papers on the problem of consciousness by Watson, Weiss, Tolman, Hunter, Lashley, and many others, were not only highly sophisticated examples of operational inquiry, they showed a willingness to deal with a wider range of phenomena than do current streamlined treatments, particularly those offered by logicians (e.g., Carnap) interested in a unified scientific vocabulary. But behaviorism, too, stopped short of a decisive positive contribution—and for the same reason: it never finished an acceptable formulation of the "verbal report." The conception of behavior which it developed could not convincingly embrace the "use of subjective terms."

A considerable advantage is gained from dealing with terms, concepts, constructs, and so on, quite frankly in the form in which they are observed —namely, as verbal responses. There is then no danger of including in the concept that aspect or part of nature which it singles out. (Several of the present questions seem to mix concept and referent; at least they seem to become trivial when, in order to make the mixture less likely, *term* is substituted for *concept* or *construct*.) Meanings, contents, and references are to be found among the determiners, not among the properties, of response. The question "What is length?" would appear to be satisfactorily answered by listing the circumstances under which the response "length" is emitted (or, better, by giving some general description of such circumstances). If two quite separate sets of circumstances are revealed, then there are two responses having the form "length," since a verbal response-class is not defined by phonetic form alone but by its functional relations. This is true even though the two sets are found to be intimately connected. The two responses are not controlled by the same stimuli, no matter how clearly it is shown that the different stimuli arise from the same "thing."

What we want to know in the case of many traditional psychological terms is, first, the specific stimulating conditions under which they are emitted (this corresponds to "finding the referents") and, second (and this is a much more important systematic question), why each response is controlled by its corresponding condition. The latter is not necessarily a genetic question. The individual acquires language from society, but the reinforcing action of the verbal community continues to play an important role in maintaining the specific relations between responses and stimuli which are essential to the proper functioning of verbal behavior. How language is acquired is, therefore, only part of a much broader problem.

We may generalize the conditions responsible for the standard "semantic" relation between a verbal response and a particular stimulus without going into reinforcement theory in detail. There are three important terms: a stimulus, a response, and a reinforcement supplied by the verbal community. (All of these need more careful definitions than are implied by current usage, but the following argument may be made without digressing for that purpose.) The significant interrelations between these terms may be expressed by saying that the community reinforces the response only when it is emitted in the presence of the stimulus. The reinforcement of the response "red," for example, is contingent upon the presence of a red object. (The contingency need not be invariable.) A red object then becomes a discriminative stimulus, an "occasion," for the successful emission of the response "red."

This scheme presupposes that the stimulus act upon both the speaker and the reinforcing community; otherwise the proper contingency cannot be maintained by the community. But this provision is lacking in the case of many "subjective" terms, which appear to be responses to *private* stimuli. The problem of subjective terms does not coincide exactly with that of private stimuli, but there is a close connection. We must know the characteristics of verbal responses to private stimuli in order to approach the operational analysis of the subjective term.

The response "My tooth aches" is partly under the control of a state of affairs to which the speaker alone is able to react, since no one else can establish the required connection with the tooth in question. There is nothing mysterious or metaphysical about this; the simple fact is that each speaker possesses a small but important private world of stimuli. So far as we know, his reactions to these are quite like his reactions to external events. Nevertheless the privacy gives rise to two problems. The first difficulty is that we cannot, as in the case of public stimuli, account for the verbal response by pointing to a controlling stimulus. Our practice is to *infer* the private event, but this is opposed to the direction of inquiry in a science of behavior in which we are to predict response through, among other things, an independent knowledge of the stimulus. It is often supposed that a solution is to be found in improved physiological techniques. Whenever it becomes possible to say what conditions within the organism control the response "I am depressed," for example, and to produce these conditions at will, a degree of control and prediction characteristic of responses to external stimuli will be made possible. Meanwhile, we must be content with reasonable evidence for the belief that responses to public and private stimuli are equally lawful and alike in kind.

But the problem of privacy cannot be wholly solved by instrumental invasion. No matter how clearly these internal events may be exposed in the laboratory, the fact remains that in the normal verbal episode they are quite private. We have not solved the second problem of how the community achieves the necessary contingency of reinforcement. How is the response "toothache" appropriately reinforced if the reinforcing agent has no contact with the tooth? There is, of course, no question of whether responses to private stimuli are possible. They occur commonly enough and must be accounted for. But why do they occur, what is their relation to controlling stimuli, and what, if any, are their distinguishing characteristics?

There are at least four ways in which a verbal community which has no access to a private stimulus may generate verbal behavior in response to it:

(1) It is not strictly true that the stimuli which control the response must be available to the community. Any reasonably regular accompaniment will suffice. Consider, for example, a blind man who learns the names of a trayful of objects from a teacher who identifies the objects by sight. The reinforcements are supplied or withheld according to the contingency between the blind man's responses and the teacher's visual stimuli, but the responses are controlled wholly by tactual stimuli. A satisfactory verbal system results from the fact that the visual and tactual stimuli remain closely connected.

Similarly, in the case of private stimuli, one may teach a child to say "That hurts" in agreement with the usage of the community by making the reinforcement contingent upon public accompaniments of painful stimuli (a smart blow, tissue damage, and so on). The connection between public and private stimuli need not be invariable; a response may be conditioned with merely periodic reinforcement and even in spite of an occasional conflicting contingency. The possibility of such behavior is limited by the degree of association of public and private stimuli which will supply a net reinforcement sufficient to establish and maintain a response.

(2) A commoner basis for the verbal reinforcement of a response to a private stimulus is provided by collateral responses to the same stimulus. Although a dentist may occasionally be able to identify the stimulus for a toothache from certain public accompaniments as in (1), the response "toothache" is generally transmitted on the basis of responses which are elicited by the same stimulus but which do not need to be set up by an environmental contingency. The community infers the private stimulus, not from accompanying public stimuli, but from collateral, generally unconditioned and at least non-verbal, responses (hand to jaw, facial expressions, groans, and so on). The inference is not always correct, and the accuracy of the reference is again limited by the degree of association.

(3) Some very important responses to private stimuli are descriptive of the speaker's own behavior. When this is overt, the community bases its instructional reinforcement upon the conspicuous manifestations, but the speaker presumably acquires the response in connection with a wealth of additional proprioceptive stimuli. The latter may assume practically complete control, as in describing one's own behavior in the dark. This is very close to the example of the blind man; the speaker and the community react to different, though closely associated, stimuli.

Suppose, now, that a given response recedes to the level of covert or merely incipient behavior. How shall we explain the vocabulary which deals with this private world? (The instrumental detection of covert behavior is again not an answer, for we are interested in how responses to private stimuli are normally, and non-instrumentally, set up.) There are two important possibilities. The surviving covert response may be regarded as an accompaniment of the overt (perhaps part of it), in which case the response to the private stimulus is imparted on the basis of the public stimulus supplied by the overt response, as in (1). On the other hand, the covert response may be *similar to,* though probably less intense than, the overt and hence supply the *same* stimulus, albeit in a weakened form. We have, then, a third possibility: a response may be emitted in the presence of a private stimulus, which has no public accompaniments, provided it is occasionally reinforced in the presence of the same stimulus occurring with public manifestations.

Terms falling within this class are apparently descriptive only of behavior, rather than of other internal states or events, since the possibility that the same stimulus may be both public and private (or, better, may have or lack public accompaniments) seems to arise from the unique fact that behavior may be both covert and overt.

(4) The principle of transfer or stimulus induction supplies a fourth explanation of how a response to private stimuli may be maintained by public reinforcement. A response which is acquired and maintained in connection with public stimuli may be emitted, through induction, in response to private events. The transfer is not due to identical stimuli, as in (3), but to coinciding properties. Thus, we describe internal states as "agitated," "depressed," "ebullient," and so on, in a long list. Responses in this class are all metaphors (including special figures like metonomy). The term *metaphor* is not used pejoratively but merely to indicate that the differential reinforcement cannot be accorded actual responses to the private case. As the etymology suggests, the response is "carried over" from the public instance.

In summary, a verbal response to a private stimulus may be maintained in strength through appropriate reinforcement based upon public accompaniments or consequences, as in (1) and (2), or through appropriate reinforcement accorded the response when it is made to public stimuli, the private case occurring by induction when the stimuli are only partly similar. If these are the only possibilities (and the list is here offered as exhaustive), then we may understand why terms referring to private events have never formed a stable and acceptable vocabulary of reasonably uniform usage. This historical fact is puzzling to adherents of the "correspondence school" of meaning. Why is it not possible to assign names to the diverse elements of private experience and then to proceed with consistent and effective discourse? The answer lies in the process by which "terms are assigned to private events," a process which we have just analyzed in a rough way in terms of the reinforcement of verbal responses.

None of the conditions which we have examined permits the sharpening of reference which is achieved, in the case of public stimuli, by a precise contingency of reinforcement. In (1) and (2) the association of public and private events may be faulty; the stimuli embraced by (3) are of limited scope; and the metaphorical nature of those in (4) implies a lack of precision. It is, therefore, impossible to establish a rigorous scientific vocabulary for public use, nor can the speaker clearly "know himself" in the sense in which knowing is identified with behaving discriminatively. In the absence of the "crisis" provided by differential reinforcement (much of which is necessarily verbal), private stimuli cannot be analyzed. (This has little or nothing to do with the availability or capacity of receptors.)

The contingencies we have reviewed also fail to provide an adequate check against fictional distortion of the relation of reference (e.g., as in rationalizing). Statements about private events may be under control of the drives associated with their consequences rather than antecedent stimuli. The community is skeptical of statements of this sort, and any attempt by the speaker to talk to himself about his private world (as in psychological system making) is fraught with self-deception.

Much of the ambiguity of psychological terms arises from the possibility of alternative or multiple modes of reinforcement. Consider, for example, the response "I am hungry." The community may reinforce this on the basis of the history of ingestion, as in (1), or collateral behavior associated with hunger, as in (2), or as a description of behavior with respect to food, or stimuli previously correlated with food, as in (3). In addition the speaker has (in some instances) the powerful stimulation of hunger pangs, which is private since the community has no suitable connection with the speaker's stomach. "I am hungry" may therefore be variously translated as "I have not eaten for a long time" (1), or "That food makes my mouth water" (2), or "I am ravenous" (3) (compare the expression "I was hungrier than I thought" which describes the ingestion of an unexpectedly large amount of food), or "I have hunger pangs." While all of these may be regarded as synonymous with "I am hungry," they are not synonymous with each other. It is easy for conflicting psychological systematists to cite supporting instances or to train speakers to emit the response "I am hungry" in conformity with a system. With the balloon technique one might condition the verbal response exclusively to stimulation from stomach contractions. This would be an example of either (1) or (2) above. Or a speaker might be trained to make nice observations of the strength of his ingestive behavior, which might recede to the covert level as in (3). The response "I am hungry" would then describe a tendency to eat, with little or no reference to stomach contractions. Everyday usage reflects a mixed reinforcement. A similar analysis could be made of all terms descriptive of motivation, emotion, and action in general, including (of special interest here) the acts of seeing, hearing, and so on.

When public manifestations survive, the extent to which the private stimulus takes over is never certain. In the case of a toothache, the private event is no doubt dominant, but this is due to its relative intensity, not to any condition of differential reinforcement. In a description of one's own behavior, the private component may be much less important. A very strict external contingency may emphasize the public component, especially if the association with private events is faulty. In a rigorous scientific vocabulary private effects are practically eliminated. The converse does not hold. There is apparently no way of basing a response entirely upon the private part of a complex of stimuli. *A differential reinforcement cannot be made contingent upon the property of privacy.* This fact is of extraordinary importance in evaluating traditional psychological terms.

The response "red" is imparted and maintained (either casually or professionally) by reinforcements which are contingent upon a certain property of stimuli. Both speaker and community (or psychologist) have access to the stimulus, and the contingency may be made quite precise. There is nothing about the resulting response which should puzzle anyone. The greater part of psychophysics rests upon this solid footing. The older psychological view, however, was that the speaker was reporting, not a property of the stimulus, but a certain kind of private event, the sensation of red. This was regarded as a later stage in a series beginning with the red stimulus. The experimenter was supposed to manipulate the private event by manipulating the stimulus. This seems like a gratuitous distinction, but in the case of some subjects a similar later stage could apparently be generated in other ways (by arousing an "image"), and hence the autonomy of a private event capable of evoking the response "red" in the absence of a controllable red stimulus seemed to be proved. An adequate proof, of course, requires the elimination of other possibilities (e.g., that the response is generated by the procedures which are intended to generate the image).

Verbal behavior which is "descriptive of images" must be accounted for in any adequate science of behavior. The difficulties are the same for both behaviorist and subjectivist. If the private events are free, a scientific description is impossible in either case. If laws can be discovered, then a lawful description of the verbal behavior can be achieved, with or without references to images. So much for "finding the referents"; the remaining problem of how such responses are maintained in relation to their referents is also soluble. The description of an image appears to be an example of a response to a private stimulus of class (1) above. That is to say, relevant terms are established when the private event accompanies a controllable external stimulus, but responses occur at other times, perhaps in relation to the same private event. The deficiencies of such a vocabulary have been pointed out.

We can account for the response "red" (at least as well as for the "experience" of red) by appeal to past conditions of reinforcement. But what about expanded expressions like "I *see* red" or "I am *conscious* of red"? Here "red" may be a response to either a public or a private stimulus without prejudice to the rest of the expression, but "see" and "conscious" seem to refer to events which are by nature or by definition private. This violates the principle that a reinforcement cannot be made contingent upon the privacy of a stimulus. A reference cannot be narrowed down to a specifically private event by any known method of differential reinforcement.

The original behavioristic hypothesis was, of course, that terms of this sort were descriptions of one's own (generally covert) behavior. The hypothesis explains the establishment and maintenance of the terms by supplying natural public counterparts in similar overt behavior. The terms are in general of class (3). One consequence of the hypothesis is that each term may be given a behavioral definition. We must, however, modify the argument slightly. To say "I see red" is to react, not to red (this is a trivial meaning of "see"), but to one's reaction to red. "See" is a term acquired with respect to one's own behavior in the case of overt responses available to the community. But according to the present analysis it may be evoked at other times by *any private accompaniment* of overt seeing. Here is a point at which a non-behavioral private seeing may be slipped in. Although the commonest private accompaniment would appear to be the stimulation which survives in a similar covert act, as in (3), it might be some sort of state or condition which gains control of the response as in (1) or (2).

The superiority of the behavioral hypothesis is not merely methodological. That aspect of seeing which can be defined behaviorally is basic to the term as established by the verbal community and hence most effective in public discourse. A comparison of cases (1) and (3) will also show that terms which recede to the private level as overt behavior becomes covert have an optimal accuracy of reference, as responses to private stimuli go.

The additional hypothesis follows quite naturally that being conscious, as a form of reacting to one's own behavior, is a social product. Verbal behavior may be distinguished, and conveniently defined, by the fact that the contingencies of reinforcement are provided by other organisms rather than by a mechanical action upon the environment. The hypothesis is equivalent to saying that it is only because the behavior of the individual is important to society that society in turn makes it important to the individual. The individual becomes aware of what he is doing only after society has reinforced verbal responses with respect to his behavior as the source of discriminative stimuli. The behavior to be described (the behavior of which one is to be aware) may later recede to the covert level, and (to add a crowning difficulty) so may the verbal response. It is an ironic twist, considering the history of the behavioristic revolution, that as we develop a more effective vocabulary for the analysis of behavior we also enlarge the possibilities of awareness, so defined. The psychology of the other one is, after all, a direct approach to "knowing thyself."

The main purpose of this discussion has been to define a definition by considering an example. To be consistent the psychologist must deal with his own verbal practices by developing an empirical science of verbal behavior. He cannot, unfortunately, join the logician in defining a definition, for example, as a "rule for the use of a term" (Feigl); he must turn instead to the contingencies of reinforcement which account for the functional relation between a term, as a verbal response, and a given stimulus. This is the "operational basis" for his use of terms; and it is not logic but science.

The philosopher will call this circular. He will argue that we must adopt the rules of logic in order to make and interpret the experiments required in an empirical science of verbal behavior. But talking about talking is no more circular than thinking about thinking or knowing about knowing. Whether or not we are lifting ourselves by our own bootstraps, the simple fact is that we *can* make progress in a scientific analysis of verbal behavior. Eventually we shall be able to include, and perhaps to understand, our own verbal behavior as scientists. If it turns out that our final view of verbal behavior invalidates our scientific structure from the point of view of logic and truth-value, then so much the worse for logic, which will also have been embraced by our analysis.

The participants in the symposium were asked to comment upon all the papers submitted. Their comments were included in the same issue of the Psychological Review. *My contribution follows.*

In the summer of 1930, two years after the publication of Bridgman's *Logic of Modern Physics,* I wrote a paper called "The concept of the reflex in the description of behavior" [see page 475]. It was later offered as the first half of a doctoral thesis and was published in 1931. Although the general method, particularly the historical approach, was derived from Mach's *Science of Mechanics,* my debt to Bridgman was acknowledged in the second paragraph. This was, I think, the first psychological publication to contain a reference to the *Logic of Modern Physics,*[2] and it was the first explicitly operational analysis of a psychological concept.

Shortly after the paper was finished, I found myself contemplating a doctoral examination before a committee of whose sympathies I was none too sure. Not wishing to wait until an unconditional surrender might be

[2] Lyle H. Lanier has called my attention to the fact that Harry M. Johnson summarized Bridgman's argument and applied the operational criterion to the concept of intensity of sensation almost a year before my article appeared (*Psychol. Rev.,* 1930, 37, 113–123).

necessary, I put out a peace feeler. Unmindful or ignorant of the ethics of the academy, I suggested to a member of the Harvard department that if I could be excused from anything but the most perfunctory examination, the time which I would otherwise spend in preparation would be devoted to an operational analysis of half-a-dozen key terms from subjective psychology. The suggestion was received with such breathless amazement that my peace feeler went no further.

The point I want to make is that at that time—1930—I could regard an operational analysis of subjective terms as a *mere exercise in scientific method*. It was just a bit of hack work, badly needed by traditional psychology, which I was willing to engage in as a public service or in return for the remission of sins. It never occurred to me that the analysis could take any but a single course or have any relation to my own prejudices. The result seemed as predetermined as that of a mathematical calculation.

In spite of the present symposium, I am of this opinion still. I believe that the data of a science of psychology can be defined or denoted unequivocally, and that some one set of concepts can be shown to be the most expedient according to the usual standards in scientific practice. Nevertheless, these things have not been done in the field which was dominated by subjective psychology, and the question is: Why not?

Psychology, alone among the biological and social sciences, passed through a revolution comparable in many respects with that which was taking place at the same time in physics. This was, of course, behaviorism. The first step, like that in physics, was a re-examination of the observational bases of certain important concepts. But by the time Bridgman's book was published, most of the early behaviorists, as well as those of us just coming along who claimed some systematic continuity, had begun to see that psychology actually did not require the redefinition of subjective concepts. The reinterpretation of an established set of explanatory fictions was not the way to secure the tools then needed for a scientific description of behavior. Historical prestige was beside the point. There was no more reason to make a permanent place for "consciousness," "will," "feeling," and so on, than for "phlogiston" or *"vis anima."* On the contrary, redefined concepts proved to be awkward and inappropriate, and Watsonianism was, in fact, practically wrecked in the attempt to make them work.

Thus it came about that while the behaviorists might have applied Bridgman's principle to representative terms from a mentalistic psychology (and were most competent to do so), they had lost all interest in the matter. They might as well have spent their time in showing what an eighteenth-century chemist was talking about when he said that the Metallic Substances consisted of a vitrifiable earth united with phlogiston. There was no doubt that such a statement could be analyzed operationally or translated into modern terms, or that subjective terms could be operationally defined. But such matters were of historical interest only. What was wanted was a fresh set of concepts derived from a direct analysis of the newly emphasized data, and this was enough to absorb all the available energies of the behaviorists. Besides, the motivation of the *enfant terrible* had worn itself out.

I think the Harvard department would have been happier if my offer had been taken up. What happened instead was the operationism of Boring and Stevens. This has been described as an attempt to climb onto the behavioristic bandwagon unobserved. I cannot agree. It is an attempt to acknowledge some of the more powerful claims of behaviorism (which could no longer be denied) but at the same time to preserve the old explanatory fictions. It is agreed that the data of psychology must be behavioral rather than mental if psychology is to be a member of the United Sciences, but the position taken is merely that of "methodological" behaviorism. According to this doctrine the world is divided into public and private events; and psychology, in order to meet the requirements of a science, must confine itself to the former. This was never good behaviorism, but it was an easy position to expound and defend and was often resorted to by the behaviorists themselves. It is least objectionable to the subjectivist because it permits him to retain "experience" for purposes of "non-physicalistic" self-knowledge.

The position is not genuinely operational because it shows an unwillingness to abandon fictions. It is like saying that while the physicist must admittedly confine himself to Einsteinian time, it is *still true* that Newtonian absolute time flows "equably without relation to anything external." It is a sort of *E pur si muove* in reverse. What is lacking is the bold and exciting behavioristic hypothesis that what one observes and talks about is always the "real" or "physical" world (or at least the "one" world) and that "experience" is a derived construct to be understood only through an analysis of verbal (not, of course, merely vocal) processes.

The difficulties which arise from the public-private distinction have a prominent place in the present symposium, and it may be worthwhile to consider four of them.

(1) The relation between the two sets of terms which are required has proved to be confusing. The pair most frequently discussed are "discrimination" (public) and "sensation" (private). Is one the same as the other, or reducible to the other, and so on? A satisfactory resolution would seem

to be that the terms belong to conceptual systems which are not necessarily related in a point-to-point correspondence. There is no question of equating them or their referents, or reducing one to the other, but only a question of translation—and a single term in one set may require a paragraph in the other.

(2) The public-private distinction emphasizes the arid philosophy of "truth by agreement." The public, in fact, turns out to be simply that which can be agreed upon because it is common to two or more agreers. This is not an essential part of operationism; on the contrary operationism permits us to dispense with this most unsatisfying solution of the problem of truth. Disagreements can often be cleared up by asking for definitions, and operational definitions are especially helpful, but operationism is not primarily concerned with communication or disputation. It is one of the most hopeful of principles precisely because it is not. The solitary inhabitant of a desert isle could arrive at operational definitions (provided he had previously been equipped with an adequate verbal repertoire). The ultimate criterion for the goodness of a concept is not whether two people are brought into agreement but whether the scientist who uses the concept can operate successfully upon his material—all by himself if need be. What matters to Robinson Crusoe is not whether he is agreeing with himself but whether he is getting anywhere with his control over nature.

One can see why the subjective psychologist makes so much of agreement. It was once a favorite sport to quiz him about inter-subjective correspondences. "How do you know that O's sensation of green is the same as E's?" And so on. But agreement alone means very little. Various epochs in the history of philosophy and psychology have seen whole-hearted agreement on the definition of psychological terms. This makes for contentment but not for progress. The agreement is likely to be shattered when someone discovers that a set of terms will not really work, perhaps in some hitherto neglected field, but this does not make agreement the key to workability. On the contrary, it is the other way round.

(3) The distinction between public and private is by no means the same as that between physical and mental. That is why methodological behaviorism (which adopts the first) is very different from radical behaviorism (which lops off the latter term in the second). The result is that while the radical behaviorist may in some cases consider private events (inferentially, perhaps, but none the less meaningfully), the methodological operationist has maneuvered himself into a position where he cannot. "Science does not consider private data," says Boring. (Just where this leaves my contribution to the present symposium, I do not like to reflect.) But I contend

that my toothache is just as physical as my typewriter, though not public, and I see no reason why an objective and operational science cannot consider the processes through which a vocabulary descriptive of a toothache is acquired and maintained. The irony of it is that, while Boring must confine himself to an account of my external behavior, I am still interested in what might be called Boring-from-within.

(4) The public-private distinction apparently leads to a logical, as distinct from a psychological, analysis of the verbal behavior of the scientist, although I see no reason why it should. Perhaps it is because the subjectivist is still not interested in terms but in what the terms used to stand for. The only problem which a science of behavior must solve in connection with subjectivism is in the verbal field. How can we account for the behavior of talking about mental events? The solution must be psychological, rather than logical, and I have tried to suggest one approach in my present paper. The complete lack of interest in this problem among current psychological operationists is nicely demonstrated by the fact that the only other members of the present panel who seem to be interested in a *causal* analysis of verbal behavior are the two non-psychologists (one of them a logician!).

My reaction to this symposium, then, is twofold. The confusion which seems to have arisen from a principle which is supposed to eliminate confusion is discouraging. But upon second thought it appears that the possibility of a genuine operationism in psychology has not yet been fully explored. With a little effort I can recapture my enthusiasm of fifteen years ago. (This is, of course, a private event.)

The Alliteration in Shakespeare's Sonnets: A Study in Literary Behavior

I have omitted articles from this collection when their substance has already appeared in book form—for example, the series of experimental papers brought together in The Behavior of Organisms. *It has not been easy to dispose of several papers on verbal and literary behavior according to this principle. The paper on Gertrude Stein was only briefly mentioned in* Verbal Behavior *and is therefore reprinted. Much of "The operational definition of psychological terms" was included in* Verbal Behavior *and in* Science and Human Behavior, *but the issue of operationism seemed to justify reprinting the whole article. A paper called "The verbal summator and a method for the study of latent speech"* (Journal of Psychology, *1936, 2, 71-107) has been omitted because part of it was covered in* Verbal Behavior *and the remaining part, concerning a relation between rank order and word frequency, did not seem worth salvaging. This was true of two other studies of the same relation—"The distribution of associated words"* (Psychological Record, *1937, 1, 71-76) and "Some factors influencing the distribution of associated words" written with Stuart W. Cook* (Psychological Record, *1939, 3, 178-184). Three other papers were not fully covered in* Verbal Behavior *because of a decision not to review experimental or statistical studies. One of these appeared in the* Psychological Record (*1939, 3, 186-192), and is reproduced here by permission of the editor.*

Alliteration is one of the most familiar forms of sound-patterning in poetry and prose. It is said to exist when two or more syllables beginning with the same consonant occur near each other in a given passage. Examples of alliteration are frequently cited as contributing to the effect of a literary work, and it is usually implied that they represent deliberate acts of arrangement on the part of the writer. If this is true, alliteration should throw some light on the dynamics of verbal behavior and especially upon a process which may be called "formal perseveration" or, better, "formal strengthening." Studies of word-association, latent speech, and so on, have indicated that the appearance of a sound in speech raises the probability of occurrence of that sound for some time thereafter. Stated in a different way: the emission of a verbal response temporarily raises the strength of all responses of similar form. The principal characteristics of poetry (alliteration, assonance, rhyme, and rhythm) seem to be exaggerated cases of the tendency toward formal strengthening, and they should supply useful information with regard to it.

In order to determine the existence or the importance of any process responsible for a characteristic pattern in a sample of speech, it is necessary to allow for the amount of patterning to be expected from chance. We cannot assert, for example, that any one instance of alliteration is due to a special process in the behavior of the writer rather than to an accidental proximity of words beginning with the same sound. Proof that there is a process responsible for alliterative patterning can be obtained only through a statistical analysis of all the arrangements of initial consonants in a reasonably large sample. In the case of alliteration what we want to know is the extent to which the initial consonants are not distributed at random. If the distribution turns out to be random, then no process by virtue of which words come to be arranged on a formal basis can be attributed to the behavior of the writer, even though selected instances still show the grouping commonly called alliteration.

If there is any process in the behavior of the writer by virtue of which the occurrence of an initial consonant raises the probability of occurrence of that sound for a short time thereafter, then the initial consonants in a sample of writing will be grouped. Methods are, of course, available for detecting a tendency toward grouping, but in the case of poetry a more appropriate technique can be based upon the use of the line as a natural unit. In any large sample of poetry certain lines will contain no occurrences of a given initial consonant, and others will contain one, two, three, and so on, occurrences. From the relative frequency of the consonant we may calculate these numbers if we assume that the probability of occurrence remains unchanged and that each occurrence is an independent event. A process of alliteration, if it existed, would violate these assumptions and yield a greater number of lines containing more than one occurrence and also a greater number of empty lines.

This paper presents some facts concerning the alliterative patterns in a block of one hundred Shakespeare sonnets. The material is drawn from a more extensive research on a number of different kinds of sound-patterns, to be reported in full later. The sonnets were first scanned according to a set of arbitrary rules, designed to prevent unintentional selection and at the same time to single out the most important syllables in each of the 1,400 lines. The average number of syllables per line thus designated was 5.036, which agrees well with the pentametric form of the poems. The range, however, was from three to eight. A tabulation of initial consonants by line was then made.[1] The results were expressed for each consonant separately

---

[1] The tabulation was made by Miss Marian Kruse and Miss Janette Jones, Federal Aid Students at the University of Minnesota.

in the form of (1) the number of lines containing no occurrences, (2) the number containing one occurrence, (3) the number containing two occurrences, and so on.

The formula for the number of lines containing 0, 1, 2, . . . occurrences of a given initial consonant involves the binomial expansion $N(q + p)^n$, where N is the number of lines examined, n the number of syllables per line, p the probability of occurrence of the consonant under consideration (obtained from its frequency in the whole sample), and q the probability of occurrence of any other sound, or $1 - p$. The successive terms in the expansion give the numbers required. A good approximation could have been obtained by letting $n = 5$, which is close to the average number of important syllables, but a more accurate estimate was obtained by calculating separately for lines of different length according to the lengths in the sample. Calculations were made for 277 lines of four syllables (including a few in the original sample which contained only three), 830 lines of five syllables, 252 of six, and 41 of seven (including a few originally of eight).[2] By adding the occurrences obtained from these separate calculations, the total chance expectancy for that consonant was obtained.

Before the observed and calculated frequencies may legitimately be compared for our present purposes, a spurious alliterative effect in the observed values must be taken into account. Shakespeare, perhaps more than most other English poets, tends to repeat a word (or to use an inflected form) within the space of a line. There are two repetitions, for example, in the line:

Suns of the world may stain when heaven's sun staineth

In tabulating initial consonants, this line must be counted as containing four *s*'s. It is clear, however, that the last two must be attributed not only to formal strengthening but to some thematic source. The line as heard is strongly sibilant, but two of the *s*'s are due to something beyond a simple alliterative process.

In a line containing a repeated word it is at present impossible to determine how the responsibility for the similarity of sound is to be divided between formal and thematic factors. To omit all repeated words from the present tabulation would obviously not be justified; at the same time we cannot accept at full value the instances of alliteration for which they are responsible. In the following summary the raw data (obtained by counting all initial sounds regardless of repetition of the whole word) are presented

---

[2] The formula for the five-syllable lines, for example, is
$$830\ (q^5 + 5q^4p + 10q^3p^2 + 10q^2p^3 + 5qp^4 + p^5),$$
the successive terms giving the number of lines containing 0, 1, 2, 3, 4, and 5 occurrences of the consonant for which p and q were calculated.

TABLE I

| Consonant | NUMBER OF OCCURRENCES PER LINE | | | | | | | | | | | | P |
	0 Shakes.	0 Calc'd.	1 Shakes.	1 Calc'd.	2 Shakes.	2 Calc'd.	3 Shakes.	3 Calc'd.	4 Shakes.	4 Calc'd.	5 Shakes.	5 Calc'd.	
qu	1377	1377	23	23	0	0	0	0	0	0	0	0	. .
z	1371	1371	29	28	0	0	0	0	0	0	0	0	< .05
j	1370	1369	29	31	0	1	0	0	0	0	0	0	< .05
ch	1350	1348	47	51	1	2	0	0	0	0	0	0	< .05
hw	1334	1331	63	68	3	4	0	0	0	0	0	0	< .05
v	1311	1310	84	88	5	9	0	0	0	0	0	0	< .05
y	1281	1277	112	118	7	15	0	0	0	0	0	0	< .05
r	1235	1233	151	159	14	15	0	0	0	0	0	0	< .05, < .10
n	1190	1176	182	208	27	18	1	0	0	0	0	0	< .05
k	1184	1176	194	208	22	18	0	1	0	0	0	0	< .02, < .05
g	1160	1158	220	223	18	22	1	1	0	0	0	0	< .001
d	1158	1134	237	244	23	29	2(0)	1	1	0	0	0	< .50
p	1138	1093	259	276	38	30	2(0)	1	1	1	0	0	< .05, < .10
h	1102	1093	246	281	40	31	1	2	0	0	0	0	< .001
w	1108	1087	264	286	35	33	5(3)	2	1	0	0	0	< .05, < .10
t	1096	1082	256	295	42	34	4(2)	2	0	0	0	0	< .05
f	1093	1071	280	299	45	44	9(3)	3	1	1	0	0	< .001, < .01
b	1074	1065	280	332	60	46	2(1)	5	1	1	0	0	< .02, < .05
m	1038	1020	299	336	48	46	4(2)	3	0	0	0	0	< .50
l	1017	1015	331	377	64	61	13(6)	4	1	1	0	0	< .001
th	981	957	341	366	52	57	6(2)	5	1	2	0	0	< .50
s	702	685	501	523	161	162	29(24)	26	7(4)	2	0	0	< .10, < .20

first. The revised values obtained by subtracting the instances arising from repetition are then given.

In Table 1 the initial consonants are arranged in order according to the frequency with which they occur in the block of 100 sonnets. The numbers of lines containing 0, 1, 2, 3, 4, or 5 occurrences per line observed for Shakespeare and calculated as described above are shown in their respective columns. The last column gives the significance of the difference between observed and calculated values expressed in terms of the probability that the difference is due to sampling.

From the table it will be seen that the least frequent sound (*qu*) occurs only 23 times and never more than once per line, as we should expect from chance. At the other extreme the sound *s* (which occurs 938 times) fails to occur in 702 lines (the expected number of empty lines being 685) but occurs once in 501 lines (expected: 523), twice in 161 lines (expected: 162), three times in 29 lines (expected: 26), and four times in seven lines (expected: two). If we omit the cases which arise from repeated words, we obtain the figures in parentheses in the table, which show a better agreement. The corrections required in the two-per-line column have merely been estimated and are not shown in the table. An examination of every tenth line showing two occurrences indicates that about 19% of such lines are due to repetition. When this correction is made for *s*, it appears that Shakespeare falls about 30 lines *short* of the expected number of lines containing two *s*'s.

Other consonants in the table show varying degrees of agreement. The estimates of significance (which are in every case based upon the raw data) indicate a possible "use of alliteration" with *n, k, h, t, f, b,* and *l;* but these all involve repetition, and the corrected values give very little support to the popular notion. There is possibly a trend in the direction to be expected from a process of alliteration, but the absolute excess of "heavy" lines is very slight. Some indication of this excess may be obtained from the following statements regarding the table as a whole:

Lines containing four like initial consonants. (Ex.: *B*orne on the *b*ier with white and *b*ristly *b*eard.)

Of these lines there are only eight more than would be expected from chance, and four of these are due to the repetition of the same word or words. Not more than once in twenty-five sonnets (350 lines) does Shakespeare lengthen a series of three like consonants into four, except when he repeats a word.

Lines containing three like initial consonants. (Ex.: *S*ave that my *s*oul's imaginary *s*ight.)

Of these lines there are thirty-three too many, but twenty-nine of these are due to repetition of the same word. Only four are, therefore, "pure" alliteration. Except when he repeated a whole word, Shakespeare changed a line of two like consonants into one of three not oftener than once in twenty-five sonnets.

Lines containing two like initial consonants.

There are ninety-two excess lines of this sort, but the correction for repetition gives a *shortage* of approximately forty lines. Allowing for eight lines extended to contain three or four occurrences, we may say that once in about every three sonnets Shakespeare *discarded* a word because its initial consonant had already been used.

These corrections probably go too far, since a repetition of the same word may in part exemplify an alliterative process. Moreover, when instances have been thrown out because they belong to repeated words, the whole table should be recalculated on the basis of a reduced total frequency. This recalculation would affect chiefly the values for the empty lines and for the lines containing one occurrence. As the table indicates, Shakespeare shows in general an excess of empty lines, but most, if not all, of this difference would disappear under recalculation with a smaller total frequency. Similarly, Shakespeare's shortage of one-occurrence lines would be reduced. These changes cannot be made without an arbitrary estimate of the share contributed by alliteration when a word is repeated, but by taking the raw data as the upper limit and the fully corrected data as the lower, the main question proposed in this study may be answered.

In spite of the seeming richness of alliteration in the sonnets, there is no significant evidence of a process of alliteration in the behavior of the poet to which any serious attention should be given. So far as this aspect of poetry is concerned, Shakespeare might as well have drawn his words out of a hat. The thematic or semantic forces which are responsible for the emission of speech apparently function independently of this particular formal property.

It is scarcely convincing to argue that Shakespeare may have arranged certain alliterative patterns and discarded an equal number due to chance, since it is unlikely that the expected frequencies would be so closely approximated. It is simpler to believe that we have been misled by the selection of instances and that no process of alliteration should ever have been attributed to the poet. If "formal strengthening" proves to be a real characteristic of normal speech, we shall have to look for the key to Shakespeare's genius in his ability to resist it, thereby reversing the usual conception of this kind of poetic activity.

Shakespeare's "philosophy of composition" might well be expressed in the words of the Duchess, who said to Alice, "And the moral of *that* is, 'Take care of the sense, and the sounds will take care of themselves.' "

A Quantitative Estimate of Certain Types of Sound-Patterning in Poetry

The technique used in estimating certain verbal processes in the composition of the Shakespeare sonnets was extended to other aspects of sound-patterning in analyzing the work of a poet known to have favored formal devices. The following paper is reprinted with permission of the editor of The American Journal of Psychology *(1941, 54, 64-79).*

The phonetic elements which compose a representative sample of normal speech are not distributed at random but are to some extent grouped. This characteristic cannot always be accounted for by the repetition of meaningful material; and it must therefore be regarded as an example of "formal perseveration" or "formal strengthening." It may be described by saying that when a speech sound is once emitted, the probability of emission of that sound is temporarily raised. In addition to normal speech, formal strengthening is observed in word associations, in speech obtained *in vacuo* with the verbal summator, and in the verbal behavior characteristic of certain psychopathic disorders. In literature it appears in an exaggerated form as rhyme, assonance, alliteration, and (if we include stress-pattern as a formal phonetic characteristic) rhythm. These extreme cases are in themselves worthy of investigation, and they may also be expected to throw some light on the general process.

A satisfactory demonstration of formal strengthening in poetry or prose cannot be made by pointing to instances, although this is common practice in the field of literary criticism. Seven or eight different initial consonants, for example, will usually account for more than half the instances, and many accidental "alliterations" are to be expected. The assertion that any sample of speech demonstrates alliteration *as a process in the behavior of the writer* must rest upon a statistical proof that the existing patterns are not to be expected from chance.

One method of analyzing a poem is to examine the number of lines containing two or more occurrences of a given initial consonant and to

437

determine whether this exceeds the expectation based upon the general frequency of the consonant in the whole sample. In a study of 100 Shakespearean sonnets it was found that the slight excess of lines containing more than one occurrence was largely accounted for by the repetition of whole words, where the strengthening or perseveration seemed to be principally derived from thematic rather than formal factors [see page 431]. Little or nothing could be learned of the nature of alliteration in such a case, and it seemed advisable to turn to a poet who almost certainly exemplifies the process in an extreme degree. The present report is an analysis of the first 500 iambic pentameter lines of Swinburne's "Atalanta in Calydon." Both alliteration and assonance are considered.

Not all the sounds in a poem contribute equally to its effect, nor do they represent equal opportunities of selection and manipulation on the part of the writer. The formal analysis of a poem is facilitated by a preliminary choice of the principal sounds, especially the syllables receiving emphasis when the line is scanned, as well as a number of other obviously important words. The omitted material may be regarded either as not contributing in any effective way to the sound pattern or as not permitting any variation in the behavior of the writer. In order to avoid unconscious prejudice with regard to patterning, the material must be selected by rule, even though the best interpretive reading is perhaps not always obtained. In the present case each line was first scanned strictly as iambic pentameter. When the accent fell on a weak syllable (e.g., preposition, auxiliary, possessive pronoun, article, copula, or such an ending as *-ness, -ing, -ance,* or *-ment*), it was shifted forward or backward whenever possible to an adjacent strong syllable not included in the scanning. Otherwise it was omitted. For example, in the line "Bite to the blood and burn into the bone," a strict scansion gave "Bite *to* the *blood* and *burn* in*to* the *bone.*" The accent on *to* was shifted backward, according to rule, to the syllable *bite.* However, the accent on *to* in *into* could not be so shifted because there was no adjacent strong syllable, and it was hence eliminated, leaving a line of four accents. This first stage generally yielded four or five selected syllables per line. Each line was then examined for strong syllables not yet receiving stress, and all accented parts of nouns, verbs, adjectives, and adverbs were added The result was a scanned line which gave an important place to practically every significant syllable. A few specific exceptions were made. For example, the prepositions *across, because, above, about, against* and *upon* were allowed to retain the beat in the first scanning. The adverbs which were later added did not include *not, no, then, thus, so, but, only, all,* nor did the adjectives include *no, some, all, none,* and *such.* Interrogative and personal pronouns were added when they were the subjects or objects of verbs. The procedure yielded 27 lines of four syllables, 211 lines of five syllables, 193 of six, 54 of seven, and 15 of eight, or a total of 2,819 syllables.

Alliteration by line. In determining Swinburne's alliteration by line, the lines containing one, two, three, four, or five occurrences of the same initial consonant were counted, and the frequencies were compared with the expected mean frequencies. The latter were obtained from the binomial expansion $N (q + p)^n$, where N is the number of lines examined, n the number of syllables per line, p the probability of occurrence of the consonant under consideration (calculated from its frequency in the sample), and q the probability of occurrence of any other sound, or $1 - p$. Separate calculations were made for the lines of various lengths given above, except that the lines of seven and eight syllables were grouped and treated as if they contained seven syllables. The total expectation was obtained by adding the resulting frequencies. The data for the ten most frequent consonants ($p > 0.03$) are given in Table 1.

TABLE I

LINES IN A SAMPLE OF SWINBURNE CONTAINING VARIOUS NUMBERS OF CERTAIN
CONSONANTS COMPARED WITH FREQUENCIES EXPECTED IN RANDOM SAMPLING

Number of occurrences per line

Conso-nant	0		1		2		3		4		5	
	Swin.	Exp.	Swin.	Exp.	Swin	Exp.	Swin.	Exp.	Swin.	Exp.	Swin.	Exp.
b	370	353	97	127	27(24)	19	4	2	2	0	0	0
d	399	395	88	95	11(9)	10	2	1	0	0	0	0
f	338	312	107	153	47(39)	31	5(4)	3	3	0	0	0
g	396	391	89	98	13(11)	10	2	1	0	0	0	0
h	312	328	139	143	43(38)	26	4	3	2	0	0	0
l	349	331	110	141	32(24)	25	9	2	0	0	0	0
m	355	352	122	127	19(14)	19	4	2	0	0	0	0
s	237	222	173	192	66(61)	70	19	14	5	2	0	0
th	360	347	107	130	29(23)	21	3(2)	2	1	0	0	0
w	366	357	105	124	27(24)	18	2	1	0	0	0	0
All			314(267)	249	54(52)	31		13	2	0	0	

Practically without exception, Swinburne has too many lines containing two, three, and four instances of the same consonant. For example, according to Table 1, there are 27 lines containing pairs of *b*'s in place of the expected 19, four containing three *b*'s in place of the expected two, and two containing four *b*'s where none is expected. There is a consequent shortage of lines containing only one *b* (97 in place of 127) and an excess of empty lines. The alliterative effect is especially strong for *b, f, h, l,* and *w.* The consonant *s* shows a preponderance of lines containing three and four instances but an actual shortage of lines containing two. The effect for *th* (voicing ignored) is slight, and that for *m, g,* and *d* negligible. For the 10 consonants combined, there is an excess of 65 lines containing two instances of the same consonant, 23 containing three, and 11 containing four.

As in the case of Shakespeare, it is difficult to interpret repetitions of whole words. These involve formal perseveration, but presumably the meaning of the passage is of considerable importance in determining the second emission in each case. The numbers in parentheses in the table are the corrected frequencies obtained by subtracting all cases of the repetition of a whole word. The correction operates to reduce the evidence for alliteration, perhaps unduly, but significant differences are still obtained.

Although the initial consonants in this sample of 500 lines are unquestionably not distributed at random, an actual estimate of the amount of arrangement on the part of the poet is not easily made. A definite meaning can be given to the statement that the sample contains so-and-so many extra lines containing two, three, or four instances of the same consonant, but in the face of an evident grouping the expected mean frequencies used here are called in question. If some instances of the repetition of a consonant are due to formal strengthening, the total frequency used in the calculation of p is not representative, and the value of p is too high. This defect in the calculation will be roughly proportional to the amount of grouping and will operate to obscure some of the alliteration actually present. Thus, if we conclude that there are eight excess lines containing two instances of the sound *b* and two excess lines each containing three and four instances, and that these lines would otherwise have contained only one *b* (this is suggested by the frequency of the one-occurrence lines), then there are at least 18 instances which are due to formal strengthening, and the frequency used in calculating the value of p which applies to the sample in general should have been, not 171, but at least as low as 153. Ignoring the effect of this elimination on the size of the total sample, we obtain a value of p equal to 0.05428 rather than 0.06066, and we then expect only 16 lines containing two instances, and only one line containing three instances, instead of 19 and two, respectively. The excess exhibited by the table is thus less than the real excess in the poem.

When little alliteration is indicated, no correction is called for in the present degree of approximation. This is generally true of the Shakespeare data. Where an excess of "heavy" lines is demonstrated, it has probably been underestimated. For practical purposes the calculation based upon the total frequency of each consonant provides for a satisfactory measure of alliteration.

Alliterative span. The analysis of alliteration *by line* has a certain value in the criticism of poetry, but it is not an exhaustive survey of alliterative strengthening. There may be a detectable grouping in some shorter unit within the line or in a large unit of, say, two or three lines which would not necessarily appear with the preceding method. Moreover, where alliteration has clearly been demonstrated, it is desirable to determine the actual alliterative range or span by taking the size of the analyzed unit into account. The perseverative strengthening which follows the emission of a consonant must eventually die out, and the course of the effect should provide an indication of its nature. This course may be traced by inquiring how often the repetition of a consonant follows immediately in the next syllable, how often a single syllable intervenes, how often two syllables intervene, and so on.

In collecting the necessary data, the initial consonants (or initial vowels, where these occurred) of all selected syllables were placed in order on a long tape. The breaks caused by the omission of two choruses were ignored. The tape was then passed under cards in which windows were cut to display consonants with any desired number of intervening syllables, beginning with adjacent pairs. The numbers of pairs of each consonant at distances up to that of eight intervening syllables were tallied by moving the tape under each card one space at a time throughout its length. The figures for the 10 commonest consonants are given in Table 2, together with the expected values. The latter were approximated by squaring the frequency for each consonant and dividing by the number of syllables in the total sample. Thus, when every *b* on the tape is compared with some other letter in a constant relative position, we expect to obtain, in round numbers, 10 pairs; for there are 171 *b*'s, and the probability of finding a second *b* in each case is approximately $171/2819$ or 0.06066.

When the second consonant immediately follows the first (with no syllable intervening between the syllables being compared), 20 pairs of *b*'s are actually observed instead of the expected 10. When the position compared is the next but one (one syllable intervening), 21 pairs are observed. It is only when four syllables intervene that the observed value drops to the chance level. (The standard error of the expected mean frequency is in

TABLE 2

NUMBER OF REPETITIONS OF A CONSONANT AT VARIOUS DISTANCES FROM THE FIRST
OCCURRENCE COMPARED WITH THE EXPECTATION FROM CHANCE

Conso-nant	Ex-pected	Observed (No. intervening syllables)								
		0	1	2	3	4	5	6	7	8
b	10	20	21	18	21	9	9	12	9	11
d	5	8	10	7	7	6	5	•6	7	7
f	18	36	32	18	17	17	22	18	21	19
g	5	11	8	9	9	11	5	1	4	4
h	15	22	20	20	19	16	16	9	18	20
l	14	24	25	22	18	15	21	17	14	15
m	11	20	14	22	12	9	11	7	13	7
s	52	66	59	57	52	58	52	49	55	57
th	12	15	19	12	21	18	16	10	12	13
w	10	13	15	14	8	10	8	14	8	6
Total	152	235	223	201	184	169	165	143	160	159

each case approximately the square root of the frequency, and this may be
used in estimating the significance of the observed figures.) The separate
values for each consonant are based upon too small a sample to be very illuminating, but the total frequencies for all 10 consonants show a very clear
trend from a maximal influence upon the immediately following syllable
to approximately a chance effect after the intervention of four syllables.
These totals have been plotted as Curve A in Figure 1, in which the chance
level is also indicated with broken line. The solid circles represent columns
in Table 2 which differ significantly from the column of expected frequencies; the observed frequencies being likely to occur less than once in 100
trials under random sampling (χ^2 test).

The curve clearly demonstrates that the strengthening effect of the emission of a consonant is greatest in its immediate vicinity and drops to zero at
a distance of about four strong syllables. There are, however, certain qualifications to be applied to this statement. In the sample here examined only
certain consonants show the effect. Moreover, the repetition of whole
words, presumably due in part to considerations of meaning, must be
allowed for. In this sample the number of pairs of whole words [1] with no

---

[1] Throughout, "whole words" is to be understood as including inflected forms, nouns,
and adjectives from the same root, or any case where a similarity of form can be related to
a single subject matter.

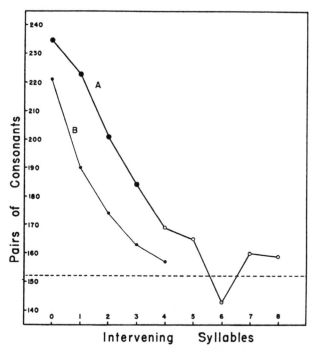

Fɪɢ. ɪ. Swinburne's alliterative span. *Curve A:* The sum of the number of pairs of the 10 commonest initial consonants is plotted against the number of syllables intervening between the syllables examined. The dotted line indicates the sum of the mean frequencies expected under random sampling. The solid circles are for frequencies differing significantly from the expected frequencies. *Curve B:* All instances of the repetition of whole words (including all forms with a common root which determines the initial consonant) have been subtracted to show the least possible effect of formal strengthening. The dotted line is slightly high for comparison with this curve.

intervening syllables is 14; with one intervening syllable, 33; with two, 27; with three, 21; and with four, 12. Curve B in Figure 1 shows the span obtained after all these instances have been subtracted. Without defining the share contributed by purely formal strengthening to the repetition of a whole word, these curves give at least the upper and lower limits of the effect. In the case of the lower curve the line indicating the sum of the expected mean frequencies is somewhat too high, since if we eliminate some of the observed cases, we must recalculate with smaller frequencies.

When one syllable intervenes, the indicated sum of the expected mean frequencies may be as much as five points too high. The effect of subtracting pairs of whole words from the curve for alliterative span is thus not quite so drastic as Figure 1 may suggest.

Three adjacent instances of the same consonant. Further evidence of formal strengthening is provided by the presence of groups of three adjacent instances of the same consonant. The values of p lead us to expect very few cases, but a considerable number should result from formal strengthening because both members of a pair of consonants presumably contribute to the heightened probability of occurrence in the third position. In Table 3 the

TABLE 3

GROUPS OF THREE ADJACENT INSTANCES OF THE SAME INITIAL CONSONANT

	Consonant										Total
	b	d	f	g	h	l	m	s	th	w	
Expected	1	0	1	0	1	1	1	7	1	1	14
Observed	3	2	10	1	5	2	3	15	1	0	42

observed and expected frequencies of groups of three instances of the same consonant are compared for the 10 commonest consonants. The excess of 28 "triples" over the expected 14 is of sufficient magnitude to confirm the cumulative action of formal strengthening. A similar result has been obtained by tabulating groups of three consonants which contain one syllable of a different sort, as in the sequences *b-b-r-b* or *b-r-b-b.*

Shakespeare's alliterative span. A comparison of instances of the same consonants without regard to linear position may be used to examine the 100 Shakespeare sonnets which previously yielded only very slight evidence of alliteration when tested by line.

It was impossible to construct a single long tape in this case, since the end of one sonnet and the beginning of another could not be supposed to have any relation, even if we had known the order of composition. Hence a tape for each sonnet was constructed and tabulated separately. All pairs up to and including those with four intervening syllables were examined. The principal effect of breaking the sample into short parts was to reduce the number of pairs with one or more intervening syllables; at the end of each sonnet there were syllables with which no succeeding syllable could be compared, and there were more of these the greater the number of in-

tervening syllables. Full allowance for this was made by calculating a separate mean frequency in comparing consonants separated by different
numbers of intervening syllables. The uncorrected data (no allowance being
made for the repetition of whole words) are shown in the upper curve in
Figure 2. The sums of the expected mean frequencies are also shown with

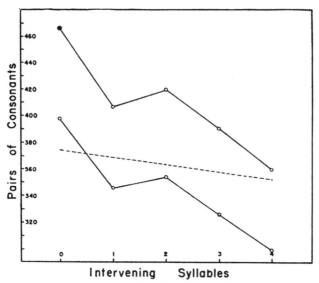

FIG. 2. Shakespeare's alliterative span. *Upper Curve:* The sum of the numbers
of pairs of the 10 commonest initial consonants is plotted against the number of
syllables intervening between the syllables examined. The dashed line indicates
the sums of the expected mean frequencies; the slope is due to the fact that with
each additional intervening syllable fewer pairs are available for comparison. The
solid circle represents a set of frequencies significantly different from the corresponding expected frequencies. *Lower Curve:* All instances of the repetition of
whole words have been subtracted. The dotted line is somewhat too high for
comparison with this curve.

a dashed line. The sums decline because of the reduction in the number of
pairs available for examination, as just noted.

At first sight the upper curve in Figure 2 may seem to indicate a considerable alliterative effect. Only the first point, however, is significantly different from the expected frequency. The observed numbers of pairs when

no syllables intervene would be expected about once in 100 trials under random sampling. The other points show a plausible trend but are not statistically significant. The lower curve is for the data corrected by subtracting instances of the repetition of whole words. As with Swinburne, the "expected" line is somewhat too high for comparison with the corrected curve because of the need of recalculation with reduced frequencies, but the curve is safely within the range of values characteristic of random sampling.

In order to provide a rough comparison of Shakespeare and Swinburne, the data obtained with this method were converted to percentages of the expected mean frequencies. The alliterative spans of the two poets are represented together in Figure 3. It is obvious that with Swinburne alliteration

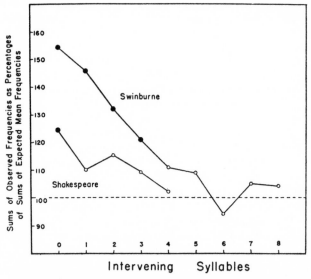

FIG. 3.   Comparison of the alliterative spans of Shakespeare and Swinburne. The sums plotted in Fig. 1 and Fig. 2 have been converted to percentages of the sums of the expected mean frequencies. The solid circles indicate significant values. No correction has been made for the repetition of whole words; the required correction would be slightly more extensive for Shakespeare.

is not only much more common, but extends over a considerably wider span, than in the Shakespeare sonnets.

Assonant span. A perseverative strengthening of vowels (or "assonance") is also to be expected from the casual observation of many poems, and the possibility may be investigated with the present method.

A tape was prepared for the vowels in the selected syllables of the Swinburne poem. In order to avoid the necessity of making relatively fine distinctions in pronunciation and to obtain larger frequencies, the phonemic boundaries were somewhat enlarged. All vowels marked in Webster's *International Dictionary* as ŭ, ẽr, and o͡o, were counted as a single *"vowel"* for present purposes. The same was true of the sounds marked ô and ä, *ou* and *oi*, and *ū* and o͞o. The other vowels tabulated were ā, ă, ē, ĕ, ī, ĭ, and ō. The resulting numbers of pairs of the nine most frequent vowels at various distances, compared with the expected numbers, are presented in Table 4 and in the lower curve of Figure 4.

The result differs considerably from that for consonants. A (barely significant) excess of pairs appears only when three syllables intervene. The frequencies in this column (Table 4) would be expected fewer than

TABLE 4

REPETITION OF A VOWEL AT VARIOUS DISTANCES FROM THE FIRST OCCURRENCE, COMPARED WITH EXPECTATION FROM CHANCE

Vowel	Expected	Observed (No. intervening syllables)										
		0	1	2	3	4	5	6	7	8	9	10
ā	20	12	17	26	22	20	28	26	25	23	21	15
ä	18	16	14	22	33	19	25	17	22	24	19	20
ē	32	29	26	39	35	21	32	33	32	25	29	31
ĕ	33	30	42	31	33	27	28	26	27	29	28	29
ī	32	35	39	25	32	27	39	36	31	33	37	31
ĭ	45	36	36	43	54	42	55	50	44	39	49	42
ō	10	12	7	12	15	14	2	15	8	14	12	11
ô, ä	40	40	41	42	39	35	27	48	37	38	43	45
ŭ, er, o͡o	51	56	55	61	59	50	54	55	50	38	44	38
Total	281	266	277	301	322	255	290	306	276	263	282	262

five times but more than twice in 100 trials under random sampling. A uniform trend toward this point is evident beginning (where the vowels are adjacent) slightly below the chance expectation. The fifth point of the curve, however, is below chance and is the lowest point in the curve as a whole. Such a rapid change from a point significantly above, to one

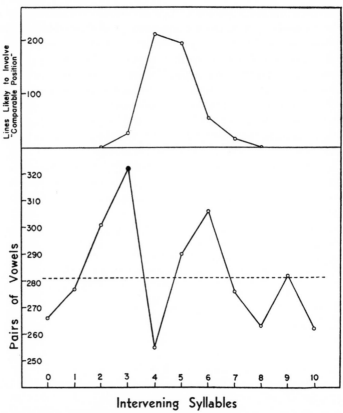

Fig. 4.   Swinburne's assonant span. *Lower Curve:* The sum of the numbers of pairs of the nine commonest vowels is plotted against the number of syllables intervening between the syllables examined. The dotted line indicates the sum of the expected mean frequencies. The solid circle represents a set of frequencies significantly different from the expected frequencies. *Upper Curve:* Distribution of lines of different length, placed on the horizontal axis in a position to indicate the numbers of lines likely to bring two syllables into a comparable position in successive lines when the indicated number of syllables intervene. It is suggested that the effect of this distribution is, to some extent at least, to fill in the sharp break in the lower curve.

probably below, chance would be puzzling were it not for the fact that it occurs in that part of the curve which represents syllables occurring in approximately the same position in successive lines. It would appear that there is a tendency not to use the same vowel in comparable position in succeeding lines, and that this conflicts with a tendency to repeat a vowel after the intervention of three or four syllables.

A test of this hypothesis was made by comparing syllables on the basis, not of a given number of intervening syllables, but of position within the line. The first and last syllables in successive lines were optimal for this purpose, because the question of the definition of "comparable position" in the case of lines which did not have the same number of syllables was avoided.

In the 499 pairs of either initial or final syllables, we should expect 53 pairs of the same vowel, but the number observed in the initial position is only 43 and in the final, only 34. The greater sensitivity of the final position is perhaps related to the avoidance of perfect or imperfect rhymes. If this tendency of syllables in comparable position not to contain the same vowel is typical of the other syllables in the line, much of the sudden change in the curve for assonant span is accounted for.

It may be noted that a correction for the repetition of whole words brings the first two points of this curve to a position which is probably significantly below the expected mean, and that the peak of the curve at three intervening syllables is brought down well into the range of values to be expected from random sampling.

Although the result is by no means as clear-cut as in the case of alliteration, a tentative conclusion may be stated. There is apparently no process acting to increase the number of pairs of vowels which fall within a few syllables of each other; on the contrary there is apparently some suppression of similar words at those distances. Some formal strengthening is perhaps indicated after three or four intervening syllables. An observed tendency to avoid the same vowel in comparable position in successive lines interferes with the evidence for assonant strengthening. There seems to be no similar effect of comparable linear position upon the agreement of consonants.

Non-alliterative grouping. Alliteration does not, of course, exhaust the possibility of consonant-patterning. A more subtle arrangement may well exist without revealing itself in a consideration of single sounds. A preliminary check on this possibility was made by examining all successive pairs of consonants regardless of whether they were the same or not. A complete tabulation was made from which it could be determined how many times any given consonant was immediately followed by any other given consonant in the sample of 500 lines. Expected frequencies were calculated by multiplying the frequency of the first consonant by the p of the second. The standard error used in estimating the significance was computed as the square root of Npq, where N is taken as the frequency of the first consonant, and p and q are the usual probabilities of occurrence and non-occurrence, respectively, of the second. No difference between observed and expected frequencies was found as great as three times the standard error. A number of cases, however, yielded differences greater than twice the standard error, and it may be well to record them here for the sake of any future comparison.

All combinations of which at least five occurrences were expected are given in Table 5. Thus, there is some tendency for b to be followed by l

TABLE 5

ALL NON-ALLITERATIVE COMBINATIONS OF CONSONANTS OF WHICH AT LEAST FIVE
OCCURRENCES ARE EXPECTED AND IN WHICH THE DIFFERENCE BETWEEN THE
OBSERVED AND EXPECTED FREQUENCIES IS GREATER THAN TWICE
THE STANDARD ERROR

Consonant	Tends to be followed by:	Tends not to be followed by:
b	l	p, s
d	l	
f		th
g	h	
l	n	
m	g	l
p		s
s	f	
t	b	
th	d	b
w	s	

and not to be followed by p and s, and so on. It should be noted that a tendency for a consonant not to be followed by another consonant may be in part the result of the observed tendency of consonants to be followed by themselves. (In other words, we face the same difficulty in estimating p in the presence of grouping.) For example, if b is not followed by s as often as we should expect, it is partly because b is too often followed by b

and partly because many of the *s*'s are tied up with other *s*'s. A positive tendency toward association, however, is all the more significant.

Table 5 does not indicate any consistent sound-patterning over and above alliteration. There seems to be no tendency for one type of sound (dental, labial, and so on) to be followed by another or not to be so followed. Taking similarity of sound very loosely, we may note that *b* may tend to avoid *p* and *f* to avoid *th,* but, contrariwise, *s* apparently accumulates *f*'s.

Non-assonant grouping. A similar attempt was made to discover combinations of vowels, in addition to repetitions, which showed exceptional frequencies. The only sequence which exceeded the expected frequency by more than three times its standard error was that in which *ā* was followed by *ĕ*. In two other sequences the excess was greater than twice the standard error: *ā* tended to be followed by *ă* and *ă* by *ō*. Two sequences showed a deficiency which was greater than twice the standard error: *ĭ* tended not to be followed by *ā* and the group *ū, ōō* not to be followed by *ĭ*. The evidence is barely reliable, only a few sounds are involved, and no consistent trend (e.g., from low to high, or from back to front) is exhibited.

A "coefficient of alliteration." A numerical "coefficient of alliteration" would enable us to make a practical comparison of poems in the extent to which they indicate alliterative selection or arrangement in the behavior of the poet. A convenient and meaningful form would represent the number of sounds in some unit number of lines which produce an excess of lines containing two, three, four, or five instances of the same consonant. The value assumed by such a coefficient would depend upon the mean length of line and the range of lengths, as well as upon the arbitrary rules used in selecting syllables. Where these are comparable, a suitable coefficient may be set up by allowing one credit for every excess line containing two consonants, two credits for every excess line containing three, and so on, and by converting the total excess of the 10 commonest consonants into a (probably fractional) excess per line. The procedure is complicated by the presence of repetitions of whole words, but a practical compromise may be made by attributing to purely formal perseveration one-third of the repetitions of whole words. The precise magnitude of the excess, in any event, is obscured by factors already considered concerning the value of *p*.

In calculating the coefficient of alliteration for Swinburne, we find that the number of lines containing two instances of the same consonant, corrected by subtracting all repetitions of whole words, is 267. If we add to this one-third of the lines accounted for by the repetition of whole words, we get an observed frequency of 285, which gives us an excess of 36 lines over the expected 249, or a credit of 36. Similarly the corrected excess of 21 lines containing three instances of the same consonant may be increased by one line (approximately one-third of the two lines containing repetitions of whole words) to yield an excess of 22 lines or 44 credits. There is a similar excess of 11 lines containing four instances of the same consonant, or 33 credits. The total number of credits for Swinburne is therefore 113. Dividing this by the number of lines (500), we obtain 0.226 as Swinburne's coefficient of alliteration. A similar calculation for Shakespeare yields a value of only 0.007. If there were no alliteration whatsoever on the part of a poet, the mean coefficient would be zero, and it is clear that Shakespeare is very close to this. The upper limit of the coefficient would be obtained when all the consonants were grouped in solid blocks, but this is a case which need not be considered. It is probable that Swinburne's coefficient of 0.226 is very near the upper limit to be found in poetry which is not deliberately constructed (say, for humorous effect) upon a principle of alliteration or where alliteration is not the chief poetic device, as in Anglo-Saxon poetry.

To argue from the structure of a poem to the behavior of the poet is difficult. The pattern of a poem (insofar as it *is* patterned) is possibly due to something more than a process of formal strengthening. Contemporary standards or personal verbalizations concerning the function or structure of poetry will have their effects. When alliteration is in fashion as an ornament, the poet may deliberately seek it out, presumably through a kind of controlled association practiced at various points in the act of composition, or through the use of such an artificial device as a word book. On the other hand, where current taste is opposed to alliteration, instances which naturally arise from chance (as well as from formal strengthening) may be rejected. No statistical analysis of a poem will supply direct information concerning these activities, but it may nevertheless be regarded as a prerequisite to saying very much about them. We cannot trust the poet himself regarding his practices. He may be unaware of his own behavior in encouraging or eliminating alliterative words. Many poems written "automatically" exhibit various kinds of formal patterning. In any event the poet's conception of a random order of sounds is probably inaccurate, and we may assume him incapable of estimating the extent of either process even if he is aware of it. Thus, although we may be supplied with a statement of the poet's philosophy of composition or an autobiographical account of his behavior as a poet, we are still not provided with an accurate statement of the structure of his poems. The selection of instances in illustration of the principles which he expresses is wholly unreliable.

We have no reason to assume that the amount or range of formal strengthening here exhibited is characteristic of the normal speech of either Shakespeare or Swinburne. The value of the research is not in supplying a rigorous measurement of the general process of formal strengthening but rather in estimating the length to which we may go in citing these poetic devices as examples of certain processes. The fact that rhyme, rhythm, alliteration, and assonance (the four principal elements of sound-patterning in poetry) can be reduced to the single principle of formal strengthening is surely not an accident, nor is it an insignificant fact, but some such analysis as the present is required in order to relate these characteristics of poetry to normal verbal behavior.

It is to be hoped that this statement will allay the fears of those who react to such research as an intrusion into the field of criticism.[2] It is difficult to see how an analysis of this sort can have any bearing upon questions of taste, "sensitivity of ear," or, in short, upon any evaluative estimate of poem or poet. The question at issue is simply the objective structure of a literary work and the validity of certain inferences concerning literary behavior.

[2] Stoll, E. E. Poetic alliteration. *Modern Language Notes*, 1940, *55*, 388–390.

The Processes Involved in the
Repeated Guessing of Alternatives

From September, 1937, to January, 1938, the Zenith Foundation (with the support of the Zenith Radio Corporation) conducted an experiment in "telepathy" over a national network. A group of senders in the studio concentrated on one of a pair of characters or subjects selected at random. From five to seven characters were sent during each broadcast. Each member of the radio audience was asked to write down the impressions he received and mail them to the studio. The first broadcast was reported to have revealed startling evidence for telepathy: the radio audience scored far above chance. Several later broadcasts produced a similar result. But several showed equally good evidence for negative telepathy: the radio audience was far below chance. The results were analyzed by Louis D. Goodfellow (Journal of Experimental Psychology, *1938, 23, 601–632*), *who demonstrated that "neither coincidence or telepathy, but the natural response of an audience to secondary cues, caused the 'highly successful' results of the Zenith Radio experiment in telepathy." Goodfellow pointed to many conditions of the experiment which could conceivably have influenced the audience in choosing between, say, a cross or a star. He also pointed out that when asked to predict a series of random events, such as tosses of coin, people show certain preconceived notions of a chance sequence. When the actual selecting mechanism yielded a sequence similar to a preferred pattern, the responses of the audience appeared to show telepathy. When the selecting mechanisms chose an unlikely sequence, negative telepathy seemed to be shown. The present paper is an effort to account for the observed patterns of guessing in terms of tendencies to alternate calls. It is reprinted with the permission of the editors of the* Journal of Experimental Psychology, *in which it first appeared (1942, 30, 495–503).*

In reporting the data from the Zenith experiments on telepathy, Goodfellow [1] has pointed out that the sixteen patterns which result when subjects are asked to make five guesses between two alternatives occur with frequencies which are related to their symmetry. Goodfellow defines symmetry in a special way and makes no claim for it as a psychological process. Nevertheless, the term has recently appeared in a paper by Yacorzynski [2] as if it referred to a property of perceptual configuration, and patterns have been obtained from psychotics in order to follow the disintegration of "perceptual processes." To speak of a series of five guesses as a single organized act is perhaps in line with one trend in modern psychology, but a possible alternative view, in which a unit of behavior is taken at a lower level of analysis, needs to be stated. It is also important to compare the two levels with respect to descriptive power.

Guessing is a special kind of (usually verbal) behavior in which two or more responses are about equally likely to be emitted. In guessing "heads or tails," for example, the conditions of the experiment strengthen these two verbal responses, but no circumstance strengthens one to the exclusion of the other. The responses may have slightly different resting strengths, so that one will be "preferred" in the long run, or some such circumstance as a biased instruction may momentarily alter the balance; but there is no clear determiner of either response such as exists, say, in the case of reading a coin already tossed. Guessing repays study because it throws into relief certain minor variables in the determination of verbal behavior which are normally obscured by variables of greater moment.

The first guess in a series of five, as in the Zenith experiments, is apparently controlled by an abiding preference, by biased preliminary conditions, or by trivial circumstances which cancel out in the long run and are spoken of as "chance." The second guess raises a different problem, for it is under the additional control of the first. Likewise, the third guess is under the control of the second and perhaps the first, and so on. Goodfellow notes the fact that subsequent guesses depend upon the preceding but dismisses the relation apparently as too complex for analysis. However, if we are not to fall back upon the whole series as a configurational unit, we must account for each guess in turn, and this demands a statement regarding the effect of one guess upon another. The additional variables noted in the preceding paragraph are presumably operative upon

[1] In the reference given above.

[2] Yacorzynski, G. K. Perceptual principles involved in the disintegration of a configuration formed in predicting the occurrence of patterns selected by chance. *J. Exp. Psychol.*, 1941, *29*, 401–406.

all five guesses, but we may eliminate them by following Goodfellow's practice of expressing all sequences in terms of the first call. Thus, both "heads-tails-heads" and "tails-heads-tails" are recorded as "*121.*" Our problem is to describe the percentages of the final patterns expressed in this way in terms of the effects of each guess upon subsequent guesses.

In Table 1 the whole guessing process in the Zenith experiment has been reconstructed. The bold-faced numbers not in parentheses in the right-hand column are from Goodfellow's tables and represent in each case the frequency of the call-pattern shown just below in italics. Thus, 4.34 percent of the persons replying to the broadcasts reported the sequence *12121* and 5.70 percent the sequence *12122.* The sum of these two figures (10.04) gives the percentage who guessed *1212* on the first four calls, and this figure (also in bold-face and without parentheses) is entered in the second column from the right. Its corresponding four-place pattern is indicated just below. All four-place percentages have been entered in this manner. From them we are able to calculate percentages for the three-place calls and in turn for the two-place. Thus, 21.94 percent guessed *121* on the first three calls and 52.93 percent guessed *12* on the first two. In Table 1 each of these figures has also been converted into a percentage of the figure at the immediately preceding stage. The results are given to one decimal place in parentheses (and also in bold-face). Thus, the 21.94 percent who called *121* represent 41.5 percent of those who called *12,* and this figure is shown in parentheses just before 21.94 in the table. The corresponding percentage for those who called *122* is not needed in what follows.

A further step is to describe each call in terms of whether it involves alternation from the preceding. The sequence *12* shows alternation and is accordingly marked A in Table 1; the sequence *11* does not and is marked O. The designation AOAA means that the sequence *12212* shows alternation followed by a failure to alternate followed by two alternations.

We are now able to collect together the various percentages of alternation according to the history of alternation. In the column headed "Zen." in Table 2 the percentages have been grouped according to the conditions which precede the last A. They reveal a significant uniformity. There is an original tendency which produces alternation 52.9 percent of the time on the second guess. (This tendency is actually very slight, since 50 percent would indicate none at all.) When a call follows an alternation already made, the percentage of alternation drops to the low forties (Lines 2, 3, and 4, Table 2), but it rises to the seventies when the preceding call has

TABLE 1

RECONSTRUCTION OF THE GUESSING PROCESS IN THE ZENITH EXPERIMENTS

The italics indicate the patterns of guesses; the preceding A's and O's describe each in terms of the alternations involved. The Zenith-Goodfellow data are in bold-face; the numbers in parentheses indicate the percentage of alternation from the preceding stage. The numbers not in bold-face are constructed from the four selected percentages in Table 2, Lines 16-19.

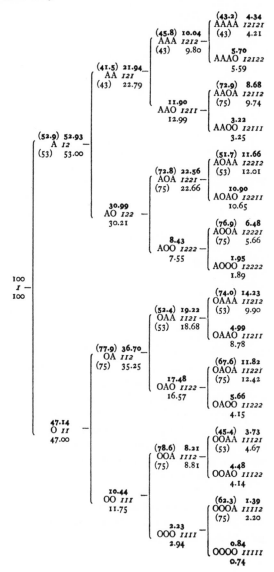

TABLE 2

PERCENTAGES OF ALTERNATION AT VARIOUS STAGES IN THE GUESSING PROCESS

		Zen.	Con.	M.-D.	Schiz.	M.-D. and Schiz.
1	First A	52.9	49.8	61.3	52.6	57.0
2	A A	41.5	37.4	59.2	66.7	62.6
3	A A A	45.8	60.2	58.7	64.4	61.7
4	A A A A	43.2	55.4	82.2	83.2	82.7
5	O A	77.9	76.4	48.5	64.6	53.5
6	O O A	78.6	89.9	56.0	56.5	56.2
7	A O A	72.8	70.2	90.4	64.6	80.0
8	O O O A	62.3	—	43.2	28.7	36.4
9	A O O A	76.9	87.1	50.0	80.7	71.7
10	O A O A	67.6	60.0	100.0	83.8	92.0
11	A A O A	72.9	83.8	66.0	60.0	64.5
12	O A A	52.4	67.2	60.1	73.0	67.6
13	A O A A	51.7	40.2	61.1	66.4	63.0
14	O O A A	45.4	47.2	44.6	66.4	55.8
15	O A A A	74.0	58.6	66.4	44.0	52.0
	Selected Constants					
16	First A	53	50	61	53	(60)
17	A–A	43	45?	59?	65?	(60)
18	O–A	75	76?	52?	64?	(60)
19	O A–A	53	60?	61?	70?	(60)

not shown alternation (Lines 5–11, Table 2). (The two exceptions in the sixties are for fifth-place calls.)

We can give a fairly good account of the table by rounding out the three constants in Lines 16, 17, and 18, which state the percentage alternations which obtain according to whether there is an immediately preceding call and whether it involves alternation or not. It would be surprising if it were not necessary to go farther back than the immediately preceding call, but the only cases which call for special treatment are those in which a preceding A is itself preceded by an O (Lines 12–14). The presence of the O apparently prevents the reduction to 43 percent which A otherwise implies. At least this is true for OAA and AOAA, and in order to avoid multiplying constants we may let the same value of 54 percent apply to this group. OAAA is an outstanding exception, to be discussed later.

The adequacy of the selected percentages at the bottom of Table 2 may be estimated by reconstructing Table 1 exclusively through their use. By beginning with 100 percent and taking the percentages dictated by the conditions of alternation, we obtain sixteen final percentages. These, together with various percentages *en route,* are shown in Table 1 directly below the corresponding Zenith figures, with which they should be compared. With two exceptions the correspondence is satisfactory.

The failure to describe one pair of percentages is a curious one. Calls beginning with *1121* are satisfactorily accounted for at OAA, but the subjects who have reached this point tend to alternate about 74 percent of the time instead of 43 or 53 percent as expected. The preceding OAA has had the same effect as O (although the similarity in magnitude may be a coincidence). There seems to be no special characteristic of the sequence *11212* to explain this anomaly. It cannot be interpreted as an avoidance of the conspicuous symmetry of *11211* (not to be confused with Goodfellow's symmetry, which shows a difference of only one point between *11212* and *11211*), since there is only negligible evidence of such avoidance elsewhere.[3] Similarly, no appeal can be made to the fact that *11212* works toward evening the score between *1*'s and *2*'s, since the table shows no tendency to exceed the calculated figures in the direction of equalizing calls. If we wish to use statements concerning alternation to account for the major part of the table, we cannot appeal to these additional processes to explain an atypical case since they are incompatible. (This does not exclude the possibility of accounting for the whole table with some other set of statements, possibly involving symmetry or the balancing of *1* and *2.*) If we accept the Zenith-Goodfellow figures as a valid indication of general tendencies (as the size of the sample seems to warrant), our only course is to set up a separate statement for the case of OAAA.

The effect of an alternation must be distinguished from that of a single guess. It is not altogether the preceding response which determines the response to be made but in addition whether this response has involved alternation. This is a distinction of some importance. Studies of formal patterning in speech have frequently indicated a substantial tendency to *repeat* a response already made (see, for example, page 385), and various lines of evidence suggest that this is a primary characteristic of verbal behavior. Nevertheless, a tendency is set up in the growing child, through readily

---

[3] If it were operative, *122* ought to be favored over *121*, *12122* over *12121*, and *12222* over *12221*, but although the percentages for these non-symmetrical sequences exceed the calculated percentages, the average excess is only 0.3 per cent above the slight average excess of the symmetrical sequence. This will not go very far toward accounting for an excess of 4.33 per cent at OAAA.

observable processes of conditioning, which opposes repetition.[4] In a universe limited to two responses, not-repeating is, of course, alternating. In the present case the first guess may be supposed to strengthen the *same* response for a second emission. But the effect of reinforcement opposing repetition is to counteract this tendency so that alternations occur 53 percent of the time. When this figure is compared, not with a chance 50 percent, but with a probable tendency to repeat the same form, greater importance may be attached to the process which produces alternation. The present data demonstrate the additional fact that alternation is more likely to occur after failure to alternate and less likely after previous alternation. This may plausibly be attributed to the conditions of reinforcement which establish the tendency to alternate, since the verbal community which provides the reinforcement opposing repetition will presumably react more vigorously to repeated failure to alternate and less vigorously to failure which follows due alternation.

The statements extracted from Table 2 require little or no interpretation, since they have a very direct reference to behavior and describe processes which are quite plausibly explained. For this reason the correspondence between the Zenith and the calculated percentages is more significant than a correspondence with symmetries. It is also probably a more complete correspondence. Although symmetry may be said to give the correct rank order of the percentages, there are as many as five cases with the same number of symmetries, and the relative order of their corresponding frequencies is not predicted. Nor does symmetry give any clue as to magnitude.

The additional data supplied by Yacorzynski cannot be as adequately accounted for with a few numerical statements. The percentages of alterr.ation exhibited by his control group, under conditions which were intended to approximate those of the Zenith experiments, are given in Table 2 under "Con." The original percentage alternation is lower (49.8 percent) and, in fact, shows no tendency to alternate whatsoever. The drop following alternation (to 37.4 percent) is comparable with that in the Zenith case, and the rise following failure to alternate is of the same or even slightly greater magnitude. But in spite of this rough agreement, the control figures are much less consistent, and it is impossible to select rounded values which give a good account of the final percentages. The

---

[4] Reinforcements applied to speech to oppose prior tendencies are fairly common and, indeed, give rise to some of the most important properties of verbal behavior. There is a special problem involved in separating opposed effects for measurement, but it is not insoluble.

difficulty seems to be in the smallness of sample and is one which especially besets the fifth-place calls where the percentages are of very small groups. The anomalous result at OAAA in the Zenith-Goodfellow data also appears, but less strikingly, in Yacorzynski's control group.

Yacorzynski has shown that the sequences given by psychotics differ significantly from his own controls and from the Zenith-Goodfellow figures. Does the interpretation just advanced for the normal case throw any light on the difference between normal and psychotic behavior? The percentage alternations under "Schiz." and "M.-D." in Table 2 provide whatever answer is available from these small samples.

The schizophrenics begin with a normal tendency to alternate but this is *not* decreased when one or more alternations have been made. On the contrary the percentages rise, reaching 83.2 in the case of AAAA (if the figure is reliable). Such an increase would result in part from a mixed population, in which there were some members who invariably alternated. In any event, the normal tendency not to alternate following alternation is lacking. The other conspicuous feature of the normal case—the increase in percentage-alternation after failure to alternate—is also lacking. It is true that the value for OA is 64.6, an increase over 52.6, but it is less than the value for AA, and the value for OOA is considerably lower. In general, there may be some increase in alternation as the guessing proceeds, but this holds regardless of the nature of preceding calls. Essentially the same may be said of the manic-depressive group, except that the original tendency to alternate is high (61.3). The reduction produced by earlier alternations (to 59.2 and 58.7) is probably not significant and, as in the case of the schizophrenics, a very high value (though of doubtful significance) is reached for AAAA. Any increase in tendency to alternate following failure to alternate (see the group ending OA) is also clearly lacking; indeed, a decrease might be claimed. So far as these small samples warrant generalization, we may summarize the percentages of Table 2 by saying that the psychotics show no effect of past alternation upon alternation in the call to be made.

This is equivalent to saying that the percentages can be described with a *single* statement, giving a permanent tendency to alternate, rather than with the three or four demanded in the case of the normal subject. From the combined percentages for the present groups (last column in Table 2) this tendency will be seen to be in the neighborhood of 60 percent, although there are large deviations. The adequacy of a single statement may be tested by constructing final percentages on the basis of a constant 60 percent alternation. The resulting sixteen percentages, together with the observed, are given in Table 3. About half the cases show a close approximation. The others differ chiefly on the fifth call, where the sample is smallest. For example, the largest differences appear in the first two pairs of percentages, yet their sums show a very good correspondence (22.0 and 21.6). All calls beginning with *1212* are adequately described, although

TABLE 3

PERCENTAGES FOR THE SIXTEEN PATTERNS OBTAINED FROM PSYCHOTICS AND PERCENTAGES CALCULATED ON THE BASIS OF A CONSTANT TENDENCY TO ALTERNATE

	12121	12122	12112	12111	12212	12211	12221	12222	11212	11211	11221	11222	11121	11122	11112	11111
M.-D. and Schiz.	18.2	3.8	8.7	5.0	10.7	6.3	3.1	1.2	8.2	7.5	6.9	0.6	6.3	5.0	3.2	5.6
Calculated	13.0	8.6	8.6	5.8	8.6	5.8	5.8	3.8	8.6	5.8	5.8	3.8	5.8	3.8	3.8	2.4

the final call is not. The discrepancy is of such a sort as to be produced by a small group who invariably alternate, although the correspondence at *1212* places this in question. The only other serious discrepancy is for *11111*, which may represent a small perseverative group who do not alternate at all.

One might conceivably describe this sort of psychotic behavior as showing a disintegration of perceptual processes, but by analyzing the pattern of a series of guesses (with its dubious status as an aspect of behavior) into the discrete events which make it up, a simpler and more useful statement may be reached. In making a series of five calls between two alternatives the psychotic differs from the normal in being uninfluenced by his own past behavior. The statement is plausible enough in view of what is known about psychotic behavior in general.

A Note on Method

In a matter of this sort it is very easy to drop into the jargon of postulational method. We might say that we *assume* certain tendencies to alternate and then validate our assumptions by predicting the final percentages correctly. But these "assumptions" are actually nothing but descriptive statements. We examine percentages of alternation at various stages and note that they are related to certain anterior conditions. Thus, we assert that a subject tends to alternate 75 percent of the time if he has just failed to alternate, but at no time does the assertion appear as an assumption. It is, rather, the approximate statement of a fact. Our net result is, not that certain assumptions have been tested and shown to be adequate, but that we have found it possible to talk about sixteen patterns of behavior with a few comprehensive statements.

It is possible that any example of postulational method in the empirical sciences may be interpreted in the same way and that "predicting" a fact from a set of assumptions is never intended to mean more than describing it. But if this is the case, the pretense of deduction should be abandoned, at least by those who are interested in a descriptive science of thought and who wish, therefore, to see the number of thought processes reduced to a minimum.

Summary

Participants in the Zenith experiments on telepathy were asked to make a series of five guesses between two alternatives. The percentages of the sixteen resulting patterns have been reported by Goodfellow and are here interpreted in terms of a tendency to alternate calls. Quantitative estimates of such a tendency are made for each of several conditions of alternation, and these are tested by constructing percentages for sixteen patterns to be compared with the Goodfellow percentages. Yacorzynski's data from psychotics differ from the normal merely in showing no effect of past alternations.

These interpretations are offered as more satisfactory than references to "symmetry" or, in the case of the psychotics, to the disintegration of perceptual principles.

PART VIII

Theoretical Considerations

Why Are the Behavioral Sciences Not More Effective?

It is often said that science has become the religion of the twentieth century—with its Book, its prophets and priests, and its communicants, not to mention its apostates. Like most religions, it also has its apocalyptic vision: our way of life, and possibly mankind itself, may not long survive if we continue on our present course. An expanding population will exhaust our resources and pollute the environment and sooner or later (sooner if we suffer a nuclear holocaust) put an end to the kind of world in which the species can live. The vision is not divine revelation but an inference from facts, and although the speed with which we are moving toward destruction may be debated, few scientists question the direction. Salvation may come spontaneously from some kind of inbuilt corrective process, but it is more likely that we shall save ourselves only if we solve our problems in a quite deliberate fashion. To do so we need a much clearer understanding of why people behave as they do. We need, in short, a science and technology of behavior which will permit us to deal with the behavioral aspects of our problems as effectively as other technologies deal with their physical and biological aspects.

Nothing of the sort is, of course, at hand. What we have are the so-called social or behavioral sciences—among them psychology, sociology, anthropology, political science, and economics. They are clearly not adequate to the uses we should like to make of them. Why not? Philip Handler, president of the National Academy of Sciences, has said that they are "too young," but they are actually much older than many branches of physics, chemistry, and biology which have proved very helpful. A common explanation is that there is something about human behavior

From *The Listener,* September 30, 1971.

467

which puts it beyond the reach of science. That would be disastrous if true, but the argument points in a useful direction. There *is* something about human behavior which has made a scientific analysis difficult and delayed the development of a technology.

With any other species we should explain behavior by pointing to a genetic endowment—to the anatomy and physiology of the species—and to events in the history of its members. But there is something special about the human case: we are members of the species we are studying. That fact should not be troublesome. On the contrary, it should mean that we are in a particularly favorable position in accumulating facts about behavior and about the relation of behavior to genetic and environmental histories. Moreover, to the extent that we can observe our own bodies, it should mean that we have a special kind of information—inside information, as it were—about the effects of those histories on an organism. A long time ago, however, that information was woven into a very different kind of explanation: the kind we give when we attribute what a person does to his feelings, thoughts, states of mind, purposes, expectancies, and so on. I shall not go into the standard objections to that kind of thing, but I hope to show that the behavioristic position has taken on a new significance in its bearing on current problems. I shall argue, in short, that the social sciences are not more effective precisely because they are not fully behavioral, and for that reason not really scientific, and for *that* reason not commensurate with the problems they are asked to solve.

Consider the fact that increasingly large numbers of young people are behaving in ways which deeply disturb their elders. They stay aloof from their families or leave home altogether. They neglect the social amenities: they are poorly dressed, dirty, and rude. They take time off from school or the university, or drop out completely. They work, if at all, irregularly and indifferently, and many are content to beg for the things they need. They steal and condone stealing, call the police "pigs" and attack them when they enforce the law, desecrate flags, burn draft-cards, refuse to serve in the armed services, and sometimes defect to other governments. Such behavior is shocking and incomprehensible to almost everyone and a matter of concern even for young people themselves when they have sampled the way of life to which it leads.

And what have the behavioral sciences to say about it? In general, this: there is something wrong with people who behave that way. The young person is said to be suffering from a disturbed personality. He is alienated and rootless. He lacks purpose. He is suffering from "misperception" of the world around him. He has no sense of achievement. He is frustrated and discouraged. He has no sense of identity. He can find nothing that interests him (technically speaking, he is suffering from anhedonia). He lacks rules to live by (technically speaking, he is suffering from anomie). His values are wrong.

According to such an explanation, our task is to correct disturbed personalities, change troubled states of mind, make people feel wanted, give them purpose or a sense of pride in their work, allay their frustration, and teach them the value of order, security, and affluence. But we have no direct access to states of mind, feelings, purposes, attitudes, opinions, or values. What we do is try to change the behavior from which we infer things of that sort, and we change it only by changing the environment, verbal and nonverbal, in which young people live. By responding in certain ways to what a person does, we may change the behavior from which we infer that he does not feel wanted, and it is quite possible that he may then feel wanted. By teaching a person to produce things of which he can be proud, we may make him productive and indirectly create "a sense of craftsmanship." By arranging better incentive conditions, we may induce him to behave more industriously, and what he feels will probably also change. By making sure that he will be generously reinforced for working for a cause, we may create the kind of behavior we call loyal, and, incidentally, create a condition which may be felt as a "sense of loyalty." By reinforcing nonverbal and verbal behavior in particular ways, we change what a person says or does, but what he says or does is not due to his opinions or attitudes but to the contingencies of reinforcement we have arranged.

The traditional view misrepresents our task. It suggests that by changing an environment we first change feelings or states of mind, and that these, in turn, determine what a person does. The feeling or state of mind seems to be a necessary link in a causal chain, but the fact is that we change behavior by changing the environment, and, in doing so, change what is felt. Feelings and states of mind are not causes, they are by-products.

By turning directly to the environmental history, rather than to its perceived or felt effects, we may take advantage of certain recent advances in the experimental analysis of behavior. In hundreds of laboratories throughout the world, complex environments are arranged and their effects studied. The evidence grows more and more convincing that a person behaves as he does because of (1) what has happened in the distant past as his species evolved, and (2) what has happened to him in his lifetime as an individual. Practical solutions of some important problems then follow.

One fact has become particularly clear: people do things because of the consequences. It has long been recognized that some effects of a person's behavior are satisfying or rewarding, but a special significance is emphasized when we call these effects "reinforcing": they strengthen the behavior they are contingent upon, in the sense of making it more likely to occur again. (Other consequences are said to be punishing, and their effects are rather more complex.) The behaviorist is often said to treat behavior simply as response to stimuli, but that view has long been out of date. Three things must be taken into account: the situation in which behavior occurs, the behavior itself, and its consequences. These three things are interrelated in very intricate ways in what are called the "contingencies of reinforcement." Some extremely complex contingencies have been analyzed, and the results help in interpreting some of the contingencies which prevail in daily life.

How reinforcing is a young person's home simply as a physical place? How does it look or sound or smell? How often do other members of his family reinforce him with attention, approval, or affection—and for what behavior? How often do they disapprove of him and punish him? What competing contingencies await him elsewhere? Do the approval and disapproval of the people he meets from day to day shape and maintain the kind of behavior which, as we say, observes the social amenities, or do they make him rude and selfish? Contingencies of this sort, rather than any feeling of commitment or alienation, create the problem we are examining. Alienation is not a state of mind; it is a state of behavior attributable to defective contingencies of reinforcement. What is felt is a by-product.

How reinforcing is a school simply as a physical place? How does it look, sound, or smell? What happens when a student behaves well toward his teachers and other students, and what happens when he behaves badly? Does he study mainly to avoid the consequences of not studying or are there positive effects—such as conspicuous progress toward the mastery of a subject or skill? How long will it be before the behavior acquired in school has reinforcing consequences elsewhere which will contribute to its strength? What contingencies in the outside world compete with those in school? The answers bear directly on our problem. If a young person often stays away from school or drops out, it is not because he is shiftless, or lacks curiosity, or is dull; it is because the contingencies of reinforcement do not keep him at school.

How reinforcing is the place in which a young person works? How do his supervisors and fellow workers treat him? Is what he does dangerous or exhausting? Does it lack variety? Is there any reinforcing connection with a final product? Is what he is paid sensitively contingent upon how hard or how carefully he works? How reinforcing to him is money? How serious is the loss when he takes a day off or changes jobs or quits work altogether? The answers are crucial. If a young person does not work productively, it is not because he does not like his job or is lazy; it is because the contingencies are defective. His feeling about his job, and the traits of character he displays in it, are by-products of the same contingencies.

And so with governmental sanctions. People obey the law primarily to avoid punishment, and they may avoid it or escape in other ways, such as by defecting. The extent to which a person *uses* the law also depends upon the consequences. Whether he turns to the government or takes the law into his own hands depends, in part, upon the results; are they quick and are they reinforcing? The consequences of *participating* in government are also important. What is the effect of casting a vote? Is a person reinforced by what a government does with his help when he joins the armed services or accepts a draft call? Behavior traditionally attributed to loyalty or disloyalty, affection or disaffection, commitment or anomie, is the product of specifiable contingencies. How a person feels about his government is a by-product.

So much for a rough interpretation. Let us turn to a practical solution. Disaffection and revolt could scarcely be better illustrated than by the behavior of young offenders living in a school for juvenile delinquents. Few have had families they have lived with closely, almost all have dropped out of school with little or no education, few have ever held a job for any length of time, and all have broken the law so often or so violently that it has been necessary to lock them up. It is hard to imagine a group of young people more completely out of control of the culture of their country. But they are not out of control of their own culture, and they may be brought under the control of a better one.

A group of about forty juvenile offenders—teenage armed robbers, rapists, and murderers—who were at the time "students" in the National Training School in Washington, D.C., since relocated at the Robert F. Kennedy Center in Morgantown, West Virginia, participated in an experiment directed by Harold Cohen of the Institute for Behavioral Research in Silver Spring, Maryland. A new social environment was constructed in which no boy was required to do anything. He could sleep on a pad in a dormitory, eat nutritious if not very palatable food, and sit on a bench all day. But he could greatly improve his lot by earning points exchangeable for more delicious food at mealtimes, admission to games rooms, the rental of a private room or television set, or even a short vacation away from the school. He could earn points by doing simple chores, but much more easily by learning things. Correct responses to programmed instructional materials and correct answers in examinations after studying other kinds of material meant points.

The results were dramatic. Boys who had been convinced by the school system that they were unteachable discovered that they were not. They learned reading and writing and arithmetic, and acquired other verbal and manual skills. They did so without compulsion, and the hostile behavior characteristic of such institutions quickly disappeared. They discovered that it was possible to earn rather than steal the things they wanted, and they began to participate in the organization and management of the school. As a result, they were prepared to lead more socially acceptable lives after they left. In the normal course of events, 85 percent of them would have been back in the school by the end of one year because of further violations, but the figure was only 25 percent. At the end of another year it had risen to 45, but the normal figure would have been practically 100 percent.

It would be pleasant to report that the change was permanent, but after three or four years there was little evidence of any further effect. The boys had been exposed to this exceptional environment for only a few months or at most a year, which was apparently not enough to offset deficiencies in the environments to which they returned. But while they were in school, and for some time thereafter, the designed culture had its predicted effects. In a better world, they lived better lives. The world gave them better reasons for behaving well, for working to produce some of the goods they needed, and for acquiring behavior which made them successful in other ways.

A training school is a culture in miniature. It can be successfully designed. And so can the culture in the world at large. Hundreds of experiments are now in progress exploring the range of what has come to be called "behavior modification." New practices in child care, in the management of institutionalized retardates and psychotics, in individual psychotherapy, in classroom management, in the design of incentive systems in industry and elsewhere are being tested. We are, I think, on our way to the technology we need to solve many of our problems.

But progress is dishearteningly slow. Social scientists have not yet fully understood the significance of the behavioristic position. Most of them still look for solutions to their problems inside the people they study. In psychotherapy, the medical analogy persists: the problem is mental illness, and it is the patient who must be cured. The therapist tries to reach his patient by making an inter*personal* contact, not by changing an environment. Educators place their bets on the natural curiosity of the student, his love of learning, his creative spirit. The teacher is at best a midwife who helps the student give birth to knowledge and wisdom. Schools and universities still *select* good students; they have not yet begun to create them. And industry still selects workers who are industrious, skilled, and careful; it has not given serious attention to the design of contingencies under which everyone works hard and carefully and enjoys his work. Governments still hold the *individual* responsible and are said to be best if they govern least, because a person is then free to behave well because of inner virtues. All this continues to divert attention from the task of building a social environment in which people behave well with respect to each other, acquire effective repertoires, produce the goods they need, and enjoy life. It obscures the fact that the problem is to design better cultures—not better people.

The behavioral sciences have been slow to take this step for many reasons, among them a characteristic response to the possibility of a technology of behavior comparable in power with the technologies of physics and biology. Perhaps human behavior can be controlled via the environment, but who will exert the control? Those who ask that question do not expect to be given a proper name. It is not the person they are worried about but his intentions, his purposes, his good will or benevolence. But this is only another example of what is wrong. They are still looking for assurance to the states of mind or the feelings of potential controllers. What they should be asking is: "What kinds of cultural contingencies induce people to engage in the control of other people? Under what contingencies do people act like tyrants? Under what contingencies do they act like 'men and women of good will'?" We must hope that a culture will emerge in which those who have power will use it for the general good. Such a culture would probably be most likely to survive, and that is an important point. Geneticists are beginning to speak of changing the course of human evolution, but we have long been able to change the evolution of cultures. As we begin to understand what a culture is, we may begin to move toward better designs.

A technology of behavior may give aid and comfort to cultures which breed despots, but it will not give them an advantage unless the cultures which breed men of good will refuse to accept the aid and comfort which are also offered them. A science of behavior has emerged in the kind of culture we like to call free, but it is quite possible that it will not be put to use there. A historical parallel may be significant. In the fifth century B.C., China was as advanced in physical technology as any other part of the world, and it retained its position until about 1400 A.D. Among its great contributions were the compass, gunpowder, and movable type. But for the next three hundred years, very little use was made of them. Military power remained ceremonial, astrological, and geomantic, long voyages were forbidden, and an ideographic system of notation gained little from movable type. A neo-Confucianist system of thought emphasized passive knowing. The West seized upon these Chinese inventions, however, and made fantastic progress. The compass enabled men to explore the globe, and gunpowder to conquer it. Movable type led to a flood of books which brought about a revival of learning. Meanwhile, China remained a medieval society. The difference was not in the availability of technological means but in the cultural contingencies governing their use. Something of the same sort could happen again. It is possible that our current aggrandizement of the individual will obscure the possibility of building a better way of life. The evolution of our democratic culture will then have taken a disastrous turn.

The Concept of the Reflex in
the Description of Behavior

This paper, written in the summer of 1930, still seems to me important for three reasons. In the first place, it was an early example of the operational analysis of terms describing behavior. *I believe the clue to the definition of reflex came from Bertrand Russell. Somewhere, possibly in a series of articles in the* Dial *in the late 20's, Russell pointed out that the concept of the reflex in physiology had the same status as the concept of force in physics. Add that to Bridgman's treatment of force in* The Logic of Modern Physics *and you have the present point. I supported the argument with a Machian analysis of the history of the reflex to explain the traditional definition as* unconscious, involuntary, *and* unlearned behavior. *The operational analysis of Sherrington's synapse and the more generalized statement in Chapter 12 of* The Behavior of Organisms, *in which I suggested that C.N.S. might be taken to stand for the Conceptual Nervous System, have been interpreted as showing an anti-physiological or anti-neurological bias. I was, however, merely protesting the use of inferences from behavior to explain behavior, while arguing for the solid status of behavioral facts apart from imagined physiological counterparts. An important point is that operational definitions are suggested not only for* reflex, *but for* drive, emotion, *and other terms appropriate to the intact organism.*

Secondly, the article insists upon the appropriateness of the concept of the reflex in describing behavior. *One consequence is a statement of behavioral facts in a form which most readily makes contact with physiological concepts and methods. In this sense the paper is, I believe, a positive contribution to physiology.* True, the term reflex *proved too rigid. It implied a complete specification of properties of behavior which was not in fact supported by the data either from whole or surgically subdivided organisms (a point which was made subsequently in the paper on page 504), and it insisted upon a demonstrable and presumably controllable stimulus as the principal independent variable (a point eventually rejected in the paper on page 535 and in* The Behavior of Organisms). *But a similar sharp reference to behavior in physical terms was maintained by the concept of the "operant" introduced to*

475

remedy these defects, and a further elaboration of this concept in interpreting, for example, verbal behavior presents the behavioral facts to be accounted for by the physiologist in the simplest possible way. Psychological facts remain on the plane of the physical and biological.

Thirdly, the paper offers a program and a general formulation of a scientific analysis of behavior. *As to program, the last paragraph on page 501 describes with considerable accuracy a subsequent investigation of "conditioning," "emotion," and "drive," some results of which are sketched in the paper on page 132. As to formulation, the observable facts underlying the concept of the reflex permit us to write the equation:*

$$R = f(S)$$

where R = *response and* S = *stimulus. Changes in this function provide another sort of datum. For example, if we repeatedly elicit a response, the reflex undergoes "fatigue." We may rewrite the equation:*

$$R = f(S, A).$$

In my paper the letter A *is noncommittally referred to as a "third variable," a point which is relevant to current controversies about intervening variables. The variable* A *is merely another variable to be taken into account; it does* not *intervene even though the traditional practice is to assign the change in the function which it accounts for to some inner state or condition. Some experimental studies on rate of eating (offered, together with the present paper, as my doctoral thesis) exemplified this distinction. The concept of "hunger" as an inner state may be useful for certain purposes, but in a strictly operational definition we must confine ourselves to changes in "reflex strength" as a function of deprivation, satiation, and similar operations.*

Edward C. Tolman missed this point when, five years later, he attempted to set up his own version of an "operational behaviorism."[1] *Tolman's equation:*

$$B = f(SPHTA)$$

is patterned after the equations above (with B for "behavior" in place of R for "response," and S for "environmental stimulus condition" rather than "stimulus"). But what about P, H, T, and A? Tolman is sufficiently operational in saying that groups of these variables are all he finds in the way of mental processes (thus disposing of the mentalistic nature of such processes),

---

[1] Tolman, E. C. Operational behaviorism and current trends in psychology. In *Proc. 25th Anniv. Celebr. Inaug. Grad. Stud.* Los Angeles: Univ. South. Calif. Press, 1936. Reprinted in Marx, Melvin H. *Psychological theory:* Contemporary Readings. New York: Macmillan, 1951.

but he is still looking for substitutes and hence (and for no other reason) calls the additional variables "intervening."

The present paper was published in the Journal of General Psychology, *(1931, 5, 427-458) and is reprinted here by permission of the editor.*

Introductory Note

The extension of the concept of the reflex to the description of the behavior of intact organisms is a common practice in modern theorizing. Nevertheless, we owe most of our knowledge of the reflex to investigators who have dealt only with "preparations," and who have never held themselves to be concerned with anything but a subsidiary function of the central nervous system. Doubtless, there is ample justification for the use of relatively simple systems in an early investigation. But it is true, nevertheless, that the concept of the reflex has not emerged unmarked by such a circumstance of its development. In its extension to the behavior of intact organisms, that is to say, the historical definition finds itself encumbered with what now appear to be superfluous interpretations.

The present paper examines the concept of the reflex and attempts to evaluate the historical definition. It undertakes eventually to frame an alternative definition, which is not wholly in despite of the historical usage. The reader will recognize a method of criticism first formulated with respect to scientific concepts by Ernst Mach [in *The Science of Mechanics*] and perhaps better stated by Henri Poincaré. To the works of these men and to Bridgman's excellent application of the method [in *The Logic of Modern Physics*] the reader is referred for any discussion of the method *qua* method. Probably the chief advantage, first exploited in this respect by Mach, lies in the use of a historical approach. But the reader should understand that in the present case no attempt is made to give an exhaustive account of the history of the reflex. Certain historical facts are considered for two reasons: to discover the nature of the observations upon which the concept has been based, and to indicate the source of the incidental interpretations with which we are concerned.

I

It was Descartes [2] who first proposed a mechanism by which the characteristics of the living organism could plausibly be produced. He came very near describing its action as the true mode of operation of the animal body, but the criticism of his contemporary, Nicolas Stensen, probably expressed his intention correctly. "Descartes," said Stensen, "was too clever in exposing the errors of current treatises on man to undertake the task of expounding the true structure of man. Therefore in his essay on Man he does not attempt such a delineation, but is content to describe a machine capable of performing all the functions of which man is capable." This interpretation is borne out by the text of the *Traité,* where, although parts of the anatomy are again and again pointed out as suitable for the functions of the mechanism, and the machine and body are, indeed, almost identified, the reader is, nevertheless, invited only to suppose the truth of the details. Descartes' interest lay primarily in furthering his philosophical notions, and the invention which is usually taken as the earliest expression of the reflex was little more than an instrument of persuasion.

In designing a convincing model of the living organism Descartes faced a peculiar difficulty. Movement in itself was easily enough obtained, for there were many mechanisms available as sources of energy. There was, for example, the current explanation of muscular contraction upon a hydraulic analogy, which, in fact, Descartes adopted. But if the energy itself was conveniently accounted for, the direction and order of its release were, on the contrary, critical. In meeting this difficulty Descartes introduced a novel device—the mechanism of the stimulus, by means of which external forces released the movements of the machine. The stimulus distinguished the model of *la bête machine* from that of a mere activated doll. It enabled the model to simulate the appropriateness and the apparent spontaneity of the movements of the living organism. So far as Descartes' purpose was concerned, it was successful in supplanting certain metaphysical concepts as causal agents leading to movement. Heretofore, the supposition had been that an animal moved because of the action of, let us say, a "soul." Descartes proposed that the body be regarded as a system of stored energy,

---

[2] Descartes' account is to be found in the *Traité de l'homme,* which differs in many respects from the earlier *Passions de l'âme* in its representation of the action of the nervous system.

A convenient account of Descartes as physiologist is given by Sir Michael Foster in his *Lectures on the History of Physiology* (London, 1901). The quotations from Nicolas Stensen and the translation from Descartes are taken from this work.

and he pointed to minute, hitherto unobserved forces which acted upon the organism in such a way as to serve as releasing mechanisms.

The principle of the stimulus was, of course, little more than a guess. With an enthusiasm for the new physics, Descartes contended that the movements of an organism were functions of the forces acting upon it, but he could in practice point to only the roughest demonstration of this relationship. Subsequent investigation of the reflex has revealed the extraordinary difficulty of identifying the stimulating forces correlated with particular movements. The information available in Descartes' time was so scant, and the principle so far-reaching that one is tempted to regard the discovery of the stimulus simply as another example of the insight with which Descartes anticipated later thought. But this would be to overlook the influence of an unusual analogy.

Descartes sought a mechanical model of the living organism for the support of an argument. For other reasons, namely, for the sake of the entertainment which they afforded, suitable models (utilizing the action of a stimulus as a source of spontaneity and appropriateness) had already been constructed by the engineers of the royal fountains in France. Descartes describes two of these fountain figures and the action of their releasing mechanisms, which are operated unwittingly by the observers.

> For in entering they necessarily tread on certain tiles or plates, which are so disposed that if they approach a bathing Diana, they cause her to hide in the rose-bushes, and if they try to follow her, they cause a Neptune to come forward to meet them threatening them with his trident. Or if they pass in another direction they occasion the springing forward of a marine monster who spouts water into their faces or things of a like sort according to the caprice of the engineers who constructed them.

A contemporary engineer, Salomon de Caus,[3] published an account of the operation of similar figures, although he did not describe the two groups referred to by Descartes. The mechanical principles are few in number, but among them can be found all of those used by Descartes in his "reflex arc." In Descartes' proposed model the organ of sense is set in motion "even ever so little" by the external object and pulls upon a thread, which in turn, acting like a bell rope, opens a valve at a central reservoir, letting the contained fluid flow outward along a pipeline into the muscles, which it activates. With a plate or lever substituted for the organ of sense and a waterwheel or similar device for the muscles, the

---

[3] de Caus, *Les raisons des forces mouvantes avec diverse machines . . . de grottes et de fontaines.* The date (1624) is considerably earlier than that of the *Traité*, and the examples treated by de Caus are, in general, simpler than those described by Descartes.

description applies as well to the fountain figures. So slightly does Descartes depart from the details of the fountain mechanism that its position as the prototype of his model seems unquestionable.

It was the accident of a convenient analogy which led Descartes to the discovery of an important principle, and so great a mutation was it in the evolution of human thought that it proved lethal. In spite of frequent assertions to the contrary, Descartes seems to have exerted no influence upon the development of the reflex. Instead, the discovery of the stimulus was made again, with great difficulty, as the culmination of a century of experimentation, and another century and a half had elapsed before the principle had again been comparably extended to the behavior of the total organism. This lack of historical influence may be variously explained. Descartes was, as Foster has said, a "retrograde" physiologist, who accepted the more convenient theory, as against the more accurate, for the sake of a broader consistency. His interest was ultimately philosophical, even in his physiological explanations, and he did not attempt to discover the true action of the nervous system.

Descartes is important to an understanding of the reflex, not because of an organic connection with subsequent history, but as a symbol. The stimulus is an essential part of a mechanistic theory of behavior, whether the notion is arrived at through observation, as it was with Marshall Hall, for example, or argued from physical necessity or mechanical analogy, as it was with Descartes. Furthermore, the analysis of behavior which is accomplished in the mere descriptive phrase, "withdrawing the foot from fire," became a critical part of later method. But a further characteristic of Descartes' position must be noted: although he substituted the stimulus for a metaphysical concept in his description of the animal, Descartes could not eliminate metaphysical concepts from his description of man. Here he regarded the mechanical principles as at work, but under the control of the soul, which might suspend the physical necessities much as the engineer might modify the activity of the fountain figures.

Descartes reserved a field of action for the concept of soul, not because the physical facts were any more lacking in the case of man than elsewhere, but because of the pressure of certain metaphysical notions. Fragments of similar reservations still prevail. But the history of the reflex can almost be told by describing the progressive encroachment of the stimulus upon them. The line which Descartes drew between the fields of action of his physical and metaphysical concepts was a temporal one only. A movement might follow at one time the action of a stimulus and at another the action of soul. The later distinction which was first definitely established by

Marshall Hall set in part an anatomical boundary. But both lines were drawn for the same purpose, namely, to resolve, by compromise, the conflict between an *observed necessity* and *preconceptions of freedom* in the behavior of organisms. In one form or another, this compromise accounts almost wholly for the aspects of the historical definition of the reflex which we are attempting to reconsider.

II

The concept of the reflex arose again from investigations which had already begun during Descartes' lifetime. They were concerned with animal movement and represented a sudden turn in the history of the concepts dealing with that phenomenon. It is a generalization sufficiently accurate for our purposes to say that the movements of an organism had generally been taken as coexistent with its life and as necessarily correlated with the action of some such entity as soul. The necessary relationship between the action of soul and the contraction of a muscle, for example, was explicit. As a consequence, it was disturbing to find, experimentally, that a muscle could be made to contract after it had been severed from a living organism or even after death. This, however, was the contention of the new physiology.

The demonstration that the volume of a muscle does not appreciably increase during contraction was made by Francis Glisson [4] in the middle of the seventeenth century. He was, as Fulton has shown, probably anticipated here by the Dutch naturalist, Swammerdam, whose influence was less immediately felt. Swammerdam's experiments on excised nerve and muscle were more clear-cut than those of Glisson on the intact limb, but either procedure was convincing and was something more than a mere disproof of the "animal spirits" hypothesis of muscular contraction. The experiment pointed to the existence of a "property of contractility" resident in the muscular tissue and independent of any remote source of energy. Contemporary and subsequent experimentation was of the same import. Glisson himself experimented upon intestinal and skeletal muscle

---

[4] For an account of the events antecedent to the explicit formulation of the concept of the reflex see: (*a*) Foster, *op. cit.*; (*b*) the historical introduction in J. F. Fulton's *Muscular Contraction and the Reflex Control of Movement*. Baltimore, Md.: Williams & Wilkins, 1926; (*c*) Ch. 1 in Verworn's *Irritability: A Physiological Analysis of the General Effect of Stimuli in Living Substances*. New Haven, Conn.: Yale Univ. Press, 1913; and, for many quotations from the sources, (*d*) F. Fearing's *Reflex Action: A Study in the History of Physiological Psychology*. Baltimore, Md.: Williams & Wilkins, 1930.

after death, when metaphysical concepts had supposedly ceased to act. Swammerdam's experiments indicated a characteristic activity in excised nerve and muscle, and in 1700 Giorgio Baglivi, the Italian physician, reporting the contractions of isolated muscular tissue, emphasized that this was "without the soul's having any share in it, or even being sensible of it." The experiments published by von Haller in 1739 and 1742 permitted him to make the following claims:

> By my experiments I separated this irritable nature on the one hand from a mere dead force, and on the other hand from the nervous force and from the power of the soul. I shewed that the movement of the heart and the irritable nature of the intestines depended on it alone. I confined it entirely to the muscular fibre. . . . I also shewed that that force was something perpetually living, and that it often broke out into movement though no external stimulus such as could be recognized by us was acting. By a stimulus, however, it could at any time be called back from rest into action. In a movement produced through it I distinguished between the stimulus which might be very slight, and the movement called forth by the stimulus which might be very powerful.

The doctrine of irritability was the theoretical accompaniment of this experimentation. As a property assigned to living tissue, irritability was from the first clearly defined in terms of the experimental operations which revealed it. In his fundamental experiment, Glisson noted that the gall bladder and the biliary duct bring about a greater secretion when they are irritated. "He argues," as Foster has noted, "that they cannot be irritated unless they possess the power of being irritated. This power of being irritated he proposes to denote by the term *irritability*." Although the concept was not immediately freed of non-physical counterparts, it was essentially a physical hypothesis, which ultimately led to the science of the general physiology of nerve and muscle. Movement, far from being the objective manifestation of the activity of soul, had become an organic process subject to experimental investigation.

As Verworn has said, stimulation and irritability cannot be separated. Irritability, by its definition, implies the action of a stimulus. The doctrine of irritability, moreover, assigns an autonomy of function to the parts of an organism. These were the prerequisites for a formulation of the concept of the reflex. The first expression in harmony with the experimental material was made by Robert Whytt.[5] The genesis of the idea is apparent in a single sentence from that work. The observation is made that muscles will contract not only upon direct stimulation but *"whenever a stimulus is applied to the coats or membranes covering them, to the nerves which are*

[5] "An essay on the vital and other involuntary motions of animals." Edinburgh, 1751.

sent to them, or to some neighboring or even distant part.[6] Step by step, the point of stimulation recedes from the locus of the phenomenon with which it is identified. When the stimulus has been spatially distinguished from the response, the inference of a conducting medium is necessary, and a further experiment by Wyatt, suggested to him by Stephen Hales, showed that the spinal marrow was a necessary part of this conducting path, which could not function if the marrow were destroyed. We shall need to return later to discuss the significance of these experiments and certain points of method which they exemplify.

Whytt, it is true, regarded the conducting force as a "sentient principle," which, if it was non-rational, was also non-physical. He thus followed the example of Glisson in his compromise with older concepts. Nevertheless, the observations themselves were independent of Whytt's interpretation. His psychical qualifications, moreover, were in this sense useful: that they permitted him to generalize his principle to various functions of the intact organism, free of the resistance which would have been encountered if the principle had been wholly physical. The application to the vegetative functions was easily made, for it had already been strongly foreshadowed. He extended his doctrine also to the field of action of some of the departments of the soul.

III

Whytt left the concept of reflex action very much as Glisson had left irritability: in the position partly of a description of observed fact and partly of a superfluous interpretation. What von Haller had done in establishing irritability as a physiological datum independent of any aspect of soul, Marshall Hall [7] now repeated on behalf of the reflex. Not only, he suggested, could muscular tissue contract solely by virtue of its property of contractility, but a given muscle *in situ* could be brought into action by a train of nervous events which were in themselves acting only by virtue of an intrinsic property. "This principle," he said, "is that termed *vis nervosa* by Haller, *motorische Kraft* or *vis motoria* by Professor Müller, and *excitabilité* by M. Flourens." [8] To describe the series of events which

---

[6] The quotation is from the second edition, published in 1763, page 267. The first edition omits "to the nerves which are sent to them."

[7] Hall, M. On the reflex function of the medulla oblongata and medulla spinalis. London, 1833, *Phil. Trans. Roy. Soc.*, read June 20, 1833.

[8] From Hall's *Memoirs on the Nervous System. Memoir II. On the True Spinal Marrow and the Excito-motory System of Nerves*, London, 1837. Whytt had distinguished between the action of the will and the action of a stimulus, but by the latter he probably intended only "mechanical action" upon a muscle. Whytt also used the word *spontaneous* to aid in the distinction, but in the reverse sense! *Reflex* movements were for him spontaneous, since they are performed by the several organs "as it were of their own accord."

a single instance of this activity comprised Hall accepted the word *reflex,* and he spoke of the principle in general as "the reflex function."

The hypothesis that the phenomena of the reflex arc are only aspects of irritability seems to have been original with Marshall Hall. Of the contributions which he claimed to have made it resisted most successfully the charge of plagiarism leveled against him by his contemporaries and was most often cited in his defense. The hypothesis involved, not a denial of the operation of non-physical concepts, but an exclusion of their operation from the reflex field. In Hall's own estimation, as Sherrington [9] has pointed out, "his chief advance lay in the doctrine of separateness in the central nervous system of the great sub-system for unconscious reflex action, and another great sub-system for sensation and volition." This estimate of himself has been more or less confirmed historically. He is, it seems fair to say, the acknowledged author of the almost immutable distinction between voluntary and reflex action and of the resulting negative definition of the reflex as a form of movement *un*conscious, *in*voluntary, and *un*learned. The emphasis which this brief account has thus far placed upon the relation of the reflex to non-physical concepts may now appear more reasonable. Hall's basic hypothesis was simply a restatement of the relationship and must be understood accordingly.

Hall distinguished between four modes of muscular action. *Volition,* he said, acts through the cerebrum, is spontaneous, and affects the muscles in a direct line through the spinal marrow and motor nerves. *Respiration* acts in the same way, is also spontaneous (sic), but its seat is in the medulla. *Involuntary* action is the response of a muscle to direct stimulation (the phenomenon of irritability). The fourth mode (the *reflex function*) involves the spinal marrow and differs from volition and respiration in that it is neither spontaneous nor direct in its course.

> It is, on the contrary, *excited* by the application of appropriate stimuli, which are not, however, applied immediately to the muscular or nervo-muscular fibre, but to certain membranous parts, whence the impression is carried to the medulla (spinalis), *reflected,* and reconducted to the part impressed, or conducted to a part remote from it, in which muscular contraction is effected.

We may neglect the second class, which seems to have been included because of the current knowledge of the respiratory center but was exclusive of neither voluntary nor reflex action, and the third (unfortunately called involuntary), which was only a statement of irritability. For the

[9] Quoted by Stirling, W. *Some Apostles of Physiology.* London, 1902.

distinction between the two remaining classes (volition and reflex action), we may consider Hall's available evidence.

Hall defined volition as a form of movement which was (*a*) spontaneous, and (*b*) dependent upon the integrity of the cerebrum. The second characteristic was not in itself sufficiently distinguishing. Hall was familiar with the segmental nature of the spinal functions, and it was a fair supposition that the differential activity found in so uniform a structure might be accentuated in the higher segments. If it was a matter of observation that characteristic movements of the animal disappeared upon ablation of the cerebrum, this was also true for any given part of the cord. Spontaneity, on the other hand, was the more critical factor in the delimitation of volition. But spontaneity, as Hall used it, described in effect only those movements for which no appropriate stimuli could be observed, and the word seems to have had no other meaning. The distinction between reflex and voluntary action rested, then, upon the possibility or the impossibility of the experimental demonstration of stimulating forces.

To the support of his distinction Hall mustered a variety of other facts. He noted that drugs (such as opium or strychnine) discriminate in their action between voluntary and reflex activity, that the brain sleeps, while the spinal marrow never sleeps, and so on. He was, of course, describing an observable phenomenon, which we recognize as the differential functioning of separate reflex systems.[10] The observations do not, however, indicate an essential difference between brain and cord, especially since the brain-cord distinction is seldom strictly respected physiologically. Hall's appeal to physiology, like that to anatomy, lacked cogency. His distinction rested primarily upon the single item of spontaneity.

In defining volition as the hypothetical antecedent of movement for which no corresponding stimulus could be observed, Hall left the concept open to extensive modification, for it was implicit in the nature of the reflex that it should, in the course of its growth, disfranchise volition. So far as it concerns behavior, the history of the reflex has been, in fact, essentially the account of the discovery of stimuli and of the concurrent passage of the corresponding behavior from the field of volition into the field of reflex action. Furthermore, in opposing volition and reflex action as mutually exclusive terms, Hall identified the reflex with scientific necessity, and volition with unpredictability. This was the pattern for future controversy, of which we may note two instances.

---

[10] An exhaustive account of the discriminating action of drugs upon separate reflex systems is available in R. Magnus's *Körperstellung*. Berlin: Springer, 1924.

In 1853, Pflüger,[11] as is well known, questioned the reflex nature of the movements of the spinal frog on the basis of unpredictability. In separate instances of the flexion reflex, he pointed out, the movement of the leg varies widely, although the stimulus is held constant. On the basis of the observed variability, Pflüger postulated a spinal mind, his famous *Rücken-markseele*. Note that the experimental justification for mind (as for Hall's volition) was the absence of demonstrable necessity, that the function of the non-physical concept was, as heretofore, to account for variability. Refutation of Pflüger's criticism needed only a demonstration that the observed variability was itself a function of collateral stimulation. The necessary observations were first supplied by von Uexküll, and the principle (*Shaltung*) has been elaborated by Magnus. Briefly, they have shown that a given response may be modified through proprioceptive stimulation arising from the posture of the animal. The effects which Pflüger observed in the spinal frog are consequently subject to adequate prediction, and, in this particular instance at least, the variability has disappeared. With it disappeared also its corresponding *Seele*.

Shortly before the beginning of the century Pavlov was engaged in the investigation of the activity of the digestive glands. For much of this activity it was possible to identify the necessary antecedent events (the mechanical or chemical changes acting directly or reflexly upon the glands). The greater part of the normal secretion, however, was unfortunately not under the control of the experimenter. The reader should not be surprised that this was called "psychic" secretion. Pavlov undertook the investigation of this activity. His findings are too well known to call for more than the briefest comment here. Essentially, it was the discovery of the operation of "substitute" stimuli. The nature of the process of substitution (conditioning) and the use of the principle as a method are not important at this point. We may emphasize, however, the aspects of the discovery which exemplify the usual course of reflex investigation. *Given a particular part of the behavior of an organism hitherto regarded as unpredictable* (and probably, as a consequence, assigned to non-physical factors), *the investigator seeks out the antecedent changes with which the activity is correlated and establishes the conditions of the correlation.* He thus establishes, as we say, the reflex nature of the behavior. In traditional practice, upon

---

11 Pflüger, E. *Die sensorische Functionen des Rückenmarks der Wirbelthiere nebst einen neuen Lehre über die Leitungsgesetze der Reflexionen.* 1853. This controversy, of course, extended well beyond Pflüger's personal participation. It was, in fact, the continuation of a philosophical reaction against Hall's concept and was only accentuated by Pflüger's interpretation of his experimental findings.

the demonstration of such a correlation, non-physical concepts dealing with the same subject matter are discarded.

IV

The subsequent development of Hall's formulation could by its very nature approach only one end, namely, the hypothesis that the total behavior of the intact organism might be described in terms of the reflex. This extension was possible only upon the demonstration of necessary correlations in a large body of residual behavior, most of which was mediated by the distance receptors of the head segments. The work of Pavlov may therefore be taken as historically fundamental. His evidence was decisive, if necessarily incomplete. It led to two achievements. The principle of conditioning supplied the extended range of stimulation needed to account for the complex behavior of the total organism, and the demonstration of the reflex activity of the cortex laid siege to the last stronghold of the old anatomical distinctions. The extension of the concept has been further facilitated by the work of Magnus upon reflexes concerned with the maintenance of posture. Magnus, like Pavlov, broadened the field of operation of the stimulus by discovering a large number of specific stimulus-response correlations, and, again like Pavlov, he attacked the anatomical distinctions by demonstrating the reflex nature of the activity of the higher, although chiefly subcortical, centers. The reflex as a concept in the description of behavior has received its most extended systematic support from behaviorism.

The adequacy or inadequacy of the reflex in the description of total behavior seems to be beyond immediate experimental demonstration and, in any event, is beyond the scope of this paper. Some of its implications also need not greatly concern us, as, for example, the fate of the non-physical concepts which are deprived of their field of operation. We may regard the ultimate validity of the concept of volition (as, indeed, of that of the reflex) as beyond any immediate estimation. We are concerned with the reflex as a working concept. What is its nature and how shall it be defined? In particular, we have set ourselves to resolve certain difficulties of definition imposed by the extension to total behavior, where volition (or the practice which it represents) is important for its effects. But perhaps we have reviewed enough of its history and may turn directly to a statement of the argument.

In the history of the reflex one positive characteristic has always been given by the facts—the observed correlation of the activity of an effector (i.e., a response) with the observed forces affecting a receptor (i.e., a stimulus). The negative characteristics, on the other hand, which describe the reflex as involuntary, unlearned, unconscious, or restricted to special neural paths, have proceeded from unscientific presuppositions concerning the behavior of organisms. When Marshall Hall decapitated his famous newt, he pointed quite correctly to the reflex activity of the parts of the headless body, to the observed fact that movement followed, inevitably, the administration of specific stimuli. But his assumption that he had imprisoned in the head of the newt the source of another kind of movement was irrelevant and unsupported. The fact before him was a demonstrable necessity in the movement of the headless body; his failure to observe similar necessities in the movement of the intact organism was the accident of his time and of his capabilities.

Tentatively, then, we may define a reflex as an observed correlation of stimulus and response. When we say, for example, that Robert Whytt discovered the pupillary reflex,[12] we do not mean that he discovered either the contraction of the iris or the impingement of light upon the retina, but rather that he first stated the necessary relationship between these two events. So far as behavior is concerned, the pupillary reflex is nothing more than this relationship. Once given a specific stimulus-response correlation, we may, of course, investigate the physiological facts of its mediation. The information there revealed will supplement our definition, but it will not affect the status of the reflex as a correlation. These are matters, however, which will bear a more detailed treatment, for they present many problems.

V

The notions of both stimulus and response were, as we have seen, essential to the principle of irritability, so that the correlation which we are emphasizing was already present (in its most easily observed form) in the older concept. The reflex emerged as a separate principle when a correlated stimulus and response could be spatially distinguished, and we have already commented upon Whytt's insistence upon the possibility of a spatial differentiation. The observation of a correlation between two spatially discrete activities led at once to the inference of a series of intervening events, to the inference, that is, of conduction. Subsequently, the investigation of the events intervening between a stimulus and its correlated response became the particular field of reflex physiology. We shall need to review certain characteristics of its method, and we may turn first to the procedure by

[12] Disregarding the supposed discovery by Galen and Descartes.

which the anatomical structures underlying the mediation of a reflex are identified.

Even for so early an investigator as Robert Whytt convenient material from the physiology of the nervous system was available in interpreting reflex phenomena. Rough descriptions of the activity of end-organ and effector and of the conducting action of nerve were at hand. The investigators of the reflex appropriated this current knowledge but began immediately to refine the references to anatomy. Whytt, as we have already seen, first demonstrated that the necessary relationship between stimulus and response (or, as he expressed it, the "sympathy between different muscles or other parts of the body") was lacking after destruction of the cord; "from whence it seems to follow," he added, "that the nerves. . . . have no communication but at their termination in the brain or spinal marrow." His conclusion, if it was not strictly logical, was made extremely probable by Bell's subsequent differentiation between the functions of the anterior and posterior spinal roots. Although Bell did not expressly subscribe to the reflex doctrine, his experiments are more to the point in its support than in his generalization to "sensation and the power of motion." The "diastaltic arc" of Marshall Hall applied Bell's discovery more explicitly to the principle of the reflex.

The diastaltic arc (eventually spoken of as the reflex arc) embraced an "esodic" (afferent) nerve, a spinal center, and an "exodic" (efferent) nerve. It was an *anatomical* term. The experimental evidence for its close correspondence to the reflex was of the sort we have noted: the impairment of reflex function after anatomical injury (Whytt), the fractional functioning of surgically isolated parts of the arc (Bell), and so on. Subsequently (especially in the neuron theory), the argument was extended to microscopic levels. By similar procedures the gross location of the central part of a given arc is determined. The practice is essential to the doctrine of the segmental action of the cord and was utilized early in the history of nerve physiology (independently of reflex theory) in the localization of higher centers, for example, the respiratory center. Typical examples in reflex investigation may be found in the work of Magnus on various mid-brain preparations. The basic assumption is that, when the ablation of a particular part of the nervous system impairs or abolishes a reflex function, the ablated structure is essential to the reflex and includes part of the arc. That inference, of course, is not unavoidable. Moreover, in the interpretation of such experiments the probability of operative artifact must unfortunately be regarded as proportional to the degree of specificity desired. For the broader inferences, however, such as that of the participation of the spinal cord, the probability of serious artifact is negligible.

The notion of the reflex arc as the anatomical counterpart of a reflex has been generally accepted. An end-organ (or a nerve trunk acting in that capacity), an afferent nerve, an interconnection between nerves in the cord or brain, an efferent nerve, and an effector are usually regarded as essential to the mediation of a reflex. We shall have no occasion to go beyond these rather general assumptions. The method which we have referred to is not peculiar to the reflex, and we shall not need to estimate it more closely. We may note, however, that the description of a reflex in functional terms (as a correlation of stimulus and response) is always prior to the description of its arc. In any available procedure the anatomical inference must always be drawn from an experiment in which the integrity of a *function* is critical.

In its simplest form, the concept of the reflex arc satisfies the need for continuity between stimulus and response, but the arc must serve as a locus not only for a communication between end-organ and effector but for modifications in the form of the communication. The statement of any reflex (for example: "the flexion of a limb following electrical stimulation of the skin of the foot") implies the possibility of a quantitative description of both stimulus and response. The statement thus expresses the observed correlation of two events, but by describing these events it describes also the special conditions of the correlation. A given stimulus and its response differ, for example, in time of inception, in duration, and in the form and amount of energy; and these modifications and conversions must be accounted for by the intervening events.

By procedures of the sort we have already described, the characteristics of a reflex have been assigned to particular parts of the arc. The gross conversions of energy have, of course, been referred to end-organ and effector, part of the elapsed time to afferent and efferent nerve, and so on. By a process of logical and surgical isolation, however, a certain group of the conditions of a reflex correlation have been shown to be independent of the activity of end-organ, effector, and nerve-trunk. These are the special characteristics of reflex conduction. They have been classically described by Sherrington in *The Integrative Action of the Nervous System*. In Sherrington's list each characteristic is expressed as a difference between nerve-trunk and reflex-arc conduction, which means simply that certain of the inferences noted above have already been made. In reproducing the list here, we shall reword it in order to emphasize the nature of each item as an observed condition of a correlation of stimulus and response.

(1) There is a latent period between application of the stimulus and ap-

pearance of the end effect; (2) the duration of the response is greater than the duration of the stimulus; (3) if stimuli are applied rhythmically (between certain limiting rates), the rhythm of the response does not closely correspond with the rhythm of the stimulus; (4) the intensity of the response does not vary rectilinearly with the intensity of the stimulus; (5) a single brief stimulus is often not effective, but succeeding stimuli following closely upon it are; (6) afferent and efferent paths cannot function interchangeably; (7) repetition of a stimulus (with certain time specifications) evokes progressively weaker responses; (8) the strength of stimulus just sufficing to elicit a response is variable; (9) (*a*) a second stimulus is ineffective for a short interval after a first and subnormally effective for a succeeding short interval, (*b*) two stimuli at separate points of stimulation may facilitate each other, (*c*) a stimulus may act to produce the absence of a response, (*d*) injury to the nervous system may temporarily destroy or weaken the effectiveness of a stimulus which is subsequently found to be normally effective; (10) the effectiveness of a stimulus depends upon the integrity of the blood supply; (11) the effectiveness of a stimulus is partially or wholly abolished by anaesthetics.

Although all the characteristics except (6) and parts of (9) are represented to some extent in nerve conduction, the degree to which they are present in reflex conduction cannot be explained by reference to nerve-trunk alone. It has been assumed, therefore, that the characteristics represent the functioning of a special structure, which has been called the *synapse,* and which has been hypothetically located at the interconnection between neurons. Since these interconnections are grouped together in the gray matter of the cord and brain, the experimental practice associated with the other parts of the arc may be used in testing the hypothesis. It is possible, for example, to show that the synaptic characteristics are present in conduction through the cord when an afferent nerve is stimulated close to the cord and the response taken electrically from the efferent root. Again, the characteristics can be shown to vary with the temperature of the cord, but they are almost wholly independent of the temperature of either afferent or efferent nerve. Examples could be multiplied indefinitely. Moreover, as Sherrington has shown, the location of the synapse at the interconnection between neurons receives considerable support from the histology of the nervous system, from studies in nerve degeneration, from the physical chemistry of surfaces of separation, and from various other sources.

Reflex physiology seeks a physico-chemical description of the events peculiar to the mediation of a stimulus-response correlation. It regards the synapse, therefore, as a physico-chemical system. Theories of the details of that system have been of various sorts. Keith Lucas [13] sought an explanation of synaptic phenomena in terms common to nerve-trunk conduction. In his theory the synapse was regarded as a region of impaired conduction, and its description in physico-chemical terms waited only upon the description of the conduction of the nervous impulse. Sherrington has recently regarded the synapse as the locus for the depositing of excitatory and inhibitory substances or states.[14] For Lapicque the synapse is the boundary between neural structures of independent chronaxies. We shall have no need of evaluating theories of this sort, nor shall we find it necessary, in the light of our brief examination of method, to justify or discredit the hypothesis of the synapse itself. We are interested, not in the validity of that concept, but in its nature. Here we are led to one conclusion.

Our present information concerning the synapse is derived wholly from observed instances of reflex conduction. There is nothing in our description of the synapse which has not already served to describe experimental data, but we translate our descriptions of data into the laws of the synapse for convenience of expression. The synapse, that is to say, described in terms of its characteristics, is a construct. *It is the conceptual expression for the conditions of correlation of a stimulus and response, where the incidental conditions imposed by a particular stimulus and a particular response have been eliminated.*

There is nothing in the physiology of the reflex which calls in question the nature of the reflex as a correlation, because there is nothing to be found there which has any significance beyond a description of the conditions of a correlation. It may be objected that, should reflex physiology succeed in describing the synapse as a physico-chemical system, the synapse would be no longer conceptual. Actually, the description would be translated into concepts of another order, which would possess the tremendous advantage of being common to all the physical sciences. But we are here very close to certain fundamental questions of scientific method which we shall not attempt to answer.

The physiological study of the reflex supplements and restricts our definition. It begins by identifying and describing certain of the events which intervene typically between stimulus and response, and it then arbitrarily restricts the use of the word *reflex* to correlations which employ that kind of event. Physiologically, the word implies the participation of at least two neurons with a synaptic junction. The best practical criterion is irreversi-

[13] Lucas, K. *The Conduction of the Nervous Impulse.* London: Longmans, Green, 1917.

[14] Sherrington, C. S. Remarks on some aspects of reflex inhibition. *Proc. Roy. Soc.,* 1925, *97 B,* 519–544.

bility of conduction, which is not in any degree a characteristic of nerve-trunk conduction and is therefore the clearest evidence of the operation of a synapse. This restriction in the use of the word *reflex* excludes (1) the movement of the organism solely under the influence of mechanical forces (for example, the movement of the paw of a dog when it is "shaken"); (2) the activity of an effector in response to direct stimulation, a distinction which is more often of importance in dealing with the internal economy of the organism; (3) those responses mediated by other types of nervous system than the synaptic; and (4) those correlations between discrete activities which are mediated by non-nervous mechanisms, as, for example, by hormones.

The advantage of these qualifications (even of the third, which is sometimes felt to be a notable difficulty) is that they insure a uniformity of material in the investigation of the reflex. It would be impossible to state with any degree of specificity a law describing the course of reflex fatigue if it were to apply to the exhaustion of such diverse mechanisms as a neural structure and a concentration of hormonic substance. The restricted definition limits the application of the principle of the reflex, but within boundaries which may be justified upon independent grounds.

We have tried to emphasize an essential continuity between reflex physiology and the special science of the description of behavior. We must not, however, fail to recognize a well-grounded distinction between the two fields, which is based primarily upon a difference in immediate purpose. The one seeks a description of the reflex in terms of physico-chemical events, the other a description of behavior in terms of the reflex. It is assumed that the word *reflex* refers to the same thing in both instances. Historically, however, the investigation of the physiology of the reflex proceeded, as we have seen, almost independently of the description of behavior and was advanced almost to its present status at a time when the possibility of a quantitative description of behavior was considered too remote for scientific consideration. The concepts of reflex physiology, consequently, cannot be transposed to the description of behavior without modification, which will in most cases be found, however, to proceed naturally from an analysis of the physiological method, as, for example, in the discussion of the synapse given above. Moreover, many assumptions which are unimportant and therefore tacit in reflex physiology are critical in the description of behavior and must be given an explicit and independent statement. This is true of the procedure by which a single reflex is isolated, as we shall see later. Again, a number of problems which arise in the description of behavior have no parallel at all in reflex physiology. Some of these matters we have already touched upon; others will enter at one time or another into the following discussion.

VI

We may summarize this much of the argument in the following way. A reflex is defined as an observed correlation of two events, a stimulus and a response. A survey of the history discloses no other characteristic upon which a definition can legitimately be based. The physiological investigation does not question the correlative nature of the reflex, for its data and its concepts deal essentially with the conditions of a correlation; but heterogeneous instances of correlations which would be embraced by the definition, read literally, are excluded by the physiological refinements of usage. It now remains for us to deal more specifically with the reflex in the description of behavior. What is the description of behavior, and how does the reflex, as a correlation, enter into it? Here (the reader may again be warned) we shall be concerned not so much with the validity or the adequacy of the concept as with its nature and the method peculiar to it.

Lacking some arbitrary distinction, the term *behavior* must include the total activity of the organism—the functioning of all its parts. Obviously, its proper application is much less general, but it is difficult to reach any clear distinction. The definition of the subject matter of any science, however, is determined largely by the interest of the scientist, and this will be our safest rule here. We are interested primarily in the movement of an organism in some frame of reference. We are interested in any internal change which has an observable and significant effect upon this movement. In special cases we are directly interested in glandular activity, but this will usually concern us only secondarily in its effect upon movement. The unity and internal consistency of this subject matter is historical: we are interested, that is to say, in what the organism *does*.

But the description of behavior, if it is to be either scientific or satisfying, must go further. As a scientific discipline, it must describe the event not only for itself but in its relation to other events; and, in point of satisfaction, it must *explain*. These are essentially identical activities. In the brief survey at the beginning of this paper it was occasionally necessary to regard the stimulus as a newly discovered cause of movement for which various conceptual causes had previously been designed. In this way we represented a real aspect of the history of the reflex. But we may now take that more humble view of explanation and causation which seems to have been first suggested by Mach and is now a common characteristic of scientific thought, wherein, in a word, explanation is reduced to description and the notion of function substituted for that of causation. The full description of an event is taken to include a description of its functional relationship with antecedent events. In the description of behavior we are interested in the relationships within a regressive series of events extending from the behavior itself to those energy changes at the periphery which we designate as stimuli. We stop here in the regression only because further steps are beyond the field of behavior. The two end events, the behavior and the stimulus, have, moreover, a particular importance, because they alone are directly observable in an intact organism, and because they limit the series. With the relationship of these two end terms the description of behavior is chiefly concerned.

The reflex is important in the description of behavior because it is by definition a statement of the *necessity* of this relationship. The demonstration of the necessity is ultimately a matter of observation: a given response is observed invariably to follow a given stimulus, or exceptions to this rule may be independently described. In its extension to total behavior the principle generalizes the statement of the necessity observed in a particular reflex, the form of the expression remaining essentially the same. That is to say, the hypothesis that "the behavior of an organism is an exact, if involved, function of the forces acting upon the organism" states the correlation of a stimulus and a response, both of which remain wholly undifferentiated. It is, in this sense, the broadest possible statement of a reflex, but it is not an observed correlation and is therefore a hypothesis only.

It is, nevertheless, solely the fault of our method that we cannot deal directly with this single correlation between behavior as a whole and all the forces acting upon the organism stated in the hypothesis. Quantitative statements of both stimulus and response and a statistical demonstration of the correlation are theoretically possible but would be wholly unmanageable. We are led, for lack of a better approach, to investigate the correlation of parts of the stimulus with parts of the response. For the sake of a greater facility (and in this case the very possibilty) of description, we turn to analysis.

Originally, the use of analysis was quite accidental and unrecognized, but it has, nevertheless, always been necessary. The early observations were possible only after it had been achieved in some form or other. This is not difficult to understand if we remember that the correlation which we call a reflex rests ultimately upon observation. In an intact newt, to return to Hall's experiment, it would have been very nearly impossible to observe a correlation between the movement of the tail and the application of a probing needle, because the movement of the tail was also correlated with other stimuli and the action of the probing needle with other movements. *In the isolated tail,* however, one kind of movement followed a given stimulus and was absent in the absence of the stimulus. The correlation was obvious and therefore observed.

Marshall Hall and his few predecessors divided the behavior of an organism into parts by the expedient method of dividing the organism. This became, in general, the method of reflex physiology, although, for obvious reasons, the division of the nervous system supplanted the division of the whole organism. The best-known group of reflexes to be studied in surgical isolation are those surviving in the body of the organism after section of the cord just below the bulb. This is the "spinal" preparation, which has been the basis for the greater part of physiological investigation, notably that of Sherrington. Other common reflex systems are the decerebrate, in which the medulla and the cerebellum remain intact, and the various midbrain and thalamic preparations, as, for example, those of Magnus. A further extension of the method involves the surgical or physiological exclusion of end-organs, as by extirpation or anaesthetization (for example, of the labyrinth), or by section of afferent nerves. The common object of these procedures is to permit the investigation of a particular response in relation to a controlled variable, independent of other variables also related to that response.

But the same result may be obtained in another way. The experiment may be so designed that the undesired variables do not vary. The distinction between the two methods will appear in the following example from the work of Magnus. Certain postural effects in a mid-brain animal are correlated partly with the position of the labyrinths relative to the earth and partly with the condition of flexion or extension of the muscles of the neck. The correlation between the posture and the state of the neck muscles can be studied alone if the labyrinths are cocainized or extirpated. But Magnus was also able to obtain the isolation by designing his experiments in such a way that the position of the labyrinths relative to the earth did not change. Perhaps the best examples of this method, however, are to be found in the work of Pavlov. Here the organism is intact and the very active receptors of the head segments fully functional. By controlling light, sound, odor, and other conditions in the experimental chamber, it is possible to observe in isolation the correlation between a given response and a selected stimulus. Placing an animal in a dark room, that is to say, is equivalent for purposes of isolation to blinding it, to sectioning the optic tracts, or to destroying the visual projection areas in the cortex, and has the great advantage over these surgical methods of being relatively free from unknown artifacts.

The practical merits of both these methods are obvious; but we are concerned with a broader aspect of analysis. For the physiologist, the isolation of a reflex is a preliminary matter of method and is relatively insignificant. In the description of behavior it is of first importance. How legitimate, then, is the process of analysis, and what is the nature of its product?

Let us deal entirely with the flexion reflex in the spinal dog, as a familiar and convenient example. We have already analyzed, of course, when we have once named, so that we must go back for a moment to the behavior as a whole. Without regard to its correlation with stimulating forces, behavior, as we have seen, is simply part of the total functioning of the organism. The problem of analysis at this level is common to physiology and anatomy. We shall not need to solve it, but shall assume that for purposes of description the body of an organism may be divided into parts (that we may speak, for example, of a leg), and that the functioning of a particular part may be described in isolation (that we may speak, for example, of the flexion of a leg). Moreover, we shall assume that the forces acting upon the organism may be analyzed and described in the manner common to the physical sciences. Our own problem lies beyond these assumptions.

In the flexion reflex our first experimental datum is the nearly simultaneous occurrence of the flexion of a leg and, let us say, the electrical stimulation of the skin of the foot. If we measure both events very carefully and repeat the stimulation, we obtain a second flexion which closely resembles the first, and we find that we may corroborate the observation, within limits, as often as we like. We call the observed correlation a reflex and, for convenience of reference, give it a special name, the flexion reflex.

The question then arises: *what is the flexion reflex?* If we try to answer by describing in detail a stimulus and a response, we meet embarrassing difficulties. We find that the exact degree and direction of flexion may vary with many factors. We find, for example, that it was very important for our original measurements that the torso of the animal had a particular position, that the contralateral leg was, say, unsupported, and so on. But we cannot specify these incidental conditions in our description without destroying its generality. Thereupon we shall probably resort to surgical methods. Theoretically, at least, we may pare down the structures underlying the flexion reflex until the collateral variables are no longer effective. But we can never be sure that the reflex which we have thus carved out of the behavior of the organism would not have been grossly otherwise if our operative procedure had been different. We are not sure, that is to say, that what turns up at the end of our process of isolation is the flexion reflex. There is another method open to us. In the flexion reflex we are dealing essentially with a group of correlations showing many characteristics in common. They involve the same effectors acting roughly in the same way and stimuli which resemble each other at least in their gross anatomical reference. We may, therefore, if we wish, *construct* a flexion reflex by a statistical treatment of many of these separate correlations. We may, in other words, determine and state a correlation between the characteristics common to all our observed responses and the characteristics common to all our observed stimuli, and we may name this construct the flexion reflex. But the resulting description of this statistical entity will likewise depend upon our choice of observations and upon our method of analysis.

We have been proceeding, of course, upon an unnecessary assumption, namely, that there *is* a flexion reflex which exists independently of our observations and which our observations approximate. Such an assumption is wholly gratuitous, but it is remarkably insistent. It arises in part from the nature of the reflex. If we remain at the level of our observations, we must recognize a reflex as a correlation. But the immediate uncritical reaction to a definition on that basis is that a correlation, in point of satisfaction, is not enough. There is an urge toward solidification, clearly evident throughout the history. We turn instantly to the reflex arc for material support. Although our knowledge of the critical part of the arc is, as we have seen, derived wholly from the observation of a correlation, we much prefer to regard the characteristics of the correlation as properties of the synapse rather than to retain them as characteristics of a correlation. Under the same pressure, then, but with less justification, we are led to assume that there are isolated reflexes concealed in the behavior of an organism, which by proper investigatory methods we may discover, and in the description of behavior to state the corollary of this proposition, namely, that behavior is the sum or the integration of these units.

Here we are touching upon the subject of a widespread current controversy, but we may, by virtue of what we have already said, dispose of the matter briefly. Let us phrase two typical questions. Is a reflex a unitary mechanism? Is behavior a sum of such mechanisms? Then, if by reflex we mean a hypothetical entity which exists apart from our observations but which our observations are assumed to approach, the questions are academic and need not detain us; if, on the other hand, we define a reflex as a given observed correlation or as a statistical treatment of observed correlations, the questions are meaningless, for they ignore the process of analysis implied in the definition. A reflex, that is to say, has no scientific meaning apart from its definition in terms of such experimental operations as we have examined, and, so defined, it cannot be the subject of questions of this sort.

There is a certain practical advantage, it is true, in regarding a reflex as a unitary mechanism—an advantage, as Mach might have said, which may have given rise to the practice. It is only when we misconstrue a purely practical device and take it to be an integral part of our definition that the possibility of theoretical misunderstanding arises. Our sample questions deal necessarily with the reflex defined in terms which we have seen to be well beyond any observational justification. As Poincaré has said of a similar issue, *"ces questions ne sont pas seulement insolubles, elles sont illusoires et depourvues de sens."* [15] A common mistake in the present case has been to suppose that, because an answer is lacking, the principle of the reflex is somehow impeached. As we have repeatedly noted, the validity of the reflex as a scientific concept is not here in question. The reflex remains, as it has always been, an observed correlation of stimulus and response.

VII

It remains for us to consider how a reflex as a correlation is dealt with experimentally. The first step, as we have seen, is the isolation of a response and the identification of its correlated stimulus. In practice, the demonstration of the correlation is usually left at an elementary level. It is based upon the appearance of the two events together and their failure to appear separately. As an experimental datum of this sort, a reflex may be given the expression

$$R = f(S) \tag{1}$$

where R is a response and S a stimulus. Theoretically, the exact nature of the function is determinable, although for any present purpose corresponding values of S and R are obtainable by observation only. Choosing convenient measures of both stimulus and response, we may vary the strength of S and observe variations in the strength of R. This is common practice, although very little has been done toward determining how a given R varies with its corresponding S. One characteristic of the relationship is the threshold: for values below a given value of S, $R = O$. There are also temporal aspects of the function, which have been investigated under the headings of latency and after-discharge.

Threshold, latency, after-discharge, and the order of variation of S and R

---

[15] Poincaré, H. *La science et l'hypothése.* Paris, 1903.

are thus descriptions of the correlation we call a reflex. They may be investigated with only one elicitation of the reflex or, at most, with a single set of corresponding values of S and R. There is a second field of investigation, however, which is concerned with variations in any aspect of a correlation, as they may appear in the comparison of successive elicitations. If, for example, we select a value of S and repeat the elicitation of the reflex at a given rate, we shall observe a progressive decrease in the value of R. Or, again, if the interval between two successive elicitations be made brief enough, the second R may be of greatly reduced magnitude or wholly lacking. Here are significant variations in the value of the terms in Equation [1]. They do not challenge the necessity of the relationship expressed therein (as they might well do if they were less orderly), but they do require that, in the description of a reflex, account be taken of *third variables.* We may indicate the required change by rewriting our equation as

$$R = f(S,A) \tag{2}$$

where A is a variable designed to account for any given observed change in the value of R.

As it appears in such an experiment, A is properly either time or the number of elicitations at a given rate. The inference is commonly made that it represents a factor of another sort, which varies with time or the number of elicitations in the same way. In the first example noted above the phenomenon has been called reflex fatigue, which is regarded as a synaptic change—as the exhaustion of a substance or state, or as an increase in resistance, according to one's preference in synaptic theory. But in the description of behavior, where we are only secondarily interested in these physiological inferences, reflex fatigue is nothing more than an orderly change in some measured aspect of a given correlation. A law describing the course of that change, where the independent variable is time or the number of elicitations or some other condition of the experiment, is peculiarly a law of behavior. It may become a law of the synapse, by virtue of certain physiological inferences, but it has by that time passed beyond the scope of the description of behavior.

Nevertheless, if we are to follow current usage, a definition of reflex fatigue as an observed variation in *one* aspect of a correlation is too narrow, for we know from observation that, when such a change has taken place, the other aspects of the correlation have also changed. If we have observed, for example, a change in the ratio of a particular R and S, we may expect to find all other ratios, as well as the threshold, latency, and after-discharge of the reflex, likewise changed. It is usual, therefore, to regard the particular change which we chance to observe as a sample of a greater process. Occasionally, where a change in one aspect of a correlation is alone important (as in summation, which is chiefly a matter of threshold), the characteristic may possibly be defined in terms of a single change. But such a characteristic as reflex fatigue, or the refractory phase, or facilitation, is by intention a description of a group of concurrent changes.

If we are to speak in terms of these group changes, it is almost necessary to have a term describing the *state* of a correlation at any given time with respect to all its aspects. The physiologist, of course, may use the synapse for this purpose. When he has once described reflex fatigue as the exhaustion of a synaptic substance, for example, he may attribute a change in *any* aspect of a correlation to that exhaustion. Although he may observe and measure at one time a change in after-discharge and at another a change in the magnitude of R, he may reasonably consider himself to be dealing with the same process in both cases. Fortunately, there is also a term serving the same purpose at the level of behavior. If, in a given reflex, the threshold is low, the latency short, the after-discharge prolonged, and the ratio R/S large, the reflex is ordinarily said to be strong. If, on the other hand, the threshold is high, the latency long, the after-discharge short, and the ratio R/S small, the reflex is said to be weak. An attribute of *strength* is imputed to the reflex. The strength of the response, of course, is not meant; a weak response may indicate a strong reflex if it be elicitable with a very weak stimulus.

"Reflex strength" expresses in a very general way the state of a given correlation at a given time with respect to many of its characteristics. It is a useful term, for it permits us to deal with reflex fatigue, for example, as a *change in reflex strength,* without stopping to specify the particular changes which compose it. Nevertheless, its usefulness does not extend beyond this qualitative level. The concept is subject to a major objection, which holds as well for the parallel use of the synaptic state. We do not know, since it has never been determined, whether the changes which compose such a characteristic as reflex fatigue all proceed at the same rate. If the threshold, let us say, and the magnitude of R do not vary in precisely the same way, we are not justified in taking either as a measure of a supposed common variable, nor, indeed, in continuing to regard reflex fatigue as a unitary process.

The study of the reflex, then, leads to the formulation of two kinds of law. The first are laws describing correlations of stimulus and response. A reflex, as we have defined it, is itself a law, and of this sort. It has a considerable generality in spite of the specificity of its terms, but it must be supplemented by other laws describing the exact conditions of a correlation. Secondly, there are laws describing changes in any aspect of these primary relationships as functions of third variables, where the third variable in any given case is a condition of the experiment. These secondary laws may be dealt with in groups, according as they involve the same experimental third variable, and they may be spoken of, for convenience, as describing changes in reflex strength. In the behavior of intact organisms the apparent variability of specific stimulus-response relationships emphasizes the importance of laws of the second sort. Conditioning, "emotion," and "drive," so far as they concern behavior, are essentially to be regarded as changes in reflex strength, and their quantitative investigation may be expected to lead to the determination of laws describing the course of such changes, that is, to laws of the second sort.[16]

It is difficult to discover any aspect of the behavior of organisms which may not be described with a law of one or the other of these forms. From the point of view of scientific method, at least, the description of behavior is adequately embraced by the principle of the reflex.

Summary

The present analysis of the reflex as a concept in the description of behavior follows the method first formulated with respect to scientific concepts by Mach and Poincaré. It examines the source of the historical definition and points out the incidental nature of most of its criteria. Eventually, it offers an alternative definition and considers in detail some of the questions which arise from the nature of the concept so defined.

I. Descartes "discovered the stimulus" and designed a mechanism which could account for animal movement upon the basis of the appropriate release of stored energy. But he was interested less in describing the action of the nervous system than in supporting metaphysical contentions of the automaticity of animals. He advanced the stimulus as a substitute for soul, but only within a field which omitted the greater part of the activity of man.

II. The notion of the reflex developed, independently of Descartes, from the investigation of "irritability." The action of a stimulus was implicit in the concept of irritability, which also assigned an autonomy of function to the parts of an organism. The concept of the reflex arose quite naturally when a stimulus and its related response were to be spatially dis-

---

[16] The second half of my thesis, of which this paper was the first half, describes experiments on "hunger drive" from this point of view.

tinguished. Robert Whytt made the first historically effective observations.

III.   It remained for Marshall Hall to clear the concept of psychical counterparts. This he did by setting up a distinction between reflex and voluntary action, which resulted eventually in the unfortunate historical definition of the reflex as a form of movement unconscious, involuntary, and unlearned. Volition, in Hall's sense, was essentially the hypothetical antecedent of movement for which no corresponding stimulus could be observed, a definition which served to identify the reflex with scientific necessity and volition with unpredictability.

IV.   The history of the reflex has known only one positive characteristic by which the concept may be defined: the observed correlation of two events, a stimulus and a response. The negative characteristics, on the other hand, which describe the reflex as involuntary, unconscious, and unlearned, have proceeded from unscientific presuppositions concerning the behavior of organisms. The reflex is tentatively defined herein as an observed correlation of stimulus and response.

V.   Reflex physiology undertakes to describe the events which intervene between a stimulus and a response. The physiological usage does not question the definition of a reflex as a correlation, for the synapse is only a conceptual expression for the "reduced" characteristics of a given correlation.

VI.   The essence of the description of behavior is held to be the determination of functional laws describing the relationship between the forces acting upon, and the movement of, a given system. The reflex is, by definition, the precise instrument for this description. Its analytical nature is discussed, and existing methods of analysis are examined. Current objections to analysis are held to have no scientific meaning.

VII.   The experimental study of the reflex may be divided into two parts. There is, first, the investigation of the characteristics of a correlation —latency, threshold, after-discharge, and the order of variation of S and R. Secondly, there is the investigation of variations in these characteristics as functions of third variables. The notion of reflex strength is useful in dealing with this second group. The question of third variables is of extreme importance in the description of the behavior of intact organisms.

From the point of view of scientific method, any law describing the behavior of organisms must be reducible to one of the forms herein discussed. The description of behavior, that is to say, is adequately embraced by the principle of the reflex.

The Generic Nature of the
Concepts of Stimulus and Response

In extending the concept of the reflex to the behavior of the organism as a whole, it was necessary to abandon the surgical procedures which had traditionally been used to generate "preparations" yielding orderly data. The specification of stimulus and response became a crucial issue. This paper, which appeared in The Journal of General Psychology, *1935, 12, 40-65, was an effort to resolve it by appealing to the lawfulness of changes in reflex strength as a criterion for the specification of properties.*

I

In the description of behavior it is usually assumed that both behavior and environment may be broken into parts, which may be referred to by name, and that these parts will retain their identity from experiment to experiment. If this assumption were not in some sense justified, a science of behavior would be impossible; but it is not immediately clear to what extent it is supported by our observations. The analysis of behavior is not an act of arbitrary subdividing, and we cannot define the concepts of stimulus and response quite as simply as "parts of behavior and environment" without taking account of the natural lines of fracture along which behavior and environment actually break.

If we could confine ourselves to the elicitation of a reflex upon a single occasion, this difficulty would not arise. The complete description of such an event would present a technical problem only; and, if no limit were placed upon apparatus, an adequate account of what might be termed the stimulus and the response could in most cases be given. The advantage would be that we should be free of the question of *what* we were describing. But when we insist upon a reproducible unit, as we cannot help doing if we are to have a science of behavior, the account of a single elicitation, no matter how perfect, is inadequate. For it is very difficult to find a stimulus and response which maintain precisely the same properties upon two successive occasions. The possible (and very rare) exceptions to this rule concern only very simple stimulating forces acting upon simple (and usually simplified) preparations. In the intact and unhampered organism (to which our laws must, eventually at least, apply) most stimuli are subject to the momentary orientation of receptors or to similar factors; and especially where the stimulus is selected through the action of prepotency (which is the case in the greater part of normal behavior), it is extremely difficult to give any clear account of how the stimulating energies are going to act. The reasons are not quite the same on the side of the response, since the stimulus-response relationship is not symmetrical, but the rule is equally well obeyed. Even in such a relatively simple example as the flexion reflex, two successive responses will be found to differ widely if the character of the movement is closely enough examined.

We are accustomed to deal with this problem by main force. We confine our study to a reflex in which the response is originally of a very simple sort or may be easily simplified (flexion, for example, or salivation) and in which the stimulus is of a convenient form, may be localized sharply, and is applied, rather than selected through prepotency. It is easier to restrict the stimulus than the response, since the stimulus presents itself as the independent variable, but we are able by technical means to control some of the properties of the response also. In this way we devise a sort of reproducibility; that is to say, we are frequently able to describe a restricted preparation in which a stimulus is correlated with a response and all properties of both terms are capable of specification within a satisfactorily narrow range.

For many purposes a preparation of this kind may be an adequate solution of the problem of reproducibility. As we shall see later, some degree of restriction is probably always required before successful experimentation can be carried on. But severe restriction must be rejected as a general solution. It necessarily implies an arbitrary unit, which does not fully correspond to the material originally under investigation because its exact character depends in part upon the selection of properties. Likewise, it is not a solution which can be extended to a very large number of reflexes. Above all, it suppresses, by virtue of the very act of restriction, an important characteristic of the typical reflex. It is with this last objection that we shall be especially concerned.

II

One way to show the inadequacy of the restricted preparation is to determine how much of either the stimulus or the response is essential or relevant to the correlation between them. In a preparation of the flexion reflex we are able, by reason of certain technical restrictions, to state a correlation between two terms fairly completely described. But on the side of the stimulus we must admit that, so far as a mere correlation is concerned, the exact location which we have given is unimportant—that the correlation could be shown even though the stimulus were applied elsewhere within a rather wide range. Similarly, we need not specify the form of the energy (whether it is heat, for example, or pressure, or electric current) or the duration of its administration or its amount within rather wide limits. A reduction to terms of afferent nervous impulses would eliminate part of the problem of the form of energy but not that of the irrelevance of the other properties. On the side of the response, likewise, we need not specify the rate or degree of flexion; and if we have not simplified, we cannot specify the exact direction or, having simplified, we cannot justify the selection of one direction as against others. Most of the properties of the two events in the correlation are, so far as the mere elicitation of the reflex is concerned, irrelevant. The only relevant properties are flexion (the reduction of the angle made by adjacent segments of a limb at a given joint) and a given ("noxious") kind of stimulation applied within a rather large area.

If we turn, then, from the exact reproducibility of stimulus and response to the criterion of simple elicitability, we arrive at nothing more than a correlation of two defining properties. In ordinary practice these properties alone maintain their identify from experiment to experiment. But it would be inconvenient to regard a reflex as a correlation of properties. We cannot produce one defining property at a given elicitation without giving incidental values to the non-defining properties which compose the rest of the event. A stimulus or a response is an *event,* that is to say, not a property; and we must turn, therefore, to a definition on the principle of classes. Accordingly, if we are to continue to regard the flexion reflex as a single entity, both the stimulus and the response must be taken (tentatively, at least) as class terms, each of which embraces an indefinitely large number of particular stimuli or responses but is sufficiently well defined by the specification of one or two properties.

The alternative to acknowledging this generic nature is to argue that every possible restricted correlation is an independent unit in itself. On this hypothesis there are practically an infinite number of flexion reflexes, corresponding to the product of the number of ways in which an effective stimulus can be applied into the number of particular responses which can be obtained through different methods of restriction. We may contrast these two views by saying that either a reflex is a broad term expressing the correlation of a class of stimuli with a class of responses (where the reproducibility of non-defining properties is unimportant) or it applies to any one of a group of particular correlations (where the terms have been severely restricted to obtain the reproducibility of all properties). In the second case we may still group our specific correlations together on the basis of a defining property without implying the functionally generic nature of either stimulus or response: even if there are practically an infinite number of flexion reflexes, for example, they all have something in common not shared by any other, in that their responses are examples of flexion. If we wish to assign the term reflex for the moment to a group of this sort, rather than to a particular example, our problem may be stated in the following form: is a reflex a correlation of classes or a class of correlations?

There is a statement of the subject which differs only slightly from the present (although it is much less flexible), in which what we have called the irrelevance of the non-defining properties of a stimulus is expressed by speaking of a group of stimuli, all of which are *equivalent* in the elicitation of a response. The kind of proof usually given for this view is based upon the fact that in the process of conditioning (Pavlov's type) a new reflex is created. It is then possible to prove the irrelevance of certain properties (or the equivalence of stimuli) in the following way. Let a conditioned reflex be established to a light, for example, which is so placed that only a limited region in the retina of one eye is illuminated. Then it may be shown that, after the conditioning is complete, a beam of light striking other parts of either retina will elicit the response. The effectiveness of the newly conditioned stimulus is independent of the property of location, and so far as the simple correlation of stimulus and response is concerned, we need not specify its location in our description, at least within wide limits. We may also find that the properties of brilliance, hue, shape, and size may not be significant over considerable ranges, and that the only important properties are, indeed, those denoted roughly by "spot" and "light." Here, then, we have a class of stimuli, defined by two properties, the members of which are equivalent so far as the elicitation of a response is concerned.

The advantage in using a conditioned reflex lies in being able to show that members of the group differing from the particular stimulus used for conditioning cannot be eliciting responses "on their own account" since they were not able to do so before the conditioning was set up. But unfortunately this proof is of limited scope. It is not easily applied to the case of the response and is of no value for unconditioned reflexes or conditioned reflexes the history of which is not known. An infinitely large number of stimuli may, through the use of conditioning, be made to evoke the same response (a spot of light and a tone, for example, may both elicit salivation), but there need be no common property among them except that of being a stimulus, which is not in itself a property which guarantees the effectiveness of an untried stimulus known to possess it. The "equivalence" of a spot of light and a tone is the product of an experimental procedure and is clearly not the equivalence found in the case of two spots of light; but the ability to elicit a common response does not distinguish between the two sorts, and no distinction is, as we have said, possible when we do not know the history of the organism.

A better proof, which is applicable to all cases, makes use of the secondary laws of the reflex [see page 502]. It is often true in the investigation of these laws that the *number* of elicitations of a reflex is important, as, for example, when we are measuring a rate. It is then possible to test the irrelevance of a non-defining property by showing that two responses, one of which possesses the property, the other not, contribute equally well to a total number. Suppose that we are studying the behavior of such an organism as a rat in pressing a lever. The number of distinguishable acts on the part of the rat which will give the required movement of the lever is indefinite and very large. Except for certain rare cases they constitute a class, which is sufficiently well-defined by the phrase "pressing the lever." Now it may be shown that under various circumstances the rate of responding is significant—that is to say, it maintains itself or changes in lawful ways.[1] But the responses which contribute to this total number-per-unit-time are not identical. They are selected at random from the whole class—that is, by circumstances which are independent of the conditions determining the rate. Not only, therefore, are the members of the class all equally elicitable by the stimulation arising from the lever, they are *quantitatively mutually replaceable*. The uniformity of the change in rate excludes any supposition that we are dealing with a group of separate reflexes and forces the conclusion that "pressing the lever" behaves experimentally as a unitary thing.

An almost parallel argument could be made from the same data on the side of the stimulus, yielding a stimulus-class sufficiently well denoted for our present purposes by the term *lever*. The proof by appeal to secondary laws is much stronger than the argument for equivalence of stimuli based upon the behavior of newly conditioned reflexes. It is of general validity and goes beyond the use of mere "ability to elicit" to a quantitative measure. Thus in our test case we could distinguish between the separate correlations of a single response with a tone and a spot of light by showing,

[1] The original paper referred here to several experimental reports later included in *The Behavior of Organisms*.

for example, that the extinction of one of them does not modify the state of the other.

An exception may be taken to this last example on the ground that there will probably be *some* influence between the two, and this brings us abruptly to an important point. The argument on the basis of secondary laws would be unanswerable if it were as clear-cut as we have given it, and it would decide the question clearly on the side of the reflex as a correlation of two generic terms rather than as a class of distinct correlations or any one member of such a class. But unfortunately the argument must be qualified, and in such a way as to strengthen the opposite view. For it is true that the non-defining properties are often not wholly negligible and that the members of our classes are consequently not exactly mutually replaceable. On the side of the response, of which we have less control, our data will not show this in most cases because of the present lack of precision. But it is certain that there are outlying members of a class which have not a full substitutive power; that is to say, there are "flexions" and "pressings" which are so unusual because of other properties that they do not fully *count as such*. It ought to be supposed that lesser differences would be significant in a more sensitive test. If we should examine a large number of responses leading to the movement of the lever, most of these would be relatively quite similar, but there would be smaller groups set off by distinguishing properties and a few quite anomalous responses. It is because of the high frequency of occurrence of the first that they are typical of the response "pressing the lever," but it is also because of this frequency that any lack of effectiveness of atypical responses is not at present sufficiently strongly felt to be noted.

On the side of the stimulus, on the other hand, small differences may be demonstrated. Since we may here control the values of our non-defining properties, we may mass the effect of a given example. Thus we can show that in the flexion reflex fatigue from one locus of stimulation does not result in complete fatigue of the reflex from another locus. Here we have segregated particular stimuli into two groups on the basis of the property of location, and have shown the relevance of the property to the course of a secondary change. A similar and very important example of the use of segregation arises in the behavior of the intact organism in the process of discrimination. Suppose we have established a conditioned response to a lever, as in the above example. Upon any one occasion the stimulus is, as we have seen, any member of an indefinitely large class of stimuli arising from the lever and the surrounding parts of the apparatus. It is possible to control some of the properties of these members. For example, the lever may be made to stimulate either in the light or in the dark, so that all properties which arise as visible radiation can be introduced or removed at will. We require to show that they are not wholly irrelevant. This may be done by setting up a discrimination, so that the strength of the response to the lever-plus-light remains at a given (say, nearly maximal) value, while the strength of the response to the lever alone declines to another value (say, nearly zero). Although a discrimination of this sort is in part the development of a distinction which did not originally exist, it can be shown that some significance originally attached to the differentiating property.[2]

In either of these cases if we had allowed the stimulus to vary at random with respect to the non-defining property, we should have obtained reasonably smooth curves for the secondary process, according to our present standards of smoothness. It is only by separating the stimuli into groups that we can show their lack of complete equivalence. But once having shown this, we can no longer disregard the importance of the property, even in the absence of grouping. A similar argument would apply, of course, if our criterion were simply ability to elicit. Here the relevance of non-defining properties (or lack of equivalence) can perhaps be shown only at near-threshold states of the reflex, since the measure is all-or-none and therefore crude, but we cannot assume that at other states a similar relevance would not be detected with a more sensitive measure. In neither case have we a clear indication that the argument for a generic definition is wholly valid.

In regarding every discrete correlation as a separate entity, both of the above proofs may be explained away by appeal to "induction"—a process through which a change in the state of one reflex is said to induce a similar change in the state of another. The apparent mutual replaceability of a number of flexion reflexes in the course of a secondary change is explained by holding that something done to one of them (in fatigue, for example) is done to others also through induction. The principle is obviously designed to deal with the effects we have just appealed to, and it has the advantage that where the argument for equivalence or a generic term falls short of complete experimental support, the argument for induction is strengthened: for it might be expected that a mutual influence of this sort would be only partial, as it proves to be, and would, moreover, depend upon the degree of community of properties, as it can be shown to depend. On the other hand induction is under the present circumstances clearly an

---

[2] Here again, reference was made to experiments later reported in *The Behavior of Organisms*.

ad hoc device, and its use should lead us to suspect the view that every particular correlation is a discrete and autonomous entity.

We have, in short, no clear basis for choosing either of these two views, and the decision we are likely to make is free to follow our personal prejudices. If we are interested in the physiological events mediating a reflex we shall very probably want to deal with severely restricted preparations and we shall be willing to explain away the proofs for the generic nature of the reflex by bringing in the device of induction. If, on the other hand, we are interested in the behavior of the intact organism, where restriction is much more difficult and in many cases impossible unless the material is seriously disturbed, we shall be anxious to prove the irrelevance of non-defining properties and shall want to define our unit without respect to them. But it ought to be clear from our failure to find a valid proof for either of these extreme views that the truth lies between them. There is no reason why a clear definition of a unit of this sort is not possible in our present state of knowledge. The problem of definition is, after all, an experimental one, and the entities which we are to use in the description of behavior are experimental entities. We have placed ourselves at a great disadvantage in trying to find among our data evidence for a preconceived term, when our primary concern ought to be simply with putting the data in order; and we may well suspend for a moment the question of the nature of these terms and turn directly to an examination of the available experimental material.

III

1. One fact which seems to be sufficiently well established is that there are defining properties. Nothing we have considered of the importance of non-defining properties modifies this in the least, nor are we prejudging the present issue, since a property may be taken, as we have seen, to define either one reflex or a class of reflexes. A defining property appears on the side of the response in the first step toward what is called the discovery of a reflex. Some aspect of behavior is observed to occur repeatedly under general stimulation, and we assign a name to it which specifies (perhaps not explicitly) a defining property. Our control over the response is almost exclusively of this sort—specification. We have the refusal of all responses not falling within the class we have set up. Since we are completely free in this first choice, it is easy to select a wrong defining property, but the following steps cannot then be taken successfully. When a defining property has been decided upon, the stimuli which elicit responses possessing

it are discovered by exploration. One stimulus may be enough to demonstrate the sort of correlation sought for, but (either deliberately or through lack of control) the properties are usually varied in later elicitations and other members of the class thus added. Subsequently the defining property of the stimulus is inferred from the part common to the different stimuli which are thus found to be effective.

There must be defining properties on the sides of *both* stimulus and response; otherwise our classes will have no necessary reference to real aspects of behavior. If the flexion reflex is allowed to be defined simply as the class of all reflexes having flexion as a response (or as a reflex having for its response a class defined by flexion), there is nothing to prevent the definition of an infinite number of reflexes upon similar bases. For example, we could say that there is a reflex or class of reflexes defined by this property: that in the elicitation the center of gravity of the organism moves to the north. Such a class is experimentally useless, since it brings together quite unrelated activities. But we must be ready to show that all flexions are related in a way in which all movements of the center of gravity are not, and to do this we must appeal to the observed fact that all flexions are elicitable by stimuli of a few classes. As soon as this relation is apparent our tentative response-class begins to take on experimental reality as a characteristic of the behavior of the organism.

It is difficult, however, to say precisely what defining properties are. We frequently define the stimulus by the very doubtful property of its ability to elicit the response in question rather than by any independent property of the stimulus itself. Thus, in the behavior of the unhampered organism with respect to some object in its environment, we often cannot describe the actual stimulating energies, but we assume that, whenever a response is elicited, some member of the class of effective stimuli has acted. Similarly in the flexion reflex the basis for our definition of the property "noxious" is probably only the effectiveness of a certain form of energy in eliciting a response. It is always implied, of course, that a parallel definition in terms peculiar to the stimulus can be given. An exception is the case already noted of the type of conditioned reflex in which we cannot define the stimulus except by ability-to-elicit or by appeal to the history of the organism. Fortunately we do not reverse the direction of this argument and define a response as any behavior elicited by a given stimulus. Behavior is less under experimental control than environment, and it would be more difficult to detect a significant correlation in that direction. But at this level of analysis the response is seldom clearly defined in *any* way. A rigorous definition without regard to non-defining properties is, in fact, probably impossible because, as we have seen, the defining property can be made to fail by taking extreme values of other properties. Nor are the actual members of either class ever exhaustively investigated; so that it may be said that these broad terms are defined neither by specification of properties nor by enumeration.

2. Aside from avoiding a wrong defining property, which will not yield a correlation with a single stimulus-class, we have a certain freedom in specifying the response. By including other non-defining properties in our specification we may set up other and less comprehensive classes, for which corresponding stimulus-classes may be found. The latter will be less comprehensive also since, as we have seen, the stimulus-class which we arrive at is always closely adjusted to the response. For example, if we begin with "flexion in a specific direction only," we obtain a stimulus-class embracing a smaller stimulating area. Now, there is nothing to prevent our taking such a restricted unit at the start, so long as for any such class a stimulus-class may be found, and if a restricted unit is taken first the very broadest term can be arrived at only by removing restrictions.

Our second experimental fact is that within the class given by a defining property we may set up subclasses through the arbitrary restriction of other properties. This procedure yields a series of responses, generated by progressive restriction, each member of which possesses a corresponding stimulus in a more or less parallel series. At one end we approach as a limit the correlation of a completely specified response and a stimulus which is not necessarily strictly constant but may be held so experimentally. If at this point both terms are in fact unit classes, one part of our problem vanishes, since with a perfectly restricted preparation there is no practical difference between a class of correlations and a correlation of classes. But this state is, as we have argued, probably always impractical and in any event never fully representative. Our interest in it here is as an ideal limit. The other end of the series, the unrestricted class, we have also seen to be ideal, so that any experimentally valid unit must be sought for among the partially restricted entities lying between these extremes.

In speaking of a *series* generated by restriction we are, of course, using too simple a term. Our technique of restriction must respect the defining property, but that is our only important limitation. Through the selection of different non-defining properties we may set up different restricted entities within a single class; for example, in restricting the flexion reflex by fixing the locus of stimulation, we may obtain separate entities by selecting different loci. There is no unique set of non-defining properties peculiar to a given defining property, and we have to deal, not with a single series, but with a complex set of ramifications from a single virtual source, approaching as limits an indefinite number of different completely restricted entities.

Part of the difficulty of definition which we encounter in dealing with a single defining property (point 1 above) may disappear in the partially restricted preparation. Usually the first restrictions are designed to protect the defining property by excluding extreme cases. They clarify the definition and add weight to the expressed correlation with a stimulus-class. In general, as we progressively restrict, our description comes to include more and more of the two events and is consequently so much the more successful. At the same time a greater and greater restriction of the stimulus-class is demanded, so that the increase in the validity and completeness of the correlation is paid for with added experimental effort.

3. Our third fact is induction, which it is now possible for us to demonstrate without raising the question of a unit. We have seen that it is possible to obtain various kinds of entities within a single class through the restriction of non-defining properties and that many of these may exist at the same time. They are experimentally real and operable, and there can be shown between two given examples some degree of mutual influence of the sort we have already examined. A change taking place in one of them is found to have taken place also in the other. The only important rule of induction that we need to note is that the extent of the mutual influence is a function of the degree to which the entities possess their non-defining properties in common. We shall not review other information in any detail. The literature is very large, especially if we include (as we rightfully may) all work on discrimination. It is an important field of analysis, although its relation to the problem of the definition of a reflex has usually not been made clear.

4. In turning to induction we have necessarily taken up new criteria. Classes or subclasses may be demonstrated simply by showing correlations of stimuli and responses and by listing the properties of these events, but the influences exerted by one restricted entity upon another are felt principally in the course of secondary changes. Our fourth point is that, in the measurement of these more advanced aspects of a correlation, movement along a series in the direction of a completely restricted entity is accompanied by an increase in the simplicity and consistency of our data. If we are measuring fatigue, for example, we shall not obtain too smooth a curve if our stimulus varies in such a way as to produce at one time one direction of flexion and at another time another; but as we restrict our stimulus to obtain a less variable response, the smoothness of the curve increases.

This is not really a separate point but rather a special case of point 3. In such a secondary process as fatigue or extinction we are examining the effect of one elicitation upon another following it. But this is only induction, since we are not yet assuming any kind of identity from one occasion to another. We look for this effect to follow the main rule of induction: it will be a function of the degree of community of properties. In a completely restricted preparation we should therefore have complete induction, since two successive elicitations would be identical. Each elicitation would have its full effect upon a secondary change, and the curve for the secondary change would be smooth. But if we are using only a partially restricted entity, successive elicitations need not have identically the same properties, and secondary processes may or may not be advanced full steps through induction. From our third point, therefore, we could have deduced a form of the fourth, namely, that an improvement in data follows from any change which makes successive elicitations more likely to resemble each other.

5. If induction followed properties quite literally and without prejudice, its study would not add anything to our knowledge of the relationship between two entities which we could not infer from a comparison of properties alone. But properties are not all equally important so far as the induction between two members is concerned. The structure we have set up has so far been based solely on community of properties. Any distinction whatsover between responses has been allowed, so long as the test of correlation with a stimulus-class was forthcoming. Now, it may have been noticed that an attempt to distinguish between two response-classes on the basis of some property has failed. It may not have been possible to find two corresponding stimulus-classes which elicited them separately. But if we have one stimulus-class corresponding with two response-classes, we cannot be sure of confirming either correlation on a given occasion to the exclusion of the other. We must conclude, therefore, that the property upon which the two classes have been distinguished is not effective. This variable importance comes out clearly in the study of induction, and it is important enough to be stated separately as our fifth point.

The most general form of the rule, in agreement with the present ordering of experimental data, is as follows: practically complete induction may prevail between two entities differing even widely with respect to some non-defining properties. As we have just seen, it may be stated in relation to our second point in this way: some non-defining properties do not establish subclasses. A more limited expression, which takes the form of a qualification of point 4, is as follows: as we proceed with the gradual restriction of a preparation, noting a corresponding improvement in the consistency of our data, the point at which an adequate consistency is reached does not coincide with the final complete restriction of all properties of the preparation. The proofs for this very important rule (especially the proof by appeal to secondary laws) have been given above in arguing for the generic nature of the reflex, and we shall not need to repeat them. We are now, however, including some non-defining properties in the terms to which they apply, and we therefore avoid the objections previously raised. In fact, it will be apparent that we have based our selection of non-defining properties upon just the criterion appealed to in those objections—namely, completeness of induction.

This is a practical rule, which does not pretend to go beyond the limits of our present degree of precision. But its main features are too well marked to be seriously disturbed under limiting conditions. A practical consistency may appear at such a relatively unrestricted level—and, as one might say, so suddenly—that extrapolation to complete consistency appears to fall far short of complete restriction. It would be idle to consider the possibility of details which have at present no experimental reality or importance. It may be that the location of the spot of light or the identity of the muscle-fibres which contract as the lever is pressed are somehow significant up to the point of complete specification; but we are here interested only in the degree of consistency which can be obtained while they are still by no means completely determined. This consistency is so remarkable that it promises very little improvement from further restriction.

As a matter of fact, when we have reached the point at which orderly secondary changes appear, we cannot go beyond it with further restriction without destroying this desired result. In the example of the lever, we may obtain smooth curves by restricting up to a certain point only; if we further limit the response by excluding all examples except those of one given kind (pressing with a certain muscle-group, for example), we destroy our curves by eliminating many instances contributing to them. The set of properties which gives us "pressing the lever" is uniquely determined; specifying either fewer or more will destroy the consistency of the result obtained. This follows naturally from the nature of our control over response specification and refusal to accept.

IV

These, then, are the important aspects of the analysis of behavior which bear upon the definition of a unit. We have listed them, not in relation to a definition, but in the order in which they appear in actual experimentation. But the problem of definition has now been practically solved. We have arrived at a structure of entities having an experimental foundation, and we have only to decide to what part of it we are to assign the term *reflex*.

The two extreme views with which we began may be related to the present result without difficulty. The extreme generic view is that a stimulus or a response is the whole class given by a defining property. But we have seen that this is probably never sharply defined without appeal to secondary properties, and its members are never exhaustively investigated. As a structure it may become prodigious: in the behavior of the intact organism the number of subclasses which could be set up through discrimination is often practically infinite. This kind of unit yields a sort of reproducibility (that of its defining property), but it is not enough to insure uniform secondary processes. It is not, in short, an experimental concept, and although it might be well to give it a name ("surreflex" for example), we ought to reserve the term *reflex* itself for an observable entity. For the same reason we cannot accept the definition proposed by the extreme particularist; the fully determined entity approached with the technique of restriction is also, as we have seen, ideal. The material which we actually observe, and which exhibits significant uniformity, is the behavior of the preparation restricted to the point of giving simple and consistent data. Here, if anywhere, it will be convenient to apply our term.

We may restrict a preparation for two quite different reasons, either to obtain a greater precision of reference for our terms (so that our description of a response, for example, will describe it more completely and accurately) or to obtain consistent curves for secondary processes. The increase in precision gives a greater authority to our statement of a correlation, which is desirable; but it will not help us in deciding upon a unit. It leads ultimately to a completely restricted entity, which we have seen to be usually unreproducible and otherwise impractical, and to obtain a unit we should be forced to stop at some arbitrary level—for example, at a compromise between precision of reference and the experimental effort of restriction. Our second criterion, the orderliness of secondary processes, gives us, on the other hand, a unit which is in no sense arbitrary. As we have seen, the appearance of smooth curves in secondary processes marks a unique point in the progressive restriction of a preparation, and it is to this uniquely determined entity that the term *reflex* may be assigned. *A reflex, then, is a correlation of a stimulus and a response at a level of restriction marked by the orderliness of changes in the correlation.*

In certain respects this is not as simple a definition as one might wish for. It means that since many equally consistent preparations may be set up within a single class, there will be a large number of reflexes passing under a single name. This may seem to rob the principle of the reflex of much of its simplicity, but it is a necessary consequence of the complexity of the material, which cannot be changed by theoretical considerations. If we shall not be able to refer unequivocally to a single experimental entity with the term *flexion reflex,* at least we may know that this has never really been possible. A great deal of misunderstanding has arisen from the practice of naming reflexes, which an insistence upon a supplementary list of specifications may avoid.

Likewise, it is not necessarily true that the entities resulting from this definition are so uniform that a law based upon one example will have complete generality. A certain latitude is allowed by our present degree of precision. It is not always easy to prove from the degree of orderliness of a change that a significant property is not varying at random, although the presence of such a variable will probably affect the shape of the curve for the change. Aside from this matter of precision, it is also probable that preparations having different controlled values of a given property will yield different curves. In the case of restriction through the removal of properties (where this is possible), we have a series of preparations of increasing simplicity and of increasing ease of control but not necessarily of increasing constancy. We should not expect an increase in smoothness along such a series, but it is probable that the nature of a curve will show a change. These are, however, experimental questions and our only present task (formulation) has been sufficiently well carried out. Our definition is not, in any event, dependent upon the generality of the laws obtained with a single example, although the greatest possible generality is obviously desirable.

In deciding upon this definition we choose simplicity or consistency of data against exact reproducibility as our ultimate criterion, or rather we temper the extent to which exact reproducibility is to be demanded and use the consistency of our data in our defense. This would be only good scientific method if we were not forced to it for other reasons. To insist upon the constancy of properties which can be shown not to affect the measurements in hand is to make a fetish of exactitude. It is obvious why this has so often been done. What is wanted is the "necessary and sufficient" correlation of a stimulus and a response. The procedure recommended by the present analysis is to discover the defining properties of a stimulus and a response and to express the correlation in terms of classes. The usual expedient has been to hold all properties of a given instance constant so far as this is possible. In a successful case all properties *seem* to be relevant because they invariably occur upon all occasions. (It is almost as if, faced with the evident irrelevance of many properties, we had invented the highly restricted preparation to make them relevant.) In giving a complete account of an arbitrarily restricted preparation, we describe at the same time too little and too much. We include material irrelevant to our principal datum, so that part of our description is superfluous, and we deliberately ignore the broader character of the stimulus and the response. The complete description of one act of pressing a lever would have very little usefulness, since most of the information would be irrelevant to the fact of elicitation, with which we are chiefly concerned, and would tell us nothing about the set of properties yielding a consistent result.

We do not, of course, avoid or wish to avoid restriction. It is an indispensable device, for it has the merit of holding a defining property constant even though the property has not been indentified. Until we have discovered a defining property, it is necessary to resort to restriction to guarantee ultimate validity. And since, as we have seen, it is often difficult to designate defining properties clearly, especially where extreme values of other properties interfere, some measure of precautionary restriction is usually necessary. It is not often obvious that it is being used. We have spoken of the number of ways in which a lever may stimulate a rat and the number of ways in which the rat may respond. We should find it very difficult to define either of these classes without considerable precautionary restriction of essentially non-defining properties—concerning the size of the lever and so on. The use of a uniform lever from experiment to experiment is in itself a considerable act of restriction and is apparently necessary to assure a consistent result.

Assigning the term *reflex* to the entities in this part of our structure means, of course, that the reflex is a generic term. That is to say, the "stimulus" and the "response" entering into a given correlation are not to be identified with particular instances appearing upon some given occasion but with classes of such instances. In this sense the generic view has been borne out as against the autonomy of the completely restricted preparation. This is perhaps the most important characteristic of the definition. Freedom from the requirement of complete reproducibility broadens our field of operation immeasurably. We are no longer limited to the very few preparations in which some semblance of completeness is to be found, for we are able to define "parts of behavior and environment" having experimental reality and reproducible in their own fashion. In particular the behavior of the intact organism is made available for study with an expectation of precision comparable with that of the classical spinal preparation. (Indeed, if smoothness of curve is to be taken as an ultimate criterion, the intact organism often shows much greater consistency than the usual spinal preparation, even though the number of uncontrolled non-defining properties is much smaller in the latter case. That is to say, the generic character is more marked in reflexes peculiar to the intact organism.)

V

The generic nature of stimulus and response is in no sense a justification for the broader terms of the popular vocabulary. We may lay it down as a general rule that no property is a valid defining property of a class until its experimental reality has been demonstrated. This excludes a great many terms commonly brought into the description of behavior. For example, suppose that it be casually observed that a child hides when confronted with a dog. Then it may be said, in an uncritical extension of the terminology of the reflex, that the dog is a stimulus and hiding a response. It is obvious at once that the word *hiding* does not refer to a unique set of movements nor *dog* to a unique set of stimulating forces. In order to make these terms validly descriptive of behavior it is necessary to define the classes to which they refer. It must be shown what properties of a stimulus give it a place in the class "dog" and what property of a response makes it an instance of "hiding." (It will not be enough to dignify the popular vocabulary by appealing to essential properties of "dogness" and "hiding-ness" and to suppose them intuitively known.) The resulting classes will meanwhile have been shown to be correlated experimentally, but it ought also to be shown that secondary changes in the correlation are lawful. It is not at all certain that the properties we should thus find to be significant are those now supposedly referred to by the words *dog* and *hiding,* even after allowing for the vagueness inevitable in a popular term.

For reasons to be noted shortly, the existence of a popular term does create some presumption in favor of the existence of a corresponding experimentally real concept. But this does not free us from the necessity of defining the class and of demonstrating the reality if the term is to be used for scientific purposes. It has still to be shown that most of the terms borrowed from the popular vocabulary are validly descriptive—that they lead to a consistent and reproducible experimentation. We cannot legitimately assume that "riding a bicycle," "seeing one's friends," or "heart-break" are responses in any scientific sense.

This restriction upon the use of the popular vocabulary in behaviorism is often not felt because the partial legitimacy of the popular term frequently results in some experimental consistency. The experimenter is more likely than not to hit upon experimentally real terms, and he may have some private set of properties resulting from his own training which will serve. Thus the word *hiding* may always be used *by him* in connection with events having certain definite properties, and his own results will be consistent by virtue of this definition *per accidens*. But it is a mistake for him to suppose that these properties are communicated in his use of the popular term. If no more accurate supplementary specification is given, the difficulty will become apparent whenever his experiments are repeated by someone with another set of private defining properties and will be the greater the wider the difference in background of the two experimenters.

We are here very close to a problem in epistemology, which is inevitable in a field of this sort. For the relation of organism to environment with which we are primarily concerned must be supposed to include the special case of the relation of scientist to subject-matter. If we contemplate an eventually successful general extension of our methods, we must suppose ourselves to be describing an activity of which describing itself is one manifestation. It is necessary to raise this epistemological point in order to explain why it is that popular terms so often refer to what are later found to be experimentally real entities. The reason is that such terms are in themselves responses of a generic sort: they are the responses of the populace of which the experimenter is a member. Consequently, when the organism under investigation fairly closely resembles man (for example, when it is a dog), the popular term may be very close to the experimentally real entity. We may hit immediately upon the right property of the stimulus, not because we have manipulated it experimentally in the manner described above, but because we ourselves react in a measure similarly to the dog. On the other hand, if the organism is, let us say, an ant or an amoeba, it is much more difficult to detect the "real" stimulus without experimentation. If it were not for this explanation, the partial legitimacy of the popular term would be a striking coincidence, which might be used (and indeed has been used) as an argument for the admission of a special method (such as "empathy") into the study of behavior. In insisting that no amount of reality in the popular terms already examined will excuse us from defining a new term experimentally if it is to be used at all, we are of course rejecting any such process. Our rule that the generic term may be used only when its experimental reality has been verified will not admit the possibility of an ancillary principle, available in and peculiar to the study of behavior, leading to the definition of concepts through some other means than the sort of experimental procedure here outlined.

VI

Throughout this discussion we have kept to our intention of dealing with the reflex and its associated processes solely at the level of behavior. We have made no reference to intermediating events in the central nervous system, and, here as elsewhere, this has apparently not caused the slightest inconvenience. But the reader may feel that the present case has involved a special difficulty: the definition we arrive at may seem to be logical or statistical rather than physiological. To take a simple example, what we should call the defining property of a stimulus is actually the logical product of all observed instances. This is easily said, so far as a consideration of the stimulus is concerned; but when we come to deal with what this means in terms of a central nervous system, it is much more difficult.

The answer of the student of behavior ought to be that this is not his problem. He is interested in a set of concepts adapted to the description of behavior. The notion of a class or of a defining property is justified in a description of this sort because, so far as behavior is concerned, all problems arising from its use are soluble. We have techniques available for demonstrating defining properties, for showing the relative importance of non-defining properties, and for measuring induction. The problem of discrimination, with its subsidiary problem of the establishment of new classes (or, in a broad sense, concepts), can be formulated equally well without reference to a central nervous system. And if these are real aspects of behavior (if nothing has gone wrong in our analysis), they must also be aspects of the activity of the central nervous system, which it is the business of the reflex physiologist to discover—through some other means, incidentally, than inference from behavior. This is a division of labor which ought to be as pleasing to the physiologist as to the behaviorist. A rigorous formulation of the present problem at the level of behavior should be the most desirable starting point for a physiological study and is a necessary condition for the eventual synthesis of the two fields.

VII. Summary

1. In breaking behavior and environment into parts for the sake of description, we cannot take a single instance of the elicitation of a response as a unit because it is not a fully reproducible entity. The usual solution of this problem through forced simplification is inadequate.

2. In a reflex preparation the observed correlation is never between all properties of both stimulus and response. Some properties are irrelevant.

The relevant properties are accordingly taken to define classes, and the reflex is regarded as a correlation of generic terms. The alternative view is that every possible correlation of a particular stimulus and a particular response is a unit in itself. One argument against this alternative, frequently offered in support of the notion of "equivalence of stimuli," is incomplete. A better proof of the generic view is based upon the secondary laws of the reflex. If smooth curves can be obtained in secondary changes while the stimulus and response vary in composition with respect to given properties, these properties may legitimately be regarded as non-defining. In the examples given, however, the non-defining properties can be shown in several ways to be not wholly irrelevant. This failure adds weight to the alternative view, but the device used to explain away the proofs for the generic view makes the particular unit equally doubtful as an autonomous entity.

3. The observed facts are: (*a*) that there are defining properties (not rigorously described) which establish gross classes of stimuli and responses; (*b*) that by specifying other properties we may set up other and less comprehensive classes in a progressive series or set of ramifications extending from the gross class to completely restricted entities (the latter not necessarily operable); (*c*) that between any two members of such a family we may demonstrate induction and show that it is a function of the degree to which the entities possess their properties in common; (*d*) that in restricting a preparation we obtain greater consistency of result because, from (*c*), we make two successive elicitations more likely to resemble each other; but (*e*) that some properties are largely irrelevant so far as induction is concerned, so that in the progressive restriction of a preparation a point may be reached beyond which further restriction does not yield an improvement in consistency and may yield the opposite.

4. These phenomena, properly considered, lead to a definition of stimulus and response. Both extremes of a series of preparations are non-experimental. There is only one other point in such a series uniquely determined: that at which smooth curves for secondary processes are obtainable. A reflex is accordingly defined as a correlation of a stimulus and a response at a level of restriction marked by the orderliness of changes in the correlation. If this is not an ideally simple definition, it is at least in accord with our data. It is based upon consistency of result rather than exact reproducibility; and it utilizes restriction only in moderation.

5. The generic nature of stimulus and response is not a justification for the use of a popular term until it has been defined experimentally. The

objection is not often felt because the popular term may have some legitimacy, due to the fact that the term is itself a generic response—of the populace. Its partial legitimacy is consequently no coincidence, nor an argument for the admission of a principle peculiar to the study of behavior which will allow for the definition of concepts through other than experimental means.

Two Types of Conditioned Reflex
and a Pseudo-type

The principle of conditioning had been advanced by Pavlov to explain all learned behavior. Many American psychologists, particularly the behaviorists, had come to use the term in the same comprehensive sense. But an act acquired through what Thorndike called "Law of Effect" learning could not be interpreted as a conditioned reflex without straining the Pavlovian notion of signalization or substitution of stimuli. The following paper pointed out that a reinforcement may have two kinds of effects. Both of them may be called learning, but only one follows the Pavlovian pattern. In listing differences between the two types, I was still trying to preserve the notion of the reflex, with its eliciting stimulus. The types were distinguished, however, in terms of temporal and other kinds of relations among observable events, and the distinction survived the later revision discussed on page 535. The paper appeared in The Journal of General Psychology *(1935, 12, 66-77) and is reprinted by permission.*

A conditioned reflex is said to be conditioned in the sense of being dependent for its existence or state upon the occurrence of a certain kind of event, having to do with the presentation of a reinforcing stimulus. A definition which includes much more than this simple notion will probably not be applicable to all cases. At almost any significant level of analysis a distinction must be made between at least two major types of conditioned reflex. These may be represented, with examples, in the following way (where S = stimulus, R = response, $(S—R)$ = reflex, $\rightarrow$ = "is followed by," and [ ] = "the strength of" the inclosed reflex):

TYPE I

$$S_0 \text{——————} R_0 \text{——————} \rightarrow S_1 \text{——————} R_1$$

(A) lever ——— pressing   food ——— salivation, eating
(B)   " ———   "   shock ——— withdrawal, emotional change

Given such a sequence, where $[S_1—R_1] \neq 0$, conditioning occurs as a change in $[S_0—R_0]$—an increase in strength (positive conditioning) in (*a*) and a decrease (negative conditioning) in (*b*).[1]

[1] Later, in *The Behavior of Organisms*, the reality of a decrease in (*b*) was questioned.

525

TYPE II

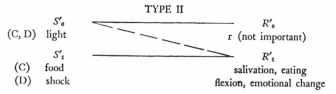

	S'_0		R'_0
(C, D)	light		r (not important)
	S'_1		R'_1
(C)	food		salivation, eating
(D)	shock		flexion, emotional change

Given the simultaneous or successive presentation of S'_0 and S'_1, where $[S'_1 — R'] \neq o$, conditioning occurs as an increase in $[S'_0 — R'_1]$.

Differences between the types are as follows:

1. In Type I, $S_0 \rightarrow R_0 \rightarrow S_1$, where R_0 necessarily intervenes between the stimuli; in Type II, $S'_0 \rightarrow S'_1$, where R'_0 is ignored.[2] In I, R_0 is important; it becomes the conditioned response. In II, R'_0 is irrelevant (except when it is relevant in another sense by conflicting with R'_1) and may actually disappear.

Since conditioning of the second type may take place even when S'_1 occurs after R'_0, Paradigm II, Example (C), may be written for this case as follows:

light ———————— r ————————→ food ———————— salivation,

when it is identical with I. But the result is not to reduce the two types to a single form. Both kinds of conditioning proceed simultaneously but separately. If r is "turning toward the light," for example, and if the food is withheld until turning takes place, [light — turning] will increase according to I while [light — salivation] will increase according to II. The same result is obtained with negative conditioning. Example (D) gives, upon delaying S'_1,

light ———————— r ————————→ shock ———————— flexion, etc.,

where [light — r] will decrease according to I, while [light — flexion] increases according to II.

In the special case in which R'_0 *and* R'_1 are of the same form, the two kinds can apparently not be separated. If, for example, some unconditioned salivation is supposed to be elicitable by a light,[3] we may substitute "salivation" for r, to obtain

light — salivation I ———————→ food — salivation II.

Both [light — salivation I] and [light — salivation II] will increase, with apparently no possible distinction.[4] This is a very special case and is also in no sense a reduction to a single type.

[2] For convenience we omit the case of simultaneous stimuli in Type II.

[3] See Difference 4 below for this general requirement in Type I.

[4] In *The Behavior of Organisms* the suitability of an autonomic response such as salivation for what is here called Type I conditioning was questioned.

2. In I, $(S_0—R_0)$ occurs normally in the absence of $(S_1—R_1)$, and its strength may be measured without interfering with the reinforcing action of S_1. In II S'_1 must be withheld whenever a measurement of $[S'_0—R'_1]$, the conditioned reflex, is taken, because S'_1 also evokes R'_1. Some amount of extinction necessarily ensues in the second case.

3. Since S'_1 must be withheld in measuring $[S'_0—R'_1]$, R'_1 must be independent of any property of S'_1 not possessed by S'_0. In Example (C) salivation may become attached to the light as a conditioned response of Type II; but seizing, chewing, and swallowing, which are also responses to S'_1, must not be included in the paradigm since they require the presence of parts of S'_1 which cannot be supplied by S'_0.

A special restriction on Paradigm II is therefore necessary. Where S'_0 is of a very simple sort (a tone, for example), the properties possessed in addition to S'_0 by S'_1 are practically equal to S'_1, and we may express the restriction in terms of a general distinction between two kinds of responses. The first kind require no external point of reference in their elicitation or description. Typical examples are: glandular activities (salivation), local muscular responses (flexion, wink, breathing movements, production of sounds), and facilitation and inhibition.[5]

The second kind require points of reference for their elicitation or description which are not supplied by the organism itself, but by the stimulus. Examples are: orientation toward the source of a sound, approaching a light, and touching, seizing, and manipulating objects (such as a lever or food). Our present rule is that responses of the second kind cannot be substituted for R'_1 in Paradigm II, unless S'_0 also supplies the required points of reference.

4. In Type I, $[S_0—R_0] \neq 0$ before conditioning takes place. The reflex-to-be-conditioned must be elicited at least once as an unconditioned "investigatory" reflex. In Type II, $[S'_0—R'_1]$ may begin at zero and usually does. In Type I the *state* of the reflex is "conditioned" by the occurrence of the reinforcing sequence, but its *existence* is not. A distinction between a conditioned and an unconditioned reflex is here less significant, because all examples of the former have necessarily been examples of the latter. There are no exclusively conditioned reflexes in this type.

Since $[S'_0—R'_1]$ may begin at zero, a new reflex may be created in conditioning of the second type. And since practically any stimulus may be attached to R'_1 in Paradigm II, a very large number of new reflexes can

[5] Where conditioned facilitation and inhibition are defined by substituting for R' in Paradigm II the expressions "Incr. $[S''—R'']$" and "Decr. $[S''—R'']$" respectively. (Incr. $=$ "increase in"; Decr. $=$ "decrease in").

thus be derived. Conditioning of Type I, on the other hand, is not a device for increasing the repertory of reflexes; R_0 continues to be elicited by the one stimulus with which it began.

There are three reflexes in Paradigm II, but only two in I.

5. The significant change in Type I may be either an increase or a decrease in strength; in Type II it is an increase only, even when $[S'_0—R'_1]$ does not begin at zero.

In Type I stimuli may be divided into two classes, positively and negatively conditioning, according to whether they produce an increase or decrease when used as reinforcement.[6] The distinction cannot be made in Type II, where a reflex may be negative in another sense (a reflex of "avoidance," for example), but where its strength only increases during conditioning.

6. In Type I the conditioned reflex $(S_0—R_0)$ may be associated with any drive; in Type II the reflex $(S'_0—R'_1)$ is necessarily attached to the drive specified by R'_1.

This point may require some comment. In the present use of the term a drive is an inferred variable of which the strength of a group of reflexes is a function.[7] Hunger, for example, is a variable (H) a change in which is responsible for concurrent changes in the strength (a) of all unconditioned reflexes concerned with the ingestion of food, (b) of all conditioned reflexes (of either type) in which the reinforcing stimulus is concerned with the ingestion of food, and (c) to a much lesser extent of all "investigatory" reflexes. In Paradigm I, Example A (lever—pressing) is originally a function of H to some slight extent under (c) above. After conditioning it varies with H according to (b), over a wide range probably equal to that of any unconditioned reflex under (a). Conditioning of Type I is really the becoming attached to a group of reflexes varying as a function of some drive. This is a much more comprehensive description of the process than to define it as an increase in strength, where the drive is assumed to remain constant at a significant value. But the identity of H in the present case is determined only by our choice of a reinforcing reflex. Given $(S_1—R_1)$ of another drive, say thirst, then $(S_0—R_0)$ will become conditioned by attaching itself to the group varying with thirst, and will not vary with H except to some slight extent under (c).

This is a characteristic wholly lacking in Type II. Here R'_1 is originally part of the unconditioned reflex and the drive to which it belongs is definitely fixed.

---

[6] See footnote 1 on page 525.

[7] Skinner, B. F. Drive and reflex strength: I. *J. Gen. Psychol.*, 1932, 6, 22–37.

7. A minor difference is in the way in which the stimulus-to-be-conditioned usually acts. In Type I, S_0 is usually part of a larger field, and R_0 occurs as the result of the eventual prepotency of S_0 over other stimuli. In Type II, S'_0 is usually suddenly presented to the organism. The significance of this difference, which is not absolute, will appear later.

We shall now consider a third type of relation which involves a discrimination. It may be based upon a conditioned reflex of either type, but we shall begin with I. To establish a discrimination subdivide S_0 into two classes on the basis of a selected property or component member.[8] For example, let the lever stimulate either in the presence of a light (L), when the stimulus may be written as $S_{AB..L..}$ (subscripts indicate properties or components), or in the dark, when the stimulus is $S_{AB..}$ Continue to reinforce the response to one of them, say $S_{AB..L..}$, and extinguish or negatively condition the response to the other by breaking the sequence at S_1 or by introducing an S_1 of the negatively conditioning kind (Difference 5). When this has been done, $[S_{AB..L..}—R_0] > [S_{AB..}—R_0]$. And at any value of the underlying drive such that ($S_{AB..L..}—R_0$) is usually elicited but ($S_{AB}—R_0$) is not, there exists the following condition: given an organism in the presence of $S_{AB..}$ ordinarily unresponsive, the presentation of L will be followed by a response. For the sake of comparison we may set up a paradigm in imitation of II as follows:

The relation between the light and the response to the lever might be called a pseudo-conditioned reflex. It has some of the characteristics of Type II: the original response to the light is irrelevant (Difference 1); the relation may be wholly absent prior to the "conditioning" (Difference 4); it changes in a positive direction only (Difference 5); and the "stimulus" is usually of the presented kind (Difference 7). In all these respects it differs from Type I, although the example is based upon a reflex of that type. In many other respects it differs from both types. A reinforcing reflex is not included in the paradigm, but must be added as a third or fourth reflex. The response is not principally to the light, but to the lever; the light is only a component member of the whole stimulus, and "light—pressing" is not legitimately the expression of a reflex. The

---

[8] Reference was originally made here to a paper describing experiments on discrimination later reported in *The Behavior of Organisms* and to the paper on page 504.

lever cannot be removed to show the conditioned effectiveness of the light as in Type II; instead, the response to the lever alone must be extinguished —a characteristic we have not met before.

In spite of these differences it is often said (in similar cases) that the light becomes the "conditioned stimulus for the response to the lever" just as it becomes the stimulus for salivation. This is a confusion with Type II which obviously arises from a neglect of the extinguished reflex. The relation of pressing the lever to the lever itself is ignored and only the relation to the light taken into account. The lever comes to be treated, not as a source of stimulation, but as part of the apparatus, relevant to the response only for mechanical reasons. When the discrimination is based upon a response not requiring an external point of reference (Difference 3), the chance of this neglect increases enormously. If we substitute "flexion of a leg" for "pressing a lever" (and continue for the moment with Type I), S_0 in Paradigm I is not directly observable; we simply wait until a flexion appears, then reinforce. Having established $(S_0 - R_0)$ as a conditioned reflex of some strength, we subdivide our inferred S_0 as before, extinguish $(S_{AB..} - R_0)$, and reinforce $(S_{AB..L..} - R_0)$. When the discrimination has been set up, we have a condition in which the organism is ordinarily unresponsive but immediately responds with flexion upon presentation of the light.

Our inability to demonstrate S_0 makes it difficult to show the discriminative nature of this relation; but it is by no means impossible to find other grounds, as we may see by comparing it with a true reflex of Type II. Let the presentation of the light be followed by a shock to the foot until the light alone elicits flexion. The resulting reflex is superficially similar to the relation of light and flexion which we have just examined, but fundamentally the two cases are unlike. Assuming that no immediate difference can in fact be detected,[9] we may still show differences by referring forward or backward to the history of the organism. The two relations have been established in different ways and their continued existence depends upon reinforcement from different stimuli. The discriminative relation also varies with an arbitrarily chosen drive, while the conditioned reflex is necessarily attached to the drive to which shock-flexion belongs.

These differences are chiefly due, however, to the use of a conditioned reflex of Type I in setting up the discrimination. In a pseudo-conditioned

---

[9] This is a generous assumption since some evidence for the presence of S_0 can usually be found. A difference in the character of the response might also be shown (in the case of the true reflex it may be accompanied by changes in breathing rate, for example, which would be lacking in the pseudo-reflex).

reflex based upon Type II the distinction is much less sure. Here we are invariably able to neglect the extinguished member because R'_1 is of the kind not requiring an external point of reference (Difference 3), and we can minimize its importance in other ways. Given a conditioned reflex of this kind:

if we establish a discrimination between the tone and the tone-plus-a-light (reinforcing the response to the latter), we obtain the following condition: an organism in the presence of the tone, ordinarily unresponsive, will respond upon presentation of the light. The only difference between this relation and a true reflex of Type II is the extinction of the response to the tone, which is evidence that a discrimination has taken place. The reinforcement of tone and light should condition responses to both of these stimuli; but we observe that the organism is unresponsive in the presence of the tone alone.

Now, this surviving difference may be reduced at will by reducing the significance of S'_0 in the basic reflex of the pseudo-type. If we lower the intensity of the tone or choose another stimulus of a less important kind, we may approach as closely as we please to a conditioned reflex of Type II. We cannot actually reach Type II in this way, but we can easily reach a point at which our pseudo-reflex is identical with any actual experimental example of that type. This is true because some amount of discrimination is practically always involved in cases of Type II. When we put a dog into a stand, present a light and then food, the food reinforces not only the light but the stimulation from the stand. Merely putting the dog into the stand again should elicit salivation according to Paradigm II. In practice this is a disturbing effect, which must be eliminated through extinction. So long as it occurs, any actual case of Type II must be formulated as a pseudo-conditioned reflex. If S_G is the stimulation affecting the organism in addition to S_0, then S_0 in Paradigm II should read $S_G + S_0$. The effect upon S_G is extinguished through lack of reinforcement in the absence of S_0, and the result is a discrimination: an organism in the presence of S_G, ordinarily unresponsive, responds when S_0 is added. The importance of this criticism will depend upon the relative magnitudes of S_G and S_0. In the optimal experiment S_G may be reduced to a value insignificant in comparison with ordinary values of S_0.

The partially discriminative nature of Type II is inevitable. It is not important in Type I because of Difference 1. Paradigm I contains an implicit specification that S_0 is active or has just acted at the moment of reinforcement, since it specifies that S_1 is to be withheld until R_0 has occurred. The reinforced stimulus is really S_0 and not $S_G + S_0$ (it is the lever, in our example, not the whole stimulating field presented by the apparatus). Paradigm II contains no specification of the activity of S_0; and the reinforcing action of S'_1 must be supposed to extend to S_G as well as to S_0. In practice an active state at the moment of reinforcement is usually insured by presenting S_0 suddenly.[10] This might be included as an additional provision in Paradigm II, but the provision really required is that S_0, and no part of S_G, be active at the moment of reinforcement. This is not easily arranged. We cannot wholly avoid the generalized action of the reinforcement in Type II because of the lack of dependence of S'_1 upon R'_0.

One characteristic of the pseudo-conditioned reflex is the variety of the forms of its "stimulus." We have assumed that in our two fundamental paradigms any stimulus had ultimately the dimensions of energy (although we have often used the shorthand device of speaking of the source of the energy—as, for example, "lever"). In the pseudo type, however, the "stimulus" can be a single property. It can be the intensity of the stimulus, or some such qualitative aspect as pitch or hue. It can be a change from one value of a property to another, or the absence of a property, or a duration. The reason why this is possible is that the other properties of the stimulus can be relegated to S_G for extinction. If the *pitch* of a tone is to be a conditioned "stimulus," the tone itself must first become one also, and the response to its other properties must be extinguished by extinguishing the responses to tones of other pitches. In a true conditioned reflex this cannot be done. Although it is common to speak of properties as stimuli [as Pavlov, for example, does], the presence of a property in the position of a stimulus is a certain indication that a pseudo-conditioned reflex is really in question. A property alone cannot be used in either true type because it implies extinction; most of the real stimulus must be relegated to S_G, and the requirement that the value of S_G be negligible cannot therefore be satisfied.

The position of a pseudo-conditioned reflex may be summarized as follows. When the pseudo-reflex is based upon a reflex of Type I and when R_0 requires external points of reference, there are important practical and

---

[10] This is our explanation of Difference 7. Another explanation might be added. If S'_0 is active for any length of time prior to S_1 it will have an extinguishing effect. This cannot be said of Type I.

theoretical reasons why a separate formulation is demanded. When R_0 does not require external points of reference, there are fewer differences, but a separate formulation is still necessary. When the pseudo-type is based upon a reflex of Type II, the distinction is weakened but should still be made, except when S_G can be reduced to a very low value relative to S'_0. In the last case a practical distinction is impossible, not because of an identity of types, but because of the failure of Type II to appear experimentally in a pure form.

It is a tempting hypothesis that II is not an authentic type but may be reduced to a discrimination based on Type I. But this has not been shown; we have not reduced the pseudo-type to Type II or *vice versa*. Nor have we come very near it. The present pseudo-reflex which resembles II most closely requires a reflex of that type for its establishment. It is probably more than a coincidence that a discrimination based upon Type I has so many of the properties of II, but the reduction to a single type appears from our present evidence to be highly improbable, desirable though it would be as an immense simplification. The differences we have noted are not easily disposed of. Still more improbable is a reduction of I to II, since the first step supplied by the pseudo-type is then lacking.

To the differences we have listed might be added differences in the parts played by the two types in the economy of the organism. The essence of Type II is the substitution of one stimulus for another, or, as Pavlov has put it, signalization. It *prepares* the organism by obtaining the elicitation of a response before the original stimulus has begun to act, and it does this by letting any stimulus which has *incidently* accompanied or anticipated the original stimulus act in its stead. In Type I there is no substitution of stimuli and consequently no signalization. Type I acts in another way: the organism selects from a large repertory of unconditioned reflexes those of which the repetition is important with respect to certain elementary functions and discards those of which it is unimportant. The conditioned response of Type I does not prepare for the reinforcing stimulus, it *produces* it. The stimulus-to-be-conditioned is never in any sense incidental.

Type I plays the more important role. When an organism comes accidentally (that is to say, as the result of weak investigatory reflexes) upon a new kind of food, which it seizes and eats, both kinds of conditioning presumably occur. When the visible radiation from the food next stimulates the organism, salivation is evoked according to Paradigm II. This secretion remains useless until the food is actually seized and eaten. But seizing and eating will depend upon the same accidental factors as before unless conditioning of Type I has also occurred—that is, unless the strength of the reflex (food—seizing) has increased. Thus, while a reflex of Type II prepares the organism, a reflex of Type I obtains the food for which the preparation is made. And this is in general a fair characterization of the relative importance of the two types. As Pavlov has said, conditioned stimuli are important in providing saliva before food is received, but "even greater is their importance when they evoke the motor component of the complex reflex of nutrition, i.e., when they act as stimuli to the reflex of seeking food." [11] Although "the reflex of seeking food" is an unfortunate expression, it refers clearly enough to behavior characteristic of Type I.

[11] Pavlov, I. P. *Conditioned Reflexes.* Trans. & ed. by G. V. Anrep. London: Oxford Univ. Press. 1927, p. 13. This is a doubly interesting statement because Pavlov has confined his own investigations practically exclusively to conditioned reflexes of the second type. It ought to be said that he usually regards this type as adequate for the whole field. Thus he says that the "function of the hemispheres" is signalization (p. 17), although signalization is, as we have seen, a characteristic of Type II only.

Two Types of Conditioned Reflex:
A Reply to Konorski and Miller

A distinction between two types of conditioned reflex had been made as early as 1928 by two Polish physiologists, Jerry Konorski and S. Miller, with whose work I was not familiar when the preceding paper was written. In The Journal of General Psychology *(1937, 16, 264-272) they questioned the characterization of my Type I, citing several of their experiments. In one of these a dog placed in an experimental stand and shocked lightly in one foot eventually lifted the foot before the shock was administered. In another the same movement in response to electric shock was reinforced with food and eventually occurred without the shock. The principal issue was the status of the stimulus originally responsible for the conditioned movement.*

Two years intervened between my paper and the Konorski and Miller comment on it. My answer (which appeared in the same issue, thanks to the kindness of the authors in providing me with an advance copy) referred to "a work now in preparation." This was The Behavior of Organisms, *in writing which I had already abandoned the notion of an eliciting stimulus in the analysis of operant behavior. My answer was, therefore, less a comment on the points raised by Konorski and Miller than a revision-in-progress of my earlier formulation. In it the operant-respondent distinction was made for the first time. The paper is reprinted by permission from* The Journal of General Psychology *(1937, 16, 272-279). A translation of the paper by Miller and Konorski ("On a Particular Form of Conditioned Reflex") may be found in* The Journal of the Experimental Analysis of Behavior, *1969, 12, 187–189.*

Before considering the specific objections raised by Konorski and Miller against my formulation of a second type of conditioned reflex, I should like to give a more fundamental characterization of both types and of the discrimination based upon them.

Let conditioning be defined as a kind of change in reflex strength where the operation performed upon the organism to induce the change is the presentation of a reinforcing stimulus in a certain temporal relation to behavior. All changes in strength so induced come under the head of conditioning and are thus distinguished from changes having similar dimensions but induced in other ways (as in drive, emotion, and so on). Different types of conditioned reflexes arise because a reinforcing stimulus may be presented in different kinds of temporal relations. There are two fundamental cases: in one the reinforcing stimulus is correlated temporally with a response and in the other with a stimulus. For "correlated with" we might write "contingent upon." These are the types I have numbered I and II respectively. Konorski and Miller refer to the second as Type I and to a complex case involving the first (see below) as Type II. To avoid confusion and to gain a mnemonic advantage I shall refer to conditioning which results from the contingency of a reinforcing stimulus upon a *stimulus* as of Type *S* and to that resulting from contingency upon a *response* as of Type *R*.

If the stimulus is already correlated with a response or the response with a stimulus, a reinforcement cannot be made contingent upon the one term without being put into a similar relation with the other. That is to say, if a reinforcing stimulus is correlated temporarily with the *S* in a reflex, it is also correlated with the *R,* or if with the *R,* then also with the *S*. It is not possible to avoid this difficulty (which seems to destroy the validity of the foregoing definition) by specifying a kind of temporal relation. If, for example, we should distinguish between the cases in which the reinforcing stimulus precedes *S* (and hence also precedes *R*) and those in which it follows *R* (and hence also follows *S*), the resulting classes would be close to those of Types *R* and *S* but they would not be identical with them, and the basis for the definition would not permit a deduction of the other characteristics of the types. The contingency of the reinforcing stimulus upon a *separate* term is necessary.

It may be noted, therefore, that in both paradigms of conditioning as previously given [page 525] the connection between the term to be correlated with the reinforcing stimulus and another term is irrelevant. No connection need exist at the start. In Type *S* we may use a stimulus (S_0) eliciting no observable response and in Type R a response (R_0) elicited by no observable stimulus (for example, the "spontaneous" flexion of a leg). Or, if a connection originally exists, it may disappear during conditioning. In Type S, if S_0 elicits a definite response [say, where $(S_0\text{---}R_0)$ is (shock — flexion)], R_0 may disappear (Eroféeva); and in Type R, if R_0 is apparently elicited by a definite stimulus [say, where $(S_0\text{---}R_0)$ is the same], R_0 will eventually appear without S_0, as Konorski and Miller have shown. The paradigms may therefore be rewritten as follows:

Type S

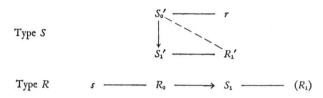

Type R s ———— R_0 ——→ S_1 ———— (R_1)

where the arrows indicate the temporal correlation responsible for conditioning,[1] and where the terms written in lower case either (*a*) cannot be identified, (*b*) may be omitted, or (*c*) may disappear. The correlation of the reinforcing stimulus with a separate term is here achieved and from it the properties of two (and, incidentally, *only* two) types of conditioned reflex may be deduced. The differences between the types given in my paper, which need not be repeated here, are no longer useful in defining the types, but they serve as convenient hallmarks.

This solution depends upon the statement that there are responses uncorrelated with observable stimuli—a statement which must not be made lightly but cannot, so far as I can see, be avoided. It is a necessary recognition of the fact that in the unconditioned organism two kinds of behavior may be distinguished. There is, first, the kind of response which is made to specific stimulation, where the correlation between response and stimulus is a reflex in the traditional sense. I shall refer to such a reflex as a *respondent* and use the term also as an adjective in referring to the behavior as a whole. But there is also a kind of response which occurs spontaneously in the absence of any stimulation with which it may be specifically correlated. We need not have a complete absence of stimulation in order to demonstrate this. It does not mean that we cannot find a stimulus which will elicit such behavior but that none is operative at the time the behavior is observed. It is the nature of this kind of behavior that it should occur without an eliciting stimulus, although discriminative stimuli are practically inevitable after conditioning. It is not necessary to assume specific identifiable units prior to conditioning, but through con-

---

[1] The uncommon case in which S_1 follows S_0 is a minor exception to the direction of the arrow, which may be accounted for with the notion of the trace.

ditioning they may be set up. I shall call such a unit an *operant* and the behavior in general, operant behavior. The distinction between operant and respondent behavior and the special properties of the former will be dealt with at length in a work now in preparation. All conditioned reflexes of Type *R* are by definition operants and all of Type *S*, respondents; but the operant-respondent distinction is the more general since it extends to unconditioned behavior as well.

A formulation of the fundamental types of discrimination may also be carried out in terms of the contingency of the reinforcing stimulus. Discrimination differs from conditioning because the existing correlation cannot be unequivocally established with any one set of properties of the stimulus or response. The effect of a given act of reinforcement is necessarily more extensive than the actual contingency implies, and the relation must be narrowed through extinction with respect to the properties not involved in the correlation. There are three basic types of discrimination.

1. *Discrimination of the Stimulus in Type S.*

    a. S_1 is contingent upon less than all the aspects or properties of S_0 present upon any given occasion of reinforcement. For example, let S_1 be contingent upon the pitch of a tone. Before this relation (and not merely a relation between the response and the tone itself) can be established, responses to tones of other pitches which have been conditioned through induction must be extinguished.

    b. S_1 is contingent upon a group of stimuli but not upon subgroups or supergroups. For example, let S_A and S_B be reinforced together but not separately. Before the relation will be reflected in behavior, the responses to either stimulus alone which are strengthened through induction must be extinguished.

2. *Discrimination of the Stimulus in Type R.* S_1 is contingent upon R_0 in the presence of a stimulus S_D. For example, let the pressing of a lever be reinforced only when a light is on. Before this relation can be established in the behavior, the responses in the absence of the light developed through induction from the reinforcement in the presence of the light must be extinguished.

3. *Discrimination of the Response in Type R.*[2] S_1 is contingent upon an R_0 having a given value of one or more of its properties. For example, let S_1 be contingent upon a response above a given level of intensity. Responses of lower intensity strengthened through induction must be extinguished.

(There is no fourth case of a discrimination of the response in Type *S*.)

---

[2] Later referred to as "differentiation" of *R*.

Both discriminations of the stimulus (but not that of the response) yield what I have called pseudo-reflexes, in which stimuli are related to responses in ways which seem to resemble reflexes but require separate formulations if confusion is to be avoided.[3] In Type S (Case b, above), given the organism in the presence of S_A, the presentation of S_B will be followed by a response. The superficial relation $(S_B — R)$ is not a reflex, because the relevance of S_A is overlooked. Similarly in Type R, the superficial relation between the light and pressing the lever is not a reflex and exhibits none of the properties of one when these are treated quantitatively.

The distinction between an eliciting and a discriminative stimulus was not wholly respected in my earlier paper, for the reflex (lever—pressing) was pseudo. As a discriminated operant the reflex should have been written ($s + lever — pressing$). Since I did not derive the two types from the possible contingencies of the reinforcing stimulus, it was not important that R_0 in Type R be independent of an eliciting stimulus. But the treatment of the lever as *eliciting* an unconditioned response has proved inconvenient and impracticable in other ways, and the introduction of the notion of the operant clears up many difficulties besides those immediately in question. It eliminates the implausible assumption that all reflexes ultimately conditioned according to Type R may be spoken of as existing as identifiable units in unconditioned behavior and substitutes the simpler assumption that all operant responses are generated out of undifferentiated material. Certain difficulties in experiments upon operants are also avoided. Operant behavior cannot be treated with the technique devised for respondents (Sherrington and Pavlov) because in the absence of an eliciting stimulus many of the measures of reflex strength developed for respondents are meaningless. In an operant there is properly no latency (except with respect to discriminative stimuli), no after-discharge, and most important of all no ratio of the magnitudes of R and S. In spite of repeated efforts to treat it as such, the magnitude of the response in an operant is not a measure of its strength. Some other measure must be devised, and from the definition of an operant it is easy to arrive at the *rate of occurrence* of the response. This measure has been shown to be significant in a large number of characteristic changes in strength.

[3] Not all pseudo-reflexes are discriminative, if we extend the term to include all superficial correlations of stimulus and response. For example, let a tetanizing shock to the tail of a dog be discontinued as soon as the dog lifts its left foreleg. The discontinuance of a negative reinforcement acts as a positive reinforcement; and when conditioning has taken place, a shock to the tail will be consistently followed by a movement of the foreleg. Superficially the relation resembles a reflex, but the greatest confusion would arise from treating it as such and expecting it to have the usual properties.

There is thus an important difference between the Konorski and Miller sequence *"shock — flexion → food"* and the sequence *"s + lever — pressing → food."* The first contains a respondent, the second an operant. The immediate difference experimentally is that in the second case the experimenter cannot produce the response at will but must wait for it to come out. A more important difference concerns the basis for the distinction between two types. Since there is no eliciting stimulus in the second sequence, the food is correlated with the response but not with the lever as a stimulus. In the first sequence the food is correlated as fully with the shock as with the flexion. The Konorski and Miller case does not fit the present formula for Type R, and a divergent result need not weigh against it. The case does not, as a matter of fact, fit either type so long as the double correlation with both terms exists. Conditioning of Type S will occur (the shock-salivation reflex of Eroféeva), but there is no reason why conditioning of Type R should occur so long as there is a correlation between the reinforcement and an *eliciting* stimulus. Nothing is to be gained in such a case; the original sequence operates as efficiently as possible.

The case comes under Type R only when the correlation with S_0 is broken up—that is, when a response occurs which is not elicited by S_0. The complex experiment described by Konorski and Miller may be formulated as follows. In the unconditioned organism there is operant behavior which consists of flexing the leg. It is weak and appears only occasionally. There is also the strong respondent (*shock — flexion*), which has more or less the same form of response. In Konorski and Miller's experiment we may assume that an elicitation of the respondent $(S — R)$ brings out at the same time the operant $(s — R)$, which sums with it. We have in reality two sequences: (A) *shock — flexion,* and (B) *s — flexion → food.* Here the respondent (A) need not increase in strength but may actually decrease during conditioning of Type S, while the operant in B increases in strength to a point at which it is capable of appearing without the aid of A. As Konorski and Miller note, ". . . the stimulus S_0 [shock] plays only a subsidiary role in the formation of a conditioned reflex of the new type. It serves only to bring about the response R_0 [by summation with the operant?], and once the connection $S_G — R_0$ is established [read 'once the operant is reinforced'], it loses any further experimental significance."

The existence of independent composite parts may be inferred from the facts that B eventually appears without A when it has become strong enough through conditioning and that it may even be conditioned without the aid of A, although less conveniently.

Konorski and Miller seem to imply that a scheme which appeals to the spontaneous occurrence of a response cannot be generally valid because many responses never appear spontaneously. But elaborate and peculiar forms of response may be generated from undifferentiated operant behavior through successive approximation to a final form. This is sometimes true of the example of pressing the lever. A rat may be found (very infrequently) not to press the lever spontaneously during a prolonged period of observation. The response in its final form may be obtained by basing the reinforcement upon the following steps in succession: approach to the site of the lever, lifting the nose into the air toward the lever, lifting the fore-part of the body into the air, touching the lever with the feet, and pressing the lever downward. When one step has been conditioned, the reinforcement is withdrawn and made contingent upon the next. With a similar method any value of a single property of the response may be obtained. The rat may be conditioned to press the lever with a force equal to that exerted by, say, 100 grams (although spontaneous pressings seldom go above 20 grams) or to prolong the response to, say, 30 seconds (although the lever is seldom spontaneously held down for more than two seconds). I know of no stimulus comparable with the shock of Konorski and Miller which will elicit "pressing the lever" as an unconditioned response or elicit it with abnormal values of its properties. There is no S_0 available for *eliciting* these responses in the way demanded by Konorski and Miller's formulation.

Where an eliciting stimulus is lacking, Konorski and Miller appeal to "putting through." A dog's paw is raised and placed against a lever, and this "response" is reinforced with food. Eventually the dog makes the response spontaneously. But a great deal may happen here which is not easily observed. If we assume that tension from passive flexion is to some extent negatively reinforcing, anything which the dog does which reduces the tension will be reinforced as an operant. Such a spontaneous response as moving the foot in the direction of the passive flexion will be reinforced. We thus have a series of sequences of this general form:

$$s + S_D \text{ (touching and flexing of leg)} - R \text{ (movement of leg in certain direction)} \rightarrow S_1 \text{ (relief of tension)}.$$

The effect of "putting through" is to provide step-by-step reinforcement for many component parts of the complete response, each part being formulated according to Type R. The substitution of food as a new reinforcement is easily accounted for.

This interpretation of "putting through" is important because Konorski and Miller base their formulation of the new type upon the fact that proprioceptive stimulation from the response may become a conditioned stimulus of Type S since it regularly precedes S_1. One of the conditions for this second type is that "the movement which constitutes its effect is a conditioned food stimulus." That conditioning of this sort does take place during conditioning of Type R was noted in my paper, but its relevance in the process of Type R does not follow. Perhaps the strongest point against it is the fact that conditioning of Type R may take place with one reinforcement, where a prerequisite conditioning of Type S could hardly have time to occur. Any proprioceptive stimulation from R_0 acts as an *additional* reinforcement in the formula for Type R. Where it is possible to attach conditioned reinforcing value to a response without eliciting it, the reinforcement is alone in its action, but the case still falls under Type R. In verbal behavior, for example, we may give a sound reinforcing value through conditioning of Type S. Any sound produced by a child which resembles it is automatically reinforced. The general formula for cases of this sort is

$$s - R_0 \rightarrow \textit{stimulation from } R_0 \textit{ acting as a conditioned reinforcement.}$$

I assume that this is not a question of priority. The behavior characteristic of Type R was studied as early as 1898 (Thorndike). The point at issue is the establishment of the most convenient formulation, and I may list the following reasons for preferring the definition of types given herein. (1) A minimal number of terms is specified. This is especially important in Type R, which omits the troublesome S_0 of Konorski and Miller's formula. (2) Definition is solely in terms of the contingency of reinforcing stimuli—other properties of the types being deduced from the definition. (3) No other types are to be expected. What Konorski and Miller give as variants or predict as new types are discriminations. (4) The distinction between an eliciting and a discriminative stimulus is maintained. Konorski and Miller's variants of their Type II are pseudo-reflexes and cannot yield properties comparable with each other or with genuine reflexes.

Two separate points may be answered briefly. (1) It is essential in this kind of formulation that one reflex be considered at a time since our data have the dimensions of changes in reflex strength. The development of an antagonistic response when a reinforcement in Type R is negative requires a separate paradigm, either of Type R or Type S. (2) That responses of smooth muscle or glandular tissues may or may not enter into Type R, I am not prepared to assert. I used salivation as a convenient hypothetical instance of simultaneous fused responses of both types, but a skeletal response would have done as well. The child who has been conditioned to cry "real tears" because tears have been been followed by positive reinforcement (e.g., candy) apparently makes a glandular conditioned response of Type R, but the matter needs to be checked because an intermediate step may be involved. Such is the case in the Hudgins' experiment,[4] where the verbal response *"contract"* is an operant but the reflex (*"contract"*—contraction of pupil) is a conditioned respondent. The question at issue is whether we may produce contraction of the pupil according to s — *contraction* $\rightarrow$ *reinforcement,* where (for caution's sake) the reinforcing stimulus will not itself elicit contraction. It is a question for experiment.

[4] Hudgins, C. V. Conditioning and the voluntary control of the pupillary reflex. *J. Gen. Psychol.,* 1933, *8,* 3–51.

A Review of Hull's
Principles of Behavior

When Clark L. Hull first approached behavior theory in earnest, more than a decade ago, the science of behavior was in a difficult position. Twenty years of the "natural science method" heralded by Behaviorism had failed to provide a consistent and useful systematic formulation. The commonest laboratory instruments were still the maze and the discrimination box, and experimental data reflected many arbitrary properties of the apparatus. Acceptable conclusions of any degree of generality referred to aspects, characteristics, or limiting capacities. While many of these were valid enough, few were logically compelling, and individual preferences had led to many individual "sciences" of behavior. Hull saw the need for a logical analysis of the vocabulary of behavior, for an explicit definition of fundamental terms and an unambiguous statement of principles. He adopted the rather extreme procedures of "postulate theory," and proposed to put order into the science of behavior by carefully defining certain primitive terms and setting up a (necessarily rather large) number of postulates, from which thousands of theorems could be deduced and experimentally tested. It is clear from his early memoranda that he first regarded his postulates as in general not directly testable, a condition which gives point to the postulate method. Deduced *theorems* were to be checked against the facts, but the validity of a postulate was to be established by the success of the theorems to which it gave rise.

The cogency of the postulate method may be said to vary inversely with the accessibility of a subject matter. When a process cannot be directly investigated, its properties may often be inferred from a study of consequences. This condition prevailed in the field of behavior in the early

From *The American Journal of Psychology*, 1944, 57, 276–281. The book reviewed is Clark L. Hull, *Principles of Behavior*. New York: Appleton-Century-Crofts, 1943.

30's, and Hull's proposal was therefore justified. The situation was, however, changing. The growing influence of Pavlov and other developments in the field at this time revealed the possibility of a direct attack upon fundamental processes which would lead to a different sort of analysis. Hull was one of the first to recognize this possibility and to encourage relevant research. Moreover, he was not insensitive to its bearing upon postulational procedures. In a memorandum of November 28, 1936, he confesses that "the 'geometrical' type of deduction does not permit the ready use of the calculus and thus has limitations not characteristic of the higher forms of scientific theory."

Instead of abandoning the postulate method and turning to the higher forms of theory appropriate to a functional analysis, Hull attempted to salvage his program by combining the two methods. In 1937 he wrote that "the postulates of the theoretical constructs are to be the basic laws or principles of human behavior. These laws are to be determined directly by experiment, so far as feasible, in advance of their use in theoretical constructs. . . . The experimental determinations will be quantitative, designed to reveal functional curves of basic relationships. Mathematical equations will be fitted to . . . these curves; such equations constitute the postulates of the system." This program, which he called "logical empiricism," proved to be an unstable blend of two widely different principles of analysis. Any demonstrated functional relation between behavior and its controlling variables is not a postulate but a law, and there is little reason to continue with the ritual of postulates. The resulting split in Hull's thinking has left its mark on his *Principles of Behavior*. At one time he appears to be working within a formal postulate system; at another he is considering behavior as a dependent variable and relating it to controlling variables in the environment. These activities are not always supplementary; on the contrary they are often mutually harmful.

The transition from "principle" to "process," or from aspect to functional relation, may be traced in the changing postulate systems which Hull has sponsored. He began, in the case of rote learning, with a selected set of current hypotheses, assembled for purposes of clarification and held together by a common relation to a field of research. By 1939 a rough precursor of the present set had been constructed. It revealed the new interest in functional analysis by referring to a group of basic processes (e.g., stimulus excitation, conditioning, motivation) in presumably an exhaustive way (the current Postulate 16 is said to *complete* "the statement of primary principles"). Some of these postulates were in effect inverted definitions; others described quantitative processes. The method was now being used, not merely for the logical rectification of existing principles, but for the isolation of a system of variables.

The new postulates proved embarrassingly un-hypothetical, however, and sometime after 1939 Hull retreated to a more speculative level of analysis —the neurological. This is a surprising change, for we are told that the *Principles* will remain at the molar level, as that term is used by Tolman. "The object of the present work," Hull writes (p. 17), "is the elaboration of the basic molar behavioral laws underlying the social sciences." Yet Postulate 1 begins, "When a stimulus energy impinges upon a suitable receptor organ, an afferent impulse is generated . . . ," and the other postulates hold essentially to the same level. Hull is not always at home in writing of neurology (as, for example, in the careless statement, on page 54, that in reciprocal innervation one muscle receives a neural discharge which is inhibitory rather than excitatory in nature), and we can scarcely explain the maneuver except by assuming that he is determined to keep his postulates hypothetical at any cost. The exigencies of his method have led him to abandon the productive (and at least equally valid) formulation of behavior at the molar level and to align himself with the semi-neurologists.

The same pressure has led to a misrepresentation of many of his scientific procedures. His "deductions" are often concerned merely with showing that complicated instances of behavior may be analyzed into simpler instances which have been, or are at least capable of being, studied experimentally. This is an unavoidable task in a science of behavior, but to regard the simple case as postulate and the complicated as theorem (or *vice versa*) is to extend the postulational framework beyond its sphere of usefulness. In the case of the postulates which are merely quantitative predictions of processes yet to be studied, "deduction" often turns out to refer to a direct experimental determination, but this should not be confused with the testing of postulates via deduced theorems. To force simple scientific inferences into the postulative mold does not contribute to clarity, but rather to awkwardness and confusion.

Because of the unsuccessful attempt to embrace a functional analysis, the book will hardly stand as an example of postulate method. Since it is likely to be received primarily as an example of method, a few defects from a more strictly logical point of view may be listed. (1) There are no formal definitions, although Hull originally recognized this responsibility. (2) Some postulates contain as many as five separate statements, so that references to a postulate during the course of a proof are ambiguous. (3) The symbols never "pay off" in convenience or progress. Six and one-half pages are needed to define them, but they are used only to paraphrase what has already been said in words. There is apparently no instance in the book of a productive manipulation of symbols. (4) Although the distinction between primary and derived principles is frequently invoked, there is no adequate discussion of the criteria of primacy or of the level of analysis of the language of the postulates. (5) The grounds for admission of a new postulate are not stated. Postulates are generally brought in when facts cannot otherwise be accounted for, but this is not always the case. The tendency is now toward a minimal set, but this is not explicitly discussed. (At least two postulates, which refer to "inhibition," could be dispensed with on logical grounds. Although they are carefully evaluated with respect to the status of inhibition as an "unobservable," no question is raised as to whether they are needed. Inhibition, as the obverse of excitation, requires no separate reference, and none of the facts in Hull's chapter demands the term in any other sense.)

Two postulates must be objected to on more than general grounds. The Postulate of Afferent Neural Interaction asserts that the impulses generated by a stimulus energy are changed by each other into "something different." Since no provision is made for determining what this something is, the postulate may be adequately paraphrased by saying that it is impossible to predict behavior from the *physical* stimulus. This is a well-known difficulty in behavior theory, but we have come to expect from Hull something more than an explanatory fiction. Until the properties of the resulting psychological or behavioral stimulus are at least suggested, the postulate serves merely to account for failure to achieve a rigorous analysis and makes no positive contribution. The same objection applies to the Postulate of Behavioral Oscillation, which asserts the presence of an oscillatory "inhibitory potentiality" (it might as well have been "excitatory") which blurs "the concrete manifestation of empirical laws." This is another neural fiction, with the single negative function of accounting for failure to predict. In his introductory chapter Hull inveighs against certain traditional psychological ghosts, but it is doubtful whether any of them is quite so ghostlike in function as Afferent Neural Interaction or Behavioral Oscillation.

Predilection for a given method is not in itself objectionable. In the present case, however, it has unquestionably diverted the author from a frontal attack on crucial issues. The important task of formulating behavior as a system of variables is performed only indirectly. The "pivotal theoretical construct" is Effective Reaction Potential, which is said to be manifested by probability of reaction evocation, latency, resistance to extinction, and reaction amplitude. These measures do not, unfortunately, always vary together, and in the face of this difficulty Hull selects "probability" as the best single indicator. This notion appears very late in the book, and almost as an afterthought. It is not included in an earlier list of the manifestations of habit strength (where, incidentally, the lack of covariation of the other measures is dismissed as unimportant), yet these manifestations should be identical with those of effective reaction potential. Probability lacks the physical dimensions of latency, amplitude, and so on, and might better be described as the thing manifested. Effective reaction potential could, in fact, be usefully defined as the probability of evocation. Although Hull would doubtless wish to retain some reference to a physical substratum, the concept does little more than assert that the business of a science of behavior is to predict response. This prediction is to be achieved by evaluating the strength of a response (the probability that it will occur) and relating this to other variables, particularly in the fields of reinforcement and motivation ("emotion" does not appear in the index). Following Tolman, Hull prefers to fractionate this probability, identifying one part with reinforcement (which is then called "habit strength") and another with motivation (called "drive").

A similarly glancing and ineffective treatment of other current problems seems due to the same methodological difficulties. We expect something new and helpful in the analysis of conditioning, but are presented instead with three demonstrational experiments which are intended to reveal essential relations in learning. By using the complicated and unexplored motive of escape (which is likely to confuse eliciting and reinforcing stimuli), Hull tries to steer a middle course between Pavlovian and operant conditioning. But the essential characteristics are admittedly difficult to find in the Pavlovian experiment, and the highly verbal resolution is unsatisfactory. Similarly, the chapter on patterning is heavily methodological but to no real effect, since the problem is virtually disposed of in the original definition, which limits patterning to the compounding of stimuli in the Pavlovian manner.

Although the book is not intended as a factual survey, the quantitative relations which the author would like to see in a science of behavior are extensively illustrated. Except for a certain autistic tendency to create appropriate data (one-third of the graphs represent hypothetical cases), Hull shows his characteristic willingness to abide by experimental facts. The present volume probably sets a record for the use of experimental material in a primarily theoretical work. The heavy use of mathematics does not imply, as one might suppose, a more rigorous insistence upon a factual correspondence, for Bengt Carlson, who is responsible for the "complicated equations" at the end of many chapters, has been given too much freedom in his curve fitting. The fact that he is able to find "simple growth functions" which approximate a number of selected sets of data offers little assurance of the ultimate usefulness of that function, since he has been allowed to use three constants to which fresh values are assigned at will. (In one instance—p. 276—Carlson describes three experimental points with an equation containing three constants!) The mathematics is also occasionally rather wishful, as, for example, when detailed instructions are given for "calculating habit strength," although no techniques have been discovered for making the necessary measurements.

In spite of an extensive period of development, the *Principles* reveals a program still in transition. There is every evidence that the postulate method is being sloughed off (compare the earlier *Mathematico-deductive Theory*), but Hull has not yet made full use of an outright functional analysis. The uncertain theoretical position of the book will not lessen its stimulating effect in the field of behavior theory. More important perhaps, is the research which will certainly follow. The book is wide open to experimental attack, and it is only fair to add that the author planned it that way.

A Review of Bush and Mosteller's
Stochastic Models for Learning

As the preface of this interesting book points out, there are those who "feel that answers to the important questions of psychology are to be found . . . in the collection of more and better data rather than in mathematical formulas." The reviewer is one of these. The book was not written for the day-to-day worker in the field of learning, but here is the reaction of one for what it may be worth.

The word *stochastic* is a newcomer in mathematical statistics and is not yet fully naturalized. It appears only a few times in the present text (mainly in connection with "stochastic matrices") and seems to have been added to the title almost as an afterthought. The authors speak of stochastic processes as identical with the field of probability and state that they use the word *stochastic* to emphasize the temporal nature of the probability problems they consider, but there are at least four different senses in which the word probability may be applied to their work.

Probability–1. In the *American Scientist* for April 1955 Linus Pauling explains his use of *stochastic* to describe a particular scientific method. The Greek στοχαστικος means "good at hitting a target or at guessing." Scientific hypotheses which are little more than guesses about the results of future inquiry are to be distinguished from those which may never be directly confirmed but which merely lead to possibly confirmable theorems. In this context *stochastic* refers to statements made in advance of adequate information and means 'currently probable' as distinguished from 'eventually certain.'

Although this may not be the sense in which the present authors would

From *Contemporary Psychology*, 1956, *1*, 101–103. The book reviewed is Robert R. Bush and Frederick Mosteller, *Stochastic Models for Learning*. New York: John Wiley & Sons, 1955.

wish to use the term, it does in fact describe their method. They point out that they are not interested in setting up a model *of the organism.* Such a model would be a set of hypotheses leading at best to the deduction of theorems to be tested. Instead, they are constructing models for experiments. They prepare the way for the experimenter by supplying him with equations which he may find useful. (Meanwhile they test their luck on a few available cases.) If we are to have mathematical theories of learning —and the four foundations which supported the work in this book, like many others in a position to determine the course of scientific research, appear to be determined that we shall—then it is to be hoped that more and more theorists will practice the stochastic method in this sense.

Probability–2. The authors reject a position of strict determinism with respect to behavior and its prediction and express their belief that behavior is intrinsically probabilistic. That is to say, the macroscopic facts of behavior seem to them to suggest the operation of random, chance, or stochastic factors. In this use of the term they are still close to etymology, but they are talking not about the aim of the marksman but about the scatter of hits on a target from which direction of aim may be inferred. Thus the authors set the proposition, "behavior is statistical by its very nature," against the alternative form, behavior "appears to be so because of uncontrolled or uncontrollable conditions." In describing the application which the experimental psychologist may make of their book, they characterize themselves as presenting "procedures for estimating parameters from data." How the parameters so estimated depend upon experimental variables can be determined only by parametric studies, which they do not undertake. Actually, not much of the book is concerned with estimating parameters from data suffering from stochastic or random disturbances.

Probability–3. If probability–1 may be said to refer to the behavior of the experimenter and probability–2 to the behavior of the organism, then probability–3, to which most of the book is devoted, does not refer to either, although the authors contend that they are considering processes in the organism. In order to deal with probability–3 it is necessary to make some arbitrary and highly restrictive assumptions.

First, it is necessary to define a trial. The authors suggest: "an opportunity for choosing among a set of mutually exclusive and exhaustive alternatives or responses." The sum of the probabilities of all such responses at any given moment add to 1—a numerical elegance not commanded by the first two probabilities. Separate probabilities are sometimes arrived at by an analysis of the responses possible in a given apparatus, as one analyzes any discrete sample space. For example, in a T maze "we assume that

none of the rats has an initial position preference, and so we let $p_1 = 0.5$."
Such a probability describes an opportunity presented to a rat but has no
reference to the rat's inclination. Perhaps the rat will not go either way;
but in that case there has been no trial, and hence probability–3 is not
applicable.

When separate possibilities depend upon the rat's history in the apparatus, the sample space loses cogency. Since the authors define the learning
process as any "systematic *change* in behavior" (thus, incidentally, missing
the attractive stable states which prevail under particular conditions of
reinforcement), they cannot evaluate probabilities from observed frequencies. There is, unfortunately, only one 'tenth trial.' A rat may turn right
on this trial, but what is the probability that it will do so? Here the authors
fall back upon a rather discredited device: "The obvious way to test a
model is to collect data on a large number of nearly identical rats, say one
hundred." Identical at birth, or just before the first trial, or on the tenth
trial? And where can such rats be purchased? Although the authors supply
a chapter on *Distributions of Response Probabilities,* they never succeed in
supporting their assumption that on any given trial a rat may be conceived
of as spinning a disk or drawing a ball from an urn to determine its choice
of right or left. When we say that the probability of turning right moves
from 0.5 to 1.0 as a rat learns a T maze to complete mastery, these explicit
values are only spuriously reassuring. They bear no useful relation to the
magnitude of the change taking place in the rat.

Conceive of a coin dropped vertically a short distance onto a horizontal
surface, and define a trial as any case in which the coin falls on one face.
Make the coin 'learn' in the following way: When it falls with a given
face up, tilt it slightly in that direction before dropping it the next time.
Let 'speed of learning' be represented by how much the coin is tilted at
each trial. Eventually, of course, the coin will always fall with one face up.
Arguing from frequencies before and after learning, we could say that the
probability has moved from 0.5 to 1.0, but what does that tell us, quantitatively, about the final tilt of the coin? A mathematical analysis of the
possibilities in a sample space is no substitute for, and may be of little help
in, the empirical study of a scientific subject matter.

Probability–4. Professors Bush and Mosteller explain in their introduction that they are attempting "to describe response tendencies by sets of
probability variables." The reader is likely to suppose that they mean
tendencies to respond, such as the determining or excitatory tendencies of
psychological theory. But such is not the case. That kind of probability—
number 4 in our series—is dealt with only indirectly in a very short chapter.

The authors' "tendency" refers to probability–3—to a choice among mutually exclusive responses. The question of the inclination to make any response whatsoever is excluded by the definition of a trial—the mathematics do not apply until a response has occurred. An effort is made to account for bar-pressing (which the authors describe as "the simplest type of learning"!) within this framework by defining "bar-pressing" and "not-bar-pressing" as mutually exclusive and exhaustive classes of responses.

The difficulty here might be expressed by saying that "not-bar-pressing" requires infinite time for its completion. The notion of a trial is not applicable. The time problem in probability estimates is discussed only in reference to latency and rate of running on a runway. If time is "quantized" into intervals of a given length, responding and not-responding become meaningful alternatives. The authors admit, however, that "our task is to construct a model for the runway by creating a choice situation in our minds, even though there may not be one in the rat's."

The procedures described in this chapter contribute little toward the much more difficult problem of rate of responding, which is dismissed in this single sentence: "Rate of responding can also be related to probabilities of appropriate response classes, as has been demonstrated in the literature." The references are to a paper by Estes and an early paper by the authors. It is unfortunate that something more along this line was not included, since the models actually presented are seldom applicable to behavior outside the laboratory, where trials satisfying the authors' definition are almost unknown.

The authors undertook to make this extensive study upon discovering the "large bulk of empirical information on learning" which was available. They have tried to help psychologists make the most of this information. It would be unfortunate if their book were instead to obscure a more attractive possibility—namely, that of discarding all such early work as crude exploration and proceeding to the collection of fresh data with new instruments and more rigorous methods. One of the great disservices of statistics to science is likely to be just this: in showing the scientist that *something* may be significantly inferred from a set of data, statistics encourages him to hold on to these data, and the methods responsible for them, long after they might better have been discarded in favor of more expedient measures. It is to be hoped that in adding the prestige of mathematics to early work in learning, the authors have not inadvertently retarded progress in the field.

A day-to-day researcher can scarcely object to the activities of mathematicians as such—even to their rewriting the first line of the gospel according to St. John in this form: "First there must be a mathematical theory or system" (p. 1). If science has seldom, if ever, begun with a model, it does not follow that models are not worth while, or that someone cannot profitably begin with one. Nevertheless those who are concerned with progress in the field of learning should not worry if their practices follow a different pattern. It is well to underscore the many frank disclaimers scattered through such a book as this. We are told in an early chapter, for example, that "close agreement does not prove that the model is correct, but suggests that it may be useful; poor agreement indicates that the specific model, including the identification, is inappropriate." This is only one example of the authors' modest evaluation of their contribution. Indeed, they would probably agree that for one who is primarily concerned with finding out more about the learning process, the Baconian admonition still holds: "Study nature, not books."

PART IX

A Miscellany

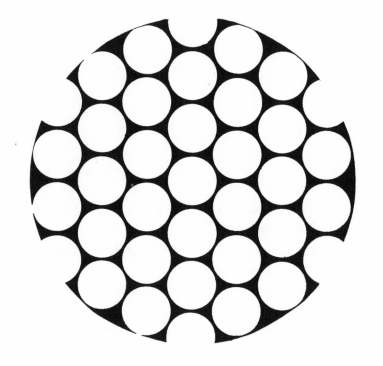

FIG. 1

A Paradoxical Color Effect

When the accompanying figure is held about two feet from the eye and looked at under low white-light illumination, the discs appear as if colored. A suitable illumination can be conveniently obtained by viewing the figure in room light through a pinhole. The colors are usually of low saturation but are quite definite. Most of the persons I have tested have reported a rose or a purplish red, a yellow, and a green or blue-green. Others have reported only a blue and yellow. Each disc takes on a single color and retains it as long as the fixation is not changed. Adjacent discs may be and usually are, of different colors.

An explanation suggests itself in terms of a functional-element theory of color vision. At the necessary low illumination the number of functional cones within the retinal image of a single disc cannot be very large. If the number is sufficiently low, a proportionate distribution of elementary types is improbable or even impossible. But a disproportionate activity is, by hypothesis, the characteristic effect of stimulation by colored light.

It should not be difficult to test this explanation. A quantitative investigation of the optimal illumination and the optimal visual angle subtended by a disc is being planned. The distribution of the several hues and possible differences in saturation are also of obvious significance in color vision theory.

So far as I am aware, no comparable effect has been reported.

From *The Journal of General Psychology*, 1932, 7, 481–482.

Some Quantitative Properties of Anxiety

(WITH W. K. ESTES)

The "mechanization of the Latin Square" referred to on page 120 was described in detail in a paper published jointly with W. T. Heron in the Psychological Record *(1939, 3, 166-176). Steel wires leading from 24 cumulative recorders were divided into four groups, each of which entered a system of pulleys as shown in Fig. 1. The six wires at* A, A. . . . . , *all of which move upward as the organisms respond, contribute equally to the movement of* B, *which is 1½ times the averaged movement of all the A's. This much of the system gives a mean curve for a subgroup of six rats. By combining*

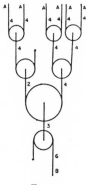

FIG. 1

four mean curves in various ways other curves are obtained. Leads from Groups I and II, passing over a single pulley, record the mean for twelve rats (again actually one and one-half times the mean). Four mean curves are obtained for groups I and II, I and III, and III and IV, and II and IV. Leads from the first and third of these groups, passing over another pulley, give the mean curve for all twenty-four rats.

Mean cumulative curves, even when arranged in subgroups, conceal more facts than they clarify. Moreover, the whole system suffers if any one of the twenty-four apparatuses breaks down, or if any one of the twenty-four animals is carelessly handled or fed, or otherwise incorrectly treated. It is not surprising, therefore, that the system did not prove productive. The present paper is one of a few examples of an apparently legitimate and successful use.

The "conditioned suppression" of behavior (as it is now generally called) has proved to be a useful baseline in studying measures which "relieve anxiety" in human subjects (see page 153). The paper appeared in the Journal of Experimental Psychology *(1941, 29, 390-400) and is reprinted with the permission of the editor of the journal and of the co-author.*

Anxiety has at least two defining characteristics: (1) it is an emotional state, somewhat resembling fear, and (2) the disturbing stimulus which is principally responsible does not precede or accompany the state but is "anticipated" in the future.

Both characteristics need clarification, whether they are applied to the behavior of man or, as in the present study, to a lower organism. One difficulty lies in accounting for behavior which arises in "anticipation" of a future event. Since a stimulus which has not yet occurred cannot act as a cause, we must look for a *current* variable. An analogy with the typical conditioning experiment, in which S_1, having in the past been followed by S_2, now leads to an "anticipatory" response to S_2, puts the matter in good scientific order because it is a current stimulus S_1, not the future occurrence of S_2, which produces the reaction. Past instances of S_2 have played their part in bringing this about, but it is not S_2 which is currently responsible.

Although the temporal relationships of classical conditioning provide for an acceptable definition of anticipation, the analogy with anxiety is not complete. In anxiety, the response which is developed to S_1 need not be like the original response to S_2. In a broader sense, then, anticipation must be defined as a reaction to a current stimulus S_1 which arises from the fact that S_1 has in the past been followed by S_2, where the reaction is not necessarily that which was originally made to S_2. The magnitude of the reaction to S_1 at any moment during its presentation may depend upon the previous temporal relations of S_1 and S_2.

The concept of "emotional state" also needs clarification in view of the experiments to be described. It has been suggested [in the *Behavior of Organisms*] that in treating emotion purely as *reaction* (either of the autonomic effectors or of the skeletal musculature), a very important influence upon operant behavior is overlooked. In practice we are most often interested in the effect of a stimulus in altering the strength of behavior which is frequently otherwise unrelated to the emotion. A stimulus giving rise to "fear," for example, may lead to muscular reactions (including facial expression, startle, and so on) and a widespread autonomic reaction of the sort commonly emphasized in the study of emotion; but of greater importance in certain respects is the considerable change in the tendencies of the organism to react in various other ways. Some responses in its current repertoire will be strengthened, others weakened, in varying degrees. Our concern is most often with anxiety observed in this way, as an effect upon the normal behavior of the organism, rather than with a specific supplementary *response* in the strict sense of the term.

The experiments to be described follow this interpretation. An emotional state is set up in "anticipation" of a disturbing stimulus, and the magnitude of the emotion is measured by its effect upon the strength of certain hunger-motivated behavior, more specifically upon the rate with which a rat makes an arbitrary response which is periodically reinforced with food. Such a rate has been shown to be a very sensitive indicator of the strength of behavior under a variety of circumstances, and it is adapted here to the case of emotion. Mowrer's recent summary of techniques for measuring the 'expectation' of a stimulus does not include a comparable procedure.[1]

In these experiments the disturbing stimulus to be "anticipated" was an electric shock delivered from a condenser through grids in the floor of the experimental box. The stimulus which characteristically preceded the disturbing stimulus and which therefore became the occasion for anxiety was a tone, produced by phones attached to a 60 cycle A.C. transformer.

The apparatus, which provided for the simultaneous investigation of twenty-four rats, has been described in detail elsewhere. Each rat was enclosed during the experimental period in a light-proof and nearly sound-proof box containing a lever which could be easily depressed. A curve (number of responses vs. time) for each rat and mechanically averaged curves for the group and for certain sub-groups of six or twelve rats were recorded. Under the procedure of periodic reconditioning, the control clock was set to reinforce single responses to the lever every four minutes, intervening responses going unreinforced. The rats came to respond at a relatively constant rate during the one-hour experimental period, and the summated response curves tended to approximate straight lines, except for local cyclic effects resulting from a temporal discrimination based upon the four-minute period of reinforcement. Curves *A* and *C* in Figure 5 are for

[1] Mowrer, O. H. Preparatory set (expectancy)—some methods of measurement. *Psychol. Monogr.*, 1940, *52*, 43.

groups of twenty-four rats and represent the sort of baseline available for the observation of the effect of anxiety.

The subjects were twenty-four male albino rats under six months of age, taken from an unselected laboratory stock. Records were taken for one hour daily during the entire experiment. After preliminary conditioning of the pressing response, two sub-groups were formed; one group of twelve rats was kept at a relatively high drive, while the other twelve were held at a drive which produced a very low rate of responding. The sound and shock were first introduced after two weeks of periodic reinforcement.

Conditioning of a State of Anxiety

The averaged periodic curve for twelve rats on a high drive on the occasion of the first presentations of the tone (T) and shock (S) is shown in Figure 2. On this first presentation the tone was allowed to sound for three

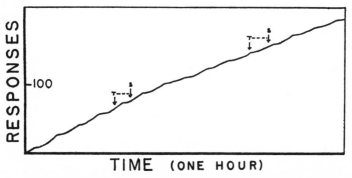

FIG. 2. First presentations of tone and shock. Mechanically averaged curve for twelve rats under periodic reinforcement. The tone was turned on at T, and at S the shock was administered and the tone turned off. There is no noticeable effect of either tone or shock upon the rate of responding at this stage.

minutes. Each rat was then given a shock and the tone was stopped. It will be observed that neither the tone nor the shock (at the intensity used throughout the experiment) produced any disturbance in the mean periodic rate at either presentation. This orderly baseline made it possible to follow with ease the development of the "anticipation" of the shock during subsequent repetitions of the situation.

The tone-shock combination was presented twice during each of six consecutive hourly periods. Then, in order to clarify any changes in the behavior, the period of the tone was lengthened to five minutes and the combination was given only once during each ensuing experimental hour.

The principal result of this part of the experiment was the conditioning of a state of anxiety to the tone, where the primary index was a reduction in strength of the hunger-motivated lever-pressing behavior. The ratio of the number of responses made during the period of the tone to the average number made during the same fraction of the hour in control experiments was 1.2 : 1.0 [2] for the first experimental hours; it had dropped to 0.3 : 1.0 by the eighth.

The changes in behavior accompanying anticipation of the shock are shown in Figure 3, which gives the averaged curves for the group of six rats with the highest periodic rate during the first four days of the five-minute tone. A number of characteristics of these records should be noted.

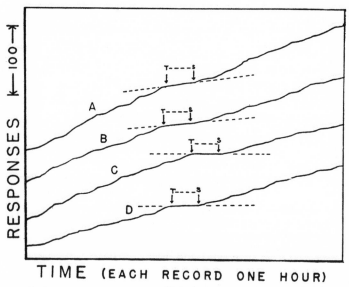

FIG. 3.   Reduction in rate of responding during successive periods of anxiety. Averaged curves for six rats on four consecutive days. By the third or fourth day responding practically ceases during the presentation of the tone.

[2] The ratio is not expected to be exactly 1 : 1 since the number of responses made during a period of five minutes will depend upon where the period begins with respect to the four-minute interval of reinforcement.

The progressively more marked reduction in periodic rate during the anticipatory period is obvious. The effect upon the rate is felt immediately after the presentation of the tone and remains at a constant value until the shock is given. (This constancy might not be maintained if the situation were repeated often enough to allow the rat to form a temporal discrimination.) Effects also appear after the shock which were not present in Figure 2 as the result of the shock alone. Especially in Curves *A* and *B* of Figure 3, the shock is seen to be followed by a depression and irregularity of rate which are at least much greater than any effect in the control records. With continued repetition of the experiment, this disturbance tends to adapt out, although not completely. In Curves *C* and *D* of Figure 3, the distortion is much less marked. Curve *B* of Figure 5 gives a similar example at a relatively late stage of conditioning.

The modification in behavior correlated with the anticipation of a disturbing stimulus cannot be attributed to a negative reinforcement of the response to the lever, since the shock was always given independently of the rat's behavior with respect to the lever. Only upon rare occasions could the shock have coincided with a response. This was especially true in the experiments upon the group at a lower drive, where a similar effect was obtained. Figure 4 shows averaged curves for a group of six rats which had been subjected to the procedure just described except that their drive was so low during conditioning that the rate of responding was virtually zero. The lower curve in Figure 4 is for the first day on which the five-minute rather than the three-minute period was given. Up to and including this record, no effect of the anticipation of the shock could be detected, since the animals were not responding at a significant rate. The drive was then raised, and the upper curve of Figure 4 shows the performance of the same group on the following day. By sighting along the curve, one may observe a marked depression in the rate of responding during the period of the tone. Comparison with Curve *B* in Figure 3 shows that, although the baseline at the higher drive is more irregular, a depression of relatively the same magnitude is obtained. In this case, coincidental presentations of shock and response may safely be ignored, yet the tone has acquired the same depressing effect upon the behavior.

Another characteristic which deserves attention is the compensatory increase in periodic rate following the period of depression. This appears to some extent in all records obtained; but it may be seen most clearly in Curve *B* of Figure 5, a periodic curve for all 24 rats after the emotional conditioning was quite complete. The curve was obtained about two weeks after the records in Figure 3. Curves *A* and *C* are controls taken (at a

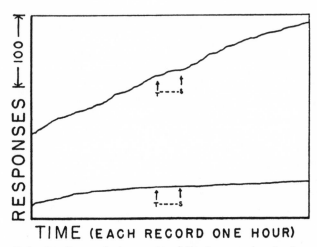

TIME (EACH RECORD ONE HOUR)

FIG. 4. Reduction in rate during anxiety following experiments at a very low drive. The lower record is a curve for six rats at a very low drive but otherwise comparable with the curves in Figs. 2 and 3. The upper curve is for the same group at a higher drive on the following day. The tone has an obvious effect, although all previous presentations have been made at a drive so low that no effect was observable.

slightly higher drive) on adjacent days. By sighting along Curve *B,* one may observe a clear-cut increase in rate subsequent to the shock, which continues until the extrapolation of the curve preceding the break is reached. Evidently the effect of the emotional state is a temporary depression of the strength of the behavior, the total amount of responding during the experimental period (the "reserve") remaining the same. Similar compensatory increases have been described under a number of circumstances, including physical restraint of the response.

Effects of Anxiety upon Extinction

When reinforcement with food is withheld, the rat continues to respond, but with a declining rate, and describes the typical extinction curve. The effects of anxiety upon this curve have been investigated. The first hour of a typical extinction curve, during which the combination of tone and shock was presented, is shown in the group curves of Figure 6 and the individual

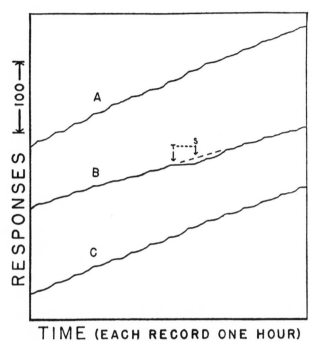

FIG. 5. Subsequent compensation for the reduction in rate during anxiety. The curves are averages for twenty-four rats taken on three consecutive days. *A* and *C* were taken under periodic reinforcement, while *B* shows the effect of the tone at a late stage in the experiment. The reduction in rate is followed by a compensatory increase, bringing the curve back to the extrapolation of the first part.

curves of Figure 7. By sighting along either curve in Figure 6, one may observe a distinct depression in rate during the period of the tone, and (following the shock) an equally distinct compensatory increase, which appears to be maintained until an extrapolation to the first part of the curve is approximated. Figure 7 contains sample records from four rats which showed different degrees of depression during the tone.

During extinction, then, a state of anxiety produces a decrease in the rate of responding and the terminating stimulus is followed by such a compensatory increase in rate that the final height of the curve is probably not modified.

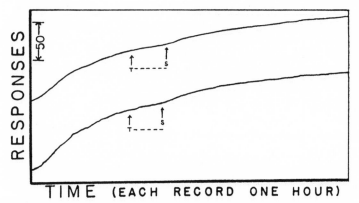

FIG. 6.   Effects of anxiety upon extinction. The lower curve is an average for six rats, the upper for twelve. The tone, which had previously been followed by shock during periodic reinforcement, depresses the slope of the extinction curves, and a compensatory increase follows the administration of the shock.

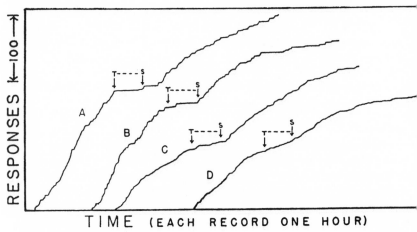

FIG. 7.   Effects of anxiety upon extinction. Individual records from the experiment represented in Fig. 6.

The Extinction of a State of Anxiety

A further property of anxiety was investigated by presenting the tone for a prolonged period without the terminal shock. In one experiment, while the rats were responding under periodic reinforcement, the tone was turned on after twenty-seven minutes of the experimental period had elapsed and allowed to sound for the remainder of the hour. The result is shown in Figures 8 and 9. It will be observed that the recovery of a normal periodic rate

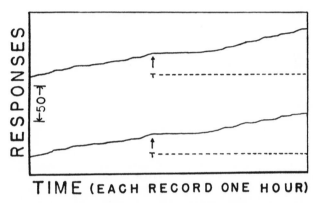

FIG. 8. Extinction of the effect of a tone when the terminating shock fails to appear. The upper record is the average curve for twelve rats under periodic reinforcement. The tone was turned on at T and continued to sound during the rest of the hour. No shock was given. The rate of responding returns to normal (and perhaps shows some compensatory increase) within ten minutes. The lower curve shows a repetition of the experiment ten days later.

is delayed considerably beyond the accustomed five-minute period of the tone. When the time is taken from the onset of the tone to the point at which the rat again reaches his previous periodic rate (measurements being made on individual curves), the mean period required for recovery is found to be 8.6 minutes. The group curve for twelve rats (the upper record in Figure 8) shows a definite compensatory increase in rate later in the hour, although the extrapolation of the first part of the curve is not quite reached by the end of the period.

The same experiment was repeated ten days later at a somewhat lower drive with the result shown in the lower curve in Figure 8. The mean delay

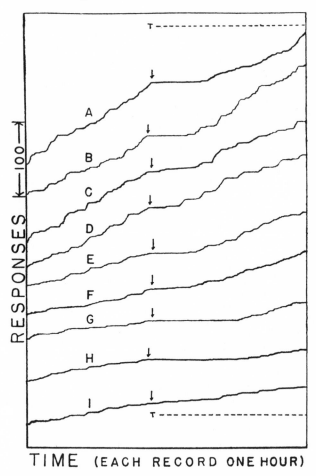

FIG. 9. Individual curves from the experiment described in Fig. 8.

in recovery is here 9.1 minutes, and recovery is less complete. Except for the effects of the difference in motivation, the two records appear quite similar and exemplify the reproducibility of behavior of this sort.

Because the period of depressed activity varies among rats, individual records are needed in order to observe the course of the recovery of normal strength during the extinction of anxiety. Figure 9 shows a number of individual records with different periodic rates, the differences being attributable mainly to differences in hunger. The lag in recovery appears in nearly all records, and the compensatory increase in periodic rate in the majority. In some curves, notably *E, F,* and *G,* an extrapolation of the first part is reached before the end of the hour. It is not clear that this would have been the case with the other rats if the experimental period could have been prolonged, but the curves in general appear to be positively accelerated.

Spontaneous recovery from the extinction of the anxiety is fairly complete. The daily record which preceded the upper figure in Figure 8 showed a ratio of 0.6 : 1.0 between the average periodic rate during the period of the tone and the normal rate for such an interval. On the day following the figure, the ratio was 0.7 : 1.0 for a similar period, indicating that little or no effect of extinction survived.

Summary

Anxiety is here defined as an emotional state arising in response to some current stimulus which in the past has been followed by a disturbing stimulus. The magnitude of the state is measured by its effect upon the strength of hunger-motivated behavior, in this case the rate with which rats pressed a lever under periodic reinforcement with food. Repeated presentations of a tone terminated by an electric shock produced a state of anxiety in response to the tone, the primary index being a reduction in strength of the hunger-motivated behavior during the period of the tone. When the shock was thus preceded by a period of anxiety, it produced a much more extensive disturbance in behavior than an "unanticipated" shock. The depression of the rate of responding during anxiety was characteristically followed by a compensatory increase in rate.

During experimental extinction of the response to the lever the tone produced a decrease in the rate of responding, and the terminating shock was followed by a compensatory increase in rate which probably restored the original projected height of the extinction curve.

The conditioned anxiety state was extinguished when the tone was presented for a prolonged period without the terminating shock. Spontaneous recovery from this extinction was nearly complete on the following day.

"Superstition" in the Pigeon

The following article is reprinted with permission from The Journal of Experimental Psychology (*1948,* 38, *168–172*).

To say that a reinforcement is contingent upon a response may mean nothing more than that it follows the response. It may follow because of some mechanical connection or because of the mediation of another organism; but conditioning takes place presumably because of the temporal relation only, expressed in terms of the order and proximity of response and reinforcement. Whenever we present a state of affairs which is known to be reinforcing at a given level of deprivation, we must suppose that conditioning takes place even though we have paid no attention to the behavior of the organism in making the presentation. A simple experiment demonstrates this to be the case.

A pigeon is reduced to 75 per cent of its weight when well fed. It is put into an experimental cage for a few minutes each day. A food hopper attached to the cage may be swung into place so that the pigeon can eat from it. A solenoid and a timing relay hold the hopper in place for five sec. at each presentation.

If a clock is now arranged to present the food hopper at regular intervals *with no reference whatsoever to the bird's behavior,* operant conditioning usually takes place. In six out of eight cases the resulting responses were so clearly defined that two observers could agree perfectly in counting instances. One bird was conditioned to turn counter-clockwise about the cage, making two or three turns between reinforcements. Another repeatedly thrust its head into one of the upper corners of the cage. A third developed a "tossing" response, as if placing its head beneath an invisible bar and lifting it repeatedly. Two birds developed a pendulum motion of the head and body, in which the head was extended forward and swung from right to left with a sharp movement followed by a somewhat slower return. The body generally followed the movement and a few steps might be taken when it was extensive. Another bird was conditioned to make incomplete pecking or brushing movements directed toward but not touching the floor. None of these responses appeared in any noticeable strength during adaptation to the cage or until the food hopper was periodically presented. In the remaining two cases, conditioned responses were not clearly marked.

The conditioning process is usually obvious. The bird happens to be executing some response as the hopper appears; as a result it tends to repeat this response. If the interval before the next presentation is not so great that extinction takes place, a second "contingency" is probable. This strengthens the response still further and subsequent reinforcement becomes more probable. It is true that some responses go unreinforced and some reinforcements appear when the response has not just been made, but the net result is the development of a considerable state of strength.

With the exception of the counter-clockwise turn, each response was almost always repeated in the same part of the cage, and it generally involved an orientation toward some feature of the cage. The effect of the reinforcement was to condition the bird to respond to some aspect of the environment rather than merely to execute a series of movements. All responses came to be repeated rapidly between reinforcements—typically five or six times in 15 sec.

The effect appears to depend upon the rate of reinforcement. In general, we should expect that the shorter the intervening interval, the speedier and more marked the conditioning. One reason is that the pigeon's behavior becomes more diverse as time passes after reinforcement. A hundred photographs, each taken two sec. after withdrawal of the hopper, would show fairly uniform behavior. The bird would be in the same part of the cage, near the hopper, and probably oriented toward the wall where the hopper has disappeared or turning to one side or the other. A hundred photographs taken after 10 sec., on the other hand, would find the bird in various parts of the cage responding to many different aspects of the environment. The sooner a second reinforcement appears, therefore, the more likely it is that the second reinforced response will be similar to the first, and also that they will both have one of a few standard forms. In the limiting case of a very brief interval the behavior to be expected would be holding the head toward the opening through which the magazine has disappeared.

Another reason for the greater effectiveness of short intervals is that the longer the interval, the greater the number of intervening responses emitted without reinforcement. The resulting extinction cancels the effect of an occasional reinforcement.

According to this interpretation the effective interval will depend upon the rate of conditioning and the rate of extinction, and will therefore vary with the deprivation and also presumably between species. Fifteen sec. is a very effective interval at the level of deprivation indicated above. One min. is much less so. When a response has once been set up, however, the interval can be lengthened. In one case it was extended to two min., and a high rate of responding was maintained with no sign of weakening. In another case, many hours of responding were observed with an interval of one min. between reinforcements.

In the latter case, the response showed a noticeable drift in topography. It began as a sharp movement of the head from the middle position to the left. This movement became more energetic, and eventually the whole body of the bird turned in the same direction, and a step or two would be taken. After many hours, the stepping response became the predominant feature. The bird made a well-defined hopping step from the right to the left foot, meanwhile turning its head and body to the left as before.

When the stepping response became strong, it was possible to obtain a mechanical record by putting the bird on a large tambour directly connected with a small tambour which made a delicate electric contact each time stepping took place. By watching the bird and listening to the sound of the recorder it was possible to confirm the fact that a fairly authentic record was being made. It was possible for the bird to hear the recorder at each step, but this was, of course, in no way correlated with feeding. The record obtained when the magazine was presented once per minute resembles in every respect the characteristic curve for the pigeon under fixed-interval reinforcement of a standard selected response. A well-marked temporal discrimination develops. The bird does not respond immediately after eating, but when 10 or 15 or even 20 sec. have elapsed, it begins to respond rapidly and continues until the reinforcement is received.

In this case it was possible to record the "extinction" of the response when the clock was turned off and the magazine was no longer presented at any time. The bird continued to respond with its characteristic side to side hop. More than 10,000 responses were recorded before "extinction" had reached the point at which few if any responses were made during a 10 or 15 min. interval. When the clock was again started, the periodic presentation of the magazine (still without any connection whatsoever with the bird's behavior) brought out a typical curve for reconditioning after fixed-interval reinforcement, shown in Figure 1. The record has been essentially horizontal for 20 min. prior to the beginning of this curve. The first reinforcement had some slight effect and the second a greater effect.

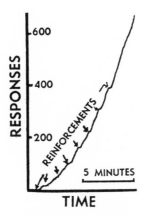

FIG. 1. "Reconditioning" of a superstitious response after extinction. The response of hopping from right to left had been thoroughly extinguished just before the record was taken. The arrows indicate the automatic presentation of food at one-min. intervals without reference to the pigeon's behavior.

There is a smooth positive acceleration in rate as the bird returns to the rate of responding which prevailed when it was reinforced every minute.

When the response was again extinguished and the periodic presentation of food then resumed, a different response was picked up. This consisted of a progressive walking response in which the bird moved about the cage. The response of hopping from side to side never reappeared and could not, of course, be obtained deliberately without making the reinforcement contingent upon the behavior.

The experiment might be said to demonstrate a sort of superstition. The bird behaves as if there were a causal relation between its behavior and the presentation of food, although such a relation is lacking. There are many analogies in human behavior. Rituals for changing one's luck at cards are good examples. A few accidental connections between a ritual and favorable consequences suffice to set up and maintain the behavior in spite of many unreinforced instances. The bowler who has released a ball down the alley but continues to behave as if he were controlling it by twisting and turning his arm and shoulder is another case in point. These behaviors have, of course, no real effect upon one's luck or upon a ball halfway down an alley, just as in the present case the food would appear as often if the pigeon did nothing—or, strictly speaking, did something else.

It is perhaps not quite correct to say that conditioned behavior has been set up without any previously determined contingency whatsoever. We have appealed to a uniform sequence of responses in the behavior of the pigeon to obtain an over-all net contingency. When we arrange a clock to present food every 15 sec., we are in effect basing our reinforcement upon a limited set of responses which frequently occur 15 sec. after reinforcement. When a response has been strengthened (and this may result from one reinforcement), the setting of the clock implies an even more restricted contingency. Something of the same sort is true of the bowler. It is not quite correct to say that there is no connection between his twisting and turning and the course taken by the ball at the far end of the alley. The connection was established before the ball left the bowler's hand, but since both the path of the ball and the behavior of the bowler are determined, some relation survives. The subsequent behavior of the bowler may have no effect upon the ball, but the behavior of the ball has an effect upon the bowler. The contingency, though not perfect, is enough to maintain the behavior in strength. The particular form of the behavior adopted by the bowler is due to induction from responses in which there is actual contact with the ball. It is clearly a movement appropriate to changing the ball's direction. But this does not invalidate the comparison, since we are not concerned with what response is selected but with why it persists in strength. In rituals for changing luck the inductive strengthening of a particular form of behavior is generally absent. The behavior of the pigeon in this experiment is of the latter sort, as the variety of responses obtained from different pigeons indicates. Whether there is any unconditioned behavior in the pigeon appropriate to a given effect upon the environment is under investigation.

The results throw some light on incidental behavior observed in experiments in which a discriminative stimulus is frequently presented. Such a stimulus has reinforcing value and can set up superstitious behavior. A pigeon will often develop some response such as turning, twisting, pecking near the locus of the discriminative stimulus, flapping its wings, and so on. In much of the work to date in this field the interval between presentations of the discriminative stimulus has been one min. and many of these superstitious responses are short-lived. Their appearance as the result of accidental correlations with the presentation of the stimulus is unmistakable.

A Second Type of "Superstition" in the Pigeon

(WITH W. H. MORSE)

The following article is reprinted with permission from The American Journal of Psychology (*1957, 70, 308-311*).

When food is given to a hungry organism, any behavior in progress at the moment must be assumed to be reinforced by this event. When small amounts of food are repeatedly given, a "superstitious ritual" may be set up. This is due not only to the fact that a reinforcing stimulus strengthens any behavior it may happen to follow, even though a contingency has not been explicitly arranged, but also to the fact that the change in behavior resulting from one accidental contingency makes similar accidents more probable. In an earlier experiment the automatic operation of a food-magazine every 15 sec. was found to induce hungry pigeons to engage in such ritualistic behavior as bowing, scraping, turning, and dancing [see page 570]. In some cases the behavior was stable, in others the topography slowly changed; but in all cases superstitious effects survived indefinitely. Similar effects from the adventitious reinforcement arising from the presentation of discriminative stimuli have recently been observed.[1] Such effects must always be allowed for in designing experiments on complex behavior.

Accidental, but nevertheless effective, relationships may arise in the *sensory* control of operant behavior. For example, a stimulus present when a response is reinforced may acquire discriminative control over the response even though its presence at reinforcement is adventitious. Suppose, for example, that an organism is responding at a moderate rate on a variable-interval schedule of reinforcement, and let an incidental stimulus (A) occasionally appear for a brief period. Even though there is no explicit temporal relation between the appearance of A and the program of reinforcement, a response will occasionally be reinforced in the presence of A.

[1] Morse, W. H. An analysis of responding in the presence of a stimulus correlated with periods of non-reinforcement. Unpublished doctoral dissertation, Harvard University, 1955.

For a brief period the frequency of such reinforcement may be appreciably greater than in the absence of A. An organism which is sensitive to slight differences in rate of reinforcement will form a discrimination; its rate of responding in the presence of A will become greater than in the absence of A. This might be called a positive sensory superstition. If, on the other hand, reinforcements happen to occur relatively infrequently in the presence of A, a discrimination will develop in the opposite direction, as the result of which the rate in the presence of A will be relatively low—a sort of negative sensory superstition.

When an accidental contingency has produced a higher or lower rate of responding in the presence of an incidental stimulus, a second effect follows. If the rate has fallen in the presence of A (because reinforcements have been relatively infrequent), responses will be even less likely to be reinforced in the presence of A. In the limiting case no responses will be made in the presence of A, and no response, of course, reinforced. Moreover, reinforcements which are made available during A are not obtained because responses are not made. The first response following the withdrawal of A is then reinforced, and the discrimination is further strengthened. Similarly, when the rate is increased during A because of favorable accidental reinforcements, all reinforcements set up during A are likely to be obtained, and if the preceding condition commands a relatively low rate, some reinforcements set up at that time may actually be obtained after A has appeared, to strengthen the discrimination.

Both types of "sensory superstition" have been demonstrated experimentally in the pigeon. The apparatus consisted of the usual experimental space $13 \times 22 \times 16$ in. A small translucent plastic plate was mounted behind a 1-in. circular opening at head height on one wall. It was lighted from behind by an orange 6-w. bulb. The pigeon pecked this disk to operate the controlling circuit. Food was presented for reinforcement in an opening below this key. Water was available.

Three pigeons, two of which had previously been reinforced on other schedules, were placed on a variable-interval schedule of reinforcement with a mean interval of 30 min. The shortest interval between reinforcements was 1 min., the longest 59 min. Daily experimental sessions varied between 6 and 20 hr. in length. Body weight was maintained at approximately 80% of the *ad lib* weight, and a reinforcement consisted of access to mixed grain for 5 sec. The resulting performance was at a low mean rate of responding with some local irregularity. Against this baseline, an incidental stimulus consisting of a blue light projected on the key instead of orange was introduced for 4 min. once per hour. The schedule of occurrence of this stimulus was independent of the programming schedule. The rate of responding was recorded continuously in the usual cumulative curve. Brief downward movements of the pen marked reinforcements, and the pen remained down during the 4-min. period of the incidental stimulus, thus slightly displacing the record made in the presence of the stimulus without changing its slope.

Segments of records showing superstitious differences in rate under the control of the incidental stimulus are shown in Figure 1. Except for the

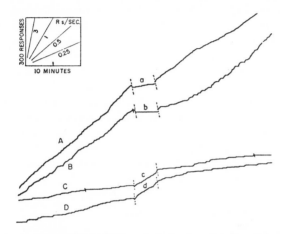

Fig. 1. Superstitious discriminative control of responding by an incidental stimulus. The stimulus is presented for 4 min. once per hour, and is marked by the downward displacement of the recording pen (*a, b, c,* and *d*). Curves *A* and *B* are segments of cumulative response-curves on a variable-interval schedule (mean interval = 30 min.) for a pigeon with a *lower* rate when the incidental stimulus is present than when it is absent—a "negative superstition." Curves *C* and *D* are segments for another pigeon on the same schedule with a *higher* rate in the presence of the incidental stimulus—a "positive superstition."

portions *a, b, c,* and *d,* the curves are characteristic of the baselines obtained on the schedule described above. Curves *A* and *B* are for a pigeon which showed sustained periods of negative superstition. The over-all rate generated by the schedule is relatively high (of the order of 0.5 responses per sec.). Whenever the incidental stimulus appears, the rate drops to a low value or to zero (*a* and *b*). Records *C* and *D* are for another pigeon showing a positive superstition. The base rate is relatively low, and the rate in the presence of an incidental stimulus at c and d is clearly of a much higher order.

The direction of the superstition is not necessarily stable. In a long experimental session a positive superstition may give way to a negative form, or vice versa. Such changes are usually easily explained in terms of adventitious reinforcement or failure to receive reinforcement in the presence of the incidental stimulus. All three birds showed periods of both positive and negative superstition.

There are several arbitrary features of such an experiment. In the present case the incidental stimulus was present 1/15 of the time during a session. A relatively shorter period would be less likely to receive reinforcements on a given schedule, and might be expected to produce negative superstition more frequently. At the other extreme, an incidental stimulus which occupied half the experimental session would presumably share so nearly equally in the reinforcements that there would be no substantial separation of rates. The schedule and the performance generated are also relevant in determining the frequency of adventitious reinforcement. Finally, the nature and intensity of the incidental stimulus also may have their effect.

Pending an investigation of these parameters, it may at least be said that incidental stimuli adventitiously related to reinforcement may acquire marked discriminative functions.

Two "Synthetic Social Relations"

About 10 years ago, two demonstration experiments were designed for a General Education course in Human Behavior at Harvard. They were briefly described in an illustrated weekly and are occasionally referred to in the psychological literature. It seems advisable to publish a somewhat more explicit account.

The "Ping-Pong" Playing Pigeons

There were several versions of this apparatus, in one of which a motor-driven device returned the ping-pong ball to the playing surface so that the apparatus ran without attention. In a less mechanized version, the "ping-pong" table was approximately 8 in. wide, 16 in. long, and 8 in. high (Fig. 1). A pigeon standing at one end could conveniently peck a ball as it arrived at the edge of the table. If the ball rolled off the edge, it fell into a trough and tripped a switch which operated a food dispenser under the opposite edge and thus reinforced the pigeon which "won the point." Light metal rails prevented the ball from falling off the sides of the table. The surface was slightly canted, sloping from a center line toward each edge so that the ball would not stop on it. Wire barriers prevented the pigeons from jumping up on the table but did not interfere with play.

In the finished performance, the demonstrator would start a ball near the middle of the table. It rolled to one edge and the pigeon on that side pecked it, driving it back across the table. At the other edge it was pecked by the other pigeon and thus returned. The pigeons usually watched the course of the ball as it crossed the table, and maneuvered into position to meet the return. They developed considerable skill in sending the ball

From *Journal of the Experimental Analysis of Behavior*, 1962, 5, 531–533. This research was supported by NSF Grant G18167.

579

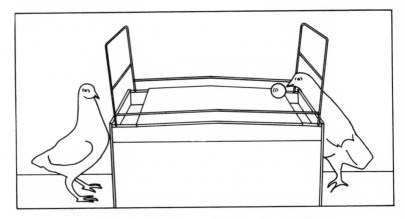

FIG. 1.   Two pigeons "playing ping-pong."

straight across. Moving pictures show rallies of as many as five or six shots before a point was made. There is no evidence, however, that either pigeon reached the stage of placing or changing the pace of its shots so that the opponent would miss.

Conditioning was begun with one pigeon at a time. A standard table tennis ball was fastened at the edge of the table, and a hungry pigeon was reinforced with food when it pecked it. At this stage the ball was not a powerful controlling stimulus; when it was moved to a different part of the edge, the pigeons often pecked the air where it had been. Eventually, however, they pecked the ball regardless of its position. The ball was then made free to roll away from the pigeon when struck. A mechanical reinforcing system was set up in which the ball, rolling up a slight grade, struck a cross-bar operating the food dispenser. The distance to the bar was gradually increased. If the ball failed to reach the bar, it rolled back and came to rest against a raised molding along the edge. The molding was later removed.

As the distance between the pigeon and the reinforcing bar was increased, reinforcement was more and more delayed, and the behavior occasionally suffered. Eventually, however, mediating behavior arose to bridge the temporal gap. Even so, in the final game, in which two pigeons participated, the delay between striking the ball and the successful outcome of getting the ball past the opponent was occasionally troublesome. A deteriorating performance could be rescued by reinforcing a pigeon with a hand-switch at the moment it struck the ball. Eventually the behavior was sustained not only for rallies of several shots at a time but for a full "game."

The demonstration offers a convenient example of competition. One bird is reinforced at the expense of another. If one is repeatedly successful, the other suffers extinction ("discouragement"). It was possible to maintain a reasonable balance in successful play by lowering the weight of the relatively unsuccessful bird or raising that of the successful, the principal effect being to sustain attention rather than alter accuracy or power.

Cooperating Pigeons

Two pigeons in adjacent compartments were separated by a pane of glass. Three red buttons were arranged in a vertical row on each side of the glass, as shown in Fig. 2. The buttons were approximately 10 in., 7½ in., and 5 in. from the floor, respectively. By pecking a button the pigeon closed a switch. In the final performance, both pigeons were reinforced with food (Fig. 2, below) when they pecked a corresponding pair of buttons so nearly simultaneously that the brief closures of the circuits (each lasting perhaps a tenth of a second) overlapped. At any given time, however, only one pair of buttons was operative, and the effective pair was scheduled in a roughly random way.

It was necessary for the pigeons to cooperate in two tasks: (1) discovering the effective pair and (2) pecking both buttons at the same time. In general, no pattern of exploration could be observed. The pigeons tested all three pairs of buttons in what was evidently an unsystematic way. In general, there was a division of labor with respect to the two tasks. One pigeon (the "leader") explored—that is, it struck the three buttons in some order. A similar performance could have been generated in one pigeon alone in the apparatus by requiring simply that a given one of three buttons be struck. The other pigeon (the "follower") struck the button opposite that being struck by the leader. Similar behavior could have been generated in one pigeon alone in the apparatus if one button after another had been marked by a discriminative stimulus.

A well-marked leader-follower relation could be established or reversed by altering the relative level of food deprivation, the more deprived bird assuming the position of leader by moving more alertly to the buttons. However, even a decisive leader was probably to some extent following. A deprived pigeon would usually "wait to be followed" by one less deprived before exploring the buttons vigorously. Under levels of deprivation at which both birds responded quickly and without interruption, perform-

FIG. 2.   Above: Two pigeons cooperating by pecking corresponding buttons at the same moment. Below: Pigeons eating from food dispensers.

ance became so perfect that it gave the impression of one pigeon seen in a mirror.

The performance was established by conditioning each bird separately to peck the three buttons, reinforcement being roughly randomized. When sustained behavior occurred on all three buttons, two birds could be put in the adjacent spaces for the first time. The presence of another bird temporarily disturbed the performance, but both birds eventually began to respond to the buttons. At this stage responses to corresponding buttons within, say, half a second of each other would trigger both food-dispensers.

These contingencies sufficed to build cooperative behavior without further attention. The visual stimulation supplied by one pigeon pecking on a button became a discriminative stimulus controlling a response to the corresponding button on the part of the other.

Prolonged exposure to these conditions made pigeons strongly imitative in other respects. They would often drink from glasses of water in the compartments at the same time, for example. The extent to which their behaviors were mutually controlled was informally demonstrated when the experiment was shown to a group of biologists, one of whom suggested putting the birds in the opposite compartments. The birds immediately lined up alongside the glass plate, facing away from the buttons. They thus assumed their previously effective positions relative to each other, but were now facing the audience through the transparent front wall of the apparatus. Though no buttons were available, they immediately began to cooperate in exploring a corresponding area, bobbing up and down in a perfect mirror-image pattern under the control of each other's behavior. Possibly because the leader-follower relation had frequently been shifted, each bird was evidently largely controlled by the behavior of the other.

Concurrent Activity Under Fixed-Interval Reinforcement

(WITH W. H. MORSE)

Under many schedules of reinforcement there are significant periods of time during which the organism does not display the behavior under investigation. For example, on a fixed-interval schedule there is commonly a period of no responding after reinforcement. The behavior which actually occurs at such times is apparently unrelated to any explicit reinforcement, yet the schedule is at least effective in controlling the time of its occurrence. Interesting examples are found in the field of psychotic behavior, where the patient engages in compulsive or other idiosyncratic ways only when he is not executing the behavior under the control of a given schedule. What the organism is doing when it is not showing the behavior produced by a schedule of reinforcement is especially important when we come to set up complex behavior in which two or more responses are studied at the same time.

Method

Unreinforced behavior accompanying the performance generated by a common schedule of reinforcement was studied in the following way. A standard rat lever and food magazine were installed alongside the open face of an aluminum running wheel. The wheel was 13 in. in diameter, had a low moment of inertia, and turned in only one direction against friction which was just overcome by a tangential force of 30 gm. Through a gear-reduction and pulley system the rotation of the wheel advanced a pen across the moving paper tape of a modified cumulative recorder. Scales were chosen so that the commonest speed of running produced a slope in the neighborhood of 45°. Responses to the lever operated a standard cumulative recorder.

From *Journal of Comparative and Physiological Psychology*, 1957, 30, 279–281.

Two rats were conditioned to respond to the operation of the magazine until they quickly seized and ate the .1-gm. pellet of food delivered. At this stage the wheel was immovable. After three sessions of magazine training all responses to the lever were reinforced for several sessions. A fixed-interval schedule was then put into effect, under which a reinforcement was set up every 5 min. (FI5) during a session of 3 hr. and 20 min. Both rats developed marked "scallops" during the first session, and the fixed-interval performance was allowed to develop during several sessions until the pause after reinforcement was well marked. At the beginning of the ninth experimental session on FI5 the wheel was unlocked. The rat could now respond to the lever or run in the wheel. (It could not do both at the same time because it faced away from the lever when running.) Because of its low inertia the wheel could be stopped and started instantly; hence a change could readily be made from one form of behavior to the other. Responses to the lever continued to be reinforced on FI5; no reinforcement was explicitly contingent upon running.

Results

The first performance when the wheel was unlocked is shown for one rat in Fig. 1. Segments *A* and *A'* comprise a continuous record of the move-

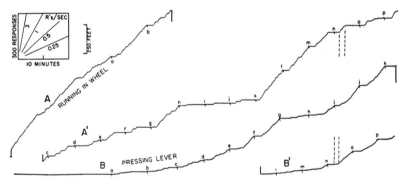

FIG. 1

ment of the wheel. Segments *B* and *B'* show the concurrent activity on the lever. Reinforcements are marked by small hatches. Reinforcement *a* in Record *A* is the same event as that marked at *a* in Record *B*, and the same correspondence is maintained throughout the figure. It will be seen that the movable wheel occupies the rat for nearly 20 min. (beginning of Record *A*), during which no responses were made to the lever (beginning of Record *B*). A first response to the lever is reinforced at *a*. The rat continues to show a high rate of running on the wheel between reinforcements *a* and *c* in Records *A* and *A'*, with corresponding low activity on the lever shown between reinforcements *a* and *c* in Record *B*. A few responses are made to the lever, however, and reinforcements are received approximately on schedule.

Before the end of the session the over-all rate of running has fallen off considerably (end of *A'*), and a fairly normal fixed-interval performance has been restored (end of *B'*). Running during each interval already begins to show a temporal pattern, which became consistent in later sessions. After reinforcement the rat neither runs nor presses the lever for a short period of time, which is much longer than the time required to eat the pellet of food. It then runs actively for distances of the order of 100 to 200 ft. before returning to the lever to resume a fairly standard-interval performance. After the reinforcement marked *n*, for example, a short horizontal section appears in both records. There is then a short burst of running in the wheel, marked by the vertical dotted lines in *A'*. The corresponding period in the lever record is indicated in *B'*. Running in the wheel ceases during the second half of the interval, when fairly constant responding on the lever is shown, leading to the reinforcement at *o*.

In order to obtain a collateral measure of the rate of unreinforced running, the following program was instituted. At the beginning of each session the rat had access to the wheel for approximately ½ hr., during which no responses to the lever were reinforced. A 6-w. lamp, previously used for general illumination in the apparatus, was off during this period, and responses to the lever were quickly extinguished in the absence of the light. The light was then turned on for 100 min., during which 20 responses were reinforced on FI5. The light was then turned off, and further running in the absence of responding to the lever was recorded.

The end of such a session for the rat in Fig. 1 is shown in Fig. 2. The curve at *B* shows the last five segments of the fixed-interval performance prevailing at this stage of the experiment. The segments at *A* and *A'* comprise a continuous record of the performance in the wheel during the five intervals and, beginning at *a*, after the light has been turned off and responding to the lever has ceased. Corresponding portions are connected by broken lines. The fixed-interval segments in *B* are now relatively "square" and suggest that responding is being postponed by the activity in the wheel. When pressing begins, however, a fairly stable, uniform rate is assumed until reinforcement. For a substantial period of time after each reinforcement, the lever is not pressed and running does not occur. Sustained run-

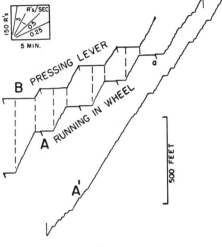

FIG. 2

ning then takes place for 2 or 3 min., yielding to the behavior on the lever for the rest of the interval.

The beginning of a daily session for the other rat at the same stage as Fig. 2 is shown in Fig. 3. Segment *A* and the first part of *A'* show the

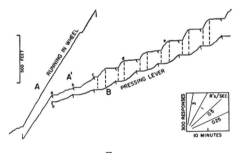

FIG. 3

relatively fast spontaneous running in the absence of the light, when responses to the lever are not reinforced. When a first response is reinforced in the presence of the light at *a*, a performance appropriate to FI5 is begun (Record *B*). Note that, although there is little activity on the lever during the first two intervals, running in the wheel is greatly suppressed (compare the segments preceding *b* and *c* with Record *A*). A stable performance persists for the balance of the session, not all of which is shown in the figure. For a short period of time after reinforcement the rat does not respond to either lever or wheel. A burst of running then follows. This yields to responding to the lever in a somewhat more continuous fashion than in the case of the other rat. The rate of running falls off in a particularly smooth curve at *d* and *e*. The segments of Record *B* showing concurrent activity on the lever have a corresponding positive curvature which is absent in Fig. 2. A continuous change as in Fig. 3 was occasionally shown by the first rat, although the more rapid shift from wheel to lever seen in Fig. 2 was characteristic.

Since responding on the wheel falls off to zero or very nearly zero late in each interval, few if any adventitious reinforcements of running could occur as the result of quick shifts from wheel to lever. We may therefore suppose that activity in the wheel remains essentially unconditioned with respect to food reinforcement.

Summary

When a rat is free to run in a low-inertia running wheel or to press a lever for food on a fixed-interval schedule, the resolution of the competition between running and pressing can be expressed in the following way. When the schedule normally generates a substantial rate of responding, running in the wheel is suppressed. When the schedule does not generate a substantial rate, running in the wheel occurs. Shortly after reinforcement, however, both behaviors are absent.

Sustained Performance During Very Long Experimental Sessions

(WITH W. H. MORSE)

Operant behavior is usually studied in experimental sessions separated by periods when the organism is not closely observed in its home cage. Even though technical advances are now available for maintaining responding for extended periods of time, the behavior under observation is seldom followed continuously 24 hours per day. The possibility of decrements in behavior (such as occur in "mental fatigue") prompted us to see just how long an animal could be kept responding in a continuous session.

The schedule of positive reinforcement best suited to maintain responding continuously is the differential reinforcement of very low rates. In the pigeon, this schedule can sustain behavior with a frequency of reinforcement below that required to maintain body weight.[1] The effect of sustained responding on several different performances can be observed by combining other schedules with the differential reinforcement of low rates in a multiple program, provided that reinforcement on these other schedules occurs infrequently enough to prevent satiation.

In the present experiment a multiple schedule was used which had the following components: a basic schedule, DRL, maintained responding at a fairly constant, low rate under the control of one key-color. Once every hour the color of the key changed to that designating another schedule, which was then in effect until reinforcement occurred. The other schedule was, alternately, either FR or FI. In this way, three different performances could be studied during continuous experimental sessions lasting many days or even weeks. The bird remained continuously in the experimental space,

From *Journal of the Experimental Analysis of Behavior,* 1958, *1,* 235–244.

[1] Herrnstein, R. J., and Morse, W. H. Some effects of response-independent positive reinforcement on maintained operant behavior, *J. Comp. Physiol. Psychol.,* 1957, *50,* 461–467.

and the over-all rate of reinforcement maintained the body weight, with only a slow drift toward satiation or a more extreme deprivation.

Procedure

A standard pigeon box was modified to accommodate a considerable quantity of grain in the food hopper. The magazine presented grain for 5 seconds. Fresh water was supplied from the outside of the box through a tube. Two adult male White Carneau pigeons were magazine-trained, and all responses to the key were reinforced (*crf*) during three sessions for a total of 180 reinforcements per bird. The color of the key changed after each reinforcement to white, red, or green in random order. The birds were then run for 12 daily sessions lasting from 4 to 7 hours each on DRL 1 min. in the presence of the white key-light—that is, a response was reinforced only if it followed a period of 1 minute without a response. If a response occurred before 1 minute had elapsed since the previous response, the timer programming reinforcement was reset to zero, and the next response was reinforced only if it occurred after another minute or more had elapsed.

When a stable performance had developed on the DRL schedule, the multiple schedule was introduced. At 1-hour intervals the color of the key was changed from white (DRL) to either red or green: when it was red, the 50th response was reinforced (FR 50); when green, the first response after 10 minutes was reinforced (FI 10). After reinforcement on either the fixed-ratio or fixed-interval component, the key-color changed to white and the DRL schedule was again in effect. Three cumulative records were taken: one of the DRL performance (the recorder stopping when the other schedules were in force), one of the alternating FR and FI performances (the recorder stopping during DRL), and one of the DRL performance on a recorder with greatly reduced scales (one-twelfth the usual coordinates) to provide a short summarizing record of the whole experiment. When the multiple schedule was first introduced, each pigeon was run for several sessions approximately 3 days long. Later, the session was allowed to continue until the bird stopped responding because of satiation (or until the apparatus failed).

Results

It was found that a pigeon could sustain a continuous performance indefinitely if precautions were taken to prevent satiation. During a long session the fixed-interval performance of the multiple schedule occasionally showed unusual properties, and all three performances changed in expected directions if satiation occurred. Typical effects are shown in the cumulative records which follow.

ACQUISITION OF THE DRL PERFORMANCE

In the transition to DRL from *crf* for Pigeon 162 (Fig. 1), a first re-

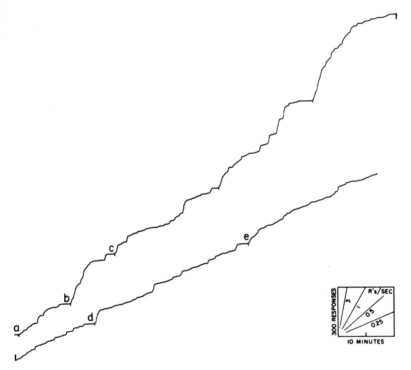

FIG. 1. Pigeon 162. Cumulative-response curve during the 1st session of DRL 1 minute after *crf*. See text for explanation of letters.

sponse was preceded by a pause of more than 1 minute and was reinforced (at *a*). A pattern of responding typical of extinction then followed, as expected from the previous *crf*. A pause sufficiently long to meet the DRL requirement finally occurred, and a second response was reinforced (at *b*).

An extinction curve beginning at a higher rate followed, and the DRL contingency was again met at *c*. The over-all rate gradually fell to a fairly steady, low level, but occasional pauses were long enough to set up reinforcements, as at *d* and *e*. The latter part of the session is not shown.

The development of the 1-minute DRL performance for Pigeon 163 is shown in Fig. 2. Curve *B* is the summarizing record from the recorder with

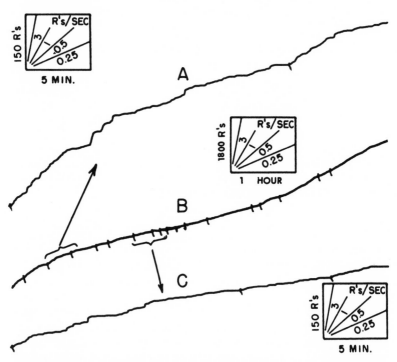

FIG. 2.   Pigeon 163. Performance during 1st session of DRL 1 min. after *crf*. Records A and C are enlarged segments of Record B.

reduced scales. Records A and C, segments from the other DRL record, are located as indicated on Record B. The early performance of this bird is similar to the early stages of Fig. 1. By the end of the session the over-all rate has declined, but the requirement of a 1-minute pause is met only infrequently.

Further development of the DRL performance is shown in Fig. 3. Curve

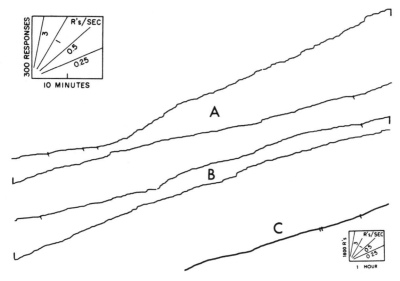

FIG. 3. Performance on DRL 1 min. Record A (Pigeon 163) and Record B (Pigeon 162) are from the middle of the third session. Record C (Pigeon 163) is the complete 12th session on DRL greatly reduced.

A is for Pigeon 163, Curve *B* is for Pigeon 162. Both curves are taken from the middle of the third session, approximately 10 hours after the beginning of DRL. Although the prevailing rate fluctuates, few pauses of greater than 1 minute occur. Curve *C,* shown on reduced coordinates, is the last DRL session for Pigeon 163. Note that the rate here is so uniformly sustained above 1 response per minute that only three reinforcements are received during the 5½-hour session. A rate of this order is needed for uninterrupted experimental sessions of the multiple schedule since 24 reinforcements will be received each day on the hourly ratio and interval components, and not more than an additional 10 reinforcements per day is needed to maintain the pigeon in the range of its experimental body weight.

PROLONGED PERFORMANCE DURING CONTINUOUS SESSIONS

The reduced summary record of the performance on the DRL component of the multiple schedule for Pigeon 162 during a single continuous session 154 hours long is shown in Fig. 4. This was the sixth long session

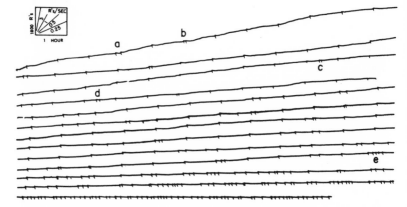

FIG. 4.   Pigeon 162. Performance on DRL component of mult FI 10 FR 50 DRL 1 min. during 6th extended session (6½ days long).

for this bird, earlier sessions having been from 7 to 17 days long. (The summary record for the first long session for this bird has been published elsewhere.[2]) In Fig. 4 the recorder was stopped while the other schedules were in effect, but all reinforcements are shown. Those received on FR or FI can generally be identified because they occurred exactly 1 hour apart. It will be seen that only an occasional reinforcement is received on DRL. Reinforcements on DRL frequently occurred either after changing from the FR or FI schedule (as at *a* and *b*), or in pairs during the DRL component, as at *c* or *d*. (It is fairly characteristic of responding on DRL that reinforcements are received in pairs.)

In the session shown in Fig. 4 the rate fell because of an increase in body weight. Reinforcement occurred more frequently as satiation progressed because the DRL contingency was more frequently met. The last two lines of Fig. 4 show a frequency of reinforcement which produced such complete satiation that the experiment was stopped. Note that even when the over-all frequency of reinforcement is fairly high, reinforcements still tend to be grouped together, as at *e*.

During the long session shown in Fig. 4, performances on the fixed-ratio and fixed-interval components were recorded in a single cumulative curve. Record A of Fig. 5 shows the initial performance on the first day. The first interval shows no scalloping. A shallow scallop is characteristic of the start of the session on FI, but the present curve is unusually straight. This may

---

[2] Skinner, B. F.; see page 132.

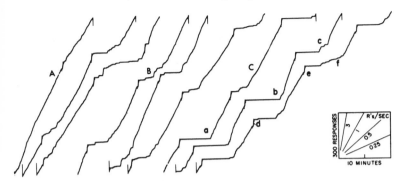

Fɪɢ. 5.   Pigeon 162. Performance on FI and FR components of mult FI 10 FR 50 DRL 1 min. during 6th extended session. Record A begins after 1 hour, Record B after 45 hours, and Record C after 105 hours from the beginning of the experiment.

be due in part to the fact that the bird had not been in the apparatus for 5 days (while the other bird had been studied). The shallow scalloping of later intervals in Fig. 5A may be partly due to the fact that the interval components are separated by 2 hours of other schedules. This fact may also have a bearing on the rather irregular performance shown in Record B (a segment beginning 45 hours after the start of the experiment) and Record C (beginning after 105 hours). Many of the intervals show a long pause followed by a high initial rate, as at *a* and *b*. "Knees" are common in Records A and B, and are seen later (as at *c*). In general, the terminal rate of the intervals is rather low and the curves are frequently negatively accelerated just before reinforcement. Some of this irregularity may be due to induction from DRL. In multiple schedules containing DRL components, superstitious "marking time" behavior is occasionally observed in other interval components. Occasionally, however, the more gradual increase in rate typical of fixed-interval reinforcement can be seen (as at *f*).

The fixed-ratio performance scarcely changed during the part of the session shown in Fig. 5. Slight pauses sometimes occur at the beginning of the ratio (as at *d* and *e*), but the terminal rate remains high throughout.

Both the fixed-ratio and fixed-interval performances change markedly toward the end of the long session. Figure 6, recorded immediately after Fig. 5C, shows the fixed-ratio and fixed-interval performances for more than a full day. Prolonged pauses now occur in interval components (as at *a*), and terminal rates in the intervals vary widely (compare intervals at

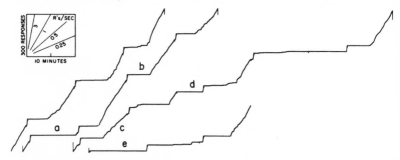

Fɪɢ. 6. Pigeon 162. Performance on FI and FR components of mult FI 10 FR 50 DRL 1 min. during 6th extended session. Record begins 125 hours after the beginning of the experiment.

b and *c*). The ratio performance frequently begins with a pause (as at *d* and *e*), but the rate remains high after responding has begun. The altered performance shown in Fig. 6 is presumably due to satiation; the record is similar to those obtained during progressive satiation on multiple fixed-ratio and fixed-interval schedules. The bird had begun the experiment weighing 390 grams (80% free-feeding weight) and weighed 440 grams (about 90%) when removed from the experimental box 7 days later.

Satiation can be prevented by changing the DRL value or by presenting the other schedules less frequently. In another extended session the bird shown in Fig. 4–6 responded for 28 days continuously. The value of DRL was varied between 3 and 4 minutes, as needed, to prevent extreme satiation or deprivation. During the first 2 days there was a slight increase in satiation and the bird paused for more than 10 minutes upon nine different occasions. During the next 6 days, however, no pause lasted for as long as 10 minutes. Subsequently, one pause of 11 minutes and one of 23 minutes appeared, but the bird did not pause for as long as 10 minutes during the next 6 days. Near the end of the experiment it again responded for 4 days with no pause longer than 12 minutes.

The fixed-ratio and fixed-interval performances during this 28-day session are sampled in Fig. 7 and 8. Figure 7A begins 56 hours after the start of the session. Occasional "knees" appear in the interval curves (as at *a* and *c*), and many intervals show the abrupt shift to a terminal rate following the initial pause (as at *b*). Sustained responding at a rate appropriate to the ratio component occurs at *d*, which is unusual in an ordinary multiple schedule. The ratio performance, meanwhile, shows a characteristic high rate with little or no pausing at the start.

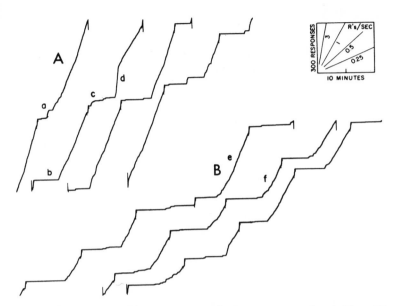

FIG. 7. Pigeon 162. Performance on FI and FR components of mult FI 10 FR 50 DRL 1 min. during 7th extended session (28 days long). Record A begins after 56 hours, and Record B after 264 hours.

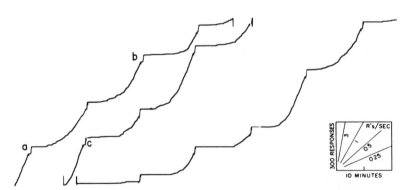

FIG. 8. Pigeon 162. Performance on FI and FR components of mult FI 10 FR 50 DRL 1 min. during 7th extended session. Record begins 474 hours after the beginning of the experiment.

Figure 7B was recorded after 264 hours. Although prolonged pauses and abrupt shifts to a moderate terminal rate still appear, some fairly characteristic interval curves may be seen (as at *e* and *f*). A series of reasonably normal interval scallops appear later in the session, as shown in Fig. 8, which begins after 474 hours of continuous responding. Both the interval and ratio performances are normal except for an occasional slight pause at the beginning of the ratio, as at *a, b,* and *c.* The performance in Fig. 8 shows little or no effect of the intervening hours on DRL or of sustained responding for almost 500 hours.

The other subject, Pigeon 163, showed more marked irregularities on the other components of the multiple schedule. Figure 9A, from the beginning

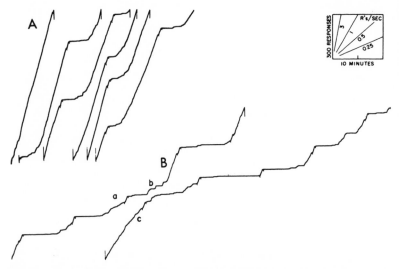

Fɪɢ. 9. Pigeon 163. Performance on FI and FR components of mult FI 10 FR 50 DRL 1 min. during 2nd extended session (24 days long). Record A begins 1 hour, and Record B 175 hours after the beginning of the session.

of an extended session, shows a relatively low rate on the ratio component, but a fairly good scallop on the interval component. The ratio rate is still low in Fig. 9B, 175 hours later, although it is now usually higher than the terminal rate in many of the intervals. "Knees" are common, as at *b,* and the interval curves tend to show negative acceleration, as at *a* and *c.* At this time the bird was responding at a steady sustained rate on DRL.

During another long session with Pigeon 163, the DRL rate was so consistently above that required for reinforcement that at one point in the experiment no reinforcement was received on DRL for over 31 hours. In other words, the pigeon never paused for as long as 3 minutes during that period. The sustained performance on the DRL component must have been due at least in part to induction from the intervening FR and FI components; no comparable performance has ever been observed on a simple DRL schedule. As with the other bird, however, induction was observed in the other direction. Figure 10 shows the FR and FI performances begin-

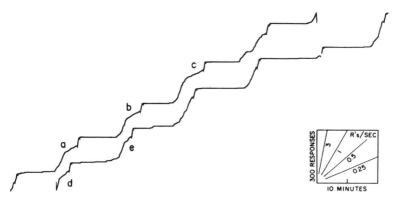

Fig. 10. Pigeon 163. Performance on FI and FR components of mult FI 10 FR 50 DRL 1 min. during the 3rd extended session (65 days long). Record begins 984 hours after the beginning of the session.

ning 984 hours after the start of the session. In general, the ratio performances are typical, and many of the interval curves are also fairly normal. A series of interval segments, however (at *a*, *b*, and *c*, and again at *d* and *e*), shows a drop to a low rate during the interval. This suggests interference from the DRL.

Summary

The behavior of pigeons has been studied continuously for sessions of many days or weeks by using a multiple schedule in which slow but continuous responding is maintained with few reinforcements on DRL, while FI and FR schedules alternate at hourly intervals. To a remarkable degree the performance on the ratio and interval components after hundreds of hours resembles that obtained using a conventional daily session. The major deviations in the ratio and interval performance during these long sessions are mostly attributable either to changes in deprivation or to a slight failure in stimulus control. Possible induction from DRL to FI is occasionally shown by a low rate in FI. Induction from FR to FI may explain an occasional unusually high rate in FI. Induction from both FR and FI components appears to sustain performance for many hours on DRL without reinforcement on that schedule, although "superstitious" reinforcements from the change to other key-colors may also be relevant. The combined schedule provides a base line of continuous responding which should be useful in studying the effects of physiological, pharmacological, or other variables acting over long periods of time.

John Broadus Watson, Behaviorist

John Broadus Watson, self-styled "the behaviorist," died on 25 September 1958 at the age of 80. His scientific life had come to a close a third of a century earlier, and he was unknown personally to a whole generation of younger men whose field of scientific activity he had defined and vigorously developed. His place in the history of science, and something of his stature, are indicated by three names—Darwin, Lloyd Morgan, and Watson—which represent three critical changes in our conception of behavior.

In establishing the continuity of species Darwin had attributed mental processes to lower organisms. He was supported by a host of anecdotal naturalists who recounted instances of reasoning, sympathy, and even artistic enjoyment on the parts of dogs, cats, elephants, and so on. The inevitable reaction was epitomized in the writings of Lloyd Morgan, who argued that such evidences of mental processes could be explained in other ways. A third step was inevitable, and it was Watson who took it: If there were other explanations of mental processes in lower organisms, why not also in man?

In dispensing with mentalistic explanations of behavior, Watson cleared the way for a scientific analysis. In doing so he acknowledged his debt both to Lloyd Morgan and to Thorndike, who, though he remained a mentalist, supplied a classical alternative explanation of "reasoning" in his experiments on trial-and-error learning. The epistemological issue was also in the air. Watson never took to philosophy (though, as he later said, his "milk teeth were cut on metaphysics"), but it was George Herbert Mead's great personal interest in Watson's animal experiments which supplied an immediate and crucial contact with relevant philosophical issues. A behavioristic interpretation of mental processes was later adopted by operationists and logical positivists, but the issue was to remain primarily empirical rather than logical.

From *Science*, 1959, *129*, 197–198.

Born in Greenville, South Carolina, Watson was to remember himself as a below-average and troublesome schoolboy with little to show for his early education except a love for manual skills. (He later built a ten-room house with his own hands.) His five years at Furman University, where he received an A.M. instead of an A.B., were also remembered as a bitter disappointment. But his educational luck suddenly improved when an interest in philosophy took him to the University of Chicago. Few men have made as many fortunate contacts during their graduate careers: with John Dewey (though Watson later complained "I never knew what he was talking about and, unfortunately, still don't"); with Angell (who taught him to write); with Jacques Loeb (whom Angell thought "unsafe" as Watson's thesis advisor); and, particularly, with Mead. Under the Chicago influence his interests turned to biology, and he always regretted that, in addition to his Ph.D., he was not able to finish work for the M.D. degree at Chicago. At the age of 29 he went to Johns Hopkins University as professor of psychology, where he came into even closer contact with biologists and medical men, particularly Jennings and Adolph Meyer. Among psychologists he worked with Knight Dunlap and Robert Yerkes (who were later to formulate their own variety of "psychobiology") and with Curt Richter and Lashley, the latter fresh from Jennings' laboratory.

From all this exceptional stimulation Watson emerged with a burning recognition of the need for a science of behavior. In 1912, when he first outlined his "behaviorism," there was no scientific discipline devoting itself to this important aspect of nature. Sociologists and economists frequently considered the behavior of men, but seldom of man as an individual. Psychology, in spite of the early American movement of functionalism, was dominated by an introspective "science of mind" which Watson viewed with an impatience which was never to be satisfied. In his most important book, *Psychology from the Standpoint of a Behaviorist,* published in 1919, Watson defined the field he wanted to see studied and assembled available techniques and facts. A second edition in 1924 contained a clearer and bolder programmatic statement. The emphasis was necessarily on the program, for not more than one-third of even the 1924 edition contained facts strictly relevant to the science of behavior the author was proposing. Anatomical and physiological material were used to complete the book. Watson's own contributions were not great, and he was to have no opportunity to extend them. His studies on maze behavior and his concept of "habit" made an uneasy marriage with Pavlov's principle of conditioning, then just beginning to attract attention in this country. His frequency theory of learning was short-lived.

In spite of its shortcomings the book had a tremendous effect. The new movement immediately attracted attention and adherents. Dissenters fell into line on the other side. In the controversy which followed, Watson's taste for, and skill in, polemics led him into extreme positions from which he never escaped. He could not content himself with prosecuting an empirical study of behavior simply as such, for he believed that psychology was the science destined to deal with that subject matter, and he wanted to reform it accordingly. He had another reason for crusading against the strongly entrenched introspectionists, since they claimed to offer direct evidence of the mental processes he wanted to discard. Watson seized upon laryngeal and other covert verbal activities as the "thought processes" of the introspective psychologists and refused to acknowledge sensory aspects of behavior which could also be observed by the behaver himself. It has been suggested that he might not himself have had visual or auditory imagery. In any case his sweeping denial of the existence of self-observed sensory events (the acknowledgment of which would not, as we now know, have implied the dualism he was so anxious to avoid) occupied him in what he later described as "a continual storm."

The same taste for polemics led him into an extreme environmentalistic position. In *Psychology from the Standpoint of a Behaviorist* he had devoted two chapters to hereditary behavior. Like all those who want to do something about behavior, he had emphasized the possibility of environmental modification, and this was widely misunderstood. Under the stress of battle he was led at last to the well-known cry: "Give me a dozen healthy infants, well-formed, and my own specified world to bring them up in and I'll guarantee to take any one at random and train him to become any type of specialist I might select—doctor, lawyer, artist, merchant-chief, and yes, even beggar-man and thief, regardless of his talents, penchants, tendencies, abilities, vocations, and race of his ancestors. I am going beyond my facts and I admit it, but so have the advocates of the contrary and they have been doing it for many thousands of years."

Watson also went beyond his facts, and in the same crusading spirit, in his views on child training. Experiments on the behavior of infants had shown him that emotional patterns could often be traced to conditioned emotional reflexes (a term he took from Pavlov via Lashley). He thought he saw the seeds of many behavior problems in early home experiences, and in his *Psychological Care of the Infant and Child*—a book he later publicly regretted—he cautioned parents against the unconsidered display of affection. (Current "mother love" theories are the other swing of that pendulum.)

And so it came about that Watson was to be remembered for a long time, by both laymen and psychologists alike, for a too narrow interpretation of self-observation, for an extreme environmentalism, and for a coldly detached theory of child care, no one of which was a necessary part of his original program. His brilliant glimpse of the need for, and the nature and implications of, a science of behavior was all but forgotten. Perhaps history is ready to return a more accurate appraisal. A year before his death he had the satisfaction of dedicating a paperback edition of his popular book *Behaviorism* to the American Psychological Association, which on 7 September 1957 cited him as follows: "To Dr. John B. Watson, whose work has been one of the vital determinants of the form and substance of modern psychology. He initiated a revolution in psychological thought, and his writings have been the point of departure for continuing lines of fruitful research."

How to Teach Animals

The "power of positive reinforcement" is probably never fully appreciated until one has seen an actual demonstration. Several suggestions for casual experiments are made in this article from the Scientific American *(1951, 185, 26-29), which is reprinted here by permission.*

Teaching, it is often said, is an art, but we have increasing reason to hope that it may eventually become a science. We have already discovered enough about the nature of learning to devise training techniques which are much more rapid and give more reliable results than the rule-of-thumb methods of the past. Tested on animals, the new techniques have proved superior to traditional methods of professional animal trainers; they yield more remarkable results with much less effort.

It takes rather subtle laboratory conditions to test an animal's full learning capacity, but the reader may be surprised at how much he can accomplish even under informal circumstances at home. Since nearly everyone at some time or other has tried, or wished he knew how, to train a dog, a cat, or some other animal, perhaps the most useful way to explain the learning process is to describe some simple experiments which the reader can perform himself.

"Catch your rabbit" is the first item in a well-known recipe for rabbit stew. Your first move, of course, is to choose an experimental subject. Any available animal—a cat, a dog, a pigeon, a mouse, a parrot, a chicken, a pig —will do. (Children or other members of your family may also be available, but it is suggested that you save them until you have had practice with less valuable material.) Suppose you choose a dog.

The second thing you will need is something your subject wants, say food. This serves as a reward or—to use a term which is less likely to be misunderstood—a "reinforcement" for the desired behavior. Many things besides food are reinforcing—for example, simply letting the dog out for a run—but food is usually the easiest to administer in the kind of experiment to be described here. If you use food, you must of course perform the experiment when the dog is hungry, perhaps just before his dinnertime.

The reinforcement gives you a means of controlling the behavior of the animal. It rests on the simple principle that whenever something reinforces a particular form of behavior, it increases the chances that the animal will repeat that behavior. This makes it possible to shape an animal's behavior almost as a sculptor shapes a lump of clay. There is, of course, nothing new in this principle. What is new is a better understanding of the conditions under which reinforcement works best.

To be effective a reinforcement must be given almost simultaneously with the desired behavior; a delay of even one second destroys much of the effect. This means that offering food in the usual way is likely to be ineffective; it is not fast enough. The best way to reinforce the behavior with the necessary speed is to use a "conditioned" reinforcer. This is a signal which the animal has observed in association with food. The animal is always given food immediately after the signal, and the signal itself then becomes a reinforcer. The better the association between the two events, the better the result.

For a conditioned reinforcer you need a clear signal which can be given instantly and to which the subject is sure to respond. It may be a noise or a flash of light. A whistle is not recommended because of the time it takes to draw a breath before blowing it. A visual signal like a wave of the arm may not always be seen by the animal. A convenient signal is a rap on a table with a small hard object or the noise of a high-pitched device such as a "cricket."

You are now ready to start the experiment with your dog. Work in a convenient place as free as possible from distraction. Let us say that you have chosen a "cricket" as your conditioner reinforcer. To build up its reinforcing power begin by tossing a few pieces of food, one at a time and not oftener than once or twice a minute, where the dog may eat them. Use pieces so small that 30 or 40 will not appreciably reduce the animal's hunger. As soon as the dog eats pieces readily and without delay, begin to pair the cricket with the food. Sound the cricket and then toss a piece of food. Wait half a minute or so and repeat. Sound the cricket suddenly, without any preparatory movement such as reaching for food.

At this stage your subject will probably show well-marked begging behavior. It may watch you intently, perhaps jump on you, and so on. You must break up this behavior, because it will interfere with other parts of the experiment. Never sound the cricket or give food when the dog is close to you or facing you. Wait until it turns away, then reinforce. Your conditioned reinforcer will be working properly when the dog turns immediately and approaches the spot where it receives food. Test this several times.

Wait until the dog is in a fairly unusual position, then sound the signal. Time spent in making sure the dog immediately approaches the food will later be saved manyfold.

Now, having established the noise as a reinforcer, you may begin teaching the dog. To get the feel of the technique start with some simple task, such as getting the dog to approach the handle on a low cupboard door and touch it with its nose. At first you reinforce any activity which will be part of the final completed act of approaching and touching the handle of the cupboard. The only permissible contact between you and the dog is via the cricket and the food. Do not touch the dog, talk to it, coax it, "draw its attention," or interfere in any other way with the experiment. If your subject just sits, you may have to begin by reinforcing any movement, however slight. As soon as the dog moves, sound the cricket and give food. Remember that your reaction time is important. Try to reinforce as nearly simultaneously with the movement as possible.

After your subject has begun to move about, reinforce when it turns to the cupboard. Almost immediately you will notice a change in its behavior. It will begin to face toward the cupboard most of the time. Then begin to reinforce only when the dog moves nearer the cupboard. (If you withhold reinforcement too long at this stage, you may lose the facing response. If so, go back and pick it up.) In a very short time—perhaps a minute or two —you should have the dog standing close to the cupboard. Now begin to pay attention to its head. Reinforce any movement which brings the nose close to the handle. You will have to make special efforts now to reduce the time between the movement and the reinforcement to the very minimum. Presently the dog will touch the handle with its nose, and after reinforcement it will repeat this behavior so long as it remains hungry.

Usually it takes no more than five minutes, even for a beginner, to teach a dog this behavior. Moreover, the dog does not have to be particularly "smart" to learn it; contrary to the usual view, all normal dogs learn with about equal facility with this conditioning technique.

Before going on with other experiments test the effect of your conditioned reinforcer again two or three times. If the dog responds quickly and eats without delay you may safely continue. You should "extinguish" the response the dog has already learned, however, before teaching it another. Stop reinforcing the act of touching the cupboard handle until the dog abandons this activity.

As a second test, let us say, you want to teach the dog to lift its head in the air and turn around to the right. The general procedure is the same, but you may need some help in sharpening your observation of the behavior to be reinforced. As a guide to the height to which the dog's head is to be raised, sight some horizontal line on the wall across the room. Whenever the dog, in its random movements, lifts its head above this line, reinforce immediately. You will soon see the head rising above the line more and more frequently. Now raise your sights slightly and reinforce only when the head rises above the new level. By a series of gradual steps you can get the dog to hold its head much higher than usual. After this you can begin to emphasize any turning movement in a clockwise direction while the head is high. Eventually the dog should execute a kind of dance step. If you use available food carefully, a single session should suffice for setting up this behavior.

Having tested your ability to produce these simple responses, you may feel confident enough to approach a more complex assignment. This time suppose you try working with a pigeon. Pigeons do not tame easily. You will probably want a cage to help control the bird, and for this you can rig up a large cardboard carton with a screen or lattice top and windows cut in the side for observing the bird. It is much less disturbing to the bird if you watch it from below its line of vision than if you peer at it from above. In general keep yourself out of the experimental situation as much as possible. You may still use a cricket as a conditioned reinforcer, and feed the bird by dropping a few grains of pigeon food into a small dish through a hole in the wall. It may take several daily feedings to get the bird to eat readily and to respond quickly to the cricket.

Your assignment is to teach the pigeon to identify the visual patterns on playing cards. To begin with, hang a single card on a nail on the wall of the cage a few inches above the floor so that the pigeon can easily peck it. After you have trained the bird to peck the card by reinforcing the movements which lead to that end, change the card and again reinforce the peck. If you shuffle the cards and present them at random, the pigeon will learn to peck any card offered.

Now begin to teach it to discriminate among the cards. Let us say you are using diamonds and clubs (excluding face cards and aces) and want the bird to select diamonds. Reinforce only when the card presented is a diamond, never when it is a club. Almost immediately the bird will begin to show a preference for diamonds. You can speed up its progress toward complete rejection of clubs by discontinuing the experiment for a moment (a mild form of punishment) whenever it pecks a club. A good conditioned punishment is simply to turn off the light ["blacking out"] or cover or remove the card. After half a minute replace the card or turn on the light and continue the experiment. Under these conditions the response which is positively reinforced with food remains part of the repertoire of the bird, while the response which leads to a blackout quickly disappears.

There is an amusing variation of this experiment by which you can make it appear that a pigeon can be taught to read. You simply use two printed cards bearing the words PECK and DON'T PECK, respectively. By reinforcing responses to PECK and blacking out when the bird pecks DON'T PECK, it is quite easy to train the bird to obey the commands on the cards.

The pigeon can also be taught the somewhat more "intellectual" performance of matching a sample object. Let us say the sample to be matched is a certain card. Fasten three cards to a board, with one above and the two others side by side just below it. The board is placed so that the bird can reach all the cards through windows cut in the side of the cage. After training the bird to peck a card of any kind impartially in all three positions, present the three chosen cards. The sample to be matched, say the three of diamonds, is at the top, and below it put a three of diamonds and a three of clubs. If the bird pecks the sample three of diamonds at the top, do nothing. If it pecks the matching three of diamonds below, reinforce it; if it pecks the three of clubs, black out. After each correct response and reinforcement, switch the positions of the two lower cards. The pigeon should soon match the sample each time. Conversely, it can also be taught to select the card which does not match the sample. It is important to reinforce correct choices immediately. Your own behavior must be letter-perfect if you are to expect perfection from your subject. The task can be made easier if the pigeon is conditioned to peck the sample card before you begin to train it to match the sample.

In a more elaborate variation of this experiment we have found it possible to make a pigeon choose among four words so that it appears to "name the suit" of the sample card. You prepare four cards about the size of small calling cards, each bearing in block letters the name of a suit: SPADES, HEARTS, DIAMONDS, and CLUBS. Fasten these side by side in a row and teach the pigeon to peck them by reinforcing in the usual way. Now arrange a sample playing card just above them. Cover the name cards and reinforce the pigeon a few times for pecking the sample. Now present, say, the three of diamonds as the sample. When the pigeon pecks it, immediately uncover the name cards. If the pigeon pecks DIAMONDS, reinforce instantly. If it pecks a wrong name instead, black out for half a minute and then resume the experiment with the three of diamonds still in place and the name cards covered. After a correct choice, change the sample card to a different suit while the pigeon is eating. Always keep the names covered until the sample card has been pecked. Within a short time you should have the bird following the full sequence of pecking the sample and then the appropriate name card. As time passes the correct name will be pecked more and more frequently and, if you do not too often reinforce wrong responses or neglect to reinforce right ones, the pigeon should soon become letter-perfect.

A toy piano offers interesting possibilities for performances of a more artistic nature. Reinforce any movement of the pigeon that leads toward its pressing a key. Then, by using reinforcements and blackouts appropriately, narrow the response to a given key. Then build up a two-note sequence by reinforcing only when the sequence has been completed and by blacking out when any other combination of keys is struck. The two-note sequence will quickly emerge. Other notes may then be added. Pigeons, chickens, small dogs, and cats have been taught in this way to play tunes of four or five notes. The situation soon becomes too complicated, however, for the casual experimenter. You will find it difficult to control the tempo, and the reinforcing contingencies become very complex. The limit of such an experiment is determined as much by the experimenter's skill as by that of the animal. In the laboratory we have been able to provide assistance to the experimenter by setting up complicated devices which always reinforce consistently and avoid exhaustion of the experimenter's patience.

The increased precision of the laboratory also makes it possible to guarantee performance up to the point of almost complete certainty. When relevant conditions have been controlled, the behavior of the organism is fully determined. Behavior may be sustained in full strength for many hours by utilizing different schedules of reinforcement. Some of these correspond to the contingencies established in industry in daily wages or in piece-work pay; others resemble the subtle but powerful contingencies of gambling devices, which are notorious for their ability to command sustained behavior.

The human baby is an excellent subject in experiments of the kind described here. You will not need to interfere with feeding schedules or create any other state of deprivation, because the human infant can be reinforced by very trivial environmental events; it does not need such a reward as food. Almost any "feedback" from the environment is reinforcing if it is not too intense. A crumpled newspaper, a pan and a spoon, or any convenient noisemaker quickly generates appropriate behavior, often amusing in its violence. The baby's rattle is based upon this principle.

One reinforcer to which babies often respond is the flashing on and off of a table lamp. Select some arbitrary response—for example, lifting the hand. Whenever the baby lifts its hand, flash the light. In a short time a well-defined response will be generated. (Human babies are just as "smart" as dogs or pigeons in this respect.) Incidentally, the baby will enjoy the experiment.

The same principle is at work in the behavior of older children and adults. Important among human reinforcements are those aspects of the behavior of others, often very subtle, which we call "attention," "approval" and "affection." Behavior which is successful in achieving these reinforcements may come to dominate the repertoire of the individual.

All this may be easily used—and just as easily misused—in our relations with other people. To the reader who is anxious to advance to the human subject a word of caution is in order. Reinforcement is only one of the procedures through which we alter behavior. To use it, we must build up some degree of deprivation or at least permit a deprivation to prevail which it is within our power to reduce. We must embark upon a program in which we sometimes apply relevant reinforcement and sometimes withhold it. In doing this, we are quite likely to generate emotional effects. Unfortunately the science of behavior is not yet as successful in controlling emotion as it is in shaping practical behavior.

A scientific analysis can, however, bring about a better understanding of personal relations. We are almost always reinforcing the behavior of others, whether we mean to be or not. A familiar problem is that of the child who seems to take an almost pathological delight in annoying its parents. In many cases this is the result of conditioning which is very similar to the animal training we have discussed. The attention, approval, and affection which a mother gives a child are all extremely powerful reinforcements. Any behavior of the child which produces these consequences is likely to be strengthened. The mother may unwittingly promote the very behavior she does not want. For example, when she is busy she is likely not to respond to a call or request made in a quiet tone of voice. She may answer the child only when it raises its voice. The average intensity of the child's vocal behavior therefore moves up to another level—precisely as the head of the dog in our experiment was raised to a new height. Eventually the mother gets used to this level and again reinforces only louder instances. This vicious circle brings about louder and louder behavior. The child's voice may also vary in intonation, and any change in the direction of unpleasantness is more likely to get the attention of the mother and is therefore strengthened. One might even say that "annoying" behavior is just that behavior which is especially effective in arousing another person to action. The mother behaves, in fact, as if she had been given the assignment of teaching the child to be annoying! The remedy in such a case is simply for the mother to make sure that she responds with attention and affection to most if not all the responses of the child which are of acceptable intensity and tone of voice and that she never reinforces the annoying forms of behavior.

Baby in a Box

Since publication of this article in the Ladies Home Journal *in October, 1945, several hundred babies have been reared in what is now known as an "Air-Crib." The advantages reported here have been generously confirmed. Although cultural inertia is perhaps nowhere more powerful than in child-raising practices, and in spite of the fact that the device is not easy to build, its use has steadily spread. The advantages to the child and parent alike seem to be too great to be resisted. One early user, John M. Gray, sent a questionnaire to 73 couples who had used Air-Cribs for 130 babies. All but three described the device as "wonderful." The physical and psychological benefits reported by these users seem to warrant extensive research.*

In that brave new world which science is preparing for the housewife of the future, the young mother has apparently been forgotten. Almost nothing has been done to ease her lot by simplifying and improving the care of babies.

When we decided to have another child, my wife and I felt that it was time to apply a little labor-saving invention and design to the problems of the nursery. We began by going over the disheartening schedule of the young mother, step by step. We asked only one question: Is this practice important for the physical and psychological health of the baby? When it was not, we marked it for elimination. Then the "gadgeteering" began.

The result was an inexpensive apparatus in which our baby daughter has now been living for eleven months. Her remarkable good health and happiness and my wife's welcome leisure have exceeded our most optimistic predictions, and we are convinced that a new deal for both mother and baby is at hand.

We tackled first the problem of warmth. The usual solution is to wrap the baby in half-a-dozen layers of cloth—shirt, nightdress, sheet, blankets. This is never completely successful. The baby is likely to be found steaming in its own fluids or lying cold and uncovered. Schemes to prevent uncovering may be dangerous, and in fact they have sometimes even proved fatal. Clothing and bedding also interfere with normal exercise and growth and keep the baby from taking comfortable postures or changing posture during sleep. They also encourage rashes and sores. Nothing can be said for the system on the score of convenience, because frequent changes and launderings are necessary.

Why not, we thought, dispense with clothing altogether—except for the diaper, which serves another purpose—and warm the space in which the baby lives? This should be a simple technical problem in the modern home. Our solution is a closed compartment about as spacious as a standard crib (Figure 1). The walls are well insulated, and one side, which can be raised

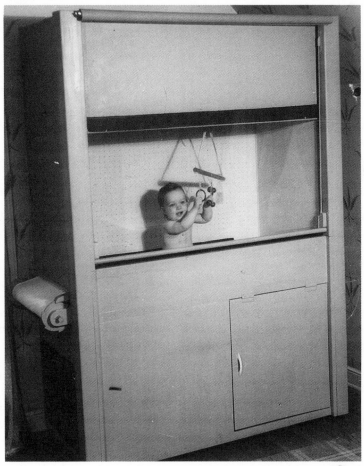

Stuart

Fig. 1

like a window, is a large pane of safety glass. The heating is electrical, and special precautions have been taken to insure accurate control.

After a little experimentation we found that our baby, when first home from the hospital, was completely comfortable and relaxed without benefit of clothing at about 86° F. As she grew older, it was possible to lower the temperature by easy stages. Now, at eleven months, we are operating at about 78°, with a relative humidity of 50 per cent.

Raising or lowering the temperature by more than a degree or two produces a surprising change in the baby's condition and behavior. This response is so sensitive that we wonder how a comfortable temperature is ever reached with clothing and blankets.

The discovery which pleased us most was that crying and fussing could always be stopped by slightly lowering the temperature. During the first three months, it is true, the baby would also cry when wet or hungry, but in that case she would stop when changed or fed. During the past six months she has not cried at all except for a moment or two when injured or sharply distressed—for example, when inoculated. The "lung exercise" which so often is appealed to to reassure the mother of a baby who cries a good deal takes the much pleasanter form of shouts and gurgles.

How much of this sustained cheerfulness is due to the temperature is hard to say, because the baby enjoys many other kinds of comfort. She sleeps in curious postures, not half of which would be possible under securely fastened blankets.

When awake, she exercises almost constantly and often with surprising violence. Her leg, stomach, and back muscles are especially active and have become strong and hard. It is necessary to watch this performance for only a few minutes to realize how severely restrained the average baby is, and how much energy must be diverted into the only remaining channel—crying.

A wider range and variety of behavior are also encouraged by the freedom from clothing. For example, our baby acquired an amusing, almost apelike skill in the use of her feet. We have devised a number of toys which are occasionally suspended from the ceiling of the compartment. She often plays with these with her feet alone and with her hands and feet in close co-operation.

One toy is a ring suspended from a modified music box. A note can be played by pulling the ring downward, and a series of rapid jerks will produce Three Blind Mice. At seven months our baby would grasp the ring in her toes, stretch out her leg and play the tune with a rhythmic movement of her foot.

We are not especially interested in developing skills of this sort, but they are valuable for the baby because they arouse and hold her interest. Many babies seem to cry from sheer boredom—their behavior is restrained and they have nothing else to do. In our compartment, the waking hours are invariably active and happy ones.

Freedom from clothes and bedding is especially important for the older baby who plays and falls asleep off and on during the day. Unless the mother is constantly on the alert, it is hard to cover the baby promptly when it falls asleep and to remove and arrange sheets and blankets as soon as it is ready to play. All this is now unnecessary.

Remember that these advantages for the baby do not mean additional labor or attention on the part of the mother. On the contrary, there is an almost unbelievable saving in time and effort. For one thing, there is no bed to be made or changed. The "mattress" is a tightly stretched canvas, which is kept dry by warm air. A single bottom sheet operates like a roller towel.[1] It is stored on a spool outside the compartment at one end and passes into a wire hamper at the other. It is ten yards long and lasts a week. A clean section can be locked into place in a few seconds. The time which is usually spent in changing clothes is also saved. This is especially important in the early months. When we take the baby up for feeding or play, she is wrapped in a small blanket or a simple nightdress. Occasionally she is dressed up "for fun" or for her play period. But that is all. The wrapping blanket, roller sheet, and the usual diapers are the only laundry actually required.

Time and labor are also saved because the air which passes through the compartment is thoroughly filtered. The baby's eyes, ears, and nostrils remain fresh and clean. A weekly bath is enough, provided the face and diaper region are frequently washed. These little attentions are easy because the compartment is at waist level.

It takes about one and one-half hours each day to feed, change, and otherwise care for the baby. This includes everything except washing diapers and preparing formula. We are not interested in reducing the time any further. As a baby grows older, it needs a certain amount of social stimulation. And after all, when unnecessary chores have been eliminated, taking care of a baby is fun.

An unforeseen dividend has been the contribution to the baby's good health. Our pediatrician readily approved the plan before the baby was

---

[1] The canvas and "endless" sheet arrangement was soon replaced with a single layer of woven plastic, which could be cleaned and instantly wiped dry.

born, and he has followed the results enthusiastically from month to month. Here are some points on the health score: When the baby was only ten days old, we could place her in the preferred face-down position without danger of smothering, and she has slept that way ever since, with the usual advantages. She has always enjoyed deep and extended sleep, and her feeding and eliminative habits have been extraordinarily regular. She has never had a stomach upset, and she has never missed a daily bowel movement.

The compartment is relatively free of spray and air-borne infection, as well as dust and allergic substances. Although there have been colds in the family, it has been easy to avoid contagion, and the baby has completely escaped. The neighborhood children troop in to see her, but they see her through glass and keep their school-age diseases to themselves. She has never had a diaper rash.

We have also enjoyed the advantages of a fixed daily routine. Child specialists are still not agreed as to whether the mother should watch the baby or the clock, but no one denies that a strict schedule saves time, for the mother can plan her day in advance and find time for relaxation or freedom for other activities. The trouble is that a routine acceptable to the baby often conflicts with the schedule of the household. Our compartment helps out here in two ways. Even in crowded living quarters it can be kept free of unwanted lights and sounds. The insulated walls muffle all ordinary noises, and a curtain can be drawn down over the window. The result is that, in the space taken by a standard crib, the baby has in effect a separate room. We are never concerned lest the doorbell, telephone, piano, or children at play wake the baby, and we can therefore let her set up any routine she likes.

But a more interesting possibility is that her routine may be changed to suit our convenience. A good example of this occurred when we dropped her schedule from four to three meals per day. The baby began to wake up in the morning about an hour before we wanted to feed her. This annoying habit, once established, may persist for months. However, by slightly raising the temperature during the night we were able to postpone her demand for breakfast. The explanation is simple. The evening meal is used by the baby mainly to keep herself warm during the night. How long it lasts will depend in part upon how fast heat is absorbed by the surrounding air.

One advantage not to be overlooked is that the soundproofing also protects the family from the baby! Our intentions in this direction were misunderstood by some of our friends. We were never put to the test, because there was no crying to contend with, but it was never our policy to use the compartment in order to let the baby "cry it out."

Every effort should be made to discover just why a baby cries. But if the condition cannot be remedied, there is no reason why the family, and perhaps the neighborhood as well, must suffer. (Such a compartment, by the way, might persuade many a landlord to drop a "no babies" rule, since other tenants can be completely protected.)

Before the baby was born, when we were still building the apparatus, some of the friends and acquaintances who had heard about what we proposed to do were rather shocked. Mechanical dish-washers, garbage disposers, air cleaners, and other laborsaving devices were all very fine, but a mechanical baby tender—that was carrying science too far! However, all the specific objections which were raised against the plan have faded away in the bright light of our results. A very brief acquaintance with the scheme in operation is enough to resolve all doubts. Some of the toughest skeptics have become our most enthusiastic supporters.

One of the commonest objections was that we were going to raise a "softie" who would be unprepared for the real world. But instead of becoming hypersensitive, our baby has acquired a surprisingly serene tolerance for annoyances. She is not bothered by the clothes she wears at playtime, she is not frightened by loud or sudden noises, she is not frustrated by toys out of reach, and she takes a lot of pommeling from her older sister like a good sport. It is possible that she will have to learn to sleep in a noisy room, but adjustments of that sort are always necessary. A tolerance for any annoyance can be built up by administering it in controlled dosages, rather than in the usual accidental way. Certainly there is no reason to annoy the child throughout the whole of its infancy, merely to prepare it for later childhood.

It is not, of course, the favorable conditions to which people object, but the fact that in our compartment they are "artificial." All of them occur naturally in one favorable environment or another, where the same objection should apply but is never raised. It is quite in the spirit of the "world of the future" to make favorable conditions available everywhere through simple mechanical means.

A few critics have objected that they would not like to live in such a compartment themselves—they feel that it would stifle them or give them claustrophobia. The baby obviously does not share in this opinion. The compartment is well ventilated and much more spacious than a Pullman berth, considering the size of the occupant. The baby cannot get out, of course, but that is true of a crib as well. There is less actual restraint in the compartment because the baby is freer to move about. The plain fact is that she is perfectly happy. She has never tried to get out nor resisted being put back in, and that seems to be the final test.

Another early objection was that the baby would be socially starved and robbed of the affection and mother love which she needs. This has simply not been true. The compartment does not ostracize the baby. The large window is no more of a social barrier than the bars of a crib. The baby follows what is going on in the room, smiles at passers-by, plays "peek-a-boo" games, and obviously delights in company. And she is handled, talked to, and played with whenever she is changed or fed, and each afternoon during a play period which is becoming longer as she grows older.

The fact is that a baby will probably get more love and affection when it is easily cared for, because the mother is not so likely to feel overworked and resentful of the demands made upon her. She will express her love in a practical way and give the baby genuinely affectionate care.

It is common practice to advise the troubled mother to be patient and tender and to enjoy her baby. And, of course, that is what any baby needs. But it is the exceptional mother who can fill this prescription upon demand, especially if there are other children in the family and she has no help. We need to go one step further and treat the mother with affection also. Simplified child care will give mother love a chance.

A similar complaint was that such an apparatus would encourage neglect. But easier care is sure to be better care. The mother will resist the temptation to put the baby back into a damp bed if she can conjure up a dry one in five seconds. She may very well spend less time with her baby, but babies do not suffer from being left alone but only from the discomforts which arise from being left alone in the ordinary crib.

How long do we intend to keep the baby in the compartment? The baby will answer that in time, but almost certainly until she is two years old, or perhaps three. After the first year, of course, she will spend a fair part of each day in a play-pen or out-of-doors. The compartment takes the place of a crib and will get about the same use. Eventually it will serve as sleeping quarters only.

We cannot, of course, guarantee that every baby raised in this way will thrive so successfully. But there is a plausible connection between health and happiness and the surroundings we have provided, and I am quite sure that our success is not an accident. The experiment should, of course, be repeated again and again with different babies and different parents. One case is enough, however, to disprove the flat assertion that it can't be done. At least we have shown that a moderate and inexpensive mechanization of baby care will yield a tremendous saving in time and trouble, without harm to the child and probably to its lasting advantage.

A Word About Boxes

The title "Baby in a Box" was not mine; it was invented by the editors of the Journal. *Nevertheless, the Air-Crib is a sort of box, and this is also true of the apparatus known as the "Skinner Box"—an expression which I have never used and which my friends accept as* verboten. *(I believe the term was first popularized by Hull and his students in the form "Modified Skinner Box.") Helplessly, I have watched the teaching machines gradually assume the form of boxes. (There is consolation in the fact that in this case the organism remains on the outside).*

I confess to one extension of the term, though I plead irresistible circumstances. At the dedication of the Renard Hospital in St. Louis, at which the paper on page 303 was given, there was a summarizing round-table discussion. Someone mentioned the "Skinner box" and a discussion ensued. I took no part in it, and Alan Gregg, sitting next to me, evidently shared my discomfiture. Finally he leaned over and whispered, "Box et praeterea nihil." It was doubly appropriate: (1) we had been hearing about "nothing but boxes" for several minutes, and (2) the gist of the argument had been that one could have an effective science about the facts observed in the box and nothing more.

At that point someone asked me to comment on the way in which my utopian novel, Walden Two, *had been received. I could not resist the variables, intraverbal and otherwise, which were playing upon my behavior and therefore replied that I had evidently been accused of wanting to build a* box populi. *I do not believe the remark has seriously damaged the notion of an experimental community. Nevertheless, it is surprising how often a proposal to remedy some defect in current cultural designs is brushed aside with a reference to boxes.*

The Psychology of Design

In the Spring term, I again taught a course in the psychology of aesthetics which I had given two years before, and I began to be interested in the field. An instant authority, I was invited to discuss Picasso on the radio and to write an article on "The Psychology of Design" for Art Education Today *[1941].* Guy Buswell had published records showing how people looked at a picture, their eyes darting from one point to another, and it occurred to me that successive fixations should produce the apparent movement called the Phi Phenomenon. Pictures with lines at different angles should appear lively, and those with parallel lines quiet. The movement might even be related to the subject. . . . *[from Skinner, B. F. (1979).* The Shaping of a Behaviorist: Part Two of an Autobiography. *New York: Knopf, p. 238.]*

Any design, considered as a simple objective thing, can be described in physical mathematical terms, but this will not suffice for an understanding of the place of design in art. The artist is not so much interested in the physical structure of a design as in the effect it has upon the one who looks at it. This happens also to be the concern of the psychologist. We might say that a design is what it *is* only because of what it *does,* and, if this is true, some knowledge of the various kinds of effects which visual patterns have should help us in understanding the nature of design.

The Behavior of Looking

One kind of effect of a visual pattern is that which it has on the simple behavior of looking. A uniform surface (so large that some central part need not be regarded as bounded by a frame or border) does not cause the observer to behave in any very definite way. However, if we place upon it a single dot of contrasting color or value, we may be said to have established a rudimentary design, for more or less uniform behavior will be induced when the surface is placed before an observer. It is not likely that the dot will first strike the region of clearest vision, but the eye will turn, almost inevitably, in the direction of the dot and stop there, at least momentarily.

621

This is a very elementary design, for its possibilities are limited. But if we introduce a second dot, we immediately enhance the effect. The eye now tends to move from one dot to the other, not so inevitably as in the first case, but with considerable uniformity. This movement has certain properties (of which the observer may or may not be aware) which contribute to the total effect: it establishes a "direction" and a "distance." If we add a third or fourth dot, we greatly increase the variety of the resulting activity, although we are less able to predict how or where the eye will move. And, in general, an increase in the number of dots reduces the predictability of the effect and weakens the design, although there are many exceptions to this rule. A number of dots arranged in a line or at the corners of an imaginary regular polygon will yield a more predictable effect than the same number scattered at random.

When we reach the order of complexity exhibited by most of the designs actually used in art, we can say very little about a uniform behavior of looking. By photographing the activity of the eye in the presence of various pictures, Buswell[1] has demonstrated this lack of uniformity in a convincing way. We can no longer explain the effect of a design by contending that the eye follows contours, or falls with a rhythmic beat upon the repeated elements of a border, or performs any of the other feats which used to be attributed to it from self-observation. This does not mean that there are no gross differences in the movement of the eye in looking at different pictures. The movement may be localized or scattered, directed or aimless, and so on; and these properties have an obvious bearing upon the character of the picture. But now that something is known about them, eye movements have lost much of their earlier importance in the explanation of design.

What many people think of as eye movements are apparently movements of attention, and this brings us to another kind of effect which a design may have. As everyone knows, it is possible to hold the eye fixed upon some object and at the same time to "attend to" objects in neighboring parts of the field of vision. One may test this with a simple experiment. If the reader will look at the letter at the left end of this line, he will find it possible to examine nearby letters (say, those above or below it) without noticeably moving the eye. This kind of behavior is not clearly understood, but it seems to involve very slight (perhaps merely potential) movements of looking toward or reaching toward other parts of the field. One may be aware of this while

---

[1]Buswell, Guy T. *How People Look at Pictures.* University of Chicago Press, 1935.

performing the experiment. The tendency toward movement may be so strong as to break into a full shift of the center of vision, or into a modified posture of the whole body. We may suppose, then, that while the eye does not actually follow a curved line, there may be a tendency for various other muscles of the body to move as if the line were being followed, and this kind of behavior will contribute to the total effect.

The Phi Phenomenon

Our modern knowledge of eye movements, while weakening their explanatory value, compensates for this to some extent by setting up certain new and interesting possibilities. When one is looking at a picture, the eye may be roughly likened to a camera which is taking a number of still photographs of different parts of the canvas. These pictures are thrown upon the eye in rapid succession. Unlike the successive frames of a film, the pictures are usually quite diverse. Under exceptional circumstances, as in looking at a strongly contrasted checkerboard, there may be a noticeable "flicker," but this is fortunately not the usual case. The rapid succession of pictures has, however, a number of effects which make an important contribution to design. The principal example is the production of "apparent movement"— the kind of movement which makes moving pictures move and which is called by psychologists the "Phi phenomenon."

The simplest demonstration of apparent movement is provided by two successive neighboring spots of light projected upon a screen. If one spot is removed just before the second one is thrown on the screen, it appears as if a single spot had moved from one position to the other through the intervening space. Traffic lights, if satisfactorily timed, give the effect in spite of the difference in color. Now, a similar effect can be obtained when the successive positions of the light are provided by the movement of the eye itself. In Figure 1, a kind of apparent movement is obtained if one looks quickly from one of the birds to the other. The effect is best if the eye falls upon the same relative position (near the beak) in both pictures. The bird on the left appears as if its beak were just being closed, and the one on the right as if its beak were just being opened. By looking very rapidly from one to he other, a lively "movement" is seen.

Many compositions are designed, either intentionally or otherwise, to encourage an effect of this sort. The movement is most obvious if the composition contains two or more principal masses having approximately the same nature but differing slightly in attitude or in

Fig. 1

the position of minor appendages. In such case the required alternate fixations of the eye are likely to be evoked without explicit instructions, and a considerable similarity to real movement or to a moving picture may result. In Figure 2, when the eye moves from the figure of Sancho Panza, with its inclination to the upper right, to that of Don Quixote, which is inclined to the upper left, a real movement is suggested. The picture appears as if Sancho Panza had just drawn himself back into the position he now holds and as if Don Quixote had just thrown himself forward on his horse. If either half of the picture is covered, this effect is destroyed. Each figure still *represents* a kind of movement; we recognize each figure as in motion but the lively and forceful contribution which is provided by the Phi phenomenon when the figures are viewed alternately is missing.

This picture also exemplifies the related effect of an apparent change of size. If a spot of light is thrown upon the screen and then replaced by a larger spot, it appears as if a single spot had suddenly *grown* larger. If it is replaced by a smaller spot, there is an apparent shrinking in size. In Figure 2, when the figures are viewed alternately, this effect makes Sancho Panza appear as if he were moving toward the observer and (what is more important for the effect of the picture as a whole) it makes Don Quixote appear as if he were riding rapidly away. All of this occurs in addition to the regular represented movement of the picture.

The possibility of apparent movement in a still picture has not to my knowledge been pointed out in its bearing upon design. But it will account for a great deal of the animation of many works of art. Some of the dancing girls of Degas (when at least two figures appear) offer excellent examples. Portraits (of two or more people) generally provide

FIG. 2. Don Quixote with Sancho Panza Wringing His Hands
Artist: Honoré Daumier. Collection of Mrs. Charles S. Payson. Courtesy of M. Knoedler & Co., NY

FIG. 3. Daughters of Revolution
Artist: Grant Wood. Collection of Edward G. Robinson. Courtesy of Museum of Modern Art

interesting cases. If the eyebrows of one face are a little higher than those of another, a peculiar lifting and lowering movement may be generated as one looks from one face to the other. Figure 3, Grant Wood's "Daughters of Revolution," makes use of this, as well as of a similar apparent stretching and shrinking of the necks of the women portrayed.

Even though apparent movement is not always as pronounced as in these examples, it may nevertheless contribute a good deal to the total effect of a picture. When it supplements a represented movement, the nature of the gain is clear; but a design need not deal with a moving object, and it may even be abstract, while at the same time receiving a considerable contribution from the Phi phenomenon. In any canvas in which all the principal lines lie in approximately the same direction, it is not likely that the successive still pictures taken as the eye moves from one point to another will differ in direction in sufficient magnitude to produce any considerable "Phi." Other things being equal, the painting will be quiet. On the other hand, in a canvas in which there are pronounced curves or an assortment of directions, it is very probable that two successive "still photographs" will contain lines differing in slope in such a way as to produce some movement of this sort. The canvas will be animated—quite apart from any animation inherent in its subject matter.

Effect of Learned Reactions

One other kind of effect which a design may have arises from various learned or acquired reactions. These constitute the greater part of the "meaning" of the design. It is quite unlikely that any arrangement of lines or areas is wholly unfamiliar to the adult observer, and hence wholly without meaning. No "abstraction" is completely free from a resemblance to previously observed forms, and representative designs are frankly based upon such resemblances. In the latter case, the relation to our previous experience is usually easily identified, but some contribution to the total effect of a design must not be overlooked in the former as well. For example, an architectural painting may, with its converging lines and overlapping surfaces, give an excellent representation of a three-dimensional world. We have moved about in such a world all our lives, and we have come to know that parallel lines converge when they stretch away from us, that the smaller of two similar objects is probably the more distant, that distant colors are usually of lower saturation, and so on. Our response to such a painting cannot escape the influence of this training. This will also be true in an abstraction, since converging lines cannot wholly free themselves from their commonest meaning in the everyday world about us, bright and dull colors are likely to take their characteristic relative positions, and so on. Although some psychologists doubt that our perception of the third dimension is learned, the heightening of this perception through our experiences with similar designs in the practical world about us can scarcely be denied.

Effect of Emotional Reactions

Of greater importance in the field of art than any of these reactions are the emotional reactions with which we respond to many visual patterns. To much of the world about us we are perhaps relatively indifferent, but there are many situations in which more or less vigorous emotional reactions are common. A design may acquire some of its effect through a resemblance to an emotional stimulus, and it is the contention of many psychologists that this may be true of pure design as well, even though we are not aware of the resemblance or do not understand the origin of our reactions.

Figure 4 is a picture of an object to which very few people remain wholly indifferent. Whether there is an inherited fear of snakes is perhaps questionable, but it is nevertheless true that this particular pattern

FIG. 4. Night Snake
Plate 26 from *Snakes of the World* by Raymond L. Ditmars.
The Macmillan Company, 1932. Courtesy of the publisher.

frequently arouses a strong reaction. A snake is not a common subject matter in Western art, perhaps because the reaction is too obvious, but it is an effective subject in the sense that few people would be indifferent to a realistic painting of a snake on the walls of a museum.

The reaction to a picture of this sort is easily attributed to the reaction which would be made to its subject matter in real life. But what are the precise characteristics of the pattern which evoke the reaction? The head of the snake could be concealed without much loss, the scales need not be visible, and a snake of a different marking would give the same effect. The "snake-ness" of the picture is apparently simply the coiling and curving of the main lines. But a picture of a coil of rope, of a cracking whip, or of the tendril of a grapevine would also satisfy this condition. If it is true that we need not recognize the snake as a snake in order to obtain the emotional effect, as many psychologists contend, we must suppose that the reaction made to snakes in real life carries over to many similar designs in art, even of an abstract nature. This example is, of course, an extreme one, but some at least of the otherwise unexplained emotional effect of good design can reasonably be attributed to an overlap with visual patterns to which we have acquired, or at least to which we possess emotional reactions.

This is not an exhaustive list of the kinds of effects which a design may have, but it must suffice. The list is long enough to suggest that complete interpretation of any given design is perhaps impossible. The design itself, as an objective geometrical factor, is only a small part of the story, and we can look for little help from the "formalists," who seek a solution in that direction. A design is a psychological and cultural object of enormous complexity. But if it is idle to attempt to account fully for any one example it is at least important to know the kinds of effects which are involved, and this is all that has been attempted here. It is no paradox that we have a better chance of understanding the nature of design in general than of accounting for the effects of any given example.

There is nothing in what has been said that is not familiar to the practicing artist, even though he does not put it into words. Nor is it likely that an understanding of processes of this sort will supplant the artist by generating a calculated or scientific art. Even though we may eventually achieve an exhaustive list of the processes involved in the practice of design, the production of a work of art will probably still require that mass of unverbalized knowledge which arises from individual experience. Similarly, on the side of the observer, it would be a mistake to identify the understanding of design with its enjoyment. The processes involved in reacting to design seem to operate freely without being recognized; and, although recognition may sharpen their effectiveness, it can hardly act as a substitute for artistic sensitivity.

Pigeons in a Pelican

This paper was presented at a meeting of the American Psychological Association at Cincinnati, Ohio, September, 1959, and was published in the American Psychologist *in January, 1960. It is reprinted with permission.*

This is the history of a crackpot idea, born on the wrong side of the tracks intellectually speaking, but eventually vindicated in a sort of middle-class respectability. It is the story of a proposal to use living organisms to guide missiles—of a research program during World War II called "Project Pigeon" and a peacetime continuation at the Naval Research Laboratory called "ORCON" from the words "organic control." Both of these programs have now been declassified.

Man has always made use of the sensory capacities of animals, either because they are more acute than his own or more convenient. The watchdog probably hears better than his master and, in any case, listens while his master sleeps. As a detecting system the dog's ear comes supplied with an alarm (the dog need not be taught to announce the presence of an intruder), but special forms of reporting are sometimes set up. The tracking behavior of the bloodhound and the pointing of the hunting dog are usually modified to make them more useful. Training is sometimes quite explicit. It is said that sea gulls were used to detect submarines in the English Channel during World War I. The British sent their own submarines through the Channel releasing food to the surface. Gulls could see the submarines from the air and learned to follow them, whether they were British or German. A flock of gulls, spotted from the shore, took on special significance. In the seeing-eye dog the repertoire of artificial signaling responses is so elaborate that it has the conventional character of the verbal interchange between man and man.

The detecting and signaling systems of lower organisms have a special advantage when used with explosive devices which can be guided toward the objects they are to destroy, whether by land, sea, or air. Homing systems for guided missiles have now been developed which sense and signal the position of a target by responding to visible or invisible radiation, noise, radar reflections, and so on. These have not always been available, and in any case a living organism has certain advantages. It is almost certainly cheaper and more compact and, in particular, is especially good at responding to patterns and those classes of patterns called "concepts." The lower organism is not used because it is more sensitive than man—after all, the kamikaze did very well—but because it is readily expendable.

Project Pelican

The ethical question of our right to convert a lower creature into an unwitting hero is a peacetime luxury. There were bigger questions to be answered in the late thirties. A group of men had come into power who promised, and eventually accomplished, the greatest mass murder in history. In 1939 the city of Warsaw was laid waste in an unprovoked bombing, and the airplane emerged as a new and horrible instrument of war against which only the feeblest defenses were available. Project Pigeon was conceived against that background. It began as a search for a homing device to be used in a surface-to-air guided missile as a defense against aircraft. As the balance between offensive and defensive weapons shifted, the direction was reversed, and the system was to be tested first in an air-to-ground missile called the "Pelican." Its name is a useful reminder of the state of the missile art in America at that time. Its detecting and servomechanisms took up so much space that there was no room for explosives: hence the resemblance to the pelican "whose beak can hold more than its belly can." My title is perhaps now clear. Figure 1 shows the pigeons, jacketed for duty. Figure 2 shows the beak of the Pelican.

At the University of Minnesota in the spring of 1940 the capacity of the pigeon to steer toward a target was tested with a moving hoist. The pigeon, held in a jacket and harnessed to a block, was immobilized except for its neck and head. It could eat grain from a dish and operate a control system by moving its head in appropriate directions. Movement of the head operated the motors of the hoist. The bird could ascend by lifting its head, descend by lowering it, and travel from side to side by moving appropriately. The whole system, mounted on wheels, was pushed across a room toward a bull's-eye on the far wall. During the approach the pigeon raised or lowered itself and moved from side to side in such a way as to reach the wall in position to eat grain from the center of the bull's-eye. The pigeon learned to reach any target within reach of the hoist, no matter what the starting position and during fairly rapid approaches.

FIG. 1.   Thirty-two pigeons, jacketed for testing.

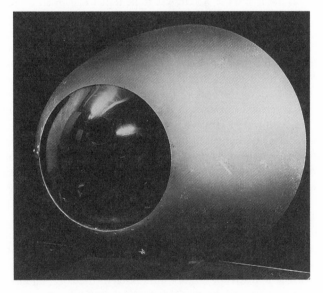

FIG. 2.   Nose of the Pelican, showing lenses.

The experiment was shown to John T. Tate, a physicist, then Dean of the Graduate School at the University of Minnesota, who brought it to the attention of R. C. Tolman, one of a group of scientists engaged in early defense activities. The result was the first of a long series of rejections. The proposal "did not warrant further development at the time." The project was accordingly allowed to lapse. On December 7, 1941, the situation was suddenly restructured; and, on the following day, with the help of Keller Breland, then a graduate student at Minnesota, further work was planned. A simpler harnessing system could be used if the bomb were to rotate slowly during its descent, when the pigeon would need to steer in only one dimension: from side to side. We built an apparatus in which a harnessed pigeon was lowered toward a large revolving turntable across which a target was driven according to contacts made by the bird during its descent. It was not difficult to train a pigeon to "hit" small ship models during fairly rapid descents. We made a demonstration film showing hits on various kinds of targets, and two psychologists then engaged in the war effort in Washington, Charles Bray and Leonard Carmichael, undertook to look for government support. Tolman, then at the Office of Scientific Research and Development, again felt that the project did not warrant support, in part because the United States had at that time no missile capable of being guided toward a target. Commander (now Admiral) Luis de Florez, then in the Special Devices Section of the Navy, took a sympathetic view. He dismissed the objection that there was no available vehicle by suggesting that the pigeon be connected with an automatic pilot mounted in a small plane loaded with explosives. But he was unable to take on the project because of other commitments and because, as he explained, he had recently bet on one or two other equally long shots which had not come in.

The project lapsed again and would probably have been abandoned if it had not been for a young man whose last name I have ungratefully forgotten, but whose first name—Victor—we hailed as a propitious sign. His subsequent history led us to refer to him as Vanquished; and this, as it turned out, was a more reliable omen. Victor walked into the Department of Psychology at Minnesota one day in the summer of 1942 looking for an animal psychologist. He had a scheme for installing dogs in antisubmarine torpedoes. The dogs were to respond to faint acoustic signals from the submarine and to steer the torpedo toward its goal. He wanted a statement from an animal psychologist as to its feasibility. He was understandably surprised to learn of our work with pigeons but seized upon it eagerly; citing it in support of his contention that dogs could be trained to steer torpedoes, he went to a number of companies in Minneapolis. His project was rejected by everyone he approached; but one company, General Mills, Inc., asked for more information about our work with pigeons. We described the project and presented the available data to Arthur D. Hyde, Vice-President in Charge of Research. The company was not looking for new products, but Hyde thought that it might, as a public service, develop the pigeon system to the point at which a governmental agency could be persuaded to take over.

Breland and I moved into the top floor of a flour mill in Minneapolis and with the help of Norman Guttman, who had joined the project, set to work on further improvements. It had been difficult to induce the pigeon to respond to the small angular displacement of a distant target. It would start working dangerously late in the descent. Its natural pursuit behavior was not appropriate to the characteristics of a likely missile. A new system was therefore designed. An image of the target was projected on a translucent screen as in a camera obscura. The pigeon, held near the screen, was reinforced for pecking at the image on the screen. The guiding signal was to be picked up from the point of contact of screen and beak.

In an early arrangement the screen was a translucent plastic plate forming the larger end of a truncated cone bearing a lens at the smaller end. The cone was mounted, lens down, in a gimbal bearing. An object within range threw its image on the translucent screen; and the pigeon, held vertically just above the plate, pecked the image. When a target was moved about within range of the lens, the cone continued to point to it. In another apparatus a translucent disk, free to tilt slightly on gimbal bearings, closed contacts operating motors which altered the position of a large field beneath the apparatus. Small cutouts of ships and other objects were placed on the field. The field was constantly in motion, and a target would go out of range unless the pigeon continued to control it. With this apparatus we began to study the pigeon's reactions to various patterns and to develop sustained steady rates of responding through the use of appropriate schedules of reinforcement, the reinforcement being a few grains occasionally released onto the plate. By building up large extinction curves a target could be tracked continuously for a matter of minutes without reinforcement. We trained pigeons to follow a variety of land and sea targets, to neglect large patches intended to represent clouds or flak, to concentrate on one target while another was in view, and so on. We found that a pigeon could hold the missile on a particular street intersection in an aerial map of a city. The map which came most easily to hand was of a city which, in the interests of international relations, need not be identified. Through appropriate schedules of reinforcement it was possible to maintain longer uninterrupted runs than could conceivably be required by a missile.

We also undertook a more serious study of the pigeon's behavior, with the help of W. K. Estes and Marion Breland, who joined the project at this time. We ascertained optimal conditions of deprivation, investigated other kinds of deprivations, studied the effect of special reinforcements (for example, pigeons were said to find hemp seed particularly delectable), tested the effects of energizing drugs and increased oxygen pressures, and so on. We differentially reinforced the force of the pecking response and found that pigeons could be induced to peck so energetically that the base of the beak became inflamed. We investigated the effects of extremes of temperature, of changes in atmospheric pressure, of accelerations produced by an improvised centrifuge, of increased carbon dioxide pressure, of increased and prolonged vibration, and of noises such as pistol shots. (The birds could, of course, have been deafened to eliminate auditory distractions, but we found it easy to maintain steady behavior in spite of intense noises and many other distracting conditions using the simple process of adaptation.) We investigated optimal conditions for the quick development of discriminations and began to study the pigeon's reactions to patterns, testing for induction from a test figure to the same figure inverted, to figures of different sizes and colors, and to figures against different grounds. A simple device using carbon paper to record the points at which a pigeon pecks a figure showed a promise which has never been properly exploited.

We made another demonstration film and renewed our contact with the Office of Scientific Research and Development. An observer was sent to Minneapolis, and on the strength of his report we were given an opportunity to present our case in Washington in February, 1943. At that time we were offering a homing device capable of reporting with an on-off signal the orientation of a missile toward various visual patterns. The capacity to respond to pattern was, we felt, our strongest argument, but the fact that the device used only visible radiation (the same form of information available to the human bombardier) made it superior to the radio-controlled missiles then under development because it was resistant to jamming. Our film had some effect. Other observers were sent to Minneapolis to see the demonstration itself. The pigeons, as usual, behaved beautifully. One of them held the supposed missile on a particular intersection of streets in the aerial map for five minutes although the target would have been lost if the pigeon had paused for a second or two. The observers returned to Washington, and two weeks later we were asked to supply data on (*a*) the population of pigeons in the United States (fortunately, the census bureau had some figures) and (*b*) the accuracy with which pigeons struck a point on a plate. There were many arbitrary conditions to be taken into account in measuring the latter, but we supplied possibly relevant data. At long last, in June, 1943, the Office of Scientific Research and Development awarded a modest contract to General Mills, Inc. to "develop a homing device."

At that time we were given some information about the missile the pigeons were to steer. The Pelican was a wing-steered glider, still under development and not yet successfully steered by any homing device. It was being tested on a target in New Jersey consisting of a stirrup-shaped pattern bulldozed out of the sandy soil near the coast. The white lines of the target stood out clearly against brown and green cover. Colored photographs were taken from various distances and at various angles, and the verisimilitude of the reproduction was checked by flying over the target and looking at its image in a portable camera obscura.

Because of security restrictions we were given only very rough specifications of the signal to be supplied to the controlling system in the Pelican. It was no longer to be simply on-off; if the missile was badly off target, an especially strong correcting signal was needed. This meant that the quadrant-contact system would no longer suffice. But further requirements were left mainly to our imagination. The General Mills engineers were equal to this difficult assignment. With what now seems like unbelievable speed, they designed and constructed a pneumatic pickup system giving a graded signal. A lens in the nose of the missile threw an image on a translucent plate within reach of the pigeon in a pressure-sealed chamber. Four air valves resting against the edges of the plate were jarred open momentarily as the pigeon pecked. The valves at the right and left admitted air to chambers on opposite sides of one tambour, while the valves at the top and bottom admitted air to opposite sides of another. Air on all sides was exhausted by a Venturi cone on the side of the missile. When the missile was on target, the pigeon pecked the center of the plate, all valves admitted equal amounts of air, and the tambours remained in neutral positions. But if the image moved as little as a quarter of an inch off-center, corresponding to a very small angular displacement of the target, more air was admitted by the valves on one side, and the resulting displacement of the tambours sent appropriate correcting orders directly to the servosystem.

The device required no materials in short supply, was relatively foolproof, and delivered a graded signal. It had another advantage. By this time we had begun to realize that a pigeon was more easily controlled than a physical scientist serving on a committee. It was very difficult to convince the latter that the former was an orderly system. We therefore multiplied the probability of success by designing a multiple-bird unit. There was adequate space in the nose of the Pelican for three pigeons, each with its own lens and plate. A net signal could easily be generated. The majority vote of three pigeons offered an excellent guarantee against momentary pauses and aberrations. (We later worked out a system in which the majority took on a more characteristically democratic function. When a missile is falling toward *two* ships at sea, for example, there is no guarantee that all three pigeons will steer toward the same ship. But at least two must agree, and the third can then be punished for his minority opinion. Under proper contingencies of reinforcement a punished bird will shift immediately to the majority view. When all three are working on one ship, any defection is immediately punished and corrected.)

The arrangement in the nose of the Pelican is shown in Figure 3. Three systems of lenses and mirrors, shown at the left, throw images of the target area on the three translucent plates shown in the center. The ballistic valves resting against the edges of these plates and the tubes connecting them with

FIG. 3.   Demonstration model of the three-pigeon guidance system.

the manifolds leading to the controlling tambours may be seen. A pigeon is being placed in the pressurized chamber at the right.

The General Mills engineers also built a simulator (Figure 4)—a sort of

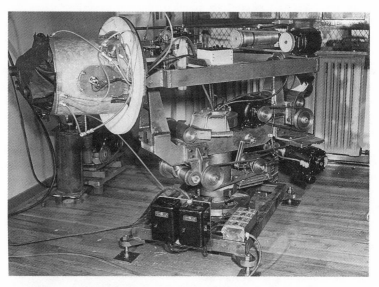

Fɪɢ. 4.   Simulator for testing the adequacy of the pigeon signal.

Link trainer for pigeons—designed to have the steering characteristics of the Pelican, in so far as these had been communicated to us. Like the wing-steered Pelican, the simulator tilted and turned from side to side. When the three-bird nose was attached to it, the pigeons could be put in full control —the "loop could be closed"—and the adequacy of the signal tested under pursuit conditions. Targets were moved back and forth across the far wall of a room at prescribed speeds and in given patterns of oscillation, and the tracking response of the whole unit was studied quantitatively.

Meanwhile we continued our intensive study of the behavior of the pigeon. Looking ahead to combat use we designed methods for the mass production of trained birds and for handling large groups of trained subjects. We were proposing to train certain birds for certain *classes* of targets, such as ships at sea, while special squads were to be trained on special targets, photographs of which were to be obtained through reconnaissance. A large crew of pigeons would then be waiting for assignment, but we developed harnessing and training techniques which should have solved such problems quite easily.

A multiple-unit trainer is shown in Figure 5. Each box contained a jack-

FIG. 5.   A trainer for four pigeons.

eted pigeon held at an angle of 45° to the horizontal and perpendicular to an 8″ × 8″ translucent screen. A target area is projected on each screen. Two beams of light intersect at the point to be struck. All on-target responses of the pigeon are reported by the interruption of the crossed beams and by contact with the translucent screen. Only a four-inch, disk-shaped portion of the field is visible to the pigeon at any time, but the boxes move slowly about the field, giving the pigeon an opportunity to respond to the target in all positions. The positions of all reinforcements are recorded to reveal any weak areas. A variable-ratio schedule is used to build sustained, rapid responding.

By December, 1943, less than six months after the contract was awarded, we were ready to report to the Office of Scientific Research and Development. Observers visited the laboratory and watched the simulator follow a target about a room under the control of a team of three birds. They also reviewed our tracking data. The only questions which arose were the inevitable consequence of our lack of information about the signal required to steer the Pelican. For example, we had had to make certain arbitrary decisions in compromising between sensitivity of signal and its integration or smoothness. A high vacuum produced quick, rather erratic movements of the tambours, while a lower vacuum gave a sluggish but smooth signal. As it turned out, we had not chosen the best values in collecting our data, and in January, 1944, the Office of Scientific Research and Development refused to extend the General Mills contract. The reasons given seemed to be due to misunderstandings or, rather, to lack of communication. We had already collected further data with new settings of the instruments, and these were submitted in a request for reconsideration.

We were given one more chance. We took our new data to the radiation lab at the Massachusetts Institute of Technology where they were examined by the servospecialists working on the Pelican controls. To our surprise the scientist whose task it was to predict the usefulness of the pigeon signal argued that our data were inconsistent with respect to phase lag and certain other characteristics of the signal. According to his equations, our device could not possibly yield the signals we reported. We knew, of course, that it had done so. We examined the supposed inconsistency and traced it, or so we thought, to a certain nonlinearity in our system. In pecking an image near the edge of the plate, the pigeon strikes a more glancing blow; hence the air admitted at the valves is not linearly proportional to the displacement of the target. This could be corrected in several ways: for example, by using a lens to distort radial distances. It was our understanding that in any case the signal was adequate to control the Pelican. Indeed, one servo authority, upon looking at graphs of the performance of the simulator, exclaimed: "This is better than radar!"

Two days later, encouraged by our meeting at MIT, we reached the summit. We were to present our case briefly to a committee of the country's top scientists. The hearing began with a brief report by the scientist who had discovered the "inconsistency" in our data, and to our surprise he still regarded it as unresolved. He predicted that the signal we reported would cause the missile to "hunt" wildly and lose the target. But his prediction should have applied as well to the closed loop simulator. Fortunately another scientist was present who had seen the simulator performing under excellent control and who could confirm our report of the facts. But reality was no match for mathematics.

The basic difficulty, of course, lay in convincing a dozen distinguished physical scientists that the behavior of a pigeon could be adequately controlled. We had hoped to score on this point by bringing with us a demonstration. A small black box had a round translucent window in one end.

A slide projector placed some distance away threw on the window an image of the New Jersey target. In the box, of course, was a pigeon—which, incidentally, had at that time been harnessed for 35 hours. Our intention was to let each member of the committee observe the response to the target by looking down a small tube; but time was not available for individual observation, and we were asked to take the top off the box. The translucent screen was flooded with so much light that the target was barely visible, and the peering scientists offered conditions much more unfamiliar and threatening than those likely to be encountered in a missile. In spite of this the pigeon behaved perfectly, pecking steadily and energetically at the image of the target as it moved about on the plate. One scientist with an experimental turn of mind intercepted the beam from the projector. The pigeon stopped instantly. When the image again appeared, pecking began within a fraction of a second and continued at a steady rate.

It was a perfect performance, but it had just the wrong effect. One can talk about phase lag in pursuit behavior and discuss mathematical predictions of hunting without reflecting too closely upon what is inside the black box. But the spectacle of a living pigeon carrying out its assignment, no matter how beautifully, simply reminded the committee of how utterly fantastic our proposal was. I will not say that the meeting was marked by unrestrained merriment, for the merriment was restrained. But it was there, and it was obvious that our case was lost.

Hyde closed our presentation with a brief summary: we were offering a homing device, unusually resistant to jamming, capable of reacting to a wide variety of target patterns, requiring no materials in short supply, and so simple to build that production could be started in 30 days. He thanked the committee, and we left. As the door closed behind us, he said to me: "Why don't you go out and get drunk!"

Official word soon came: "Further prosecution of this project would seriously delay others which in the minds of the Division would have more immediate promise of combat application." Possibly the reference was to a particular combat application at Hiroshima a year and a half later, when it looked for a while as if the need for accurate bombing had been eliminated for all time. In any case we had to show, for all our trouble, only a loftful of curiously useless equipment and a few dozen pigeons with a strange interest in a feature of the New Jersey coast. The equipment was scrapped, but 30 of the pigeons were kept to see how long they would retain the appropriate behavior.

In the years which followed there were faint signs of life. Winston Churchill's personal scientific advisor, Lord Cherwell, learned of the project and "regretted its demise." A scientist who had had some contact with the project during the war, and who evidently assumed that its classified status was not to be taken seriously, made a good story out of it for the *Atlantic Monthly,* names being changed to protect the innocent. Other uses of animals began to be described. The author of the *Atlantic Monthly* story also published an account of the "incendiary bats." Thousands of bats were to be released over an enemy city, each carrying a small incendiary time bomb. The bats would take refuge, as is their custom, under eaves and in other out-of-the-way places; and shortly afterwards thousands of small fires would break out practically simultaneously. The scheme was never used because it was feared that it would be mistaken for germ warfare and might lead to retaliation in kind.

Another story circulating at the time told how the Russians trained dogs to blow up tanks. I have described the technique elsewhere.[1] A Swedish proposal to use seals to achieve the same end with submarines was not successful. The seals were to be trained to approach submarines to obtain fish attached to the sides. They were then to be released carrying magnetic mines in the vicinity of hostile submarines. The required training was apparently never achieved. I cannot vouch for the authenticity of probably the most fantastic story of this sort, but it ought to be recorded. The Russians were said to have trained sea lions to cut mine cables. A complicated device attached to the sea lion included a motor-driven cable cutter, a tank full of small fish, and a device which released a few fish into a muzzle covering the sea lion's head. In order to eat, the sea lion had to find a mine cable and swim along side it so that the cutter was automatically triggered, at which point a few fish were released from the tank into the muzzle. When a given number of cables had been cut, both the energy of the cutting mechanism and the supply of fish were exhausted, and the sea lion received a special stimulus upon which it returned to its home base for special reinforcement and reloading.

ORCON

The story of our own venture has a happy ending. With the discovery of German accomplishments in the field of guided missiles, feasible homing systems suddenly became very important. Franklin V. Taylor of the Naval Research Laboratory in Washington, D. C., heard about our project and asked for further details. As a psychologist Taylor appreciated the special capacity of living organisms to respond to visual patterns and was aware of

[1] See page 121.

recent advances in the control of behavior. More important, he was a skill-ful practitioner in a kind of control which our project had conspicuously lacked: he knew how to approach the people who determine the direction of research. He showed our demonstration film so often that it was com-pletely worn out—but to good effect, for support was eventually found for a thorough investigation of "organic control" under the general title ORCON. Taylor also enlisted the support of engineers in obtaining a more effective report of the pigeon's behavior. The translucent plate upon which the image of the target was thrown had a semiconducting surface, and the tip of the bird's beak was covered with a gold electrode. A single contact with the plate sent an immediate report of the location of the target to the controlling mechanism. The work which went into this system contributed to the so-called Pick-off Display Converter developed as part of the Naval Data Handling System for human observers. It is no longer necessary for the radar operator to give a verbal report of the location of a pip on the screen. Like the pigeon, he has only to touch the pip with a special contact. (He holds the contact in his hand.)

At the Naval Research Laboratory in Washington the responses of pigeons were studied in detail. Average peck rate, average error rate, aver-age hit rate, and so on, were recorded under various conditions. The track-ing behavior of the pigeon was analyzed with methods similar to those employed with human operators (Figure 6). Pattern perception was stud-ied, including generalization from one pattern to another. A simulator was constructed in which the pigeon controlled an image projected by a moving-picture film of an actual target: for example, a ship at sea as seen from a plane approaching at 600 miles per hour. A few frames of a moving picture of the pigeon controlling the orientation toward a ship during an approach are shown in Figure 7.

The publications from the Naval Research Laboratory which report this work [2] provide a serious evaluation of the possibilities of organic control. Although in simulated tests a single pigeon occasionally loses a target, its tracking characteristics are surprisingly good. A three- or seven-bird unit

[2] Chernikoff, R., and Newlin, E. P. ORCON. Part III. Investigations of target acquisition by the pigeon. *Naval Res. Lab. lett. Rep.*, 1951, No. S-3600-629a/51 (Sept. 10). Conklin, J. E., Newlin, E. P., Jr., Taylor, F. V., and Tipton, C. L. ORCON. Part IV. Simulated flight tests. *Naval Res. Lab. lett. Rep.*, 1953, No. 4105. Searle, L. V., and Stafford, B. H. ORCON. Part II. Report of phase I research and bandpass study. *Naval Res. Lab. lett. Rep.*, 1950, No. S-3600-157/50 (May 1). Taylor, F. V. ORCON. Part I. Outline of proposed research. *Naval Res. Lab. lett. Rep.*, 1949, No. S-43600-157/50 (June 17). White, C. F. Development of the NRL ORCON tactile missile simulator. *Naval Res. Lab. Rep.*, 1952, No. 3917.

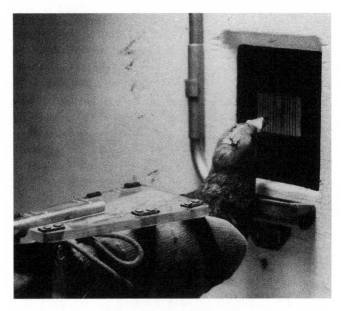

Fig. 6.   Arrangement for studying pursuit movements.

with the same individual consistency should yield a signal with a reliability which is at least of the order of magnitude shown by other phases of guided missiles in their present stage of development. Moreover, in the seven years which have followed the last of these reports, a great deal of relevant information has been acquired. The color vision of the pigeon is now thoroughly understood; its generalization along single properties of a stimulus has been recorded and analyzed; and the maintenance of behavior through scheduling of reinforcement has been drastically improved, particularly in the development of techniques for pacing responses for less erratic and steadier signals.[3] Tests made with the birds salvaged from the old Project Pigeon showed that even after six years of inactivity a pigeon will immediately and correctly strike a target to which it has been conditioned and will continue to respond for some time without reinforcement.

The use of living organisms in guiding missiles is, it seems fair to say, no longer a crackpot idea. A pigeon is an extraordinarily subtle and complex mechanism capable of performances which at the moment can be

[3] See, for example, the paper beginning on page 132.

FIG. 7. Frames from a simulated approach.

equalled by electronic equipment only of vastly greater weight and size, and it can be put to reliable use through the principles which have emerged from an experimental analysis of its behavior. But this vindication of our original proposal is perhaps the least important result. Something happened during the brief life of Project Pigeon which it has taken a long time to appreciate. The practical task before us created a new attitude toward the behavior of organisms. We had to maximize the probability that a given form of behavior would occur at a given time. We could not enjoy the luxury of observing one variable while allowing others to change in what we hoped was a random fashion. We had to discover all relevant variables and submit them to experimental control whenever possible. We were no doubt under exceptional pressure, but vigorous scientific research usually makes comparable demands. Psychologists have too often yielded to the temptation to be content with hypothetical processes and intervening variables rather than press for rigorous experimental control. It is often intellectual laziness rather than necessity which recommends the *a posteriori* statistical treatment of variation. Our task forced us to emphasize prior experimental control, and its success in revealing orderly processes gave us an exciting glimpse of the superiority of laboratory practice over verbal (including some kinds of mathematical) explanation.

The Crackpot Idea

If I were to conclude that crackpot ideas are to be encouraged, I should probably be told that psychology has already had more than its share of them. If it has, they have been entertained by the wrong people. Reacting against the excesses of psychological quackery, psychologists have developed an enormous concern for scientific respectability. They constantly warn their students against questionable facts and unsupported theories. As a result the usual PhD thesis is a model of compulsive cautiousness, advancing only the most timid conclusions thoroughly hedged about with qualifications. But it is just the man capable of displaying such admirable caution who needs a touch of uncontrolled speculation. Possibly a generous exposure to psychological science fiction would help. Project Pigeon might be said to support that view. Except with respect to its avowed goal, it was, as I see it, highly productive; and this was in large measure because my colleagues and I knew that, in the eyes of the world, we were crazy.

One virtue in crackpot ideas is that they breed rapidly and their progeny show extraordinary mutations. Everyone is talking about teaching machines nowadays, but Sidney Pressey can tell you what it was like to have a crackpot idea in that field 40 years ago. His self-testing devices and self-scoring test forms now need no defense, and psychomotor training devices have also achieved a substantial respectability. This did not, however, prepare the way for devices to be used in verbal instruction—that is, in the kinds of teaching which are the principal concern of our schools and colleges. Even five short years ago that kind of instruction by machine was still in the crackpot category. (I can quote official opinion to that effect from high places.) Now, there is a direct genetic connection between teaching machines and Project Pigeon. We had been forced to consider the mass education of pigeons. True, the scrap of wisdom we imparted to each was indeed small, but the required changes in behavior were similar to those which must be brought about in vaster quantities in human students. The techniques of shaping behavior and of bringing it under stimulus control which can be traced, as I have suggested elsewhere,[4] to a memorable episode on the top floor of that flour mill in Minneapolis needed only a detailed reformulation of verbal behavior to be directly applicable to education.

I am sure there is more to come. In the year which followed the termination of Project Pigeon I wrote *Walden Two,* a utopian picture of a properly engineered society. Some psychotherapists might argue that I was suffering from personal rejection and simply retreated to a fantasied world where everything went according to plan, where there never was heard a discouraging word. But another explanation is, I think, equally plausible. That piece of science fiction was a declaration of confidence in a technology of behavior. Call it a crackpot idea if you will; it is one in which I have never lost faith. I still believe that the same kind of wide-ranging speculation about human affairs, supported by studies of compensating rigor, will make a substantial contribution toward that world of the future in which, among other things, there will be no need for guided missiles.

[4] See page 165.

Some Responses to the Stimulus "Pavlov"

In opening the first session this morning Dr. Reese said that he felt the program showed signs of an ecumenical spirit. I don't know whether the remark was a reference to my Protestant activities, but if so, I must say it was extraordinarily generous of the College of Cardinals to have made me Pope. I shall try to learn the proper rituals. In the movie, *Zorba the Greek*, the French woman was never accepted by the islanders because she crossed herself from left to right, rather than right to left. I shall try not to make that kind of mistake. From now on it will be condition*al* reflexes.

It seems appropriate on this occasion to try to say what Pavlov has meant to me. I have to strain a bit to get back to personal reminiscences, but I can just make it. In 1929 Pavlov was enthusiastically received in Boston as President of the International Congress of Physiology. I was in my first year of graduate study in psychology at Harvard, and I turned up hero-worshipping wherever Pavlov could be expected to appear. A photographer was taking orders for an official portrait. He had asked Pavlov to write his name on a sheet of paper, and he assured prospective buyers that the signature would appear on each photograph. I offered to buy one if I could have the sheet of paper when he was through with it. I got it, and still have it. It is the only autograph I have ever collected.

It was my biology teacher at Hamilton College, Albro Morrill, who first called my attention to Anrep's translation of Pavlov. I had gone back, a year after graduation, to talk with him about graduate study in psychology. He had always hoped I would be a biologist, and perhaps that was why he showed me Pavlov's book, which he had just received. In one of his courses he had already called my attention to Jacques Loeb's *The Physiology of*

From *Conditional Reflex*, 1966, *1*, 74–78. These remarks were originally delivered at a dinner of the Pavlovian Society held on Saturday, February 12, 1966.

the Brain and Comparative Psychology. I bought Pavlov's book and took it with me to Greenwich Village, where I spent several Bohemian months before going on to Harvard. I read Pavlov by day and sowed wild oats by night. I am sure Pavlov himself would have approved of this pairing of stimuli. Even today a page of his book elicits many warm, if somewhat faded, autonomic responses.

Pavlov was particularly relevant to a rather drastic change which I had made in my plans for a career and about which I was not yet too secure. I had majored in English and had planned to be a writer. It took me a year or two to discover that although I had learned how to write, I had learned nothing worth writing about. I found I had nothing to say. I decided to go into psychology to remedy the defect. At about that time H. G. Wells wrote an article for, I believe, the Sunday *New York Times.* In it he compared Pavlov and George Bernard Shaw. They looked rather alike, with their great white beards, and it was easy for Wells to contrast the witty propagandist with the laboratory scientist. He posed a hypothetical question: If these two men were drowning, and you had only one life preserver, to which would you throw it? Wells enormously reassured me in the decision I had made by throwing it to Pavlov.

Several years later I worked for a time in the laboratory of Professor Walter B. Cannon at the Harvard Medical School. Cannon and Pavlov were close friends, and when Pavlov came to America, he stayed with the Cannons in a house on Divinity Avenue about 60 yards (I paced it off this morning) from the auditorium in which we have been meeting. Cannon told many amusing stories about Pavlov. They were gentle stories, scarcely worth telling about anyone, even of Pavlov's distinction, but here are two of them. Pavlov knew little English. He and Cannon conversed in German. One morning at breakfast Pavlov was trying to read the headlines on the sports page of a Boston paper. It appeared that a ninth inning rally of the Red Sox had fizzled. Pavlov called across the table to Cannon, "Was meint das Wort 'fizzle'?"—pronouncing it "fit—zell." Another story had to do with the episode in which Pavlov was robbed upon his arrival in New York. He and his son were in Grand Central Terminal intending to take a train for Boston. He evidently displayed his wallet a little too conspicuously as he paid for his tickets. Two young thugs bumped against him, grabbed the wallet, containing nearly $2,000, and ran. (I believe it was the Rockefeller Foundation which came to Pavlov's rescue, making him a grant of $1,000 to permit him "to study physiology in the United States.") The next day Pavlov was sitting on Cannon's front porch when Cannon suggested they walk to Harvard Square for a soda. As Cannon started down the steps, Pavlov said, "But you haven't locked your door." Cannon assured him it would be all right. "But there's no one in your house, and your door is unlocked," insisted Pavlov. "It doesn't matter," Cannon said, "we'll be back in a little while." Pavlov shook his head uncertainly. "My," he said, "what a great difference between New York and Cambridge!"

Pavlov's book proved to be enormously helpful in my graduate studies. Possibly the most important lesson I learned from it, and one easily overlooked, was respect for a fact. On December 15, 1911, at exactly 1:55 in the afternoon, a dog secreted nine drops of saliva. To take that fact seriously, and to make one's readers take it seriously, was no mean achievement. It was important too that it was a fact about a single organism. Animal psychology at that time was primarily concerned with the behavior of the *average* rat. The learning curves which appeared in textbooks were generated by large groups of organisms. Pavlov was talking about the behavior of one organism at a time.

He also emphasized controlled conditions. His soundproofed laboratory, a picture of which appears in the book, impressed me greatly, and the first apparatus I built consisted of a soundproofed chamber and a silent release-box. I suspect that the control of the environment in Pavlov's laboratory would seem rather inadequate today. I have always been suspicious of that experiment in which a dog, given food every 30 minutes without any signal, begins to salivate promptly 29 minutes after the previous delivery. I have often wondered what the experimenter did during those 30 minutes. My guess is that he left the room to attend to other matters, perhaps to have a smoke. At 29 minutes by his watch, rather than by any temporal conditioning, I imagine him tiptoeing back and noting with satisfaction that the red fluid in the glass tube shortly thereafter began to move. But whether or not the control was adequate, it was held to be of first importance.

The motto of this society is taken from Pavlov: "Observation and observation." Pavlov meant, of course, the observation of nature, not of what someone had written about nature. He was opposed to dogma and would be opposed to current dogma about himself. It is now 50 years since he was most active, and that is a long time in the history of science. His position in that history is secure, for he made extraordinary contributions; but he was not free of certain limitations. His influence upon the subsequent history of the study of behavior has not always been happy. I think I can express my respect for Pavlov in a way which he would be most likely to approve if I indicate certain points on which I think he was wrong.

He turned too quickly to inferences about the nervous system. The subtitle of the Anrep translation is "An Investigation of the Physiological Activity of the Cerebral Cortex." Pavlov never saw any of that activity; he was studying merely what he took to be its products. His facts were about behavior, and his effort to represent them as facts about the nervous system interfered with his reports and must have affected the design of his experiments. Pavlov probably took this line as a product of a nineteenth century materialism. Sherrington did the same thing at about the same time.

A different brand of materialism came into the story when the Soviets made Pavlov a national hero. There is no doubt that the nervous system is material; when it decays, it smells, and could one ask for better proof? Behavior on the other hand is evanescent. In talking about it without mentioning the nervous system, one runs the risk of being called an idealist. There has never been a separate Russian science of behavior. Perhaps that is one reason why cybernetics has been taken up so energetically. Mathematics and the machine analogy have at last permitted the Russians to talk about behavior without mentioning the nervous system. The fear of being called an idealist has led to some absurd practices. In a teacher's college in Tashkent the director told us that the college was interested in "higher nervous activities." He meant simply that they were teaching teachers.

Pavlov's physiological metaphors encouraged him to speculate about processes supposed to be going on behind his facts rather than about the facts themselves. Freud had done the same thing but much more dramatically. The various kinds of inhibition which Pavlov thought he saw in his data were logically unnecessary. A response may, for many reasons, grow weak; it is not necessarily suffering extinction. But the metaphor of a central, probably cortical, process is attractive. A prestige attaches to the statement that inhibition has spread across the cortex, a prestige which is lacking in a mere recital of the facts upon which the statement is based.

Diverted from a strict formulation of behavioral facts as such, it was easy for Pavlov to believe that conditioned reflexes comprised the whole field of learned behavior, and to overlook differences even among the kinds of behavior to which the principle seems to apply. It was extraordinarily lucky that he began with the salivary reflex. There seems to be no other response quite so simple. Other glandular secretions, for example, tears or sweat, are by no means so easy to control, and we have heard today something of the enormous complexity of conditioned cardiac responses. The extension of the Pavlovian formulation to skeletal musculature raises especially difficult questions. To insist that the Pavlovian experiment is a useful prototype in formulating all learned behavior is not really very helpful.

Two or three years ago the Moscow Circus came to Boston, and the bear trainer, Mr. Filatov, expressed an interest in talking with me about animal-training procedures. My wife invited him to dinner, together with a charming interpreter and her date for the evening, the ringmaster of the circus. When we got around to shop talk, Mr. Filatov announced the ground rules: "Now, it is all a matter of conditioned reflexes, isn't it?" he said. I replied that in America we tried to make a distinction between the case in which the reinforcing stimulus accompanied another stimulus and the case in which it followed a response.

"That doesn't matter," he insisted. "Whether the reinforcement comes before or after the response, it is still a conditioned reflex. Right?" I saw that we could not otherwise get on to the training of bears, and so I agreed.

But of course I do not agree. A careful analysis of contingencies of reinforcement in both operant and respondent behavior seems to me an absolutely essential first step. It is not a question of differences in theory, it is a matter of reaching a formulation which fits the known facts. This is a task to which Pavlov, if he were alive today, would devote himself with his characteristic enthusiasm.

Facts and formulations of facts change as science progresses. The experimental spirit and the integrity of the scientist do not change. In the abiding aspects of the life of a scientist we still have much to learn from Ivan Petrovitch Pavlov.

Squirrel in the Yard

For twenty-five years the end of the spring term at Harvard has been heralded by the sound of hammers ringing out in the Yard, as workmen reconstruct the Tercentenary Theater for another Commencement. A solid platform rises along the south side of Memorial Church and is painted a fresh gray, in a show of permanence that deceives even the grass growing beneath it, which must later be replaced with fresh sod. Fifteen thousand folding chairs are set in place in staked-out rows, fanning out from the platform to the steps of Widener Library. On the day before Commencement a great canopy is stretched above the platform, and loud-speakers are lashed to trees throughout the Yard. This is all done in the confident expectation that Commencement Day will be fair, and, indeed, no Commencement has been driven indoors by bad weather since the Tercentenary Theater was first built in 1936.

Thus reassured, Harvard has replaced the wooden platform with a permanent stone terrace, to be used this year for the first time. Nothing else about Commencement will be greatly changed. The day will begin with an early swell of excitement outside the walls of the Yard. Some of the iron gates will be closed and locked. Others will be defended by policemen with instructions to admit alumni and those about to become alumni, their families and guests, members of the Harvard Corporation and the Board of Overseers in their frock coats and silk hats, and Faculty members in their bright gowns and hoods, some in the strange regalia of foreign universities. The Governor will arrive from the State House in Boston, no longer coming on horseback himself but still escorted by the National Lancers on their spirited mounts.

By nine-thirty I shall have joined my colleagues near Massachusetts Hall. It will be my day to wear the crimson gown owned jointly by three

From *Harvard Alumni Bulletin*, May 1962.

members of my department (and unfortunately tailored to accommodate the tallest of them). We shall stand about, greeting friends whom we have possibly not seen since last year, glancing unobtrusively at a colleague's new hood and trying to guess from its colored lining the name of the university that gave it to him. We shall peer a little less cautiously at those about to receive Harvard's honorary degrees, whose identity has been kept secret until this moment, but who will now be standing about in front of Massachusetts Hall.

Eventually, the line will move. Two by two we shall shuffle forward, through a somber gauntlet of black-gowned seniors, many of them looking on their professors for the last time. (There may be a twinge of guilt as I think of the senior who is not here because he flunked my course—who is not only not there but cannot go on that all-summer honeymoon or accept the commission waiting for him in one of the services because he must come back to summer school to pass another course for his degree.) We shall move past University Hall under the flags which stir gently above the statue of John Harvard. We shall take off our mortarboards out of respect for the flag, or possibly John Harvard, and put them on again carefully, the tassles tickling. Crossing in front of the steps of Widener, we shall turn slowly down the center aisle of the Theater to the new terrace under the canopy and move carefully up the steps (carefully, because nothing is more awkward than stumbling on an academic gown; you do not fall, you simply walk up the front of the gown, forcing yourself into an ignominious genuflection).

We shall stand before our seats on the terrace for a long time as the candidates for degrees file into their designated places. Then the bell in Memorial Church will peal vigorously. The Marshal will call out, "Mr. Sheriff, pray give us order!" and the Sheriff of Middlesex County, rapping on the platform three times, will perform his verbal magic: "The meeting will be in order."

Nothing that follows will be unpredictable, or even of much interest. God will be told of our concerns and hopes. The Latin Salutatory Disquisition will be understood by some of the Faculty; the rest of us will simply wait for references to *pullae pulcherrimae Radcliffensis* and laugh heartily. The English Dissertation and the English Disquisition will, in spite of every effort of the speakers and their advisors, be period pieces, for no one orates in that style any more. Those who came to get their degrees will get them and be admitted into the society of educated men (and women). The citations for the honorary degrees may be amusing. Later that day some of the recipients of honorary degrees will make speeches from that terrace, and once in a while one of them makes history.

It is hard to explain why this is so exciting and glamorous. In any case I have lost all hope of making a proper evaluation myself, for the bell which rings out so joyously to proclaim the emancipation of these thousands of students awakens in me a compulsive memory. The bell figured prominently in a ceremony which I attended on the same spot several years before the Tercentenary Theater was built. A squirrel stole the show. In its way it deserves to make history, too.

I owe a special debt to squirrels. When I began graduate work at Harvard, another student and I ordered three of them from an animal supply house. Somehow or other they came into my exclusive charge, and for about a year I gave them the run of my laboratory. When not fencing with my rats through the screened walls of their cages, they would sit on my desk or lie in wait on top of a bookcase, leaping to the shoulders of unsuspecting visitors. Within the year they grew too destructive to be left free, but I made their cage as large as possible and added a wheel (the classical squirrel cage) to provide a semblance of freedom in the opportunity to run without interruption.

The following summer was unusually warm, and I increased the verisimilitude of the wheel as an infinitely long running space by arranging a fan so that it blew into the face of the squirrel. It was an old electric fan. The motor had gone, but I attached a pulley to the shaft of the blade and ran a belt to a larger pulley on the shaft of the running wheel. Whenever the wheel turned, the fan turned, at a higher rate. In a sense, the squirrel fanned itself as it ran.

There was a graduate student from Korea in our department, a Mr. Kim. He had found it difficult to adjust to the mechanized life in America, and the sight of an American squirrel automatically fanning itself was too much. He would come into my laboratory day after day and stand beside the squirrel cage, laughing quietly as he watched a squirrel running head-on into its self-generated breeze. Not long afterward Mr. Kim quietly returned to Korea without his degree.

I also experimented on the squirrels in the Yard. At that time there was considerable interest in the way chimpanzees and other apes solved problems—by raking in bananas through the bars of their cages with long sticks or piling boxes in order to reach them where they hung near the ceiling. We had originally bought our squirrels because they had hands which might permit them to do similar things. In the open laboratory of the Yard I would tie a peanut to a two- or three-foot length of string and hang it from a branch on a young elm. A squirrel would squat on the branch above the string and pull it in, hand over hand, as deft as any sailor pulling in a cast-off line.

This sciurine phase of my studies of animal behavior came to an end in the spring vacation of 1932. The old Appleton Chapel had been torn down, and Memorial Church was just being completed in its place. The belfry was still empty, but the bell which had hung in Harvard Hall across the Yard had been brought to the base of the tower, where it rested on an improvised platform. Cables and pulleys had been rigged, and it was to be hoisted into place at one o'clock in the afternoon. A little ceremony had been planned. President Lowell, who had given the bell to Harvard, would be present.

On the morning of that day, workmen had begun to take down a large elm near the bell. The Dutch Elm Disease had not yet struck the Yard, but the tree stood too close to the church and had been condemned. By noon workmen had cut off all the branches so that nothing remained but a heavy block Y. As they unpacked their lunches, sitting alongside the wall of the church, quiet settled over the Yard. A few minutes later a frightened squirrel looked out from a hole in the crotch of the Y. She had evidently been cowering in the tree all morning, through the shock and vibration of axe and saw. Accepting the cease-fire, she emerged from the hole, flicked her tail nervously, spiraled head-first down the tree in sudden starts, and set out to explore the Yard. A quarter of an hour later she returned, slipped into the hole in the tree, and came out carrying a struggling young squirrel. It was well grown, probably more than a month and a half old. Its tail was still rat-like, but the rest of its body was well covered with fur. It had almost certainly been weaned, but a squirrel family stays together all summer, and this one was to be no exception.

The young squirrel resisted strenuously as its mother packed it into a manageable mouthful, patting it rapidly with her forepaws. With the squirming youngster in her mouth she came awkwardly down the tree and set off for Emerson Hall a hundred and fifty yards to the East. She climbed up the well-grown ivy on the right side of the door, twisting, turning, and occasionally moving backward to get her struggling burden through the branches and leaves to a ledge above the second floor. A few minutes later she came down empty-mouthed, and went straight back to the tree. She brought out a second squirrel of the same vintage, also stoutly protesting, and started off again toward Emerson.

It was now nearly one o'clock and people had begun to gather for the ceremony. Mr. Lowell arrived with his red cocker spaniel—too old to chase squirrels (and so deaf that Mr. Lowell could call it only by waving both arms in a broad semaphore). When he was told what was happening, Mr. Lowell gave orders that the bell was not to be hoisted until the squirrel had finished.

There was a shout of "Here she comes!", and the crowd divided into two thin lines, stretching from the base of the tree well toward Emerson Hall. Completely absorbed, the squirrel entered this formidable gauntlet and proceeded to the tree and up and into the hole. She came out wrestling with another youngster, packed it into her mouth as well as she could, spiraled down the tree, and set off between the lines, a small leg kicking from her mouth in protest as she went.

It was a warm day, and she was growing tired. She would stop to flatten herself against the cool ground, then rally her forces, recompose her uncooperative burden, and set off. As she reached Emerson Hall and lost herself in the ivy, the crowd began to move uncertainly about. It was well past one. The workmen tested the ropes and cables impatiently, looking at each other and at Mr. Lowell. But Mr. Lowell had spoken, and the bell stayed in its place.

The squirrel appeared again, and the lines, denser now, reformed. She came back, pausing from time to time in growing exhaustion but looking neither to right nor to left in her dedication. She took a fourth youngster from the tree and set off toward her new quarters.

Speculation arose as to the size of squirrel litters. Unreliable rumors spread as to how many youngsters she had already transported, and small wagers were laid as to how many were still to come. The books say "three to six" in a litter for the gray squirrel, but there must be exceptions. Possibly this squirrel had had the bad luck to be taking care of a neighbor's children. In any case, she was to carry seven young squirrels from one nest to the other that day. She carried each of them nearly five hundred feet, plus two tall flights of ivy and one flight of elm.

Another speculation ran through the growing crowd. Would she, arriving on the ledge of Emerson Hall, know that she had rescued her last child? How would she know? Did she know how many children she had? Could she, in fact, count? Or would she be able to remember that she had left an empty nest behind her on her last trip?

It was nearly two o'clock when, for the last time, someone cried, "Here she comes!" The crowd, now swelled far beyond those who cared about the mere hoisting of a bell, broke into well-disciplined lines. The exhausted squirrel dragged herself back to the elm, inch by inch, and struggling slowly to the top of the trunk slipped with obvious relief into the hole. We were all silent. She reappeared empty-mouthed. She had come back once too often. She made a brief effort to cover her mistake, flicking her tail lightly as if she had known all along that the nest was empty, and then gave in. She settled herself limply, like a tiny fur piece, on the rough bark of the elm alongside the hole, looking timidly, and a little sheepishly, out over her audience for the first time.

Mr. Lowell nodded curtly to the workmen, ropes were shaken clear, and the bell moved slowly upward and was swung into place in the tower of Memorial Church.

PART X

Coda

Can Psychology Be a Science of Mind?

'Faith, I must leave thee, love, and shortly too;
My operant powers their functions leave [cease] to do.

HAMLET, III, ii

Can Psychology Be a Science of Mind?

[*This article was completed August 17, 1990, the evening before its author died. It appeared in the November 1990 issue of the* American Psychologist. *The following account of B. F. Skinner's last days was written by his daughter, Julie S. Vargas.*]

My father always spoke admiringly of his grandfather's death. "He died with his boots on," he'd say, approvingly. Sometimes he would add, "That's the way I want to go." Well, he came close. . . .

Eight days before his death, . . . my father received, from the American Psychological Association, the first APA Citation for Outstanding Lifetime Contribution to Psychology. The association officials had assured the family that they would keep my father from crowds— important because of his heightened susceptibility to infection from leukemia—and they kept their word. At 1:00 o'clock on August 10th, a limousine appeared at the Skinner home to drive our party to the convention hotel. There we were met and ushered upstairs in our own elevator to a hotel room, "like movie stars," my father remarked. A few minutes before the opening session was to begin, we were ushered back downstairs and taken by a back way to the side door of the auditorium. I was holding my father's arm as we entered. The room was packed. A second room to the side had been opened and it, too, was overflowing. When we had taken two steps into the room everyone stood up and began to applaud. My father made an awkward nod of his head in acknowledgment as he continued walking—I could tell he hadn't expected such a reception. The applause was thunderous. It continued as we made our way to the bottom of the steps at the middle of the stage. It continued, undiminished, as my father was escorted across the stage to his chair. He turned around and made a gracious bow of his head, but there was no sign of the applause letting up. Finally, APA officials interrupted the applause and started the program . . . .

I was glad that he had decided not to use a text or even notes, for the glaring light from the TV camera crews would have made it impossible for him to have seen anything. He began. "President Graham, past-President Matarazzo, distinguished guests, ladies and gentlemen. . . ."[1]   He talked smoothly, the way I had heard him talk at dozens of conventions, complete with names and dates I would have had trouble remembering. The talk turned to the split in psychology, "one part going in the direction of finding out the essence of the feeling, the essence of the cognitive process, and the other going in the direction of references to contingencies of reinforcement." He drew an analogy between the difficulty of acceptance of Darwin's natural selection and the difficulty of acceptance of Skinner's own selection by consequences, culminating in the statement, "So far as I'm concerned, cognitive science is the creationism of psychology." The whole audience gasped audibly. A sprinkling of clapping could be heard here and there. (Clearly the split was not 50–50.) Skinner continued, ending in just over 15 minutes—as he had planned. . . .

Over the weekend, my father worked on the paper from which his remarks were taken. It was to go in the American Psychologist *and he was anxious to finish it. We talked about the future—what he would work on next. He didn't feel he would have time to complete the work he had done on the derivations of words, or to put into article form material from a book on ethics he had begun but given up. As it turned out, he was right about time.*

Monday morning my father had an hour interview with Dan Bjork, a historian who had been working on a biography of him. In the afternoon, I took him for his usual platelet transfusion. That evening I was working in the den I had created out of a storeroom in the basement when I got a call. It was my father. "Julie, could you come here?" I rushed to his study to find him shivering under several blankets in his reclining chair. I panicked. The symptoms were the same as those that had put him into a coma one time before. Unable to reach a doctor, I called 911. By the time the ambulance arrived he was feeling better, although his heart was still racing. The ambulance team gave him oxygen and took all sorts of measures, conferring by phone with medical personnel from his infirmary. My father didn't want to go back to the hospital, so, because he appeared stable, the team left. The oxygen had made him feel better, so I hooked up an old tank he had saved from years ago. I encouraged him to stay sitting up because his heart was still racing, and a sitting position is less strain

---

[1] All quotes are from extemporaneous comments made by B. F. Skinner upon receiving APA's lifetime award at the opening session of the American Psychological Association's 98th Annual Convention, August 10, 1990, in Boston.

on the heart. He agreed, and took out a book to read. I set up a cot in his study and brought in my guitar. For an hour I played for him— all of the classical pieces I could play reasonably well. It pleased him. He hadn't heard me play in some time and commented on the "richness" of the sound. The oxygen and I both ran out about the same time. Later, in his bed, a Japanese-designed sleeping cubicle in the far corner of his study, we talked. I sat on the edge, holding his hand, as so many times, dewy-eyed, he had held mine when putting me to bed as a child. Only this time there were tears in both of our eyes.

I awoke the next morning to find him awake, but weak. In spite of my urging, he refused to cancel a TV crew scheduled to take footage for that night's newscast. Wednesday morning, another interview. That afternoon he went into the hospital for the last time. But the day before he died, in the hospital, he worked on the last changes in his paper for the American Psychologist.

B. F. Skinner was a member of the Hemlock Society and believed in the right to take one's own life. He had made a living will and, in the hospital, again refused "heroic" lifesaving efforts that could have prolonged the functioning of his organs. Near the end, his mouth was dry. Upon receiving a bit of water he said his last word, "Marvelous."

[From Vargas, J. S. (1990). B. F. Skinner—The last few days. *Journal of the Applied Analysis of Behavior,* 23, 409–410.]

Many psychologists, like the philosophers before them, have looked inside themselves for explanations of their behavior. They have felt feelings and observed mental processes through introspection. Introspection has never been very satisfactory, however. Philosophers have acknowledged its inadequacies while insisting that it is nevertheless the only means of self-knowledge. Psychologists once tried to improve it by using trained observers and the brass instruments of which William James had such a low opinion. Introspection is no longer much used. Cognitive psychologists may see representations and may even argue that they are the only things that can be seen, but they do not claim to see themselves processing them. Instead, like psychoanalysts who face the same problem with processes that cannot be seen because they are unconscious, they have turned to theory. Theories need confirmation, however, and for that many have turned to brain science, where processes may be said to be inspected rather than introspected. If the mind is "what the brain does," the brain can be studied as any other organ is studied. Eventually, then, brain science should tell us what it means to construct a representation of reality, store a representation in memory, convert an intention into action, feel joy or sorrow, draw a logical conclusion, and so on.

But does the brain initiate behavior as the mind or self is said to do? The brain is part of the body, and what it does is part of what the body does. What the brain does is part of what must be explained. Where has the body-cum-brain come from, and why does it change in subtle ways from moment to moment? We cannot find answers to questions of that sort in the body-cum-brain itself, observed either introspectively or with the instruments and methods of physiology.

The behavior of the organism as a whole is the product of three types of variation and selection. The first, natural selection, is responsible for the evolution of the species and hence for species behavior. All types of variation and selection have certain faults, and one of them is especially critical for natural selection: It prepares a species only for a future that resembles the selecting past. Species behavior is effective only in a world that fairly closely resembles the world in which the species evolved.

That fault was corrected by the evolution of a second type of variation and selection, operant conditioning, through which variations in the behavior of the individual are selected by features of the environment that are not stable enough to play any part in evolution. In operant conditioning, behavior is reinforced, in the sense of strengthened or made more likely to occur, by certain kinds of consequences, which first acquired the power to reinforce through natural selection.

A second fault in variation and selection is critical for operant conditioning: Selection must wait upon variation. The process is therefore usually slow. That was not a problem for natural selection because evolution could take millions of years, but a repertoire of operant behavior must be constructed during a lifetime. Operant conditioning must solve the "problem of the first instance": How and why do responses occur before they have been reinforced?

The problem was solved in part by the evolution of processes through which individuals take advantage of behavior already acquired by others. Imitation is an example. It often brings the imitator into contact with the reinforcing consequences responsible for the behavior imitated. The behavior of the imitator is "primed" in the sense of made to occur for the first time and usually when it is likely to be reinforced.

At this point the human species appears to have taken a unique evolutionary step. Other species imitate, but if they model behavior to be imitated, it is only as the product of natural selection. The consequence of modeling the behavior of the imitator is too remote to serve as an operant reinforcer. Only in the human species does the behavior of the imitator reinforce modeling.

The species underwent another unique evolutionary change when its vocal musculature came under operant control and when vocal behavior began to be shaped and maintained by its reinforcing consequences. People could then prime the behavior of others by telling them what to do as well as by showing them. (In a presumably later step, temporary reinforcing consequences were added to make the behavior more likely to remain in strength until the consequence for which it was primed could come into play. Adding temporary reinforcements in this way is teaching.)

Advice can be useful on more than one occasion, and it is then often given or taught in such a way that it is passed on from person to person or from generation to generation. Maxims ("great sayings") and proverbs ("sayings put forth") are examples. They describe rather general contingencies of reinforcement—a penny (as well as many other things) saved is a penny (as well as many other things) earned. Rules are sayings transmitted by groups, usually with stronger reinforcing consequences. The laws of governments and religions describe the contingencies of (usually negative) reinforcement maintained by those institutions. They have the effect of warnings: By obeying the law a person avoids behaving in ways that would be punished. The laws of physics and chemistry ("rules for effective action") describe the contingencies of reinforcement maintained by the physical environment.

Modeling, telling, and teaching are the functions of the social environments called cultures. Different cultures emerge from different contingencies of variation and selection and differ in the extent to which they help their members solve their problems. Members who solve them are more likely to survive, and with them survive the practices of the culture. In other words cultures evolve, in a third kind of variation and selection. (Cultures that shape and maintain *operant* behavior are exclusively human. Animal societies have many similar features, but only as the product of contingencies of survival.) Cultural evolution is not a biological process, but as a kind of variation and selection it has the same faults. The fact that a culture prepares a group only for a world that resembles the world in which the culture evolved is the source of our present concern for the future of a habitable earth.

The process of variation and selection has a third fault: Variations are random and contingencies of selection accidental. What evolved is not a single slowly developing species but millions of different species, competing with each other for a place in the world. The product of operant conditioning is not a single coherent repertoire but thousands of smaller repertoires, conflicts among which must somehow be resolved. The evolution of social environments has produced not a single culture but many often conflicting ones.

Although operant control of the vocal musculature is exclusive to the human species, it is seldom if ever cited as its distinguishing feature. The presence or absence of "consciousness" or "conscious intelligence" is more likely to be cited. The role played by the mind/brain has always been a problem in comparing species. Descartes excepted "man" from his mechanical model of an organism, and Wallace, unlike Darwin, did not believe that evolution could explain the human mind. Brain scientists have expressed similar reservations. Evolutionary theorists have suggested that "conscious intelligence" is an evolved trait, but they have never shown how a nonphysical variation could arise to be selected by physical contingencies of survival. (The suggestion simply moves the bothersome physical-metaphysical distinction a step further out of sight.) It has been said that we may never know how a conscious mind evolved because nothing would survive for palaeontologists to discover, but the operant control of the vocal musculature and the showing, telling, and teaching that follow have survived, and it is possible that they explain introspection and also what is "seen" with its help.

The root *spect* suggests vision. We say that we "look at" and "see" what is happening within ourselves, but no inner eye has ever been discovered. We can avoid specifying a kind of organ by saying *observe*, *notice*, or *note* rather than *see*, and it is significant that *observe*, *notice*, and *note,* and less commonly *remark,* mean both *say* and *see*. Much depends on what it means to sense any part of the world with any kind of organ. Input-output theories, as in stimulus-response or information-processing models, make a sharp distinction between sensing and doing. We are said to sense the world before acting upon it. The experimental analysis of behavior assigns a very different role to the stimulus, however. An operant response is more likely to occur in the presence of a stimulus that was present when it was reinforced. Sensing is as much a product of variation and selection as doing. It is a part of doing. For similar reasons, natural selection explains the readiness with which animals respond instantly to features of the environment that have been crucial to the survival of their species, such as the sight, sound, or smell of food or sexual opportunity, or a threat of danger, including the danger of the unfamiliar. Animals presumably "receive" all the stimuli that impinge upon them, but it is possible that they only respond to those that have played a part in contingencies of selection. (We cannot know whether nonverbal animals see stimuli that have never played such a part, because we should have to arrange contingencies containing such stimuli in order to find out.) We ourselves may see things with respect to which we have taken no *practical* action (we see things that are out of reach, for example) but possibly only because we have talked about them. To see things without taking further action is to be *aware* of them. (The root in *aware* is also found in *wary*; we are wary of things that have been part of negative contingencies of selection.) The word *conscious*, used more often than *aware*, means co-knowledge (Latin: *con-science*) or "knowing with others"—an allusion to the verbal contingencies needed for being conscious.

All this is particularly important when what we see is within our body, the kind of seeing to which we usually reserve the word introspection. But what do we actually see? Psychologists who are uneasy about the metaphysical nature of mental life often say that what we see through introspection must be the brain, but that is unlikely. We have no sensory nerves going to important parts of the brain; a surgeon can operate without anesthesia. No contingencies of selection would have promoted the evolution of such nerves before the advent of verbal behavior, and that was very late in the evolution of the species. It is more likely that what we see through introspection are the early stages of our behavior, the stages that occur before the behavior begins to act upon the environment.

Sensing is such a stage; we see things before we respond to them in any other way, and we see that we are seeing them when we are doing nothing else. The necessary contingencies are supplied by people who ask us whether we see things. The very beginning of action is another early stage. It does not raise any question of the availability of sensory nerves because we should be able to see early stages with the nerves needed for the complete action. (It is also possible that we are sometimes not *intro*specting at all, but are responding to the external setting, as if "I am going to go . . ." meant "In situations like this I have usually gone. . . .")

The Greeks are said to have discovered the mind, but it is more likely that they were the first to talk at great length about what they saw within themselves and thus construct the contingencies needed for introspection. The "Great Conversation" of Plato's Academy would have created contingencies under which more and more of the beginnings of behavior would be seen. It must have been a puzzling world. We see the public world about us, but we also feel, hear, taste, and smell it. We do nothing with an inner world but "see" it. It is not surprising that the Greeks called it *meta*physical.

Unfortunately, what they saw occurred at just the time and place to be mistaken for a cause of what they then did, and it was therefore easy to suppose that they had discovered an originating self or mind. If what they saw was simply an early part of what they then did, however, it was no more a cause of the rest of what they did than the backswing of a golfer is the cause of the stroke that strikes the ball. Early parts of behavior affect later parts, but it is the behavior as a whole that is the product of variation and selection.

Such an analysis of introspection and of the "consciousness" introspected needs careful consideration, of course, but every effort should be made to preserve it because it dispenses with any need to appeal to a special kind of knowing or a special kind of stuff known. It stays within the world of physics and chemistry and the sciences of variation and selection. It avoids any suggestion of a break in the processes of variation and selection.

Two established sciences, each with a clearly defined subject matter, have a bearing on human behavior. One is the physiology of the body-cum-brain—a matter of organs, tissues, and cells, and the electrical and chemical changes that occur within them. The other is a group of three sciences concerned with the variation and selection that determine the condition of that body-cum-brain at any moment: the natural selection of the behavior of species (ethology), the operant conditioning of the behavior of the individual (behavior analysis), and the evolution of the social environments that prime operant behavior and greatly expand its range (a part of anthropology). The three could be said to be related in this way: Physiology studies the product of which the sciences of variation and selection study the production. The body works *as* it does because of the laws of physics and chemistry; it does *what* it does because of its exposure to contingencies of variation and selection.

Physiology tells us *how* the body works, the sciences of variation and selection tell us *why* it is a body that works that way.

The two sciences observe very different causal principles. The body-cum-brain obeys the laws of physics and chemistry. It has no freedom and makes no choices. No other vision of "man a machine" (in this case a biochemical machine) has ever been so well supported. Some brain scientists have argued that the brain must have structural features that allow for freedom of choice, creativity, and the like, but in doing so they argue from what the brain does rather than from its structure. It has also been said that variation and selection may occur in the brain, but although the brain, like any other part of the body, undergoes variations, the selecting contingencies are in the environment.

The more we know about the body-cum-brain as a biochemical machine, the less interesting it becomes in its bearing on behavior. If there is freedom, it is to be found in the randomness of variations. If new forms of behavior are created they are created by selection. The faults in variation and selection are a source of fascinating problems. We must adapt to new situations, resolve conflicts, find quick solutions. A lawful biochemical structure does nothing of the sort.

Computer simulations of human behavior are electronic machines designed to behave as the biochemical machine of the body behaves. We know how they were designed and built, and hence we ask no questions about origin. For the same reason, however, simulations are of no particular interest to behavior analysts. The interesting things in life come from the vagaries of variation and selection, in the construction of the machine.

Behavior analysis is the only one of the three sciences of variation and selection to be studied at length in the laboratory. Ethologists observe behavior in the field and reconstruct evolution from evidence that survives from earlier times. Ethology is supported by a laboratory science, genetics, but no one has yet produced a new species with a repertoire of innate behavior under laboratory conditions. The evolution of a culture is also primarily a matter of inferences from history. It is speed that makes the difference; only operant conditioning occurs quickly enough to be observed from beginning to end. For the same reason it is the only one of the three sciences to be much used for practical purposes in daily life.

It is therefore hard to understand why operant conditioning has not attracted more attention. The role of variation and selection in the behavior of the individual is often simply ignored. Sociobiology, for example, leaps from socio- to bio-, passing over the linking individual.

Many of the psychologists who have studied behavior have also neglected variation and selection. Thorndike's Law of Effect came close, but his experiment suggested that variations were trials and consequences errors. Watson, Lashley, and Hull appealed to habit formation and stimulus and response. Tolman's purpose, like goal orientation or subjective expected utility, projected copies of past consequences into the future as attractions that seemed to pull behavior.

Behavior analysis is the youngest of the three sciences (theories of natural selection and the evolution of cultures dating from the middle of the 19th century and behavior analysis only from the end of the first third of the 20th), but immaturity will not explain why it has so often been neglected. A better explanation may be that its field had been occupied for so long by that extraordinarily intriguing theory of an internal originating mind or self.

We do not speak the languages of brain science and behavior analysis in our daily lives. We cannot see the brain and we know very little about the history of variation and selection responsible for a given instance of behavior. Instead, we use a language that came into existence long before there were philosophers or scientists of any kind. It is properly called a vernacular. The word means, as its root meant for the Romans, the language of the household, of daily life. We all speak it. It is the language of newspapers, magazines, books, radio, and television. When speaking of the behavior of the individual, it is the language of behavioral scientists—psychologists, sociologists, anthropologists, political scientists, and economists. William James wrote *Principles of Psychology* in the vernacular. Behaviorists speak it in their daily lives (and young behaviorists must learn to do so without embarrassment).

The vernacular refers to many feelings and states of mind. In English, for example, we say that we do what we *feel* like doing or what we *need* to do to *satisfy* our desires. We say that we are *hungry* and are *thinking* of getting something to eat. It is easy to suppose that the references are to an initiating mind, but, as we have seen, the useful allusions are to prior contingencies of selection or to the beginnings of action. From "I'm hungry" we infer that a person has not eaten for some time and will probably eat when food is available. From "I am thinking of getting something to eat" we infer a probability of doing something that will make food available.

Through the use of the vernacular with its allusions to personal history and probability of action, psychology has emerged as an effective, essential, and highly respected profession. The attempt to use the apparent references to an initiating mind and to convert the vernacular into the language of a science was, however, a mistake. Watson and other early behaviorists thought the mistake lay in using introspection. How well could feelings be felt or mental processes seen? Anticipating logical positivism, they argued that an event seen by only one person had no place in a science. The problem was not introspection, however. It was the initiating self or mind to which introspection seemed to gain access.

In face-to-face contact with another person, references to an initiating self are unavoidable. There is a 'you,' and there is an 'I.' I see what 'you' do and hear what 'you' say and you see what 'I' do and hear what 'I' say. We do not see the histories of selection responsible for what is done and therefore infer an internal origination, but the successful use of the vernacular in the practice of psychology offers no support for its use in a science. In a scientific analysis, histories of variation and selection play the role of the initiator. There is no place in a scientific analysis of behavior for a mind or self.

What, then, are we to make of the fact that for 100 years psychologists have tried to build just such a science of mind? What about the brilliant analyses that have been made of intelligence or the claims for the value of the concept of subjective expected utility or the equations that have been written to describe psychological space? Have these been parts of a search for something that does not exist? It appears that we must say so, but all is not lost. Intelligence, never introspectible, is clearly an inference from the behavior sampled in intelligence tests, and an analysis of different kinds of intelligence is an analysis of different kinds of behavior. Expectation, another kind of "spection," cannot possibly mean seeing the future and must be the product of past contingencies of reinforcement. Utility means usefulness or use, the act or means of doing something in such a way that consequences follow. Psychological space is real space as it enters into the control of contingencies of reinforcement; at issue is the extent to which a stimulus present when a response is reinforced generalizes in such a way that similar stimuli that were not present exert control. In short, psychologists have unwittingly been analyzing contingencies of reinforcement, the very contingencies responsible for the behavior mistakenly attributed to an internal originator.

But what about the illustrious philosophers who throughout the centuries have tried to follow the injunction of the Delphic Oracle and to know themselves through introspection? Is there a similar justification or have they been uselessly pursuing a will-o'-the-wisp? To say so would seem little short of arrogance if there were not an illuminating parallel. Equally illustrious men and women have searched much longer and with greater dedication for another Creator, spelled this time with a capital 'C,' whose reported achievements are also being questioned by science. It was Darwin, of course, who made the difference. It holds for the origin of behavior as well as for the origin of species. After almost a century and a half, evolution is still not widely understood. It is vigorously opposed by defenders of a creator. As a result, it is still impossible to teach biology properly in many American schools. A creation science has been proposed to be taught in its place. The role of variation and selection in the behavior of the individual suffers from the same opposition. Cognitive science is the creation science of psychology, as it struggles to maintain the position of a mind or self.

The history of psychology is informative. It began, 100 years ago, with an introspective search for mind. Watson attacked introspection in his behavioristic manifesto of 1913, and for that or other reasons introspection was essentially abandoned. Behaviorists turned to the study of behavior for its own sake, and nonbehavioristic psychologists turned to the behavior of teachers, students, therapists, clients, children growing older year by year, people in groups, and so on.

Cognitive psychologists tried to restore the status quo. Behaviorism, they declared, was dead. They could not have meant that psychologists were no longer studying behavior, of animals in laboratories and of teachers, students, therapists, clients, and so on. What they hoped was dead was the appeal to selection by consequences in the explanation of behavior. The mind or, failing that, the brain must be restored to its rightful position.

Because of its similarity to the vernacular, cognitive psychology was easy to understand and the so-called cognitive revolution was for a time successful. That may have accelerated the speed with which behavior analysts drew away from the psychological establishment, founding their own associations, holding their own meetings, publishing their own journals. They were accused of building their own ghetto, but they were simply accepting the fact that they had little to gain from the study of a creative mind.

Cognitive psychology was left as the scientific companion of a profession and as the scientific underpinning of educational, clinical, developmental, social, and many other fields of psychology. The help it has given them has not been conspicuous. A version of the vernacular refined for the study of mental life is scarcely more helpful than the lay version, especially when theory began to replace introspection. Much more useful would have been behavior analysis. It would have helped in two ways, by clarifying the contingencies of reinforcement to which the vernacular alludes, and by making it possible to design better environments—personal environments that would solve existing problems and larger environments or cultures in which there would be fewer problems. A better understanding of variation and selection will mean a more successful profession, but whether behavior analysis will be called psychology is a matter for the future to decide.

APPENDIX

Introductions Revised for the 1961 Edition

The introductions used in this volume are from the First Edition of *Cumulative Record*, published in 1959. In preparing the 1961 Enlarged Edition, Skinner modified many of them but none more than the two presented here. Additional information about his revisions is provided in the Foreword.

1. Has Gertrude Stein a Secret? The revised introductory comments given below first appeared on page 261 in the Enlarged Edition (1961) and then were used as a postscript on page 369 of the Third Edition. The original introduction from the First Edition (1959) appears on pages 405–406 of this volume.

I first heard about the Autobiography of Alice B. Toklas *from Mary Louise White (Aswell). It had reached her desk in the editorial offices of the* Atlantic Monthly *as a bona fide autobiography, but the last paragraph had come as no surprise: "About six weeks ago Gertrude Stein said, it does not look to me as if you were ever going to write that autobiography. You know what I am going to do. I am going to write it for you. I am going to write it as simply as Defoe did the autobiography of Robinson Crusoe. And she has and this is it." Miss White was to be the only* Atlantic *reader to enjoy Gertrude Stein's little joke for when parts of the book were published in that magazine during the summer of 1933, the author's name appeared on the title page. My article appeared in the January, 1934 number of* Atlantic Monthly *and is reprinted with permission.*

Literary critics are by no means agreed on the significance of Gertrude Stein's psychological experiments. Conrad Aiken, writing in the New Republic, *reviewed the prevailing attitude toward Miss Stein's literary revolution—"Like the splitting of the atom, or the theory of relativity, Miss Stein's destruction of meaning was inevitably going to change, if not the world, at any rate the word"—and expressed the opinion that the present article made of the whole thing a very cruel joke. "What becomes of all this precise and detached and scientific experimentation with rhythm and meaning if, after all, it has been nothing on earth but automatic writing? Is it merely one more instance of the emperor's new clothes? Have we been duped, and has Miss Stein herself, perhaps, been duped? It looks very like it—though of course it is not impossible that Miss Stein has been pulling our legs." Among those who came to the defense was Sherwood Anderson, who quite properly rejoined that "all good writing is, in a sense, automatic." But partisans of Gertrude Stein have been afraid of this answer and have generally denied that her published work was written automatically.*

2. The Concept of the Reflex in the Description of Behavior.
This revision of the original introduction appeared on pages 319–321 of the Enlarged Edition (1961) and was retained in that form on pages 429–431 in the Third Edition (1972). The introduction from the First Edition (1959) appears on pages 475–477 of this volume. [Page numbers below refer to the present volume.]

This paper, written in the summer of 1930, was an early example of the operational analysis of terms describing behavior. *The clue to the definition of* reflex *may have come from Bertrand Russell. Somewhere, possibly in a series of articles in the* Dial *in the late 20's, Russell pointed out that the concept of the reflex in physiology had the same status as the concept of force in physics. Add that to Bridgman's treatment of force in* The Logic of Modern Physics *and you have the present point. The argument could be supported with a Machian analysis of the history of the reflex to explain the traditional definition as un*conscious, *in*voluntary, *and un*learned *behavior. The operational analysis of Sherrington's synapse, and the more generalized statement in Chapter 12 of* The Behavior of Organisms *where it was suggested that C.N.S. might be taken to stand for the Conceptual Nervous System, have been interpreted as showing an anti-physiological or anti-neurological bias. The objection, however, was merely to the use of inferences from behavior to explain behavior. The paper argued for the solid status of behavioral facts apart from imagined physiological counterparts. An important point is that operational definitions are suggested not only for* reflex, *but for* drive, emotion, conditioning *and other terms appropriate to the intact organism.*

The article also insisted upon the appropriateness of the concept of the reflex in describing behavior. *One consequence is a statement of behavioral facts in a form which most readily makes contact with physiological concepts and methods. In this sense the paper is, I believe, a positive contribution to physiology. True, the term* reflex *proved too rigid. It implied a complete specification of properties of behavior which was not in fact supported by the data either from whole or surgically subdivided organisms (a point which was made subsequently in the paper on page 504), and it insisted upon a demonstrable and presumably controllable stimulus as the principal independent variable (a point eventually rejected in the paper on page 535 and in* The Behavior of Organisms). *Similarly sharp reference to behavior in physical terms was maintained by the concept of the "operant" introduced to remedy these defects (see page 535). A further elaboration of this concept in interpreting, for example, verbal behavior presents the behavioral facts to be accounted for by the physiologist in the simplest possible way. Psychological facts remain on the plane of the physical and biological.*

The paper also offered a program *and a* general formulation *of a scientific analysis of behavior. As to program, the last paragraph on page 501 describes with considerable accuracy a subsequent investigation of "conditioning," "emotion," and "drive," some results of which are sketched in the paper on page 132. As to formulation, the observable facts underlying the concept of the reflex permit us to write the equation:*

$$R=f(S)$$

where R=response and S=stimulus. Changes in this function provide another sort of datum. For example, if we repeatedly elicit a response, the reflex undergoes "fatigue." We may rewrite the equation:

$$R=f(S,A).$$

In this paper the letter A was noncommittally referred to as a "third variable," a point which is relevant to current controversies about intervening variables. The variable A is merely another variable to be taken into account; it does not intervene *even though the traditional practice is to assign the change in the function which it accounts for to some inner state or condition. Some experimental studies on rate of eating (offered, together with the present paper, as my doctoral thesis) exemplified this distinction. The concept of "hunger" as an inner state may be useful for certain purposes, but in a strictly operational definition we must confine ourselves to changes in "reflex strength" as a function of deprivation, satiation, and similar operations.*

Edward C. Tolman missed this point when he set up his own version of an "operational behaviorism."[1] *Tolman's equation:*

---

[1] Tolman, E. C. Operational behaviorism and current trends in psychology. In *Proc. 25th Anniv. Celebr. Inaug. Grad. Stud.* Los Angeles: Univ. South. Calif. Press, 1936. Reprinted in Marx, Melvin H. *Psychological theory: Contemporary Readings.* New York: Macmillan, 1951.

$$B=f(SPHTA)$$

is patterned after the equations above (with B for "behavior" in place of R for "response," and S for "environmental stimulus condition" rather than "stimulus"). But what about P, H, T, and A? Tolman is sufficiently operational in saying that groups of these variables are all he finds in the way of mental processes (thus disposing of the mentalistic nature of such processes), but he is still looking for substitutes and hence (and for no other reason) calls the additional variables "intervening."

The present paper was published in the Journal of General Psychology, *(1931, 5, 427–458) and is reprinted here by permission of the editor.*

Note: The introduction to "The Processes Involved in the Repeated Guessing of Alternatives" was modified slightly by its author for reasons unrelated to those governing changes to other papers. The following sentence appeared in both the First Edition and the Enlarged Edition but was omitted from the version used in the Third Edition: "The present paper is an effort to account for the observed patterns of guessing in terms of tendencies to alternate calls."

ACKNOWLEDGMENTS

pp. 3–18: Appeared in *American Scholar*, Winter 1955–1956.

pp. 19–24: Reprinted with permission from *Transactions of the New York Academy of Sciences*, Series II, 1955, *17*: 7, 547–551.

pp. 25–38: Reprinted with permission from *Science*, 1956, *124*, 1057–1066. Copyright © 1956 by the American Association for the Advancement of Science.

pp. 39–50: Reprinted by permission from *Daedalus*, Journal of the American Academy of Arts and Sciences, from the issue entitled "Evolution and Man's Progress," Summer 1961, Vol. 90, No. 3. Copyright © 1961 by the American Academy of Arts and Sciences.

pp. 51–57: From *Proceedings of the American Philosophical Society*, 1964, *108*, 482–485. Copyright © 1964 by the American Philosophical Society. Reprinted with permission of the publisher.

pp. 58–65: From *International Encyclopedia of the Social Sciences*, David L. Sills, ed., New York: Crowell, Collier and Macmillan, 1968. Vol. 16, pp. 271–275. Copyright © 1968 by Crowell, Collier and Macmillan, Inc. Reprinted by permission of the publisher.

pp. 69–100: From *Psychological Review*, 1950, *57*, 193–216. Copyright © 1950 by the American Psychological Association. Reprinted with permission.

pp. 101–107: Appeared with adaptations in *American Psychologist*, 1953, *8*, 69–79.

pp. 108–131: From *American Psychologist*, 1956, *11*, 221–223. Copyright © 1956 by the American Psychological Association. Reprinted with permission.

pp. 132–164: From *American Scientist*, 1957, *45*, 343–371. Reprinted by permission of the publisher.

pp. 165–175: From *American Psychologist*, 1958, *13*, 94–99. Copyright © 1958 by the American Psychological Association. Reprinted with permission.

pp. 179–191: Appeared in *Psychology and the Behavioral Sciences,* University of Pittsburgh Press, 1955.

pp. 192–216: Appeared in *Science,* 1958, 128, 969–977.

pp. 217–239: Reprinted by permission from *Harvard Educational Review*, *31*:4 (Fall 1961), pp. 377–398. Copyright © 1961 by the President and Fellows of Harvard College. All rights reserved.

pp. 240–253: From *Teachers College Record*, November 1963. Copyright © 1963 by Columbia University Press. Reprinted by permission of the publisher.

pp. 254–270: Reprinted with permission from *Science*, 1968, *159,* 704–710. Copyright © 1968 by American Association for the Advancement of Science.

680   *Acknowledgments*

pp. 271–281: Reprinted by permission from *Education*, December 1969, *90*, 93–100.

pp. 285–294: Reprinted with permission from *Scientific Monthly*, November 1964. Copyright © 1964 by the American Association for the Advancement of Science.

pp. 295–302: Appeared in *Integrating the Approaches to Mental Disease* edited by H. D. Kruse (New York: Paul B. Hoeber, Inc., 1957).

pp. 303–321: From *Theory and Treatment of the Psychoses: Some New Aspects*, F. Gildea, ed. Copyright © 1956 by Washington University Studies. Reprinted by permission of the publisher.

pp. 322–328: Appeared in *Cumulative Record* (3rd ed.). (New York: Appleton-Century-Crofts, 1972, pp. 276–282).

pp. 329–337: "Compassion and Ethics in the Care of the Retardate" reprinted by permission of the Joseph P. Kennedy, Jr., Foundation for Mental Retardation.

pp. 341–359: "Experimental Psychology" by B. F. Skinner is from *Current Trends in Psychology*, by Wayne Dennis, et al. Copyright © 1947 by University of Pittsburgh Press. Reprinted by permission of the University of Pittsburgh Press.

pp. 360–376: From *Current Trends in Psychological Theory: A Bicentennial Program* by Wayne Dennis, et al. Copyright © 1961 by University of Pittsburgh Press. Reprinted by permission of the University of Pittsburgh Press.

pp. 379–390: From *On the Future of Art* by Solomon R. Guggenheim Museum. Copyright © 1970 by the Solomon R. Guggenheim Foundation. Reprinted with the permission of The Viking Press, Inc.

pp. 391–401: Lecture given at the Poetry Center in New York City, October 13, 1971.

p. 393: Selected lines from *So Much Nearer* by I. A. Richards. Copyright © 1960 by I. A. Richards. Reprinted by permission of Harcourt Brace Jovanovich, Inc.

pp. 394–395: "Verbal Behaviour" and "For Ivor Richards" from *Encounter*, November 1962.

pp. 405–415: Appeared in *Atlantic Monthly*, January 1934.

pp. 416–430: From *Psychological Review*, 1945, *52*, 270–277. Copyright © 1945 by the American Psychological Association. Reprinted with permission.

pp. 431–436: From *Psychological Record*, 1929, *3*, 186–192. Copyright © 1929 by Psychological Record. Reprinted with permission of the publisher.

pp. 437–453: From *American Journal of Psychology*. Copyright © 1941 by the Board of Trustees of the University of Illinois. Used with permission of the University of Illinois Press.

pp. 454–463: From *The Journal of Experimental Psychology*, 1942, *30*, 495–503. Copyright © 1942 by the American Psychological Association. Reprinted with permission.

pp. 467–474: Appeared in *The Listener*, September 30, 1971.

pp. 475–503: From *The Journal of General Psychology*, 1931, *5*, 427–458. Copyright © 1931. Reprinted with permission of the Helen Dwight Reid Educational Foundation. Published by Heldref Publications, 1319 Eighteenth Street NW, Washington, DC 20036-1802.

pp. 504–524: From *The Journal of General Psychology*, 1935, *12*, 40–65. Copyright © 1935. Reprinted with permission of the Helen Dwight Reid Educational Foundation. Published by Heldref Publications, 1319 Eighteenth Street NW, Washington, DC 20036-1802.

pp. 525–534: From *The Journal of General Psychology*, 1935, *12*, 66–77. Copyright © 1935. Reprinted with permission of the Helen Dwight Reid Educational Foundation. Published by Heldref Publications, 1319 Eighteenth Street NW, Washington, DC 20036-1802.

pp. 535–543: From *The Journal of General Psychology*, 1937, *16*, 272–279. Copyright © 1937. Reprinted with permission of the Helen Dwight Reid Educational Foundation. Published by Heldref Publications, 1319 Eighteenth Street NW, Washington, DC 20036-1802.

pp. 544–549: From *The American Journal of Psychology*, 1944, *57*, 276–281. Copyright © 1944 by the Board of Trustees of the University of Illinois. Used with permission of the University of Illinois Press.

pp. 550–554: From *Contemporary Psychology*, 1956, *1*, 101–103. Copyright © 1956 by the American Psychological Association. Reprinted with permission.

pp. 556–557: From *The Journal of General Psychology*, 1932, *7*, 481–482. Copyright © 1932. Reprinted with permission of the Helen Dwight Reid Educational Foundation. Published by Heldref Publications, 1319 Eighteenth Street NW, Washington, DC 20036-1802.

pp. 558–569: From *The Journal of Experimental Psychology*, 1941, *29*, 390–400. Copyright © 1941 by the American Psychological Association. Reprinted with permission.

pp. 570–574: From *The Journal of Experimental Psychology*, 1948, *38*, 168–172. Copyright © 1948 by the American Psychological Association. Reprinted with permission.

pp. 575–578: From *The American Journal of Psychology*, 1957, *70*, 308–311. Copyright © 1957 by the Board of Trustees of the University of Illinois. Used with permission of the University of Illinois Press.

pp. 579–583: Reprinted with permission from *Journal of Experimental Analysis and Behavior*, 1962, *5*, 531–533. Copyright © 1962 by the Society for the Experimental Analysis of Behavior, Inc.

pp. 584–588: Appeared in *Journal of Comparative and Physiological Psychology*, 1957, *30*: 3, 279–281.

pp. 589–600: Reprinted with permission from *Journal of the Experimental Analysis of Behavior*, 1958, *1*, 235–244. Copyright © 1958 by the Society for the Experimental Analysis of Behavior, Inc.

pp. 601–604: Reprinted with permission from *Science*, 1959, *129*, 197–198. Copyright © 1959 by American Association for the Advancement of Science.

pp. 605–612: Reprinted with permission. Copyright © 1951 by Scientific American, Inc.

pp. 613–620: Appeared in *Ladies' Home Journal*, October 1945.

pp. 621–629: Reprinted by permission of the publisher from B. F. Skinner, "The Psychology of Design" which appeared in *Art Education Today*, (New York: Teachers College Press [formerly Bureau of Publications], copyright © 1941, Teachers College, Columbia University. All rights reserved.).

pp. 630–647: From *American Psychologist*, January 1960. Copyright © 1960 by the American Psychological Association. Reprinted with permission.

pp. 648–652: Appeared in *Conditional Reflex*, 1966, *1*, 74–78.

pp. 653–658: From *Harvard Alumni Bulletin*, May 1962. Copyright © 1962 by Harvard Alumni Bulletin (now *Harvard Magazine*). Reprinted with permission.

pp. 661–673: From *American Psychologist*, 1990, *45*, 1206–1210. Copyright © 1990 by the American Psychological Association. Reprinted with permission.

INDEX

Instructional programs, 248
Integrating the Approaches to Mental Disease, 295
The Integrative Action of the Nervous System, 490
Intelligence testing, 297, 322
Intelligibility, 413
International Congress of Physiology, 648
The International Encyclopedia of the Social Sciences, 58
Interval performance, 139, 152–153, 571–572
Introspective psychology, 301–302, 316, 318, 667
Involuntary action, 484
Irritability, 482, 488, 502
Irritability: A Physiological Analysis of the General Effect of Stimuli in Living Substances, 481

J
Jakobson, Roman, 392
James, William, 243, 364, 375, 663, 670
Jennings, Herbert S., 602
Jewitt, J. E., 208
Johns Hopkins University, 602
John Locke Lectures, 393
Johnson, Harry M., 426
Jones, Howard Mumford, 81
Jones, Janette, 432
Jones, Lawrence, 392
Joseph P. Kennedy, Jr., Foundation for Mental Retardation, 329
Journal of Applied Psychology, 149
Journal of Comparative and Physiological Psychology, 140, 145, 154, 584, 589
Journal of the Experimental Analysis of Behavior, 392, 535, 579, 589
The Journal of Experimental Psychology, 81, 454, 455, 559, 570
The Journal of General Psychology, 146, 477, 504, 525, 528, 535, 543, 557
Journal of Psychology, 431
Juvenile offenders, 471

K
Kateb, George, 396, 401
Keller, Fred S., 111, 120, 124, 140
Kennedy, Joseph P., Jr., 329
"Knees," 595, 596, 598
Koch, Robert, 359
Koch, Sigmund, 108
Knoedler, M., & Co., 625
Knowledge, 300–301, 316–317
Koestler, Arthur, 385
Konorski, Jerzy, 535–537, 540, 542
Körperstellung, 485
Kruse, Heinrich D., 295
Kruse, Marian, 432
Krutch, Joseph Wood, 11, 13–14, 22–23, 32, 54, 56
Kubie, Lawrence, 316
Kymograph, 113, 114

L
La science et l'hypothèse, 499
Laboratory research, 325
Laboratory, flight from the, 360–376
Ladies' Home Journal, 613
Language, 391, 417, 419
Language, 391
Lanier, Lyle H., 426
Lapicque, Louis, 492
Lashley, Karl, 369, 418, 602, 603, 670
Latency, 73, 74, 76–77, 539, 547, 548, 553
Latent speech, 431
Latin square, 120
The Law of Effect, 78, 179, 399, 525, 670
Leader-follower relation, 581, 583
Learning, 69–100, 126, 275, 297, 298–299, 310, 324, 353, 363, 551, 552
Learning, complex, 92
Learning, mathematical theories of, 551
Learning, theories of, 69–100, 369, 370
Learning curves, 369
Lectures on the History of Physiology, 478
Legal system, 357
Lehmann-Haupt, Christopher, 391
Leisure, 63–64, 335, 336, 379, 381–382

THE FOUR EDITIONS OF *CUMULATIVE RECORD*: INDEX TO CONTENTS

The following summarizes the contents of *Cumulative Record* by listing the inclusive page numbers of each article in each of its editions (First, Revised, Third, and this Definitive Edition, respectively abbreviated in boldface as **1**, **2**, **3** and **4**). Where pages are identical in two or more editions, the editions are listed together. For example, **3/4** 51–57 indicates that the article appears on pages 51 through 57 in both the Third Edition and this Definitive Edition. Articles new to the Revised Edition were inserted into the First Edition pagination; for example, pages 36.01 through .12 are twelve pages that appear between pages 36 and 37 in the Revised Edition. Section headings are unnumbered because the number of sections varies across editions.

The Implications of a Science of Behavior for Human Affairs

A Method for the Experimental Analysis of Behavior

The Technology of Education

The Analysis and Management of Neurotic, Psychotic, and Retarded Behavior

For Experimental Psychologists Only

Creative Behavior

Literary and Verbal Behavior

Theoretical Considerations

A Miscellany

Coda